Applications and Developments in Grid, Cloud, and High Performance Computing

Emmanuel Udoh
Sullivan University, USA

Information Science
REFERENCE

Managing Director:	Lindsay Johnston
Senior Editorial Director:	Heather A. Probst
Book Production Manager:	Sean Woznicki
Development Manager:	Joel Gamon
Assistant Acquisitions Editor:	Kayla Wolfe
Typesetter:	Jennifer Romanchak
Cover Design:	Nick Newcomer

Published in the United States of America by
Information Science Reference (an imprint of IGI Global)
701 E. Chocolate Avenue
Hershey PA 17033
Tel: 717-533-8845
Fax: 717-533-8661
E-mail: cust@igi-global.com
Web site: http://www.igi-global.com

Library of Congress Cataloging-in-Publication Data

Applications and developments in grid, cloud, and high performance computing / Emmanuel Udoh, editor.
    p. cm.
  Includes bibliographical references and index.
  Summary: "This book provides insight into the current trends and emerging issues by investigating grid and cloud evolution, workflow management, and the impact new computing systems have on the education fields as well as the industries"-- Provided by publisher.
    ISBN 978-1-4666-2065-0 (hardcover) -- ISBN 978-1-4666-2066-7 (ebook) -- ISBN 978-1-4666-2067-4 (print & perpetual access) 1. Computational grids (Computer systems) 2. Cloud computing--Research. 3. High performance computing--Research. I. Udoh, Emmanuel, 1960-
  QA76.9.C58A67 2013
  004.6782--dc23
                                    2012015946

British Cataloguing in Publication Data
A Cataloguing in Publication record for this book is available from the British Library.

The views expressed in this book are those of the authors, but not necessarily of the publisher.

Table of Contents

Section 1
Introduction

Yuyu Chou, Berlin Institute of Technology, Germany
Jan Oetting, Consileon Business Consultancy GmbH, Germany

Section 2
Scheduling

Zahid Raza, Jawaharlal Nehru University, India
Deo Prakash Vidyarthi, Jawaharlal Nehru University, India

Ahmed I. Saleh, Mansoura University, Egypt

Meriem Meddeber, University of Mascara, Algeria
Belabbas Yagoubi, University of Oran, Algeria

Section 3
Algorithms and Optimization

Section 4
High Performance Computing

Section 5
Applications

Detailed Table of Contents

Section 1
Introduction

Chapter 1

    Yuyu Chou, Berlin Institute of Technology, Germany
    Jan Oetting, Consileon Business Consultancy GmbH, Germany

The use of Cloud Computing services is an attractive option to improve IT systems to achieve rapidly and elastically provisioned capability, and also to offer economic benefits. However, companies see security as a major concern in migrating to the Cloud. To bring clarity in Cloud security, this paper presents a systematic approach to manage the risks and analyzes the full range of risk in Cloud Computing solutions. Furthermore, as a study case, Google App Engine Platform is assessed based on ISO/IEC 27002 and OWASP Top 10 Risk List in this paper. Knowing the risks of Cloud solutions, companies can execute well-informed decisions on going into the Cloud and build their Cloud solutions in a secure way, relying on a robust e-trust relationship.

Section 2
Scheduling

Chapter 2

    Zahid Raza, Jawaharlal Nehru University, India
    Deo Prakash Vidyarthi, Jawaharlal Nehru University, India

This paper presents a grid scheduling model to schedule a job on the grid with the objective of ensuring maximum reliability to the job under the current grid state. The model schedules a modular job to those resources that suit the job requirements in terms of resources while offering the most reliable environment. The reliability estimates depict true grid picture and considers the contribution of the computational resources, network links and the application awaiting allocation. The scheduling executes the interactive jobs while considering the looping structure. As scheduling on the grid is an NP hard problem, soft computing tools are often applied. This paper applies Modified Genetic Algorithm (MGA), which is an elitist selection method based on the two threshold values, to improve the solution. The MGA works on the basis of partitioning the current population in three categories: the fittest chromosomes, average fit chromosomes and the ones with worst fitness. The worst are dropped, while the fittest chromosomes of the current generation are mated with the average fit chromosomes of the previous generation to produce off-spring. The simulation results are compared with other similar grid scheduling models to study the performance of the proposed model under various grid conditions.

Chapter 3

Scheduling is an important issue that must be handled carefully to realize the "Just login to compute" principle introduced by computational grids. Current grid schedulers suffer from the haste problem, which is the inability to schedule all tasks successfully. Accordingly, some tasks fail to complete execution as they are allocated to unsuitable workers. Others may not start execution as suitable workers are previously allocated to other tasks. This paper introduces the scheduling haste problem and presents a novel high throughput grid scheduler. The proposed scheduler selects the most suitable worker to execute an input grid task. Hence, it minimizes the turnaround time for a set of grid tasks. Moreover, the scheduler is system oriented and avoids the scheduling haste problem. Experimental results show that the proposed scheduler outperforms traditional grid schedulers as it introduces better scheduling efficiency.

Chapter 4

A computational grid is a widespread computing environment that provides huge computational power for large-scale distributed applications. One of the most important issues in such an environment is resource management. Task assignment as a part of resource management has a considerable effect on the grid middleware performance. In grid computing, task execution time is dependent on the machine to which it is assigned, and task precedence constraints are represented by a directed acyclic graph. This paper proposes a hybrid assignment strategy of dependent tasks in Grids which integrate static and dynamic assignment technologies. Grid computing is considered a set of clusters formed by a set of computing elements and a cluster manager. The main objective is to arrive at a method of task assignment that could achieve minimum response time and reduce the transfer cost, inducing by the tasks transfer respecting the dependency constraints.

Section 3
Algorithms and Optimization

Task scheduling in heterogeneous parallel and distributed computing environment is a challenging problem. Applications identified by parallel tasks can be represented by directed-acyclic graphs (DAGs). Scheduling refers to the assignment of these parallel tasks on a set of bounded heterogeneous processors connected by high speed networks. Since task assignment is an NP-complete problem, instead of finding an exact solution, scheduling algorithms are developed based on heuristics, with the primary goal of minimizing the overall execution time of the application or schedule length. In this paper, the overall execution time (schedule length) of the tasks is reduced using task duplication on top of the Critical-Path-On-a-Processor (CPOP) algorithm.

Chapter 6

Apurva Shah, G H Patel College of Engg & Tech, India
Ketan Kotecha, Nirma University, India

The Ant Colony Optimization (ACO) algorithms are computational models inspired by the collective foraging behavior of ants. The ACO algorithms provide inherent parallelism, which is very useful in multiprocessor environments. They provide balance between exploration and exploitation along with robustness and simplicity of individual agent. In this paper, ACO based dynamic scheduling algorithm for homogeneous multiprocessor real-time systems is proposed. The results obtained during simulation are measured in terms of Success Ratio (SR) and Effective CPU Utilization (ECU) and compared with the results of Earliest Deadline First (EDF) algorithm in the same environment. It has been observed that the proposed algorithm is very efficient in underloaded conditions and it performs very well during overloaded conditions also. Moreover, the proposed algorithm can schedule some typical instances successfully which are not possible to schedule using EDF algorithm.

Chapter 7

Rashedur M. Rahman, North South University, Bangladesh
Ruppa K. Thulasiram, University of Manitoba, Canada
Parimala Thulasiraman, University of Manitoba, Canada

The neural network is popular and used in many areas within the financial field, such as credit authorization screenings, regularities in security price movements, simulations of market behaviour, and so forth. In this research, the authors use a neural network technique for stock price forecasting of Great West Life, an insurance company based in Winnipeg, Canada. The Backpropagation algorithm is a popular algorithm to train a neural network. However, one drawback of traditional Backpropagation algorithm is that it takes a substantial amount of training time. To expedite the training process, the authors design and develop different parallel and multithreaded neural network algorithms. The authors implement parallel neural network algorithms on both shared memory architecture using OpenMP and distributed memory architecture using MPI and analyze the performance of those algorithms. They also compare the results with traditional auto-regression model to establish accuracy.

Chapter 8

Ming-Jeng Yang, Mackay Medical College, Taiwan
Chin-Lin Kuo, National Taiwan Normal University, Taiwan
Yao-Ming Yeh, National Taiwan Normal University, Taiwan

Virtualization and partitioning are the means by which multiple application instances can share and run multiple virtual machines supported by a platform. In a Green Cloud environment, the goal is to consolidate multiple applications onto virtual machines associated by fewer servers, and reduce cost and complexity, increase agility, and lower power and cooling costs. To make Cloud center greener, it is beneficial to limit the amount of active servers to minimize energy consumption. This paper presents a precise model to formulate the right-sizing and energy-saving mechanism, which not only minimizes energy consumption of the server but also maintains a service quality through the Mt/M/Vt strategy of queuing theory. The authors map the complicated formula of the energy-saving mechanism to an approximation equation and design the fast decidable algorithms for calculating the right size of virtual machines in constant time complexity for power management systems.

Several position-based routing protocols have been developed for mobile ad hoc networks. Many of these protocols assume that a location service is available which provides location information on the nodes in the network. This paper introduces a new schema in management of mobile nodes location in mobile ad hoc networks. Fuzzy logic optimization is applied to a better management of location update operation in hierarchical location services. Update management overhead is decreased without significant loss of query success probability. One-hop-chain-technique is used for Auto compensation. A new composed method can update mobile nodes location when the nodes cross a grid boundary. The proposed method uses a dynamic grid area that solves the ping-pong problem between grids. Simulation results show that these methods are effective. The algorithms are distributed and can keep scalability in the scenario of increasing nodes density. The described solutions are not limited to a special network grid ordering, and can be used in every hierarchical ordering like GLS if the ordering can be mappable on these methods.

Grid computing came into existence as a manner of sharing heavy computational loads among multiple computers to be able to compute highly complex mathematical problems. The grid topology is highly flexible and easily scalable, allowing users to join and leave the grid without the hassle of time and resource-hungry identification procedures, having to adjust their devices or install additional software. The goal of grid computing is described as "to provide flexible, secure and coordinated resource sharing among dynamic collections of individuals, institutions and resources". AODV is an on-demand (reactive) algorithm capable of both unicast and multicast routing. In this paper, AODV has been modified by varying some of the configuration parameters used in this algorithm to improve its performance. This modified protocol i.e. A-AODV (advanced ad hoc on demand distance vector) has been compared with AODV in grid environment. The simulations have shown that A-AODV is able to achieve high throughput and packet delivery ratio and average end-to-end delay is reduced.

Chapter 11

An Intelligent Sensor Placement Method to Reach a High Coverage in Wireless Sensor

Shirin Khezri, Islamic Azad University - Mahabad, Iran

Karim Faez, Amirkabir University of Technology, Iran

Amjad Osmani, Islamic Azad University - Saghez, Iran

Adequate coverage is one of the main problems for Sensor Networks. The effectiveness of distributed wireless sensor networks highly depends on the sensor deployment scheme. Optimizing the sensor deployment provides sufficient sensor coverage and saves cost of sensors for locating in grid points. This article applies the modified binary particle swarm optimization algorithm for solving the sensor placement in distributed sensor networks. PSO is an inherent continuous algorithm, and the discrete PSO is proposed to be adapted to discrete binary space. In the distributed sensor networks, the sensor placement is an NP-complete problem for arbitrary sensor fields. One of the most important issues in the research fields, the proposed algorithms will solve this problem by considering two factors: the complete coverage and the minimum costs. The proposed method on sensors surrounding is examined in different area. The results not only confirm the successes of using the new method in sensor placement, also they show that the new method is more efficiently compared to other methods like Simulated Annealing(SA), PBIL and LAEDA.

Section 4
High Performance Computing

Chapter 12

High Performance Computing Design by Code Migration for Distributed Desktop Computing

Makoto Yoshida, Okayama University of Science, Japan

Kazumine Kojima, Okayama University of Science, Japan

Large scale loosely coupled PCs can organize clusters and form desktop computing grids on sharing each processing power; power of PCs, transaction distributions, network scales, network delays, and code migration algorithms characterize the performance of the computing grids. This article describes the design methodologies of workload management in distributed desktop computing grids. Based on the code migration experiments, transfer policy for computation was determined and several simulations for location policies were examined, and the design methodologies for distributed desktop computing grids are derived from the simulation results. The language for distributed desktop computing is designed to accomplish the design methodologies.

Chapter 13

Parallelization of Littlewood-Richardson Coefficients Computation and its Integration into the

Heithem Abbes, University of Tunis, Tunisia

Franck Butelle, LIPN/UMR 7030 - Université Paris 13, France

Christophe Cérin, LIPN/UMR 7030 - Université Paris 13, France

This paper shows how to parallelize a compute intensive application in mathematics (Group Theory) for an institutional Desktop Grid platform coordinated by a meta-grid middleware named BonjourGrid. The paper is twofold: it shows how to parallelize a sequential program for a multicore CPU which participates in the computation; and it demonstrates the effort for launching multiple instances of the solutions for the mathematical problem with the BonjourGrid middleware. BonjourGrid is a fully decentralized Desktop Grid middleware. The main results of the paper are: a) an efficient multi-threaded version of a sequential program to compute Littlewood-Richardson coefficients, namely the Multi-LR program and b) a proof of concept, centered around the user needs, for the BonjourGrid middleware dedicated to coordinate multiple instances of programsfor Desktop Grids and with the help of Multi-LR. In this paper, the scientific work consists in starting from a model for the solution of a compute intensive problem in mathematics, to incorporate the concrete model into a middleware and running it on commodity PCs platform managed by an innovative meta Desktop Grid middleware.

Chapter 14

Ahmad Awwad, Fahad Bin Sultan University, Saudi Arabia

Jehad Al-Sadi, Arab Open University, Jordan

Bassam Haddad, University of Petra, Jordan

Ahmad Kayed, Fahad Bin Sultan University, Saudi Arabia

Recent studies have revealed that the Optical Transpose Interconnection Systems (OTIS) are promising candidates for future high-performance parallel computers. This paper presents and evaluates a general method for algorithm development on the OTIS-Arrangement network (OTIS-AN) as an example of OTIS network. The proposed method can be used and customized for any other OTIS network. Furthermore, it allows efficient mapping of a wide class of algorithms into the OTIS-AN. This method is based on grids and pipelines as popular structures that support a vast body of parallel applications including linear algebra, divide-and-conquer types of algorithms, sorting, and FFT computation. This study confirms the viability of the OTIS-AN as an attractive alternative for large-scale parallel architectures.

Chapter 15

Arnab Nandi, National Institute of Technology Durgapur, India

Sumit Kundu, National Institute of Technology Durgapur, India

Energy level performances of three packet delivery schemes in Wireless Sensor Networks (WSN) are evaluated in presence of Rayleigh fading. Three different information delivery mechanisms are investigated using regenerative relays with or without error correction capability. Energy consumption for successful delivery of a data packet for each mechanism is evaluated and compared under several conditions of node density, bit rate, transmit power, and channel fading. Energy efficiencies of different retransmission schemes are also evaluated. Further, an optimal packet length based on energy efficiency is derived. Impact of optimal packet size on average number of retransmission and total energy expenditure is analyzed for each delivery scheme.

Chapter 16

Amitabha Chakrabarty, Dublin City University, Ireland

Martin Collier, Dublin City University, Ireland

Symmetric rearrangeable networks (SRN) (Chakrabarty, Collier, & Mukhopadhyay, 2009) make efficient use of hardware, but they have the disadvantage of momentarily disrupting the existing communications during reconfiguration. Path continuity is a major issue in some application of rearrangeable networks.

Using repackable networks (Yanga, Su, & Pin, 2008) is a solution to the path continuity problem in SRN. These networks provide functionality comparable to that of strict sense no blocking networks (SNB) but with minimum increase in the hardware than SRN. This paper proposes an efficient implementation of multistage symmetric repackable networks requiring optimum hardware cost than the method proposed in the literature. Cost optimization is achieved through the use of minimum number of bypass link(s). Investigated method works for networks built with more than three switching stages and shows promise of scalability.

Chapter 17

Sharing of resources by the cores of multi-core processors brings performance issues for the system. Majority of the shared resources belong to memory hierarchy sub-system of the processors such as last level caches, prefetchers and memory buses. Programs co-running on the cores of a multi-core processor may interfere with each other due to usage of such shared resources. Such interference causes co-running programs to suffer with performance degradation. Previous research works include efforts to characterize and classify the memory behaviors of programs to predict the performance. Such knowledge could be useful to create workloads to perform performance studies on multi-core processors. It could also be utilized to form policies at system level to mitigate the interference between co-running programs due to use of shared resources. In this work, machine learning techniques are used to predict the performance on multi-core processors. The main contribution of the study is enumeration of solo-run program attributes, which can be used to predict concurrent-run performance despite change in the number of co-running programs sharing the resources. The concurrent-run involves the interference between co-running programs due to use of shared resources.

Multipath fading is inherent in wireless communication systems. Diversity is the technique which takes advantage of multipath to mitigate the effect of fading and increase signal strength. Space Time Block codes (STBC) are used in MIMO systems to improve the performance by maximizing transmit and/or receive diversity. Among different schemes based on STBC, Quasi Orthogonal Space Time Block Code (QOSTBC) is able to achieve full rate transmission for more than two transmit antennas. Constellation Rotation QOSTBC (CR-QOSTBC) achieves full diversity and improves performance further along with full rate, to overcome the limitation of QOSTBC, which is unable to maintain orthogonality amongst the codes transmitted by different antennas. Higher diversity can be achieved by increasing uncorrelated paths between transmitter and receivers using higher number of receive antennas. This paper examines improvement in BER with reference to a number of receive antennas. Simulations were carried out under ideal as well as realistic environments, using least square technique with four antennas at transmitter side and variable receive antennas. Results of simulations presented in this paper indicate performance improvement of CR-QOSTBC over QOSTBC in flat fading channel environment. Simulation results also show performance degradation in BER when channel is estimated at the receiver.

Biology databases are diverse and massive. As a result, researchers must compare each sequence with vast numbers of other sequences. Comparison, whether of structural features or protein sequences, is vital in bioinformatics. These activities require high-speed, high-performance computing power to search through and analyze large amounts of data and industrial-strength databases to perform a range of data-intensive computing functions. Grid computing and Cluster computing meet these requirements. Biological data exist in various web services that help biologists search for and extract useful information. The data formats produced are heterogeneous and powerful tools are needed to handle the complex and difficult task of integrating the data. This paper presents a review of the technologies and an approach to solve this problem using cluster and grid computing technologies. The authors implement an experimental distributed computing application for bioinformatics, consisting of basic high-performance computing environments (Grid and PC Cluster systems), multiple interfaces at user portals that provide useful graphical interfaces to enable biologists to benefit directly from the use of high-performance technology, and a translation tool for converting biology data into XML format.

Chapter 20

Recently, smartphone technologies have evolved quickly and offered end users the computing power and networking capabilities required to perform useful network and multimedia applications. However, due to limited physical sizes and battery capacities, the current generation of smartphones cannot yet fulfill the requirements of sophisticated applications of which personal computers are capable. One way to solve this problem is to minimize the workload on a smartphone as much as possible by offloading portions of an application to a server. The solution is particularly attractive today as cloud computing provides the needed server resources at relatively low costs. This paper proposes a novel, lightweight application migration mechanism for the users of smartphones to suspend the execution of applications and offload them to the cloud. The authors also developed a framework to perform Android applications efficiently with virtual phones in the cloud with a virtual storage. This paper discusses the migration mechanism and evaluates its effectiveness on the Android smartphone. This approach may effectively offload workload for Android applications even with low-speed mobile network.

Wing-Ning Li, University of Arkansas, USA
Donald Hayes, University of Arkansas, USA
Jonathan Baran, University of Arkansas, USA
Cameron Porter, Acxiom Corporation, USA
Tom Schweiger, Acxiom Corporation, USA

Record linkage deals with finding records that identify the same real world entity, such as an individual or a business, from a given file or set of files. Record linkage problem is also referred to as the entity resolution or record recognition problem. To locate those records identifying the same real world entity, in principle, pairwise record analyses have to be performed among all records. Analytical operations between two records vary from comparing corresponding fields to enhancing records through large knowledge bases and querying large databases. Hence, these operations are complex and take time. To reduce the number of pairwise record comparisons, blocking techniques are introduced to partition the records into blocks. After that records in each block are analyzed against one and another. One of the effective blocking methods is the closure approach, where a "related" equivalence relation is used to partition the records into equivalence classes. This paper introduces the closure problem and describes the design and implementation of a parallel and distributed closure prototype system running in an enterprise grid.

Preface

The Magellan report on cloud computing for science (funded by the U.S. Department of Energy) highlighted the potential of cloud computing for scientific computing by emphasizing the power of virtualization and the on-demand grid/cloud service resources. One of the outcomes of this DOE project explored the cloud capabilities in the traditional high performance computing (HPC) platforms that combine the flexibility of cloud models with the performance of HPC systems. The integration of the business model of cloud computing into the well-known and optimized HPC platforms is expected to support more diverse workloads and scientific discovery. In that vein, research efforts are encouraged and geared at simplifying the cloud environments, improving Hadoop/MapReduce models and security techniques to better-fit scientific data and workflows. This book series "Applications and Developments in Grid, Cloud, and High Performance Computing" features several papers in HPC that are in line with these endeavors. It discusses research findings, gaps, and challenges that exist in the integration of the HPC applications in the grid and cloud environments in addition to other developments.

The HPC environments have witnessed great improvements from the early days of the Cray machines to the current systems that are characterized by massively parallel supercomputers with numerous processors (beyond 50,000 processors), which are opportunistically used in grid environments (e.g. Folding@ home) or deployed in close proximity in cluster or centralized formation of multi-core processors. To manage the capability of these massive and enhanced systems especially the computational and communication resources as well as the hardware failures, HPC operating systems have undergone major transformations in capacity. Linux still remains the operating system of choice for the management of the HPC environments, although other systems are also used. Major strides are also being recorded in HPC architectures such as Cyclops64 (IBM) architecture and exaflops supercomputers. The number of special purpose systems and general-purpose graphic processors (GPGPUs) continues to increase in addition to conventional processors such as SPARC-based designs. These developments portend great strides in high performance computing that will be integrated in the emerging cloud environments. As a matter of fact, these systems will be harnessed and deployed in compute intensive endeavors such as geological, biological and physical simulations as well as climate and weather research.

In sync with these research strides are the current interest and concerns about cloud adoption, as the capability of the cloud to efficiently and cost-effectively deliver information and services become more apparent. The decision of which services to deliver locally or in the cloud is not a light one, as it must be carefully considered by organizations before the leap into the cloud space. In this vein, it is worthwhile to note the description and comprehensive framework about cloud computing provided by the US National Institute of Standards and Technology (NIST) and the European Commission (Advances in Clouds – Research in Future Cloud Computing) for cloud types (private and public), adoption, interoperability and security standards.

The new advances in HPC, grid and cloud computing will greatly impact IT services resulting in improved computational and storage resources as well as service delivery. To keep educators, students, researchers and professionals abreast of advances in the cloud, grid and high performance computing, this book series *Applications and Developments in Grid, Cloud, and High Performance Computing* will provide coverage of topical issues in the discipline. It will shed light on concepts, protocols, applications, methods and tools in this emerging and disruptive technology. The book series is organized in five sections, covering wide-ranging topics such as: (1) Introduction (2) Scheduling (3) Algorithms and Optimization (4) High Performance Computing and (5) Applications.

Section 1. *Introduction* addresses the security concerns regarding the adoption of the emerging cloud technology by organizations. It is now obvious to cloud developers and vendors that adoption by users is a major component of the development process. Several surveys detail industry concerns about the security of data hosted in public clouds despite the attractive propositions of cloud computing. The chapter *Risk Assessment for Cloud-Based IT Systems* by Yuyu Chou and Jan Oetting presents a systematic approach to manage the risks with a full analysis of cloud computing solutions. To strengthen this analysis, a case study is presented whereby a Google App Engine Platform is assessed based on ISO/IEC 27002 and OWASP Top 10 Risk List. It is anticipated that a good knowledge of the risks associated with cloud solutions, will help companies to take well-informed decisions before launching into the cloud space as cloud solutions can be initiated with assuring security, by relying on a robust e-trust relationship.

Section 2. *Scheduling,* an NP hard problem, is an important and dominant process in the complex grid and cloud environments. A poorly executed task assignments or resource management can degrade grid middleware performance. Consequently, the development of efficient job-scheduling techniques still remains an active research area in computational grids and clouds as the number of pertinent research papers can attest to. Zahid Raza and Deo Vidyarthi, in the chapter *A Computational Grid Scheduling Model to Maximize Reliability Using Modified GA,* present a technique that schedules a modular job to those resources that suit the job requirements in terms of resources while offering the most reliable environment. The paper applies Modified Genetic Algorithm (MGA), which is an elitist selection method based on the two threshold values, to improve the solution. The algorithm partitions the current population of jobs in three categories: the fittest chromosomes, average fit chromosomes and the ones with worst fitness. In the elimination process, the worst chromosomes are dropped, while the fittest chromosomes of the current generation are mated with the average fit chromosomes of the previous generation to produce offspring. The authors were able to compare the simulation and performance results with other similar grid scheduling models under various grid conditions.

In another chapter, *A Novel System Oriented Scheduler for Avoiding Haste Problem in Computational Grids,* researcher Ahmed Saleh proposes a high throughput grid scheduler that can be used to resolve the haste problem in grid environment. The haste problem is a common occurrence in grid environment in which all queuing tasks cannot be scheduled successfully. Some jobs may fail to start or complete execution due to the allocation of unsuitable workers. To avoid the haste problem, the new proposed system-oriented scheduler selects the most suitable worker to execute a given job, thus minimizing the turnaround time for a set of grid tasks. The researcher presented experimental results to demonstrate the efficacy of this scheduler that outperforms traditional grid schedulers. In another study, *Dynamic Dependent Tasks Assignment for Grid Computing*, researchers Meriem Meddeber and Belabbas Yagoubi proposed a scheme to tackle resource management issues involving dependent tasks assignment. The researchers designed a hybrid assignment strategy of dependent tasks in grids, which integrate static and dynamic assignment technologies. The aim is to arrive at a method of task assignment that could achieve minimum response time and reduce the transfer cost, inducing by the tasks transfer respecting the dependency constraints. This is because in grid environment, task execution time is dependent on the machine to which it is assigned, and task precedence constraints can be represented by a directed acyclic graph.

Section 3. *Algorithms and Optimization* provide powerful tools to manage the processes, jobs and different organizational policies in the grid environments. Optimization comes in handy in extracting the best solution from the set of available alternatives. In this section, several researchers present effective algorithms and best available alternatives, mirroring the intensity of research on this topic. Rahaman, Thulasiram, and Thulasiraman, in *Performance Analysis of Sequential and Parallel Neural Network Algorithm for Stock Price Forecasting,* used a neural network Backpropagation technique for stock price forecasting of Great West Life. The researchers reduced the training time of this technique by using different parallel and multithreaded neural network algorithms on both shared memory architecture (OpenMP) and distributed memory architecture (MPI). The performance and accuracy of the algorithms were compared with traditional autoregression model. In another study, researchers Amrit Agrawal and Pranay Chaudhuri, in *An Algorithm for Task Scheduling in Heterogeneous Distributed Systems Using Task Duplication,* developed scheduling algorithms for parallel systems based on heuristics, with the primary goal of minimizing the overall execution time of the application or schedule length. The researchers demonstrated the reduction of the overall execution time of the tasks using task duplication on top of the Critical-Path-On-a-Processor (CPOP) algorithm.

There are other chapters in this section with novel algorithmic approaches. Researchers Apurva Shah and Ketan Kotecha described a useful parallel computational model that mimics the foraging behavior of ants in *ACO Based Dynamic Scheduling Algorithm for Real-Time Multiprocessor Systems*. The algorithm provides balance between exploration and exploitation along with robustness and simplicity of individual agent. The results obtained during simulation are measured in terms of Success Ratio (SR) and Effective CPU Utilization (ECU) and compared with the results of Earliest Deadline First (EDF) algorithm in the same environment. This new algorithm performs wells both in under-loaded and over-loaded conditions. In another study, that is, directed at cost and energy saving schemes for servers in grid/cloud centers, researchers Yang, Kuo, and Yeh in *Dynamic Rightsizing with Quality-Controlled Algorithms in Virtualization Environments* proposed an algorithm to minimize the number of active energy-consuming servers that also maintains a service quality through the Mt/M/Vt strategy of queuing theory. The researchers map the complicated formula of the energy-saving mechanism to an approximation equation and design the fast decidable algorithms for calculating the right size of virtual machines in constant time complexity for power management systems.

In an endeavor to better manage location update operations in ad hoc and distributed networks, researchers Amjad Osmani, Abolfazl Haghighat, and Shirin Khezri, in *Location Update Improvement Using Fuzzy Logic Optimization in Location Based Routing Protocols in MANET,* introduced a new schema based on fuzzy logic optimization. The schema decreased the update management overhead without significant loss of query success probability. The researchers used one-hop-chain-technique for Auto compensation, which are updatable when the nodes cross a grid boundary. The proposed method uses a dynamic grid area that solves the ping-pong problem between grids. Simulation results show that these methods are effective and not limited to a special network grid ordering, and can be used in every hierarchical ordering like GLS if the ordering can be mappable on these methods.

Furthermore, other researchers in this section devised algorithms and optimization schemes to improve performance in mobile grid and sensor networks. The authors Shrivastava, Tomar, and Bhadauria, in

Performance Evaluation of Reactive Routing in Mobile Grid Environment, modified AODV (ad hoc on demand distance vector)) by varying some of the configuration parameters used in the algorithm. AODV operates as an on-demand (reactive) algorithm capable of both unicast and multicast routing. The modified protocol i.e. A-AODV has been compared with AODV in grid environment. The simulation results show that A-AODV is able to achieve high throughput and packet delivery ratio with reduced average end-to-end delay. In a similar development, an attempt was made to solve the problem of adequate coverage for distributed wireless sensor networks. Researchers Khezri, Faez, and Osmani, in *An Intelligent Sensor Placement Method to Reach a High Coverage in Wireless Sensor Networks*, applied the modified binary particle swarm optimization algorithm for solving the sensor placement in distributed sensor networks. A discrete PSO was adapted for the project. The proposed algorithms consider two factors: the complete coverage and the minimum costs to solve the problem. The simulation outcomes confirm the success of the new method in sensor placement as well as its efficiency compared to other methods like Simulated Annealing (SA), PBIL and LAEDA.

Section 4. *High Performance Computing* continues to serve organizations requiring high bandwidth and compute intensive capabilities despite moves to integrate with cloud computing. Scientists and engineers increasingly run a variety of HPC applications to leverage cloud offerings such as Amazon EC2 in solving biochemical and physical problems. Presenting applications in HPC environments are researchers Arnab Nandi and Sumit Kundu in *Energy Efficient Packet Data Service in Wireless Sensor Network in Presence of Rayleigh Fading*, and researchers Amitabha Chakrabarty and Martin Collier in *Cost Efficient Implementation of Multistage Symmetric Repackable Networks*. Other researchers who address HPC issues in their works are Rai, Negi, and Wankar in *Using Machine Learning Techniques for Performance Prediction on Multi-Cores* and Shah, Parmar, Kothari, and Dasgupta in *Performance Evaluation of Full Diversity QOSTBC MIMO Systems with Multiple Receive Antenna*.

This section features further articles demonstrating the current developments in HPC applications. Researchers Awwad, Al-Sadi, Haddad, and Kayed in the paper *Structural Outlooks for the OTIS-Arrangement Network*, showcase a general method for algorithm development on the Optical Transpose Interconnection Systems (OTIS) that is implemented in HPC platform. The project shows how to map a wide class of algorithms (e.g. linear algebra, divide-and-conquer types of algorithms, sorting, and FFT) into the OTIS-Arrangement Network. The study confirms the viability of the OTIS-AN as an attractive alternative for large-scale parallel architectures.

In the chapter *High Performance Computing Design by Code Migration for Distributed Desktop Computing Grids* by Makoto Yoshida and Kazumine Kojima, the authors describe design methodologies of workload management in distributed desktop computing grids. The authors conducted several code migration experiments with simulation results, and were able determine the transfer policy for computation as well as the location policies. The language for distributed desktop computing was designed to accomplish the design methodologies. In another study, the authors - Abbes, Butelle, and Cerin, in *Parallelization of Littlewood-Richardson Coefficients Computation and its Integration into the BonjourGrid Meta-Desktop Grid Middleware*, show how to parallelize a compute intensive application in mathematics (Group Theory) for an institutional desktop grid platform coordinated by a meta-grid desktop middleware named BonjourGrid. This project parallelizes a sequential program for a multicore CPU, which participates in the computation; and demonstrates the effort for launching multiple instances of the solutions for the mathematical problem with the BonjourGrid middleware. The scientific work starts from a model for the solution of a compute intensive problem in mathematics, to incorporating the concrete model into a middleware and running it on commodity PCs platform managed by an innovative meta-desktop grid middleware.

Section 5. *Applications* features the growth of software applications in different disciplines that leverage the grid and cloud resources. Biology, especially micro-array analysis produces large and massive data sets that require the use of high-speed, high-performance computing or distributed systems like grids and clouds. Researchers Yang and Shih, in *On Construction of Cluster and Grid Computing Platforms for Parallel Bioinformatics Applications*, implemented an experimental distributed computing application for bioinformatics, consisting of basic high-performance computing environments (Grid and PC Cluster systems), multiple interfaces at user portals that provide useful graphical interfaces to enable biologists to benefit directly from the use of high-performance technology, and a translation tool for converting biology data into XML format. Further applications are also recorded in smartphone environments.

The fit of smartphones to cloud technology is becoming obvious to all developers. Cloud technology can manage and provision virtual machine profiles that execute on smartphones. As a growing trend, a virtualized smartphone environment can be launched in which a separate set of managed enterprise applications are available to connect to corporate back-end data systems via VPN. However, the limited physical sizes and battery capacities of the current generation of smartphones requires offloading the large applications on these phones to the cloud. Researchers Hung, Shieh, and Lee, in *Migrating Android Applications to the Cloud*, propose a novel, lightweight application migration mechanism for the users of smartphones to suspend the execution of applications and offload them to the cloud. The researchers also developed a framework to perform Android applications efficiently with virtual phones in the cloud with a virtual storage. The chapter discusses the migration mechanism and evaluates its effectiveness on the Android smartphone. Finally, the researchers Li, Hayes, Baran, Porter, and Schweiger in *A Grid and Cloud Based System for Data Grouping Computation and Online Service*, applied HPC methods to entity resolution or record recognition problem. The pairwise record analysis is known to be cumbersome, thus requiring HPC application. To reduce the number of pairwise record comparisons, blocking techniques are introduced to partition the records into blocks. This chapter introduces the closure problem and describes the design and implementation of a parallel and distributed closure prototype system running in an enterprise grid.

In conclusion, cloud technology is now a reality for agile organizations as HPC/distributed systems are becoming increasingly integrated. This book series captures the surge of research endeavors that are certainly useful to government, industry, institutions, and individuals that are receptive to change. It advances the frontier of science that is impactful to the global economy.

Emmanuel Udoh
Sullivan University, USA

Section 1
Introduction

Chapter 1
Risk Assessment for Cloud-Based IT Systems

Yuyu Chou
Berlin Institute of Technology, Germany

Jan Oetting
Consileon Business Consultancy GmbH, Germany

ABSTRACT

The use of Cloud Computing services is an attractive option to improve IT systems to achieve rapidly and elastically provisioned capability, and also to offer economic benefits. However, companies see security as a major concern in migrating to the Cloud. To bring clarity in Cloud security, this paper presents a systematic approach to manage the risks and analyzes the full range of risk in Cloud Computing solutions. Furthermore, as a study case, Google App Engine Platform is assessed based on ISO/IEC 27002 and OWASP Top 10 Risk List in this paper. Knowing the risks of Cloud solutions, companies can execute well-informed decisions on going into the Cloud and build their Cloud solutions in a secure way, relying on a robust e-trust relationship.

INTRODUCTION

Many companies have problems with existing systems. They need greater business agility, cost effective, stable IT infrastructures and the operation can keep pace with fast growing technology and the changing environment. However, maintenance of the current environment accounts for over 70% of the IT budget, leaving less than 30% available for new projects (Bain, Read, Thomas, & Merchant, 2009). Cloud Computing is the model that can fit their requirements, for enabling con- venient, on-demand network access to a shared pool of configurable computing resources that can be rapidly provisioned and released with minimal management effort or service provider interaction (Mell & Granc, 2009). A Cloud is the type of parallel and distributed system consisting of a collection of inter-connected and virtualized computers that are dynamically provisioned and presented as one or more unified computing re- sources based upon the service level agreements established through negotiation between service provider and service user (Buyya, Yeo, Venugopal,

DOI: 10.4018/978-1-4666-2065-0.ch001

Broberg, & Brandic, 2009). However, the security standards for Cloud Computing forms slowly, if without cautious understanding the know-how and the risk evaluation when we adapt the systems based on Cloud structures, it will become a disaster.

Not all risks of Cloud Computing can be addressed on a global level. Individual risks arise at different Cloud solutions. Before going into Clouds, a company needs to know the specific of the individual Cloud providers. Therefore, it will be very helpful if research institutes will analyze and publish individual risk profiles after intensive analysis. This paper performed such an analysis for the Google Cloud Platform (called "Google App Engine") for industry as a reference first. This analysis is based on the security domains of ISO/IEC 27002 Standard (International Organization for Standardization, 2007) and OWASP Top 10 (OWASP, 2010) risks in web application to check if using the Google Platform can alleviate these risks.

RISK MANAGEMENT

Though an IT system can be evaluated in terms of functionality, completeness, consistency, accuracy, performance, reliability, usability, fit with the organization, and other relevant quality attributes (Hevner, March, Park, & Ram, 2004), if the system is not secure enough, the whole enterprise will be exposed to the high risk of getting into vulnerable situations. Despite the promising business model, security is a major concern that could limit the Cloud Computing paradigm's impact (Jaeger & Schiffman, 2010). Owing to the fact that customers must perform their applications, or store their data on the Internet, moving application servers to Clouds means a considerable risk for enterprises. How to build up the trust in the remote execution becomes the biggest challenge. Identifying threats and vulnerabilities plays a crucial role in securing the system. Consequently, we need a

systematic approach to identify the appropriated security requirements on Clouds which can fulfill the Business Strategy and reduce risks to create an effective and efficient IT system.

Security Risk management analyses what can happen and what the possible consequences can be, before deciding what should be done and when, to reduce the risk to an acceptable level (International Organization for Standardization, 2008). Risk should be identified, assessed, and monitored regularly.

The level of risk should be estimated by the likelihood of incident scenario, mapped against the estimated negative impact (Catteddu & Hogben, 2009). After assessing the risks, priority order for the risks and treatments should be also established before hosting the system on the Cloud. The risk executive function does not make authorization decision; rather, the intent is to provide visibility into the decisions of authorizing officials and a holistic view of risk to the organization beyond that risk associated with the operation and use of individual information systems (The National Institute of Standards and Technology, 2008). Companies can follow the process that suggest by ISO/ IEC 27005, as Figure 1 shows.

RISK ANALYSIS IN CLOUD COMPUTING SOLUTIONS

The massive concentrations of resources and data present a more attractive target to attackers, but Cloud-based defenses can be more robust, scalable and cost-effective (Catteddu & Hogben, 2009) if well-organized. Outsourcing IT services has been a highly controversial topic for many years. Not only costs should be considered but also other relevant aspects. To evaluate the risks before hosting a solution on the Cloud, customers can reference the items, which shows the main considerations and the detail analysis are as below:

Figure 1. Information security risk management process (Source: International Organization for Standardization, 2008)

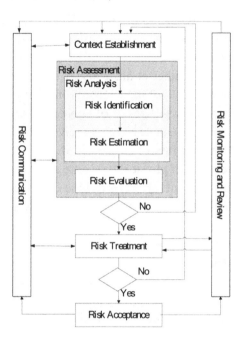

- **Investment cost:** Typical *aaS offerings are over a public network, and without purchasing hardware and serve via the Internet. The service is rented, not purchased, the cost is controlled, paid by use and the capital investment can be zero (Sun, 2009). Software is easier to install, maintain, and update than client-based computing, which requires installing and configuring software and updating it with each new release, as well as revising other programs with every update (Parikh, 2009). However, carefully balance all costs and benefits associated with Cloud Computing and the conventional system in both the short and long terms is necessary. Underestimating or overestimating the provision of resources will lead to decrease in revenue. Switching cost, sunk cost, exit cost and hidden cost, which including support, disaster recovery, application modification, data loss insurance,

etc., are especially important and need to be estimated. In addition, most of the Cloud applications are not portable across Clouds. All *aaS developers need familiar with specific APIs when deploy and manage the platforms. Software as a Service (SaaS) typically does not offer APIs other than for basic export and import functionality, which uses browsers or scripts and web URI manipulation methods (Mather, Kumaraswamy, & Latif, 2009). Therefore, this will create lock-in issues after deploying the system on the Cloud.

- **Governance and Controllability:** Although Cloud solutions can be deployed efficiently in time and cost, Cloud providers usually offer a single scalable solution for all its clients as limited customization support. For example, to make the business with global providers such as Amazon or Google, customers need to accept the unique Service Level Agreement (SLA). Therefore, losing the capability of dominate and monitor IT systems will cause great consideration for CIO and managers. To compare the basic three *as a service, SaaS is relatively more secure than Platform as a Service (PaaS) and Infrastructure as a Platform (IaaS). For that reason, it also losses more control as is shown in Figure 2. Large enterprises are not willing to support the Cloud concept if the provider cannot guarantee the locations of processing and how the system is protected. However, Cloud Computing is one type of distributed system. An important goal of a distributed system is to hide the fact that its processes and resources are physically distributed across multiple computers, which including access, location, migration, relocation, replication, concurrency, failure, and persistence (Tanenbaum, & van Steen, 2001). Hence, data may be stored and/or processed in high risk jurisdictions, if this information is not available to Cloud customers. Furthermore, external providers or partners may also outsource their services by using other suppliers. It makes the supply chain and trust relationships even more complicated and difficult to manage. Depending on the nature of the services provided or the information shared, it may be unwise for organizations to wholly trust the provider or partner (The National Institute of Standards and Technology, 2008). In consequence of these issues, the control and management methods need to be defined and negotiated as detailed as possible in Service Level Agreements.

- **Availability and Integrity:** Integrity, and availability depend on some factors, including the Cloud Service Provider's (CSP's) data centre architecture (load balancers, networks, systems), application architecture, hosting location redundancy, diversity of Internet service providers (ISPs), and data storage architectures (Mather et al., 2009). In a traditional IT environment, hardware breakdown can inflict enormous damage if there is no failover capability. Cloud Computing by contrast, keeps availability high with various methods that stay affordable through economies of scale (T-Systems, 2010). Hence, failures usually can be management. Each potential risky aspect should be carefully considered, realized, tested and then negotiated these as part of the SLAs when customers engage with Cloud providers, for example, PaaS applications may rely on other third-party web services components. Making sure the system can be availability and robust, to understand the dependency of the third-party services is essential.

- **Data Protection:** Data need to be protected against compromise in all phases of the information lifecycle, namely, data in transit, processing, at rest and also rema-

nence. Nowadays, Cloud providers use all kind of virtualisation techniques to allow dynamic scaling. Resources are shared at the network level, host level, and application level. Instead of physical separation, customer services are only separated logically (Mather et al., 2009). Consequently, in the event of the confiscation of physical hardware as a result of subpoena by law-enforcement agencies or civil suits, the centralisation of storage as well as shared tenancy of physical hardware means many more clients are at risk of the disclosure of their data to unwanted parties (Catteddu & Hogben, 2009). Hence, we need to amend traditional data protection methods in each data life cycle when adapting Cloud solutions. For example, data at rest used by a Cloud application is generally not encrypted, because encryption will be hard to index or search. But need to keep in mind, when data is being processed, Cloud providers can still know the data even if it is encrypted in storage and transmission. In addition, any algorithm that is proprietary should absolutely be avoided, included indexing, masking, redaction, and truncation because there are no accepted standards. The only data protection technique for which there are recognized standards is encryption, such as the NIST Federal Information Processing Standards (FIPS), or at least informally accepted by the cryptographic community should be used.

- **Malicious Attack:** Criminals continue to leverage new technologies to improve their reach, avoid detection, and improve the effectiveness of their activities. Successful attacks on IT systems can result in great harm in industry. Nowadays, Cloud Computing providers are actively being targeted, partially because their relatively weak registration systems facilitate anonymity, providers' fraud detection capabilities are limited (Cloud Security Alliance, 2010), can cause economic denial of service, and also can poach confidential data. We can reference the risk list of OWASP Top 10 (2010) critical web application security risks, to know the latest attack trend. Furthermore, discretion is the better part of valour. Customers may not only suffer external attacks, internal environment in Cloud service provider and customer side may also have malicious insiders. This is a serious matter should not be taken lightly!

- **Management Interface Compromise:** Although there are definitely security challenges with Cloud Computing, none of those challenges are caused specifically unique by Cloud Computing (Mather et al., 2009). Most organizations in the developing world lack IT security measures (Kinyanjui, 2009), for example, about 3 million SMEs in Brazil lacked antivirus software in 2006 (Kshetri, 2010). Therefore, Cloud-based systems are good solutions for them to build up a more robust and lower cost system. In spite of security vulnerability, patch, and configuration may be managed better in Cloud-based solutions, Cloud Computing providers expose a set of software interfaces or APIs that customers use to manage and interact with Cloud services. However, it can be a great risk for PaaS and IaaS delivery models, if the management responsibilities remain with the customers. Therefore, Cloud solutions should follow the standards, e.g., ISO/IEC 27002 type control, BSI (Bundesamt für Sicherheit in der Informationstechnik) 100-x Standard, and CobiT.
- **Policy:** In general, Cloud service providers do not publicly share information related to their host platforms, operating systems, and the processes that are in place to secure the hosts, since hackers can exploit that information when they are trying to intrude

into the Cloud service (Parikh, 2009). In addition, the multi-tenant service is one proposal fits all operating business, which means providers typically offer a standard Service Level Agreement for all customers; it may not be amenable if the hardening procedures conflict or does not meet the requirements of the users. Hence, in the Service Level Agreement of some global companies show the responsibility of host security is belong to them, e.g., Salesforces.com, and Google App Engine. However, it is impossible to list all of the responsibilities in contracts regarding to each role, process, and even in security incident. Also the regulations, standards, laws are currently not well defined for Cloud business. Therefore, to mitigate the potential risk of making wrong decisions, customers should ask vendors to share information under a nondisclosure agreement (NDA) or simply ask for certification for their level of security according to the established security management framework standard ISO/IEC 27001, SysTrust, Cobit, etc., before signing the service-level agreements because it is very hard to negotiate with vendors after signing the agreements.

- **Audit and Compliance:** Audit forces better IT system management. Running systems on Clouds may help for data and evidence-gathering. However, lack of standard technologies and solutions, official certification usually cannot available to customers. Moreover, audit cannot execute, usually because is not only lack of completeness and transparency in terms of use, but also refuse or cannot be executed by providers. For example, some services use open source hypervisors or customised versions, which cannot come up to Common Criteria certification, which is a fundamental requirement for some organizations (e.g., US government agencies).

5

• **Legal:** Legal issues perhaps are the most complex topic in Cloud Computing. Most of laws and regulations are not specific for Cloud-based services, not to mention what or how should be done. Failure to comply with a data protection law may lead to administrative, civil and also criminal sanctions, which vary from country to country. This problem is exacerbated in the case of multiple transfers of data e.g., between federated Clouds (Catteddu & Hogben, 2009). For example, Cloud providers from developing countries such as China and India might face barriers to internationalization activities, particularly because security is among the most important concerns for Cloud adoption (Kshetri, 2010). Do not need to mention it will increase the investment risk when we consider the governmental control. The worst case is that a country imposes or lifts a related ban in the near future, then the Cloud-based solutions become illegal and the influence coverage may extend worldwide immediately. In addition, in the event of a suspected security breach, the customers can take an image of a live virtual machine or virtual components for offline forensic analysis, leading to less down-time for analysis (Catteddu & Hogben, 2009). But this also increases the risk of leaking out the confidential data.

In the definition of NIST, there are four type of Cloud Computing, deployment models, namely, Private Cloud, Public Cloud, Community Cloud, and Hybrid Cloud. Due to Community Cloud and Hybrid Cloud are the composition of Private, Public Clouds and exist on premise, and each model may have variance. Therefore, this paper shows the risk comparison base on the previously described only among public, private cloud and conventional IT system solutions in Figure 3. The Private Clouds deliver some benefits of Cloud Computing with moderate the pitfalls, capitalizing on data security, corporate governance, and reliability concerns. But, organizations must buy, build, and manage them and, as such, do not benefit from lower upfront capital costs and less hands-on management. Therefore, customers need to base on their requirements and evaluations to decide which deployment models are better suitable for them.

Figure 2. Comparison of the losing governance in different services (Source: Matthew Gardiner, CA, Inc)

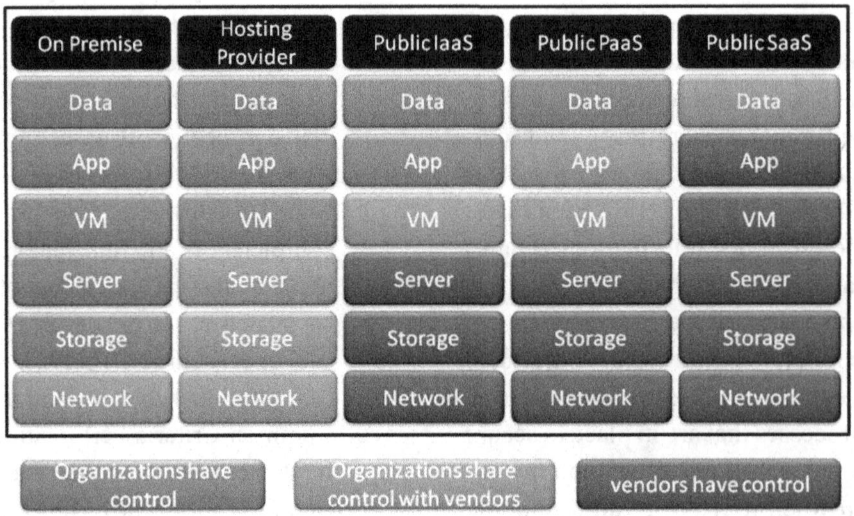

Figure 3.Risk comparison

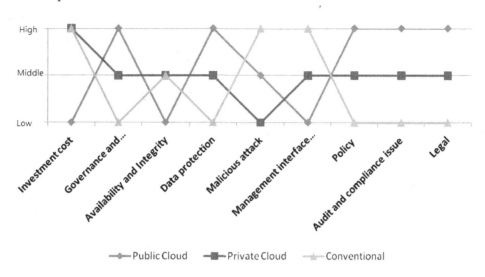

CASE STUDY- GOOGLE CLOUD PLATFORM ASSESSMENT

As mentioned before not all risks of Cloud Computing can be addressed on a global level. Individual risks arise at different Cloud solutions. Before going into Cloud a company needs to know the specific of the individual Cloud provider. Our hope is that research institutes will analyze and publish individual risk profiles after intensive analysis. This paper performed such an analysis for the Google Cloud Platform (called "Google App Engine") for reference. Although this platform is currently in its testing phase (beta), new features will evolve and probably some security controls will change, we still choose this platform because it is the currently most evolved Cloud Platform service with many promising security features.

First part based on ISO 27002 Standard, we check the eleven domains in Google Cloud Platform Google App Engine, because nowadays the ISO 2700x ISO /IEC Standard is the worldwide standard for a security management system. So we assume for the analysis that a company wants to be compliant to this standard. Therefore we checked if the Google platform can fulfill the requirements and what additional efforts the company needs to

take. Specifically for the Cloud environments the Cloud Security provides very helpful information for performing an analysis (Figure 2). The second part, we review the web application risks based on the report of the OWASP Top 10 (2010) to discuss these risks for the Google platform. These analyses are based on not only public available information, but also on our own experiences in a special security test application running in the Google App Engine.

ISO 27002 Assessment

- **Domain 1 Information Security Policy:** Using Cloud services changes IT processing and responsibilities in a major way, it is necessary to come to a strategic IT decision how to use Cloud services. This should be reflected in the customers' Information Security policy. Therefore, here should be addressed, what kind of data may be processed by other companies and in what areas. For the information security policy Cloud services do not differ from hosting services. Management needs to consider that with current technology it is not possible to prevent access to the data from the

Cloud provider even if many providers promise such encryption technology. This decision is independent from the specific platform Google App Engine. You need to be aware of the fact that the Google Cloud service is a public one, and there is no guarantee for the location of processing.

- **Domain 2 Organization of information security:** Using Cloud service doesn't affect this domain.
- **Domain 3 Asset Management:** As required by the ISO 27001 standard (International Organization for Standardization, 2005) data need to be classified. Following the strategic decision done before and documented in the information security policy data and applications may be put to a public Cloud service.
- **Domain 4 Human Resources Security:** A company who relies on Google's services put their data under control of selected Google employees. According to the information available by Google, they only allow very restricted access to their data centers and perform intensive personal background checks for their administrative personal (Google, 2010). Google provides a SAS 70 type II certification for their Google Apps data centers. The formal scope of the audit is not public, but normally includes this part. As with all outsourcing services companies need to build a trust relationship with the service provider.
- **Domain 5 Physical and Environmental Security:** There is no direct information available for the physical security of the Google App Engine Platform. This is probably due to the beta phase of this product. For the sake of this, we need to refer to the information available for their Cloud business suite (Google Apps), where they offer some more detailed information. In general, they don't ensure a certain country

for data processing. They keep the location of their data centers secret and do not allow individual customers' audits as part of their security strategy. For bigger customers (>1.000 users) it is possible to negotiate at least the continent of processing (Koppe, n.d.). They provide some basic information about the layout of their data centers including a video tour in Google Apps. Furthermore, they also provide a certification for SAS 70 Type II, for their internal control system (Google, 2011a). As for human resource security, an ISO 27001 certification would give greater confidence for the physical security.

- **Domain 6 Communications and Operations Management:** As for the physical security, there is only limited information about the internal IT infrastructure available in public (Google, 2010). A general important issue is the attack surface to other customers of the Cloud providers. The design of the Google App Engine has some interesting security aspects. Every application is running in a sandbox that only allows certain API functions via Java or Python. No direct access to memory, filesystem of the system or low level network is possible. Previous attacks to hypervisors for example on Xen or on EC2 need such access to be performed (Ristenpart, Tromer, Shacham, & Savage, 2009). This way Google provides a high security standard against OS injections to get control about system of other customers. So attacks on application running in the Google Cloud can be started only from Google internal system and from outside, not from other customers. Publicly available services are the protocols HTTP, HTTPS and the AUTH. Regarding the operation management, the current and history health status of the Google Environment is publicly visible (Google, 2009).

Figure 4. Cloud Reference Architecture (Source: Cloud Security Alliance, 2010)

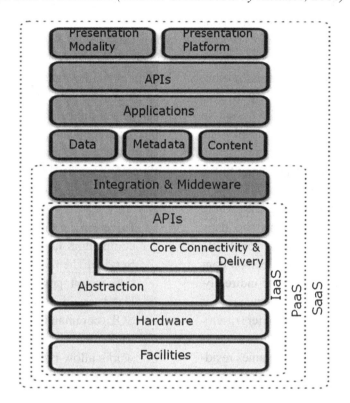

- **Domain 7 Access Control:** As mentioned previously, public access is limited to following services: HTTP, HTTPS and the AUTH. Applications run in the Google App Engine can decide between 3 protocols for authentication: OpenID, Google Authentication (technically OpenID with Google As Referring Party), and OpenAuth. Applications can implement individual access control (either declarative with Standard J2EE mechanism and programmatically). (Caveat: In current in-house solutions this is often forgotten and will cause security issues if just migrated)

- **Domain 8 Information Systems Acquisition, Development and Maintenance:** The platform is maintained by Google as provider. Customers need only to care about the application layer. This can be a big advantage of such a Cloud platform. In Cloud infrastructure services this can lead to incompatibilities to the application layer, if the interface or the implementation of the service changes. It will be interesting to watch, if this can be avoided in the Google platform. Google runs its own security team training engineers and auditing their systems. Their Google App Engine shows a great attitude regarding security as shown later.

- **Domain 9 Information Security Incident Management:** After we had found one security issue and reported it, there was no feedback until the publication deadline (3 months later) and the security issue was still present in the Cloud platform.

- **Domain 10 Business Continuity Management:** The complete infrastructure is redundant, with other data centers that can take over the job. This is one part that Cloud Computing is all about, and Google is no exception there.

- **Domain 11 Compliance:** Is it possible to use the Google Cloud platform for your company? This question cannot be answered without regarding the country's regulations and laws. For this reason, we being a IT research group will give an overview of the current discussion in Germany. Probably the biggest legal issue for Cloud services is the privacy protection law. In Europe personal data belong to the person whose data are processed. This is different from nations like the U.S. where the processing company owns the data. From this basic assumption personal data may only be processed, if the person concerned agrees either directly or indirectly. If a company lets another company process the personal data of their customers or employees, this is called order data processing" and this is limited to companies residing inside the European Union. Companies who put their data to the Google Platform conclude a contract with Google Ireland Limited. At first glance this seems to be compliant to German law. But it needs to be mentioned that these same data could also be processed by Google Incorporated, U.S. The originating company still is responsible for the complete data processing; they can't ignore the fact that data is processed outside Europe. There is no final judgment if this is legal or not. Beside the personal data there are other data that may not leave German (e.g. some financial data). Google itself has certified its internal control system according to SAS 70 type 2. For a company who wants to be itself compliant to ISO 27001, it would be a very good basis, if the Cloud provider also complied with this standard, a step that Microsoft performed (Microsoft, 2010). Without this certification a company basically would need to audit the security itself which is not allowed by Google.

Test Top 10 Web Applications Risks

Hopefully Cloud Services provided by professional IT providers have a better security profile compared to the standard level reached by many companies. To proof or disprove this thesis, we analyzed the top 10 risks (Table 1) for web applications for an application implemented in the Google Cloud. This analysis assumes the web framework offered by Google (Google Web Toolkit) is used as frontend for the Google App Engine.

- **Injection:** In this area Google shows their competitors how to build a secure Cloud Service. The number 1 attack vector injection is not possible in two main fields. Database injection with special formatted SQL commands causes the majority of hacks of web servers. All modern frameworks allow prevention of this if the programmers work carefully, validate all input and use secure database API. Still programmers are human, so they often don't follow these rules. It is better if the framework provides security regarding this aspect to avoid insecure programming. For Google, this kind of security is already implemented for BigTable-access. The database query language GQL on top of the Google database BigTable doesn't have such weaknesses. The following paragraph proves this statement for the Java using the persistence framework JDO.

First, GQL only allows for query. Create and updating recording is done via the Persistance-API JDO. The Java JDBC API only allows one statement at a time. An attack that adds a second database query can therefore not be performed. So now attacks are already restricted to expanding a query. For SQL injection such expanding is done by adding an expanding filter like ('or 1==1'). This way the result set of the database return more rows. The attacker may access more data than he

Table 1. Overview top 10 risks for web application in Google Cloud

OWASP Top 10 Risks	Risk in Google Cloud- GAE+ GWT
Injection	Partly prevented by platform (Database, OS)
Cross-Site Scripting (XSS)	-If limit to declarative layout, can be prevented -Additional Attack vector for Ajax
Broken Authentication and Session Management	Insecure Logout (affects Google Authentication and OpenID)
Insecure Direct Object References	Responsibility of application layer
Cross-Site Request Forgery (CSRF)	Responsibility of application layer
Security Misconfiguration	Configuration only in application layer (especially SSL), critical for external interfaces
Insecure Cryptographic Storage	There is no generic secure storage. OpenID can be used for authentication
Failure to Restrict URL Access	Responsibility of application layer (option available)
Insufficient Transport Layer Protection	SSL and Secure Data Connector available
Unvalidated Redirects and Forwards	Responsibility of application layer

is authorized to or may also log in without an account if the login procedure has a security failure. The left side parameter in GQL must be always an existing column name. Also, if combining two Selection-Statements, the left side parameter must be the same as before. Secondly, if combine two selection criteria, the second selection statement only allows the EQUAL-Operation. The number of combinations is restricted to 32. This way an effective SQL injection attack is not feasible. Every application running in the Cloud is limited to a white listed Java or Python API (Google, 2011b), that doesn't allow access to the file system, to low level network functions or arbitrary memory. This way the standard attacks against the virtualization environment cannot be performed.

- **Cross Site Scripting:** Many modern frameworks offer automated escaping of output. So if the layout is not based on the input, these frameworks provide sufficient security against Cross Site Scripting. With the concept of declarative layout realized in the UI-Binder-Framework, Google offers a comfortable way of preventing Cross Site Scripting. The fact remains, programmers often try to work around such framework some fancy or required feature. As other framework programmers have the freedom to build layout the way they want and may omit arbitrary HTML. That is the reason why cross site scripting still remains Top 2 Risk for web applications. Therefore, an organization has to take responsibility and check the application in deep for such exceptions as before. One thing a company can do, are audits. It is feasible to facilitate secure program are some organizational processes that forces a security discussion for every such case. This way, programmers learn to take the safe way.

- **Broken Authentication and Session Management:** Google App Engine uses in the default scenario OpenID as the authentication protocol. Analyzing the implementation we found that Google made a serious mistake in the App Engine and also in their complete product suite. Logging off a user, the session still remains valid on the server side. This way an attacker who steals a session cookie of a user (e.g. via WLAN in an Internet café) can still use the session even after the victims have logged out. Three months after reporting this issue there is still no feedback from Google and no change in the system.

- **Insecure Direct Object References.** This remains in the responsibility of the application layer.

- **Cross-Site Request Forgery (CSRF):** This remains in the responsibility of the application layer.
- **Security Misconfiguration:** The concept of a standardized J2EE container run by Google reduces the necessary configuration to a minimum. This way the main configuration is about using SSL and the authentication protocol. It can get complicated again if the application running in the Google Cloud needs to communicate with existing software. This case needs to be discussed individually.
- **Insecure Cryptographic Storage:** Other application servers like the IBM product Websphere Application Server offer so called "Secure Storages" that allows to store credentials in a secure way. This storage is maintained by an administrator. The application does not need to manage these credentials itself, so credentials handling is partly outside of the application responsibility and therefore not under control of the application development team. Such a feature is missing in the App Engine.
- **Failure to Restrict URL Access:** This remains in the responsibility of the application layer.
- **Insufficient Transport Layer Protection:** Google offers usage of SSL for communication. This is sufficient. For communication with other system a component called Secure Data Connector (SDC) can be installed in the DMZ of a company that functions as a gateway to the internal system. The security of this depends on the implementation and needs also to be supervised by an architect with knowledge in the security area.
- **Unvalidated Redirects and Forwards:** This remains in the responsibility of the application layer.

As our analysis showed Google chooses to provide a managed Cloud Service in a quite strict way and provides an environment that can exclude many common attacks. This way the Google Cloud provides a technically more secure environment compared to current industry standard. However, migrating existing software to this Cloud Service requires more effort due to the security restrictions. Their competitors (e.g. Amazon or Microsoft) offer less managed and structured services, this way providing a smoother way towards the Cloud. In addition, from a compliance viewpoint, Google is nevertheless far behind the leading competitors who can already show up ISO/IEC 27001 certifications.

CONCLUSION

Organizations can take the benefit of using Cloud Services and transfer liability to the providers, but not accountability. Every instance of trust in Cloud Computing involves taking a risk and trusting in machines, protection methods, and sociotechnical systems to hedge against future threats (Miller, Voas, & Laplante, 2010). The risk and threat profile in Cloud Computing is different from conventional on premised IT systems. Some specific risks, especially handing over control to a Third Party, are intrinsically added by Cloud Paradigm. For other risk profile of individual Cloud providers should be analyzed as done in this paper for the Google Platform. Currently we lack mature security Cloud Computing standards, metrics and measurements, but there are still some comprehensive security frameworks and generic standards (such as the ISO 2700x series, NIST guidelines, etc.) that providers and companies should refer to and follow. To sum up, companies need a clear policy addressing what kind of data may be processed by other companies and in what areas. Based on the policy and guided by risk management throughout the IT system life cycle, the IT can take the advantage of Cloud Computing and also support the mission of enterprises without hesitation.

REFERENCES

Bain, S. A., Read, I., Thomas, J. J., & Merchant, F. (2009). *Advantages of a dynamic infrastructure: A closer look at Private Cloud TCO, from IBM Rep.* Retrieved from http://ftp://public.dhe. ibm.com/common/ssi/ecm/en/zsw03126usen/ ZSW03126USEN.PDF

Buyya, R., Yeo, C. H., Venugopal, S., Broberg, J., & Brandic, I. (2009). *Future generation computer system.* Amsterdam, The Netherlands: Elsevier.

Catteddu, D., & Hogben, G. (2009). *Cloud computing, benefits, risks and recommendations for information security.* Retrieved from http://www. net-security.org/secworld.php?id=8531

Cloud Security Alliance. (2010). *Top threats to cloud computing.* Retrieved from http://www. cloudsecurityalliance.org/topthreats/csathreats. v1.0.pdf

Google Inc. (2009). *App engine.* Retrieved from http://code.google.com/status/appengine

Google Inc. (2010). *Security whitepaper Google Apps messaging and collaboration products.* Retrieved from http://static.googleusercontent. com/external_content/untrusted_dlcp/www. google.com/zh-TW//a/help/intl/en/admins/pdf/ ds_gsa_apps_whitepaper_0207.pdf

Google Inc. (2011a). *Security and privacy.* Retrieved from http://www.google.com/support/a/ bin/answer.py?answer=60762

Google Inc. (2011b). *The JRE class white list.* Retrieved from http://code.google.com/appengine/ docs/java/jrewhitelist.html

Hevner, A. R., March, S. T., Park, J., & Ram, S. (2004). Design science in information systems research. *Management Information Systems Quarterly, 28*(1), 75–105.

International Organization for Standardization. (2005). *ISO/ IEC 27001: Information technology -- Security techniques -- Information security management systems -- Requirements.* Retrieved from http://www.iso27001security.com/html/27001. html

International Organization for Standardization. (2007). *ISO/ IEC 27002: Information technology - Security techniques - Code of practice for information security management.* Retrieved from http://www.iso.org/iso/catalogue_ detail?csnumber=50297

International Organization for Standardization. (2008). *ISO/ IEC 27005: Information technology -- Security techniques -- Information security risk management.* Retrieved from http://www.27001. com/products/155

Jaeger, T., & Schiffman, J. (2010). Outlook: Cloudy with a chance of security challenges and improvements. *IEEE Security & Privacy, 8*(1), 77–80. doi:10.1109/MSP.2010.45

Kinyanjui, K. (2009 August 13). *High speed Internet exposes Kenya to cybercrime.* Retrieved from http://www.businessdailyafrica.com

Koppe, N. (n. d.). *Ektosym.* Retrieved from http:// www.ektosym.com/

Kshetri, N. (2010). Cloud computing in developing economies. *IEEE Computer, 43*(10), 47–55.

Mather, T., Kumaraswamy, S., & Latif, S. (2009). *Cloud security and privacy.* Sebastopol, CA: O'Reilly Media.

Mell, P., & Granc, T. (2009 Oct 7). *The NIST definition of cloud computing v15.* Retrieved from http:// www.nist.gov/itl/cloud/upload/cloud-def-v15.pdf

Microsoft. (2010). *Information security management system for Microsoft cloud infrastructure-online services security and compliance.* Retrieved from http://www.globalfoundationservices.com/security/documents/InformationSecurityMang-SysforMSCloudInfrastructure.pdf

Miller, K. W., Voas, J., & Laplante, P. (2010). In trust we trust. *IEEE Computer, 43*(10), 85–87.

OWASP. (2010).. . *Top (Madrid), 10,* Retrieved from http://www.owasp.org/index.php/Top_10_2010-Main.

Parikh, T. S. (2009). Engineering rural development. *Communications of the ACM, 52*(1), 54–63. doi:10.1145/1435417.1435433

Ristenpart, T., Tromer, E., Shacham, H., & Savage, S. (2009). Hey, you, get off of my cloud: Exploring information leakage in third-party compute clouds. In *Proceedings of the 16th ACM Conference on Computer and Communication Security,* Chicago, IL (pp. 199-212).

Sun Microsystems Inc. (2009). *Introduction to cloud computing architecture.* Retrieved from http://webobjects.cdw.com/webobjects/media/pdf/Sun_CloudComputing.pdf

T-Systems. (2010). *White paper security in the cloud.* Frankfurt, Germany: T-Systems International GmbH.

Tanenbaum, A. S., & van Steen, M. (2001). *Distributed systems: Principles and paradigms.* Upper Saddle River, NJ: Prentice Hall.

The National Institute of Standards and Technology. (2008). *NIST 800-39: Managing risk from information systems, an organization perspective.* Retrieved from http://www.nist.gov/index.html

This work was previously published in the International Journal of Grid and High Performance Computing, Volume 3, Issue 1, edited by Emmanuel Udoh and Ching-Hsien Hsu, pp. 1-13, copyright 2011 by IGI Publishing (an imprint of IGI Global).

Section 2
Scheduling

Chapter 2
A Computational Grid Scheduling Model to Maximize Reliability Using Modified GA

Zahid Raza
Jawaharlal Nehru University, India

Deo Prakash Vidyarthi
Jawaharlal Nehru University, India

ABSTRACT

This paper presents a grid scheduling model to schedule a job on the grid with the objective of ensuring maximum reliability to the job under the current grid state. The model schedules a modular job to those resources that suit the job requirements in terms of resources while offering the most reliable environment. The reliability estimates depict true grid picture and considers the contribution of the computational resources, network links and the application awaiting allocation. The scheduling executes the interactive jobs while considering the looping structure. As scheduling on the grid is an NP hard problem, soft computing tools are often applied. This paper applies Modified Genetic Algorithm (MGA), which is an elitist selection method based on the two threshold values, to improve the solution. The MGA works on the basis of partitioning the current population in three categories: the fittest chromosomes, average fit chromosomes and the ones with worst fitness. The worst are dropped, while the fittest chromosomes of the current generation are mated with the average fit chromosomes of the previous generation to produce off-spring. The simulation results are compared with other similar grid scheduling models to study the performance of the proposed model under various grid conditions.

INTRODUCTION

Last few decades have witnessed an enormous development in the area of computing. These advancements have led to availability and use of superior hardware and powerful efficient software.

The developments coupled with the growth in the web technologies have enabled the users at different geographic locations to fetch the information of their need, share their work and most importantly collaborating with others towards a problem solving.

DOI: 10.4018/978-1-4666-2065-0.ch002

Many a times it happens that research groups desire for a high end computational facility which is not available with them either due to the excessive cost or the investment not justifying the cost with respect to its contribution towards the whole research work. Contrary to this, a scenario could be in which a research group owning a high end computational facility but may not be able to exploit it to its full extent. The solution, in such cases, is to have an environment of cooperative engineering in which people can share their information and computational facilities. This need is addressed by a grid which is an aggregation of heterogeneous resources spread over multiple administrative domains. When a user becomes a part of the grid, it enables him to view the grid as a supercomputing computational resource with almost every computational capability available anywhere and allowing him to use them irrespective of his own computational capabilities and physical location. A grid could be of many types depending on the objectives of its usage. A computational grid is dedicated towards compute intense jobs; a data grid manages the storage retrieval and maintenance of data; a bio grid for biological applications and so on (Prabhu, 2008; Tarricone & Esposito, 2005; Taylor & Harrison, 2009).

Grid computing system is different from other computing systems like Distributed Computing Systems (DCS) and Cluster computing. The scale of operation of the grid in terms of the number of nodes involved and the heterogeneity of resources, their management policies and geographical locations is very large as compared to its peers with no Single System Image (SSI). The resources of various computers in a network are used concurrently to solve a single problem in a collaborative fashion. The grid which involves a participation of people and resources at a heterogeneous scale, presents huge challenges due to the varying system wide performance matrix and a common acceptable policy. For a computational grid, these issues may range from handling jobs of varying nature and requirements, services offered, load balancing,

interactive job handling, grid topology, robustness, job allocation, security, reliability, maintenance and commercial feasibility (Vidyarthi, Tripathi, & Sarker, 2001). As scheduling is an NP hard problem, a number of approaches have been proposed in the literature to schedule a job on the grid considering one or the other objectives. Soft computing tools are quite useful for such class of problems where sub-optimal solution is acceptable. Genetic algorithm (GA) is one such tool that is widely used for scheduling problem. GA is different from the conventional optimization techniques as it explores various peaks by considering a set of points evaluated on the basis of an objective function rather than climbing one peak. GA works on the Darwin's theory of "survival of the fittest" by reproducing the fittest members of the past generation to generate the next population. Since the new population is resulted from the best fit members of the past generation it is expected that the new members will be more fit. Thus, over the generations, the fitness of the newer generations keep on improving and the process is repeated till the result saturates. Mutation is used after every few generations to randomly alter the properties of the population, enabling it to come out of the local optima.

Since the grid involves heterogeneity at every level i.e. the computational resources, applications demanding execution, network characteristics enabling communication, the system is always prone to failures. The failure may range from hardware to software. Although many proactive and reactive approaches to deal with these failures are available, it is always desirable that the job should be scheduled with better reliable execution at that moment of time.

A number of job schedulers for the grid are available in the literature with various approaches towards scheduling the jobs. Scheduler to minimize turnaround (Raza & Vidyarthi, 2008a) has been reported. A batch scheduling scheme to minimize makespan and flowtime using Cellular Mementic Algorithms is proposed in Xhafa,

Alba and Dorronsoro (2007). A scheduling model considering the availability of the computational resources, communication delays and the resource reservation is reported in Aggarwal and Aggarwal (2006). A SLA based scheduling scheme proposing an economy driven scheduler on commodity market is presented in Ranjan, Harwood, and Buyya (2006).

Reliability of the execution is also given due importance in the literature with a reliability analysis for grid being done in Dai, Xie, and Poh (2002) and Huedo, Montero, and Llorente (2006) while a reliability based scheduler is presented in Raza and Vidyarthi (2008b, 2010a), with another one using Markov process is proposed in Tian and Yu (2008). Most of these models run short of the scheduling requirements over grid resources in the sense that nature of the job for the resource requirements and interactive job handling was not considered. Even the resource attributes like node speed and existing workload on the nodes have not been considered in the allocation strategy. Further, most of the work focuses on only a few parameters in determining the fitness function thus invariably missing the real grid picture. Majority of the models, reported in the literature, have handled the reliability based scheduling by first scheduling the job and then estimating its reliability rather than scheduling the job on the reliable resources.

GA has been extensively used for many optimization problems. The applications vary from channel allocation for mobile communication (Khanbary & Vidyarthi, 2008; Zomaya & Wright, 2002) to several other applications seeking optimization. Scheduling being an optimization problem has also attracted attention of the GA. GA based scheduler for allocation of jobs over the grid is discussed in Aggarwal, Kent, and Ngom (2005). Minimization of the turnaround for the job submitted has been reported in Raza and Vidyarthi (2009b). Maximization of reliability using GA has been reported in Raza and Vidyarthi (2009c). Many more GA based schedulers optimizing one

or more parameters are available (Amaki, Kita, & Kobayashi, 1996; Nebro, Alba, & Luna, 2006; Grosan, Abraham, & Helvik, 2007; Lin & Wu, 2005; Sarker, Tripathi, Vidyarthi, Rani, & Uehara, 2002; Tripathi, Sarker, Kumar, & Vidyarthi, 2000; Vidyarthi, Tripathi, Sarker, & Yang, 2005; Vidyarthi & Tripathi, 2001; Vidyarthi, Tripathi, Sarker, & Rani, 2003; Gao, Rong & Huang, 2005; Zomaya & Teh, 2001). Multi-objective optimization using NSGA-II for minimizing the turnaround time of the job and maximizing reliability has been reported in Raza and Vidyarthi (2008b, 2009b). Few other models using soft computing tools are also reported. A high level timed Petri net to model the workflow of grid tasks is proposed in Han, Jiang and Luo (2005) and a Game Theoretic approach used in Rzadca, Tryatram, and Wierzbicki (2007).

Since GA works best for the problems where sub-optimal solutions are acceptable. GA itself can be used in many different ways by varying the selection criterion for reproduction, the method of crossover and mutation. Khanbary and Vidyarthi (2009) has proposed a Modified GA (MGA) by proposing a new selection method for the chromosomes of a generation. In the work, they used a threshold selection method to partition the population into three categories viz. the best chromosomes with highest fitness, the ones with average fitness and the ones with fitness worst than the minimum expected value. The average chromosomes of the current generation are preserved to be later mated with the best chromosomes of the next generation. MGA is further used in Raza and Vidyarthi (2009a) to schedule a job on a computational grid to minimize the turnaround time of the job leading to further possibilities of the use of MGA on other similar problems in which threshold can be determined apriori. The current work proposes one such model employing MGA to schedule a job on a grid with the objective of maximizing the reliability of job execution.

The rest of the paper is organized as follows. Next section discusses the working of the GA and the Modified GA scheme followed by the model for scheduler using MGA. The fitness function (cost estimation) used for scheduling the jobs in the grid is elaborated next. Simulation study for the model and the performance comparison with other related models is done to establish the effectiveness of the model. Finally, the paper concludes.

GENETIC ALGORITHM

GA is a soft computing tool used for optimization problems. It works on the basis of natural selection and evolution based on the Darwin's theory of "survival of the fittest". GA works on the set of parameters encoded as chromosomes rather than working on the parameters directly. The encoding of the parameter set depends on the application domain. The chromosomes consist of various genes (alleles). A particular arrangement of genes in a chromosome corresponds to a solution with some fitness value. Based on this fitness value, the chromosomes are rated. The best chromosomes of a generation are selected using the Selection operator and are mated with the remaining population using crossover operator to generate offsprings. Since the offsprings have resulted from best chromosomes, it is expected that they have an improved fitness value as compared to parents. This process is repeated over the generations resulting in an evolving population with an improved fitness. To avoid local optima mutation is effectuated after every few generations to alter the gene pattern randomly. This leads to an unpredicted change in the fitness of the resulting chromosomes which may be fitter or weaker as compared to the previous case. The process stops when the results start saturating (Goldberg, 2007; Mitchell, 1999). A proper selection of chromosomes thus helps in ensuring that the better chromosomes are mated for reproduction. Some popular selection operators, reported in the literature, are Roulette wheel selection, Tournament selection, Sigma selection, Linear ranking selection, Best selection, Random selection etc.

Further, mating of the selected chromosomes can also take place in a number of ways depending on the application requirements. Some of the popular crossover operators in use are Arithmetic, Heuristic, Intermediate, Scattered, Single-point, Multipoint, Uniform crossover etc.

Modified Genetic Algorithm (MGA)

The selection operator defines the criterion in which the chromosomes are selected for mating. Thus selection plays a vital role in deciding the performance of the GA as it provides the seed to the process. Modified Genetic Algorithm (MGA) uses a selection method drawing its inspiration from the mother nature (Khanbary & Vidyarthi, 2009; Raza & Vidyarthi, 2009a). It is a natural practice that while selecting some product e.g. fruits, vegetables, food grain, flowers etc. we check their growth to decide on their use. If the product is ripe enough it is consumed on the very day itself else it is left for few days to get it ripe. The reason is that the product is not ripe enough for consumption today but if given some time may be used in future. The same philosophy is adopted by the MGA. It partitions the current population in three categories according to the fitness of the chromosomes with the two benchmark threshold values Th_1 and Th_2. The values of Th_1 and Th_2 depends on the domain knowledge of the application and represent maximum and minimum expectation. Thus the chromosomes with fitness below Th_2 are rated as the worst chromosomes and are discarded for any further use. This partitioning results in three groups of chromosomes viz. the ones with fittest chromosomes as Pi having fitness equal to or greater than Th_1, the other ones as Q_i with fitness better than or equal to Th_2 but less than Th_1. The set Q_i may not be fit now but are expected to be fit in the coming generations. Remaining chromosomes R_i with fitness values less than Th_2 are considered of no use. The fittest individuals of the current generation, P_i are then mated with Q_{i-1} individuals of the previous

Figure 1. Population partitioning in MGA

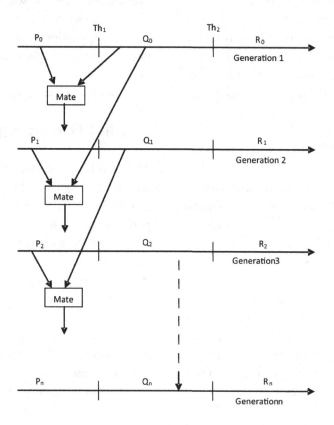

generation, which is expected to become fit by now. This process is repeated for generations till result saturates. Mutation is performed every few generations to avoid local optima. The partitioning of the population and mating mechanism in MGA is presented in Figure 1.

The algorithm of the modified GA can thus be written as in Algorithm 1 (Raza & Vidyarthi, 2009a).

THE MGA BASED SCHEDULER

The proposed work makes use of the MGA scheme to schedule a modular job on the grid with the objective of ensuring maximum reliability to the job execution. This is a two step process; in the first step the grid resources suitable to the job's

requirements are classified. In the second step the selected resources are examined for the reliability they can offer to the job. Finally, the job is submitted to the resource that offers the maximum reliability.

The Scheduler

A grid is an aggregation of heterogeneous resources spread geographically and connected by a high speed network. As shown in Figure 2, a grid is assumed to be a collection of clusters having its specialization. Each cluster, in turn, consists of a number of nodes on which the job can be executed. If the job submitted to the cluster matches the cluster specialization, it can be executed efficiently in comparison to the other clusters. A Cluster Scheduler (CS) allocates the

Algorithm 1. Modified GA algorithm

```
Mod_GA( )
{
 Generate initial population
 Evaluate the fitness of the population
 Partition the population in groups P, Q and R
 Mate the chromosomes of group 'P' with 'Q' randomly and drop R
 For each generation, do
 {
 Evaluate the fitness of the population
 Partition the population
 Mate P_i of the current population with Q_{i-1}
 Perform mutation periodically
 }
 }
```

Figure 2. Computational grid

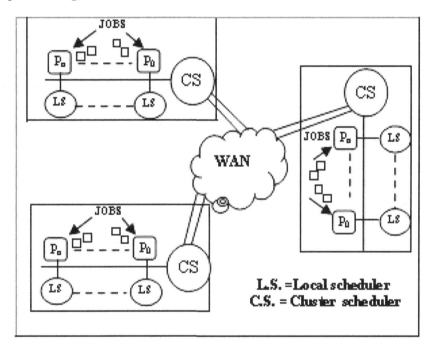

job on the cluster nodes for the job submitted. The CS contains a Cluster Table (CT) to maintain the current state of the cluster in terms of the number of resources available, their attributes and the jobs assigned to the cluster. The system is considered a multi entry point where job can be submitted at any node of any cluster.

The cluster table (CT) contains the following information which is updated periodically;

1. Number of clusters in the grid.
2. Number of nodes in each cluster.
3. Hamming Distance between the nodes of the cluster (intra cluster distance).
4. Processing speed of each node (processor) of the cluster.

Since the grid is a dynamic structure, CT updates dynamically. In case of node failure, the

Figure 3. (a) Chromosome structure (b) A sample chromosome structure

a

Node No. for Module1	Node No. for Module2	Node No. for Module3	Node No. for Module 4	Node No. for Module5

b

2	2	5	1	6

resource entries may be deleted from the cluster table in order to isolate the fault.

The scheduler accepts all types of job submitted in form of modules along with the job attributes like job specialization, number of modules in the job, size of each module, inter module communication (IMC) for interactive modules and the order of execution of these modules as Job Precedence Graph (JPG). During compilation (data flow analysis) the size of the modules and loop constructs in the modules may be determined. The scheduler checks for the clusters of the matching specialization with the job thus helping in an efficient execution of the job. If no specialized cluster is found, it is treated as an ordinary job without special needs.

The various data structures and parameters used in the model are as follows.

1. **Cluster table (CT)**: for each cluster C_n indicating the state of the cluster. It has following attributes: $C_n (P_k, S_n, f_k, T_{prk})$, where P_k is the number of nodes, S_n the cluster specialization, f_k the clock frequency of each node, and T_{prk} the time to finish already existing modules on the nodes.

2. **Job type J_j:** representing the type of the job in terms of its resource requirements for execution.

3. **E_{ijkn}:** Processing time of a module m_i (Size I_i) of job J_j on node P_k of cluster C_n. $E_{ijkn} = I_i * (1/f_k) + n * \alpha (1)$, where, n is multiplication factor to account for the loop construct in the module and α is the average time taken in the loop. E_{ijkn} expresses the time taken to execute a given module on a specific node thus reflecting the node's computational capabilities. It will be smaller for faster nodes and vice versa.

4. **B_{ihj}:** Bytes exchange between modules m_i and m_h of job J_j. This is the IMC cost of the interacting modules.

5. **Chromosome structure:** For the scheduling problem the chromosome structure should reflect the allocation of the job to various nodes. This is ensured by a chromosome structure of size (number of genes) equal to the number of modules in the job. Each gene in the chromosome thus represents the allocation of a node to a module. The order of modules is taken from left to right from first module to the last module as shown in Figure 3(a).

This structure helps in allocation of multiple modules to a single node. As shown in Figure 3(b) using an example of a job with five modules on a cluster with six nodes, the gene positions are interpreted as module 1 being allocated to node 2, module 2 on node 2, module 3 on node 5, module 4 on node 1 and module 5 on node 6.

Notation Used

The Notation used in the proposed model is as follows:

- $\mathbf{J_j}$: Submitted job J with specialization j
- $\mathbf{m_i}$: i^{th} module of the submitted job
- $\mathbf{I_i}$: Number of instructions in the module m_i
- $\mathbf{C_n}$: n^{th} cluster in the grid
- $\mathbf{S_n}$: Specialization of cluster C_n
- $\mathbf{P_k}$: k^{th} node of a cluster
- $\mathbf{f_k}$: Clock frequency of node P_k
- $\mathbf{\lambda_{kn}}$: Failure rate of a node P_k of cluster C_n
- $\mathbf{\mu_{ij}}$: Failure rate of the module m_i of job J_j
- $\mathbf{\zeta_{kln}}$: Failure rate of the link connecting nodes Pk and Pl of cluster C_n
- $\mathbf{R_i}$: Reliability of a module m_i being considered for allocation
- $\mathbf{R_{ki}}$: Reliability offered by a node P_k to module m_i
- $\mathbf{R_l}$: Reliability of the link connecting the two nodes Pk and Pl
- **N**: Number of clusters in the grid
- **M**: Number of modules in a job
- **K**: Number of nodes in the cluster
- **g**: Generation number for the population
- $\mathbf{E_{ijkn}}$: Processing time of a module m_i of job J_j on node P_k of cluster C_n
- $\mathbf{B_{ihj}}$: Communication requirements between interactive modules m_i and m_h of job J_j. It is the form of number of bytes that needs to exchange.
- $\mathbf{D_{kln}}$: Hamming distance between nodes P_k and P_l of a cluster C_n. This corresponds to the number of links between nodes P_k and P_l.
- $\mathbf{X_{ijk}}$: Vector indicating the assignment of module m_i of job J_j on node P_k. It assumes a binary value. It is 1 if the module is allocated to the node and is 0 otherwise.
- $\mathbf{T_{prk}}$: Time to finish the current modules on a node P_k of a cluster C_n. This represents the execution time needed for the execution of the modules of the jobs already assigned to the node.
- $\mathbf{ModRel_{ik}}$: Reliability of execution of module m_i on node P_k. This is the reliability with which a module can be executed on a node and is a function of the reliabil-

ity of the module, reliability of the node on which allocation is being considered and the reliability of the links which participates in data exchange for the interactive modules, residing on different nodes. Thus the same module may have a different reliability of execution over different nodes.

- $\mathbf{ChromRel_{fn}}$: Reliability with which a job can be executed as per the allocation pattern of chromosome f of cluster C_n.
- $\mathbf{f_{gn}}$: Chromosome offering the maximum reliability calculated as the maximum of $ChromRel_{fn}$ over all chromosomes f of cluster C_n for generation g. It gives the chromosome offering the highest reliability till generation g and is considered the best till that point of time. In the last generation f_{gn} becomes the best chromosome offering the maximum reliability with its corresponding allocation pattern for the modules of the job.
- $\mathbf{ClusRel_{jn}}$: Reliability of execution of a job J_j at cluster C_n.
- $\mathbf{GridRel_j}$: Reliability offered by the grid to the job.
- **Sendall**: Send modules of the job along with its attributes to all the clusters for cost evaluation.
- **Receiveall**: Receive the $ClusRel_{jn}$ from all the selected clusters at the calling node.

FITNESS FUNCTION

The objective of the model is to schedule a modular job on the grid resources such that it gets executed with better reliability. To consider the true grid picture for the reliability estimates, the fitness function should take into account the contribution from various factors that effect the reliable execution of the job. It depends on the reliability of the computing resources executing the job, the network over which the interactive modules sends the data in addition to the reliability of the application modules being considered for allocation.

The model first searches for the clusters matching the job's specialization and then schedules the modules of the job on that cluster of the grid which provides the most reliable environment to it. Considering all these factors, the reliability offered to any module m_i being considered for allocation on node P_k and desiring communication with other modules lying on nodes P_l on the same cluster C_n can be written as presented in Exhibit 1.

Where w is the scaling factor to scale the term $\sum_{h=1}^{i-1} (B_{ihj}.D_{k\,ln})\,x_{ijk}.x_{hjl}$ into time unit. This factor represents the communication cost of the module m_i with previous modules m_h and w is the scaling factor to scale this cost into time unit. x_{ijk} is the assignment vector indicating whether a node is assigned a module or not. The assignment is given by

$$x_{ijk} = \begin{cases} 1, & \text{if module } m_i \text{ of Job } J_j \text{ is assigned to node } P_k \\ 0, & \text{otherwise} \end{cases} \quad (3)$$

Thus for a module m_i allocated on node P_k, the T_{prk} of the this node is updated to

$$T_{prk} = T_{prk} + E_{ijkn} + \sum_{h=1}^{i-1} \left(B_{ihj}.D_{kl}\right) x_{ijk}.x_{hjl} \quad (4)$$

For any chromosome f, with all the modules allocated to a node, the reliability offered by the chromosome to the job becomes the equation presented in Exhibit 2.

For each selected cluster, in each generation, the chromosome f_{gn} offering the maximum reliability is treated as the best and for the last generation the reliability offered by f_{gn} becomes the reliability offered by the cluster to the job and is calculated as presented in Exhibit 3.

Therefore, the reliability offered by the grid to the job becomes

$$\text{GridRel}_j = \text{Max}\,(\text{ClusRel}_{jn})\ (\text{for all selected clusters}) \quad (7)$$

Exhibit 1.

$$\boxed{Mod\,\mathrm{Re}\,l_{ik} = \exp\left\{-\left[(m_{ij}+l_{kn})\left[E_{ijkn}.x_{ijk}\right]+(m_{ij}+x_{kl})\left[\sum_{h=1}^{i-1} w(B_{ihj}.D_{kl})x_{ijk}.x_{hjl}\right]+l_{kn}\left[T_{prk}\right]\right]\right\}} \quad (2)$$

Exhibit 2.

$$\boxed{\begin{aligned} \text{ChromRel}_{fn} &= \prod_{i=1}^{k} \text{ModRel}_{ik} \\ Chrom\,\mathrm{Re}\,l_{fn} &= \prod_{i=1}^{k} Mod\,\mathrm{Re}\,l_{ik} \\ &= \prod_{i=1}^{k} \exp\left\{-\left[(\mu_{ij}+\lambda_{kn})\left[E_{ijkn}.x_{ijk}\right]+(\mu_{ij}+\xi_{kl})\left[\sum_{h=1}^{i-1} w(B_{ihj}.D_{kl})x_{ijk}.x_{hjl}\right]+\lambda_{kn}\left[T_{prk}\right]\right]\right\} \end{aligned}} \quad (5)$$

Exhibit 3.

$$ClusRel_{jn} = Max\ (ChromRel_{fn})\ (for\ f=1\ to\ PopSize)$$
$$Clus\operatorname{Re}l_{jn} = Max\left(Chrom\operatorname{Re}l_{fn}\right)\ \left(for\ f=1\ to\ PopSize\right)$$

$$= Max\left(\prod_{i=1}^{k}\exp\left\{-\left[(\mu_{ij}+\lambda_{kn})\left[E_{ijkn}.x_{ijk}\right]+(\mu_{ij}+\xi_{kl})\left[\sum_{h=1}^{i-1}w(B_{ihj}.D_{kl})x_{ijk}.x_{hjl}\right]+\lambda_{kn}\left[T_{prk}\right]\right]\right\}\right) \quad (6)$$

$$= Chrom\operatorname{Re}l_{fgn}$$

THE ALGORITHM

The proposed model schedules the job on the grid with the objective of maximizing the reliability of the job execution. For this purpose a job awaiting allocation is accepted at any node of the participant cluster in the grid in the format mentioned in the section "The MGA Based Scheduler". The scheduler first matches the job's type with the specialization of the clusters of the grid. The matching clusters are selected for further evaluation of the reliability they can offer to the job. This helps in selection of suitable resources for the job as per its requirements.

For the job modules, for the selected clusters, a processing time matrix is generated as per Equation (1). This is followed by the threshold selection for each cluster. The selected lower threshold Th_1 in the model is equal to the reliability offered by a similar model but without using GA (non GA model) (Raza & Vidyarthi, 2010a) whereas the Threshold Th_2 is chosen to be cluster specific.

The non GA model also schedules the job but does not use GA to decide on the allocation pattern. This model evaluates the reliability as per equation (ii) offered to each job module independently and accordingly the module is allocated to the appropriate node, in the present grid conditions. The evaluation of the reliability and the allocation of the modules is done while preserving the module precedence as per the JPDG. With the allocation of each module, the reliability of the node, on which the module is allocated, also gets affected. This

is due to the fact that each allocated job module increases the workload of the node thereby increasing its T_{prk}. This increase, in turn, affects the reliability estimates of the forthcoming modules. When all the modules have been allocated, the reliability offered to the job is estimated as the product of $ModRel_{ik}$ corresponding to the nodes on which the modules are allocated. This, in turn, becomes the reliability offered by the cluster to the job. Finally, the reliability offered by all the selected clusters is compared to select the cluster with the maximum reliability for the job. Since the reliability offered by the finally selected cluster is the best reliability, it becomes the reliability offered to the job by the grid. The allocation pattern corresponds to the parallel execution of the job on the cluster and the corresponding reliability is considered as the threshold Th_2. On the other hand, threshold Th_1 is the reliability obtained by executing the job sequentially on the cluster nodes and is set according to the cluster attributes. Th_1 is obtained by independently executing the modules of the job serially on each node of the selected clusters and then calculating the reliability offered in each case. The lowest value of reliability thus obtained serves as threshold Th_1. The reliability obtained in this manner is very high and need to be relaxed to some extent depending on the domain knowledge of the application. Thus, Th_1 and Th_2 represents two extremes of selection. Using MGA, the chromosomes offering the reliability better than or equal to Th_1 serves as the better chromosomes of a population whereas the chromosomes with reliability less than Th_2 are discarded being least fit.

A population of size Popsize is randomly populated with the chromosomes. Each chromosome corresponds to an allocation pattern for the job modules. For each chromosome, corresponding to its allocation pattern, the reliability $ChromRel_{fn}$ is calculated. The population is then partitioned in three groups P_0, Q_0 and R_0 with the criterion that the chromosomes with $ChromRel_{fn}$ greater than or equal to Th_1 becomes the member of the group P_0, the chromosomes with $ChromRel_{fn}$ greater than Th_2 but less than Th_1 falls in group Q_0 and the rest falling in group R_0 is discarded for any future use.

The chromosomes of the initial population P_0 are then mated randomly with a chromosome of group Q_0 till the population gets restored to Pop-Size. The resulting population is again partitioned in the same manner in three groups named P_1, Q_1 and R_1. Hereafter, in each generation the group P_1 is mated with previous Q 1.e. Q_0 to generate new population till the result converges as explained in Figure 1. Mutation is effectuated after every few generations to avoid local optima.

For each cluster, the chromosome f_{gn} offering reliability $ChromRel_{fn}$ is treated as the best till that generation becoming the reliability offered by the cluster $ClusRel_{jn}$. The maximum value of $ClusRel_{jn}$ out of all the selected clusters finally becomes the reliability offered by the grid $GridRel_j$ to the job and the job is allocated to that cluster. A suitable updation in the Cluster Table (CT) is also done. The algorithm for the job allocation is seen in Algorithm 2.

SIMULATION EXPERIMENT

To test the effectiveness of the model, simulation experiments were conducted using MATLAB version 7 as a platform under varied grid architectures. The input parameters were generated dynamically and are depicted in Table 1.

The simulation experiments were designed to focus on the study of the variation of reliability with generation, effect of the variation of threshold values on the reliability and the effect of the degree of interaction of the job on reliability. Finally, the performance of the model is compared with other related models with the same objective. The experiments are conducted till 70 generations as the result converges satisfactorily during this range.

Effect on Reliability over the Generations

In this set of experiment, the grid architecture is varied to study the effect on reliability offered by selected clusters matching the specialization of the job. Results for few of the experiments are shown in Figures 4 through 6 for the finally selected clusters for job execution. It is observed that the reliability offered by the selected clusters increases with generations till the result saturates. Similar trend is noticed in all other experiments also. Therefore, it can be established that MGA helps in converging the result to meet the desired objective of maximizing the reliability.

Observed from Figures 4 through 6 are that reliability decreases with increase in the number of modules.

Effect of Threshold Values on Reliability

The MGA partitions the population in three groups viz. P, Q and R based on two threshold values Th_1 and Th_2. Thus, it is important to study the effect of the threshold value selection on the reliability obtained. In this set, a simulation experiments were performed first by keeping Th_2 constant and varying Th_1 and vice versa. It is found that if Th_1 is kept as suggested in the algorithm, the scheduler sometimes halts in the very beginning itself with group P falling null. This implies that the threshold selection Th_1 is quite restrictive

Algorithm 2. Algorithm for the job allocation

Alloc (Job)
{
Submit the job in form of modules // *Submit the job in form of modules* m_i *(i = 1 to M) in the*
// *desired format*
Sendall // *Send the jobs to all the clusters for evaluation of their suitability for the job execution*
For all clusters C_n (n = 1 to N) do
{
Compare the specialization of the job with the cluster
// *check for the clusters which matches the job's requirements*
Select the clusters with matching specialization
}
For the selected clusters, do
{
Compute E_{ijkn} // *Calculate the processing time of each node, for all the modules, as per eq.(i)*
Set threshold Th_1 // *equal to the least value of the reliability obtained by executing the job*
// *modules serially on all the nodes*
Set threshold Th_2 // *equal to reliability offered by the non GA model using the same allocation*
// *strategy*
Estimate_Fitness( ) // *Estimate the reliability offered by the selected clusters to the job*
{
Generate population // *Generate chromosomes of size 'PopSize' with number of genes*
// *equal to the number of modules and randomly allocate nodes to these modules*
Prepare groups $P_0/Q_0/R_0$ ( )
{
For all chromosomes, do
{
Compute $ModRel_{ik}$ // *Calculate the reliability of job execution on each node* P_k
// *(k=1 to K) on which allocation has been proposed as per eq.(ii)*
Compute $ChromRel_{fn}$ // *Calculate the reliability offered to the job by each*
// *chromosome as per eq. (v)*
Perform Selection ( ) // *Partition the population in groups* P_0 *and* Q_0, *Discard*
// *remaining chromosomes falling in group* R_0
{
For all the chromosomes 'f' (f =1 to PopSize), do
{
If ($ChromRel_{fn}$ >=Th_1)
Move 'f' to group of chromosomes P_0
If ($ChromRel_{fn}$ <Th_1 and $ChromRel_{fn}$ >Th_2)
Move 'f' to group of chromosomes Q_0
}
}
}
}
Prepare groups $P_0/Q_0/R_0$ ( )
{
For all chromosomes, do
{
Compute $ModRel_{ik}$ // *Calculate the reliability of job execution on each node* P_k *(k=1 to*
// *K) on which allocation has been proposed as per eq.(ii)*
Compute $ChromRel_{fn}$ // *Calculate the reliability offered to the job by each chromosome*
// *as per eq. (v)*
Perform Selection ( ) // *Partition the population in groups* P_0 *and* Q_0, *Discard*
// *remaining chromosomes falling in group* R_0

{

continued on following page

Algorithm 2. Continued

For all the chromosomes 'f' (f =1 to PopSize), do
{
If (ChromRel$_{fn}$ >=Th$_1$)
Move 'f' to group of chromosomes P$_0$
If (ChromRel$_{fn}$ <Th$_1$ and ChromRel$_{fn}$ >Th$_2$)
Move 'f' to group of chromosomes Q$_0$
}
}
}
}
Prepare groups P$_1$/Q$_1$/R$_1$ ( )
{
Perform Crossover // *Mate the chromosomes of group P$_0$ randomly with chromosomes of*
// *group Q$_0$ for the given crossover point(s).*
Compute ModRel$_{ik}$ // *Calculate the reliability of job execution on each node P$_k$ (k=1 to K)*
// *on which allocation has been proposed as per eq.(ii)*
Compute ChromRel$_{fn}$ // *Calculate the reliability offered to the job by each chromosome as per eq. (v)*
Perform Selection ( ) // *Partition the population again in groups P$_1$ and Q$_1$*
{
For all the chromosomes 'f' (f =1 to PopSize), do
{
If (ChromRel$_{fn}$ >=Th$_1$)
Move 'f' to group of chromosomes P$_1$
If (ChromRel$_{fn}$ <Th$_1$ and ChromRel$_{fn}$ >Th$_2$)
Move 'f' to group of chromosomes Q$_1$
}
}
}

For generations 'g', do
{
Perform Crossover // *Randomly mate chromosomes P$_1$ with Q$_0$ for the given crossover point*
Perform Mutation // *Perform mutation for every fifth generation to avoid local optima*
Compute ModRel$_{ik}$ // *Calculate the reliability of job execution on each node P$_k$ (k=1*
// *to K) on which allocation has been proposed as per eq.(ii)*
Compute ChromRel$_{fn}$ // *Calculate the reliability offered to the job by each chromosome as per eq. (v)*
Perform Selection( ) // *Partition the population again in groups P$_1$ and Q$_1$*
Mark group Q$_1$ as Q$_0$
{
For all the chromosomes 'f' (f =1 to PopSize), do
{
If (ChromRel$_{fn}$ >=Th$_1$)
Move 'f' to group of chromosomes P$_1$
If (ChromRel$_{fn}$ <Th$_1$ and ChromRel$_{fn}$ >Th$_2$)
Move 'f' to group of chromosomes Q$_1$
}
}
Mark chromosome 'f$_{gn}$' as the chromosome with best execution cost
// *offering maximum reliability*
ClusRel$_{jn}$ = ChromRel$_{fn}$; *for the selected chromosome 'f$_{gn}$' as per eq. (vi)*
} *repeat till result saturates*
Receiveall // *Receive the various 'ClusRel$_{jn}$' from the selected clusters*
Compute GridRel$_j$ & select the cluster for job execution // *Calculate 'GridRel$_j$' as per eq. (vii)*
Allocate the job to the selected cluster and update its Cluster Table (CT)
}

Table 1. Grid parameters

S. No.	Parameter	Notation Used	Range
1	Number of Clusters	N	5-10
2	Number of Nodes in a Cluster	K	5-15
3	Clock Frequency of Nodes	f_k(MHz)	10-20
4	Intra Node Distance	D_{kl}	1-10
5	Time to finish Previous Workload	T_{prk} (µS)	10-30
6	Number of Modules in a Job	M	5-15
7	Number of Instructions in a Module	I_i	500-3000
8	IMC	B_{ihj} (Bytes)	5-20
9	Population Size	PopSize	100
10	Probability of Crossover	---	100%
11	Probability of Mutation	---	20%

Figure 4. Reliability v/s generations for 5 modules

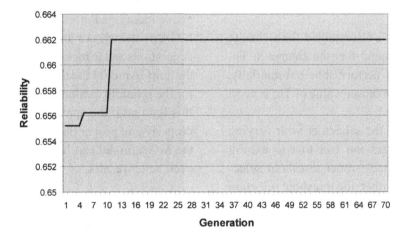

Figure 5. Reliability v/s generations for 7 modules

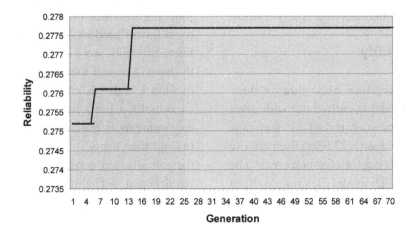

Figure 6. Reliability v/s generations for 10 modules

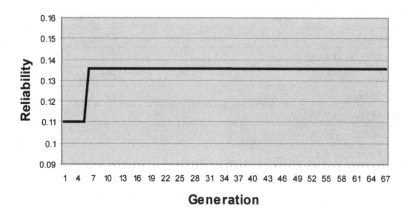

and requires to be relaxed. Subsequently, Th_1 was reduced gradually by 20-30%. It is noticed that in this range the scheduler worked well for reliable allocation.

Variation in Th_2 is also studied for a change of ±30% and it is found that the change in Th_2 does not affect the performance substantially. This implies that the chosen value of Th_2 is good enough for the model.

The behavior of the scheduler with varying thresholds emphasizes the fact that to exhibit optimum performance, proper threshold selection is necessary. Further, the threshold selection cannot be done on a trial and error basis and the domain knowledge and past experience about the application gains paramount importance for the MGA based scheduler to work properly. In other words, the model works well for those applications in which thresholds can be properly defined.

Comparative Study

To analyze the performance, a comparative study of the proposed model is carried out with other similar models. One such model for the same purpose (Raza & Vidyarthi, 2009a) does not use GA is the non GA model (briefed in section "The Algorithm"). The other model uses simple (Raza & Vidyarthi, 2009c) and does not use a threshold selection. For the comparative study, same

grid architecture is realized for all the models by keeping the input parameters same. Figures 7 through 9 represent the behavior of all these above mentioned models. It is observed that the MGA model tries to improve the reliability over generations and in most of the cases matches with the non GA model and the simple GA based model for the reliability value of first place of decimal. It is felt that if the application domain is studied properly and proper threshold selection is made, the MGA model can be further tuned to lead to even better results.

Effect of Degree of Interaction in the Job on Reliability

The jobs, executed in the grid, may range from the highly interactive jobs to the least interactive jobs. Performance of the model in terms of the reliability offered and for high interactive and low interactive jobs were studied and compared with the non GA model. One such result corresponding to a job J_0 is discussed below.

Initially a job J_0 with lower communication requirements is executed being referred as case (a) and then keeping the same grid architecture the job is again executed with communication requirements set to higher values. This is referred as case (b). Rest all parameters remains the same for both the cases.

Figure 7. Reliability v/s generations for non GA, simple GA and MGA based model for 5 modules

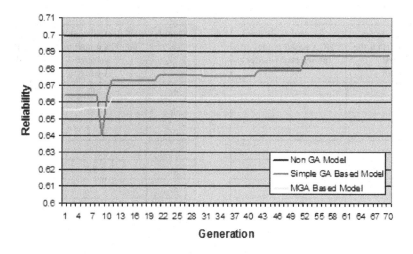

Figure 8. Reliability v/s generations for non GA, simple GA and MGA based model for 7 modules

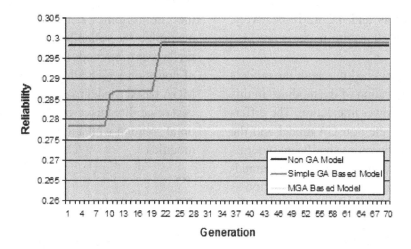

Figure 9. Reliability v/s generations for non GA, simple GA and MGA based model for 10 modules

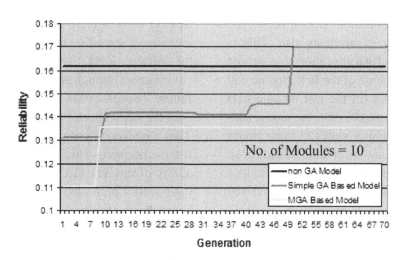

Table 2. Allocation table for the job J0 with low IMC

Module (m_i)	Selected Node for non GA model on the selected Cluster	Selected Node for MGA based model on the selected Cluster
m_{00}	10	10
m_{10}	2	2
m_{20}	13	6
m_{30}	6	3
m_{40}	12	9
m_{50}	9	13
m_{60}	10	10

Table 3. Allocation table for the job J0 with high IMC

Module (m_i)	Selected Node for non GA model on the selected Cluster	Selected Node for MGA based model on the selected Cluster
m_{00}	12	12
m_{10}	12	12
m_{20}	12	13
m_{30}	6	5
m_{40}	12	12
m_{50}	1	10
m_{60}	12	4

In case (a), the reliability for the non GA model and the proposed model for a specific job is obtained as 0.2989 and 0.2782 respectively. The corresponding allocation patterns are also shown in Table 2.

It can easily be noticed that both the models offer a uniform allocation of the modules in this case for a job with lower interaction. The difference in working of the non GA model and the MGA based model becomes significant in terms of the allocation of job modules if the job demanding execution has a high degree of interaction as per case (b) for which the allocation pattern for the job is shown in Table 3.

It is observed from Table 3 that non GA model does not offer a proper load balancing in this case. Many modules are allocated to the same node, resulting in imbalance. Similar results are obtained with other experiments also. This is understood by the fact that allocation process here starts from the allocation of the first module and the process continues till the last module gets allocated. To minimize the cost, the model tries to allocate the coming modules to those nodes which results in a minimum communication cost. In doing so, the nodes on which the previous modules have got allocated become the preferred ones. This results in a comparatively localized allocation pattern. The problem is more severe for the jobs with large number of modules. On the other hand, the MGA based model populates the chromosomes randomly and then tries to maximize the reliability. That way there is no preference to any node leading to a wider spectrum of nodes on which allocation is made. Thus the MGA based model may not result in the overall best reliability but certainly provides us a suboptimal solution with a more uniform allocation of modules.

CONCLUSION

Grid is an aggregation of heterogeneous resources in multiple administrative domains with the number of participants at an exorbitant scale. In such an environment there is always a possibility of the failures spreading from the hardware level to the software level. Scheduling a job in such an environment is tough as such systems are prone to failure. The cost of these failures can be exorbitant once the job has been allocated to these resources. Thus it is always desired to have the job allocated to those resources which have the maximum probability of survival. GA is a popular tool used for optimization purposes. The MGA based scheduler has addressed this problem by scheduling the job taking into account the grid reliability. The reliability estimates represents the true grid picture by considering the reliability of the computational resources, reliability of the application demanding execution and reliability of the network links which also contributes significantly owing to the data communicated.

Since GA itself can also be modified to suit the needs, the MGA based scheduler does the same. It works by partitioning the population into three groups using some threshold values. This results in first group containing those chromosomes which are the best fit in that generation, the second group which contains the chromosomes with average fitness and the last one with chromosomes having least fitness which are eventually discarded. The best fit chromosomes of the current generation are then mated with the chromosomes of the previous generation having average fitness.

The performance of the model is studied and compared with the other similar models by simulation. It is found that the results are same till the first place of decimal in comparison to a benchmark used. Further, it is felt that the performance of the MGA based scheduler depends on the threshold values selection which requires the proper domain knowledge. MGA provides proper load balancing with better reliability values.

The MGA based model has been tested for its performance in the past and this work is an extension of that study. In future the problem can be further explored for its use in various other application domains with various optimization objectives.

ACKNOWLEDGMENT

The authors would like to thank the anonymous reviewers for their valuable comments and suggestions to improve the quality of this paper.

REFERENCES

Aggarwal, M., & Aggarwal, A. (2006). A Unified Scheduling Algorithm for Grid Applications. In *Proceedings of the International Symposium on High Performance Computing in an Advanced Collaborative Environment (HPCS'06)* (pp. 1-7).

Aggarwal, M., Kent, R. D., & Ngom, A. (2005). Genetic Algorithm Based Scheduler for Computational Grids. In *Proceedings of the 19th International Symposium on High Performance Computing Systems and Applications (HPCS'05)* (pp. 209-215). Washington, DC: IEEE Computer Society.

Amaki, H., Kita, H., & Kobayashi, S. (1996). Multi-objective Optimization by Genetic Algorithms: A Review. In *Proceedings of the IEEE International Conference on Evolutionary Computation* (pp. 517-522). Washington, DC: IEEE Computer Society.

Dai, Y. S., Xie, M., & Poh, K. L. (2002). Reliability Analysis of Grid Computing Systems. In *Proceedings of the Pacific Rim International Symposium on Dependable Computing (PRDC'02)* (p. 97).

Fatos, X., Alba, E., & Dorronsoro, B. (2007). Efficient Batch Job Scheduling in Grids using Cellular Memetic Algorithms. In *Proceedings of the IEEE International Symposium on Parallel and Distributed Processing (IPDPS 2007)* (pp. 1-8).

Gao, Y., Rong, H., & Huang, J. Z. (2005). Adaptive Grid Job Scheduling with Genetic Algorithms. *Future Generation Computer Systems*, *21*(1), 151–161. doi:10.1016/j.future.2004.09.033

Goldberg, D. E. (2007). *Genetic Algorithms in Search, Optimization & Machine Learning*. Upper Saddle River, NJ: Pearson Education.

Grosan, C., Abraham, A., & Helvik, B. (2007). *Multiobjective Evolutionary Algorithms for Scheduling Jobs on Computational Grids*. Retrieved from http://www.softcomputing.net/ac2007_2.pdf

Han, Y., Jiang, C., & Luo, X. (2005). Resource Scheduling Model for Grid Computing Based on Sharing Synthesis of Petri Net. In *Proceedings of the Ninth International Conference on Computer Supported Cooperative Work in Design* (pp. 367-372).

Huedo, E., Montero, R. S., & Llorente, I. M. (2006). Evaluating the Reliability of Computational Grids from the End User's Point of View. *Journal of Systems Architecture*, 727–736. doi:10.1016/j.sysarc.2006.04.003

Khanbary, L. M. O., & Vidyarthi, D. P. (2008). A GA-Based Effective Fault-Tolerant Model for Channel Allocation in Mobile Computing. *IEEE Transactions on Vehicular Technology*, *57*(3), 1823–1833. doi:10.1109/TVT.2007.907311

Khanbary, L. M. O., & Vidyarthi, D. P. (2009). Modified Genetic Algorithm with Threshold Selection. *International Journal of Artificial Intelligence*, *2*(9), 126–148.

Limaye, K., Leangsuksun, B., Liu, Y., Greenwood, Z., Scott, S. L., Libby, R., & Chanchio, K. (2005). Reliability-Aware Resource Management for Computational Grid/Cluster Environments. In *Proceedings of the Sixth IEEE/ACM International Workshop on Grid Computing* (pp. 211-218).

Lin, J., & Wu, H. (2005). A Task Duplication Based Scheduling Algorithm on GA in Grid Computing Systems. In *Advances in Natural Computation* (LNCS 3612, pp. 225-234).

Mitchell, M. (1999). *An Introduction to Genetic Algorithms*. Cambridge, MA: MIT Press.

Nebro, A. J., Alba, E., & Luna, F. (2006). *Multi-objective optimization using Grid Computing*. Berlin, Germany: Springer Verlag.

Prabhu, C. S. R. (2008). *Grid and Cluster Computing*. PHI Learning Private Limited.

Ranjan, R., Harwood, A., & Buyya, R. (2006). SLA-Based Coordinated Superscheduling scheme for Computational Grids. In *Proceedings of the IEEE International Conference on Cluster Computing* (pp. 1-8).

Raza, Z., & Vidyarthi, D. P. (2008a). A Fault Tolerant Grid Scheduling Model to Minimize Turnaround Time. In *Proceedings of the International Conference on High Performance Computing, Networking and Communication Systems (HPCNCS'08)*, Orlando, FL.

Raza, Z., & Vidyarthi, D. P. (2008b). *Maximizing Reliability with Task Scheduling in a Computational Grid*. Paper presented at the Second International Conference on Information Systems Technology and Management, Dubai, UAE.

Raza, Z., & Vidyarthi, D. P. (2009a). A Computational Grid Scheduling Model To Minimize Turnaround Using Modified GA. *International Journal of Artificial Intelligence*, *3*(A9), 86–106.

Raza, Z., & Vidyarthi, D. P. (2009b). GA Based Scheduling Model for Computational Grid to Minimize Turnaround Time. *International Journal of Grid and High Performance Computing*, *1*(4), 70–90. doi:10.4018/jghpc.2009070806

Raza, Z., & Vidyarthi, D. P. (2009c). Maximizing Reliability with Task Scheduling In a Computational Grid Using GA. *International Journal of Advancements in Computing Technology*, *1*(2), 40–47.

Raza, Z., & Vidyarthi, D. P. (2010a). *Reliability Based Scheduling Model (RSM) for Computational Grids*.

Raza, Z., & Vidyarthi, D. P. (2010b). A Scheduling Model with Multi-Objective Optimization for Computational Grids using NSGA-II. *International Journal of Applied Evolutionary Computation*, *1*(2), 74–94. doi:10.4018/jaec.2010040104

Rzadca, K., Tryatram, D., & Wierzbicki, A. (2007). Fair Game-Theoretic Resource Management in Dedicated Grids. In *Proceedings of the IEEE International Conference on Cluster Computing and the Grid (CCGrid'07)* (pp. 343-350).

Sarker, B. K., Tripathi, A. K., Vidyarthi, D. P., Rani, K., & Uehara, K. (2002). Comparative Study of Task Allocation Algorithms based on A* and GA in a Distributed Computing System. In *Proceedings of the Third International Conference on Parallel and Distributed Computing, Applications and Technologies,* Kanazawa, Japan (pp. 116-121).

Tarricone, L., & Esposito, A. (2005). *Grid Computing for Electromagnetics.* Norwood, MA: Artech House.

Taylor, I. J., & Harrison, A. (2009). *From P2P and Grids to Services on the Web- Evolving Distributed Communities* (2nd ed.). New York, NY: Springer.

Tian, G.-Z., & Yu, J. (2008). Grid Workflow Scheduling Based on the Resource Combination Reliability. In *Proceedings of the Fourth International Conference on Natural Computing* (Vol. 1, pp. 207-211).

Tripathi, A. K., Sarker, B. K., Kumar, N., & Vidyarthi, D. P. (2000). A GA Based Multiple Task Allocation Considering Load. *International Journal of High Speed Computing, 11*(4), 203–214. doi:10.1142/S0129053300000187

Vidyarthi, D. P., & Tripathi, A. K. (2001). Maximizing Reliability of Distributed Computing System with Task Allocation using Simple Genetic Algorithm. *Journal of Systems Architecture, 47*(6). doi:10.1016/S1383-7621(01)00013-3

Vidyarthi, D. P., Tripathi, A. K., & Sarker, B. K. (2001). Allocation Aspects in Distributed Computing Systems. *IETE Technical Review, 18,* 449–454.

Vidyarthi, D. P., Tripathi, A. K., Sarker, B. K., & Rani, K. (2003). Comparative Study of Two GA based Task Allocation Models in Distributed Computing System. In *Proceedings of the Fourth International Conference on Parallel and Distributed Computing, Applications and Technologies,* Chengdu, China.

Vidyarthi, D. P., Tripathi, A. K., Sarker, B. K., & Yang, L. T. (2005). Performance Study of Reliability Maximization and Turnaround Minimization with GA based Task Allocation in DCS. In Yang, L. T., & Guo, M. (Eds.), *Scheduling and Resource Management, High Performance Computing: Paradigm and Infrastructure* (pp. 349–360). New York, NY: John Wiley & Sons.

Zomaya, A. Y., & Teh, Y. H. (2001). Observations on Using Genetic Algorithms for Dynamic Load-Balancing. *Proceedings of IEEE Transactions on Parallel and Distributed Systems, 12*(9), 899–911. doi:10.1109/71.954620

Zomaya, A. Y., & Wright, M. (2002). Observation on Using Genetic Algorithms for Channel Allocation in Mobile Computing. *IEEE Transactions on Parallel and Distributed Systems, 13*(9), 948–962. doi:10.1109/TPDS.2002.1036068

This work was previously published in the International Journal of Grid and High Performance Computing, Volume 3, Issue 1, edited by Emmanuel Udoh and Ching-Hsien Hsu, pp. 1-20, copyright 2011 by IGI Publishing (an imprint of IGI Global).

Chapter 3
A Novel System Oriented Scheduler for Avoiding Haste Problem in Computational Grids

Ahmed I. Saleh
Mansoura University, Egypt

ABSTRACT

Scheduling is an important issue that must be handled carefully to realize the "Just login to compute" principle introduced by computational grids. Current grid schedulers suffer from the haste problem, which is the inability to schedule all tasks successfully. Accordingly, some tasks fail to complete execution as they are allocated to unsuitable workers. Others may not start execution as suitable workers are previously allocated to other tasks. This paper introduces the scheduling haste problem and presents a novel high throughput grid scheduler. The proposed scheduler selects the most suitable worker to execute an input grid task. Hence, it minimizes the turnaround time for a set of grid tasks. Moreover, the scheduler is system oriented and avoids the scheduling haste problem. Experimental results show that the proposed scheduler outperforms traditional grid schedulers as it introduces better scheduling efficiency.

INTRODUCTION

Recently, due to the dramatic development of network technologies and the popularity of the Internet, grid computing has become an appealing research area (Jens, Martin, & Roman, 2009; Lee, Squicciarini, & Bertino, 2009). Computational grids are the next generation of computer clusters. They aim to maximize the utilization of resources owned by a set of distributed heterogeneous systems (He, Jarvis, Spooner, Bacigalupo, Tan, & Nudd, 2005; (Sacerdoti, Katz, Massie, & Culler, 2003). Moreover, grids can be considered as the recent instances of metacomputing (Wolski, Spring, & Hayes, 1999). The primary goal of grid computing is to provide a transparent access to geographically distributed heterogeneous resources owned by different individuals or organizations (Jen & Yuan, 2009). Hence, the grid provides hardware and software infrastructure to create an illusion of a virtual supercomputer that exploit the computational power aggregated from a huge

DOI: 10.4018/978-1-4666-2065-0.ch003

set of distributed workers (Buyya, 1999). This allows the execution of tasks whose computational requirements exceed the available local resources. However, although the notion of grid computing is simple and attractive, its practical realization poses several challenges and open problems that need to be addressed (Tsai & Hung, 2009; Creel & Goffe, 2008). These challenges include resource discovery, failure management, fault tolerance, resource heterogeneity, reliability, scalability, security, and more importantly the scheduling of incoming tasks among available grid resources (Tseng, Chin, & Wang, 2009).

Scheduling is the major puzzle in developing a grid based computing paradigm (Tseng, Chin, & Wang, 2009; Iavarasan, Thambidurai, & Mahilmannan, 2005). It involves the matching of task or application requirements with the available resources (Tseng, Chin, & Wang, 2009). Scheduling in grids can be carried out in three different phases which are; (i) resource discovery, (ii) scheduling, and (iii) executing (Li & Hadjinicolaou, 2008). However, to achieve the expected potentials of the available resources, efficient scheduling algorithms are required (Daoud, & Kharma, 2008). Unluckily, scheduling algorithms previously employed in computer clusters can't be used in grids as they run on homogenous and guaranteed resources over the same LAN. A Scheduler used in a computer cluster only manages such cluster; hence, it owns the resources with no ability to discover new ones (Sacerdoti, Katz, Massie, & Culler, 2003). Also it assumes both the availability and stability of resources. On the other hand, scheduling in grids is significantly complicated as a result of grid heterogeneity and dynamic nature (Kiran, Hassan, Kuan, & Yee, 2009). Unlike the cluster scheduler, a grid scheduler should have the ability to discover new computing resources over multiple administrative domains (Yan, Shen, Li, & Wu, 2005). The dynamic nature of grids is a result of both the network connectivity and grid resources. The network may be unreliable as it can't guarantee its bandwidth. Moreover, grid resources change both availability and capability over time as they may join or leave the grid without any notification (Shah, Veeravalli, & Misra, 2007; Kousalya, & Balasubramanie, 2008).

Two alternative views may be considered when developing a grid scheduling system. The first is the User View (UV) while the other is the System View (SV). On one hand, the user aims to achieve the maximum Quality of Service (QoS); hence, he asks the scheduler to elect the best currently available resources for executing his task. On the other hand, the grid system tries to manage the available resources in a way for achieving the maximum QoS for all users not for a specific one. Based on those alternative views, grid schedulers can be categorized into two major categories, which are; (i) Task Oriented Grid Schedulers (TOGS), and (ii) System Oriented Grid Schedulers (SOGS). The former supports the user's demands, and therefore, it tries to minimize the execution time of each input task. The latter category supports the system's demands, and therefore, it tries to introduce a high throughput computing. Unlike TOGS, SOGS aims to maximize the processing ability of the system over the long run. Also, it introduces a better resource management scheme by allocating the grid task to the most suitable resource, not the best available one.

To the best of our knowledge, all the proposed grid scheduling algorithms were task oriented ones (Aggarwal, Kent, & Ngom, 2005), which usually suffer from the haste problem. The haste problem is the ability of the scheduler to present a good scheduling performance in the present; however an overall degraded performance is presented in the long run. Moreover, implementing an efficient SOGS has not been addressed yet. Hence, scheduling in grids is still more complex than the proposed solutions. Many hurdles stand in the way of achieving the maximum utilization of grid resources (Liu, Yang, Lian, & Wanbin, 2006). Accordingly, scheduling in grids is still an elusive problem that attracts the interests of many researchers (Aggarwal, & Kent, 2005; Hsin, 2005).

This paper discusses the scheduling haste problem in details. Then, a novel system oriented grid scheduler is introduced as a solution for this problem, which is the first to study the scheduling by mapping the tasks to the suitable workers not the best available ones. This has a great impact in minimizing the makespan (turnaround time) of executing a set of tasks in the long run. The paper also introduces an instance of such new generation of grid schedulers. Experimental results have shown that the proposed scheduling strategy outperforms traditional grid schedulers as it introduces a better scheduling efficiency as well as avoiding the scheduling haste problem.

RELATED WORK

Tremendous amount of research had been introduced in the area of task scheduling. Early work focused in scheduling tasks against dedicated workers. An example is the Resource Reservation Strategy (RRS) (Foster, Roy, & Sander, 2000), which reserves the resource in advance for the user's task. However, RRS becomes not feasible for computational grids as it contradicts the privacy of owners who does not want their machines dedicated for grid tasks.

Enterprise (Malone, Fikes, Grant, & Howard, 1988) is a market-like scheduler for distributed computing environment. When a task is ready to execute, each idle worker sends the estimated task completion time to the task initiator. The worker claiming the earliest completion time is then selected for executing the task. Similar market based schedulers including Spawn (Waldspurger, Hogg, Huberman, Kephart, & Stornetta, 1992) and Computer Power Market (CPM) (Buyya & Vazhkudai, 2001).

A set of Agent-based techniques have also been proposed for addressing the scheduling problem such as; AppLes (Application-Level Scheduling) (Berman, Wolski, Figueira, Schopf, & Shao, 1996) and NetSolve (Casanova, Kim,

Plank, & Dongarra, 1999). AppLes uses a resident agent that employs the NWS (Network Weather Service) to predict the load and availability of the system resources at the scheduling time. It then considers the application requirements to determine the best schedule; hence, scheduling is done on a per-application basis. On the other hand, NetSolve is a client-agent-server system, which was developed to solve remotely the complex scientific problems. However, extra overhead is needed to rebuild the scheduled applications to perform RPC-like computations.

GWMS (Grid Workflow Management System) (Kadav, & Sanjeev, 2006) is a dynamic scheduler that uses a repository which stores information related to resources and application instances. Whenever a task is ready to execute, the scheduler queries the repository to get the set of workers capable of executing the task. The Approximated Turnaround Time (ATT) is calculated for each worker. Then, the worker with the minimal ATT is contacted. A similar approach was introduced in (Kiran, Hassan, Kuan, & Yee, 2009), where a novel methodology to predict the execution time of jobs using aspects of static analysis and compiler based approach.

As per our knowledge, no grid scheduling strategy till date taking the scheduler Haste problem into account. All schedulers tend to choose the best available resource for executing an input task not the suitable one. However, choosing the suitable worker for the input task guarantees the system reliability as it maximizes the capability to execute the incoming future tasks.

BACKGROUND AND BASIC CONCEPTS

In this section, a simple view for the traditional computer clusters is introduced. Then, the differences between task oriented and system oriented schedulers are verified. And finally, scheduler trap and haste problem are explained in details.

Cluster Computing

Computer clusters are three tier structural systems interconnected via two functional relationships (He, Jarvis, Spooner, Bacigalupo, Tan, & Nudd, 2005). Those tiers are; (i) clients, (ii) cluster server (master node or scheduler), and (iii) cluster workers. The server is a dedicated machine that receives incoming tasks from the clients; this is a client-server relationship. It is the server's responsibility to schedule the incoming tasks to a set of identical, dedicated, and usually fixed workers for execution; this is a master-slave relationship. Moreover, the underlying interconnection network is usually a private and high speed network, which in turn guarantees the high quality of communication service (Sacerdoti, Katz, Massie, & Culler, 2003). Certainly, this structure is quite different from computational grids which are heterogeneous and dynamic in both resource and communication availabilities.

As depicted in Figure 1, scheduling in clusters is quite simple. Initially, incoming tasks as well as their requirements are kept in an input queue. The task requirements include both the expected execution time and the number of workers needed to execute the task. The cluster server (scheduler), on the other hand, continuously reports the availability of cluster workers. Once a worker completes executing a task, it notifies the server that it is available and ready to receive a new task. Many scheduling algorithms can be used to pick a task for execution when a worker is available such as; First Come First Serviced (FCFS), Minimum Request Job First (MRJF), Shortest Job First (SJF), and Backfill (Buyya, 1999).

Task-Oriented Versus System-Oriented Grid Schedulers

Recent work in grid scheduling aims to introduce task oriented schedulers. A Task Oriented Grid Scheduler (TOGS) manages the scheduling for the benefit of the end user, who has initialized the task, with no awareness of the overall system efficiency. Form one point of view, TOGS considers only the current state of the grid system. It does not take into account the future needs of the other grid users. This behavior degrades the system performance as the newly incoming tasks may be blocked (starved) for a long period of times (as their execution requirements are not currently available). Form another point of view, TOGS is a greedy scheduler as it exploits all the currently available grid resources for the current task to be scheduled. It gives no attention to the needs of the future incoming tasks.

Although TOGS benefits the current task, it does not guarantee the system efficiency in the near future. As illustrated in Figure 2, TOGS elects the best resources for executing the current task, however, it may be more efficient for the system to allocate the task to the most suitable (not the best available) one. From these premises, it is feasible and necessary to introduce a new generation of grid schedulers that elects the most suitable worker to execute the task with the aim of maximizing both system throughput and quality of service. As it tries to maximize the scheduling system efficiency, we name such new generation, as the System-Oriented Grid Schedulers (SOGS).

Scheduler Trap and Haste Problem

Current generation of grid schedulers try to predict the execution time for the incoming task on the available grid workers, then allocate the task to the one that introduces the minimal predicted Turnaround time (TAT) (Tseng, Chin, & Wang, 2009). The predicted TAT for task T_i on worker w_j at the wall-clock time τ, denoted by $TAT(T_i, w_j, \tau)$, consists of four components as illustrated in (1);

$$\begin{aligned}
TAT(T_i, w_j, \tau) &= ET(T_i, w_j, \tau) \\
&+ MT(T_i, S, w_j, \tau) \\
&+ WT(T_i, w_j) \\
&+ RT(Res(T_i), S, w_j, \tau_{finish})
\end{aligned} \quad (1)$$

Figure 1. A clustering system infrastructure

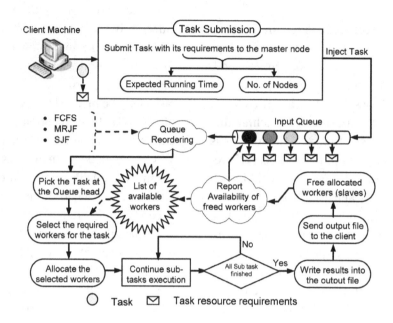

where, $ET(T_i, w_j, \tau)$ is the predicted execution time of T_i on w_j at time τ, $MT(T_i, s, w_j, \tau)$ is the time elapsed by T_i to migrate from the scheduler machine S to w_j at time τ, $WT(T_i, w_j)$ is the waiting time for T_i on w_j before it has begun its execution, and $RT(Res(T_i), S, w_j, \tau_{finish})$ is the time needed to retract the results of T_i from w_j to the scheduler machine S after T_i has finished. As illustrated in (1), $TAT(T_i, w_j, \tau)$ depends on both computation and communication latencies. The former is the time taken by w_j to execute T_i (include execution and waiting latencies). While the latter includes both; (i) the time needed to transfer T_i from the scheduler machine to the chosen worker, and (ii) the time to transfer the task's result in the opposite direction. However, those constituent components are themselves decomposed into smaller ones. As an illustration, $ET(T_i, w_j, \tau)$ depends on the cur-

Figure 2. Operational steps for the task oriented scheduler

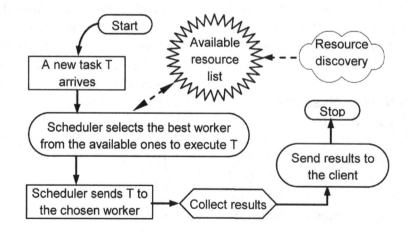

rent available resources (services) provided by the worker w_j at time τ such as CPU_Speed(w_j,τ), Current_Load(w_j,τ), and Available_Memory(w_j,τ). Also, Communication latency (including MT(T_i, S, w_j, τ) and RT(Res(T_i), S, w_j, τ_{finish})) depends on the bandwidth of the network connecting w_j to the scheduler machine at time τ.

In spite of its optimality at schedule time, traditional grid schedulers may be trapped. By other words, they may not introduce the best scheduling decisions. Scheduler trapping is due to one (or both) of the following reasons. The first is that; both the available resources of grid workers as well as the network bandwidth are dynamic parameters, which means that they change their values with time. Hence, a scheduling decision that is valid at the time τ may be invalid or becomes a costly choice after a small time period. The second reason for trapping is the scheduler haste problem.

The reason of haste problem is that; current grid schedulers are task oriented ones, which means that they look for the best worker to execute the task. From the scheduler point of view, the best worker (the selected worker w_{sel} for executing the task T_i at time τ) is the one which introduces the minimal predicted execution time for the task as illustrated in (2).

$$w_{sel} = T \arg et(T_i, \tau)$$
$$= \arg \min_{wj \in W(\tau)}[\text{TAT}(T_i, w_j, \tau)] \quad (2)$$

where, $W(\tau)=\{w_1, w_2, \ldots., w_n\}$ is the set of available workers at the scheduling time τ. However, such chosen worker w_{sel} may not be the most suitable one. The suitable worker for the input task is the one that not only introduces an acceptable Qos for the current task but also guarantees the Qos of the future incoming tasks. The haste problem is a result of the inability of the scheduler to choose the suitable worker for the grid task. Certainly, haste problem will harm the future performance

of the system. To narrate confidently, imagine a task T_i which requires a computing resource of type R that is available only at workers w_n and w_m with computational power of (for example) 5μ and 10μ respectively. Moreover, T_i needs the resource type R with power of at least 4μ. Although it is logically to allocate T_i to w_n which is more suitable, traditional schedulers are greedy ones, so they will allocate T_i to w_m. For the first time, this situation may appear trivial and has no effect on the system performance. However, it may result in future problems when, for example, another task T_j arrives and need a resource of type R with a computational power of at least 7μ. At this situation, two alternative procedures may be followed by the scheduler, which are both costly ones. The first is to interrupt T_i, reschedule it to w_n, and then allocate T_j to w_m. This is not a good choice as T_i may be executing for a long time, which requires saving its state before rescheduling, then sending such state to w_n so that T_i can resume its execution with no losses. The second alternative is to allow T_i to continue its execution, allocate T_j to w_m as soon as T_i terminates. However, this solution deemed unreliable as it increases the waiting time of T_j. Hence, it will be better to "make haste slowly" by choosing the most suitable worker to execute the task. This guarantees the system performance and service availability at the future. We claim that this paper is the first to study this issue in grid scheduling.

THE PROPOSED SCHEDULER

As depicted in Figure 3, the proposed grid scheduling system consists of three different tiers, which are; (i) Grid Clients Tier (GCT), (ii) Grid Scheduler Tier (GST), and (iii) Grid Workers Tier (GWT). GCT represents the grid users who are sitting behind a set of client machines and willing to execute their tasks using the grid computational power. On the other hand, GWT provides the infrastructure that creates an illusion of a virtual supercomputer. It exploits the computational power aggregated from a large set of geographically distributed workers. The last tier is the GST, which represents the core of the proposed scheduling framework. GST is responsible of carrying out the scheduling decisions. It determines where and when the input task T will be executed by applying a set of heuristic rules. GST also appoints when T should be interrupted and resume its execution. Moreover, GST is responsible of collecting the results of T, and then sending them to the task initiator. Executing a task T in the proposed framework is carried out in the sequential steps shown in Figure 4. As depicted in the figure, the grid scheduler standing as an interface between the two other tiers. The following sub-sections describe the internal

structure of GST as well as the functionality of its modules in more details.

Receiver Module

The first module of GST is the receiver module, which receives the incoming tasks from the GCT, then assigns the requirements (task parameters) as well as an initial priority for each incoming task. According to the receiver module, an input task T and any grid worker w_j can be represented by a set of N parameters as a point in an imaginary N-dimensional space called the Parm-Space. The orthogonal axes of such space are those N parameters. When representing a task on the Parm-Space, those N parameters illustrate the task requirements. Moreover, when a worker is being

Figure 3. The proposed 3 tier scheduling system structure

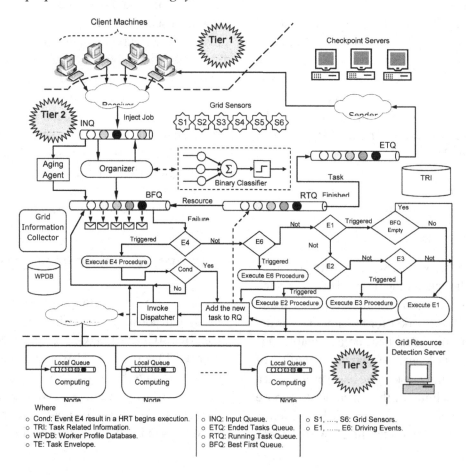

Where
- o Cond: Event E4 result in a HRT begins execution.
- o TRI: Task Related Information.
- o WPDB: Worker Profile Database.
- o TE: Task Envelope.

- o INQ: Input Queue.
- o ETQ: Ended Tasks Queue.
- o RTQ: Running Task Queue.
- o BFQ: Best First Queue.

- o S1, ..., S6: Grid Sensors.
- o E1, ..., E6: Driving Events.

Figure 4. The sequential steps to execute a task in a grid

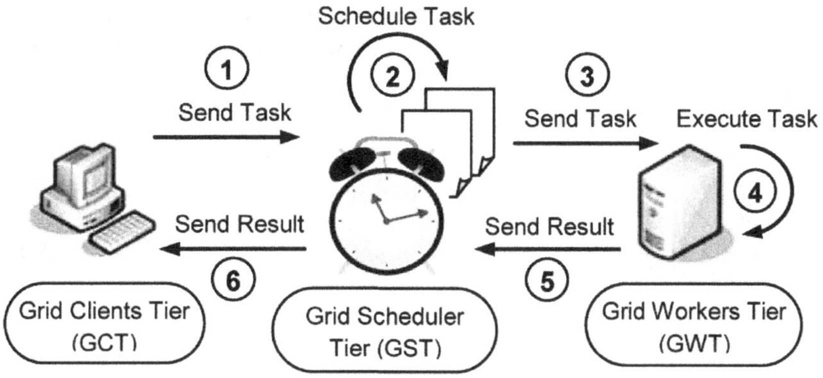

expressed in the Parm-Space, the N parameters illustrate the availabilities (current levels) of the worker resources. Although many parameters can be used to represent either task requirements or the worker availabilities, three different parameters are considered here, which are; (i) CPU power (CPU), (ii) Memory space requirement (MEM), and (iii) Storage requirements (STR). Many other parameters could be taken into account, such as the deadline requirement for each task, however, CPU, MEM, and STR are considered for illustration. Extra work could be done to enhance the performance of the scheduling system by considering more parameters.

Hence, at the receiver module, a task T_i can be represented as; $T_i = (Parm_i, P_i)$. Where, P_i is the task priority and $Parm_i$ is a set representing the different task parameters, which is written as; $Parm_i = \{CPU=x_i, MEM=y_i, STR=z_i\}$, where x_i, y_i, and z_i representing the task requirements for CPU, memory, and storage respectively. Figure 5 shows the graphical representation for the task T_i in the proposed Parm-Space. Setting (or more precisely estimating) the task's parameters (requirements) is a true challenge. However, human assistance can be exploited to solve this issue.

After representing the incoming task and setting its initial priority, a Task Envelope (TE) is attached to it. A TE for task T stores the detailed information about that task such as its type, pa-

rameters, priority, output file name, Run Before (RB) flag, and checkpoint server. A graphical representation for the envelope of task T is shown in Figure 6. Three different types of tasks are considered, which are (i) Hard real time task (T_H), (ii) Soft real time task (T_S), and (iii) Normal task (T_N). Moreover, when a task is allowed to run, a checkpoint server is attached to the task from the list of available checkpoint servers. The function of that server is to track the task execution by maintaining an output file for the task. Hence, when a task is involuntary interrupted, it can successfully resume its execution with no additional cost. Finally the incoming task is injected into the input queue (INQ) in which it will stay for a while.

As there are three different types of tasks T_H, T_S, and T_N, they are assigned different initial priorities by the receiver, which are r_H, r_S, and r_N respectively (where $r_H > r_S > r_N$). Moreover, the system interacts differently with each type. A T_H is assigned the highest initial priority r_H over all other types of tasks. Hence, it may preempt a running task (of type T_N) if it arrives with no available workers. However, choosing the victim task, which will be preempted, is a challenge. We believe that the last task (of type normal) that has immediately started its execution is the one that will minimize the cost; hence, it is the most suitable task to be interrupted. Accordingly, when it is needed to interrupt a normal task, the used

Figure 5. Task T_i in a Parm_Space of three dimensions

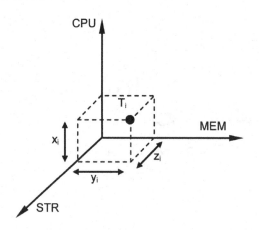

strategy is the Last Executed First Interrupted (LEFI).

On the other hand, T_S is restricted to run on a specific time period. Accordingly, when a task of type T_S arrives, it is assigned an initial priority r_S, which is higher than the initial priority of any task of type T_N. However, as the time gone, T_S will be promoted (as its deadline time becomes closer) till it treated as a hard real time one. Hence, it can preempt a working task (of type T_N) if there are no available workers. The third type is the normal task T_N, which will initially assigned the priority r_N, however, its priority is gradually increased (by the ager) in order to avoid starvation. Hence, at a specific time, it will be assigned the highest priority in the input queue (INQ), and accordingly, it will be allowed to enter the best first queue (BFQ).

Figure 6. The envelope of the task T

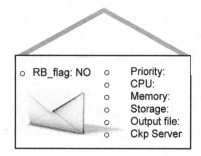

Due to its importance and time limitations, T_H is allowed to run directly with no delay. On the other hand, the priorities of T_N and T_S tasks (denoted as R_N and R_S respectively) are time dependent. R_N and R_S are calculated using (3) and (4) shown below.

$$R_s(\tau) = \alpha_s r_s + \frac{\beta_s}{\tau_c(T_s) - \tau} \qquad (3)$$

$$R_n(\tau) = \alpha_n r_n + \beta_n(\tau - \tau_0(T_n)) + \frac{\lambda_n}{1 - \sum_{i=1}^{m}(Exec\_Period_{ni}/PET_i)} \qquad (4)$$

where, $R_s(\tau)$ and $R_n(\tau)$ are the priorities of the soft real time task T_s and the normal task T_n respectively; α, β, and λ are equations constants (for simplicity, their values was taken as 1), $\tau_c(T_s)$ is the critical (deadline) time for the soft real time task T_s, $\tau_0(T_n)$ is the submission time of T_n (i.e., the time when T_n enters BFQ), $Exec\_Period_{ni}$ is the time period elapsed while T_n executed on worker w_i, PET_i is the predicted execution time of T_n on worker w_i, r_s and r_n are the initial priorities of the soft real time task T_s and the normal task T_n respectively, and m is the number of workers on which T_n has executed. It should be noticed that many factors can be employed to set the initial priority of a process. A simple rule is to set the initial priority according to the importance of the process owner and the process type.

However, since it is difficult to introduce an accurate estimation for the task execution time on different workers, (4) can be reformulated in (5);

$$R_n(\tau) = \alpha_n r_n + \beta_n(\tau - \tau_0(T_n)) + \lambda_n(Exec\_Period_{ni}) \qquad (5)$$

Organizer and Ager Modules

All incoming tasks are intentionally injected into the INQ after they had been represented by the receiver as an initial priority and a set of parameters. The organizer module stands as a distiller that elects a task from the set of ready-to-run tasks in the INQ, then injects such task into the Best First queue (BFQ) when its importance (priority) exceeds a threshold (critical) value R_C. The proposed grid organizer is a simple perceptron representing a binary classifier as illustrated in Figure 7. Another important module is the ager, which is provided mainly to avoid starvation. Its basic function is to promote continuously (increase priority of) the old tasks, so that they allowed to enter BFQ as soon as possible. As the time left, the importance of the old task will exceed the threshold value R_C, and accordingly, it will be picked by the organizer and intentionally injected into the BFQ.

Scheduler Queues (INQ, BFQ, RTQ, and ETQ)

There are four different queues in the Grid Scheduler Tier (GST), which are; (i) Input Queue (INQ), (ii) Best First Queue (BFQ), (iii) Running Tasks Queue (RTQ), and (iv) Ended Tasks Queue (ETQ). INQ receives the incoming tasks after it has been registered by the receiver as well as their envelopes. The organizer, on the other hand, allows a task to enter the BFQ when the task importance exceeds a threshold value R_C. BFQ is the place where the ready-to-run tasks reside waiting to start execution. The interrupted tasks (either voluntary or involuntary) also reside in the BFQ. Whenever a new worker is available, the best task (in the BFQ) or more precisely the most suitable task will be chosen, and then allocated to the newly available worker. The most suitable task is specified by comparing the distance among the available worker and all ready-to-run tasks in the BFQ using the Parm-Space. The closest task T_{suit},

is the most suitable one, then it will be allocated to the freed worker. T_{suit} is then cloned, the first clone is allowed to migrate towards the worker (to be executed) after assigning it a checkpoint server and an output file (if it was not run before, i.e., RB_flag=0), while the other clone (with its envelope) is forced to enter the Running Tasks Queue (RTQ), hence, an alternative copy is available, which can be used if the migrated copy is suddenly corrupted, involuntary stops running, or its hosting worker is abruptly failed. When the task finishes its execution (with one or more runs), it is allowed to enter the Ended Tasks Queue (ETQ) where it will be picked by the sender. Finally, the sender sends back the task output file to the task initiator (grid user).

In general, similarity/distance measures map the distance or similarity between the symbolic descriptions of two objects into a single numeric value. They reflect the degree of closeness or separation of the target objects. However, choosing an appropriate similarity measure is also crucial. A variety of similarity or distance measures have been proposed and widely applied, such as cosine similarity and Euclidean distance.

Euclidean distance is a standard metric for geometrical problems. Let $X=(x_1, x_2, x_3, ..., x_n)^t$ and $Y=(y_1, y_2, y_3, ..., y_n)^t$ be two vectors in n-dimensional Euclidean space. The Euclidean distance D_{Eucl} between two n-dimensional vectors is given in (6):

$$D_{Eucl}(X,Y) = \sqrt[2]{\sum_{i=1}^{n}(x_i - y_i)^2}$$
$$= \sqrt[2]{(x_1 - y_1)^2 + (x_2 - y_2)^2 + ... + (x_n - y_n)^2}$$
(6)

In a three dimensional Euclidean space, the distance can be calculated by (7);

$$D_{Eucl}(X,Y) = \sqrt[2]{(x_1 - y_1)^2 + (x_2 - y_2)^2 + (x_3 - y_3)^2}$$
(7)

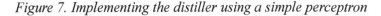

Figure 7. Implementing the distiller using a simple perceptron

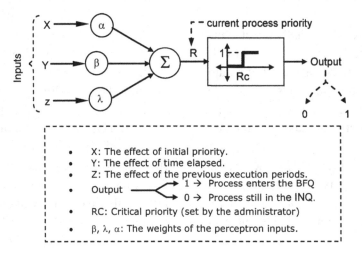

On the other hand, cosine coefficient, as illustrated in (8), measures the angle between two vectors and thus often called the angular metric (Deza, 2006). One important property is that the cosine similarity will be maximum (equal to 1) even the two vectors are not identical. Hence, it is not suitable to our case and accordingly the Euclidean distance is the chosen one.

$$S_{Cos}(X,Y) = \frac{\sum_{i=1}^{n} x_i y_i}{\sqrt{\sum_{i=1}^{n} x_i^2} \sqrt{\sum_{i=1}^{n} y_i^2}} \qquad (8)$$

Grid Checkpoint Servers

In order to insure the system reliability, a set of checkpoint servers are constantly attached to the scheduler tier. A checkpoint server is responsible of monitoring a set of currently running tasks by maintaining an output file for each running one. It also stores the output files of the involuntary interrupted tasks, so that they can successfully resume their execution. When a task T_i is attached to a checkpoint server, the server creates an output file for T_i where task's intermediate results can be stored. The name of the task's output file consists of two parts, which are name and extension. The name is the task's ID, while the extension differs according to the type of the output file. A resident agent is located at each grid worker, which is responsible of updating the output file of the task at a specific interval specified by the system administrator. Hence, before T_i starts execution, information inside its envelope should be completed by specifying the IP of its checkpoint server as well as the name of its output file. Hence, T_i can resume its execution if it has been involuntary interrupted.

Worker Profile Database (WPDB)

The aim of the Worker Profile Database (WPDB) is to maintain an up-to-date profile for each grid worker. A worker profile indicates the levels of worker's resources all the time during the day. This stored profile is helpful in predicting the levels of the available worker resources at any time during the daytime.

Usually, most of the workers that join the computational grid are enterprise owned ones. By other words, they belong to large organizations or private companies. Accordingly, resources owned by those workers usually follow an utilization histogram. For illustration, consider a working node belongs to a university; it will be available during the night time (from 12 pm to 6 am) with very low CPU utilization level. However, the situation certainly differs at the other day times. Figure 8 gives an illustration.

The machine profile is accumulative. This means that it is reported continuously and updated every time the worker is available. The profile of each worker is stored in the WPDB. A worker profile is used whenever the scheduler decides to send a task to that worker. WPDB stores the available amounts of three different parameters for each worker. Those parameters constitute the worker's profile during the daytime, which are; (i) CPU power (CPU), (ii) Memory space requirement (MEM), and (iii) Storage requirements (STR). Moreover, WPDB receives the current available amounts of those parameters whenever the worker becomes free. This could be helpful in choosing the suitable task for execution from the BFQ.

Grid Sensors

As depicted in Figure 3, a special set of dedicated sensors are employed to trigger several driving events. A grid sensor is responsible of triggering a special driving event. In turn, the triggered events induct the scheduler to take the appropriate scheduling decisions. Table 1 depicts a list of the used sensors as well as the activity that the sensor monitors. On the other hand, Table 2 illustrates the considered events as well as the corresponding sensor(s) that trigger each event. Moreover, Figures 9 through 14 explain in details the procedure followed by the scheduler when each event has been triggered.

GRID SIMULATION ARCHITECTURE

Computational grids are complex heterogeneous environments consisting of several organizational domains in which no one has the full control of all the available resources. Consequently, a true realization of computational grids is extremely complicated. Therefore, the results in this paper are based on simulating a simple grid based on the network shown in Figure 15, which consists of a set of 10 grid workers of different capabilities, 5 clients, as well as the grid scheduler.

As depicted in Figure 15, for simplicity reasons, a set of restrictions and assumptions have been suggested, which are; (i) no worker failure during the test periods, (ii) no need for checkpoint servers since we guarantee the availability of grid workers thought the test periods, (iii) we ignore the existence of the grid resource detection server since all workers are available from the beginning.

Competitors

We believe that two main categories of scheduling strategies can be considered. The first is the static (Daoud, & Kharma, 2008), while the second is the dynamic (adaptive) strategy (Shah, Veeravalli, & Misra, 2007). A static scheduler maps the task to the corresponding worker at the scheduling time. Despite its simplicity, static scheduling is not suitable for the grids' dynamic environment as the situation may differ when the task is ready to run. Hence, dynamic schedulers, which find the suitable worker to execute the task at the run time, may be more preferable in the highly dynamic environments such as the grids. For the purpose of comparing the proposed scheduling strategy, a set of scheduling techniques are chosen for the comparison, which are listed in Table 3.

Measuring the Scheduling Performance

As discussed before, measuring the scheduling performance can be considered from two different point views, which have different targets, namely; user view and system view. The former

Table 1. A list of the used sensors as well as the activity that the sensor monitors

Sensor	Activity
S_1	A new task arrives
S_2	A worker (computational node) failure
S_3	A worker performance degradation.
S_4	A task finishes its execution.
S_5	A worker w_j is allocated to a task T_i
S_6	An arrival of a hard real time task.
S_7	A soft real time task exceeds a threshold.
S_8	A new worker is detected (register itself to the grid).

Figure 8. CPU utilization of a worker owned by a university

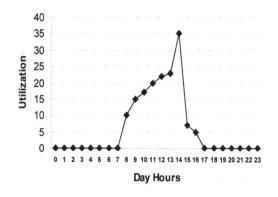

aims to minimize the turnaround time for each grid task, while the latter aims to minimize the makespan (time required to finish the execution) of an input batch of grid tasks. The next subsections measure the scheduling performance for the proposed scheduler as well as its competitors from both views.

Experiment 1: Measuring the Scheduling Efficiency (System View)

An efficient scheduler is the one that truly schedule a batch of input tasks to minimize the makespan. The makespan for a batch B of N tasks can be defined as the time elapsed between the start time of the first task in the batch and the finish time of the last task in the same batch, and can be calculated as; MakeSpan(B)= $[T_{f\_l} - T_{s\_f}]$, where; T_{f_l} is the finish time of the last task in the batch B, and T_{s_f} is the start time of the first task in the batch. Figure 16 shows the makespan (measured in milliseconds) for different input batches of different sizes (10, 20, 30, 40, and 50 tasks), in which hard real and soft real time tasks are not included. Moreover, Figure 17 illustrates the makespan against the number of scheduled tasks in a continuous fashion.

Table 2. The considered events and the corresponding sensor(s) that trigger each event

Event	Triggered by	Activated when	Result in
E_1	S_4, S_8	A new worker is available and ready to host a task (e.g., a new worker register itself to the grid or a task finishes its execution)	Begin the execution of a normal task or a soft real time task.
E_2	S_2, S_3	A worker w_j which hosts the task T_i has been failed or introduces a degraded performance (e.g., w_j becomes not ready to host a grid task)	Suspend the execution of T_i and then add it to the BFQ.
E_3	S_5	A worker w_j has been allocated to task T_i	Prepare T_i to begin or resume its execution.
E_4	S_1	Organizer adds a new task T_i to BFQ	May result in preempting a normal task if T_i is a hard real time task.
E_5	S_6	The arrival of a hard real time task T_i.	Instruct the organizer to inject T_i into BFQ.
E_6	S_7	A soft real time task T_i (in INQ or BFQ) exceeds the threshold value.	T_i is treated as a soft real time task, then it may result in preempting a normal task.

Figure 9. Procedure followed by the scheduler if E_1 is triggered

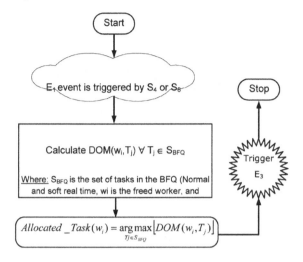

Figure 10. Procedure followed by the scheduler if E_2 is triggered

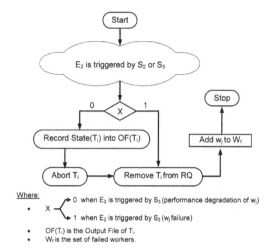

As illustrated in Figures 16 and 17, SOS scheduler introduces the best makespan for a set of input grid tasks as it allocates the suitable task to the suitable worker. On the other hand, the rest of schedulers suffer from the haste problem. They are forced, in many circumstances, to allocate a heavy task to a week worker. UDA is the closest scheduler to SOS, as it relies on some of the user experiences. The rest schedulers introduce poor performance as they ignore the dynamic nature of the grid. They don't take the load changes on the workers into their accounts.

Experiment 2: Measuring the Average Turnaround Time (User View)

This experiment, which was handled in the same scenario as the previous one, measures the Average Turnaround Time (ATAT) for a set of grid tasks. This parameter measures the scheduler performance from the user point of view. The turnaround time for a grid task T_i on worker w_j, at time τ, denoted by TAT(T_i, w_j, τ), was introduced previously by (1) as;

$$
\begin{aligned}
TAT(T_i, w_j, \tau) = {} & ET(T_i, w_j, \tau) \\
& + MT(T_i, S, w_j, \tau) \\
& + WT(T_i, w_j) \\
& + RT(Res(T_i), S, w_j, \tau_{finish})
\end{aligned}
$$

where, ET(T_i, w_j, τ) is the predicted execution time of T_i on w_j at time τ, MT(T_i, s, w_j, τ) is the time elapsed by T_i to migrate from the scheduler machine S to w_j at time τ, WT(T_i, w_j) is the waiting time for T_i on w_j before it begins execution, and RT($Res(T_i)$, S, w_j, τ_{finish}) is the time needed to retract the results of T_i from w_j to the scheduler machine S when T_i finished. Hence, the Average Turnaround Time (ATAT) for a set of n grid tasks can be calculated by (9) as;

$$
ATAT = \sum_{i=1}^{n} TAT(T_i) / n = \sum_{i=1}^{n} \left[ET(T_i) + MT(T_i) + WT(T_i) + RT(Res(T_i)) \right] \Big/ n
$$
(9)

However, MT(T_i) and RT($Res(T_i)$) can be neglected because grid tasks are often large ones, which run in the order of hours or even days. Hence, the overhead of migration costs are negligible. Examples of such grid tasks are; state-

Figure 11. Procedure followed by the scheduler if E_3 is triggered

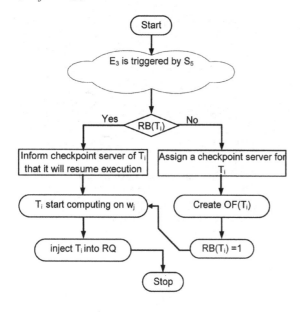

Figure 13. Procedure followed by the scheduler if E_5 is triggered

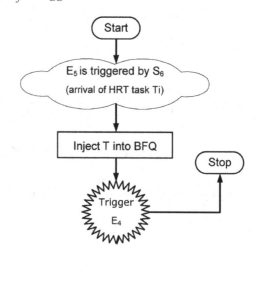

Figure 12. Procedure followed by the scheduler if E_4 is triggered

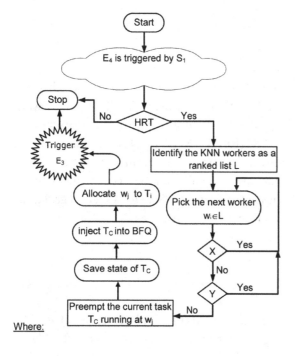

HRT: Hard Real Time Task.

Figure 14. Procedure followed by the scheduler if E_6 is triggered

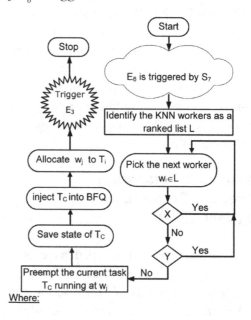

HRT: Hard Real Time Task.

Figure 15. The simple grid architecture used in the simulation

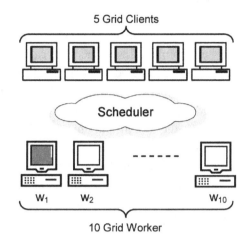

Figure 16. Makespan for different batches using in discrete fashion

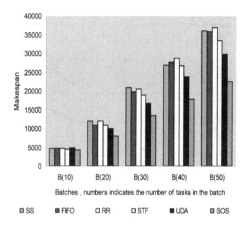

Table 3. A simple description for each competiting scheduling technique as well as the proposed one

Technique	Description	Type
Static Scheduling (SS)	Static scheduling maps the task T_i to an arbitrary worker w_j from the set of available workers immediately when T_i enters BFQ. However, when a worker is suddenly failed or becomes unavailable, its assigned tasks are rescheduled again. When static scheduling is employed, each available worker should have a private ready queue that maintains its per-assigned tasks. When the worker is available, it will be allocated to the next task in its private ready queue.	Static
First Input First Output (FIFO)	This technique assigns the next task in BFQ to the newly available worker. Hence, when a task t_i enters BFQ (a new task or an involuntary suspended one), its enter time (wall clock time when T_i enters BFQ) is registered. Then, when a new worker w_j is available, the task with the minimal enter time is allocated to w_j in order to begin (or resume) its execution.	Dynamic (Adaptive)
Round Robin (RR)	Round Robin scheduling assigns an arbitrary task $T_i \in$ BFQ to the newly available worker w_j with no other restrictions.	
User Directed Assignment (UDA)	In this scheduling technique [30], grid workers are manually categorized into M different categories (in our experiments M=3) based on the worker strength (e.g., its own resources, which are; CPU speed, memory and secondary storage size). The three considered categories are; (i) strong, (ii) medium, and (iii) weak. On the other hand, all tasks in BFQ are manually categorized into the same predefined categories according to the task requirements. By other words, BFQ is divided into three separate smaller queues in which each queue attached to one category. When a worker is available, a task from the corresponding queue is picked for execution. If the corresponding queue is empty, a task from the lower queue is picked for execution.	
Shortest Task First (STF)	This technique is sometimes called Shortest Job First (SJF) (Silberschatz, Galvin, & Gagne, 2005). Briefly, STF uses the user assistance to choose the task (from BFQ) with the minimal predicted execution time on the freed worker.	
System Oriented Scheduler (SOS) - the proposed strategy	The proposed strategy was implemented in the following scenario. On one hand, when a new task T_i enters BFQ, its required parameters (CPU, MEM, and STR) are mapped into a set of predefined distinct levels (from 0 to 10). On the other hand, when a worker w_j is free and ready to receive a grid task, its parameters are collected, then mapped into the same predefined levels (from 0 to 10). The worker is then projected into the Parm_Space as a point as well as all tasks in BFQ. An assumption that the most suitable task for w_j is one of its K-Nearest Neighbor (KNN) tasks. Using K=5, the nearest neighboring tasks are picked. However, estimating the most suitable task is a challenge. To go around such hurdle, the Worker Profile Database (WPDB) is employed to predict the most suitable task (from the available five ones) for the worker considering the worker profile in the next time periods.	

Figure 17. Makespan for different batches using in continuous fashion

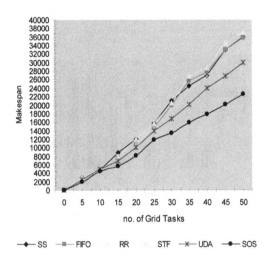

space search algorithms, long running simulations and image processing. Also, this experiment is carried out using a private LAN, which in turn guarantees a high bandwidth. Accordingly, (9) can be reformulated in (10) as;

$$ATAT = \sum_{i=1}^{n} TAT(T_i) / n = \sum_{i=1}^{n} \left[ET(T_i) + WT(T_i) \right] \Big/ n \tag{10}$$

Figure 18 illustrates the ATAT against the number of grid tasks for different scheduling strategies. It is shown that UDA and SOS schedulers demonstrate smaller ATAT than the rest of schedulers, which indicates their good scheduling performance. However, UDA outperforms the proposed SOS scheduler in some points. This is clear because UDA targets to minimize the turnaround time for each individual task with no attention for the system efficiency, which accordingly results in decreasing the average turnaround time for a batch of grid tasks.

Experiment 3: Measuring the System Slowdown Factor

One of the vital metric that indicates the latency of the system compared with the ideal case (i.e., the execution on dedicated machines) is the system slow down factor (Kousalya & Balasubramanie, 2008). The slowdown of task T_i, denoted as; $Slow(T_i)$, is the turnaround time of T_i divided by its runtime on a dedicated machine. Clearly, to measure the system slowdown factor for a batch X of n tasks, $Slow(T_i) \forall T_i \in X$ should be calculated first. Then the system slowdown for the batch X, which denoted as $S\_Slow(X)$ can be calculated by averaging the slowdown values of each task $T_i \in X$. Accordingly, $S\_Slow(X)$ can be expressed as; $S\_Slow(X) = \sum_{i=1}^{n} Slow(T_i) \Big/ n$. The slowdown of the grid system against different numbers of tasks is calculated by considering the different competing scheduling techniques. Results are illustrated in Figure 19.

Again, UDA and SOS schedulers outperform the other schedulers as they demonstrate smaller slow down factor than the other schedulers. This happened because they introduce the smaller ATAT for a set of input grid tasks.

Experiment 4: Measuring System Failure Rate

Some scheduling techniques assume guaranteed workers. However, this assumption deemed implausible because of the grid dynamic nature, which leads to a consistency problem. Many tasks may fail to finish their execution especially if the rescheduling capability is not established. An efficient parameter that measures the system consistency is the failure rate. The system failure rate is the percentage of tasks that failed to finish their execution in an input batch of tasks. Failure rate, denoted as; F_Rate and can be calculated as; F_Rate=N_f/N, where, N_f is the number of failed tasks in a batch of N input tasks. More-

Figure 18. The Average Turnaround Time (ATAT) against the number of grid tasks

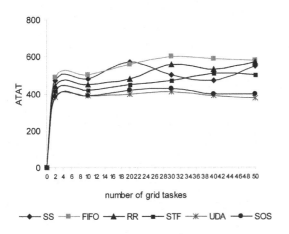

Figure 20. System failure rate against both N and n_{Sf}

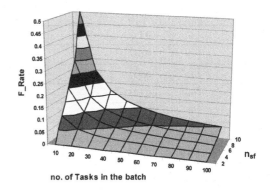

Figure 19. The slowdown of the grid system against different number of tasks

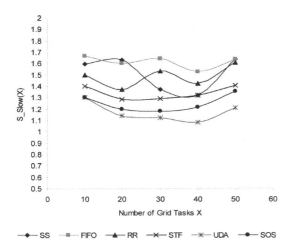

Figure 21. System failure rate against both N and n_{Hf}

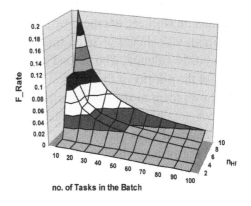

over, N_f can be subdivided into three smaller numbers, hence, $N_f = n_{Rf} + n_{Sf} + n_{Hf}$, where n_{Rf}, n_{Sf}, and n_{Hf} are the number of failed tasks of types normal, soft real time, and hard real time respectively. Accordingly, F_Rate can be calculated as F_Rate$= (n_{Rf} + n_{Sf} + n_{Hf})/N$. In the next section, we will study the effect of those three numbers n_{Rf}, n_{Sf}, and n_{Hf} on the system failure rate.

Figure 20 and Table 4 illustrate the system failure rate against both N and n_{Sf}. It is believed

that F_Rate increases by increasing n_{Sf}, this happened because as n_{Sf} increases, the number of soft real time tasks that fail to complete their execution will increase accordingly, which in turn increases the system failure rate. A soft real time task failure is due to an unexpected high load on the machine that hosts that task, which in turn minimizes the amount of local resources allocated to the grid task. Two logical solutions can be presented for that problem; the first is to reformulate the system behavior to support the re-scheduling ability. By other words, when unexpected sudden load has

Table 4. System failure rate against N and n_{Sf}

N	n_{Sf}				
	2	4	6	8	10
10	0	0.1	0.2	0.3	0.5
20	0	0.05	0.1	0.15	0.25
30	0	0.033	0.0667	0.1	0.166667
40	0	0.025	0.05	0.075	0.125
50	0	0.02	0.04	0.06	0.1
60	0	0.0166	0.0333	0.05	0.0833
70	0	0.014	0.0285	0.0428	0.0714
80	0	0.0125	0.025	0.0375	0.0625
90	0	0.0111	0.0222	0.0333	0.05556
100	0	0.01	0.02	0.03	0.05

been detected on a worker that hosts a soft real time task, the system reschedules that critical task to a new worker. However, this requires interrupting the task, saving its state. Also, if there is no available workers, another low priority (of type normal) task should be interrupted. Hence, this is a costly solution. The second solution is to increase the priority of the soft real time tasks which allows them to start executing as soon as possible. A possible scenario is to treat them as the hard real time ones.

Again, the system failure rate is illustrated in Figure 21 and Table 5 against both N and n_{Hf}. It is noticed that; n_{Hf} has smaller impact on the

system failure rate compared by the impact of n_{Sf}. This is due to the high priority of the hard real time tasks, which allows them to start executing at their submission times. Finally, the effect of n_{Rf} on the system failure rate has been neglected. Our justification is; "with our assumption that; no worker failure, all normal tasks will finish their execution even at the infinity".

CONCLUSION

In this paper, we have come up with a novel, in-advance global philosophy for classify com-

Table 5. System failure rate against N and n_{Hf}

N	n_{Hf}				
	2	4	6	8	10
10	0	0	0.1	0.1	0.2
20	0	0	0.05	0.05	0.1
30	0	0	0.0333	0.033333	0.066667
40	0	0	0.025	0.025	0.05
50	0	0	0.02	0.02	0.04
60	0	0	0.0166	0.016667	0.033333
70	0	0	0.0142	0.014286	0.028571
80	0	0	0.0125	0.0125	0.025
90	0	0	0.0111	0.011111	0.022222
100	0	0	0.01	0.01	0.02

putational grid schedulers. According to that philosophy, a grid scheduler may follow a task oriented or a system oriented strategy. We have also approved that task oriented schedulers usually suffer from a haste problem, which is presented for the first time in this article. The haste problem is the ability of the scheduler to present a good scheduling performance in the initial scheduling periods; however an overall degraded performance is presented in the long run.

To support our point of view, a novel system oriented, event driven grid scheduler is also presented in the paper. The proposed scheduler has salient properties that other scheduler do not have. On one hand, it is a high throughput scheduler as it selects the most suitable worker to execute the grid task using a set of driving heuristic rules. Hence, it minimizes the execution time for a set of grid tasks. On the other hand, it avoids the haste problem. Using simulation, we have compared the performance of our proposed scheduler with other existing grid scheduling heuristics. Experimental results have shown that the proposed scheduling strategy outperforms traditional grid schedulers as it introduces a better scheduling efficiency.

REFERENCES

Aggarwal, M., & Kent, R. (2005). An Adaptive Generalized Scheduler for Grid Applications. In *Proceedings of the 19th Annual International Symposium on High Performance Computing Systems and Applications (HPCS'05)* (pp. 15-18).

Aggarwal, M., Kent, R., & Ngom, A. (2005). Genetic algorithm based scheduler for computational grids. In *Proceedings of the International Symposium on High Performance Computing Systems and Applications* (pp. 209-215).

Berman, F., Wolski, R., Figueira, S., Schopf, J., & Shao, G. (1996). Application-Level Scheduling on Distributed Heterogeneous Networks. In *Proceedings of the 1996 ACM/IEEE Conference on Supercomputing* (p. 39).

Buyya, R. (1999). *High performance cluster computing: systems and architectures*. Upper Saddle River, NJ: Prentice Hall.

Buyya, R., & Vazhkudai, S. (2001). Compute Power Market: Towards a Market-Oriented Grid. In *Proceedings of the 1st International Symposium on Cluster Computing and the Grid* (p. 574).

Casanova, H., Kim, M., Plank, J., & Dongarra, J. (1999). Adaptive Scheduling for Task Farming with Grid middleware. *International Journal of Supercomputer Applications and High-Performance Computing, 13*(3), 231–240. doi:10.1177/109434209901300306

Creel, M., & Goffe, W. (2008). Multi-core CPUs, Clusters, and Grid Computing: A Tutorial. *International Journal of Computational Economics, 32*(4), 353–382. doi:10.1007/s10614-008-9143-5

Daoud, M., & Kharma, N. (2008). Research Note: A high performance algorithm for static task scheduling in heterogeneous distributed computing systems. *International Journal of Parallel and Distributed Computing, 68*(4), 399–409. doi:10.1016/j.jpdc.2007.05.015

Deza, E., & Deza, M. (2006). *Dictionary of Distances*. Amsterdam, The Netherlands: Elsevier.

Foster, I., Roy, A., & Sander, V. (2000). A Quality of Service Architecture that Combines Resource Reservation and Application Adaptation. In *Proceedings of the International Workshop on Quality of Service* (pp. 181-188).

Fujimoto, N., & Hagihara, K. (2004). A Comparison among Grid Scheduling Algorithms for Independent Coarse-Grained Tasks. In *Proceedings of the 2004 Symposium on Applications and the Internet-Workshops (SAINT 2004 Workshops)* (p. 674).

He, L., Jarvis, S., Spooner, D., Bacigalupo, D., Tan, G., & Nudd, G. (2005). Mapping DAG-based Applications to Multiclusters with Background Workload. In *Proceedings of the IEEE International Symposium on Cluster Computing and the Grid (CCGrid'05)* (pp. 855-862).

Hsin, C. (2005). On The Design of Task Scheduling in The Heterogeneous Computing Environments. In *Proceedings of the Computers and Signal Processing Conference (PACRIM 2005)* (pp. 396-399).

Iavarasan, E., Thambidurai, P., & Mahilmannan, R. (2005). Performance Effective Task Scheduling Algorithm for Heterogeneous Computing System. In *Proceedings of the 4th International Symposium on Parallel and Distributed Computing* (pp. 28-38).

Jen, M., & Yuan, F. (2009). Service-oriented grid computing system for digital rights management (GC-DRM). *International Journal of Expert Systems with Applications, 36*(7), 10708–10726. doi:10.1016/j.eswa.2009.02.066

Jens, V., Martin, W., & Roman, B. (2009). Services Grids in Industry - On-Demand Provisioning and Allocation of Grid-based Business Services. *International Journal of Business & Information Systems Engineering, 1*(2), 177–184. doi:10.1007/s12599-008-0009-0

Kadav, A., & Sanjeev, K. (2006). A workflow editor and scheduler for composing applications on computational grids. In *Proceedings of the 12th International Conference on Parallel and Distributed Systems* (pp. 127-132).

Kiran, M., Hassan, A., Kuan, L., & Yee, Y. (2009). Execution Time Prediction of Imperative Paradigm Tasks for Grid Scheduling Optimization. *International Journal of Computer Science and Network Security, 9*(2), 155–163.

Kousalya, K., & Balasubramanie, P. (2008). An Enhanced ant algorithm for grid scheduling problem. *International Journal of Computer Science and Network Security, 8*(4), 262–271.

Lee, W., Squicciarini, A., & Bertino, E. (2009). The Design and Evaluation of Accountable Grid Computing System. In *Proceedings of the 29th IEEE International Conference on Distributed Computing Systems (ICDCS '09)* (pp. 145-154).

Li, M., & Hadjinicolaou, M. (2008). Curriculum Development on Grid Computing. *International Journal of Education and Information Technology, 1*(2), 71–78.

Liu, L., Yang, Y., Lian, L., & Wanbin, S. (2006). Using Ant Optimization for Super Scheduling in Computational Grid. In *Proceedings of the IEEE Asia-pacific Conference on Services Computing*.

Malone, W., Fikes, R., Grant, R., & Howard, M. (1988). A Market-Like Task Scheduler for Distributed Computing Environments. In *Ecology of Computation* (pp. 177–205). Enterprise.

Sacerdoti, F., Katz, M., Massie, M., & Culler, D. (2003). Wide area cluster monitoring with Ganglia. In *Proceedings of the IEEE International Conference on Cluster Computing* (pp. 289-298).

Shah, R., Veeravalli, B., & Misra, M. (2007). On the Design of Adaptive and Decentralized Load Balancing Algorithms with Load Estimation for Computational Grid Environments. *IEEE Transactions on Parallel and Distributed Systems, 18*(12), 1675–1686. doi:10.1109/TPDS.2007.1115

Silberschatz, A., Galvin, P., & Gagne, G. (2005). *Operating System Concepts*. New York, NY: John Wiley & Sons.

Tsai, M.-J., & Hung, Y.-K. (2009). Distributed computing power service coordination based on peer-to-peer grids architecture. *International Journal of Expert Systems with Applications, 36*(2), 3101–3118. doi:10.1016/j.eswa.2008.01.050

Tseng, L., Chin, Y., & Wang, S. (2009). The anatomy study of high performance task scheduling algorithm for Grid computing system. *International Journal of Computer Standards & Interfaces, 31*(4), 713–722. doi:10.1016/j.csi.2008.09.017

Tseng, L., Chin, Y., & Wang, S. (2009). A minimized makespan scheduler with multiple factors for Grid computing systems. *International Journal of Expert Systems with Applications, 36*(8), 11118–11130. doi:10.1016/j.eswa.2009.02.071

Waldspurger, C., Hogg, T., Huberman, B., Kephart, O., & Stornetta, S. (1992). Spawn: A Distributed Computational Economy. *IEEE Transactions on Software Engineering, 18*, 103–177. doi:10.1109/32.121753

Wolski, R., Spring, N., & Hayes, J. (1999). The Network Weather Service: A Distributed Resource Performance Forecasting Service for Metacomputing. *International Journal of Future Generation Computing Systems, 15*(5-6), 757–768. doi:10.1016/S0167-739X(99)00025-4

Yan, H., Shen, X., Li, X., & Wu, M. (2005). An Improved Ant Algorithm for Job Scheduling in Grid Computing. In *Proceedings of the IEEE International Conference on Machine Learning and Cybernetics* (pp. 2957-2961).

Zhou, D., & Lo, V. (2005). Wave Scheduler: Scheduling for Fast Turnaround Time in Peer-based Desktop Grid Systems. In *Proceedings of the 11th International Workshop on Job Scheduling Strategies for Parallel Processing* (pp. 194-218).

This work was previously published in the International Journal of Grid and High Performance Computing, Volume 3, Issue 1, edited by Emmanuel Udoh and Ching-Hsien Hsu, pp. 22-41, copyright 2011 by IGI Publishing (an imprint of IGI Global)

Chapter 4
Dynamic Dependent Tasks Assignment for Grid Computing

Meriem Meddeber
University of Mascara, Algeria

Belabbas Yagoubi
University of Oran, Algeria

ABSTRACT

A computational grid is a widespread computing environment that provides huge computational power for large-scale distributed applications. One of the most important issues in such an environment is resource management. Task assignment as a part of resource management has a considerable effect on the grid middleware performance. In grid computing, task execution time is dependent on the machine to which it is assigned, and task precedence constraints are represented by a directed acyclic graph. This paper proposes a hybrid assignment strategy of dependent tasks in Grids which integrate static and dynamic assignment technologies. Grid computing is considered a set of clusters formed by a set of computing elements and a cluster manager. The main objective is to arrive at a method of task assignment that could achieve minimum response time and reduce the transfer cost, inducing by the tasks transfer respecting the dependency constraints.

INTRODUCTION

A *computational Grid* (Foster & Kesselman, 2004) is a hardware and software infrastructure that provides consistent pervasive and inexpensive access to high end computational capacity. An ideal grid environment should provide access to all the available resources seamlessly and fairly (Saleh, Deldari, & Dorri, 2008). *Grid computing* originated from a new computing infrastructure for scientific research and cooperation and is becoming a mainstream technology for large-scale resource sharing and distributed system integration. Current efforts towards making the global infrastructure a reality provide technologies on both grid services and application enabling (Cao, Spooner, Jarvis, & Nudd, 2005).

DOI: 10.4018/978-1-4666-2065-0.ch004

A *task* is defined to be a program segment that can be individually scheduled. A *grid computing element* is defined to be any processor that can receive tasks from a central scheduler and may be a single processor node or one of the processors within a multi-processor node. The problem of obtaining an optimal matching of tasks to machines in any distributed system is well known to be *NP-hard* even when the tasks are independent. The problem is much more difficult when the tasks have dependencies because the order of task execution as well as task-machine pairing affects overall completion time (Boyer & Hura, 2005).

A *precedence relation* from task *i* to task *j* means that *j* needs data from *i* before being started. If these two tasks are not assigned to the same computing element, a delay c_{ij} must be considered between the completion of *i* and the beginning of *j* to transfer the data.

Dynamic tasks assignment assumes a continuous stochastic stream of incoming tasks. Very little parameters are known in advance for dynamic tasks assignment. Obviously, it is more complex than *static tasks assignment* for implementation, but achieves better throughput. Also it is the most desired because of the application demand (Vidyarthi, Sarker, Tripathi, & Yang 2009).

In this paper, we propose a hybrid assignment strategy of dependent tasks in Grids which integrated static and dynamic assignment technologies. This strategy meets the following objectives:

1. Reducing, whenever possible, the average response time of tasks submitted to the grid,
2. Respecting the constraints of dependency between tasks, and,
3. Reducing communication costs by using a static tasks placement based on the connected components algorithm to minimize the delay c_{ij} between task *i* and task *j* and by favoring a dynamic tasks placement within the cluster rather than the entire grid.

The rest of this paper is organized as follows. We begin with the overview of some related works in Section 2. Section 3 describes the grid computing topology. In section 4, we present the tasks assignment problem. In section 5, we present Tasks assignment in Grid computing environments. In Section 6 we will presents our system model. Section 7 describes the main steps of the proposed assignment strategy. We evaluate the performance of the proposed scheme in Section 8. Finally, Section 9 concludes the paper.

RELATED WORK

There have been many heuristic algorithms proposed for the static and dynamic tasks assignment problem. Many of these algorithms apply only to the special case where the tasks are independent i.e. there are no precedence constraints (Kamalam, Maharajan, & Maheish Sundhar, 2010; Leal, Huedo, & Llorente, 2009; Jiang, Baumgarten, Zhou & Jin, 2009; Salcedo-Sanz, Xu, & Yao, 2006; Maheswaran, Ali, Siegel, Hensgen, & Freund, 1999). Many heuristic algorithms have been proposed for static scheduling of dependent tasks where task precedence constraints are modeled as a directed acyclic graph (DAG). Qu, Soininen, and Nurmi (2007) target dependent task models and propose three static schedulers that use different problem solving strategies. The first is a heuristic approach developed from traditional list based schedulers. It presents high efficiency but the least accuracy. The second is based on a full-domain search using constraint programming. It can guarantee to produce optimal solutions but requires significant searching effort. The last is a guided random search technique based on a genetic algorithm, which shows reasonable efficiency and much better accuracy than the heuristic approach. Boyer and Hura (2005), propose a non-evolutionary random scheduling (RS) algorithm for efficient matching and scheduling of inter-dependent tasks in a DHC system. RS is a succession of randomized task orderings and a heuristic mapping from task order to schedule. Randomized task ordering is effectively a topological sort where the outcome may be any possible task order for which the task precedent constraints are maintained. However static tasks assignment is performed off-line, or in a predictive manner and can be used whenever the task information is known a priori such as at compile time of a parallelized application. Although the good results that this approaches provides, they stay limited to a static assignment. Various research is examined in this issue (Falzon & Li, 2010; Nakechbandi, Colin, & Gashumba, 2007; Chen, Zhang, & Hao 2008).Large and non dedicated computing platforms as grids may require dynamic task assignment methods to adapt to the run-time changes such as increases in the workload or resources, processor failures, and link failures (Uçar, Aykanat, Kaya, & Ikinci, 2006; He & Zhao, 2008; Chtepen, Dhoedt, Turck, & Demeester, 2008).

In Yagoubi and Meddeber (2010), a distributed load balancing model is proposed; this work doesn't take into account the tasks dependencies.

We propose, in this paper, a novel assignment strategy to address the new challenges in Grid computing. Comparatively to the existing works, the main characteristics of our strategy are:

1. It addresses the problem of tasks with precedence constraints,
2. It has the advantage of being able to divide the input task graph into set of connected component,
3. It integrated static and dynamic assignment technologies for solving the placement problem.
4. It executes an inter-clusters load balancing even if the cluster is well balanced. This allows exploitation of the ability of clusters under loaded or completely free.

COMPUTING TOPOLOGY

From a topological point of view (Figure 1), (Bertis, Ferreira, & Amstrong, 2002) index the grids in three levels per ascending order of geographical scope and complexity: Intra-cluster, Extra-cluster and Inter-clusters.

- **Intra-cluster (by analogy to the Intranet):** This grid is composed of a relatively simple set of resources (computing elements and storage elements) belonging to a single organization. The main characteristics of such topology are the presence

Figure 1. Grid computing topology

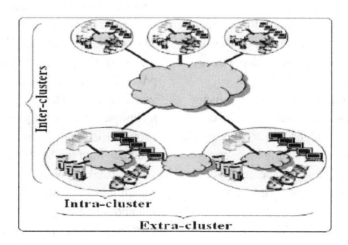

of an interconnection high-speed network and a set relatively static and homogeneous of resources.

- **Extra-cluster (by analogy to Extranet):** This type of grid topology extends the previous by aggregating several clusters. An extra-cluster is characterized by the presence of a heterogeneous high and low speed (LAN / WAN) network and a set of dynamic resources.
- **Inter-clusters (by analogy to the Internet):** This topology is to federate grids of multiple organizations into one overall grid. Its main characteristics are the presence of an interconnection network very heterogeneous high and low speed (LAN / WAN) and a highly dynamic heterogeneous resources.

TASKS ASSIGNMENT

In As Grid is a distributed system utilizing idle nodes scattered in every region, the most critical issue pertaining to distributed systems is how to integrate and apply every computer resource into a distributed system, so as to achieve the goals of enhancing performance, resource sharing, extensibility, and increase availability. Tasks assignment is very important in a distributed environment. In distributed systems, every node has different processing speed and system resources, so in order to enhance the utilization of each node and shorten the consumption of time, tasks assignment will play a critical role. On the other hand, in distributed systems, the policies and methods for keeping a tasks assignment will directly affect the performance of the system. In addition, the tasks assignment policies for distributed systems can be generally categorized into static tasks assignment policies and dynamic tasks assignment policies (Yan, Wang, Chang, & Lin, 2007).

A. Static Tasks Assignment

Static tasks assignment policies use some simple system information, such as the various information related to average operation, operation cycle, and etc., and according to these data, tasks are distributed through mathematical formulas or other adjustment methods, so that every node in the distributed system can process the assigned tasks until completed. The merit of this method is that system information is not required to be collected at all times, and through a simple process, the system can run with simple analysis. However, some of the nodes have low utilization rates. Due to the fact that it does not dynamically adjust with the system information, there is a certain degree of burden on system performance.

B. Dynamic Tasks Assignment

Dynamic tasks assignment policies refer to the current state of the system or the most recent state at the system time, to decide how to assign tasks to each node in a distributed system. If any node in the system is over-loaded, the over-loading task will be transferred to other nodes and processed, in order to achieve the goal of a dynamic assignment. However, the migration of tasks will incur extra overhead to the system. It is because the system has to reserve some resources for collecting and maintaining the information of system states. If this overhead can be controlled and limited to a certain acceptable range, in most conditions, dynamic tasks assignment policies outperform the static tasks assignment policies.

TASKS ASSIGNMENT IN GRID COMPUTING ENVIRONMENTS

Tasks assignment systems for Traditional distributed environments do not work in Grid environments because the two classes of environments are radically distinct. Tasks assignment in Grid environments is significantly complicated by the unique characteristics of Grids:

- **Heterogeneity of the grid resources:** Heterogeneity exists in two categories of resources. First, networks used to interconnect these computational resources may differ significantly in terms of their bandwidth and communication protocols. Second, computational resources may have different hardware, computer architectures, physical memory size, CPU speed and so on and also different software, such as different operating systems, cluster management software and so on. This characteristic complicates the system workload estimation because the heterogeneous resources could not be considered uniformly.
- **Grid resources are dynamic:** In traditional distributed systems, such as a cluster, the pool of resources is assumed to be fixed or stable. In the Grid, this character is not verified because of computational resources and communication networks dynamicity. Both computational resources availability and capability will exhibit dynamic behaviour.

On one hand new resources may join the Grid and on the other hand, some resources may become unavailable due to problems such as network failure. This poses constraints on applications such as fault tolerance. A resource that connects or disconnects must be detected and taken into account by the system.

SYSTEM MODEL

A. Grid Model

In our study we model a Grid as a collection of n clusters with different computational facilities.

Let $G = (C_1, C_2, ..., C_n)$ denotes a set of clusters, where each cluster C_i is defined as a vector with four parameters: $C_i = (NCE_i, M_i, Band_i, Spd_i)$,

Where NCE_i is the number of computing elements, M_i is the Manager node of the cluster C_i, $Band_i$ is the bandwidth of the network, Spd_i correspond to the cluster capability.

A cluster is a set of R computing elements $C_i = (CE_{i1}, CE_{i2}, ..., CE_{ir})$, where each computing element CE_{ij}, have it own capability. The cluster manager CM_i uses the following equation to calculate Spd_i:

$$Spd_i \sum_{j \in NCE_i} Spd_{ij} \qquad (1)$$

Figure 2 shows the Grid system model. In highly distributed systems, centralized work tasks assignment approaches become less feasible because it make use of a high degree of information, which causes a high work tasks assignment overhead. That is why we chose to develop a hybrid assignment model that is centralized *intra-cluster*, but distributed *inter-clusters*. Each cluster in the Grid has a manager, which assign tasks to the cluster computing element.

We assume that in the grid under study there is a central resource broker (*CRB*), to which every Cluster Manager (*CM*) connects and the grid clients send their tasks to the central scheduler. The central scheduler is responsible for scheduling tasks among *CMs*.

Figure 2. Grid model

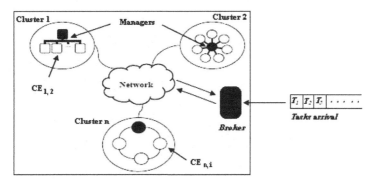

B. Application Model

DAG Model

An application can be represented by a directed acyclic graph (*DAG*) *D= (V, E)*, where *V* is a set of *v* nodes and *E* is a set of directed *e* edges. A node in the DAG represents a task which in turn is a set of instructions which must be executed sequentially without pre-emption in the same processor. The edges in the DAG, each of which is denoted by (n_i, n_j), correspond to the precedence constraints among the nodes. The weight of an edge is called the communication cost of the edge and is denoted by C_{ij}. The source node of an edge is called the *parent node* while the sink node is called the *child node*. A node with no parent is called an *entry node* and a node with no child is called an *exit node* (Kwok & Ahmad, 1999). Figure 3, shows a task precedence graph constituted by five tasks, with one entry task T_1 and three exit tasks T_3, T_4, T_5.

Task Model

We consider that tasks arrive randomly with a random computation length, an arrival time and precedence constraints. In our work, we generate randomly precedence constraints between tasks. Also, we believe that tasks can be executed on any computing element and each *CE* can only execute one task at each time point, the execution of a task cannot be interrupted or moved to another CE during execution. We also assume that a task cannot start execution before it gathers all of the messages from its parent tasks. The communication cost between two tasks assigned to the same processor is supposed to be zero.

PROPOSED STRATEGY

In order to reduce the global response time of the system and respect the tasks dependencies, this study proposed a tasks assignment policy. When a user sends his tasks, they will be assigned to appropriate computing elements to achieve the goal of placement, then, the system will be adjusted dynamically according to the clusters workload.

A. Static Tasks Placement Strategy

Central resource broker The role of the *CRB* in the system is to assign tasks placed in the task queue. For that we propose the following steps that will be executed periodically:

• Partition all tasks waiting in the queue to *x* connected component by executing the connected component algorithm. A connected component is defined as a collection of dependent tasks with inter task

Figure 3. Task precedence graph

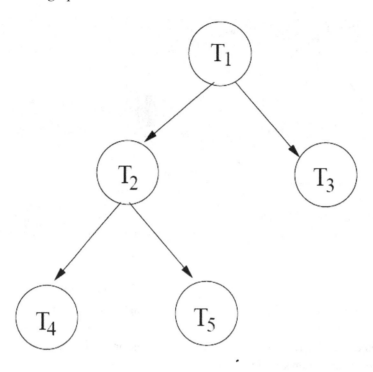

data dependencies. Figure 4 shows a set of waiting tasks composed of three connected component.

- Sends each connected component CC_k to a cluster manager CM_i using one of the following methods:
- Using a **random** strategy: assign a connected component to a randomize cluster.
- Using a **round robin** strategy, as follows:

$(CC_1, CM_1), (CC_2, CM_2),..., (CC_p, CM_n), (CC_{p+1}, CM_1),..., (CC_x, CM_j),$

- Using a **Min-Min** strategy, as follows:
  1. Selects the connected component CC_k with the maximum length,
  Computes the average Grid execution time equal to:

$$Tex_G = \frac{\sum_{i \in n} LOD_i}{\sum_{i \in N} Spd_i} \qquad (2)$$

where: n represent the number of cluster manager in the grid and LOD_i the workload of the cluster manager CM_i.

Calculates the Supply $Supply_j$ of each Clusters manager CM_j which corresponds to the load that it agrees to receive so that its processing time: TEX_r converges to TEX_G.

$$Supply_r = \frac{LOD_G \cdot SPD_r}{SPD_G} - LOD_r \qquad (3)$$

4. Sends the connected component CC_k to the cluster manager with the biggest supply.
5. Repeat the previous steps until the assignment of all connected components.

Cluster Manager

Once the cluster manager receives the connected component CC_k, it affects them to the computing elements composing the cluster:

Figure 4. Example with three connected components

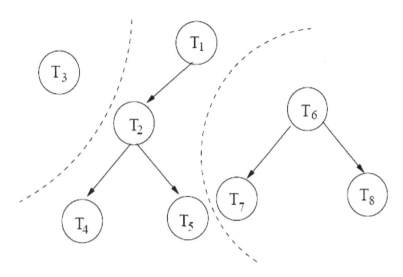

- Using a random strategy,

- Using a round robin strategy, as follows:

$(CC_1, CE_{1i}), (CC_2, CE_{2i}),..., (CC_x, CE_{ji}),$

- Using a Min-Min strategy, as follows:
  1. Selects the connected component CC_k with the maximum length,
  2. Compute the Cluster execution time which is equal to:

$$Tex_i = \frac{\sum_{j \in CNE_i} LOD_{ji}}{\sum_{j \in CNE_i} Spd_{ji}} \qquad (4)$$

where: CNE_i represent the number of computing element in the cluster and LOD_{ji} the workload of the computing element CE_{ji}.

  3. Calculates the Supply $Supply_{ji}$ of each computing element CE_{ji} which corresponds to the load that it agrees to receive so that its processing time: TEX_{ji} converges to TEX_i.

$$Supply_{ji} = \frac{LOD_i \cdot SPD_{ji}}{SPD_i} - LOD_{ji} \qquad (5)$$

  4. Sends the connected component CC_k to the computing element with the biggest supply.
  5. Repeat the previous steps until the assignment of all connected components.

B. Dynamic Tasks Placement Strategy

Computing Element

The computing element, perform these steps while its tasks queue is not empty:

- Run the first entry task T_j (with no precedence constraints) of its tasks queue.
- Updates the connected component CC_j associated to task T_j.

The computing element executes the following steps periodically:

- Executes the connected component algorithm on CC_j to obtain the new entry *tasks*. Figure 5 shows an example of a connected component with one entry task. After the end of execution of T_j, the CC_j is divided on three connected components.
- Computes its execution time tex_{ij} as follows:

$$Tex_{ij} = \sum_{c \in CCN_{ij}} \sum_{l \in L} \sum_{k \in P} \frac{length_{c,k}}{Spd_{ij}} \qquad (6)$$

where, *CCN* is the connected component number assigned to the computing element. L is the level number of connected components, and P is the tasks number of level k.

- Sends its execution time to the cluster manager and all computing element of the cluster.
- We define a threshold α, from which a resource CEij can say that it is more loaded than another. If $(Tex_{ij} > Tex_{ik} + \alpha)$ then transfer some connected components from CE_{ij} to CE_{ik} until $Tex_{ij} <= Tex_{ik} + \alpha$.

- Inform the cluster manager about the tasks movement.
- Cluster manager: The cluster manager receives periodically the execution time of each resource of the cluster and performs the next steps:
- Computes the execution time of cluster as follow:

$$Tex_i = \sum_{j \in R} Tex_{ij} \qquad (7)$$

- We define a threshold β, such as:

If $(Tex_i > Tex_k + \beta)$ **then** transfer some connected components from C_i to C_k until $Tex_i <= Tex_k + \beta$.

SIMULATION RESULTS

There are some tools available, for application scheduling simulation in Grid computing environments, such as:

- Bricks (Takefusa, Matsuoka, Aida, Nakada, & Nagashima, 1999) focus on simulating scheduling policies over the Computational Grid. It is a multiple clients

Figure 5. Example with one entry task

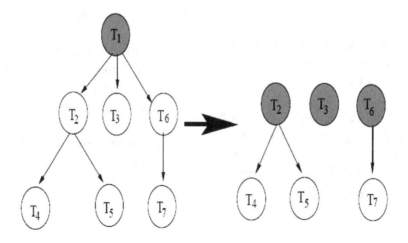

and multiple servers scenario simulator that returns average overall service rates. The network is shaped as standalone simulating entity between a Grid Computing Client and a Grid Server, without complex topology implementation.

- OptorSim (Bell, Cameron, Capozza, Millar, Stockinger, & Zini, 2003) has explicitly accounts for both dynamic provisioning and resource scheduling policies, obtaining resulting performance. Dynamic provisioning is performed in the context of replication in data Grid. Various economic market model replication strategies can be evaluated with the canonical reference.

- GangSim (Dumitrescu & Foster, 2005) have been developed to support studies of scheduling strategies in Grid environments, with a particular focus on interactions of local and global resource allocation policies. It is derived as part of the Ganglia monitoring framework, an implementation that mix simulated and real Grid components. It is the first simulator that model not only sites but also Virtual Organizations (VO) users and planners.

- SimGrid (Legrand, Marchal, & Casanova, 2003) is focus on scheduling to model the grid network topology, and simulate the data flow over the available network bandwidth. The mayor drawback of this tool is that is not modeling job decomposition and task Parallelization characteristics, or resource availability is also not modeled.

- GridSim (Buyya & Murshed, 2002) is a toolkit for analyze and compare the performance of resource scheduling algorithms of the grid. There is not Data Grid simulation, only processing is implemented on variants of the NimrodG (Buyya, Abramson, & Giddy, 2000) resource broker based on the market based economic model. GridSim is shape of heterogeneous, multi-tasking Grid resources, calendar based on dead-line and budget based constraints. It also allows evaluation of various scheduling policies in a single simulation. Each grid task is implemented as a separate thread in the Java Virtual Machine.

To test and evaluate the performance of our model, we developed our strategy under the Grid-Sim simulator. In GridSim, application tasks/jobs are modelled as Gridlet objects that contain all the information related to the job and the execution management details, such as:

- **Resources parameters:** These parameters give information about computing elements, clusters and networks. A node is characterized by its capacity, speed and networks bandwidth sizes.
- **Tasks parameters:** These parameters include the number of tasks queued at every node, task submission date, number of instructions per task, cumulative processing time, cumulative waiting time and so on.

As performance measures, we are interested in average response time and waiting time of tasks. We compute the above metric *before* and *after* execution of our strategy. To obtain results that are as consistent as possible, we repeated the same experiments more than ten 5 times.

All these experiments were performed on a PC 3 GHz Pentium IV, with 1GB of memory and running on Linux Redhat 9.0.

Experiments 1

In the first set of experiments (Table 1), we used the simulator Simgrid to test our static strategy. SimGrid is a toolkit written in C language and designed to test scheduling algorithms in grid computing and / or implementation of distributed applications. It generates platforms consisting of 2, 3 or 4 clusters. The number of processors in each cluster is randomly selected between 16 and 24.

Experiments 2

In this set of experiments we focused results relating to objective metrics, according to various numbers of tasks and clusters. We have varied the clusters number from 2 to 6 by step of 2. We supposed that each cluster involves 30 computing elements. For each node we randomly generate associated speed varying between 5 and 30 MIPS. The number of tasks has been varied from 500 to 2000 by step of 500, with sizes randomly generated between 1000 and 100000 MI (Millions of Instructions). We also generate randomly precedence constraints between tasks.

Table 2 shows the variation of the average response time (in seconds) before and after execution.

We can note the following:

- Proposed strategy allowed for very clear reduction of average response time of the tasks. We obtain a gain varying between 6\% and 55\%.
- In more than 90\% of cases, this improvement is greater than 20\%.
- The lower benefits were obtained when the number of clusters was set to 6. We can justify this by the instability of the Grid state (Most nodes are under loaded or even idle).
- The best gains were realized when the Grid is in a stable state: (For 2 and 4 clusters).

Figure 6 illustrates the improvement of the mean response time for 4 clusters:

We observe that our strategy reduce considerably the average response time of tasks submitted to the system. When increasing the tasks number,

Table 1. First experiment results

Tâches	Clusters	2	3	4
70	Aléatoire	11.42	15.415	15.635
	Par C. C.	8.2714	10.849	9.975
	Gains	28%	30%	36%
90	Aléatoire	14.558	19.815	20.09
	Par C. C.	17.044	12.534	11.812
	Gains	1%	38%	41%
100	Aléatoire	16.126	22.179	22.292
	Par C. C.	18.181	13.456	12.610
	Gains	1%	39%	45%
120	Aléatoire	19.263	26.521	26.693
	Par C. C.	20.440	15.118	14.407
	Gains	1%	43%	46%
150	Aléatoire	23.883	33.121	33.293
	Par C. C.	23.883	17.735	17.159
	Gains	1%	46%	48%
170	Aléatoire	27.105	37.579	37.529
	Par C. C.	26.020	19.585	18.946
	Gains	4%	48%	49%

Table 2. Second experiment results

#Tasks	#Clusters	2	4	6
500	*Before*	1.10E+05	0.81E+05	0.75E+05
	After	0.75E+05	0.65E+05	0.60E+05
	Gain	**23%**	**19%**	**20%**
1000	*Before*	3.13E+05	1.79E+05	1.71E+05
	After	2.21E+05	1.19E+05	1.62E+05
	Gain	**29%**	**34%**	**6%**
1500	*Before*	5.08E+05	3.48E+05	3.33E+05
	After	2.31E+05	2.21E+05	2.58E+05
	Gain	**55%**	**36%**	**23%**
2000	*Before*	6.95E+05	5.21E+05	5.52E+05
	After	4.39E+05	3.93E+05	3.40E+05
	Gain	**36%**	**26%**	**38%**

response time benefits increase. The lower benefit is obtained with 500 tasks, it is due to an under loaded state of the grid.

Experiments 3

Table 3 shows that the average waiting time of tasks is significantly ameliorated by our strategy. The gain on the waiting time varies between 23\% and 62\%, these results are very promising in the present state of our strategy.

Experiments 4

In this series of experiments, we modified the algorithm executed by the cluster manager; Instead of assigning the tasks by connected components within the cluster, the manager assigns the tasks one by one taking into account the precedence constraints connecting them (so it's an assignment by tasks and not by connected components).

Once the cluster manager receives the connected component CC_k, it affect it using one of the following methods:

Figure 6. Response time results (4 clusters)

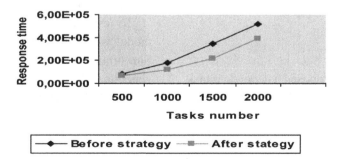

Table 3. Third experiment results

#Tasks	#Clusters	2	4	6
500	*Before*	1.03E+05	1.44E+05	1.59E+05
	After	0.66E+05	0.65E+05	0.60E+05
	Gain	35%	54%	62%
1000	*Before*	0.73E+05	0.20E+05	1.26E+05
	After	0.47E+05	0.12E+05	1.37E+05
	Gain	36%	37%	47%
1500	*Before*	6.95E+05	5.21E+05	5.52E+05
	After	4.39E+05	3.93E+05	3.40E+05
	Gain	38%	40%	38%
2000	*Before*	8.11E+05	6.57E+05	6.05E+05
	After	6.27E+05	5.01E+05	4.61E+05
	Gain	23%	24%	24%

1. Affect the first task Ti and at least one of his sons to a computing element chosen randomly, and then affect the other tasks randomly to the other computing element of the same cluster (Figure 7).
2. Affect all ready tasks (with no precedence constraints) randomly to the cluster computing elements. After their execution, the scheduler determines and affects new ready tasks and so on until the end of execution of all tasks submitted to the cluster (Figure 8).

The set of experiments is to compare the results of the three methods presented above.

The analysis of got results, allowed us to deduct that proposed approach performs very encouraging gains in terms of response time (Figure 9) and that the second method gave the best gains.

CONCLUSION

In this paper we have proposed a dependent task assignment strategy for Grid computing. This strategy integrated static and dynamic assignment technologies for solving the placement problem. A tasks placement strategy is introduced; it has the advantage of being able to divide the input task graph into set of connected component in order to:

1. Reduce, whenever possible, the average response time of tasks submitted to the grid,
2. Respect the constraints of dependency between tasks, and,
3. Reduce communication costs by using a static tasks placement based on the connected components algorithm to minimize the delay c_{ij} between task i and task j and by favoring a dynamic tasks placement within the cluster rather than the entire grid

Relatively to the existing works, our strategy is fully distributed, uses a task-level assignment and privileges, as much as possible, a local dynamic assignment to avoid the use of WAN communication.

To test and evaluate the performance of our model, we developed our strategy under the GridSim simulator written in Java. We have randomly generated clusters with different characteristics and a set of dependent tasks. The first experimental results are encouraging since we can significantly reduce the average response and waiting time.

Figure 7. Method 1

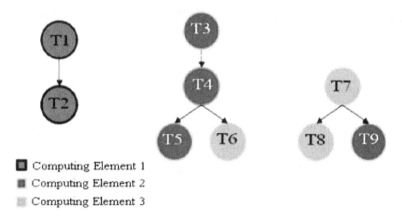

Figure 8. Method 2

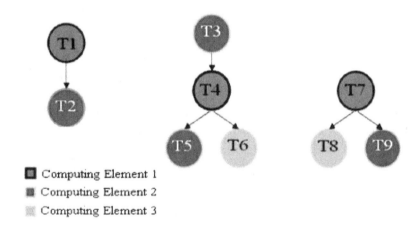

Figure 9. Average response time based on the number of cluster

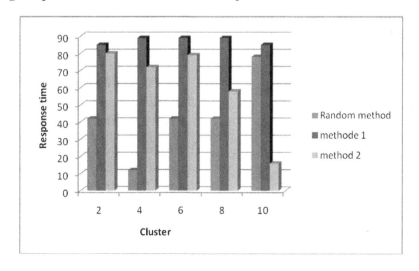

In the future we want to improve the proposed strategy by integrating the multi-agent systems. We will also define other metrics of performance to evaluate and compare our approach with other already existing.

We plan also to Integrate our algorithm into other known Grid simulators, such as SimGrid, GangSim and Bricks. This will allow us to measure the effectiveness of our algorithm in existing simulators. And finally we will integrate our strategy to the middleware GLOBUS (Foster, 2005).

REFERENCES

Bell, W. H., Cameron, D. G., Capozza, L., Millar, A. P., Stockinger, K., & Zini, F. (2003). Optorsim: A grid simulator for studying dynamic data replication strategies. *International Journal of High Performance Computing Applications.*

Bertis, V., Ferreira, L., & Amstrong, J. (2002). Introduction to grid computing with Globus. In *IBM RedBook*. Armonk, NY: IBM.

Boyer, W. F., & Hura, G. S. (2005). Non evolutionary algorithm for scheduling dependent tasks in distributed heterogeneous computing environments. *Journal of Parallel and Distributed Computing, 65*, 1035–1046. doi:10.1016/j.jpdc.2005.04.017

Buyya, R., Abramson, D., & Giddy, J. (2000). Nimrod/G: An architecture for a resource management and scheduling system in a global computational grid. In *Proceedings of the 4th International Conference and Exhibition on High Performance Computing in the Asia-Pacific Region* (Vol. 1, pp. 283-289).

Buyya, R., & Murshed, M. (2002). Gridsim: A toolkit for the modeling and simulation of distributed resource management and scheduling for grid computing. *Journal of Concurrency and Computation: Practice and Experience, 14*, 13–15.

Cao, J., Spooner, D. P., Jarvis, S. A., & Nudd, G. R. (2005). Grid load balancing using intelligent agents. *Future Generation Computer Systems, 21*(1), 135–149. doi:10.1016/j.future.2004.09.032

Chen, T., Zhang, B., & Hao, X. (2008). A dependent tasks scheduling model in grid. In Y. Zhang, G. Yu, E. Bertino, & G. Xu (Eds.), *Proceedings of the 10th Asia-Pacific Conference on Progress in WWW Research and Development* (LNCS 4976, pp. 136-147).

Chtepen, M., Dhoedt, B., Turck, F. D., & Demeester, P. (2008). Scheduling of dependent grid jobs in absence of exact job length information. In *Proceedings of the 4th IEEE/IFIP International Workshop on End-to-end Virtualization and Grid Management*, Samos Island, Greece (pp. 185-196).

Dumitrescu, C. L., & Foster, I. (2005). Gangsim: A simulator for grid scheduling studies. In *Proceedings of the Fifth IEEE International Symposium on Cluster Computing and the Grid* (Vol. 2, pp. 1151-1158).

Falzon, G., & Li, M. (2010). Enhancing list scheduling heuristics for dependent job scheduling in grid computing environments. *Journal of Supercomputing.*

Foster, I. (2005). Globus toolkit version 4: Software for service oriented systems. In H. Jin, D. Reed, & W. Jiang (Eds.), *Proceedings of the International Conference on Network and Parallel Computing*, Beijing, China (LNCS 3779, pp. 2-13).

Foster, I., & Kesselman, C. (2004). *The Grid2: Blueprint for a new computing infrastructure* (2nd ed.). San Francisco, CA: Morgan Kaufmann.

He, K., & Zhao, Y. (2008). Clustering and scheduling method based on task duplication. *Wuhan University Journal of Natural Sciences, 12*(2), 260–266. doi:10.1007/s11859-006-0028-y

Jiang, W., Baumgarten, M., Zhou, Y., & Jin, H. (2009). A bipartite model for load balancing in grid computing environments. *Frontiers of Computer Science in China*, *3*(4), 503–523. doi:10.1007/s11704-009-0036-0

Kamalam, G. K., Maharajan, R., & Maheish Sundhar, K. P. (2010). Min mean: A static scheduling algorithm for mapping meta-tasks on heterogeneous computing systems. In *Proceedings of the International Conference on Information Science and Applications*, Chennai, India.

Kwok, Y.-K., & Ahmad, I. (1999). Static scheduling algorithms for allocating directed task graphs to multiprocessors. *ACM Computing Surveys*, *31*, 406–471. doi:10.1145/344588.344618

Leal, K., Huedo, E., & Llorente, I. M. (2009). A decentralized model for scheduling independent tasks in Federated Grids. *Future Generation Computer Systems*, *25*, 840–852. doi:10.1016/j.future.2009.02.003

Legrand, A., Marchal, L., & Casanova, H. (2003). Scheduling distributed applications: The simgrid simulation framework. In *Proceedings of the 3rd IEEE/ACM International Symposium on Cluster Computing and the Grid* (pp. 138-145).

Maheswaran, M., Ali, S., Siegel, H. J., Hensgen, D., & Freund, R. F. (1999). Dynamic mapping of a class of independent tasks onto heterogeneous computing systems. *Journal of Parallel and Distributed Computing*, *59*, 107–121. doi:10.1006/jpdc.1999.1581

Nakechbandi, M., Colin, J.-Y., Gashumba, J. B. (2007). An efficient fault tolerant scheduling algorithm for precedence constrained tasks in heterogeneous distributed systems. *Innovations and Advanced Techniques in Computer and Information Sciences and Engineering*, 301-307.

Qu, Y., Soininen, J.-P., & Nurmi, J. (2007). Static scheduling techniques for dependent tasks on dynamically reconfigurable devices. *Journal of Systems Architecture*, *53*, 861–876. doi:10.1016/j.sysarc.2007.02.004

Salcedo-Sanz, S., Xu, Y., & Yao, X. (2006). Hybrid meta heuristics algorithms for task assignment in heterogeneous computing systems. *Computers & Operations Research*, *33*, 820–835. doi:10.1016/j.cor.2004.08.010

Saleh, M. A., Deldari, H., & Dorri, B. M. (2008). Balancing load in a computational grid applying adaptive, intelligent colonies of ants. *Informatica*, *32*, 327–335.

Takefusa, A., Matsuoka, S., Aida, K., Nakada, H., & Nagashima, U. (1999). Overview of a performance evaluation system for global computing scheduling algorithms. In *Proceedings of the Eighth IEEE International Symposium on High Performance Distributed Computing*.

Uçar, B., Aykanat, C., Kaya, K., & Ikinci, M. (2006). Task assignment in heterogeneous computing systems. *Journal of Parallel and Distributed Computing*, *66*, 32–46.

Vidyarthi, D. P., Sarker, B. K., Tripathi, A. K., & Yang, L. T. (2009). *Scheduling in distributed computing systems analysis, design and models*. New York, NY: Springer. doi:10.1007/978-0-387-74483-4

Yagoubi, B., & Meddeber, M. (2010). Distributed load balancing model for grid computing. *Revue Africaine de la Recherche en Informatique et Mathématiques Appliquées*, *12*, 43–60.

Yan, K. Q., Wang, S. C., Chang, C. P., & Lin, J. S. (2007). A hybrid load balancing policy underlying grid computing environment. *Computer Standards & Interfaces*, *29*, 161–173. doi:10.1016/j.csi.2006.03.003

This work was previously published in the International Journal of Grid and High Performance Computing, Volume 3, Issue 2, edited by Emmanuel Udoh and Ching-Hsien Hsu, pp. 44-58, copyright 2011 by IGI Publishing (an imprint of IGI Global).

Section 3
Algorithms and Optimization

Chapter 5
An Algorithm for Task Scheduling in Heterogeneous Distributed Systems Using Task Duplication

Amrit Agrawal
Jaypee University of Information Technology, India

Pranay Chaudhuri
Jaypee University of Information Technology, India

ABSTRACT

Task scheduling in heterogeneous parallel and distributed computing environment is a challenging problem. Applications identified by parallel tasks can be represented by directed-acyclic graphs (DAGs). Scheduling refers to the assignment of these parallel tasks on a set of bounded heterogeneous processors connected by high speed networks. Since task assignment is an NP-complete problem, instead of finding an exact solution, scheduling algorithms are developed based on heuristics, with the primary goal of minimizing the overall execution time of the application or schedule length. In this paper, the overall execution time (schedule length) of the tasks is reduced using task duplication on top of the Critical-Path-On-a-Processor (CPOP) algorithm.

1. INTRODUCTION

A heterogeneous distributed computing system (HDCS) consists of a set of processors or nodes of varying computing power, connected by a high speed network. An efficient scheduling of the tasks of an application on the available processors is one of the key factors for achieving high performance. There are two types of task allocation schemes: static and dynamic. In static task allocation scheme, the decision about which tasks should be allocated to which processors is made prior to the actual start of that job execution. In

DOI: 10.4018/978-1-4666-2065-0.ch005

dynamic task allocation scheme, the decision about the number of processors to be made available for a job and the task assignment to these processors is made during the job execution and the decision can vary according to the existing conditions (current loads, node failures, priorities, etc.) of the network. In recent years, HDCS has emerged as a popular platform to execute computationally intensive applications with diverse computing needs. The problem of mapping (including matching and scheduling) tasks and communications is a very important issue since an appropriate mapping can truly exploit the parallelism of the system thus achieving large speedup and high efficiency (Braun & Siegel, 1998). It deals with assigning (matching) each task to a machine and ordering (scheduling) the execution of the tasks on each machine in order to minimize some cost function. The most common cost function is the total schedule length. This policy has a very high overhead leading to a degradation of the overall system performance. The above situation can be avoided by the use of simple and constant time heuristics. Efficient application scheduling is critical for achieving high performance in heterogeneous computing systems. These heuristics are classified into a variety of categories such as list scheduling algorithms, task duplication based algorithms, clustering algorithms and guided random search methods. Task assignment is known to be an NP-complete problem. The natural approach, therefore, is to develop good heuristics that will allocate the tasks to the available processors and minimize the schedule length.

List based scheduling: According to their priority, list-scheduling heuristic maintains a list of all tasks of a given graph. It has two phases: task prioritizing phase for selecting the highest-priority ready task and the processor selection phase for selecting a suitable processor that minimizes a predefined cost function. Some of the examples are the Modified critical Path (MCP) (Wu & Gajski, 1990), Dynamic level Scheduling (Sih & Lee, 1993), Mapping Heuristic (MH) (Rewini

& Lewis, 1990), Insertion Scheduling Heuristic (Kruatrachue & Lewis, 1998), Earliest Time first (EFT) (Hwang, Chow & Anger, 1989), and Dynamic Critical Path (DCP) (Kwok & Ahmad, 1996) algorithms. List-scheduling heuristics are generally more practical and provide better performance results at a lower scheduling time than the other groups.

Task Duplication based Heuristics: The idea behind duplication-based scheduling algorithms is to schedule a task graph by mapping some of its tasks redundantly, which reduces the communication overhead (Ahmad & Kwok, 1994; Park, Shirazi & Marquis, 1997; Chung & Ranka, 1992). The only change is to selection strategies of the tasks for duplication in different duplication-based algorithms.

Clustering based heuristics: Another class of DAG scheduling algorithms is based on a technique called clustering (Gerasoulis & Yang, 1992; Kim & Browne, 1998; Yang & Gerasoulis, 1994). The basic idea of clustering based algorithm is to group heavily communicated tasks into the same cluster. Tasks grouped into the same cluster are assigned to the same processor in an effort to avoid communication costs.

Guided random search algorithms: The task scheduling problem is a search problem where the search space consists of an exponential number of possible schedules with respect to the problem size. Guided random search algorithms are a class of search algorithms based on enumerative techniques with additional information used to guide the search. They have been used extensively to solve very complex problems. A Genetic algorithm (GA) (Davis, 1991) is a type of evolution computations that is commonly used.

2. TASK-SCHEDULING PROBLEM

An application program can be represented by a Directed Acyclic Graph (DAG), $G = (V, E)$, where V is the set of n tasks. E is the set of e directed edges.

The directed edge $e_{i,j}$ joins nodes n_i and n_j. This also implies that n_j cannot start until n_i finishes and sends its data to n_j. In a given task graph, a task without any parent is called an entry task and a task without any child is called exit task. Data is a n x n matrix of communication data, where $data_{i,k}$ is the amount of data required to be transmitted from task n_i to task n_k. A heterogeneous computing system consists of independent different types of m processors fully interconnected by a high-speed arbitrary network. The bandwidth (data transfer rate) of the links between different processors in a heterogeneous system may be different depending on the kind of the network. The data transfer rate is represented by an m x m matrix, $R_{m \times m}$. W is a n x m computation cost matrix in which each $w_{i,j}$ gives the computation time to task n_i on processor p_j. The task executions of a given application are assumed to be non-preemptive. The communication cost between two processors p_x and processor p_y, depends on the channel initialization at both sender processor p_x and receiver processor p_y in addition to the communication time on the channel (Ilavarasan & Thambidurai, 2007). The channel initialization time is assumed to be negligible in this paper. The communication cost of the edge (i,k), which is for transferring data from task n_i to task n_k is defined by

$$C_{i,k} = data_{i,k} / R_{x,y} \ldots \ldots \ldots \quad (1)$$

Note that when n_i and n_k are both scheduled on same processor then communication cost between them is taken as zero, as we assume that intra-processor communication cost is negligible compared to the inter-processor communication cost.

Let $EST (n_i, p_j)$ and $EFT(n_i, p_j)$ are the Earliest Start Time and Earliest Finish Time of task n_i on p_j respectively. For the entry task n_{entry}, $EST(n_{entry}, p_j) = 0$ and for the other tasks in the graph, the *EST and EFT* values are computed recursively, starting from the entry task, as shown in Equations (2) and (3). In order to compute the *EFT* of

a task n_i, all immediate predecessor tasks of n_i must have been scheduled.

$$EST(n_i, p_j) = \max \{avail[j], \max \{AFT(n_i) + C(t,i) : n_t \in pred(n_i)\}\} \ldots \ldots \ldots \quad (2)$$

$$EFT(n_i, p_j) = Wi, j + EST(n_i, p_j) \ldots \ldots \ldots \quad (3)$$

Where *pred(n_i)* is the set of immediate predecessor tasks of task n_i and *avail[j]* is the earliest time at which processor p_j is ready for task execution. If n_k is the last assigned task on processor n_j, then *avail[j]* is the time that processor p_j completed the execution of the task n_k and it is ready to execute another task when we have a non insertion-based scheduling policy. After a task n_t is scheduled on a processor p_j, the earliest start time and the earliest finish time of n_t on processor p_j is equal to the actual start time $AST(n_t)$ and the actual finish time $AFT(n_t)$ of task n_t, respectively. After all tasks in a graph are scheduled, the makespan will be the actual finish time of the exit task n_{exit}.

$$Schedule \ Length = \max\{AFT (n_{exit})\} \ldots \ldots \ldots \quad (4)$$

The objective function of the task-scheduling problem is to schedule the tasks of an application to processors such that its schedule length is minimized.

3. TASK DUPLICATION SCHEDULING PROBLEM

Whenever we schedule an application on any heterogeneous system using nay of the available algorithms the scheduling is in such a way that there are always some empty slots on processors i.e. there are some time duration on processors during which no task has been scheduled. As a result the processor is not used during that time. Task duplication is an approach that tries to uses those time slots to improve the overall execution time of the application. The main focus of our work has been on implementing task duplication in the pre-existing algorithm. There are two issues to be addressed for designing an effective task duplication technique i.e. which node(s) to duplicate and where to duplicate the node(s).

3.1 Single Parent Task Duplication

Since the purpose of duplication is primarily to reduce the communication cost, whenever we try to find EST of n_i on any processor p_j then the duplication is checked only on p_j. This is because if the parent node is duplicated on any other processor then there is no improvement in EST of n_i. The start time of a node is determined by the data arrival time from its parent nodes. The parent node from which the data arrives at the latest time is called a Very Important Parent (VIP) of the candidate node (Ahmed & Kwok, 1998).

The only change that is done is in the case of calculation of EST and the function of EST is defined below.

EST (n_i, p_j)

{

Let $n_k = VIP(n_i)$

If n_k can be duplicated on p_j

then EST = EFT(n_k, p_j)

else EST = AFT$(n_k) + c_{i,k}$

}

We also made a function to check whether n_k can be duplicated on p_j or not, it checked the availability of p_j at that time as well as checked that is it really worthy to duplicate n_k. Rest of the procedure is same as it used to be in the case of classic CPOP algorithm.

3.2 All Possible Ancestor Task Duplication

Locating a proper time slot to accommodate a duplicated node is very important since duplicating a node in an improper time slot may not reduce the start time of a node. Some of the existing algorithms consider only the last idle time slot on a processor but ignore other idle time slots that may give further reduction in the schedule length (Ahmed & Kwok, 1998).

4. PROPOSED ALGORITHM

We have tried to implement the concept of Task Duplication in the pre-existing CPOP algorithm. As mentioned earlier, the CPOP algorithm has two phases: the task prioritization and processor selection phase. The application of task duplication comes in the processor selection phase. What we have done is that whenever a task is being scheduled, then we find out its VIP and check whether duplicating this on any processor will reduce the EFT of task. If yes, then we duplicate the parent task on the processor and then schedule the task.

Algorithm CPOP-TD

1. Set the computation cost of tasks and communication cost of edges with mean values.
2. Compute the rank (upward and downward) by traversing the graph, starting from exit task and entry task for upward and downward rank, respectively.
3. Compute priority by adding upward and downward rank.
4. Select the priority of n_{entry} to a critical path and set it as SET_{CP}, where SET_{CP} is the set of tasks on the critical path.
5. $n_k \leftarrow n_{entry}$
6. *while*(n_k is not the exit task) *do*
7. select n_j where$((n_j \in succ(n_k))$ and priority(n_j) == $|CP|)$

8. $SET_{CP} = SET_{CP} \cup \{n_j\}$

9. $n_k \leftarrow n_j$

10. select the critical path processor (p_{cp}) which minimizes $\sum_{n_j \tau SET_{\in p}} w_{ij}, \forall p_i \in Q$

11. initialize the priority queue with the entry task

12. **while** there is an unscheduled task in the priority queue **do**

13. select the highest priority queue task n_i from the priority queue

14. compute the computation cost of (n_i, p_j)

15. $P \leftarrow$ processor p_k which minimize the computation cost of task n_i

16. arriv_lsit $\leftarrow$ sort the data arrival time of prec(n_i) on the processor P

17. new_start_time(n_j,P) = EST(n_j,P)

18. **if** $n_i \in SET_{CP}$ **then** assign the task n_i on p_{cp}

19. **else repeat**

20. start_time = New_strat_time(n_i,P)

21. Select the task n_t from the arriv_list

22. Compute(new_start_time(n_i,P))

23. arriv_list$\leftarrow$arriv_list $-$ \{n_t\}

24. **until** (new_start_time(n_i,P) $\geq$ start_time or arriv_list = 0)

25. assign the task n_i on P at Minimize_start_time(start_time, new_start_time(n_i,P))

26. update the priority queue with the successors of n_i, if they become the ready tasks

27. **endwhile**.

Algorithm Complexity

Lines 1 - 4 take O(e + n) time. Line 5 requires O(1) time for the assignment. The rest of the algorithm consists of a while-loop. Lines 12 - 14 take the O(p $\times$ n). Lines 15 and 17 take O(1) time for the assignment statements. Line 16 requires O(d $\times$ log d) time because it sorts the immediate predecessors based on the data arrival time, where d is the indegree of the node. Since lines 19 to 24 duplicate all the possible predecessors on the selected processor and it takes d time, it has a complexity O(d $\times$ n). Lines 25 and 26 require

constant time. Since the while loop run n times, the total complexity will be O(n^2(p + d)).

5. AN ILLUSTRATIVE EXAMPLE

As an example let us consider the DAG (Figure 1(a)) used in (Topcuoglu, Hariri & Wu, 2002). The computation cost matix is provided in Figure 1(b). The schedule length as obtained by the proposed CPOP-TD algorithm is 77, whereas the same obtained by the CPOP algorithm is 86 (Figure 2).

5.1 Comparison Metrics

The following metrics are used to evaluate the scheduling algorithm.

Schedule Length Ratio (SLR)

SLR is the ratio of the parallel time to the sum of weights of the critical path tasks on the fastest processor.

$$SLR = \frac{makespan}{\sum_{n_i \in cpMIN} \min_{pj \in Q}\{w_{i,j}\}}$$

Speedup

Speed up is the ratio of the sequential execution time to the parallel execution time.

$$Speedup = \frac{\min_{p_j \in Q}\{\sum_{n_i \in v} w_{i,j}\}}{makespan}$$

Efficiency

Efficiency is the ratio of the speedup value to the number of processor used to schedule the graph.

Figure 1(a). A sample task graph (b). Computation cost matrix

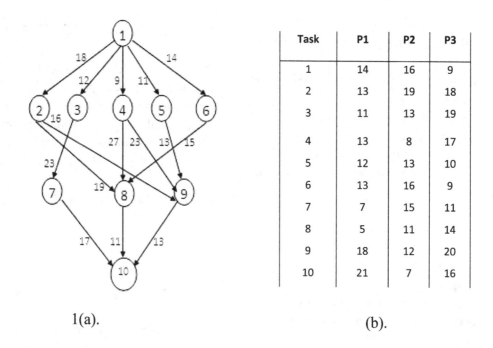

Task	P1	P2	P3
1	14	16	9
2	13	19	18
3	11	13	19
4	13	8	17
5	12	13	10
6	13	16	9
7	7	15	11
8	5	11	14
9	18	12	20
10	21	7	16

1(a).   (b).

Figure 2. Scheduling of task graph in Figure 1 with the CPOP and CPOP-TD algorithms (a) CPOP Algorithm (Schedule length=86); (b) CPOP-TD Algorithm (Schedule length = 77)

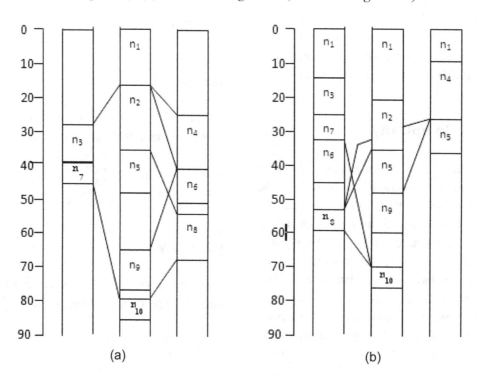

5.2 Randomly Generated Application Graphs

Our random graph generator requires the following input parameters to build weighted DAGs.

1. Number of tasks in the graph, v.
2. Shape parameter of the graph, α. We assume that the height (depth) of a DAG is randomly generated from a uniform distribution with a mean value equal to ($\sqrt{v}/\alpha$). The width of each level is randomly selected from a uniform distribution with mean equal to ($\sqrt{v}*\alpha$) If $\alpha \gg 1.0$ dense graph is generated, else if $\alpha \ll 1.0$ long graph with low parallelism degree is generated.
3. Out degree of a node, out _degree.
4. Communication to computation ratio, (CCR). It is the ratio of the average communication cost to the average computation cost. If a DAG's CCR value is very low, it can be considered as a computation-intensive application.

   As in Topcuoglu et al. (2002), the range percentage of computation costs on processor (β), is heterogeneity factor for the processor. If the percentage value is high, the differece in computation cost across the processors is significant. On the other hand, if the value is low then the computation cost of the task across procssor is almost equal. The average Computation cost of Task Graph, which it randomly selects a predefined set. The computation cost of each task n_i in the graph, i.e., w_i, is selected randomly from a uniform distribution with range [0, 2 * |Wdag|], where |Wdag| is the average computation cost of the given graph, which is set randomly by the algorithm. Then, the computation cost of each task n_i on each processor pj in the system is randomly set from the following range:

$$\overline{w}_i \times (1 - \frac{\beta}{2}) \leq w_{i,j} \leq \overline{w}_i \times (1 + \frac{\beta}{2})$$

In each experiment, the values of these parameters are assigned from the corresponding sets given below

- SET_V (10, 20, 30, 40, 50, 60, 70)
- SET_{CCR} (0.1, 0.5, 1.0, 5.0, 10.0)
- SET_α (0.5, 1.0, 2.0)
- SET_{OUT_DEGREE} (1 to v)
- SET_β (0.1, 0.25, 0.5, 0.75, 1.0)

6. PERFORMANCE RESULTS

In this section, we evaluated the quality of schedules generated by each of the algorithms for random task graphs with respect to various graph characteristics values. We have generated a large set of random task graphs with different characteristics and scheduled these task graphs on to a heterogeneous computing system consists of three processors. The average SLR and speedup generated by each of the algorithm are plotted and are shown in Figure 3(a) and Figure 3(b). The average SLR value based ranking (starting with minimum ending with maximum) of the algorithms is {CPOP-TD, CPOP} and the Speedup value based ranking (starting with maximum and ending with minimum) of the algorithms is {CPOP-TD, CPOP}. We have also evaluated the performance of the algorithm with respect to various CCR and graph structure values and the outcomes of these results are shown in Figure 3(c). These experiments also confirm that CPOP-TD algorithm substantially outperforms reported algorithms for various CCR value and for different graph structure. For this experiment, we have used 1000 numbers of randomly generated task graphs for every set of nodes like *{10, 20, 30, 40, 50, 60, 70}*.

Figure 3(a). Average Speedup (b). Average SLR (c). Average SLR with varying CCR

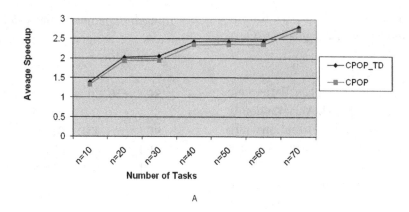

A

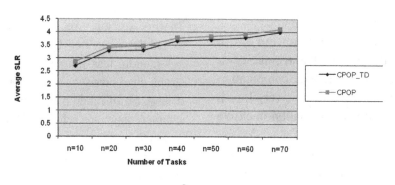

B

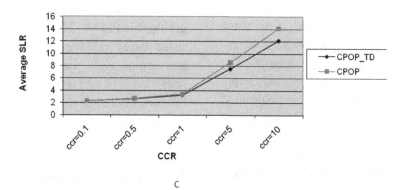

C

The CPOP algorithm gives the better results for graphs with higher CCRs than the graphs with lower CCRs. Clustering of the critical path on the fastest processor results in better quality of schedules for the graphs in which average communication cost is greater than average computation cost.

7. CONCLUSION

In this paper, we have presented a scheduling algorithm using task duplication. The proposed algorithm considered CPOP as the base algorithm on which the task duplication strategy was incorporated. The resulting algorithm (CPOP-TD) is shown to perform better than the CPOP algorithm. More specifically, the comparison study, based on randomly generated graphs, shows that the proposed scheduling algorithm significantly surpass the CPOP approach alone in terms of both quality and cost of schedules, which are determined based on the schedule length ratio, speedup, frequency of the best results and average scheduling metrics.

REFERENCES

Ahmad, I., & Kwok, Y. (1994). A New Approach to Scheduling parallel Programs Using Task Duplication. In *Proceedings of the International Conference on Parallel Processing, 2*, 47–51.

Ahmed, I., & Kwok, Y. (1998). On exploiting task duplication in parallel program scheduling. *IEEE Transactions on Parallel and Distributed Systems, 9*, 872–892. doi:10.1109/71.722221

Braun, T. D., & Siegel, H. J. (1998). A taxonomy for describing matching and scheduling heuristics for mixed-machine heterogeneous computing systems. In *Proceedings of the Seventeenth IEEE Symposium on Reliable Distributed Systems,* West Lafayette, IN (pp. 330-335).

Chung, Y., & Ranka, S. (1992). Applications and Performance Analysis of a Compile-time Optimization Approach for List Scheduling Algorithms on Distributed Memory Multiprocessors. *Proceedings of the Conference on Supercomputing* (pp. 512-521).

Davis, L. (1991). *Handbook of Genetic Algorithms.* New York, NY: Van Nostrand Reinhold.

Gerasoulis, A., & Yang, T. (1992). A comparison of clustering heuristics for scheduling directed acyclic graphs on multiprocessors. *Journal of Parallel and Distributed Computing, 16*(4), 276–291. doi:10.1016/0743-7315(92)90012-C

Hwang, J. J., Chow, Y. C., & Anger, F. D. (1989). Scheduling Precedence Graphs in Systems with Inteprocessor Communication Costs. *SIAM Journal on Computing, 18*(2), 244–257. doi:10.1137/0218016

Ilavarasan, E., & Thambidurai, P. (2007). Low complexity Performance Effective Task Scheduling Algorithm for Heterogeneous Computing Environments. *Journal of Computer Science, 3*, 94–103. doi:10.3844/jcssp.2007.94.103

Kim, S. J., & Browne, J. C. (1998). A general approach to mapping of parallel computation upon multiprocessor architectures. In *Proceedings of the International Conference on Parallel Processing, 2*, 1–8.

Kruatrachue, B., & Lewis, T. G. (1998). Grain Size Determination for Parallel Processing. *IEEE Software, 5*(1), 23–32. doi:10.1109/52.1991

Kwok, Y., & Ahmad, I. (1996). Dynamic Critical-Path Scheduling: An Effective Technique for Allocating Task Graphs to Multiprocessors. *IEEE Transactions on Parallel and Distributed Systems, 7*(5), 506–521. doi:10.1109/71.503776

Park, G., Shirazi, B., & Marquis, J. (1997). DFRN: A New Approach for Duplication Based Scheduling for Distributed Memory Mulitiprocessor Systems. In *Proceedings of the International Conference on Parallel Processing* (pp. 157-166).

Rewini, H., & Lewis, T. G. (1990). Scheduling Parallel Program Tasks onto Arbitrary Target Machines. *Journal of Parallel and Distributed Computing, 9*, 138–153. doi:10.1016/0743-7315(90)90042-N

Sih, D. C., & Lee, E. A. (1993). A Compile-Time Scheduling heuristic for Interconnection-Constrained Heterogeneous Processor Architectures. *IEEE Transactions on Parallel and Distributed Systems, 4*(2), 175–186. doi:10.1109/71.207593

Topcuoglu, H., Hariri, S., & Wu, M. Y. (2002). Performance effective and low-complexity task scheduling for heterogeneous computing. *IEEE Transactions on Parallel and Distributed Systems, 13*, 262–274. doi:10.1109/71.993206

Wu, M., & Gajski, D. (1990). Hyprotocol: A Programming Aid for Message Passing Systems. *IEEE Transactions on Parallel and Distributed Systems, 1*, 330–334. doi:10.1109/71.80160

Yang, T., & Gerasoulis, A. (1994). DSC: Scheduling parallel tasks on an unbounded number of processors. *IEEE Transactions on Parallel and Distributed Systems, 5*(9), 951–967. doi:10.1109/71.308533

This work was previously published in the International Journal of Grid and High Performance Computing, Volume 3, Issue 1, edited by Emmanuel Udoh and Ching-Hsien Hsu, pp. 89-97, copyright 2011 by IGI Publishing (an imprint of IGI Global).

Chapter 6
ACO Based Dynamic Scheduling Algorithm for Real–Time Multiprocessor Systems

Apurva Shah
G H Patel College of Engg & Tech, India

Ketan Kotecha
Nirma University, India

ABSTRACT

The Ant Colony Optimization (ACO) algorithms are computational models inspired by the collective foraging behavior of ants. The ACO algorithms provide inherent parallelism, which is very useful in multiprocessor environments. They provide balance between exploration and exploitation along with robustness and simplicity of individual agent. In this paper, ACO based dynamic scheduling algorithm for homogeneous multiprocessor real-time systems is proposed. The results obtained during simulation are measured in terms of Success Ratio (SR) and Effective CPU Utilization (ECU) and compared with the results of Earliest Deadline First (EDF) algorithm in the same environment. It has been observed that the proposed algorithm is very efficient in underloaded conditions and it performs very well during overloaded conditions also. Moreover, the proposed algorithm can schedule some typical instances successfully which are not possible to schedule using EDF algorithm.

INTRODUCTION

Real-time systems are defined as those systems in which the correctness of the system depends not only on the logical results of computations but also on the time at which the results are produced

DOI: 10.4018/978-1-4666-2065-0.ch006

(Ramamritham & Stankovik, 1994). The objective of real-time system is to guarantee the deadline of tasks in the system as much as possible when we consider soft real-time system and for achieving this goal vast research on real-time task scheduling has been conducted.

Real-time scheduling techniques can be broadly divided into two categories - Static and

Dynamic. Static algorithms assign all priorities at design time and it remains constant for the lifetime of the task. Dynamic algorithms assign priority at runtime, based on execution parameters of tasks.

The ACO algorithms are computational models inspired by the collective foraging behavior of ants. Each ant is an autonomous agent that constructs a path. There might be one or more ants concurrently active at the same time. Ants do not need synchronization. Forward ant moves to the good-looking neighbor from the current node, probabilistically. Probabilistic choice is biased by Pheromone trails previously deposited and heuristic function. Without heuristics information, algorithm tends to converge towards initial random solution. In backward mode, ants lay down the pheromone. In ACO algorithm, pheromone is added only to arcs belonging to the global best solution (Dorigo & Gambardella, 1997). Pheromone intensity of all the paths decreases with time, called pheromone evaporation. It helps in unlearning poor quality solution (Dorigo & Stutzle, 2004).

ACO based scheduling algorithm has been presented for single processor real-time system (Shah & Kotecha, 2010). Moreover, ACO has been applied for heterogeneous multiprocessor systems (Turneo et al., 2008; Chang, Wu, Shann, & Chung, 2008) and reconfigurable parallel processing system (Saad, Adawy, & Habashy, 2006). In this paper, ACO based dynamic scheduling algorithm for multiprocessor real-time operating system has been proposed.

RELATED WORK

A multiprocessor system is tightly coupled so that global status and workload information on all processors can be kept current at a low cost. The system has shared memory and generally uses centralized scheduler. If system uses separate scheduler for each processor, the decisions and actions of the schedulers of all the processors are coherent. Multiprocessor systems are divided in two basic types, homogeneous and heterogeneous. In homogeneous system, processors can be used interchangeably and in contrast, heterogeneous processors cannot be used interchangeably. Homogeneous processors can be subdivided in two types: identical and uniform. In identical processors, it is assumed that all processors are equally powerful whereas uniform multiprocessor machine is characterized by a speed (Baruah, Funk, & Goossens, 2003).

There are two main strategies when dealing with the problem of multiprocessor scheduling: partitioning strategy and global strategy (Oh & Son, 1995). In a partitioning strategy, once a task is allocated to a processor, all of its instances are executed exclusively on that processor. In a global strategy, any instance of a task can be executed on any processor, or even be preempted and moved to a different processor before it is completed (Lopez, Diaz, & Garcia. 2004).

EDF (Earliest Deadline First) and LLF (Least Laxity First) algorithms are proved optimal under the condition that tasks are preemptive, there is only one processor and it is not over-loaded (Dertouzos & Ogata, 1974; Mok, 1983). EDF is appropriate algorithm to use for on-line scheduling on uniform multiprocessors (Funk, Goossens, & Baruah, 2001). However, many practical instances of multiprocessor real-time system are NP-complete, i.e. it is believed that there is no optimal polynomial-time algorithm for them (Ramamritham, Stankovik, & Shiah, 1990; Ullman, 1973).

The scheduling is considered as on-line, if scheduler makes scheduling decision without knowledge about the task that will be released in the future. On-line scheduling algorithms cannot work efficiently in overloaded conditions. Researchers have proved that, for single processor system, the competitive factor of an on-line scheduling algorithm is at most equal to 0.25 when the system is highly overloaded and its value can't be more than 0.385 when the system is slightly over-loaded. They have further derived the upper limit of competitive factor for dual processor system and it is 0.5 during overloading condition (Liu, 2001; Baruah, Koren, Mishra,, Raghunath, Roiser, & Shasha, 1991). It has been also proved that multiprocessor system is schedulable with guarantee when utilization is below 0.37482 (Lundberg, 2002).

Advantages of ACO based systems are high parallelism and can exhibit high level of robustness, scalability, fault tolerance and effectiveness on unquantifiable data along with simplicity of individual agent (Dorigo & Caro, 1999; Ramos, Muge, & Pina, 2002). This technique combines global and local heuristics to allow step-by-step decisions by a group of cooperating agents and it seems particularly suitable to efficiently explore the search space of this class of problems that can be formulated as stochastic decisions making processes as well as the traveling salesman problem for which this method has been introduced (Dorigo & Gambardella, 1997; Dorigo, Maniezzo, & Colorni, 1996). Several characteristics make ACO a unique approach: it is constructive, population-based metaheuristic which exploits an indirect form of memory of previous performance. These combinations of characteristics are not found in any of the other metaheuristic (Dorigo & Stutzle, 2004).

EDF performs very efficiently during underloaded conditions but it has been experimentally proved that its performance is quite poor when the system is even slightly overloaded (Saini, 2005; Locke, 1986). The proposed algorithm is found quite efficient in underloaded and slightly overloaded conditions. Its performance is satisfactory in highly overloaded conditions also.

SYSTEM AND TASK MODEL

The system assumed here is tightly coupled multiprocessor real-time system with shared memory and soft timing constraints. The processors assumed are homogeneous and identical. The system has adopted global strategy along with centralized scheduler. The system permit task preemption and inter-processor migrations (i.e. a job executing on a processor may be interrupted at any instant and its execution resumed later on the same or a different processor with no cost or penalty).

A task set consists of m independent periodic tasks $\{T1,...,Tm\}$. In the periodic model of real-time task $Ti = (Ei, Pi)$, a task Ti is characterized by two parameters: an execution requirement Ei, and a period Pi - with the interpretation that the task generates a job at each integer multiple of Pi and each such job has an execution requirement of Ei units and must complete by a deadline equal to the next integer multiple of Pi (Baruah & Goossens, 2004; Liu, 2001).

In soft real-time systems, each task has a positive value. The goal of the system is to obtain as much value as possible. If a task succeeds, then the system acquires its value. If a task fails, then the system gains less value from the task (Locke, 1986). In a special case of soft real-time systems, called a firm real-time system, there is no value for a task that has missed its deadline, but there is no catastrophe either (Koren & Shasha, 1995; Kotecha & Shah, 2008). The algorithm proposed in this paper applies to firm real-time system and the value of the task has been taken same as its computation time required.

APPLICATION OF ACO IN REAL-TIME MULTIPROCESSOR SYSTEMS

Pseudo-code of the proposed algorithm is given in Box 1.

The detail flowchart of the algorithm shown in Box 1 is given in Figure 1.

Tour Construction

Each schedulable task is considered, as a node and different ants will start the journey starting from one of the node. Ants will continue to traverse till

Box 1. The_New_scheduling_algorithm

```
{
  i.    Construct tour of each  ant and produce different task execution sequences
  ii.   Analyze the task execution sequences generated for available number of processors
  iii.  Update the value of pheromone on each node
  iv.   Decide probability of each task and select the task for execution
}
```

all nodes are visited. Nodes are assumed having memory and they store the value of pheromone.

The starting point of the journey will be different node for each ant. The number of ants taken is same as number of executable tasks the system is having at that time. Therefore, from all the different nodes, one ant will start the journey. All the ants traverse through all the nodes based on probability (pi) of each node. Ants traverse in such a way that all the nodes are visited and no node is repeated.

Probability (pi) of a node at particular time t can be found using following equation:

$$p_i\left(t\right) = \frac{\left(\tau_i\left(t\right)\right)^{\alpha} * \left(\eta_i\left(t\right)\right)^{\beta}}{\sum_{l \in R_1} \left(\tau_l\left(t\right)\right)^{\alpha} * \left(\eta_l\left(t\right)\right)^{\beta}}$$

where,

- pi (t) is the probability of ith node at time t; i $\in$ R1 and R1 is set of nodes (schedulable tasks) at time t.
- $\tau_i(t)$ is pheromone on ith node at time t.
- $\eta_i(t)$ is heuristic value of ith node at time t, which can be determined by,

$$\eta_i = \frac{K}{D_i - t}$$

here, t is current time, K is a constant (suitable range is 5 to 20) and Di is absolute deadline of ith node.

α and β are constants which decide importance of τ and η.

Ants construct their tour based on the value of p of each node as per following:

Ant 1: Highest p $\rightarrow$ second highest p$\rightarrow$ third highest p$\rightarrow$…
Ant 2: Second highest p$\rightarrow$ highest p$\rightarrow$ third highest p$\rightarrow$…
Ant 3: Third highest p$\rightarrow$ highest p$\rightarrow$ second highest p$\rightarrow$…

….

Suppose at time t, there are 4 schedulable tasks. Each task will be considered as a node and from each node; one ant will start its journey. If the priorities of all the nodes are assumed in decreasing order of A, B, C, D; ants will traverse different nodes as per following:

Ant 1: A$\rightarrow$ B$\rightarrow$ C$\rightarrow$ D
Ant 2: B$\rightarrow$ A$\rightarrow$ C$\rightarrow$ D
Ant 3: C$\rightarrow$ A$\rightarrow$ B$\rightarrow$ D
Ant 4: D$\rightarrow$ A$\rightarrow$ B$\rightarrow$ C

Analyze the Journey

After all ants have completed their tour, evaluate the performance of different ants' journey for the available number of processors.

The journey of each ant gives us different possibilities of scheduling of the tasks. Find out the number of missed tasks during the journey of each ant (i.e. for possible scheduling order) and decide the best journey produced by an ant during which minimum number of tasks missed

Figure 1. Flowchart of the proposed algorithm

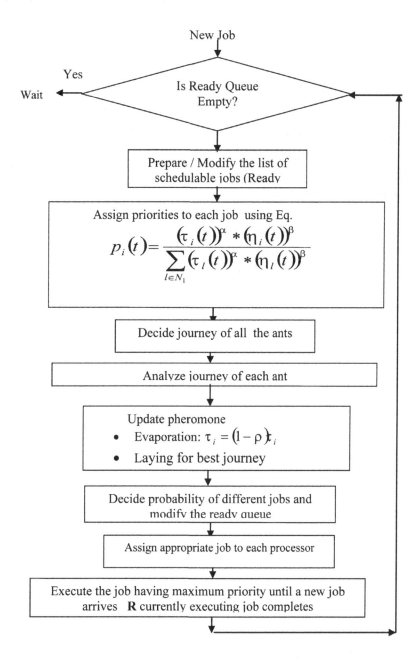

the deadline. Update the value of pheromone on each node as per following.

Pheromone Update

Pheromone updating on each node is done in two parts.

Pheromone Evaporation: Pheromone evaporation is required to forget bad journey of ants and to encourage new paths (Ramos, Muge, & Pina, 2002). Pheromone is evaporated on each node as per following equation:

$$\tau_i = \left(1 - \rho\right)\tau_i$$

where,

- ρ is a constant. (suitable range is 0.2 to 0.4)
- $i \in R2$; R2 is set of all (schedulable and non-schedulable at that time) tasks.

Pheromone Laying: Pheromone will be laid only for the best journey of ants. Select the best journey as discussed earlier and lay pheromone. Amount of pheromone ($\Delta\tau$) laid will be different at each node and it depends on the order of visited node. The nearest node will get highest amount of pheromone and far most node will get the least. Pheromone is added on each node as per following equation

$$\tau_i = \tau_i + \Delta\tau_i$$

where,

- $i \in N1$, N1 is set of nodes at time t.
- $\Delta\tau = \dfrac{ph}{s}$

Here,

- $ph = C * \dfrac{Number\ of\ Sucessed\ Tasks}{Number\ of\ Missed\ Tasks + 1}$

- s is sequence number of the node visited by the ant during the best journey.
- value of C is constant (preferably 0.1).

Selection of Task to Be Executed By Each Processor

After updating pheromone again find out the value of p for each task. Depending on the available number of processors, select the tasks for execution starting from the highest value of p to its lower values.

Important Points about the Algorithm

- Each schedulable task is considered as a node, and it stores the value of τ i.e. pheromone. Initial value of τ is taken as one.
- Number of ants required to construct the tour is an important design criteria. During simulation, we have taken number of ants same as number of executable tasks the system is having at that time. Therefore, from each node one ant will start its journey during tour construction.
- Value of α and β decide importance of τ and η. During simulation, we got best results with $\alpha = 1$ and $\beta = 2$.

Unlike the real ants, the pheromone is laid only for the best journey of ants. Amount of pheromone laid is also not uniform. Moreover, for forgetting the poor journey, pheromone is evaporated.

SIMULATION METHOD

The proposed algorithm and EDF algorithms are simulated for the real-time multiprocessor system with homogeneous processors and preemptive environment. The results are taken using periodic tasks. The relative deadline of the task is considered the same as its period i.e. before the arrival of the next job; present job is expected to be completed. The task set generated for each load value consist of 4 different values of period. For taking result at each load value, we have generated 200 task sets each one containing 3 to 90 tasks.

For periodic tasks, load of the system can be defined as summation of ratio of required computation time and period of each task. The results are taken from underloaded conditions ($0.5 \leq$ load) to highly overloaded conditions (load ≤ 3) and tested on more than 1 lakh scheduling instances.

The system is said to be overloaded when even a clairvoyant scheduler cannot feasibly schedule the tasks offered to the scheduler. A reasonable way to measure the performance of a scheduling algorithm during an overload is by the amount of work the scheduler can feasibly schedule according to the algorithm. The larger this amount the better the algorithm. Because of this, we have considered following two as our main performance criteria:

In real-time systems, deadline meeting is most important and we are interested in finding whether the task is meeting the deadline. Therefore the most appropriate performance metric is the Success Ratio (SR) and defined as (Ramamritham, Stankovik, & Shiah, 1990):

$$SR = \frac{Number\ of\ tasks\ successfully\ scheduled}{Total\ number\ of\ tasks\ arrived}$$

It is important that how efficiently the processors are utilized by the scheduler especially during overloaded conditions. Therefore the other performance metric is Effective CPU Utilization (ECU) and defined as:

$$ECU = \sum_{i \in R} \frac{V_i}{T}$$

where,

- V is value of a task and,
  - value of a task = Computation time of a task, if the task completes within its deadline.
  - value of a task = 0, if the task fails to meet the deadline.
- R is set of tasks which are scheduled successfully i.e. completed within their deadline.
- T is total time of scheduling.

An on-line scheduler has a competitive factor Cf if and only if the value of the schedule of any finite sequence of tasks produced by the algorithm is at least Cf times the value of the schedule of the tasks produced by an optimal clairvoyant algorithm (Liu, 2001). Since maximum value obtained by a clairvoyant scheduling algorithm is a hard problem, we have instead used a rather simplistic upper bound on this maximum value, which is obtained by summing up the value of all tasks (Baruah, Koren, Mishra, Raghunath, Roiser, & Shasha, 1991). Therefore, value of ECU for clairvoyant scheduler has been considered as 100%.

Finally, the results are obtained, compared with EDF algorithm in the same environment and shown in Figure 3 to Figure 5.

DEMONSTRATION OF SCHEDULING OF SOME TYPICAL INSTANCES

In this section, two cases consisting of different task sets are given and their scheduling with EDF algorithm and the proposed algorithm are discussed. First case discusses scheduling of a task set of aperiodic tasks and second case discusses the same for task set consisting of periodic tasks.

First task set is made up of aperiodic tasks and shown in Table 1. The system is considered having two processors. EDF schedule of the task set is shown in Figure 2(a) and it can be observed that task C missed the deadline

Scheduling using the proposed Algorithm:

1. At T = 0, the proposed algorithm works as shown in Table 2. Out of 3 eligible tasks, processor 1 (P1) selects task C and processor 2 (P2) selects task A for execution. Intermediate steps along with values of variables are shown in the Table 2.

Therefore, the scheduling by the proposed algorithm results as shown in Figure 2(b). We can

Table 1. Task Set for first case

Task	Arrival Time	Absolute Deadline	Required Exe. Time
A	0	10	3
B	0	10	4
C	0	11	10

observe that EDF algorithm has failed as it missed the deadline for task C, but the proposed algorithm has been succeeded.

2. Second task set is made up of periodic tasks and shown in Table 3. The system is considered having three processors and load of the system is 0.95.

Using both algorithms results are taken and measured in terms of SR and ECU. For the proposed algorithm we get SR = 100% & ECU = 95.32%, whereas EDF gives SR = 96.38% & ECU = 74.43%. For EDF algorithm, value of SR is less than 100% as it is failed to schedule all the tasks,

but the proposed algorithm has got value of SR as 100%. Therefore, it has been concluded that proposed algorithm has scheduled all the tasks successfully.

RESULTS

Figure 3 shows the results of the proposed algorithm and EDF algorithm during simulation with two processors. The results are taken from underloaded condition (load ≤ 0.5) to highly overloaded condition (load ≥ 3).

Results show that the proposed algorithm performs very well when the system is not overloaded. During overloaded condition, as expected ECU and SR of EDF fall down rapidly but proposed algorithm works exceptionally well. The number of processors is increased during simulation and the results are shown in Figure 4 and Figure 5 with number of processors is 5 and 15 respectively.

For underloaded condition (i.e. load ≤ 1), performance of the proposed algorithm is quite

Figure 2. Scheduling for First Case Using (a) EDF Algorithm (b) New Algorithm

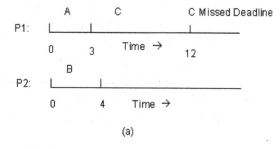 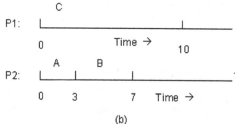

    (a)   (b)

Table 2. Steps of the proposed algorithm at time T = 0

Tour of Ant	Path	Analyze Journey		Imp. After Pheromone Update	Select Task at T=0
		Succ. Tasks	Miss. Tasks		
1	A,B,C	2	1	C(max)	P1: C
2	B,A,C	2	1	A	P2: A
3	C,A,B	3	0	B(min)	

Table 3. Task set for second case

Task No.	Arrival Time	Period	Relative Deadline	Required Exe. Time
1	0	10	10	2
2	0	10	10	2
3	1	3	3	1
4	2	5	5	1
5	3	3	3	1
6	2	10	10	1
7	2	3	3	1
8	0	11	11	10
9	0	8	8	2

well and nearer to optimal clairvoyant scheduling algorithm. As the load increases just beyond 1.00, EDF is not able to schedule. Even a spike of overload can affect the system seriously for long period of time. But we can observe that ACO based algorithm is working effectively and sustain the overload. It gives value of ECU more than 75% up to the load value 1.5. Because of this characteristic, the proposed algorithm is more suitable for the situation when future work load of the system is unpredictable. During highly overloaded situations (load ≥ 2) also the proposed algorithm works satisfactorily and gives value of ECU more than 50% up to the load value 2.50.

ECU measures that how efficiently the processors are utilized. By considering maximum value of ECU (i.e. 100%) for clairvoyant scheduler, the competitive factor achieved by the proposed algorithm as well as EDF algorithm have been found. For the proposed algorithm, competitive factor is at least 0.91 up to load value is equal to 1 whereas for EDF its value is 0.83. Moreover, we find that the competitive factor of the proposed algorithm is more than 0.75 and 0.55 when loading factor is 1.50 and 2.00 respectively where as in the same conditions competitive factor achieved by EDF algorithm is less than 0.06 and 0.04 respectively.

The algorithm is dynamic. During simulation periodic tasks are considered but it can handle aperiodic tasks as well. For periodic task, even if arrival time is changed, the algorithm can work effectively. Moreover, the algorithm can work with available number of processors. Therefore, even if one processor (except master) fails in between, the system works normally.

CONCLUSION

The algorithm discussed in this paper is dynamic (or online) scheduling algorithm for real-time multiprocessor systems using the concept of ACO. The algorithm finds importance of each schedulable task using pheromone value on a task and heuristic

Figure 3. Load Vs % SR and Load Vs %ECU with number of processor = 2

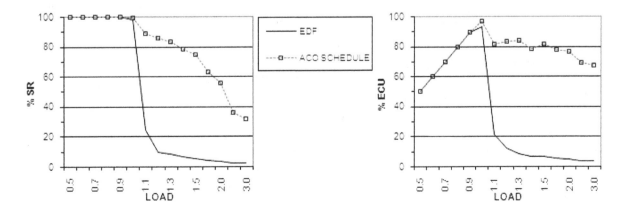

Figure 4. Load Vs % SR and Load Vs %ECU with number of processor =5

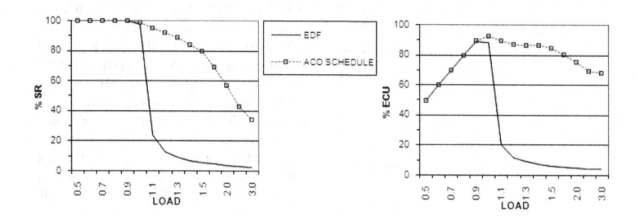

Figure 5. Load Vs % SR and Load Vs %ECU with number of processor =15

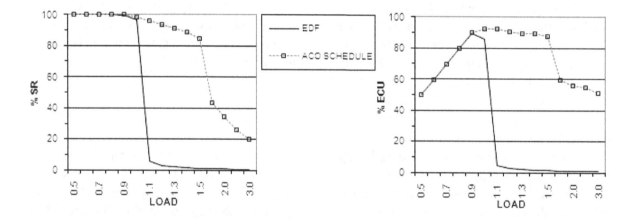

function, which is proportional to deadline of the task. We can conclude the following from results achieved during simulation:

The proposed algorithm performs efficiently for the multiprocessor system having homogenous, identical processors and soft timing constraints. The algorithm performs very well during underloaded conditions and slightly overloaded conditions. During highly overloaded conditions also it performs quite satisfactorily. Many instances, which are not possible to schedule using EDF algorithm, can be scheduled successfully using the proposed algorithm. The only disadvantage of the algorithm is: Time required for decision of scheduling is more, compared to EDF algorithm. But the inherent parallelism provided by the algorithm reduces the intensity of this disadvantage.

REFERENCES

Baruah, S., Funk, S., & Goossens, J. (2003). Robustness results concerning EDF scheduling upon uniform multiprocessors. *IEEE Transactions on Computers, 52*(9), 1185–1195. doi:10.1109/TC.2003.1228513

Baruah, S., & Goossens, J. (2004). Rate-monotonic scheduling on uniform multiprocessors. *IEEE Transactions on Computers*, *52*(7), 966–970. doi:10.1109/TC.2003.1214344

Baruah, S., Koren, G., Mishra, B., Raghunath, A., Roiser, L., & Shasha, D. (1991). On-line scheduling in the presence of overload. In *Proceedings of the 32nd Annual Symposium on Foundations of Computer Science* (pp. 100-110).

Chang, P. C., Wu, I. W., Shann, J. J., & Chung, C. P. (2008). ETAHM: An energy-aware task allocation algorithm for heterogeneous multiprocessor. In *Proceedings of the 45th Conference on Design Automation* (pp. 776-779).

Dertouzos, M., & Ogata, K. (1974). Control robotics: The procedural control of physical process. In *Proceedings of the IFIP Congress* (pp. 807-813).

Dorigo, M., & Caro, G. (1999). The ant colony optimization metaheuristic. In Corne, D., Dorigo, M., & Glover, G. (Eds.), *New ideas in optimization*. New Delhi, India: McGraw-Hill.

Dorigo, M., & Gambardella, L. M. (1997). Ant colony system: A cooperative learning approach to the traveling salesman problem. *IEEE Transactions on Evolutionary Computation*, *1*(1), 53–66. doi:10.1109/4235.585892

Dorigo, M., Maniezzo, V., & Colorni, A. (1996). The ant system: Optimization by a colony of cooperative agents. *IEEE Transactions on Systems, Man, and Cybernetics. Part B, Cybernetics*, *26*(1), 29–41. doi:10.1109/3477.484436

Dorigo, M., & Stutzle, T. (2004). *Ant colony optimization*. Cambridge, MA: MIT Press.

Funk, S., Goossens, J., & Baruah, S. (2001). On-line scheduling on uniform multiprocessors. In *Proceedings of the IEEE Real-Time Systems Symposium* (pp. 183-192).

Koren, G., & Shasha, D. (1995). DOver: An optimal on-line scheduling algorithm for overloaded real-time systems. *SIAM Journal on Computing*, *24*, 318–339. doi:10.1137/S0097539792236882

Kotecha, K., & Shah, A. (2008). Efficient dynamic scheduling algorithms for real-time multiprocessor system. In *Proceedings of the International Conference on High Performance Computation Networking and Communications* (pp. 21-25).

Liu, W. S. (2001). *Real-time systems*. New Delhi, India: Pearson Education.

Locke, C. D. (1986). *Best effort decision making for real-time scheduling*. Unpublished doctoral dissertation, Carnegie-Mellon University, Pittsburgh, PA.

Lopez, J. M., Diaz, J. L., & Garcia, D. F. (2004). Minimum and maximum utilization bounds for multiprocessor rate monotonic scheduling. *IEEE Transactions on Parallel and Distributed Computing*, *15*(7), 642–653. doi:10.1109/TPDS.2004.25

Lundberg, L. (2002). Analyzing fixed-priority global multiprocessor scheduling. In *Proceedings of the Eighth IEEE Real-Time and Embedded Technology and Applications Symposium* (pp. 145-153).

Mok, A. (1983). *Fundamental design problems of distributed systems for the hard-real-time environment*. Unpublished doctoral dissertation, Massachusetts Institute of Technology, Cambridge, MA.

Oh, Y., & Son, S. H. (1995). Allocating fixed-priority periodic tasks on multiprocessor systems. *Real-Time Systems*, *9*(3), 207–239. doi:10.1007/BF01088806

Ramamritham, K., & Stankovik, J. A. (1994). Scheduling algorithms and operating support for real-time systems. *Proceedings of the IEEE*, *82*(1), 55–67. doi:10.1109/5.259426

Ramamritham, K., Stankovik, J. A., & Shiah, P. F. (1990). Efficient scheduling algorithms for real-time multiprocessor systems. *IEEE Transactions on Parallel and Distributed Systems*, *1*(2), 184–190. doi:10.1109/71.80146

Ramos, V., Muge, F., & Pina, P. (2002). Self-organized data and image retrieval as a consequence of inter-dynamic synergistic relationships in artificial ant colonies. In *Proceedings of the Second International Conference on Hybrid Intelligent System*, Santiago, Chile (pp. 500-512).

Saad, E. M., Adawy, M. E., & Habashy, S. M. (2006). Reconfigurable parallel processing system based on a modified ant colony system. In *Proceedings of the 23rd National Conference on Radio Science*, Menoufiya, Egypt (pp. 1-11).

Saini, G. (2005). Application of fuzzy-logic to real-time scheduling. In *Proceedings of the 14th IEEE Real-Time Conference* (pp. 60-63).

Shah, A., & Kotecha, K. (2010). Dynamic scheduling algorithm for real-time operating system using ACO. In *Proceedings of the International Conference on Computing Intelligence and Communication Networks* (pp. 617-621).

Turneo, A., Pilato, C., Ferrandi, F., Sciuto, D., & Lanzi, P. L. (2008). Ant colony optimization for mapping and scheduling in heterogeneous multiprocessor systems. In *Proceedings of the International Conference on Embedded Computer Systems: Architectures, Modeling and Simulation* (pp. 142-149).

Ullman, J. D. (1973). Polynomial complete scheduling problems. *Operating Systems Review*, *7*(4), 96–101. doi:10.1145/957195.808055

This work was previously published in the International Journal of Grid and High Performance Computing, Volume 3, Issue 3, edited by Emmanuel Udoh and Ching-Hsien Hsu, pp. 20-30, copyright 2011 by IGI Publishing (an imprint of IGI Global).

Chapter 7
Performance Analysis of Sequential and Parallel Neural Network Algorithm for Stock Price Forecasting

Rashedur M. Rahman
North South University, Bangladesh

Ruppa K. Thulasiram
University of Manitoba, Canada

Parimala Thulasiraman
University of Manitoba, Canada

ABSTRACT

The neural network is popular and used in many areas within the financial field, such as credit authorization screenings, regularities in security price movements, simulations of market behaviour, and so forth. In this research, the authors use a neural network technique for stock price forecasting of Great West Life, an insurance company based in Winnipeg, Canada. The Backpropagation algorithm is a popular algorithm to train a neural network. However, one drawback of traditional Backpropagation algorithm is that it takes a substantial amount of training time. To expedite the training process, the authors design and develop different parallel and multithreaded neural network algorithms. The authors implement parallel neural network algorithms on both shared memory architecture using OpenMP and distributed memory architecture using MPI and analyze the performance of those algorithms. They also compare the results with traditional auto-regression model to establish accuracy.

DOI: 10.4018/978-1-4666-2065-0.ch007

INTRODUCTION

Forecasting is important for financial institution for two reasons: to decrease loss and to increase return on investment. Technical analysis and fundamental analysis are two techniques that could be used for forecasting. Technical analysis identifies internal and external variables that could factor the stock price. Important indicators of technical analysis are filter and momentum indicators, cycle theory, volume indicators and pattern analysis. Fundamental analysis forecasts the market direction based upon the underlying economic factors. Sometimes, decision making is not straightforward using these two techniques. Besides, it requires considerable effort from the front end traders in using these two techniques. Averages of the consecutive values of the variables are found to follow some invariant pattern and are found useful. Moving averages of some quantities are also found to be transparent for analysis and became prominent in predicting future values. In finance, moving averages were initially used for stock price forecasting. One of the important models developed is called *Auto Regressive Moving Average (ARMA)* which is more scientific with reproducible results and hence is applied successfully for decision making. The nonlinear and non-parametric behaviour of financial markets sometimes could not be captured by the time-series analysis. *Artificial Neural Networks (NN)* is one of the techniques developed from artificial intelligence research (Fausett, 1994) that can be used for stock price forecasting. The novelty of NN lies in their ability to model the nonlinear process with few prior assumptions.

NNs are applied for many problems in finance including, mortgage risk assessment, economic prediction, risk rating of exchange-traded fixed-income investments, portfolio selection/diversification, simulation of market behaviour, index construction and identification of explanatory economic factors (Trippi & Turban, 1993; Weigend et al., 1997). NN is designed to learn certain aspects

of the application to solve a given problem. To predict a future value the neural network needs to be trained. BackPropagation (BP) is one of the most commonly used training algorithms for multi-layer neural networks (McCulloch & Pitts, 1998). The standard Backpropagation algorithm employs an optimization method to map the inputs to the outputs of the network. The optimization method poses serious challenges when the network under consideration has a large number of processing elements. Sixty hours of training with certain parametric conditions is not uncommon (Hamm, Brorsen & Sharda, 1993). This huge amount of training time is sometimes unacceptable for quick decision making that is generally required in financial markets.

In our current research, we study and implement parallel algorithms for stock price forecasting. To the best of our knowledge, we first attempt to use the parallel algorithms on neural network for stock price forecasting. We implement two techniques, namely Training Set Parallelism (TSP) and Neuron Parallelism (NP) on distributed and shared memory multiprocessor architectures. Our goal in this research is to test whether parallel processing could expedite the training process of neural network to facilitate quick decision making for stock price forecasting. Our aim is not in rigorous statistical testing of the forecasted results or even study and implement our techniques in all of the different parallel architectures addressed in literature (for example PVM, Systolic Arrays, Pthreads, MPI, POSIX threads etc.). Moreover, we want to mention that the study of parallel algorithms for financial forecasting has been limited due to multi-disciplinary nature and our current attempt reveals the importance and necessity of parallel computing in the financial area.

Rest of the paper is organized as follows. We describe some of the forecasting models including time series forecasting with ARMA model in related work section, as well as the neural network and general Backpropagation algorithm. We then discuss distributed and multithreaded NN training algorithms used in this research. We present theoretical analysis of these algorithms and discuss the experimental results. Finally, we conclude and give directions of future research.

RELATED WORK

Forecasting has been applied in many areas, from weather to business and economic forecasting. Managers in businesses use forecasts in their day-to-day planning and control of company operations. Reliable forecasts help managers to make timely decisions on: company financial planning, investment in plant and machinery, acquisition of materials, human resources, set production, inventory levels and so on.

The forecasting techniques used in business, industry and finance are *surveys*, the *Delphi method* and various *extrapolation methods*. *Surveys* are commonly used in market research for industrial and financial products. This method relies on a questionnaire administered by mail, telephone or personal interview. The responses help to find out the views of consumers regarding future demand of a product and accordingly the managers could predict the future sales. On the other hand, the *Delphi method* (Rowe & Wright,1999) relies on combining the views of a number of experts. For this reason it is also called "jury of executive opinion" (Holden et al., 1990). Initially a group of experts is asked independently to forecast some particular event. The results of this outcome are collected and discussed together. These experts are then asked to explain their standing for prediction and after further discussion, a second survey is conducted, a discussion follows and the process is repeated until the experts reach a decision which is acceptable to everyone. The *extrapolation method* tries to identify the past patterns and expects that these previous patterns in the data will be repeated in the future under similar business condition. In this technique data are observed at regular time intervals; say daily,

weekly, quarterly or annually. A *Time-series* is an extrapolation method which is an important tool used for forecasting. A time series is a set of observations ordered in time. With the advent of widespread computer applications, the much more general and statistically based methods of time-series analysis known as *autoregressive moving averages (ARMA)* (Box, Jenkins & Reinsel, 1994) are developed and applied in forecasting. ARMA is a statistical tool that is used to explain the behaviour of time-series data using only past observations on the variable in question. In ARMA analysis, we use the statistical concept of correlation to measure the relationships between observations within the series.

Though neural networks have been studied since 1940s they are relatively new methods for modeling and forecasting financial data, for example, stock/asset price. Using neural networks, it is possible to search for regularities in the historical data that could help predict the current asset price. Kimoto et al. (1990) introduced modular neural networks that could learn the relationships between the past technical and economic indices and predict the timing to buy and sell a stock. Simulation of buying and selling stocks using the prediction system showed an excellent profit. Stock price fluctuation factors could be extracted by analyzing the neural networks. Yoon and Swales (1993) illustrated the neural networks approach to predict stock price performance and compared its predictive power with that of multiple discriminant analysis (MDA) methods. Inputs for the network were a list of nine variables: confidence, economic factors outside the firm's control, growth, strategic gains, new products, anticipated loss, anticipated gain, long-term optimism, and short-term optimism. The outputs of the network were the predicted stock price performance of the firm; a firm whose stock price performed well was classified as Group 1 and a firm whose stock price performed poorly was classified as Group 2. The neural network outperforms the

MDA method with more correct classifications into Group1 and Group 2.

Dutta and Shekar (1994) rated different industrial bonds using neural networks. Valueline Index and S&P Bond guide identified ten financial variables that had influence on the bond rating. These ten variables were used as input for the neural network. Various neural network configurations (two-layered, three-layered, different number of hidden nodes etc.) were experimented with the Berkeley ISP (the Interactive Statistical Package developed at the University of California, Berkeley), which is normally used for multiple regression analysis. Neural network consistently outperformed the regression model in prediction for bond rating. Besides, the total squared error for both training and testing samples for regression analysis was about an order of magnitude higher than that for neural network.

White (1990) used neural networks for predicting one-day of return for holding IBM common stock. Of the available 5000 days of return data, 1000 days were selected for training purposes, whereas samples of 500 days before and after the training period were used for testing the neural network's performance. The three-layer neural network trained on the 1000 days detected the nonlinear structure of the market and a positive correlation coefficient was found between the actual rate of daily return and predicted rate of return. Kanas (2001) compared out-of-sample forecasts of monthly return for Dow Jones (DJ) and Financial Times (FT) indices generated by a nonlinear neural network and linear model. This comparison was carried out on the basis of two approaches: directional accuracy and forecast encompassing. Though the two models did not produce good performance in terms of predicting the directional change of the two indices, the neural network forecasts could explain the forecast errors of the linear model whereas the linear model could not explain the forecasts errors of the neural network for both indices.

In addition, neural networks have been applied to many problems in finance, including mortgage risk assessment, economic prediction, risk rating of exchange-traded fixed income investments, portfolio selection/diversification, and simulation of market behaviour, index construction and identification of explanatory economic factors (Trippi & Turban, 1993; Weigend et al., 1997).

In the next section we briefly introduce neural network and sequential Backpropagation algorithm.

NEURAL NETWORK AND BACKPROPAGATION ALGORITHM

Neural networks are one of the techniques developed from artificial intelligence research (Fausett, 1994) that can be used in different applications. Neural networks were developed through studies of neuron perceptions. In a sense neural networks are computer programs that are trained to learn analogously to a human brain remembering some information from the past. A network is built with many neurons called nodes which are modeled on neurons from biological organisms. It is a system composed of many simple processing elements whose function is determined by network structure, connection strengths, and the processing performed at computing elements or nodes. The network learns the patterns and develops the ability to forecast. BackPropagation (BP) is one of the most commonly used training algorithms for multi-layer neural networks.

A fully connected, layered, feed-forward network is depicted in Figure 1, where x_i, h_i, o_i represent unit activation levels of input, hidden, and output units, respectively. Weights on the connections between the input and hidden layers are denoted by $w1_{ij}$, while weights on connections between the hidden and output layers are denoted by $w2_{ij}$. The neurons marked with "1" are threshold neurons and their activation value is set to 1.

Figure 1. A multilayer feed-forward neural network

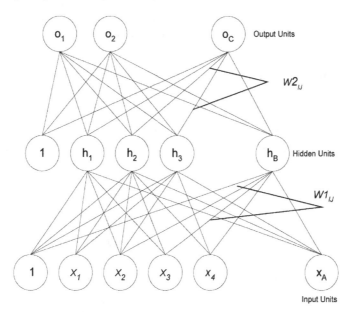

The BP networks with supervised learning rules are the most popular and useful in many forecasting applications. Standard Backpropagation employs an optimization method called the gradient descent method (Rich & Knight, 1993) to map the inputs to the outputs of the network. The steps of a BP algorithm for training the neural network are summarized as follows:

a. Randomize the weights to small arbitrary values and initialize the activations neurons. The neurons marked as "1" in Figure 1 are activation neurons. Their values are set to 1 in this step.

b. Select a training pair from the training set. A training pair consists of an input and output vectors.

c. Apply the input vector to the network input neurons. An input vector consists of stock prices for last m days where m is the number of input neurons for the neural network under consideration.

d. Propagate the activations from the input neurons of the input layer to the hidden neurons of the hidden layer using the activation function.

e. Propagate the activations from the neurons of the hidden layer to the neurons of the output layer.

f. Calculate the error, the difference between the network output, and the desired output. The desired output is the output vector from the training pair and the network output is calculated by activation of output neurons. These errors are the errors of the neurons in the output layer.

g. Compute the errors of the neurons in the hidden layer.

h. Adjust the weights of the network between the hidden layer and output layer.

i. Adjust the weights between the input layer and the hidden layer. The error adjustment in steps h-i use the gradient decent method.

Repeat steps b-i for each pair of input-output vectors in the training set until the error for the entire system is acceptably low.

The sequential Backpropagation algorithm runs well and has a good running time for a small network but when the network is large it takes a longer time to converge. Therefore, the main drawback of a BP algorithm is its training time. For example, 50 input variable combinations tested over three different hidden neurons with five sets of randomly selected starting weights and a maximum number of 4 thousand runs, results in 3 million iterations. The training time of 60 hours is not uncommon (Hamm, Brorsen & Sharda, 1993) for such problems. Parallel processing could definitely help in accelerating the training time of the network. The BP algorithm is computationally intensive and training times on the order of days and weeks are not uncommon. As a result, some studies have been focused, though not for finance applications, on efficient parallel implementations of the BP algorithm (Takefuji, 1992). Two main paradigms used to parallelize the BP learning algorithm are: partitioning the neural network called *network-based parallelism* and partitioning the training set of neural network called *training-set parallelism* (Sundararajan & Saratchandran, 1998). In network-based parallelism, the neural network is partitioned and distributed among different processors. Each processor then simulates a group of neurons belonging to different layers of the neural network over the whole training set. In training-set parallelism the neural network is duplicated on every processor of the parallel machine, and each processor works with a subset of the training set. Each processor has a local copy of the complete weight matrix of the neural network and accumulates weight change values for the given training patterns. Pipelining is another technique (Petrowski et al., 1993) that allows the training patterns to be "pipelined" between the layers. That is, the hidden and output layers are computed on different processors. While the output layer processor calculates the output and error values for the present training set, the hidden layer processor processes the next training set. The forward and backward phase of BP algorithm could also be parallelized. However, the study of parallel algorithms for financial forecasting has been limited due to multi-disciplinary nature. In general, parallel computing is expected to increase the overall efficiency of the NN algorithms.

The main objective of this paper is to study the stock price forecasting problem by developing parallel algorithms for Backpropagation neural network. The next section presents parallel neural network algorithms.

PARALLEL NEURAL NETWORK ALGORITHMS

To expedite the training process, we have developed parallel neural network algorithms in this research and implemented them on distributed and multithreaded architectures and conducted various experiments to study the performance.

In the distributed version of neural network we have followed a very coarse-grained approach, where the data is partitioned and distributed among the processors. In the multithreaded approach, we experimented with parameters such as thread size and number of threads in the system. We describe the details of these two algorithms in the following sections.

Distributed Approach

We have developed and implemented two types of parallelism in the distributed approach: *neuron parallelism* (NP) and *training set parallelism* (TSP). In NP, the neurons are subdivided and distributed among the processors. In TSP, the input data is divided among the processors but the network is replicated on every processor. Each processor trains its own part of the network on its local data set examples, and the weights are resolved by propagating the weights among the processors. The algorithms are implemented on a Beowulf cluster using MPI.

Neuron Parallelism

In our implementation we have used only one hidden layer; however for general understanding we describe the algorithm here with multiple hidden layers. In the BP algorithm, the nodes within a hidden layer i are independent of one another. There is no communication required among these nodes. This lends itself easily to a parallel implementation. However, the nodes between the two hidden layers h_j and h_{j+1} (j refers to the number of hidden layers in the network) are dependent on one another and therefore, require communication. Figure 2 shows the technique of NP for a network with one hidden layer and one output. The total training data set is N. We present $n < N$ subsets of data to the network at a time. We assume P processors and the number of nodes at each hidden layer is M. Every processor has a replicated copy of the input nodes. We partition and distribute $\dfrac{M}{P}$ hidden neurons to each of the processors. The edge weights corresponding to the $\dfrac{M}{P}$ nodes local to each processor, reside within that processor.

Each node i in a given hidden layer h_{j+1}, requires the value of all the nodes in h_j. Therefore, each processor has to distribute its local node values calculated at h_j to its neighbouring nodes in different processors to calculate the value of output neuron at layer h_{j+1}. This communication can be performed as one *broadcast* operation. However, to proceed from one hidden layer to the next layer requires barrier synchronization. The following steps comprise the parallel implementation.

1. The processors calculate the activations for the hidden layer neurons residing locally.
2. Each processor sends the activations of its neurons to all other processors as soon as these are computed.
3. Once the activations of all the hidden neurons are received, each processor calculates the output value for the output layer neuron.
4. All processors calculate the *deltas* for the output neuron residing in them (*delta* is error computed in the output layer based on the network's actual output and the target output value. This error is directly proportional to the derivative of activation function

Figure 2. Parallelization of the neural network-neuron parallelism

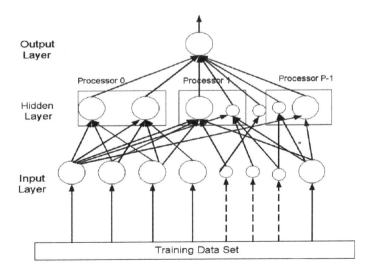

with respect to the weights, the constant of proportionality being the learning rate. In other words, delta is defined as the product of learning rate and the rate of change of the squared error in the output neuron with respect to the change in the weights of the connections).

5. All processors send these delta values to all other processors.

6. The processors calculate the deltas for all the hidden neurons residing in them as soon as they receive the deltas for the output neuron.

7. Finally the processors calculate the weight increments and update the incoming and outgoing weights for those neurons that reside in them.

8. Repeat steps 1-7 to present N data set to the network to complete one epoch.

Training Set Parallelism

We describe here the TSP technique for training a parallel network. Each processor maintains its own copy of the neural network and local weights. This style of parallelism is different from neuron parallelism in the sense that the input data is partitioned, rather than the hidden nodes. Figure 3 illustrates the TSP technique. Given N data set, and P processors, we partition the data set into $\frac{N}{P}$ data sets and distribute each set to the processors. Each processor iterates through every data in its local data set $\frac{N}{P}$ and calculates the error gradients or weight changes to the network. Upon completion of computation, each processor broadcasts the error gradients to the other processors. Once each processor receives the entire gradient information from all the other processors, it updates the weights of its network. This process continues for many epochs or until the error is acceptably low. In effect, each network looks as if it had been trained with the entire data set. For training set parallelism, the complete training set

data is distributed among different processors. In this paradigm, each processor maintains its own network and own local weights. For example, in our case of 2080 data sets, we could distribute first 520 data sets among P processors so that each processor gets $(520/P)$ data points. Weights remain the same for the first $(520/P)$ data sets. Each processor accumulates the weight changes for each training pair (data-set) and keeps weight changes in its own local memory. After completing the weight updates of the network for $(520/P)$ data sets, each processor broadcasts its local weights and weight changes to other processors. Each processor calculates an average of the initial weights of P processors and required weight change for the first 520 data sets. The new weight of the network is calculated by adding the average weight change to the average weight. Each processor broadcasts these updated weights to other processors so that for the next 520 data sets each processor works with this new weight. This process continues until one epoch is completed, that is, 2080 data sets are presented to the network. After one epoch, the algorithm described above repeats itself until the error is acceptably low.

Shared Memory Approach

OpenMP supports both *fine-grained parallelism* (FGP) and *coarse-grained parallelism* (CGP) using the concept of parallel regions. We describe in this section the neural network multithreaded algorithms for these types of parallelism.

Fine-Grained/Loop Level Parallelism

This structure exploits the inherent loop structure in the program by parallelizing the loops individually. The iterations of a loop are divided among the threads. In this approach, we flood the system with as many threads as we require and allow the dynamic scheduler in the system to allocate the threads among the processors. These threads can be executed concurrently and asynchronously.

Figure 3. Parallelization of the neural network- training set parallelism

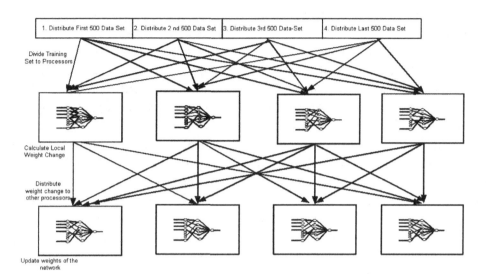

The parallel/distributed version of the neural network algorithm described in the previous section, (for N input data, M hidden neurons and one output) requires a barrier synchronization to perform the reduction operation at the output layer. Hence, all processors have to broadcast their final values to the master processor before the master processor can compute the output. In a shared memory model, this extra overhead is not required. Instead, we explicitly synchronize the output variable by placing it in a *critical section* and allow each processor to access this critical section without any read-write conflicts.

A portion of the actual computations of the neural network algorithm using loops for the activation calculations of the hidden neurons (the

Figure 4. Pseudo code for loop-level parallelism

```
#pragma omp parallel for
  {
        for(j = 0; j < M; j++)
        {
                for (i = 0; i < n; i++)
                {
                  /* Some Computation is performed here*/
                }
        }

  #pragma omp critical
    {
        /* Output is calculated here*/
    }
  }
```

weight update calculations are also performed using loop-level parallelism without critical section) in OpenMP is given below.

In the above code, there are *n* input data and *M* hidden nodes. This code can be easily explained through the execution diagram in Figure 5. Each vertical arrow represents an executable thread. The master thread starts the algorithm and executes the serial portion of the code before encountering the *parallel for* directive. The master thread invokes the loop creating *X-1* slave threads; *X* may be specified by the user. We assume in this diagram that $X = m$. The *X-1* slave threads together with the master thread creates *X* threads. These *X* threads divide the iterations of the *for loop* among themselves, with each thread executing a portion of the iterations. The parameter *X* can be varied according to the needs of the application. In this algorithm, when $X = M$, we obtain pure fine-grained parallelism.

At the end of each iteration, the slave threads enter the mutually exclusive critical section to calculate the output. Note that we have explicitly inserted this directive for synchronization purposes to control access to the shared variable. After each thread has completed its portion of the iterations, the thread waits at the end of the *parallel for construct* for all the other threads to finish. OpenMP adds an implicit barrier at the end of the parallel constructs. The threads are released of this barrier condition, once all the threads finish and synchronize at the barrier. At this point, the slave threads no longer exist and the master thread resumes execution of the code at the end of the *parallel for* construct.

Coarse-Grained Parallelism

In this approach, we explicitly intervene by partitioning the workload into various sections and

Figure 5. Loop level parallelism in OpenMP

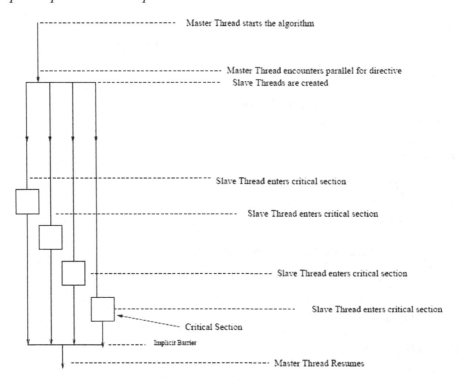

distributing them to the threads. This is performed in OpenMP using the concept of *parallel region*. The *parallel* directive defines a parallel region shown below. The number of threads to execute the parallel region can be defined by the user within the code. The code within the *parallel* directive is executed concurrently and asynchronously by the threads. For example, with T threads and n nodes, each thread can be allowed to execute on $\dfrac{n}{T}$ nodes. The same code is replicated on each thread. Each thread, therefore, has its own data environment. The threads and the data environments disappear at the end of the parallel region and the master thread resumes execution.

There are two parallel regions and one sequential region. The above code can be best explained using Figure 6. The master thread starts the serial execution as before. When it encounters the first parallel region to compute the activations of the hidden neurons, a team of slave threads is created to execute this parallel region concurrently. The code within this parallel region is replicated on every thread. At the end of the parallel region, the master thread performs the activation calculations of the output neuron and the error calculations of the output and hidden neurons sequentially. When the master thread encounters the parallel region for the second time, a team of slave threads are again created. The code within this parallel region, updating weights of its neurons, is replicated on each slave thread as before. The amount of computation and communication required for the neural network training process is determined theoretically first. This is done in order to get an idea of the feasibility of implementation of the algorithms on parallel architectures for their practicality. In the next chapter we derive the theoretical limits of these four algorithms based on the computation and communication requirements (Figure 7).

Figure 6. Parallel region in OpenMP

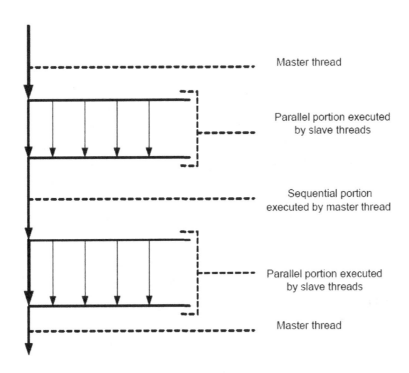

Figure 7. Pseudo code for coarse-grained parallelism

```
for i = 1 to number_of_epochs do
  {
    #pragma omp parallel
        {
                id=omp_get_thread_num()
                /* number of the thread
                    specified by user*/
                /* Calculation of activations of hidden neurons done in
                parallel fashion */
            }
        /* Activation calculation of output neuron and error*/
        /* calculation of output and hidden neurons are done*/
        /* sequentially by the master processor */

    #pragma omp parallel
        {
                id=omp_get_thread_num();
                /* Weight update of the weights connecting to*/
                /* hidden-input and hidden-output neurons are done in parallel fashion.*/
        }
  }
```

THEORETICAL ANALYSIS

In this section we present some of the analytical results of the algorithms.

Distributed Approach

The processors in a Beowulf cluster are connected by a ring and every processor requires to broadcast its message to every other processor, say to P-1 processors. To analyze the time complexity for two algorithms in the distributed approach, we assume that is t_s the start-up time and t_c is the communication cost for a fixed length message (floating point) to traverse the interconnection network. We also assume that t_b is the average time required for the parallel machine to complete barrier synchronization.

The training process consists of several batches of inputs from initial data set to the network. This requires several epochs. The training time is the product of the number of epochs and the time consumed for each epoch. During each epoch, the following computations are performed: calculation of the activation for each neuron; calculation of error gradient with respect to weight; and updating the weights. Given n neurons in the input layer and M neurons in the hidden layer, each hidden neuron computes a weighted sum with n inputs and evaluates a bipolar sigmoid activation function. Each hidden neuron is connected by an edge from all n input neurons with a weight w_i. Therefore, for M neurons, the total number of weights connecting the input layer to the hidden layer is $Mn = W_1$. The number of weights connecting from the hidden layer to the output is $M = W_2$. Since W_2 is essentially much less than W_1, we will ignore W_2. Therefore, the total number of weights in the network is $W = Mn$. The computation of the error gradient at each neuron, involves each weight in the network, which is approximately W. The time required to update each weight, in the final step, is therefore W.

Training Set Parallelism

For accuracy of the neural network results, each of the $\frac{N}{P}$ data set is further subdivided into l sets and distributed to the P processors. The computation time T_{c1}, for evaluation the network and computing error gradient is $\Theta\left(\frac{N}{P}W\right)$. Each processor then broadcasts the calculated error gradient to each of the $P-1$ processors to update every weight in the network. The total communication time is, therefore, $T_{comm} = \Theta\left(Wl(P-1)(t_s + t_c)\right)$. The total time required to update the weights, W, for l steps is $T_{c2} = \Theta\left(Wl(P-1)\right)$. Time required for barrier synchronization is l. Therefore, the total time for the training set parallelism (TSP) approach, including communications and computations is:

$$Total_{TSP} = T_{c1} + T_{c2} + T_{comm} + T_{barrier}$$

$$= \Theta\left(\frac{N}{P}W\right) + \Theta\left(Wl(P-1)(t_s + t_c)\right)$$
$$+ \Theta\left(Wl(P-1)\right) + \Theta\left(lt_b\right)$$

Neuron Parallelism

In this algorithm, M hidden neurons are partitioned so that $\frac{M}{P}$ hidden neurons are distributed to P processors. The total computation time is $\Theta\left(\frac{W}{P}N\right)$. Each processor accumulates the values

of its hidden neurons and distributes the sum to the other $P-1$ processors for activation calculation of output neuron. This communication phase takes $\Theta\left((t_s + t_c)(P-1)N\right)$. Before broadcasting the accumulated sum, a barrier is introduced to perform the final computation at the output neuron. The total synchronization required is Nt_b. Thus, the total time for the NP is:

$$Total_{NP} = T_{comp} + T_{comm} + T_{barrier}$$

$$=$$

$$\Theta\left(\frac{W}{P}N\right) + \Theta\left((t_s + t_c)(P-1)N\right) + \Theta\left(Nt_b\right)$$

Shared-Memory Multithreaded Approach

In this section we derive the time complexity of both fine-grained/loop level parallelism and coarse-grained parallelism.

Fine Grained or Loop-Level Parallelism

For the code discussed in Figure 4, the number of threads created is the number of hidden neurons, M. Only the outer loop is parallelized. In loop-level parallelism, the scheduler within the system distributes the work load among the processors trying to evenly balance the load. Each thread then enters a critical section. However, OpenMP does not provide fair access to the critical section, meaning that the threads are not guaranteed access in some fashion such as first-in first-out or round robin. OpenMP makes sure that a thread will be granted access to the critical section eventually. Under this circumstance, a thread may be starved since other threads may get repeated access to the critical section. In our problem, threads enter the critical section only once. In the worst case, a thread T, will enter the critical section after all the other $M-1$ threads have had access. Then the waiting time to compute the critical section (CS) is the product of the time to compute the instructions within the section, t_{CS}, and the number of threads ahead of $T (= T \times t_{CS})$.

In shared memory, there is no communication between processors or barrier synchronization. Each thread is fine-grained and performs computation independently and concurrently. As mentioned in previous section, all threads have an implicit barrier (IB), however. This is additional overhead. Let us assume that each thread T takes time t to finish the whole algorithm. Let t_{IB} be the associated time for all threads to reach the end of the loop. As we explain later, the overhead of the critical section waiting time and the implicit barrier, play a major role in the performance of the multithreaded algorithm in loop-level parallelism.

Therefore, the total computation time for fine-grained/loop level parallelism (LLP) with the overhead incurred is:

$$Total_{LLP} = T_{comp} + T_{CS} + T_{overhead}$$

$$= \left(t + t_{CS} * \left(M - 1\right) + t_{IB}\right) N$$

Coarse-Grained Parallelism

In this approach, given M neurons, we predetermine the number of threads required and allocate data to these threads. For example, with T threads and n nodes, each thread can be allowed to execute on $\dfrac{n}{T}$ nodes. Each thread executes the same code. In previous section, we have shown the code for this approach. We notice that there are two parallel regions and one sequential region. The activation calculation of the hidden neurons is performed in parallel. The time required for this is $\dfrac{W}{T} N$. At the end of the activation calculations, all threads join the master thread. At this point the master thread resumes execution of the serial part.

OpenMP implicitly adds a barrier at the end of the parallel region directive. Let t_{PRT} be the time required by all threads to join the master thread. The time taken for sequential step to calculate the activations of output neuron and error calculation of output and hidden neurons is $2M$. Finally the weight updates are done in parallel. This takes time $\dfrac{W}{T} N$. Since there is no critical section, there is no additional overhead and there is no communication because of shared-memory. Therefore, the total computation time for coarse-grained parallelism (CGP) for N data set is:

$$Total_{CGP} = T_{parallel} + T_{serial} + T_{overhead}$$

$$= \left(2 \times \dfrac{W}{T} + 2M + t_{PRT}\right) N$$

This is a first attempt of neural network implementation on OpenMP. It is very difficult to analyze the multithreaded algorithm in general. We use the above derived complexity results as a basis to analyse the performance results we present in the next section.

PERFORMANCE RESULTS

In this section we describe the performance results of the parallel implementations on an 8 node Beowulf cluster with MPI and on an 8 processor SMP with OpenMP. Each node in a Beowulf cluster consists of two Pentium III processors with speed of 501.146 MHz and has a memory of 526 MB with cache size of 512 KB. The SMP has Pentium III processors with speed of 700.011 MHz and has a memory of 764 MB with cache size 1024 KB. The inputs for the neural network for NP approach are daily stock prices for 200 consecutive days. The output is the predicted stock price for the following day. The number of hidden neurons is about 75% of input neurons that is 152 neurons. For TSP we use a small network of 25 input nodes representing stock prices of 25 days, 16 hidden nodes and 1 output node that predicts the output for the following day. We used bipolar sigmoid as the activation function. Using the data set of 2080 daily prices for a real-life stock with a mean and standard deviation, the inputs are normalized and fed to the input units of the neural network. The data are obtained from Great-West Life. We initialize the weights using Nguyen-Widrow initialization (Fausett, 1994) which helps the neural network for fast learning rather than a fully random initialization.

ARMA Model

Time-series data refers to observations on a variable that occurs in a time sequence. We use the symbol X_t to stand for the numerical value of an observation; the subscript t refers to the time period when the observation occurs. Thus, a sequence of n observations could be represented as: ($X_1, X_2, X_3, ..., X_n$). ARMA is a statistical tool that is used to explain the behaviour of time-series data using only past observations on the variable in question.

In ARMA analysis, the time-sequenced observations in the data $\left(...., X_{t-1}, X_t, X_{t+1}\right)$ are statistically dependent. We use the statistical concept of correlation to measure the relationships between observations within the series. In auto regression analysis we would like to examine the correlation between X at time t $\left(X_t\right)$ and X at all earlier time periods.

A general Auto Regression AR (p) model is defined as follows (Makridakis & Wheelright, 1978):

$$X_t = \varphi_1 X_{t-1} + \varphi_2 X_{t-2} + \varphi_3 X_{t-3}$$
$$+ .... + \varphi_p X_{t-p} + e_t$$

Where the φ_i's are the autoregression coefficients, X's are the series under investigation and p is the order of the model. Before an AR model can be used, its order p must be specified. The appropriate value for p specifies the number of terms to be included and it is much less than the length of the series. The noise term or residue e_t is known as Gaussian white noise.

The current term of the series can be estimated by a linear weighted sum of previous terms in the series. The weights are the autoregressive coefficients φ_i's. The problem in AR analysis is to derive the "best" values for φ_i given a series X_t. The autoregressive coefficients could be found using nonlinear least square methods. The most common method for deriving the coefficients involves multiplying the definition above by X_{t-p} and taking the expectation values and normalizing. This gives a set of linear equations called the Yule-Walker system of linear equations that can be solved numerically (Makridakis & Wheelright, 1978).

Method of Adaptive Filtering

Adaptive Filtering can be applied as an AR method of the form described above. This method starts with an initial set of φ_i values that are calculated with the procedure described above and proceeds to adjust them according to the method of steepest descent

$$\varphi_{it} = \varphi_{it-1} + 2Ke_t X_{t-i}$$

$$i = 1, 2, ..., p$$

$$t = p+1, p+2, ..., n$$

where φ_{it} is the new adaptive parameter, φ_{it-1} is the old parameter, K is the learning constant that determines the speed of adaptation, and e_t and

X_{t-i} have same definitions as before. It is shown (Makridakis & Wheelright, 1978) that by repeatedly using the above equation under the necessary conditions, parametric values (φ_i's) that give successively smaller Mean Squared Error (MSE) can be easily estimated.

Figure 8 shows the testing and training errors for traditional time-series models namely the ARMA model. The figure depicts the error with respect to order p of the AR (p) model. The order p is the total number of previous stock prices included for the prediction of the current stock price. We run the adaptive filtering AR model 1000 times to get the optimal set of autoregressive coefficients. It clearly shows that the testing error decreases as we consider more lagged variables. For our 2080 data set, we get the lowest training error when we consider 152 lagged variables. The error in this case is only 0.076. With the help of autoregressive coefficients, we tried to predict stock prices for successive seven days and obtained a testing error of 0.061463. Both these errors are calculated from the difference of square of the predicted stock and the actual stock price for that day. We get an optimal test error for successive seven days with 10 lagged variables with an error

of 0.043908. One important observation from this figure is that the testing errors are better than the training errors, a counter intuitive phenomenon. This could be due to the fact that test data size is small and very structured. Since our aim is only on the parallel neural network results, we do not pay attention to this phenomenon.

Distributed Approach

Figure 9 presents the execution time of the NP in MPI with respect to the number of processors at various epochs. There is a gradual decrease in execution time as we increase the number of processors for different epochs. In NP, we partition and distribute the hidden neurons to the processors. The processors execute the neural network algorithm on their local data sets for a set of 200 data each time until all the data is fed in. In this approach, there is a communication overhead of $(ts + tc)*7*2080 = 14560*(ts + tc)$ for 8 processors and 2080 data. This communication is required in each of the 1000 epochs and hence leads to a very large overhead for the overall performance of the algorithm.

Figure 8. Autoregression model with varying order

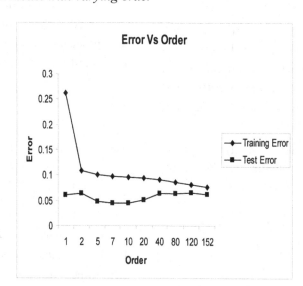

Figure 9. Execution time vs number of processors for neuron parallelism in MPI

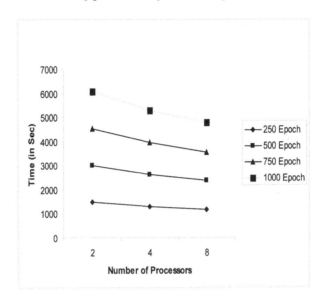

Also, the time required for synchronization per epoch is $2080\,t_b$. Again, for 1000 epochs (last epoch) this is a large overhead. However, the parallel implementation does produce good performance as we increase machine size from 2 to 8 processors. Figure 10 presents the execution time of the TSP algorithm for MPI with respect to number of processors for various epochs. In this approach, the input data set (2080) is partitioned and distributed to the processors. We observe a significant difference in execution time compared to the NP algorithm in MPI shown in Figure 10. On 8 processors, the execution time for TSP with 15000 epochs (last epoch) is only 700 seconds and in NP with only 1000 epochs, it is already close to 5000 seconds (see Figure 9). The communication time (for 25 inputs and 16 hidden neurons) is only

$$Wl(P-1)(t_s + t_c) = (25*16)\,\mathrm{X}\,(4)\,\mathrm{X}\,(7)\,\mathrm{X}\,(t_s + t_c),$$

where l is 4 and the synchronization time compared to NP is $4\mathrm{X}t_b$. This has a significant impact on the overall execution time of algorithm. In addition, since the network size is small, due to domain decomposition, the computation time is smaller than that of a larger network as in NP. This implies better scalability of the TSP algorithm.

A useful indication of the convergence of a neural network is the monitoring of the *correlation* between the target and observed output layer values over each epoch during training given by (Fausett, 1994):

$$r = \frac{\sum_{i=1}^{N_e} T_i O_i - N_e \overline{T}\,\overline{O}}{\sqrt{\left(\sum_{i=1}^{N_e} O_i^2 - N_e \overline{O}^2\right)\left(\sum_{i=1}^{N_e} T_i^2 - N_e \overline{T}^2\right)}}$$

Where O_i is defined as the input dataset i, T_i is defined as the target output for input dataset i, N_e is the total number of input datasets, $\overline{O}$ is the average output and $\overline{T}$ is the average output. The coefficient r will lie in the range $\left[-1, 1\right]$. A small value of r near 0 implies no association and $+1$ means output and target values are strongly correlated and indication of the convergence of neural network towards a global minimum.

Figure 10. Execution time vs number of processors for training set parallelism in MPI

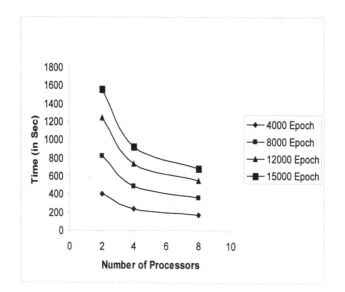

Experiments with NP in MPI indicated that the correlation coefficient gradually increases as we increase the number of epochs. For example, in the second epoch, the correlation coefficient is 0.77 while at the last epoch (1000), the correlation is 0.999005. Also note that the coefficients are positively correlated which implies that the neural network converges as desired.

Shared Memory Multithreaded Approach

Figure 11 shows the timing results for fine-grained algorithm for NP in OpenMP for five epochs. We achieve the best performance with approximately 60 threads after which the execution time starts to increase. This we attribute to the load imbalance and the synchronization cost of entering the critical section. In loop-level parallelism, only the outer loop is parallelized. Also, there is an explicit barrier at the end of each loop, which is added by the system (OpenMP compiler).

The critical section that we need to add explicitly for synchronization purposes is an additional overhead. For a large number of threads, the implicit barrier time t_{IB} is greater than that required for a small number of threads. The computation time decreases when we adopt a large number of threads. However, the overhead incurred due to synchronization barrier dominates the entire computation, for example if we used 100 threads. All threads have to wait until the critical section is completed. The time taken for this is $152*t_{CS}$ for 152 threads. One of the reasons for the downtrend in the execution time for this approach is that the parallelized loops are not distributed evenly (by OpenMP scheduler) among the processors. Due to the poor performance results of this approach, we have conducted all our experiments (training and testing) with coarse-grained algorithm in OpenMP and compared our results with MPI on this algorithm. Note that since we did not find any significant improvement in the accuracy of the results for more epochs, the experimental results are given using 5 epochs.

Figure 12 presents the timing results for coarse-grained parallelism in OpenMP with respect to number of processors and various epochs. We notice in relation to the NP in MPI (Figure 9), the execution time decreases as we increase the number of processors. The execution time for

Figure 11. Execution time vs number of processors for fine-grained parallelism in OpenMP

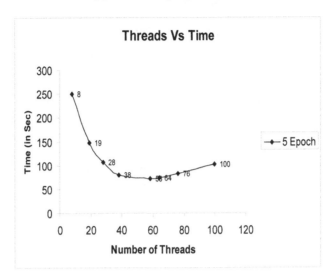

1000 epochs (last epoch) on 8 processors is approximately the same in both cases.

Comparison

Figures 13 through 16 capture the training and testing errors in four different implementations against epochs. Since the number of epochs required in neuron and training-set parallelism is different, the training errors are plotted in different figures. However, the idea is to capture the trend of the error in comparison with the AR model and to show that neural network gives better accuracy when compared to the traditional AR model. Figures 13 and 14 demonstrate the training error for the parallel implementations

Figure 12. Execution time vs. number of processors for coarse-grained parallelism in OpenMP

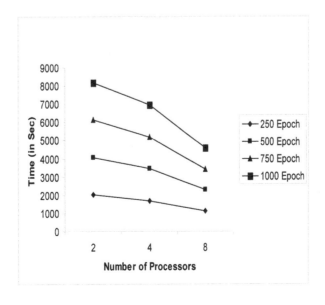

Figure 13. Training errors for neuron, training set, coarse grained parallelisim and AR model

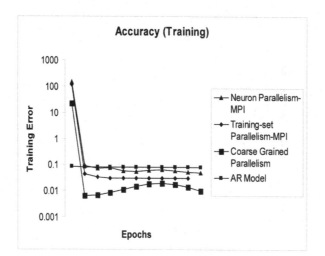

in MPI, OpenMP and the AR model at various epochs. We notice that OpenMP produces the best training results. The AR model stagnates at about 0.08. Adaptive filtering of the AR model gives a good acceleration if the coefficients are randomly chosen. Here, the coefficients for regression analysis given by Wales Yulker (Makridakis & Wheelright, 1978) equation yields good estimation of the coefficients for regression analysis. We see that adaptive filtering does not improve the initial estimation of coefficients. Further, in order to remove discrepancies, the data was normalized

by taking the difference from the mean. For the calculation of coefficients of regression analysis, we used the difference values of successive stock prices mean. For the calculation of coefficients of regression analysis, we used the difference values of successive stock prices.

We observe from this figure that all three algorithms train the neural network with better accuracy. In other words, our algorithms do not compromise on the training errors of the neural network. However, since the focus is on the development of parallel algorithms for neural net-

Figure 14. Training errors for training-set parallelism

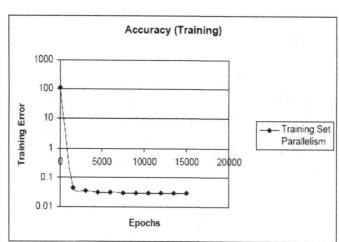

Figure 15. Testing errors for neuron, training set, coarse grained parallelism and AR model

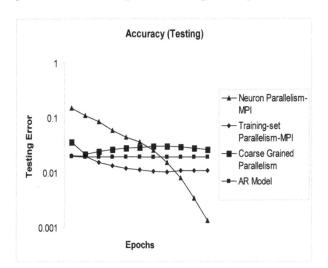

work training process we do not pay attention to the training error as depicted in Figure 14.

Figures 15 and 16 demonstrate the testing error with 8 processors at various epochs. The network was trained with 2080 data sets but tested with 7 data sets each with 200 inputs. The network training depends on the weight initialization as well as gradient error. We notice that in MPI, NP version converges very fast. For NP, each processor initializes its weight matrix and updates its weights in each iteration independently. Since the

data is distributed among the processors in MPI implementation, the independent weight initialization helps in reducing the error accumulation and hence helps in faster convergence. In other words, with independent weight initialization, successive stock price computations produce higher correlation value in relation to the target value. Figure 17 presents the comparison of the three algorithms on 8 processors and at the end of the last epoch in each case. For NP in MPI and CGP in OpenMP, the last epoch is 1000 and

Figure 16. Testing errors for training-set parallelism

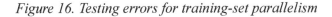

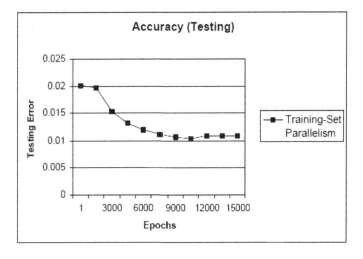

Figure 17. Execution time vs. number of processors for all three parallelisms

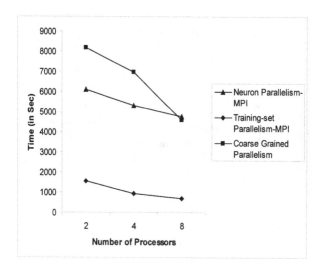

for the TSP, the last epoch is 15000 (for 1000 epochs we noticed that this approach was too fast, with very small execution time). Even with 15000 epochs, we notice that the TSP gives the best execution time.

For NP in MPI and OpenMP the backpropagation algorithm trains a big network of 200 input nodes, 152 hidden nodes and one output node, which requires a large computation. On the other hand, in TSP, the network is of small size, so the computation time is less than that of a bigger network. For NP in OpenMP, we get a better execution time than NP in MPI because there is less associated communication cost in the shared memory architecture as broadcast is eliminated by a common shared variable in critical section.

Table 1 shows the comparison of the three algorithms at the end of the last epoch in each case for 8 processors. The learning rate for NP

and CGP is 0.01 and the momentum is 0.04; for TSP the learning rate is 0.7 and the momentum is 0.6. We define the learning rate as a scale factor that informs how far to move in the direction of gradient. Momentum is a parameter that can be defined as the fraction of previous weight change that should be added to the current weight to proceed with a constant weight change in the same direction. The absolute speedup for TSP with 15000 epochs is 2.32 while for NP in MPI and OpenMP it is 2.4 and 2.5 respectively.

For a given architecture of neural network and backpropagation algorithm we have to work with a fixed problem size (for TSP) or fixed hidden neurons (for NP). In order to get a close to linear speed up, the problem size (or neurons) should be increased significantly in proportion to the machine size (number of processors) so that a large amount of computation will compensate the

Table 1. Comparison of three techniques

Type of Algorithm	Exec. Time (sec)	Speedup	Training Error	Testing Error
MPI (NP) 1000 Epoch	4773.65	2.4	0.048	0.00132
MPI (TSP) 15000 Epoch	683.28	2.32	0.029	0.01808
OpenMP(CGP) 1000 Epoch	4574.23	2.5	0.01	0.019

increased communication overhead. Accuracy is another concern of neural network. In TSP, data is divided into smaller chunks and distributed among a large number of processors. As a result, the computation time decreases but the communication cost dominates the overall efficiency. So we get a less speedup with TSP. Since the network is large, each processor has to do a large amount of computation; we get a better speed up of 2.4 for NP in MPI. The large computation compensates for the communication cost to some extent in this case. The same argument can be made for NP in OpenMP. Moreover, a relatively better speedup is achieved due to absence of broadcast operations and communication delay that are inherent with distributed approach in MPI. However, it does not provide very good speedup as the shared memory machine has its own problems like context switching between the threads, implicit synchronization, barrier for parallel regions, and improper load balance, which contribute to the overall performance degradation.

CONCLUSION AND FUTURE WORK

We implemented Training Set Parallelism (TSP) and Neuron Parallelism (NP) in two multiprocessor paradigms namely Distributed-Memory MIMD Multiprocessors and Shared-Memory MIMD Multiprocessors. In the TSP algorithm, training datasets are distributed among processors whereas the training algorithm is replicated on every processor. After processing a certain amount of datasets each processor needs to broadcast its weights to other processors so communication increases the cost of this algorithm and hence leads to a reduced overall performance with a speedup of only 2.32. On the other hand, in NP technique, neurons are partitioned among processors and each processor performs the calculations of neurons (e.g., activation calculations, error propagations etc.) under its control. However, to calculate the activation value of output neuron and propagate

delta values from output neurons to hidden neurons synchronizations are required for every training pattern. Therefore, we did not achieve a linear speedup; the speedup is only 2.4 for NP. We can achieve a linear speedup if we can avoid extensive communications. However, when we increase processor numbers in our experiment the computation time decreases but the communications time increases and a large number of parameters (weights) need to be propagated to more number of processors for TSP and more processors need to be synchronized for output and delta calculations for NP. This synchronization latency is expensive. This is the reason behind the observed non-linear speedup in the NP and TSP algorithms with MPI.

The fine-grained algorithm did not produce good results in OpenMP. This is because we do not have control over the number of iterations that could be allocated to a particular thread. This is performed dynamically by the system. In OpenMP, there are implicit barriers added by the system for the synchronization purposes and they add to the total overhead. The performance stagnated after 60 threads. For this application having more than 60 threads does not improve the performance. In the coarse-grained algorithm for OpenMP, we experimented with different thread sizes. We distributed data to the threads. In other words, distribution of data to the threads is left to the user. The speedup of 2.5 in this case is slightly higher than the NP version with MPI. This is due to the shared memory architecture, where broadcasting is not necessary. While this is good, neural network still has synchronization step as mentioned before and this, we feel is the primary bottleneck for all the algorithms. Synchronization consumes a significant portion of the execution time of the algorithms.

There are opportunities to improve the performance with other types of algorithms such as pipelining the network. For example, in *pipelining*, the different weight layers are computed in different processing elements. First, the hidden layer processor computes output values of training pattern (a). The output processor reads the values and computes and the error values of (a). The hidden layer processor concurrently processes the next training pattern (b). Then it reads the hidden error for (a) and both processors accumulate the weight change values for (a). This method pipelines the forward phase with the backward phase and therefore, improves the concurrency in the application. This requires a major modification in the algorithm and left as future work. The theoretical analysis could be studied in depth to find the cost of the execution for a given platform on which the algorithm is implemented. This requires a study of the system level details to calculate the actual theoretical timings of the parameters mentioned previously, such as t_s, t_c, t_{IB} etc. A rigorous statistical testing of the results is in order for practicability of the algorithms. In other words, the testing results need to be substantiated further which is left as our important extension of this research work.

REFERENCES

Box, G., Jenkins, G. M., & Reinsel, G. C. (1994). *Time Series Analysis: Forecasting and Control* (3rd ed.). Upper Saddle River, NJ: Prentice-Hall.

Dutta, S., & Shekhar, S. (1994). Bond rating: a non consecutive application of neural networks. In *Proceedings of the IEEE International Conference on Neural Networks* (pp. 527-554).

Fausett, L. (1994). *Fundamentals of Neural Network: Architecture, Algorithms and Applications*. Upper Saddle River, NJ: Prentice Hall.

Hamm, L., Brorsen, B. W., & Sharda, R. (1993). Futures trading with a neural network. In *Proceedings of the NCR-134 Conference on Applied Commodity Analysis, Price Forecasting and Market Risk Management* (pp. 486-496).

Holden, K., Peel, D. A., & Thompson, J. L. (1990). *Economic Forecasting: an Introduction*. New York, NY: Cambridge University Press.

Kanas, A. (2001). Neural network linear forecasts for stock returns. *Financial Economics, 6*, 245–254.

Kimito, T., Asakawa, K., & Takeoka, N. (1990). Stock market prediction system with modular neural networks. In *Proceedings of the IEEE International Joint Conference on Neural Networks* (pp. 11-16).

Kumar, V., Grama, A., Gupta, A., & Karypis, G. (1994). *Introduction to Parallel Computing*. Redwood City, CA: Benjamin/Cummings.

Makridakis, S., & Wheelright, S. (1978). *Forecasting Methods and Applications*. New York, NY: John Wiley & Sons.

McCulloch, W. S., & Pitts, W. (1998). A logical calculus of the ideas imminent in nervous activity . In Anderson, J., & Rosenberg, E. (Eds.), *Neurocomputing: Foundations and Research* (pp. 18–28). Cambridge, MA: MIT Press.

Petrowski, A., Dreyfus, G., & Girault, C. (1993). Performance analysis of a pipelined back-propagation parallel algorithm. *IEEE Transactions on Neural Networks, 4*(6), 970–981. doi:10.1109/72.286892

Rich, E., & Knight, K. (1993). *Artificial Intelligence*. New Delhi, India: Tata McGraw Hill.

Rowe, G., & Wright, G. (1999). The Delphi technique as a forecasting tool: issues and analysis. *International Journal of Forecasting, 15*(4), 353–375. doi:10.1016/S0169-2070(99)00018-7

Sundararajan, N., & Saratchandran, P. (1998). *Parallel Architectures for Artificial Neural Networks-Paradigms and Implementation*. Los Alamitos, CA: IEEE Computer Society Press.

Takefuji, Y. (1992). *Neural Network Parallel Computing*. Norwell, MA: Kluwer Academic.

Trippi, R., & Turban, E. (1993). *Neural Networks in Finance and Investing*. Chicago, IL: Probus.

Weigend, A. S., Abu-Mostafa, Y. S., & Refenes, A. P. N. (1997). *Decision Technologies for Financial Engineering*. New York, NY: World Scientific.

White, H. (1990). Economic prediction using neural networks: the case of IBM daily stock returns. In *Proceedings of the IEEE International Conference on Neural Networks* (pp. 451-458).

Yoon, Y., & Swales, G. (1993). A comparison of discriminate analysis vs. artificial neural network. *Operational Research Society, 1*, 51–60.

This work was previously published in the International Journal of Grid and High Performance Computing, Volume 3, Issue 1, edited by Emmanuel Udoh and Ching-Hsien Hsu, pp. 45-68, copyright 2011 by IGI Publishing (an imprint of IGI Global).

Chapter 8
Dynamic Rightsizing with Quality–Controlled Algorithms in Virtualization Environments

Ming-Jeng Yang
Mackay Medical College, Taiwan

Chin-Lin Kuo
National Taiwan Normal University, Taiwan

Yao-Ming Yeh
National Taiwan Normal University, Taiwan

ABSTRACT

Virtualization and partitioning are the means by which multiple application instances can share and run multiple virtual machines supported by a platform. In a Green Cloud environment, the goal is to consolidate multiple applications onto virtual machines associated by fewer servers, and reduce cost and complexity, increase agility, and lower power and cooling costs. To make Cloud center greener, it is beneficial to limit the amount of active servers to minimize energy consumption. This paper presents a precise model to formulate the right-sizing and energy-saving mechanism, which not only minimizes energy consumption of the server but also maintains a service quality through the $M/M/V_t$ strategy of queuing theory. The authors map the complicated formula of the energy-saving mechanism to an approximation equation and design the fast decidable algorithms for calculating the right size of virtual machines in constant time complexity for power management systems.

1. INTRODUCTION

A 2010 article "A View of Cloud Computing" by Armbrust et al. (2010) defined the cloud computing as refers to both the applications delivered as services over the Internet and the hardware and systems software in the data centers that provide those services. The cloud itself comprises many services running on a set of highly configurable and dynamically configurable hardware and software resources (Winkler, 2009). The cloud technology offers a wide range of services such as infrastructure-as-a-service (IaaS), software-as-a-service (SaaS), and platform as a service (PaaS)

DOI: 10.4018/978-1-4666-2065-0.ch008

(Prodan & Ostermann, 2009). In the characteristic view, the cloud technology has ultra-large-scale, virtualization, high reliability, versatility, high extendibility, on demand service, as well as non-expensive, etc. (Zhang, Zhang, Chen, & Huo, 2010).

Basically, Cloud Computing is a model in which IT infrastructure and software are offered as services to users over the Internet. Winkler (2009) mentioned that cloud computing holds great promise in energy reduce and greenhouse effect. Cloud computing, he said, was the "green computing option". The potential and the reasons are as follows (Winkler, 2009):

- Shared resources in cloud can "eliminate redundancies".
- "Dynamically-assigned resource pools" means that spare capacity isn't sitting around drawing power in as many places or as many configurations.
- "Location independence" could mean the ability to move services to physical facilities where power is cleaner or used more efficiently. The tyranny of the speed of light will certainly limit "follow the moon" - changing longitudes daily to take advantage of evening cooling. But it could work for some applications; more will be able to "follow the seasons"; shifting biannually by latitude to take advantage of winter cooling.
- "Properly instrumented", clouds will be able to inform consumers of their environmental (energy, carbon, etc.) impact, to enable them to be accountable for their choices.
- Clouds can provide an "elastic infrastructure" to enable retro-commissioning of more traditional infrastructure.
- Clouds hold the potential for rapid connection between disparate sources of people and data to "accelerate innovation" to address all sorts of environmental challenges.

The above potential means that if we put it on the action and take advantage of cloud computing, we could integrate environment resources to reduce energy consumption. However, as the cloud computing is available and popularized, the data center energy consumption in cloud is growing. Therefore it is imperative to reduce energy consumption of servers of cloud's data center. Since the server is considered as a vital supply resource, the work pattern of the servers is to keep open and turning regardless of if they actual perform of the services. But now we must face the green efficiency considerations (Blackburn, 2008) required to abandon the above concept.

Recently, Cloud services have driven the growth of server farms in Cloud centers. Most of these servers are vastly over-provisioned. The analysis of server usage patterns will reveal the potential for 'right-sizing'. Unneeded capacity can be turned off, but the server farm can still provide sufficient resiliency for agreed upon service levels. Modern Cloud centers use virtualization (Xen, VMware, and Hyper-V) to get better performance through resource consolidation and live migration (Beloglazov & Buyya, 2010). Consolidating multiple servers running in different virtual machines (VMs) on physical machines (PMs) increases the overall utilization and efficiency of the equipment across the whole deployment.

In this paper, we present the Mt/M/Vt strategy of queuing theory model to address how to efficiently manage energy in virtual servers. Also the formulations are calculated to show the best way that can control some of the virtual machines into the energy-saving states. In addition, Abdelsalam et. Al. (2010) have proposed schemes by calculating model in the data center through validating average distribution of workload to achieve overall minimum energy consumption for servers. In this paper, we propose an energy-saving strategy of cloud data center by rightsizing the virtual machine supported by virtual platform. Based on efficient consideration, we develop computational models to minimize energy consumption of server but also to maintain a service quality through the Mt/M/Vt strategy of queuing theory. In the next section, a description of the right-sizing and energy-saving system architecture is provided. In section 3, problem formulation is described. In section 4, we discuss some relationships among these parameters and develop our algorithms. In section 5, we apply the Square-root Law to fast determining the action of all VMs at each discrete time. Finally, in section 6, we draw conclusions based on our research.

2. SYSTEM ARCHITECTURE

In this section, we give the part of the servers for energy-saving control to achieve better energy efficiency. In cloud computing, users deliver their works through the internet, which are submitted to the job broker that is responsible for the disposal of delivery of the works. These works are cut into smaller instances that are assigned to the virtual machines to execute. In our system architecture, there has a power management unit system (PMU) that supports active and idle states that enable improved power management, and a service scheduler that includes instance broker unit and VM-status monitoring unit (VMU). The

instance broker fetches the front instance from waiting queue and assigns a suitable VM. The service scheduler supports applications to scale resource usage and performance. Coordination between PMU and service scheduler has been set up to jointly control the power and job management. During the peak of workloads, most virtual machines are created and assigned appropriate works. During the periods of not heavy workloads, power management system is started as the agent for reducing energy consumption by first turning off virtual machines and then power down the physical servers when there is unneeded capacity. Servers are powered back on when the capacity is required. This feature automatically shrinks or expands the pool of virtual machines and the physical servers running at any given time without reducing service levels. The entire system architecture is shown in Figure 1.

3. PROBLEM FORMULATION

The system consists of abstract four layers, waiting queue (1st) layer, control (2nd) layer, virtual machine (3rd) layer and physical server (4th) layer. After submitting to the cloud system, the service instance is arranged in the waiting queue for be-

Figure 1. System architecture

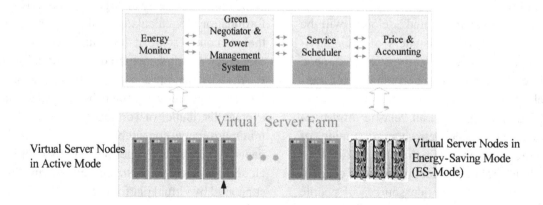

ing assigned, which is called "birth". The second layer includes power management unit (PMU), instance broker unit and VM-status monitoring unit (VMU). The instance broker fetches the front instance from waiting queue and assigns a suitable VM in third layer to execute and then respond. Such process means the "death" of the instance. We model the entering and leaving operations of instances as a specific type of continuous-time Markov-chain.

The second layer is responsible for distributing instances to VMs, calculating the number of active VMs required to achieve negotiated quality of service (QoS), monitoring and switching VM states, and maintaining energy efficiency, etc. All components in third layer are virtual machines with their unique status respectively, whether in active or energy-saving (ES) mode. We concentrate the energy saving on the virtual machine working mode. The fewer active VMs execute service on the premise of maintaining QoS, the more energy can be economized.

3.1. Queuing Model

We apply the queuing model, *M/M/V*, to obtaining measures of power-saving effectiveness for the cloud system outlined in above Figure 2. There are totally *C* servers in which *V* virtual machines are needed to be active for proceeding service instances and others can be set to ES-mode. The queue discipline is first come, first served (FCFS) and consists of a set of states $\{0,1,2,3,\cdots\}$, typically denoting the number of service instances in the system. State transitions occur as unit jumps up or down from the current state (Figure 3).

In the model, we denote some terms:

- λ: arrival-rate of service instances. Instance arrivals follow the Poisson distribution with mean rate λ.

- $P(i)$: stead-state probability of the system having i service instances.

- μ: service-rate for each VM. Each VM has an independently and identically distributed exponential service time distribution with mean $1/\mu$.

- $r = \lambda/\mu$: expected number of instances in service, called offered work load rate.

- V: the number of active VMs. The combined service completion rate is $V\mu$.

- N: the mean number of instances in the system.

- N_q: the mean number of instances in waiting queue.

- T_{dw}: the dwell time which includes T_q, the time an instance spent waiting in queue, and T_{sv}, the service time. T_{dw} is often used for measuring system performance.

- α: the probability that an instance has *nonzero* delay in queue before receiv-

Figure 2. The abstract concept describing queuing model, M/M/V

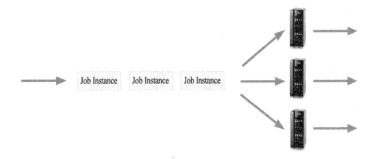

Figure 3. State transition diagram for the M/M/V queue

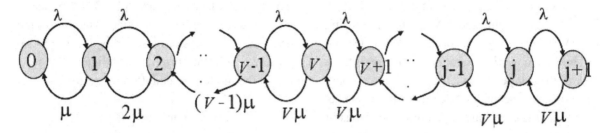

ing service. It is an example performance measure.

- $\rho = r / V$: traffic intensity denoting a measure of traffic congestion for V active virtual machines.

In the "quality and efficiency domain" (QED), there is an emphasis on providing a balance between the QoS and service efficiency. We adopt the probability α that an instance has *nonzero* delay in queue as the measure of QoS. With the help of Square-root Law (Halfin & Whitt, 1981), we can fast calculate the number V of required active virtual machines by the instance arrival-rate, VM service-rate and α.

Usually it is impractical to keep constant instance arrival-rate over the entire day. In fact, the arrival-rate in cloud service may be highly time-varying. On the other hand, it can be possible fortunately to apply stationary models in a non-stationary manner. That is, we partition time into segments with equal length Δt, use stationary model in each segment and then calculate the new V at the end of each Δt, which can be achieved by utilizing a *timer* to be in charge of counting time. The number of active VMs keeps constant within each of these intervals.

If the current number of active VMs exceeds the calculated V, then the redundant active VMs should be switched to energy-saving mode (ES-mode). On the other hand, if it is smaller than V, there should be some sleeping VMs to be awaked. Whenever the *timer* expires, which means at the

end of a unit time slot, the PMU needs to recalculate V and coordinate state changes of VMs based on the new V. Each VM can decide whether its mode is going to change or to keep in the next time slot.

Due to the hypothesis of queuing model, the minimum number V required to guarantee a steady-state must be calculated immediately for satisfying $\rho < 1$. Hence we only discuss the power-saving performance subject to the constraint. Given the instance arrival-rate λ, VM service-rate μ and α, we can fast calculate the minimal number V of parallel VMs. Then the cloud system can determine how many active VMs should be switched into ES-mode or sleeping VMs should be waked up.

3.2. Formulas

In Figure 3, the queue can be modeled as a birth-death process. We can apply the queuing theory to obtain the following equations. Little (1961) described the steady-state mean system sizes to the steady-state average customer waiting times as follows.

$$N = \lambda \cdot E(T_{dw}) \tag{1}$$

$$N_q = \lambda \cdot E(T_q) \tag{2}$$

From above equations, a result derived immediately is

$$N - N_q = \lambda \cdot (E(T_{dw}) - E(T_q)) = \lambda E(T_{sv}) = \lambda / \mu \tag{3}$$

which means the expected number of instances in service in steady state. (i.e. the amount of instances accepting service in the system per unit time.) The value of $\lambda / (\mu V)$ means the average amount of instances assigned to each active VM per unit time.

$$\begin{cases} \lambda P(0) = \mu P(1), & i = 0, \\ (\lambda + i\mu)P(i) = \lambda P(i-1) + (i+1)\mu P(i+1), & 1 \le i < V, \\ (\lambda + V\mu)P(i) = \lambda P(i-1) + V\mu P(i+1), & i \ge V. \end{cases} \tag{4}$$

Note that only if the condition $\rho = \lambda / (\mu V) < 1$ holds, the steady state can exist. Furthermore, the steady-state probability $P(i)$ is

$$P(i) = \begin{cases} \dfrac{r^i}{i!} \cdot P(0), & i < V, \\[2mm] \dfrac{r^S}{V!}\left(\dfrac{r}{V}\right)^{i-S} \cdot P(0), & i \ge V. \end{cases} \tag{5}$$

To find $P(0)$, we use the property that the probabilities must sum to 1 and get

$$P(0) = \left[\sum_{i=0}^{V-1} \frac{r^i}{i!} + \frac{r^V}{V!} \cdot \frac{V}{(V-r)} \right]^{-1}. \tag{6}$$

The expected queue size is

$$N_q = \frac{(r/V)r^V P(0)}{V!(1 - r/V)^2}. \tag{7}$$

By Little's formula, $T_q = \dfrac{N_q}{\lambda}$ and the average number of instances in the system is

$$N = \sum_{i=0}^{\infty} iP(i) = \frac{\lambda}{\mu} + N_q = \frac{\lambda}{\mu} + \frac{(\lambda / (V\mu))(\lambda / \mu)^V P(0)}{V!(1 - \lambda / (V\mu))^2}. \tag{8}$$

Therefore, the average dwell time of a service instance in the system is deduced.

$$\begin{aligned} E(T_{dw}) &= E(T_q) + E(T_{sv}) = \frac{N}{\lambda} \\ &= \frac{r^V P(0)}{\mu V \cdot V!(1 - r/V)^2} + \frac{1}{\mu} \end{aligned} \tag{9}$$

The minimum of T_{dw} is $1/\mu$, that is, the waiting time of an instance in queue is 0. Intuitively, $E(T_q)$ will decrease strictly when the number V increases. In order to plan and care for quality control of service and energy saving, it is often desirable to determine the appropriate number V in the cloud system. We now can obtain the probability $P(T_q = 0)$ that an instance has *zero* delay in queue. $P(T_q = 0) = \sum_{i=0}^{V-1} P(i) = P(0) \cdot \sum_{i=0}^{V-1} \frac{r^i}{i!}$.

By (6), $\sum_{i=0}^{V-1} \dfrac{r^i}{i!} = \dfrac{1}{P(0)} - \dfrac{r^V}{V!(1 - r/V)}$, which implies

$$P(T_q = 0) = P(0)\left(\frac{1}{P(0)} - \frac{r^V}{V!(1-\rho)} \right) = 1 - \frac{r^V P(0)}{V!(1-\rho)} \tag{10}$$

So, the probability that an arriving instance has a *nonzero* wait in queue is

$$\alpha = 1 - P(T_q = 0) = \frac{r^V \cdot P(0)}{V!(1-\rho)}. \tag{11}$$

Putting this result together with (9), we can get their relationship,

$$E(T_{dw}) = \frac{1}{\mu} + \frac{1}{V\mu(1-\rho)} \cdot \alpha \qquad (12)$$

4. RELATIONSHIPS AND ALGORITHMS

In this section, we discuss some relationships among these parameters and develop our algorithms.

4.1. Relationships

The relationship between α and V is illustrated in Figure 4 plotted by (11). In general, many customers demand the quality of service, α, in SLA (service level agreement) to be bounded by the range of small-to-moderate values $0 \leq \alpha \leq 0.5$. It clearly appears that small α close to 0 yields larger V and the increasing of α cannot reduce V significantly.

In closing here, we point out that the calculation value of $V!$ in the formulas of queuing model may exceed the computing range of mathematical software (e.g. MatLab, Mathematica). This fact motivates us to give an approximation for easily computing and reducing time complexity.

4.2. Square-Root Law and Approximation

Basically, choosing the number of active VMs is the most important but not simple via the formulas of queuing theory. The problem of finding V should focus on adequately balancing the quality and cost of service. In "quality and efficiency domain" (QED), we use a constant measure of congestion, denoted as α probability, to approximate to V. The following Square-root Law (Halfin & Whitt, 1981; Borst, Mandelbaum, & Reiman, 2004) provides an approximate formula to determine V.

$$V \approx r + \beta\sqrt{r}, \qquad (13)$$

Figure 4. The relationship between α and V

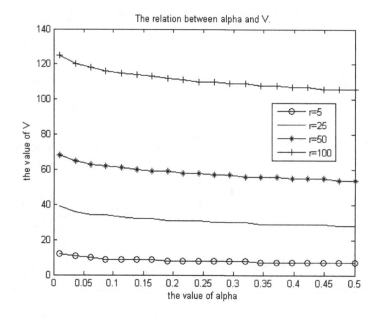

where β is a constant related to α via the relationship,

$$\alpha = \frac{\phi(\beta)}{\phi(\beta) + \beta \cdot \Phi(\beta)} \qquad (14)$$

called the Halfin-Whitt delay function. $\phi(\ )$ and $\Phi(\ )$ are the *PDF* and the associated *CDF* of the standard normal distribution respectively. Although the Law looks simple while estimating V, it is not easy to directly get β from α. We need an explicit function formula for $\beta(\alpha)$. A similar approximation is to let β equal the $1-\alpha$ quantile of the standard normal distribution (Kolesar & Green, 1998). But its estimate is rough. Instead of applying it, we use the numerical method in (14) to list and draw their relationship as Figure 5.

Then we can build an approximate β function of α by the steps, outlined below. The curve in Figure 5 includes 200 given distinct points (α_i, β_i).

Step 1: Compute $x_i = \ln(\alpha_i)$ and plot the graph of (x_i, β_i) as in Figure 6.

Step 2: Make the curve of (x_i, β_i) s transform into a line as far as possible. (The value of β must be decreased.) Assume $0 \leq \beta \leq 4$ and observe that the *deviation*s are about 0, 0.6 and 0 when $\beta = 0, 2$ and 4 respectively. Set *deviation* $= 0.6 - 0.15 \cdot (\beta - 2)^2$ by interpolating second-degree polynomial. Thus, let $y_i = \beta - deviation = 0.15\beta_i^2 + 0.4\beta_i$ and obtain the line in Figure 7.

Step 3: According to these 200 points, (x_i, y_i), apply Least-Squares to determining the best-fit line, $y = A + Bx = -0.0263 - 0.3934x$.

Step 4: Given x, get an approximate $approxi\_y$ (if the $approxi\_y < 0$, then let $approxi\_y = 0$) by the formula of step 3 and substitute the $approxi\_y$ for the y in the equation of step 2. Solve the equation for β.

Step 5: Recapitulate the above 4 steps,

Figure 5. The relationship between α and β

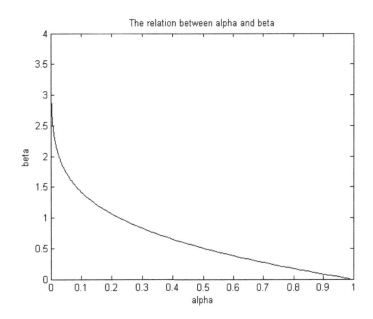

$$approxi\_\beta =$$

$$\frac{-0.4 + \sqrt{0.16 + 0.6 \times (-0.0263 - 0.3934 \times \ln(\alpha))}}{0.3}$$

$$= \frac{-0.4 + \sqrt{0.14422 - 0.23604 \ln(\alpha)}}{0.3} \qquad (15)$$

The value of β lies about in the interval (0,4). The yielding errors are plotted in Figure 8 showing that they are sufficiently small, in which the error is defined as

$$error = approximate\ value - exact\ value.$$

$$(16)$$

4.3. Algorithms

Given λ, μ and α, the system must calculate the number V of needed active VMs as fast as possible. We apply the Square-root Law and (15) to obtaining V within constant time. The procedure, *Calculate_V*, describes how to calculate it for the next Δt.

Procedure *Calculate_V* (λ, μ, α) (abbreviated by CVA)

1: let $r = \lambda / \mu$ and obtain β by (15)

2: $v = \left\lceil r + \beta \sqrt{r} \right\rceil$.

3: return (v)

End

Figure 9 plots the V variation with various offered loads, rs, in CVA scheme. Apparently, smaller α leads larger V, which is consistent with our conjecture.

At the initialization stage of the cloud system, $\lambda = 0$ and all VMs are set to be in ES-mode. The parameters, μ and α are also initialized in advance. Once the monitoring unit detects service instances arrival, it immediately measures the arrival-rate and transmits the data to PMU for calculating V. The unit of monitoring the service instances arrival-rate must be responsible all the time for checking the variation of λ. For the implementation of our algorithm, we assume the $M_t / M / V_t$ model is more appropriate for the non-homogeneous Poisson arrival process (the

Figure 6. The relationship between ln(α), β and y

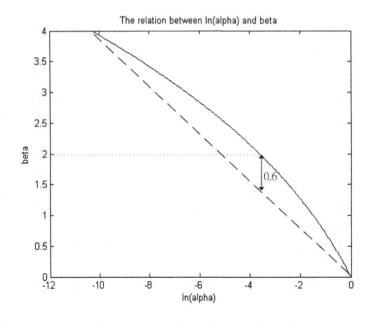

Figure 7. The relationship between ln(α), β and y

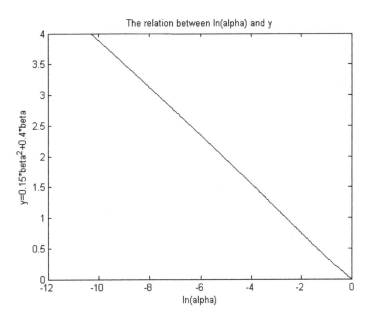

M_t) with time-varying arrival-rate $\lambda(t)$, which possibly changes the number V of needed active VMs (the V_t).

The strategy of deciding which VMs should be switched is based on the simple rule: The longer these VMs have been activated, the more priority they switch to ES-mode. On the other hand, the longer the VMs have been in ES-mode

Figure 8. The error of β approximation in our algorithm

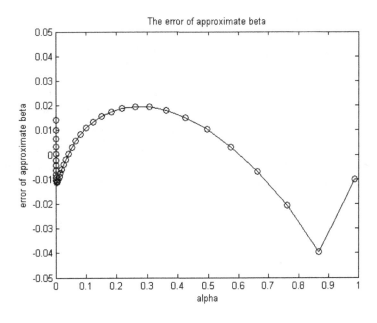

Figure 9. Given different α values, the V calculated by CVA with various offered loads

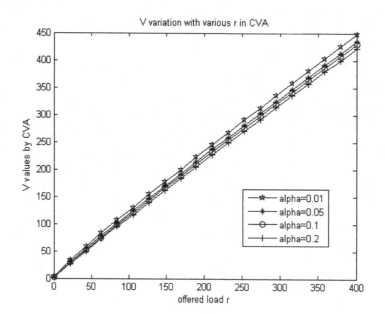

(sleep mode), the more priority they should be awaked. Such mechanism is proceeded by the PMU in which contains a *sleep-active* data structure recording the latest time of switching mode of each VM from activation to sleep mode or vice versa and how long it has been in active or sleep mode. Whenever the modes of VMs were switching, their *sleep-active* data were simultaneously updated and sorted. After finishing changing modes, the PMU updates the number of active VMs and service instances arrival-rate to be V' and λ' respectively. The following pseudo-code describes our algorithm detailed, which iteratively performs 3 steps.

Algorithm CACA (Cloud Approximate Control Algorithm) When the *timer* expires, do
step 1: calculates the new number of active VMs,
$V' = Calculate\_V(\lambda', \mu, \alpha)$,
step 2: compares V' with the current V.
case $V' > V$: awakes $(V' - V)$ sleeping VMs, which have been in ES-mode longest.

case $V' < V$: switches $(V - V')$ active VMs to ES-mode, which have activated longest.
case $V' = V$: does nothing.
step 3: updates the number of active VMs and service instances arrival-rate to be V' and λ' respectively.

End

5. DYNAMIC ADAPTATION AND ANALYSIS

We emphasize the importance of adaptive property of CVA and CACA. Due to the dynamic characteristic of service instance arrival-rate in practical cloud or other business environments, the corresponding calculation of V must be valid and efficient. Hence we apply the Square-root Law to fast determining the action of all VMs at each discrete time. Meanwhile, the condition of energy-saving in each time interval can also be revealed and analyzed.

5.1. Adaptation For Dynamic Arrival-Rate

Nowadays, cloud computing centers currently fall into the data-poor category. Without sufficient data, we imagine a mathematical arrival-rate function, $\lambda(t)$, of time to describe the workload in cloud system. It is reasonable that the correlation between $\lambda(t)$ and workload is intimate. We emphasize that the fictitious $\lambda(t)$ in (17) is only an example for explanation convenience. Indeed, our algorithm can dynamically adapt itself to arbitrary variation of instance arrival-rate since it executes the *Claculate_V* procedure periodically according to the new parameters. Let $\Delta t = 1$ unit time and the $\lambda(t)$ is assumed to be of the following form:

$$\lambda(t) = 60 + 30\sin(t\pi / 4),\ 0 \le t \le 8, \qquad (17)$$

in which there is a complete sinusoidal cycle as Figure 10. Figure 11 illustrates its corresponding V values at time t with different αs when $\mu = 1$. It

matches with the intuition that smaller α leads larger V. In addition, we can find the two figures are basically similar and V are highly correlative with $\lambda(t)$.

The example cannot represent the actual situation of instance arrival-rate, but it can explain its non-homogeneous characteristic and our adaptive scheme. No matter what $\lambda(t)$ looks like, our adaptation can efficiently manipulate mode switch of all VMs and reduce unnecessary energy consumption.

5.2. Error of CVA

Recall from sections 4.2 and 4.3 that procedure CVA is to find the minimal V such that the probability of a service instance delaying in the queue is equal to or smaller than α. Each step in CVA takes only $O(1)$ time, yielding the total running time of constant.

To analyze the error of CVA, we need to specify the accuracy of its approximation. We have an integer programming problem to solve,

Figure 10. A fictitious arrival-rate function (left) and its corresponding V with various αs

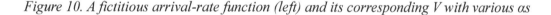

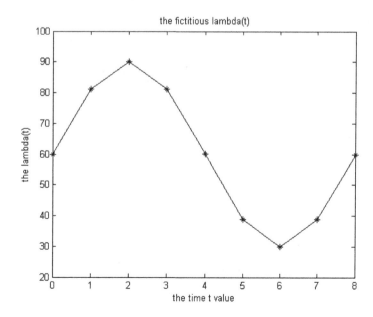

Figure 11. A fictitious arrival-rate function (left) and its corresponding V with various αs

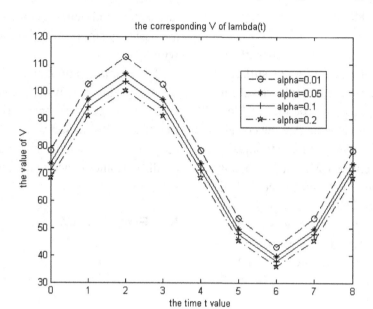

Figure 12. The error of V generated by CVA

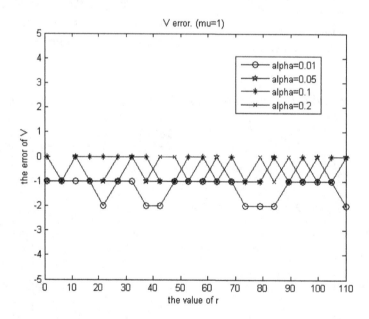

which can be done by stepping V from $\lceil r \rceil + 1$ and finding the exact V that satisfies the probability of non-zero delay $\leq \alpha$ by referring to (11), since it can be shown that smaller α will yield larger V and vice versa. Figure 12 illustrates how close the approximation to the exact value. The error of V by CVA is certainly small enough, where error is as (16).

Figure 13. The conditions of energy-saving, w=5, 10

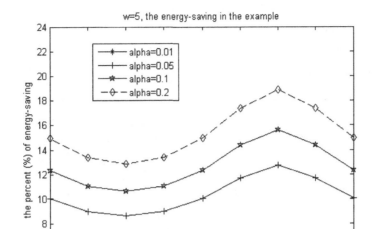

Figure 14. The conditions of energy-saving, w=5, 10

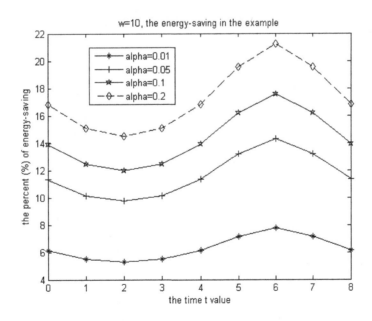

5.3. Energy Saving Analysis

The running modes of VM in this paper are classified by energy consumption. Server virtualization makes it possible to concurrently execute several VMs on top of a single physical machine. A VM means a kind of resource that needs to consume energy. We simply differentiate two modes: active and energy-saving modes, where the energy consumption within a period of time under the two modes is symbolized by E_{act} and E_{slp} respectively. So far, there is no clear answer to the energy consumption ratio of E_{act} to E_{slp}. We assume it to be $w/1$ and analyze our scheme with various w values.

An energy-saving protocol puts a VM into the sleep mode to save energy. A sleeping VM cannot provide service for instances but its unavailability may save much energy. Our scheme therefore seeks to maximize energy saving, while minimizing impact on throughput, latency and quality of service.

Figures 13 and 14 illustrate the effectiveness of energy-saving with different ws, 5 and 10 (Niyato, Chaisiri, & Bu Sung, 2009), respectively. We suppose the QoS is 100% when α is set to be 0.001. Then the V generated by the α could be taken as the pivoting object to be compared. We compute the energy consumed by V VMs in active-mode and other VMs in ES-mode when given distinct values of α. Larger α leads smaller V and consequently allows more energy-saving. We propose the following formula defining the energy-saving percent when $\alpha > 0.001$.

$$EngySave = (1 - \frac{V \cdot E_{act} + (V_{\alpha=0.001} - V)E_{slp}}{V_{\alpha=0.001} \cdot E_{act}}) \times 100\%$$

(18)

The two figures plot the comparison of energy-saving generated by various αs. Larger α can save more energy. As a general observation, if we were to sacrifice QoS about 10%, we could save up to 6% ~ 22% energy. However, such savings are obtained at quite moderate offered work load rate, $r < 100$; as offered load increases, the available savings will decline slowly.

Energy consumption is the main criterion in evaluating a power-save protocol, but factors such as throughput and QoS must also be taken into consideration.

6. CONCLUSION

As energy climbs the list of corporate priorities, "Green Cloud" solutions are proliferating. Improper energy management, Cloud servers not only fail to improve overall efficiency, but also cause waste of resources and could not be sustainable operation. How to make the cloud servers to achieve efficient management of energy consumption is an important issue. In this research, we use a feature called Cloud Approximate Control Algorithm (CACA) to reduce energy consumption by first turning off virtual machines and then power down the physical servers when there is unneeded capacity. Servers are powered back on when the capacity is required. This feature automatically shrinks or expands the pool of virtual machines and the physical servers running at any given time without reducing service levels.

REFERENCES

Abdelsalam, H. S., Maly, K., Mukkamala, R., Zubair, M., & Kaminsky, D. (2009). Analysis of energy efficiency in clouds. In *Proceedings of Computation World: Future Computing, Service Computation, Cognitive, Adaptive, Content* (pp. 416–421). Patterns. doi:10.1109/ComputationWorld.2009.38

Armbrust, M., Fox, A., Griffith, R., Joseph, A. D., Katz, R., & Konwinski, A. (2010). A view of cloud computing. *Communications of the ACM*, *53*(4), 50–58. doi:10.1145/1721654.1721672

Beloglazov, A., & Buyya, R. (2010). Energy efficient allocation of virtual machines in cloud data centers. In *Proceedings of the 10th IEEE/ACM International Conference on Cluster, Cloud and Grid Computing* (pp. 577-578).

Blackburn, M. (2008). *Five ways to reduce data center server power consumption.* Retrieved from http://www.thegreengrid.org/en/sitecore/content/ Global/Content/ white-papers/Five-Ways-to-Save-Power.aspx

Borst, S., Mandelbaum, A., & Reiman, M. I. (2004). Dimensioning large call centers. *Operations Research, 52*(1), 17–34. doi:10.1287/opre.1030.0081

Halfin, S., & Whitt, W. (1981). Heavy-traffic limits for queues with many exponential servers. *Operations Research, 29*(3), 567–588. doi:10.1287/opre.29.3.567

Kolesar, P., & Green, L. (1998). Insights on service system design from a normal approximation to Erlang's formula. *Production and Operations Management, 7*(3), 289–293.

Little, J. D. C. (1961). A proof for the queuing formula $L = \lambda W$. *Operations Research, 9,* 383–387. doi:10.1287/opre.9.3.383

Niyato, D., Chaisiri, S., & Bu Sung, L. (2009). Optimal power management for server farm to support green computing. In *Proceedings of the 9th IEEE/ACM International Symposium on Cluster Computing and the Grid* (pp. 84-91).

Prodan, R., & Ostermann, S. (2009). A survey and taxonomy of infrastructure as a service and web hosting cloud providers. In *Proceedings of the 10th IEEE/ACM International Conference on Grid Computing* (pp. 17-25).

Winkler, K. (2010). *Green clouds.* Retrieved from http://interconnected world.typepad.com/ my_weblog/2009/10/green-clouds.html

Zhang, S., Zhang, S., Chen, S., & Huo, X. (2010). Cloud computing research and development trend. In *Proceedings of the Second International Conference on Future Networks* (pp. 93-97).

This work was previously published in the International Journal of Grid and High Performance Computing, Volume 3, Issue 2, edited by Emmanuel Udoh and Ching-Hsien Hsu, pp. 29-43, copyright 2011 by IGI Publishing (an imprint of IGI Global).

Chapter 9
Location Update Improvement Using Fuzzy Logic Optimization in Location Based Routing Protocols in MANET

Amjad Osmani
Islamic Azad University - Saghez, Iran

Abolfazl Toroghi Haghighat
Islamic Azad University - Qazvin, Iran

Shirin Khezri
Islamic Azad University - Mahabad, Iran

ABSTRACT

Several position-based routing protocols have been developed for mobile ad hoc networks. Many of these protocols assume that a location service is available which provides location information on the nodes in the network. This paper introduces a new schema in management of mobile nodes location in mobile ad hoc networks. Fuzzy logic optimization is applied to a better management of location update operation in hierarchical location services. Update management overhead is decreased without significant loss of query success probability. One-hop-chain-technique is used for Auto compensation. A new composed method can update mobile nodes location when the nodes cross a grid boundary. The proposed method uses a dynamic grid area that solves the ping-pong problem between grids. Simulation results show that these methods are effective. The algorithms are distributed and can keep scalability in the scenario of increasing nodes density. The described solutions are not limited to a special network grid ordering, and can be used in every hierarchical ordering like GLS if the ordering can be mappable on these methods.

DOI: 10.4018/978-1-4666-2065-0.ch009

1. INTRODUCTION

Ad Hoc networks consist of autonomous nodes that collaborate in order to transport information. Usually, these nodes act as end systems and routers at the same time (Mauve, Widmer, & Hartensteinm, 2001). Due to node mobility, the network topology changes frequently which makes the design of a scalable and robust routing protocol with low message overhead, one of the challenging task in this kind of networks. Routing a packet from a source to a destination in a mobile ad hoc network is a challenging problem, since nodes in the network may move and cause frequent, unpredictable topological changes (Camp, Bolengm, & Davies, 2002). Location services are used in mobile ad hoc and hybrid networks either to locate the geographic position of a given node in the network or to locate a data item. One of the main usages of position location services is in location based routing algorithms.

2. RELATED WORK

Figure 1 shows the classification of the location services proposed so far. Location services can be divided into flooding-based and rendezvous-based approaches. Flooding-based protocols can be further divided into dissemination and reactive approaches. In the dissemination approach, each node periodically floods its location to all nodes in the network. Thus, when a given node requires location information on another node, the information is found in the node's location table, i.e., the dissemination services usually do not send query messages. They can be classified as an all for-all approach. In the reactive approach, nodes do not send update messages; instead they query location information of a specific node only if needed. The location query is flooded to the whole network. The reactive services belong to all-for some category. In rendezvous-based approach, all nodes agree on the set of location servers.

Reactive and dissemination services represent the two extremes of the update strategy and they are not scalable. We focus in the following on the rendezvous based services. Two approaches are used to select the location servers, quorum-based and hashing based (Camp, Boleng, & Wilcox, 2001; Luo, X., Camp, & Navidi, 2005).

One of the main problems in location service problem is time of sending of location update packets. As per available methods, we can classify those to: 1) Time based, 2) Distance based, 3) Distance deviation based, 4) Combination based, 5) Grid based and 6) parametric based methods. The proposed classification is available in Figure 2.

2.1. Time Based (Periodic)

In this category, after a special time each node generates a packet (with new location information) and sends that. We can address ADLS (Seet, Pan, Hsu, & Lau, 2005), DQS (Bae, 2007) and DREAM (Basagni, Chlamtac, Syrotiuk, & Woodward, 1998). It is possible that a node sends a packet (after a special time) but without long passed distance.

(Basagni, Chlamtac, Syrotiuk, & Woodward, 1998) has proposed the Distance Routing Effect Algorithm for Mobility (DREAM) in which nodes maintain a location table using the distance effect. Nodes maintain location information of all other nodes in the network proactively. However, the location of a node is updated (by the node) to its nearer neighbors more frequently than nodes that are farther. To send a packet to the destination a source node estimates the expected zone of the destination based on the destinations' location (using its location table) and floods data packets within the expected region. An intermediate node upon receiving the packet re-broadcasts the data packet if it is within the expected region and this continues until the destination receives the packet.

(Seet, Pan, Hsu, & Lau, 2005) proposes ADLS, an Adaptive Demand-driven Location Service

Figure 1. Location services classification

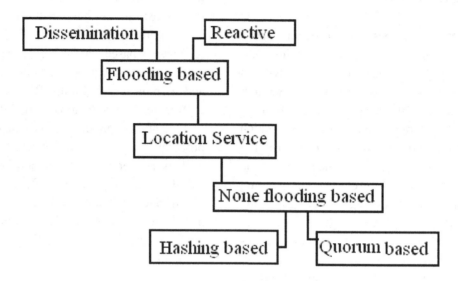

– a multi-home region scheme that creates and maintains beyond a single home region for each node *on-demand*, based on the actual location demand for each node and the locality of the querying sources.

In Bae (2007) the author designs an adaptive location service on the basis of diamond quorum considering the gravity of locality of a mobile node in a MANET. In the protocol, the topology of the ad-hoc network is divided into several logical regions of 2-layered grid structure, and single home region is selected from each two dimensional region by using the mapping function. Then, the logically spread surface quorum system is composed from these selected N home regions, and the diamond quorum system (DQS) is constructed from this system. If one mobile node updates its location, a quorum is selected from the DQS by considering the gravity of locality of that mobile nodes, the location information of that mobile node is stored to the nodes in the selected quorum.

Figure 2. Time of update classification

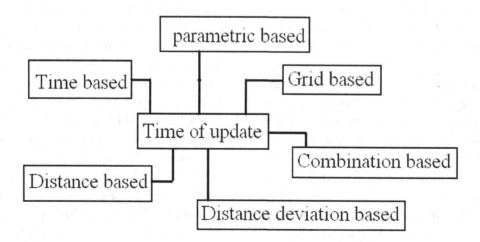

2.2. Distance Based

In this category, the nodes after a special distance generate a packet (with new location information) and send that. We can address GLS (Li, Jannotti, De Couti, Karger, & Morris, 2000), GHLS (Das, Pucha, & Hu, 2005) and KCLS (Leng, Zhang, Rao, & Yang, 2006). It is possible that a node sends a packet (after a special distance) but without long passed time.

The GHLS protocol proposed in (Das, Pucha, & Hu, 2005) shares the nature of geographic hashing with GHT (Ratnasamy, Karp, Yin, Yu, Estrin, Govindan, & Shenker, 2002). However, GHT is proposed to support data storage in dense sensor networks which are typically static. Additionally, storage and replication strategies are fundamentally different for GHT since it stores sensed data where reliability and storage costs are a bigger concern.

The GLS (Grid Location Service) (Li, Jannotti, De Couti, Karger, & Morris, 2000) divides the area containing the ad hoc network into a hierarchy of square, forming a quad-tree. Each node selects one node in each element of the quad-tree as a location server. Therefore the density of location servers for a node in areas close to the node is high and becomes exponentially less dense as the distance to the node increases. The update and request mechanisms of GLS require a chain of nodes based on node IDs is found and traversed to reach an actual location server for a given node. The chain leads from the updating or requesting node via some arbitrary and some dedicated nodes to a location server.

The KCLS protocol (Leng, Zhang, Rao, & Yang, 2006) is based on a single level k -hop cluster structure to provide location service. A k -hop cluster is a set of hosts under the cluster-head and any host in the cluster has a distance of equal to or less than k hops to the cluster-head. Every cluster consists of one cluster-head, ordinary cluster members that are located inside of a cluster, and gateways which are located on the cluster border to connect the neighboring clusters. It is supposed that each host has a unique host ID. The cluster ID is determined by the host ID of the cluster-head.

2.3. Distance Deviation Based

In this category, the nodes after a special time (for example 1 second) check predicted location and real location and if distance deviation be greater than a special value then generate a packet (with new location information) and send that. We can address DRM (Kumar & Das, 2004), SaLAM (Osmani & Haghighat, 2010), H2SaLAM (Osmani, Haghighat, & Khezri, 2010) and SHGRID (Osmani, Haghighat, & Khezri, 2010).

SaLAM (Osmani & Haghighat, 2010) (Scalable @ Location Advertisement Management in MANET) has designed based on some phases such that some of them are used in SaLAM-ON-HGRID and some of that are used in SaLAM-ON-SLALoM and SaLAM-ON-SLURP. The phases are used to decreasing control overhead and solutions are not limited to a special network grid ordering.

H2SaLAM (Osmani, Haghighat, & Khezri, 2010) uses a dynamic hierarchy between location servers such that ping-pong problem between rings. SHGRID (Osmani, Haghighat, & Khezri, 2010) using one hop chain technique has prevented decreasing of data delivery rate and it has increased the delay experienced by data packets. Both of them use location prediction method, near to destination.

2.4. Combination Based

This category can be a composed of Time based and Distance based methods. We can address GrLS (Cheng, Cao, & Chen, 2007).

GrLS (Cheng, Cao, & Chen, 2007) consists of two components: individual location management and group location management. In the protocol, the network coverage area is partitioned into equal circle-shaped regions, which are selected as home regions by nodes. For each node with individual mobility, it sends location updates to the location servers in its home region and the location server handles all the location queries for it. For nodes with group mobility, group location management is designed, which consists of micro and macro group location management. With micro group location management, each group member is aware of the locations of all other group members. With macro group location management, a designated group leader updates its location to the location servers in a specified group home region and replies all the location queries for other group members in its group. Thus, the overhead of location updates to the home regions can be saved for all the other group members.

2.5. Grid Based

In this category, each time a node crosses a grid boundary, it generates a packet (with new location information) and sends that. We can address HGRID (Philip, Ghosh, & Qiao, 2005) and SLURP (Woo & Singh, 2001), SLALoM, HLS (Liu & Hwang, 2006), SaLAM, H2SaLAM, SHGRID, NGRID (Jomeiri & Dehghan, 2008).

In Cheng, Lemberg, Philip, van den Berg, and Zhang (2002) they present an algorithm, called Hierarchical Location Service (HLS), which can efficiently provide position information about nodes in ad hoc networks. HLS is a hierarchical architecture to maintain the location information of nodes. Cheng, Lemberg, Philip, van den Berg, and Zhang (2002) also mention some update/query problem of location service would be happened in hierarchical manner, and Cheng, Lemberg, Philip, van den Berg, and Zhang (2002) discuss how HLS can solve these problems when providing the location service.

In HGRID (Philip, Ghosh, & Qiao, 2005), Hierarchical leader nodes serve as location servers, and are updated by other nodes on crossing grid boundaries, via location update packets. A lower order leader notifies its leader only if the location

update requires it to update its leader. Thus, while the leaders in the highest level of the hierarchy know the approximate locations of all the nodes in the network, location information in servers becomes more accurate as one traverse down the hierarchy. Location servers can now be queried by source nodes who wish to know the location of the destination, in an on demand fashion.

In SLURP (Woo & Singh, 2001), the network area is divided into a flat grid of squares. Node A selects its location servers by applying a hash function to A's ID and obtains the (x, y) coordinate of a point in the entire area. The square containing that point is called the home square for node A. All nodes in that square store A's exact location information. Every time node A moves to a different square, it updates its home square with new location information. For any node B wishes to communicate with node A, the same hash function is applied to node A's ID to obtain A's home square. A query packet is then forwarded to A's home square to retrieve A's location information. One of the major drawbacks of this design is that the query latency grows as the network size grows. Even if the querying node B is relatively close to the target node A, node B may still need to query A's home region that is far away. Furthermore, nodes may be far away from their home square and their updates may have to travel long distances.

To address the problems of the flat-based approach, SLALoM (Cheng, Lemberg, Philip, van den Berg, & Zhang, 2002) uses a two-level structure. The entire network is first divided into a flat grid of level-1 squares as in SLURP. The network is then partitioned into various level-2 squares with each level-2 square containing many level-1 squares. Node A selects its location servers by hashing to the same point in each of the level-2 squares. Node A thus has a home square in every level-2 square. SLALoM defines home squares near A as the nine level-1 home squares closest to A (i.e., the home square in the level-2 square where A is in, plus the eight home squares in the surrounding level-2 squares). It employs a two-level grained location information, i.e., all the home squares of A know which level-2 square A resides in, and all the home squares near A know the exact location of A. As A moves around, only closer servers need to be updated frequently, whereas remote servers require only infrequent updates. To query node A, node B sends query packet to A's home square in the level-2 square B is in. If that home square is the one near A, B can retrieve A's exact location. Otherwise, the servers in that home square know which level-2 square A is in. The two-level structure reduces the location query cost but increases the cost of updating location servers.

2.6. Parametric Based

In this category, the nodes will check other parameters (instead of time and distance). We can address SaLAM and Column/Row (Stojmenovic, Liu, & Jia, 2008).

In the Column/Row Location Service (CRLS) (Stojmenovic, Liu, & Jia, 2008) the location of each node is propagated in the north–south direction, while any location queries are propagated in the east–west direction. When a node decides a location update is needed, it propagates the location update along the north–south direction, i.e., with the goal of reaching all the nodes in the same column in the geographic area. Each node selected as a location server in the north or south direction broadcasts the update to its one hop neighbors. The update contains the identifier of the next location server in the update direction. When a source node initiates a location request for a destination node, the query is propagated along the east–west direction, i.e., along its row of nodes in the geographic area. The query contains the time of the most recent location known to the source. If a node along the row has a cached location for the destination node that is more recent than the time in the query, it sends a reply packet via geographic forwarding back to the source.

The rest of this article is organized as following. In Section 3, we briefly review the basic concept of FLS. Section 4 details the FLS-algorithms design for distributed location service. Simulations are presented in Section 5. Section 6 concludes this paper through a summary.

3. ABOUT FUZZY LOGIC OPTIMIZATION

Figure 3 shows the structure of a rule-based type-1 FLS (Mendel, 1995). It contains four components: fuzzifier, rules, inference engine and defuzzifier. When an input is applied to a FLS, the inference engine computes the output set corresponding to each rule. The defuzzifer then computes a crisp output from these rule output sets. Rules are the heart of a FLS and may be provided by experts or can be extracted from numerical data. In either case, the rules that we are interested in can expressed as a collection of IF-THEN statements, e.g. (Mendel, 2001). The IF-part of a rule is its antecedent and the THEN-part of a rule is its consequent. The process of making a crisp input fuzzy is called fuzzification. The most widely used fuzzification is the singleton fuzzification. All fuzziness for a particular fuzzy set is essentially characterized by the membership functions (MFs). The shapes used to describe the fuzziness have very few restrictions but with the help of mathematical structure, some standard terms related to the shape of MFs have been developed over the years. The most common forms of MFs are those that are normal and convex. Consider a type-1 FLS having p inputs and one output. Let us suppose that it has M rules, there the lth rule has the form: R^l :IF x_1 is F_1^l and x_2 is F_2^l and ... and x_p is F_p^l THEN y is G^l .l=1,... ,M

Assuming singleton fuzzification is used, when an input $x' = \{x_1',...,x_p'\}$ is applied, the degree

Figure 3. The structure of a fuzzy logic system

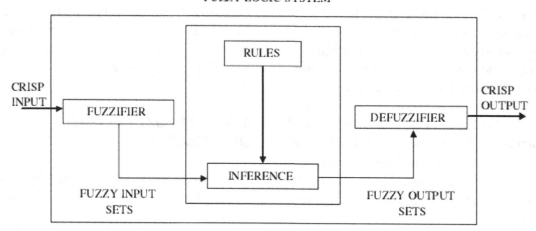

of firing corresponding to the lth rule is computed as

$$\mu_{F_1^l}(x_1') * \mu_{F_2^l}(x_2') * ... * \mu_{F_p^l}(x_p') = \Gamma_{i=1}^p \mu_{F_i^l}(x_i')$$

$$(1)$$

Where * and Γ both indicate the chosen t-norm. The last but not the least process in a FLS is called defuzzification. Defuzzification is the conversion of fuzzy output sets to crisp output sets. There are many defuzzification methods including maximum, mean-of-maxima, centroid, center-of-sums, height, modified height and center-of-sets. In this paper, we focus on the maximum defuzzifier. At first, we multiply the values in each rows of rules table and then select the row with maximum value.

4. SUGGESTED PROTOCOLS

We apply Fuzzy logic to our distributed location services (FLS (1, 2, 3): Fuzzy-based Location Service).This section is divided to three parts: 1) grid ordering, 2) Location update, 3) location query based data transferring.

a. Hierarchical Partitioning

Our location services use a partitioned network based on unit square regions of side $r_t / \sqrt{2}$ (L0), where r_t is the transmission range of a node such that any two nodes within a L0 grid can directly communicate with each other. The grid hierarchy is defined as Figure 4 shows which is grid based and hierarchical. Note that this may not be the only way to form clustering using unit grid (L0)

Figure 4. Squares area that are maintained by each level location server

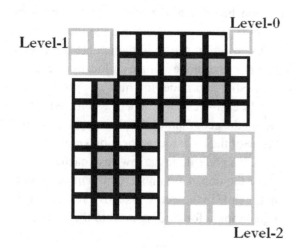

Figure 5. Location servers in hierarchically mode

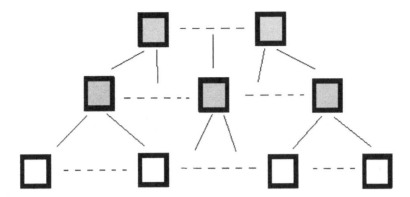

regions and we just use it to setup our location service. We can simplify Figure 4 in Figure 5. We want to propose a system which is based on fuzzy logic to a better management of update operation in hierarchical location services.

b. Location Update

In FLS (1, 2) each time a node crosses a *L0* grid boundary, it sends a location update packet to its current location servers in location server area (*L0*) in current *L1* grid.

In FLS 3, each node each time crosses a *L0* grid it runs algorithm in Figure 6 and based on result of that will send location update packet to its location server.

The algorithm in Figure 6 has two modes. The first is *no-prediction mode* that operates when a node's destination is in its current L0 or its distance from predicted value is greater than a threshold

value (j). The second one is *prediction mode.* When a node is in *prediction mode,* it does not send update packet to its server. Location server in *L1* grid uses the Formula 1 to prediction mobile nodes location (in Figure 7):

$$\begin{cases} y2 = y1 + Vy \times (t2 - t1) \\ x2 = x1 + Vx \times (t2 - t1) \end{cases} \quad (1)$$

Where in Formula 1 *Vy* and *Vx* are equal to Formula 2:

$$\begin{cases} Vy = v \times SIN(\hat{\alpha}) \\ Vx = v \times COS(\hat{\alpha}) \end{cases} \quad (2)$$

Where *v* in Formula 2 is equal to Formula 3:

Figure 6. To trigger update when Each node crosses a L0

if *(node crosses an L0)* **then**
    if *(node is in prediction mode)* **then**
        //nothing
    else
        if *(destination is in current L0)* **then**
            trigger update with no-prediction mode
        else
            trigger update with prediction mode

Figure 7. To prediction mobile node location

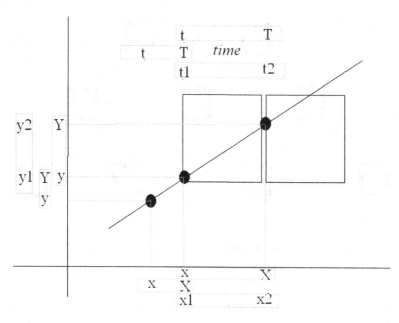

$$v = \frac{\sqrt{(Y-y)^2 + (X-x)^2}}{T-t} \qquad (3)$$

And $\hat{\alpha}$ is equal to Formula 4:

$$\hat{\alpha} = \begin{cases} ArcCOS(\frac{X-x}{\sqrt{(Y-y)^2 + (X-x)^2}})\ldots\cdots\ldots\ldots\cdots When(Y-y \geq 0) \\ 2 \times \Pi - ArcCOS(\frac{X-x}{\sqrt{(Y-y)^2 + (X-x)^2}})\cdots\ldots\cdots When(Y-y < 0) \end{cases}$$

$$(4)$$

In FLS (1, 2, 3) each time a node crosses a *L1* grid boundary (+ danger area), two location-update packets are generated, one to the *L1* grid of its current *L0* grid to indicate its arrival, and another packet to the L_1 grid of its previous *L1* grid, indicating its departure from the region and indicating location of its new leader in new *L1* grid. Each packet contains information to make the location servers consistent in their view of the network. The location-update packets are processed at each level of the hierarchy in the following manner:

In scenario of *b* under Figure 8, node u sends a location-update packet to its leader in *L1* grid

of its current L_0 grid and the leader that receives location-update packet updates its own location database.

In scenario of *a* under Figure 8, node u sends a location-update packet to its new leader in *L1* grid of its new *L0* grid and new leader that receives location-update packet updates its own location

Figure 8. Two scenarios in Location-update-part

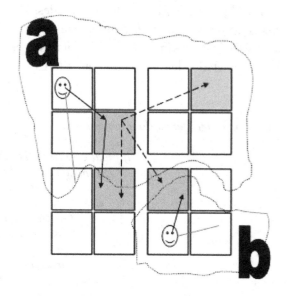

database and sends notification to *L1* grid of previous *L0* grid such that it makes a one-hop-chain between two leaders that if new location-update is not received (seldom) by hierarchical leader then new server can be achievable for data transfer. The new leader also checks the location-update packet to see whether the boundary under *L1* grid of previous *L0* grid has crossed and whether its hierarchical leader requires to be alerted then it uses fuzzy rules under Table 1 and if the consequent is one (it means trigger) it sends the location-update packet to its next hierarchical leader else waits to arrive adequate time to trigger (maybe another time). If the movement is within the area covered by the current hierarchical leader then the leader decides to stop the registration process. Thus the location registration process continues until the location-update packet reaches one of the four *L* leaders. In FLS (1, 2, 3) each node has a counter that presents number of call-References (d_{NCNN}) that recently has had. Each time a node crosses a *L1* grid boundary, it sends its d_{NCNN} and new location to new leader and new leader add d_{NCNN} to $\sum d$. Addition to storing counter, each node stores the time of last call-Reference (T_{LCNN}). So each time each node that has crossed the L_1 grid of previous L_0 grid and hierarchical leader requires to be alerted, leader waits and uses fuzzy rules under Table 1.

We have two algorithms for this section. The first is Timer based and second is Cross based. At first we describe Timer based algorithm and then Cross based.

We want to aggregate the location update packets in first location server in each *L1* grid. For example if we have *n* location update packets that location server is needed to forward them to hierarchical server, we can show in here that our solution has lower overhead related to normal mode that server will send all packets to hierarchical server. So:

Table 1. Simulation parameters for FLS

simulator	Glomosim (Zeng, Bagrodia, and Gerla, 1998)
MAC model	IEEE 802.11
Simulation time	300s
Each side of L0	100 m
$(\alpha 2 - \alpha 1)$ (sec)	8
β	7
δ (sec)	15
ω	1
λ	0
transmission range	144m

- **In normal mode:** we have *n* packets to forward so it means *n*(data + header)* that is *(n*data + n* header)*.
- **In our phase 2:** we have *1* packets to forward so it means *1*(n*data + header)* that is *(n*data +1* header)*.

Data means location of a mobile node and *header* is header section of a packet that is sent.

It means leader aggregates location-update packets and each time that is essential, instead of all packets sends a location-update packet to hierarchical leader. It decreases the number of location-update packets that are generated but some of that are essential for responsiveness in operation of location- query while the other in another time maybe are used and we want to distinguish between them.

Timer based algorithm uses fuzzy rules in Table 1 and if probability of trigger is one then the algorithms decide for trigger else wait, where R is a random number between zero and one. Under Table 1 e is neperian number and if $\sum d$ is high then probability of trigger is high and vice versa.

Figure 9. Relationship between $\sum d$ and probability of trigger

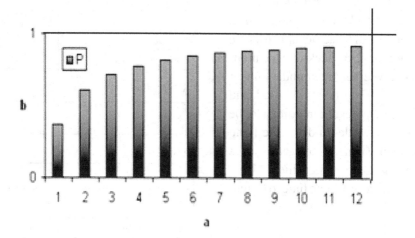

a

For example if T_{LCNN} is equal to 0.4 (for High-Urgency) and 0.1 (for Low-Urgency) and 0.0 (for None-Urgency) and if $\sum d$ is equal to 0.6 (for Wait) and 0.3 (for Trigger) then the values in each rows of Table 1 are multiplied and respect to the result of each rows decision will be make. It means the row with the maximum value is selected for probability of sending location update packet to hierarchical server. You can see relationship between $\sum d$ different values and probability of sending in Figure 9.

As you can see, Figure 9 shows the probability of trigger in rows of 3 and 4 in Table 1. In the Figure 9, a means $\sum d$ value and p is the probability.

We mainly focus on the nodes that recently are referenced (by call). Recently means the time of last call-Reference is related to first and second fuzzy sets in Figure 10. It means the nodes that recently are referenced with high probability, in future again are referenced relative to other. Maybe in future other nodes are referenced too, so the leader set a timer and every δ seconds add the value of $(\omega \times (N / 2) + \lambda)$ to $\sum d$ (where N is the number of nodes that have entered to new

L_1 grid up to now and (ω, λ) are for tuning of proposed value) and Figure 11 is checked, if $\sum d$ is in trigger-mode then triggers an update packet, else waits to trigger in another time. It means the timer, in the time, increases weight of $\sum d$ such that other nodes which recently are not referenced do not be forgotten. So in FLS, firstly, update operation for low-essential nodes is delayed and

Figure 10. Membership function for the time of last call-reference

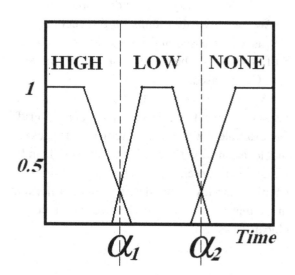

Figure 11. Membership function for the number of call-references

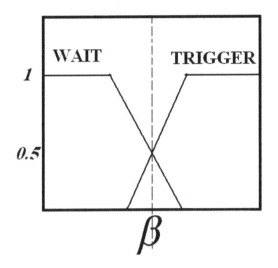

secondly, location-update packets are aggregated and one packet is sent instead of all. The algorithms that we have introduced and proposed timer

guaranty that we do not have significant loss of query success probability. In FLS (2), if a leader decides to trigger to hierarchical leader then it will send update packet to hierarchical leader and other leaders that are in the same level and same hierarchical grid but in FLS (1, 3) trigger-operation will stop in hierarchical leader.

In Cross based algorithm location server runs the algorithm in Figure 12 and based on result of that will send location update packet to its hierarchical location server in L2 grid. The algorithm uses Figure 13 to map the *time* variable to the *urgency* in *high* or *low*. Note that if *t(now) – t(last-call)* be between *zero and beta* then we say *high-urgency* else we say *low-urgency*. Note that, this can be using a kind of fuzzy logic and we can simplify fuzzy rules in Table 2. In here we describe the algorithm parameters:

T(now) is current time. *T(last-call)* is time of last call reference to receive data. *N(call)* is number of call reference heretofore. *N(cross-level-1)*

Figure 12. Fuzzy Rules for Trigger or Not and Consequent in the Timer based algorithm

T_{LCNN}	Σd	**Probability of Trigger**
HGH-URGENCY	TRIGGER	1
HGH-URGENCY	WAIT	1
LOW-URGENCY	TRIGGER	$e^{-\left|\frac{1}{\sum d}\right|} > R$
LOW-URGENCY	WAIT	$e^{-\left|\frac{1}{\sum d}\right|} > R$
NON-URGENCY	TRIGGER	1
NON-URGENCY	WAIT	0 (means Wait)

Figure 13. Fuzzy Rules for Trigger or Not and Consequent in the Cross based algorithm

n (cross-level-1)	T(now)– t(last-call)	**Probability of Trigger**
EVEN	ANY	1
ODD	HIGH-URGENCY	1
ODD	LOW-URGENCY	$e^{-\left| \frac{1}{N(Call)} \right|} > e^{-\left| \frac{1}{N(cross\text{-}level\text{-}1)} \right|}$

is number of crossing of *L1* grids heretofore. Note that "Trigger update to hierarchical location server" in the algorithm means that sending a location update that is contained all previous hoarded location update packets such that packet is contained *(n*data +1* header)*.

When a node leaves or enters a grid, it needs to update the corresponding location server. It may happen that a node leaves a grid for a very short while, and then it enters the grid again. In this case, the node has to update its position information with location servers repeatedly. This phenomenon of updating position information continuously is called the ping-pong (Flury & Wattenhofer, 2006) effect. The system resource is consumed rapidly when the ping-pong effect occurs.

Table 2. Comparison parameters between FLS and GLS

GLS	FLS	Comparison parameter/Method
All for some	All for some	Mauve classification(Mauve, Widmer, and Hartensteinm, 2001)
Yes	Yes	Hierarchical based?
Grid based	Grid based + parametric based + Combination based	Time of update?
No	Yes	Dynamic organizing Static grids?
No	Yes	Solving ping-pong Problem?

Figure 14. The Cross based algorithm

Figure 15. To map time variable to urgency in high or low

If n (cross-level-1) is an even number

Trigger update to hierarchical location server

Else

If t (now) – t (last-call) means high-urgency

Trigger update to hierarchical location server

Else

If t (now) – t (last-call) means low-urgency

$$If \quad e^{-\left|\frac{1}{N(Call)}\right|} > e^{-\left|\frac{1}{N(cross\text{-}level\text{-}1)}\right|}$$

Trigger update to hierarchical server

Else

WAIT

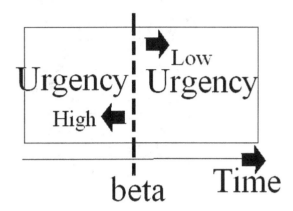

We change L1 grid area and organize that dynamically. We define a danger area out of each L1 grid. The idea is simple. When a node enters a danger area it sends location update to location server in previous L1 grid not to new server. That is effective in decreasing location update overhead because the node delays firing location update to location server in new L1 grid (it is contained at least two packets. one to previous location server in previous L1 grid and one to location server in new L1 grid and probably one to Hierarchical server) and in danger area just sends a packet to location server in previous L1 grid. Also this phase can solve ping-pong problem between L1 grids.

As per Figure 14, we can divide the network area to four partitions and then we divide left-button partition to four partitions. Each partition has four L0 grids that one of them is related to server-area and all of nodes at them are server. We propose two methods for binding of client node to server node: 1-Time based Late Binding (TLB); 2-Grid based Late Binding (GLB).

Our methods are based on late binding. Binding means client node *a* (for example) at an area related to server node *b* (for example) sends loca-tion update to it, so client node *a* binds to server *b*.

In TLB method, when a node crosses a *L0* grid boundary, it waits for a special time (for example c seconds) and then will send location update packet.

In GLB method, the nodes use a danger area outer than original grid. When a node enters a danger area it sends location update to location server in previous L1 grid not to new server. Danger area is virtual and dynamic. It means the danger area for a L1 grid is organized when the node leaves the current L1 grid.

For example, as per Figure 15, the node moves in directions of 2, 3, 4, 5, 6, and 7, and in our algorithms 7 packets are generated but in other grid based protocols like HGRID 16 packets are generated.

c. Location Query and Data Transferring

Considering FLS (1, 2, 3) we suggest two methods for location query and data transferring. In FLS 1, as Figure 16 shows, when s1 in scenario of *b* wants to send data to d1, it sends data to its leader then if leader does not find location of destination in its database it sends a query-packet to hierarchical

Figure 16. Danger area schema

leader and as soon as possible that receives reply packet it sends data to destination location. In FLS 2, as Figure 16 shows, when s1 in scenario of *a* wants to send data to d1, it sends data to its leader then leader with considering specifications of FLS 2 if it finds location of destination in its database then it sends data to d1. If leader does not find the location of destination in its database then it sends a query-packet to hierarchical leader and as soon as possible that receives reply packet it sends data to destination location, but this situation is happened when destination is in one of other three grids with level of two. In FLS 3, location server (in last L1 grid that destination exists) that receives data sends data to destination based on the algorithm in Figure 17. If the node is in prediction mode server predicts location of destination in L1 grid by formula one and sends data to destination.

5. SIMULATION RESULTS

In this section, we study the performance of the proposed algorithms using *Glomosim* (Zeng, Bagrodia, & Gerla, 1998). When location information is available, geographic forwarding can be used in the place of establishing a route from a source node to a destination node. There are different methods for forwarding packets in geographic way, for instance flooding, restricted flooding, hierarchical methods and greedy forwarding. Greedy methods seem to be better for geographic routing, because these methods just need local information for choosing route. We use a composed method for geographic routing

Figure 17. An example for danger area application

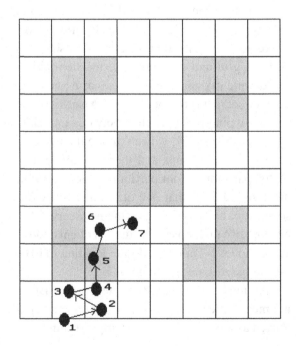

Figure 18. Two scenarios in location query and data transfer

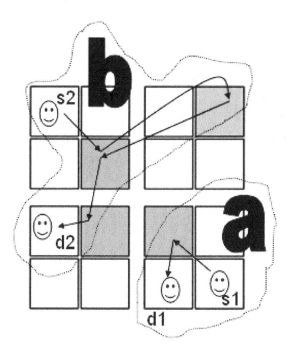

Figure 19. Send data to destination

if *(node is in no-prediction mode) then*

  send data to destination in without prediction

else

  send data to destination with prediction of its location

of packet through network. This method has two sections. Assume that we have three type nodes that have main roles in geographic routing in one hop forwarding to destination, node S that is source node, node I that is intermediate node and D which is destination node.

At first node S finds the closest node to D related itself between its neighbors.

But the first phase is based on a greedy algorithm and sometimes may fail for the sake of void-space (or hole-space) such that the node cannot find closest neighbor node and packet is dropped. In Ad-hoc networks this problem is completely temporary because of node mobility, consequently further attempts leads to success. In this work we use a simple way (in Figure 18 and Figure 19). The way is finding hindmost node between neighbors. This strategy leads to turn around the face. Since the I nodes keep records of visited nodes, loops are prevented.

In this section, we study the performance of the proposed services. They move according to

the waypoint mobility model. In this model, a node randomly selects a location and moves toward it with a constant speed uniformly distributed between zero and a maximum speed Vmax, and then it stays stationary during a pause time before moving to a new random location. Simulation time in second is 300. Each side of grid (level 0) is 100 m. Our Hierarchical partitioning comprises 3 levels (0, 1 and 2). Maximum speed (m/s) is 10 (to 15). Traffic pattern is random. We have evaluated the performance of the FLS (1, 2, 3) in terms of location overhead, query-cost, location discovery count and query success probability. Table 2 shows the parameter values for the simulation. At beginning of setup of network, counter of each node sets to one and after that reach to β /2 at everywhere of network, it will be set to one again.

Figure 20 shows average update overhead in packets per node per second for all the protocols. FLS (1, 2, 3) have low overhead related to GLS and FLS 1 has overhead lower than FLS 2 because of different in last step of Location update process. We at all (as Figure 20 shows) have decreased

Figure 20. The algorithm of forwarding of packets

If *(s find closest node to d)* ***thwn***

  // Forward the packet to closest node to d

Else

  // Forward the packet to hindmost neighbor

Endif

Figure 21. Forwarding of packets schema

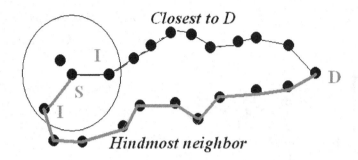

Figure 22. Average update cost vs. #nodes

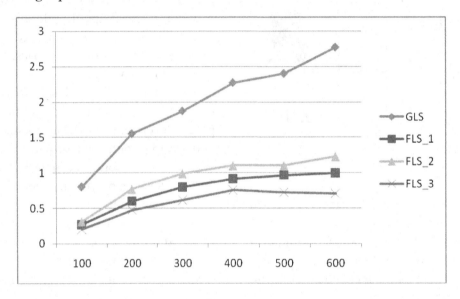

Figure 23. Average query cost vs. #nodes

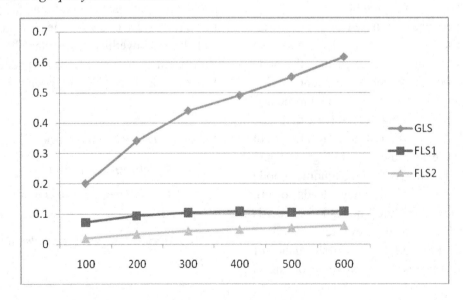

Figure 24. Average total cost vs. #nodes

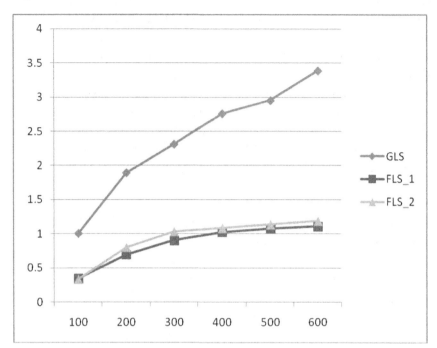

Figure 25. Query success rate vs. #nodes

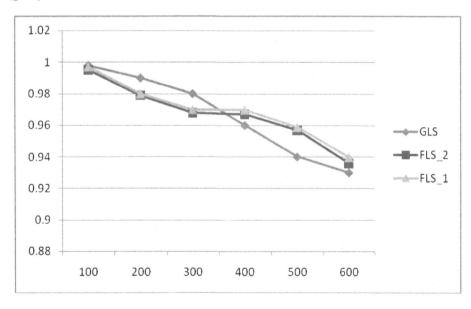

overhead of update operation. FLS 3 has low overhead related to FLS (1, 2), because the nodes use two modes (predictive and no-predictive) in *L1* grids.

Figure 21 shows average query overhead for all three protocols. This term in FLS 1 is lower than FLS 2, because in FLS 2, if leader decide to trigger to hierarchical leader update packet is sent to leaders (including hierarchical leader and leaders that are in the same level and are in the same hierarchical grid) and request for location (and data transferring) goes to first leader and it (mostly) finds destination location and transfers data to destination.

Figure 22 shows total cost for three protocols. It means average update cost and average query cost. Average update cost (Figure 24) in FLS 1 is lower than FLS 2 and average query cost in FLS 2 is lower than FLS 1 but at all total cost in FLS 1 is lower than FLS 2.

Figure 23 shows the query success probability of location for the three protocols. Query success probability (Figure 25) in our services at first is lower than GLS because our algorithms wait and immediately do not trigger location-update to hierarchical leader, so databases in hierarchical leaders are not consistent and this decreases query success probability related to GLS but that is not significant, as you see in Figure 23, because our algorithms using fuzzy logic and one-hop-chaining do not let to significant decreasing of success probability of location. In continue of increasing nodes success probability in our methods will be greater than GLS. One of the reasons can be significant increasing of location-update-packets in GLS related to FLS1,2. Result of that is congestion and exact locations will not arrive (on time) to leaders, so locations will not be precise related to FLS 1,2 (by increasing of nodes). We want to make an algorithm (in current work) such that location overhead be lower than GLS while reaching the good query success probability of location without significant loss of that related to GLS and we will work (in our other works) on simulation of other parts that are important for improving of mobility management and location service in mobile ad hoc networks.

Table 2 shows comparison parameters between FLS (1, 2, and 3) and GLS.

6. CONCLUSION AND FUTURE WORKS

In this article, we have introduced some methods to better management of location update operation. Simulation results show that our methods decrease location-update-overhead without loss of Query Success Rate. Note that our algorithms are distributed and can keep scalability in scenario increasing nodes density.

ACKNOWLEDGMENT

This work was supported by Islamic Azad University (Saghez branch).

REFERENCES

Bae, I.-H. (2007). An adaptive location service on the basis of diamond quorum for MANETs. In *Proceedings of the Third IEEE International Conference on Natural Computation* (p. 781).

Basagni, S., Chlamtac, I., Syrotiuk, V., & Woodward, A. B. (1998). A distance routing effect algorithm for mobility (dream). In *Proceedings of the 4th Annual ACM/IEEE International Conference on Mobile Computing and Networking* (pp. 76-84).

Camp, T., Boleng, J., & Wilcox, L. (2001). Location information services in mobile ad hoc networks. In *Proceedings of the IEEE International Conference on Communications* (pp. 3318-3324).

Camp, T., Bolengm, J., & Davies, V. (2002). A survey of mobility models for ad hoc network research. *Wireless Communications and Mobile Computing, 2*(5), 483–502. doi:10.1002/wcm.72

Cheng, C. T., Lemberg, H. L., Philip, S. J., van den Berg, E., & Zhang, T. (2002). SLALoM: A scalable location management scheme for large mobile adhoc networks. In *Proceedings of the IEEE Conference on Wireless Communications and Networking* (pp. 574-578).

Cheng, H., Cao, J., & Chen, H. H. (2007). GrLS: Group-based location service in mobile ad hoc networks. In *Proceedings of the IEEE International Conference on Communications* (pp. 4734-4740).

Das, S. M., Pucha, H., & Hu, Y. C. (2005). Performance comparison of scalable location service for geographic ad hoc routing. In *Proceedings of the 24th Annual IEEE Joint Conference INFOCOM* (pp. 1228-1239).

Flury, R., & Wattenhofer, R. (2006). MLS: An efficient location service for mobile ad hoc networks. In *Proceedings of the 7th ACM Conference on Mobile Ad Hoc Networking and Computing* (pp.226-237).

Jomeiri, A., & Dehghan, M. (2008). Performance improvement of a grid based location service in manet. In *Proceedings of the Second IEEE International Conference on Mobile Ubiquitous Computing, Systems, Services, and Technologies* (pp. 165-170).

Kumar, V., & Das, S. R. (2004). Performance of dead reckoning-based location service for mobile ad hoc networks. *Wireless Communications and Mobile Computing, 4*(2), 189–202. doi:10.1002/wcm.163

Leng, S., Zhang, L., Rao, J., & Yang, J. (2006). A novel k-hop cluster-based location service protocol for mobile ad hoc networks. In *Proceedings of the 6th IEEE International Conference on ITS Telecommunications* (pp. 695-700).

Li, J., Jannotti, J., De Couti, D. S. J., Karger, D. R., & Morris, R. (2000). A scalable location service for geographic ad hoc routing. In *Proceedings of the 6th Annual ACM International Conference on Mobile Computing and Networking* (pp. 120-130).

Liu, T. N., & Hwang, S. I. (2006). On design of an efficient hierarchical location service for ad hoc network. In *Proceedings of the 1st IEEE International Symposium on Wireless Pervasive Computing* (pp. 1-6).

Luo, X., Camp, T., & Navidi, W. (2005). Predictive methods for location services in mobile ad hoc networks. In *Proceedings of the 19th IEEE International Symposium on Parallel and Distributed Processing* (p. 6).

Mauve, M., Widmer, J., & Hartensteinm, H. (2001). A survey on position-based routing in mobile ad hoc networks. *IEEE Network, 15*(6), 30–39. doi:10.1109/65.967595

Mendel, J. M. (1995). Fuzzy logic systems for engineering: A tutorial. *Proceedings of the IEEE, 83*(3), 345–377. doi:10.1109/5.364485

Mendel, J. M. (2001). *Uncertain rule-based fuzzy logic systems*. Upper Saddle River, NJ: Prentice Hall.

Osmani, A., & Haghighat, A. T. (2010). SALAM: Scalable @ location advertisement management in ad hoc networks. In *Proceedings of the Second IEEE International Conference on Computational Intelligence, Communication Systems and Networks* (pp. 355-360).

Osmani, A., Haghighat, A. T., & Khezri, S. (2010). Performance improvement of two ble location services in MANET. In *Proceedings of the IEEE International Conference on Computational Intelligence and Communication Networks* (pp. 172-176).

Philip, S. J., Ghosh, J., & Qiao, C. (2005). Performance evaluation of a multilevel hierarchical location management protocol for ad hoc networks. *Computer Communications*, *28*(10), 1110–1122. doi:10.1016/j.comcom.2004.07.015

Ratnasamy, S., Karp, B., Yin, L., Yu, F., Estrin, D., Govindan, R., & Shenker, S. (2002). GHT: A geographic hash table for data-centric storage in sensornets. In *Proceedings of the 1st ACM International Workshop on Wireless Sensor Networks and Applications* (pp. 78-87).

Seet, B.-C., Pan, Y., Hsu, W.-J., & Lau, C.-T. (2005). Multi-home region location service for wireless ad hoc networks: An adaptive demand-driven approach. In *Proceedings of the 2nd IEEE Annual Conference on Wireless On-demand Network Systems and Services* (pp. 258-263).

Stojmenovic, I., Liu, D., & Jia, X. (2008). A scalable quorum based location service in ad hoc and sensor networks. *International Journal of Communication Networks and Distributed Systems*, *1*(1), 71–94. doi:10.1504/IJCNDS.2008.017205

Woo, S.-C. M., & Singh, S. (2001). Scalable routing protocol for ad hoc networks. *Wireless Networks*, *7*(5), 513–529. doi:10.1023/A:1016726711167

Zeng, X., Bagrodia, R., & Gerla, M. (1998). Glomosim: A library for parallel simulation of large scale wireless networks. *ACM SIGSIM*, *28*(1), 154–161. doi:10.1145/278009.278027

This work was previously published in the International Journal of Grid and High Performance Computing, Volume 3, Issue 3, edited by Emmanuel Udoh and Ching-Hsien Hsu, pp. 1-19, copyright 2011 by IGI Publishing (an imprint of IGI Global).

Chapter 10
Performance Evaluation of Reactive Routing in Mobile Grid Environment

L. Shrivastava
Madhav Institute of Technology and Science, Gwalior, India

G. S. Tomar
Machine Intelligence Research Labs, India

S. S. Bhadauria
Madhav Institute of Technology and Science, India

ABSTRACT

Grid computing came into existence as a manner of sharing heavy computational loads among multiple computers to be able to compute highly complex mathematical problems. The grid topology is highly flexible and easily scalable, allowing users to join and leave the grid without the hassle of time and resource-hungry identification procedures, having to adjust their devices or install additional software. The goal of grid computing is described as "to provide flexible, secure and coordinated resource sharing among dynamic collections of individuals, institutions and resources". AODV is an on-demand (reactive) algorithm capable of both unicast and multicast routing. In this paper, AODV has been modified by varying some of the configuration parameters used in this algorithm to improve its performance. This modified protocol i.e. A-AODV (advanced ad hoc on demand distance vector) has been compared with AODV in grid environment. The simulations have shown that A-AODV is able to achieve high throughput and packet delivery ratio and average end-to-end delay is reduced.

DOI: 10.4018/978-1-4666-2065-0.ch010

1. INTRODUCTION

Wireless grids are wireless computer networks (Anastasi, Borgia, Conti, & Gregori, 2003; Murthy & Manoj, 2004) consisting of different types of electronic devices with the ability to share their resources with any other device in the network in an ad-hoc manner. A definition of the wireless grid can be given as: "Ad-hoc, distributed resource-sharing networks between heterogeneous wireless devices" The following key characteristics further clarify this concept:

- No centralized control
- Small, low powered devices
- Heterogeneous applications and interfaces
- New types of resources like cameras, GPS trackers and sensors
- Dynamic and unstable users / resources

Mobile Grid, in relevance to both Grid and Mobile Computing, is a full inheritor of Grid with the additional feature of supporting mobile users and resources in a seamless, transparent, secure and efficient way (Nilsson, 2005). It has the ability to deploy underlying ad-hoc networks and provide a self-configuring Grid system of mobile resources (hosts and users) connected by wireless links and forming arbitrary and unpredictable Mobile Grid enables both the mobility of the users requesting access to a fixed Grid and the resources that are themselves part of the Grid. Both cases have their own limitations and constraints that should be handled. In the first case the devices of the mobile users act as interfaces to the Grid to monitor and manages the activities in 'anytime, anywhere' mode, while the Grid provides them with a high reliability, performance and cost-efficiency. Physical limitations of the mobile devices make necessary the adaptation of the services that Grid can provide to the users' mobile devices. In the second case of having mobile Grid resources, we should underline that the performances of current mobile devices are significantly increased. Laptops and

PDAs can provide aggregated computational capability when gathered in hotspots, forming a Grid on site (Abdullah, Ramly, Muhammed, & Derahman, 2008; Usop, Abdullah, & Abidin, 2009). This capability can advantage the usage of Grid applications even in places where this would be imaginary.

In this paper, an Advanced AODV (A-AODV) has been proposed in which some of the configuration parameters of AODV (Perkins, Royer, & Das, 2003) have been modified. These parameters are net diameter, node traversal time, active route timeout, hello interval, allowed hello loss and rreq retries. This new protocol A-AODV has been compared with AODV in grid environment. The comparison is made using the performance metric such as throughput, packet delivery ratio, average end-to-end delay and average jitter.

The remainder of this paper is organized as follows: II part describes AODV, III part develops proposed routing protocol i.e. A-AODV, IV part describes simulation scenarios and performance parameter, IV part describes the scenarios result and V part describes the conclusion and future work.

2. AD HOC ON DEMAND DISTANCE VECTOR (AODV)

AODV (Ad hoc On-demand Distance Vector routing) (Perkins, Royer, & Das, 2003) is a distance vector routing protocol, i.e. routes are advertised as a vector of direction and distance. To avoid the Bellman-Ford "counting to infinity" problem and routing loops, sequence numbers are utilized for control messages. Operation of the protocol here is also divided in two functions – route discovery and route maintenance. At first all the nodes send Hello message on its interface and receive Hello messages from its neighbors. This process repeats periodically to determine neighbor connectivity. When a route is needed to some destination, the protocol starts route discovery. The source node sends Route Request to its neighbors. If a neighbor has no information on the destination, it will send message to all of its neighbors and so on. Once request reaches a node that has information about the destination (either the destination itself or some node that has a valid route to the destination), that node sends Route Reply Message to the Route Request (RREQ) Message initiator. In the intermediate nodes (the nodes that forward Route Request Message), information about source and destination from Route Request Message is saved. Address of the neighbor that the Route Request Message came from is also saved. In this way, by the time Route Request Message reaches a node that has information to answer Route Request Message; a path has been recorded in the intermediate nodes. This path identifies the route that Route Request Message took and is called reverse path. Since each node forwards Route Request Message to all of its neighbors, more than one copy of the original Route Request Message can arrive at a node. When a Route Request Message is created at the initiator, it is assigned a *unique id*. When a node receives Route Request Message, it will check this *id* and the address of the initiator and discard the message if it had already processed that request.

A node that has information about route to the destination sends Route Reply Message to the neighbor from which it received Route Request Message. This neighbor then does the same. This is possible because of the reverse path created by the Route Request Message. While the Route Reply Message travels back using reverse path, that path is being transformed into forward path, by recording the node that Route Reply Message came from (i.e. same procedure as mentioned above just in opposite direction). When Route Reply Message reaches the initiator, the route is ready, and the initiator can start sending data packets.

If one of the links on the forward path breaks, the intermediate node just above the link that failed sends new Route Reply Message to all the

sources that are using the forward path to inform them of the link failure. It does this by sending the message to all neighbors using the forward path. In turn, they will send to their neighbors until all upstream nodes that use forward path are informed. The source nodes can then initiate new route request procedures if they still need to route packets to the destination.

3. A-AODV (ADVANCED AD HOC ON DEMAND DISTANCE VECTOR) ROUTING PROTOCOL

In this paper, the ad hoc on demand distance vector routing protocol (AODV) has been modified. This modification has been done by varying some of the following configuration parameters used in AODV:

- **NET DIAMETER:** This parameter specifies the maximum possible number of hops between two nodes in the network.
- **NODE TRAVERSAL TIME:** This parameter specifies the maximum possible number of hops between two nodes in the network.
- **ACTIVE ROUTE TIMEOUT:** This parameter specifies in QualNet Time Format the value of the lifetime field that a destination node places in Route Reply Packets.
- **HELLO INTERVAL AND ALLOWED HELLO LOSS:** These parameters specify the value of the lifetime field for Hello Packets. This lifetime value equals AODV-HELLO-INTERVAL multiplied by AODV-ALLOWED-HELLO-LOSS (an integer).
- **RREQ RETRIES:** This parameter specifies the number of times AODV will repeat an expanded ring search for a destination if no Route Reply Packet is received within the specified amount of time.

Figure 1. Throughput for different pause time

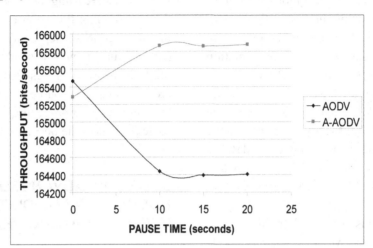

Figure 2. Average end-to-end delay for different pause time

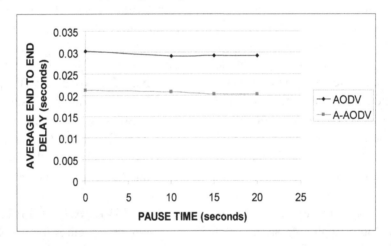

So the new routing protocol A-AODV is obtained after modification in AODV. The Simulation results of AODV & A-AODV are carried out by the Qualnet 4.5 simulation tool.

4. DESIGN OF THE EXPERIMENT & SIMULATION SETUP

In this scenario, terrain size of 500mX500m has been taken in which 50 mobile nodes are randomly placed with random way point mobility model (Gowrishankar, Basavaraju, & Sarkar, 2007). Fixed simulation time of 100 seconds is taken for all the running simulations. The simulation used fixed number of source nodes which are 50 nodes (*50 sources*), packet size of 512 bytes and a packet rate of 4 packets per seconds with varying pause time of 0, 5, 10, 15 and 20 sec at speed of 20 m/s and also with varying speed of 0, 5, 10, 15, 20 and 25 m/s at pause time of 20 sec. The traffic type used in this experiment is constant bit rate (CBR), here 10 CBR connections have been used.

Figure 3. Packet delivery ratio for different pause time

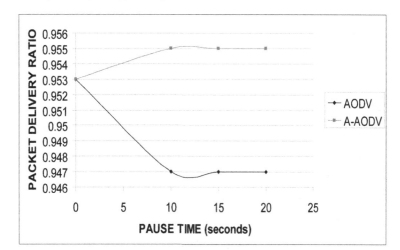

Figure 4. Average jitter for different pause time

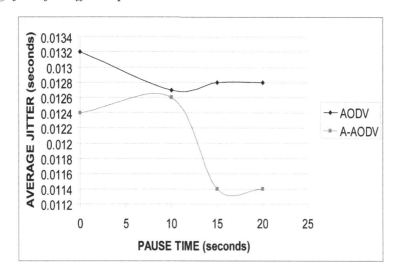

5. RESULTS AND DISCUSSION

The performance has been analyzed for different pause time and speed using the performance metrics (Pirzada, McDonald, & Datta, 2006): Throughput, Average End to End Delay, Packet Delivery Ratio (PDR) and Average Jitter.

- **Throughput** is measured by the total amount of packets which is received by a destination node. It is measured by byte/ sec or bit/sec. High throughput is always expected for any routing protocol.

- **Average End To End Delay** is the average delay of data packets from source to destination. It is also called data Latency. It is measured by the time taken between the generation of data packet and the last bit of arrival at the destination.

- **Packet Delivery Ratio (PDR)** is the ratio between the number of packet originated by the CBR sources and the number of

Figure 5. Throughput for different speed

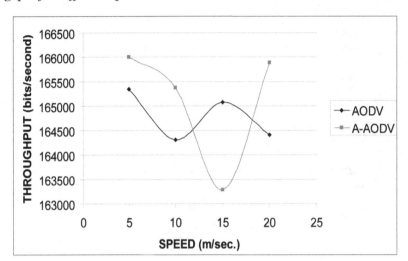

Figure 6. Average end-to-end delay for different speed

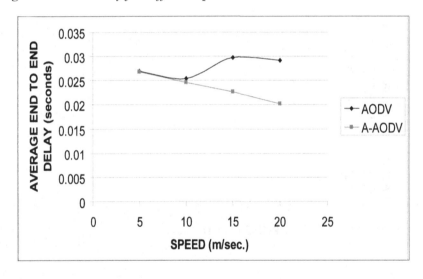

packet received by the CBR sink at the final destination.

- **Average Jitter** is the variation in the time between packets arriving, caused by network congestion, timing drift, or route changes. A jitter buffer can be used to handle jitter.

Performance analysis with varying pause time is shown in Figure 1, Figure 2, Figure 3, and Figure 4.

PDR will describe the loss rate that will be seen by the transport protocols, which in turn affects the maximum throughput that the network can support. This simulation chooses 0, 5, 10, 15, 20, and 25 seconds pause time. This simulation generates 50 nodes. At pause time 0 seconds (high mobility) environment, PDR of both A-AODV and AODV is same in high mobility environment, topology change rapidly and both protocols can adapt to the changes quickly since they only maintain one route that is actively used. In low

Figure 7. Packet delivery ratio for different speed

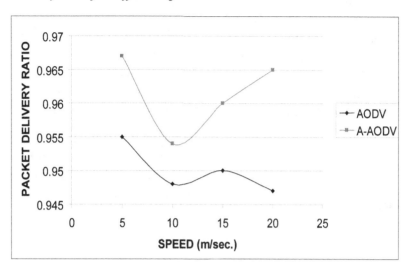

Figure 8. Average jitter for different speed

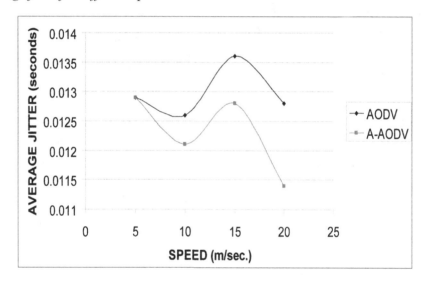

mobility environment, A-AODV out performs AODV. AODV delivers less data packet compare to A-AODV because it is not as adaptive to route changes in updating its table.

The buffers become full much quicker, so the packets have to stay in the buffers a much longer period of time before they are sent. The delay is slightly high for AODV irrespective of changes in mobility. This is because of extremely high data rate and in AODV, since routes are established on demand and destination sequence numbers are used to find the latest route to the destination.

Throughput of A-AODV is high due to packet loss on AODV side. This is because when a link fails, a routing error is passed back to a transmitting node and the process repeats and information on new Routes, broken Links, metric change is immediately propagated to neighbors.

Performance analysis with varying speed is shown in Figure 5, Figure 6, Figure 7, and Figure 8.

By varying speed of nodes, there is much improvement in the performance of A-AODV over AODV. As speed increase, there is rapid change in the network topology even though the performance of A-AODV is much better as compared to AODV with respect to throughput, packet delivery ratio, end-to-end delay, and average jitter because A-AODV is more adaptive to change in network topology.

6. CONCLUSION

There are a large number of different kinds of routing protocols in Mobile ad hoc networks. In this paper, AODV has been modified and compared with the original protocol in grid environment and analyzed for different pause time and speed which affects the performance metrics parameters: Throughput, Average end to end delay, Packet delivery ratio & Average jitter. The results showed that the modifications made in the configuration parameters of AODV have improved its performance. It is concluded that A-AODV showed improved performances in throughput, average end to end delay, packet delivery ratio and average jitter as compared to AODV.

FUTURE WORK

In the future, several other Enhancements and comparison also can be done to other routing protocols of MANET. This experiment can be done on other Network simulators for different terrain size, simulation time and for increasing large number of nodes. VANET (vehicular ad hoc networking) which is the new concept is also the most significant one to work with in the future.

REFERENCES

Abdullah, A., Ramly, N., Muhammed, A., & Derahman, M. N. (2008). Performance comparison study of routing protocols for mobile grid environment. *International Journal of Computer Science and Network Security, 8*(2), 82–88.

Anastasi, G., Borgia, E., Conti, M., & Gregori, E. (2003). IEEE 802.11: Ad-hoc networks: Performance measurements. In *Proceedings of the IEEE Workshop on Mobile and Wireless Networks* (pp. 758-763).

Broch, J., Maltz, D. A., & Johnson, D. B. (1998). A performance comparison of multi-hop wireless ad-hoc network routing protocols. In *Proceedings of the 4th Annual ACM/IEEE Conference on Mobile Computing and Networking* (pp. 85-97).

Geetha, J., & Gopinath, G. (2007). Ad hoc mobile wireless networks routing protocols – A review. *Journal of Computer Science, 3*(8), 574–582. doi:10.3844/jcssp.2007.574.582

Gowrishankar, S., Basavaraju, T. G., & Sarkar, S. K. (2007). Effect of random mobility models pattern in mobile ad hoc networks. *International Journal of Computer Science and Network Security, 7*(6), 160–164.

Murthy, C. S. R., & Manoj, B. S. (2004). *Ad hoc wireless networks architectures and protocols.* Upper Saddle River, NJ: Prentice Hall.

Naserian, M., Tepe, K. E., & Tarique, M. (2005, August). Routing overhead analysis for reactive routing protocols in wireless ad hoc networks. In *Proceedings of the IEEE International Conference on Wireless and Mobile Computing, Networking, and Communications*, Windsor, ON, Canada (Vol. 3, pp. 87-92).

Nilsson, T. (2005). *Resource allocation and service differentiation in wireless local area networks.* Umea, Sweden: Umea University.

Perkins, C. E., Royer, E. M. B., & Das, S. R. (2003). *Ad hoc on-demand distance vector (AODV) routing.* Retrieved from http://www.ietf.org/rfc/rfc3561.txt

Pirzada, A. A., McDonald, C., & Datta, A. (2006). Performance comparison of trust based reactive routing protocols. *IEEE Transactions on Mobile Computing, 5*(6), 695–710. doi:10.1109/TMC.2006.83

Usop, M., Abdullah, A., & Abidin, A. (2009). Performance evaluation of AODV, DSDV & DSR routing protocol in grid environment. *International Journal of Computer Science and Network Security, 9*(7), 261–268.

Yadav, N. S., & Yadav, R. P. (2007). Performance comparison and analysis of table- driven and on-demand routing protocols for mobile ad hoc networks. *International Journal of Information Technology, 4*(2), 101–109.

This work was previously published in the International Journal of Grid and High Performance Computing, Volume 3, Issue 3, edited by Emmanuel Udoh and Ching-Hsien Hsu, pp. 45-53, copyright 2011 by IGI Publishing (an imprint of IGI Global).

Chapter 11
An Intelligent Sensor Placement Method to Reach a High Coverage in Wireless Sensor Networks

Shirin Khezri
Islamic Azad University - Mahabad, Iran

Karim Faez
Amirkabir University of Technology, Iran

Amjad Osmani
Islamic Azad University - Saghez, Iran

ABSTRACT

Adequate coverage is one of the main problems for Sensor Networks. The effectiveness of distributed wireless sensor networks highly depends on the sensor deployment scheme. Optimizing the sensor deployment provides sufficient sensor coverage and saves cost of sensors for locating in grid points. This article applies the modified binary particle swarm optimization algorithm for solving the sensor placement in distributed sensor networks. PSO is an inherent continuous algorithm, and the discrete PSO is proposed to be adapted to discrete binary space. In the distributed sensor networks, the sensor placement is an NP-complete problem for arbitrary sensor fields. One of the most important issues in the research fields, the proposed algorithms will solve this problem by considering two factors: the complete coverage and the minimum costs. The proposed method on sensors surrounding is examined in different area. The results not only confirm the successes of using the new method in sensor placement, also they show that the new method is more efficiently compared to other methods like Simulated Annealing(SA), PBIL and LAEDA.

DOI: 10.4018/978-1-4666-2065-0.ch011

INTRODUCTION

Wireless sensor networks consist of certain amount of small and energy constrained nodes (Chong & Kumar, 2003; Pottie, 1998; Pottie & Caiser, 2000). A typical wireless sensor network consists of thousands of sensor nodes, deployed either randomly or according to some predefined statistical distribution, over a geographic region of interest. A sensor node by itself has severe resource constraints, such as low battery power, limited signal processing, limited computation and communication capabilities, and a small amount of memory. However, when a group of sensor nodes collaborate with each other, they can accomplish a much bigger task efficiently. One of the primary advantages of deploying a wireless sensor network is its low deployment cost and freedom from requiring a messy wired communication backbone (Chong & Kumar, 2003; Akyildiz, Su, Sankarasubramaniam, & Cayirci, 2002).

For instance, a sensor network can be deployed in a remote island for monitoring wildlife habitat and animal behavior (Mainwaring, Polastre, Szewczyk, Culleradn, & Erson, 2002; Qi, Iyengar, & Chakrabarty, 2001), or near the crater of a volcano to measure temperature, pressure, and seismic activities. In many of these applications the environment can be hostile where human intervention is not possible and hence, the sensor nodes will be deployed randomly or sprinkled from air and will remain unattended for months or years without any battery replacement. Therefore, energy consumption or, in general, resource management is of critical importance to these networks. Sensor deployment strategies play a very important role in providing better QoS, which relates to the issue of how well each point in the sensing field is covered. Three types of coverage have been defined by Gage (1992):

1. **Blanket coverage:** to achieve a static arrangement of sensor nodes which maximizes the detection rate of targets appearing in the sensing field.

2. **Barrier coverage:** to achieve a static arrangement of sensor nodes which minimizes the probability of undetected penetration through the barrier.

3. **Sweep coverage:** to move a number of sensor nodes across a sensing field, such that it addresses a specified balance between maximizing the detection rate and minimizing the number of missed detections per unit area.

We will focus mainly on the Blanket coverage, where the objective is to deploy sensor nodes in strategic ways such that optimal area coverage is achieved according to the needs of the underlying applications.

In the distributed sensor networks, the issue of sensor placement is an importance paramount in researches. A sensor network can be arranged in two ways, one as a random placement and the second as a grid-based placement. Once the surrounding is unknown the random placement is the only option and the sensors may be disintegrated everywhere but when the features of the network were known before, then the sensor placement could be done with great scrutiny and we could guarantee the quality of providing services along with satisfying the limitations. The strategy of sensor placement depends on the application of the distributed sensor network (DNS). In this article the focus is on the grid-based placement. Here we applied the modified binary PSO algorithm for solving these NP-complete problems (Rostami & Nezam Abadi, 2006).

Considering the existence of many networks with high velocity and computational capabilities of these sensor networks, we can say that they have different applications for example in aviation, military, medical, robot, air forecasting, security and anti terrorism applications and also we can use them in very important infrastructures like power plants, environmental and natural resource monitoring, and military applications like communication systems, commanding, reconnaissance patrols, looking –out etc (Chong & Kumar, 2003; Akyildiz, Su, Sankarasubramaniam, & Cayirci, 2002).

RELATED WORK

Several deployment strategies have been studied for achieving an optimal sensor network architecture which would minimize cost, provides high sensing coverage, be resilient to random node failures, and so on. Random placement does not guarantee full coverage because it is stochastic in nature, hence often resulting in accumulation of nodes at certain areas in the sensing field but leaving other areas deprived of nodes. Some of the deployment algorithms try to find new optimal sensor locations after an initial random placement and move the sensors to those locations, achieving maximum coverage (like our approach). These algorithms are applicable to only mobile sensor networks. Research has also been conducted in mixed-sensor networks, where some of the nodes are mobile and some are static and approaches are also proposed to detect coverage holes after an initial deployment and to try to heal or eliminate those holes by moving sensors.

Zou and Chakrabarty (2004) proposed an algorithm as a sensor deployment strategy to enhance the coverage after an initial random placement of sensors. It is assumed that sensors can move by "virtual force" with the force's strength determined by node distance. Cao, Wang, La Porta, and Zhang (2006) considered the problem of moving some sensors from their initial random placement in order to cover some areas which were not covered by either the nature of randomness or some other effects such as wind. It is also assumed that sensors can move after gathering some information from neighbors. The algorithm proceeds in rounds. In each round, each sensor then subtracts its sensing area from its Voronoi polygon, and moves in the direction of the largest uncovered piece of area. The process repeats until no further improvement is possible. The approach appears suitable when robots, equipped with sensors, are monitoring an area, which can also be monitored by some static sensors. An alternative approach may be to use face routing (Bose, Morin, Stojmenovic, & Urrutia, 2001) to estimate the size of a hole, find its centroid, estimate the number of sensors which should move toward the centroid, and provide the best possible information to sensors for their move.

Wang, Cao, and La Porta (2004) proposed a proxy-based sensor deployment protocol. Instead of moving iteratively, sensors calculate their target locations based on a distributive iterative protocol. Current proxy sensors advertise the service of mobile sensors to their neighborhoods (up to certain parameter distance), searching for a better coverage location. They collect bidding messages and choose the highest bid. Then they delegate the bidder as the new proxy. Actual movement only occurs when sensors determine their final locations. If the bidding process is local, the sensor movement and the area-coverage gains may be restricted. If the bidding process includes neighbors at several hops distance, the communication overhead for bidding becomes significant. Bidding decisions are based on price (number of logical movements made so far) and distance that the moving sensors are physically supposed to move altogether. A procedure to prevent multiple healing is described, which includes some message overhead. The bidding criterion does not include lost area coverage for moving out of the current position. It is not certain whether the described procedure is always loop-free and always converging. The difference between sensing and transmission radii has a direct impact on message complexity.

Yang, Li, and Wu (2007) proposed a scan-based movement-assisted sensor deployment method (SMART) which uses scan and dimension exchange to achieve a balanced state. In SMART, a given rectangular sensor field is first partitioned into a 2-D mesh through clustering. Each cluster corresponds to a square region and has a cluster head which is in charge of bookkeeping and communication with adjacent cluster heads. Clustering is a widely used approach in sensor networks for its support for Design simplification.

Another idea has been described in Stojmenovic (1999) for the purpose of providing location service. If the network of static sensors is disconnected, then mobile sensors will send one message to each connected component and search several perimeters.

In (WU, CHO, AURIOL and LEE, 2007) three sensor relocation algorithms were proposed according to the mobility degree of sensor nodes. The first one, PSOA, regards the sensors in the network as a swarm and reorganizes the sensors by PSO, in the full sensor mobility case. The other two, relay shift based algorithm (RSBA) and energy–efficient fuzzy optimization algorithm (EFOA), assume relatively limited sensor mobility, i.e., the movement distance is bounded by a threshold, and to further reduce energy consumption.

In Rahman, Razzaque, and Hong (2007) for the exposure estimation the whole network is thought to be a Voronoi diagram (Meguerdichian, Koushanfar, Potkonjak, & Srivastava, 2001) based network which is formed considering all the cluster head of the network as a single point. The clustering algorithm used here is based on Delaunay triangulated sensor nodes. The key idea of this clustering method is taken from the clustering method used for key frame-based video summarization technique (Padmavathi, Yong, & Yelena, 2006). Some recent work focus on sensors with limited mobility, which is motivated by the DARPA project called Intelligent Mobile Land Mine Units (IMLM) (http://www.darpa.mil/ato/progarms/shm/index.html, 2007). In IMLM, the mobility system is based on a hopping mechanism. Chellapan et al. (2005) studied a special hopping model in which each sensor can flip (or flop) to a new location only once. In addition, the flip distance is bounded. The deployment problem is

then formulated as a minimum cost, maximum-flow problem.

In Dhillon, Chakrabarty, and Iyengar (2002) and Dhillon and Chakrabarty (2003), they presented a resource-bounded optimization framework for sensor resource management under the constraints of sufficient grid coverage of the sensor field. In (Chakrabarty, Iyengar, Qi, and Cho (2002), they formulated the sensor placement problem in terms of cost minimization under coverage constraints. In Sasikumar, Vasudevan, Vivek, and Subashri (2009) Node placement in heterogeneous WSN is formulated using a generalized node placement optimization problem to minimize the network cost with lifetime constraint, and connectivity.

In Rajagopalan, Niu, Mohan, Varshney, and Drozd (2008) they formulated and solved the sensor placement problem for efficient target localization in a sensor network. They developed a mathematical framework for the localization of the missile using multiple sensors based on Cramer-Rao Lower Bound (CRLB) analysis. In Indu, Chaudhury, Mittal, and Bhattacharyya (2009) they presented the practical problem of optimally placing the multiple PTZ cameras to ensure maximum coverage of user defined priority areas with optimum values of parameters like pan, tilt, zoom and the locations of the cameras. Moreover in Lin and Chiu (2005) a heuristic algorithm is proposed based on Simulation Annealing Algorithm to solve this problem considering the coverage and cost limitations.

In Osmani, Haghighat, Dehghan, and Emdadi (2010) and Osmani, Dehghan, Pourakbar, and Emdadi (2009), they applied Fuzzy Logic System (FLS) to re-deploy the sensors. Each individual mobile sensor uses a FLS to self-adjust its location. Therefore the deployment scheme based on FLSs is a fully distributed approach.

In Osmani, Haghighat, Dehghan, and Emdadi (2010) and Osmani, Dehghan, Pourakbar and Emdadi (2009), the algorithms after random deployment of sensors at the beginning of network setup, start to redeployment of sensors to increase the coverage on the sensor field. FSPNS (Osmani, Haghighat, Dehghan, & Emdadi, 2010) after deciding for movement use one of three policies depend on fuzzy rules based on neighbors density and average distance from them. FSPNS is simple and simulation shows coverage enhancement. FRED (Osmani, Dehghan, Pourakbar, & Emdadi, 2009) uses neighbor's information about location and state to decide on movement.

In Khezri, Osmani, and Gholami (2011) they have used the Distribution Estimation Algorithms named LAEDA on sensor placement. In Learning Automata Estimation Distributed Algorithm (LAEDA), the independency of genome variables is assumed. In these algorithms a Learning Automata is used for each variable in genome. The number of actions of Learning Automata equals to number of permitted values for the corresponding variable of Learning Automata. For production of each genome sample, the Learning Automata of each variable is asked to select its own suitable action; afterwards, they give a corresponding value of selected action to the corresponding variable. Though, they can calculate the probability of a genome's production $X = (x_1, ..., x_n)$ based on Equation (1).

$$P\left(X = x\right) = \prod_{i=1}^{n} P(X_i = x_i) = \prod_{i=1}^{n} Grad_i^j \quad (1)$$

Where, $1 \leq j \leq r_i$, so $Grad_i^j$ equals to probability of action of corresponding j to value of x_i by i^{th} Learning Automata. By applying Automata in each stage, a number of N individual genomes are created, which is compatible with the number of population. Then the new population of genomes is evaluated using Evaluation Function, and Se genomes which are considered as the best genomes are chosen from this population. After applying some mechanisms which are dependent on Learning Automata Environment Model, a reinforcement signal vector is created and we apply the

Learning process in each Learning Automata. Having accomplished the learning process, a new generation is produced and the above stages will be continued until a terminal condition is satisfied.

Another model of probability distribution estimation algorithms is Population Based Incremental Learning (Khezri, Meybodi, & Osmani, 2011) that is a technique which combines aspects of Genetic Algorithms and simple competitive learning. Like the GA, PBIL represents the solution set as a population set of solution vectors. In general, each solution vector in the population set, called an individual, is a possible solution of the problem. The population is produced randomly according to the probabilities specified in the probability vector. The population is evaluated and the knowledge about composing of the best individual in the population is acquired and then the probability vector is updated by pushing it towards generating good individuals in the population. After the probability vector being updated, a new generation population is produced according to the updated probability vector, and the cycle is continued until the termination condition is satisfied.

The rest of this work is organized as following. First we describe PSO briefly. Next, we state the sensor placement problem and the proposed algorithm. The performance evaluations and conclusion are then presented.

ABOUT PSO

The PSO algorithm is an optimization technique based on statistical rules which were proposed by Eberhart and Kennedy in 1995 and the proposed algorithm inspired by the social behavior of birds and fishes in searching for food (Kennedy & Eberhart, 1995). Suppose a group of birds are searching for food in a place randomly and food is available in one part of searching area and the birds have no information about the place where the food is available and they only know their distance to the food source. The adopted strategy by birds is that they follow the bird which has minimum distance to the food source.

In PSO algorithm, each answer to the problem is considered as a bird in the search space which is called a particle. Each particle has its own fitness determined by the fitness function. A bird which is close to food source has a better fitness. This algorithm has a continuous nature and it proved its performance in different applications (Firip & Goodman, 2004; Lip, Tang, Meng, & Jp, 2004; Al- Kazemi & Mohan, 2002). There are many subjects who have discrete nature and because there are many problems which have a discrete nature and also because many of both discrete and continuous problems can be solved in a discrete space so there is a need to use the binary PSO algorithm. A copy of binary algorithm was proposed by its designers in 1997 which unfortunately lacks enough convergence (Kennedy & Eberhart, 1997).

DEFINITION OF PROBLEM

The sensor network based on grid-based could be considered as a two or three dimensional network (Dhillon, Chakrabarty, & Iyengar, 2002). A set of sensors are settled on different points of grid points in order to monitor the sensor field. In this section we defined a power vector for each point of the field to show whether these sensors could cover that point on the field or not, for which the number of components are as many as the number of sensors available.

Now if the Euclidean distance between each grid point and the corresponding sensor is less than the coverage radius of the sensor ($d<r$), then the coverage is assumed to be full (1), and it becomes a parallel component of that sensor on the power vector, Otherwise, the coverage is ineffective and the parallel components equaled to (0). If each point on the grid point in a sensor field can be covered by at least one sensor so that the sum of the vector components of that field equals to one, then the field is called completely covered. In Figure 1, a complete and discriminated sensor field of 4*4 with radius =1 is illustrated, in which a target can be detected at any place in the field.

For example in Figure 1 the power vector for point 7 equals to (0, 1, 0, 0) which is calculated based, Hyperbolic function showed in Figure 2, to the velocity component according to Equations (4). The v_{id} in high value indicates that particle's position is unfit, so it causes the value of x_{id} to be changed from 0 to 1 or vice versa, and a low value for x_{id} decreases the probability of changes in the value of x_{id}. Finally if the value of v_{id} is zero, the value of x_{id} is unchanged according to Equations (3).

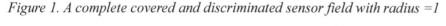

Figure 1. A complete covered and discriminated sensor field with radius =1

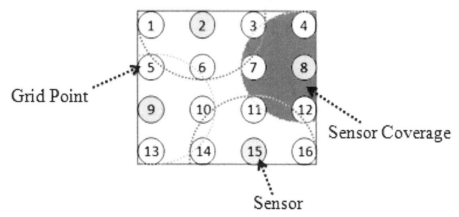

$$V_{id}^d \left(t+1\right) = w\left(t\right) * V_{id}^d \left(t\right) + c_1 * rand\left(p\_best_{id}^d - x_{id}^d\right) +$$
$$c_2 * rand\left(g\_best_{id}^d - x_{id}^d\right), \ d \in 1,...,N_d$$
$$(2)$$

In Equation (2) *Rand* is a random number in the range $(0, 1)$, c_1 and c_2 are learning coefficients. Usually $c1$ is equal to $c2$, and they are in the range $(1, 2)$; the inertia factor w usually is a number in the range $(0, 1)$. Also the v_{id} final value for velocity of each particle is limited to a span to avoid the divergence of each algorithm: $v_{id} \in [-v_{max}, v_{max}]$. And finally the only condition to end an algorithm, we need algorithm convergence or finishing it after several repetitions. Figure 3 shows MDPSO algorithm in pseudo code.

$$if \ rand < S^{'} \left(v_{id} \left(t+1\right)\right) \ then$$
$$x_{id} \left(t+1\right) = exchange\left(x_{id} \left(t\right)\right) \qquad (3)$$
$$else \quad x_{id} \left(t+1\right) = x_{id}(t)$$

$$Sigmoid \left(v_{id}\right) = \frac{1}{1+e^{-v_{id}}}$$
$$S^{'} \left(v_{id}\right) = 2 \times | \left(Sigmoid \left(v_{id}\right) - 0.5 \right|$$
$$(4)$$

MATHEMATICAL MODEL

The sensor placement problem is formulated here as a combinatorial optimization problem. The formulation forms a sensor network which provides either complete or high discrimination depending on the cost limitation. Complete discrimination requires that the minimum Hamming Distance of the power vectors associated with any pair of grid points be at least one. Available parameters in this problem are defined in Table 1.

Figure 2. Hyperbolic function $S^{'} \left(v_{id}\right) Grad_i^j$

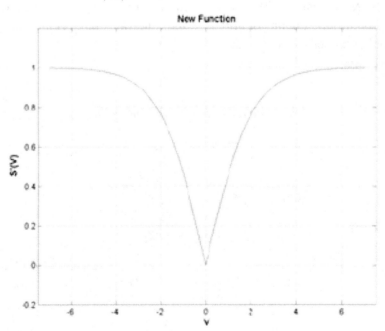

Figure 3. MDPSO pseudo code for Sensor Placement

For each particle $id \in 1,\ldots,s\, do$

    Initialize v_{id} (set v_{id} to 0.5)

    Repeat

      Calculate particle position according equation (3)

      Until *coverage* is satisfied according equation (5)

    Set $p\_best_{id} = x_{id}$

End for

Repeat

    For each particle $id \in 1,\ldots,s\ do$

      Evaluate the fitness of particle $id, f(x_{id})$

      Update p_best_{id} using $p\_best_{id}(t+1)$

$$= \begin{cases} p\_best_{id}(t) & if\ f\left(x_{id}\left(t+1\right)\right) \geq f\left(p\_best_{id}\left(t\right)\right) \\ x_{id}\left(t+1\right) & if\ f\left(x_{id}\left(t+1\right)\right) < f\left(p\_best_{id}\left(t\right)\right) \end{cases}$$

      Update g_best_{id} using

$$p\_best_{id} \in \left\{p\_best_0, p\_best_1, \ldots, p\_best_s\right\} = min\left\{f\left(p\_best_0\left(t\right)\right), \ldots, f\left(p\_best_s\left(t\right)\right)\right\}$$

      For each dimension $j \in 1,\ldots,\mathrm{N}_d\ do$

        Apply velocity update using equation (2)

      End loop

      Repeat

        Apply position update according equation (3)

        Until *coverage* is satisfied according equation (5)

    End loop

Until some convergence criteria is satisfied

SIMULATION RESULTS

This section presents the simulation results. Firstly, the performance of our proposed algorithm is evaluated when small sensor fields are deployed. The purpose of the experiment is whether the algorithm can find the optimal solution under a minimum cost constraint. Then, the performance results in the case of larger sensor fields are presented under various cost constraints.

Here we assume that the population value is 30, $c_1 = c_2 = 2$ and $v_{max} = 6.0$. The value of w from 0.9 to 0.2 is considered as decreasing values. The proposed method is examined on sensor field with different area. The results confirm the superiority of the proposed algorithm against the Simulated Annealing algorithm (Lin & Chiu, 2005) considering the convergence factor. In LAEDA and PBIL algorithms, a high value of *Se* genomes was chosen for updating the genome's probability model. In all experiments, we assume the value of *Se* as a value equals to half of population of each generation and Learning Rate is 0.01.

Table 1. The parameters for defined Mathematical Model

Given Parameters	
$A=\{1, 2,\dots m\}$	Index set of the sensor's candidate locations.
$B=\{1, 2\dots n\}$	Index set of the location in the sensor field, $m \leq n$
r_k	Detection radius of the sensor located at k, $k \in A$.
d_{ij}	Euclidean distance between location i and j, $i, j \in B$.
C_k	The cost of the sensor located at k, $k \in A$.
G	Total Cost limitation
Decision Variables	
y_k	is 1, if a sensor is allocated at location k and 0 otherwise, $k \in A$.
(5) pv_i $=(pv_{i1}, pv_{i2},\dots,pv_{ik})$	The power vector of location i, where pv_{ik} is 1 if the target at location i can be detected by the sensor at location k and 0 otherwise, where $i \in B$, $k \in A$.
Objective Function	
Objective Function is cost limitation and the complete coverage that cost limitation formula is:	$$\sum_{k=1}^{m} c_k y_k \leq G$$

In SA algorithm, the parameters of the cooling schedule are $\alpha=0.75$ and $\beta=1.3$. The initial value of r and t are $5n$ and 0.1 and n is the number of grids in the sensor field. The frozen temperature t_f is $t_0/30$ and the cost of each sensor is equal to one.

At first each algorithm is run for five times and average results for different areas are calculated and compared in Table 2, then each algorithm is run for 20 times and average results for different areas are calculated and compared in Table 3.

A. Experiment I

Experiment I, evaluates the performance of our proposed algorithm for smaller rectangular sensor fields which have no more than 30 grid points. The results are compared with those obtained in SA, PBIL and LAEDA.

Firstly, we find a minimum sensor density for a complete covered and discriminated sensor field.

Then, an attempt is made to obtain the better result by using the proposed algorithm under a sensor density constraint.

Table 2 and Table 3 show the number of sensors in four algorithms when they cover the sensor field with various areas. At first each algorithm is run 5 times and the average results for different areas are calculated and compared in Table 2. Then each algorithm is run 20 times and the average results for different areas are calculated and compared in Table 3.

Simulation results show that the algorithms in Table 2, 3 generate alike solutions across low runs number but our proposed algorithm reach to better solutions across more runs number. Note that MDPSO is more rapid than other algorithms in Tables 2, and 3.

Table 3 shows, in all cases, that our proposed algorithm achieves the best deployment of sensor fields with a minimum sensor density. The required sensor density is between 25% and 33%. Results of simulation of placement problem show

Table 2. Comparison between three algorithms and the proposed algorithm for some target area values (average of 5 runs)

Area	# of Sensors				
	SA	LAEDA	PBIL	MDPSO	MDPSO's Sensor Density
4*3	6	5	6	4	0.33
4*4	7	4	7	4	0.25
6*3	8	6	8	6	0.33
6*4	10	9	10	8	0.33
7*3	9	7	9	7	0.33
8*3	10	9	10	9	0.37
9*3	11	9	11	10	0.37
5*3	6	5	6	5	0.33
5*5	10	9	10	10	0.4
6*5	12	10	12	11	0.36
7*4	12	11	12	10	0.357
10*3	12	11	12	11	0.366

that Modified Discrete PSO Algorithm improves PBIL. The proposed algorithm for sensor field of 10×3 finds the solution in a few minutes.

Figure 4 confirms the superiority of the proposed algorithm against the SA, PBIL and LAEDA algorithms considering Sensor density (in #Sensors) vs. target area parameter, and Figure 5

Table 3. Comparison between three algorithms and the proposed algorithm for some target area values (average of 20 runs)

Area	# of Sensors				
	SA	LAEDA	PBIL	MDPSO	MDPSO's Sensor Density
4*3	6	4	6	4	0.33
4*4	7	4	6	4	0.25
6*3	8	6	8	5	0.27
6*4	10	7	9	7	0.29
7*3	9	7	8	7	0.33
8*3	10	9	10	7	0.27
9*3	11	9	10	8	0.296
5*3	6	5	5	4	0.26
5*5	10	9	10	7	0.28
6*5	12	10	11	9	0.3
7*4	12	9	11	8	0.28
10*3	12	11	12	9	0.3

Figure 4. Sensor density (in #Sensors) vs. target area parameter

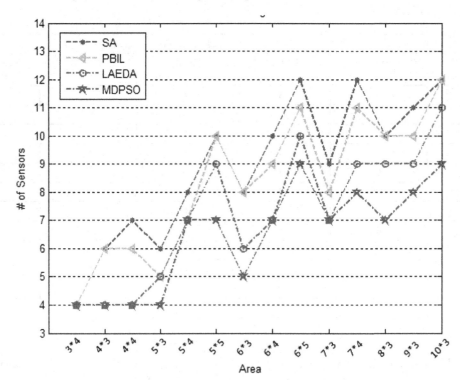

Figure 5. Sensor density (in percent) vs. target area parameter

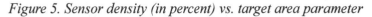

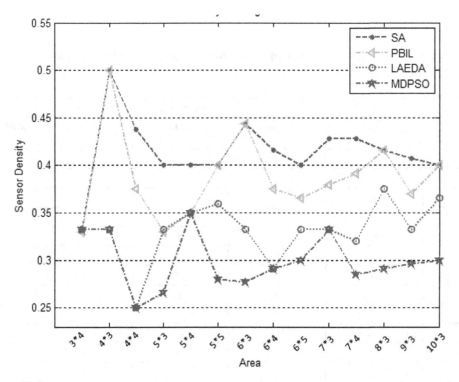

Figure 6. Sensor density (in #Sensors) for 15*15 sensor field

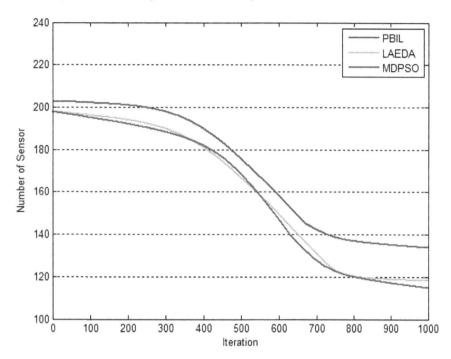

Figure 7. Sensor area with 9 × 3 grid points

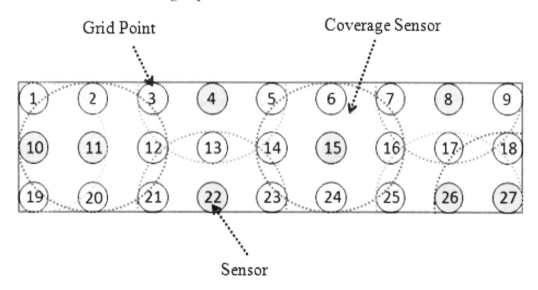

confirm the superiority of the proposed algorithm against the SA, PBIL and LAEDA algorithms considering Sensor density (in percent) vs. target area parameter.

B. Experiment II

In this experiment, a large sensor field, with 15 × 15 grid points is considered. The radius of

Figure 8. Sensor area with 6 × 4 grid points

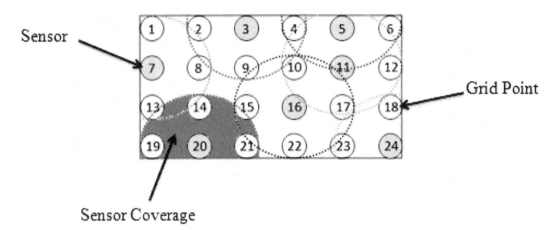

the each sensor is one. Obtained results using the proposed algorithm are compared with the best solution obtained by the SA, LAEDA and PBIL approaches. The best solution which has a minimum objective value is founded in 1000 arbitrarily generated solutions.

Figure 6 shows that the required density for obtaining the desired solution using the proposed algorithm is 50% in 1000 arbitrarily generations

but other approaches are associated with a relatively high density (58% and 62%). The proposed algorithm can reach to a completed coverage with a very low sensor density.

Sensor density formula is:

$$Sensor\,density\left(\%\right) = \left(\sum_{k=1}^{m} \frac{y_k}{n}\right) \times 100\% \qquad (6)$$

Figure 9. Sensor area with 5 × 5 grid points

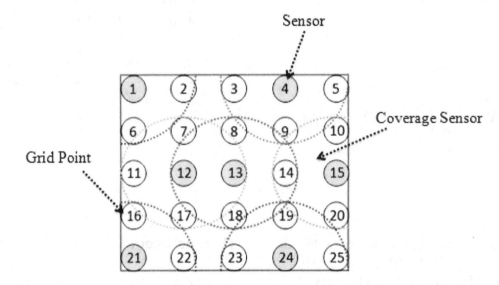

Where

$$y_k = \begin{cases} 1, \text{if a sensor is allocated at location k} \\ 0, otherwise \end{cases}$$

and n is the number of grids in sensor field

Figures 7, 8, and 9 show sensor area with 9×3, 6×4 and 5×5 grid points after that MDPSO reaches to its solution.

CONCLUSION

This paper considers the sensor placement problem for locating targets under constraints (complete coverage of sensor network with minimum costs). Firstly, we defined this NP-complete problem as a combinatorial optimization model then the modified binary PSO algorithm expanded for solving the problem. The results show that our algorithm compared to simulated annealing algorithm, is more able to detect the optimization solution in a limited time and costs, which provides placement of sensors to increase the coverage on the sensor field. Also it improves the chance of escaping of local optimal. In addition the proposed algorithm is more useful and scalable than PBIL, LAEDA and SA. Since sensor placement in the Wireless Sensor Networks (WSN) is important, we should find better intelligent algorithms.

ACKNOWLEDGMENT

This research is a bridged group work in subject to sensor placement.

REFERENCES

Akyildiz, I. F., & Su, W., Sankarasubramaniam, & Cayirci, E. (2002). Wireless sensor networks: A survey. *Computer Networks*, *38*(4), 393–422. doi:10.1016/S1389-1286(01)00302-4

Al-Kazemi, B., & Mohan, C. K. (2002). Training feed forward neural networks using multi-phase particle swarm optimization. In *Proceedings of the 9th International Conference on Neural Information* (Vol. 5).

Bose, P., Morin, P., Stojmenovic, I., & Urrutia, J. (2001). Routing with guaranteed delivery in adhoc wireless networks. *Wireless Networks*, *7*(6). doi:10.1023/A:1012319418150

Chakrabarty, K., Iyengar, S. S., Qi, H., & Cho, E. (2002). Grid coverage for surveillance and target location in distributed sensor networks. *IEEE Transactions on Computers*, *51*(12). doi:10.1109/TC.2002.1146711

Chellappan, S., Bai, X., Mam, B., & Xuan, D. (2005). Mobility limited flip-based sensor networks deployment. *IEEE Transactions on Parallel and Distributed Systems*, *18*(2), 199–211. doi:10.1109/TPDS.2007.28

Chong, C. Y., & Kumar, S. P. (2003). Sensor networks: Evolution, opportunities, and challenges. *Proceedings of the IEEE*, *91*(8), 1247–1256. doi:10.1109/JPROC.2003.814918

Darpa. (2007). *Creating & preventing strategic surprise*. Retrieved from http://www.darpa.mil/default.aspx

Dhillon, S. S., & Chakrabarty, K. (2003). Sensor placement for effective coverage and surveillance in distributed sensor networks. *IEEE Wireless Communications and Networking*, *3*, 1609–1614.

Dhillon, S. S., Chakrabarty, K., & Iyengar, S. S. (2002). Sensor placement for grid coverage under imprecise detections. In *Proceedings of the Fifth International Conference on Information Fusion* (Vol. 2, pp. 1581-1587).

Firip, H. A., & Goodman, E. (2004). Swarmed feature selection. In *Proceedings of the 33rd Applied Imagery Pattern Recognition Workshop* (pp. 112-118).

Gage, D. W. (1992). Command control for many-robot systems. In *Proceedings of the 19th Annual AUVS Technical Symposium.*

Indu, S., Chaudhury, S., Mittal, N. R., & Bhattacharyya, A. (2009). Optimal sensor placement for surveillance of large spaces. In *Proceedings of the Third International Conference on Digital Object Identifier* (pp. 1-8).

Kennedy, J., & Eberhart, R. C. (1995). Particle swarm optimization. In *Proceedings of the IEEE International Conference on Neural Networks* (pp. 1942-1948).

Kennedy, J., & Eberhart, R. C. (1997). A discrete binary version of the particle swarm algorithm. In *Proceedings of the Conference on Systems, Man, and Cybernetics* (pp. 4104-4108).

Khezri, S., Meybodi, M., & Osmani, A. (2011). Fuzzy adaptive PBIL based sensor placement in WSN. In *Proceedings of the International Symposium on Computer Networks and Distributed Systems* (pp. 216-221).

Khezri, S., Osmani, A., & Gholami, M. (2011). Estimation of distribution algorithm based on learning automata for sensors placement in wireless sensor networks. In *Proceedings of the 3nd National Conference on Computer/Electrical and IT Engineering.*

Lin, F. Y. S., & Chiu, P. L. (2005). A near-optimal sensor placement algorithm to achieve complete coverage/discrimination in sensor networks. *IEEE Communications Letters, 9*(1), 43–45.

Lip, H. B., Tang, Y. Y., Meng, J., & Jp, Y. (2004). Neural networks learning using vbest model particle swarm optimization. In *Proceedings of the 3rd International Conference on Machine Learning and Cybernetics* (pp. 3157-3159).

Mainwaring, A., Polastre, J., Szewczyk, R., Culler, D., & Anderson, J. (2002). Wireless sensor networks for habitat monitoring. In *Proceedings of the 1st ACM International Workshop on Wireless Sensor Networks and Applications* (pp. 88-97).

Meguerdichian, S., Koushanfar, F., Potkonjak, M., & Srivastava, M. B. (2001). Coverage problems in wireless ad-hoc sensor networks. In *Proceedings of the International Conference on Mobile Computing and Networking* (pp. 1380-1387).

Osmani, A., Dehghan, M., Pourakbar, H., & Emdadi, P. (2009). Fuzzy-based movement-assisted sensor deployment method in wireless sensor networks. In *Proceedings of the International Conference on Computational Intelligence, Communication Systems and Networks* (pp. 90-95).

Osmani, A., Haghighat, A. T., Dehghan, M., & Emdadi, P. (2010). FSPNS: Fuzzy sensor placement based onstate. In *Proceedings of the International Conference on Computer Modeling and Simulation.*

Padmavathi, M., Yong, R., & Yelena, Y. (2006). Key frame-based video summarization using Delanunay clustering. *International Journal on Digital Libraries, 6*, 219–232. doi:10.1007/s00799-005-0129-9

Pottie, G. J. (1998). Wireless sensor networks. In *Proceedings of the Information Theory Workshop* (pp. 139-140).

Pottie, G. J., & Caiser, W. (2000). Wireless sensor networks. *Communications of the ACM, 43*(5). doi:10.1145/332833.332838

Qi, H., Iyengar, S. S., & Chakrabarty, K. (2001). Distributed sensor fusion – a review of recent research. *Journal of the Franklin Institute, 338*, 655–668. doi:10.1016/S0016-0032(01)00026-6

Rahman, M. O., Razzaque, M. A., & Hong, C.-H. S. (2007). Probabilistic sensor deployment in wireless sensor network: A new approach. In *Proceedings of the 9th International Conference on Advanced Communication Technology* (pp. 12-14).

Rajagopalan, R., Niu, R., Mohan, C. K., Varshney, P. K., & Drozd, A. L. (2008). Sensor placement algorithms for target localization in sensor networks. In *Proceedings of the IEEE Radar Conference* (pp. 1-6).

Rostami, M., & Nezam Abadi, H. (2006). Modified binary PSO. In *Proceedings of the IEEE 14th International Conference on Electrical Engineering*, Iran.

Sasikumar, P., Vasudevan, S. K., Vivek, C., & Subashri, V. (2009). Heuristic approaches with probabilistic management for node placement in wireless sensor networks. *International Journal of Recent Trends in Engineering, 2*(4).

Stojmenovic, I. (1999). *A scalable quorum based location update scheme for routing in ad hoc wireless network* (Tech. Rep. No. TR-99-09). Ottawa, ON, Canada: University of Ottawa.

Wang, G., Cao, G., & La Porta, T. (2004). Proxy-based sensor deployment for mobile sensor networks. In *Proceedings of the 1st IEEE International Conference on Mobile Ad-hoc and Sensor Systems* (pp. 493-502).

Wang, G., Cao, G., & La Porta, T. (2006). Movement-assisted sensor deployment. *IEEE Transactions on Mobile Computing, 5*(6). doi:10.1109/TMC.2006.80

Wu, X., Cho, J., Auriol, B. J. D., & Lee, S. (2007). Mobility-assisted relocation for self-deployment in wireless sensor networks. *IEICE Transactions on Communications, 90*(8), 2056–2069. doi:10.1093/ietcom/e90-b.8.2056

Yang, S., Li, M., & Wu, J. (2007). Scan-based movement-assisted sensor deployment methods in wireless sensor networks. *IEEE Transactions on Parallel and Distributed Systems, 18*(8).

Zou, Y., & Chakrabarty, K. (2004). Sensor deployment and target localization in distributed sensor networks. *IEEE Transactions on Embedded Computer Systems, 3*(1).

This work was previously published in the International Journal of Grid and High Performance Computing, Volume 3, Issue 3, edited by Emmanuel Udoh and Ching-Hsien Hsu, pp. 54-68, copyright 2011 by IGI Publishing (an imprint of IGI Global).

Section 4
High Performance Computing

Chapter 12
High Performance Computing Design by Code Migration for Distributed Desktop Computing Grids

Makoto Yoshida
Okayama University of Science, Japan

Kazumine Kojima
Okayama University of Science, Japan

ABSTRACT

Large scale loosely coupled PCs can organize clusters and form desktop computing grids on sharing each processing power; power of PCs, transaction distributions, network scales, network delays, and code migration algorithms characterize the performance of the computing grids. This article describes the design methodologies of workload management in distributed desktop computing grids. Based on the code migration experiments, transfer policy for computation was determined and several simulations for location policies were examined, and the design methodologies for distributed desktop computing grids are derived from the simulation results. The language for distributed desktop computing is designed to accomplish the design methodologies.

INTRODUCTION

Grid system is a type of distributed systems, and it can be categorized into three classes: computing grid, data grid and service grid (Krauter et al., 2002; Choi et al., 2008). This article deals with

DOI: 10.4018/978-1-4666-2065-0.ch012

the computing grid. The purpose of the computing grid is to use the existing computing powers effectively, those scattered around in one or more organizations. Several hundred PCs, such as Note PCs, Desktop PCs and WSs, are assumed in our model. User jobs, namely transactions, can be executed on the local or remote computer systems depending upon the workload in the system. If the workload of the system that the job entered is heavy enough for processing, it must be properly migrated to the other site through migration. However, the effectiveness of the code migration against the migration overhead must be evaluated (Coulouris et al., 2005).

The network of the computing grids we modeled is shown in Figure 1. It consists of many computing nodes and one information server. On decentralized control, it does not have the information server. Figure 2 shows the taxonomy of the distributed computing systems (Venugopal et al., 2006; Theotokis & Spinellis, 2004). The shadow area is the topics of this article. For migrating the transactions, both the transfer policy that determines the migration decision and the location policy that determines the site to be migrated must be properly provided according to the application environment (Shah et al., 2007). The environment of the system is getting more complex with the increasing and diversifying applications.

However, little work for the code migration has been associated with the application environment. Depending upon the migration policy and the environment situated, the performance of the system greatly varies. The scales of transactions and networks, the workload patterns, the power of computers, code migration algorithms, all of these characterize the performance of the system. The relations of these characteristics, the pros and cons, must be analyzed, and the boundaries of the code migration must be specified in designing the distributed computing grids.

We need some methodologies to design the workload of transactions in various complex application environments to have a good performance system. Shah (2007) has shown the theoretical approach for code migration. We develop the practical approach in this article. Code migration overhead was exemplified by implementing the code migration system. Based on the experiments, several centralized and decentralized al-

Figure 1. Computing grid model

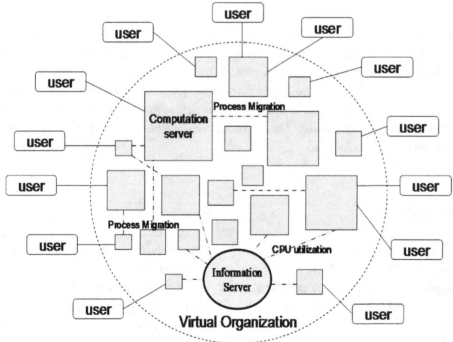

Figure 2. Taxonomy of distributed computing systems

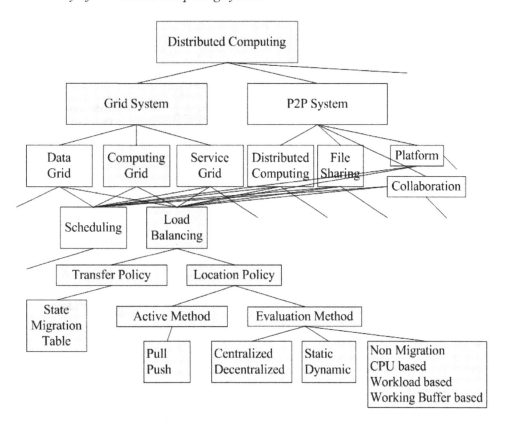

gorithms for various location policies are simulated and evaluated. And, design methodologies for distributed desktop computing grids in various environments are derived from several simulation results. The language for distributed computing was also designed to carry out the methodologies derived.

EXPERIMENTAL MODEL

The experimental system that migrates objects among PCs was implemented to measure the migration overhead. The system structure is shown in Figure 3. A transaction can be transferred to the other site to perform the computation by the agent. The performance of the two systems, the one that was executed at the local site without migrating object code and the other that was executed at the remote site, was measured and compared (Yoshida & Sakamoto, 2007).

Some results are shown in Table 1, Table 2, and Table 3. These were obtained by varying the transaction workload and the CPU utilization. Each Table shows the response time of a transaction executed at the local site, the response time executed at the remote site, the transmission time and the migration overhead. Figure 4 summarizes the results. The right side of the box in Figure 4 indicates the workload of a transaction, and "R" indicates remote. So, for example, 20R means the workload of the transaction is 20 percent and it was executed at the remote site. The threshold point; that is the intersection of the two response time graphs, the one for local processing and the other for remote processing by migrating the object code to remote site, was obtained varying the CPU utilization and the transaction workload. The change of threshold points varying the

Figure 3. System structure

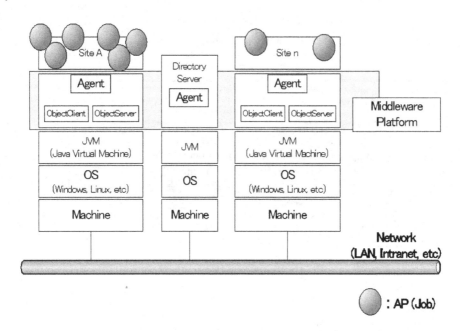

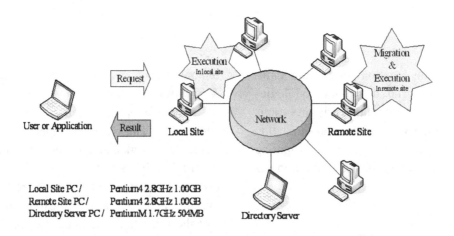

Local Site PC /   Pentium4 2.8GHz 1.00GB
Remote Site PC /   Pentium4 2.8GHz 1.00GB
Directory Server PC /   PentiumM 1.7GHz 504MB

transaction workload is depicted as squares in Figure 4. From Figure 4, we obtained the migration state table, MST, shown in Figure 5. We divided the graph in Figure 5 into three states: busy state, normal state and idle state, through setting some widths around threshold points (Santos, 1996). The axis X indicates the workload of a transaction and the axis Y indicates the average CPU utilization of the site. When the transaction comes in and the CPU utilization of the site was in normal or busy state, the object code of the transaction can be moved to the remote site in which the migration state in the computer is in the idle state, by negotiating with the information server. MST, shown in Figure 5, works as a decision table for code migration at each site, and it is used for carrying out the transfer policy in the following simulations

Table 1. Response time (10% AP workload)

CPU (%) utilization	Local (msec)	Remote	transmission	migrration
0	1078	1219	16	188
10	1250	1234	16	282
20	1422	1344	32	219
30	1531	1281	31	296
40	1672	1375	16	235
50	1843	1360	15	343
60	2031	1390	47	298
70	2438	1407	47	359
80	3265	1656	16	281
90	5718	1594	47	360
99	13875	1672	94	294

Table 2. Response time (60% AP workload)

CPU (%) utilization	Local (msec)	Remote	transmission	migration
0	78	234	15	250
10	78	281	47	235
20	110	297	16	219
30	79	344	31	234
40	78	343	31	235
50	94	375	32	219
60	125	407	47	250
70	282	438	47	265
80	547	547	31	235
90	781	469	78	329
99	1593	594	47	598

LOAD BALANCING ALGORITHMS

The transfer policy and the location policy must be properly defined for computing grid (Shah et al., 2007). The transfer policy in our model is determined by the migration state table; that was obtained by implementing and evaluating the experimental model, previously described. To satisfy the location policy, the algorithm for load balancing to find out the appropriate site for object migration must be provided. Many load balancing algorithms have been proposed (Coulouris et al., 2005, Choi & Buyya, 2008, Shah et al., 2007): pull and push approach for active method, and several algorithms for evaluation method exist, as is shown in Figure 2. However, little work has been associated with the application environments.

We compared four centralized algorithms, including the working buffer algorithm (Yoshida & Sakamoto, 2007), and one decentralized algorithm, by varying transaction patterns, workloads, network scales and network delays.

Centralized Algorithm

There exists several centralized location policy algorithms (Yoshida & Sakamoto, 2008): the random based selection algorithm, the CPU power based selection algorithm, the traffic based selection algorithm and the working buffer based selection algorithm. The random based algorithm (RB) selects the site randomly from available sites. The CPU based algorithm (CB) selects the site by the order of CPU powers, and the traffic based algorithm (TB) selects the site by the order of workloads at each site. The working buffer algorithm (WB) selects the site by the number of available working buffer at each site. The literature (Yoshida & Sakamoto, 2008) showed that the number of the available working buffer must be chosen carefully.

The protocol of each algorithm is shown in Figure 6. Figure 6(a) shows the sequences based on RB. Figure 6(b) is the sequences based on CB. Figure 6(c) is the sequences based on TB. The CB algorithm uses the multicast message to have the traffic information at each site. Figure 6(d) shows the sequences based on WB. The available buffer size at each site is given statically, and maintained at each site. The information server asks the value of the current WB at each site when the request for migration arrived.

Table 3. Response time (AP workload 99%)

CPU (%) Utilization	Local (msec)	Remote	transmission	migration
0	1641	1828	15	219
10	1906	1812	46	282
20	2140	1813	62	297
30	2468	1796	47	250
40	2578	1937	31	203
50	2781	1829	31	250
60	3156	1922	31	281
70	3156	2000	47	313
80	5093	2079	47	328
90	6890	2063	63	265
99	14078	2515	93	360

Decentralized Algorithm

This section describes the autonomous decentralized control algorithm (DC) adopted at each site. Figure 6(e) shows the sequences of DC, and 6(f) shows the algorithm adopted at each site. Each site determines the migration site autonomously by using the DC algorithm described in Figure 6(f). Both the sender and the receiver processes, shown in Figure 6(f), exist at each site. The sender broadcasts the migration request to the grid members when the state is not in the idle state, and waits the acknowledgements from the members. If several acknowledgements are returned, it selects the site that has the earliest timestamp attached, and migrate the code to that site. On the other hand, if the receiver receives the migration request and if its state is in the idle state, it returns the acknowledgement with its current timestamp. After the acknowledgement, if it has received Move_Transaction message with earlier timestamp or it has not received Move_Transaction message, then it cancels the migration request, as is described in Figure 6(f).

SIMULATION

A simulation model of each site of the system is designed based on the prototype experiment. Figure 7 shows the simulation model. Each site runs transaction manager that directs a transaction which has just originated from that site. If the processor is idle, a transaction is processed at that site. Otherwise, a transaction must wait in the queue to finish the other transactions, or must move to the other site to finish computing. The judge of the migration is determined by checking the Migration State Table situated at each site. The agent negotiates the movement of the transaction with the information server if it were the centralized control. The simulation was carried out by using the event based algorithm.

Simulation Model

The simulation model, shown in Figure 7, was organized and several simulations are carried out. The parameters we selected for the model are the following.

1. **Site number:** 50 to 500 sites for computing are assumed, and 1 site for information server is assumed for centralized control.
2. **Average arrival time:** The arrival transaction patterns at each site follow one of the three different distributions: a Normal distribution, a Poisson distribution, and a Uniform distribution. From 1000 to 15000 transactions at each site are assumed.
3. **Processing time:** The processing time of transactions at each site is assumed to follow a normal distribution. The average processing time is assumed to have 2 simulation units.
4. **CPU power:** The CPU power at each site follows a normal distribution.
5. **Transmission time**: The time taken to transmit a message from one site to another for

Figure 4. Threshold points

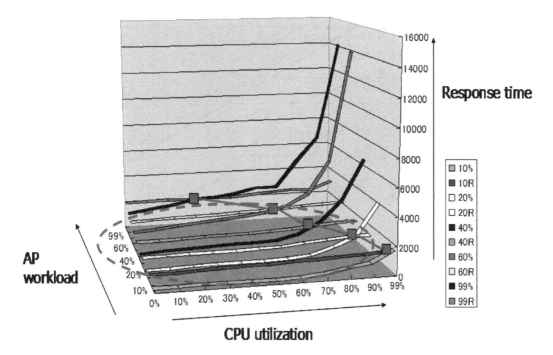

migration is assumed to vary from 1 unit to 20 simulation units.

6. **Object migration time:** The time taken to migrate object code of a transaction to the remote site is assumed to be constant. 10 simulation units are assumed.

7. **Transfer policy:** The migration state table given in Figure 5 was provided at each site.

8. **Location policy:** Six location policy algorithms are compared; these are the random based algorithm (RB), the CPU power based algorithm (CB), the traffic based algorithm (TB), the working buffer based algorithm (WB), the decentralized control algorithm (DC), and the non-migration algorithm (NM).

The resulting statistics collected are the following.

1. **Average response time:** The average time lapse between the moment a transaction is requested, and the moment it obtains an answer.

2. **Average throughput:** The average transactions processed per unit time.

3. **Remote processing rate:** The rate of transactions processed at remote sites.

4. **Rejected transaction rate:** The rate of transactions rejected for processing at remote sites.

5. **Average messages transferred:** The average number of messages used to process a transaction.

Several simulations were performed, and several statistics were collected. In the literature (Yoshida & Sakamoto, 2007, 2008), the statistics collected were evaluated. In this article, we focus the evaluation factor to the response time.

Figure 5. Migration state table

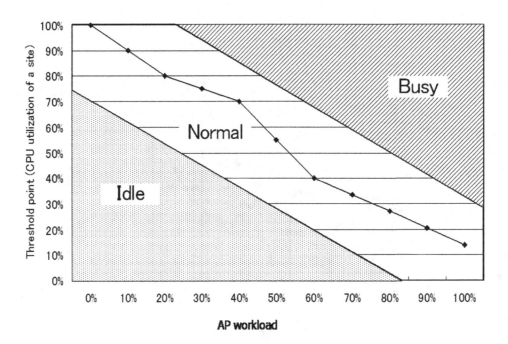

Simulation1: Performance Comparison of Various Load Balancing Algorithms

Several load balancing algorithms for location policy were evaluated. Figures 8 and 9 show the comparison of the response time. The results are summarized as follows.

1. The performance of the centralized location policy algorithms for load balancing is shown in Figure 8. The result was as follows.

```
(good) WB > {TB, CB} > RB > NM (bad)
```

Comparing the NM with the WB that is the best algorithm in the centralized control, the WB was 8.85 times better than the NM.

2. The decentralized control algorithm (DC) and the WB algorithm are compared in the simulation. Figure 9 shows the response time compared. When the traffic is not heavy, the

WB works very efficiently. When the traffic is 7000, the WB is 10.42 times faster than the NM, and 19% faster than the DC when traffic is 6500. However, as the traffic increases, the best algorithm changes from the WB to the DC. In heavy traffics, the DC is faster 25% than the WB when the traffic is 7500, and 2.95 times faster than the NM when the traffic is 8000. And, when the traffic is very heavy, both algorithms, the DC and the WB, have almost converged to the same response time.

Simulation2: Performance Comparison of Response Time Varying Transaction Patterns

The distribution of transactions at each site was varied and evaluated. Three distributions are assumed: a Normal distribution, a Poisson distribution and a Uniform distribution. And the response time was compared. Figure 9 shows the response time for the Normal distribution. Figure 10 is the

Figure 6(a) RB protocol;(b) CB protocol;(c) TB protocol;(d). WB protocol; (e) DC protocol;(f) Decentralized control algorithm

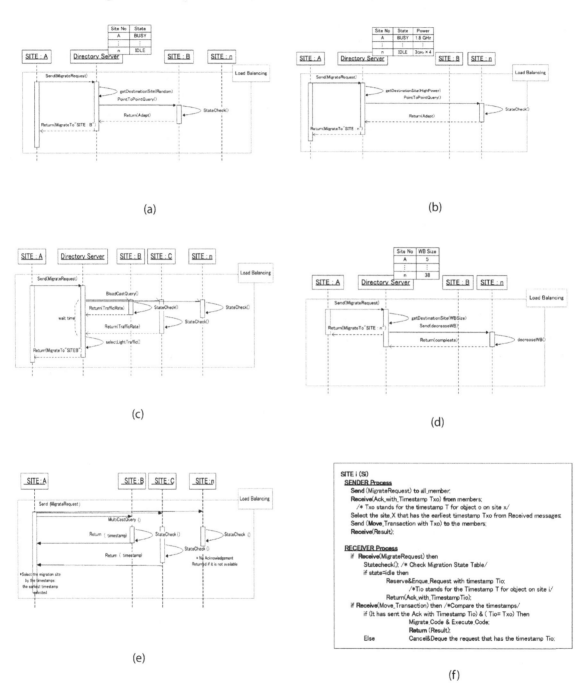

response time for the Poisson distribution, and Figure 11 is the response time for the Uniform distribution.

The pattern of transaction distributions affects greatly the response time, especially in heavy traffic environment. It gets worsen exponentially as the traffic increases. However, we can observe

Figure 7. Simulation model of each site

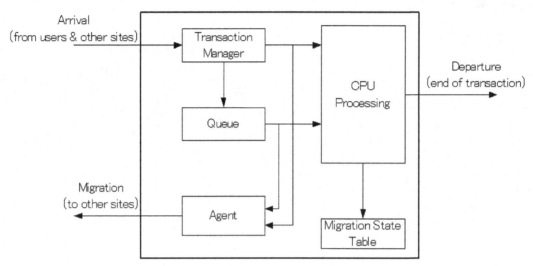

that the increase of the workload by the Uniform distribution pattern does not influence the response time so much; it has the best response time comparing to the other transaction patterns, and the worst is the Normal distribution pattern. The effectiveness of the transaction patterns can be ordered as follows.

```
(good) Uniform > Poisson > Normal
(bad)
```

The non migration policy get worsen the response time immediately when the traffic increases. The DC and WB have a threshold at which the response time gets worsen; it is around

Figure 8. Response time (centralized)

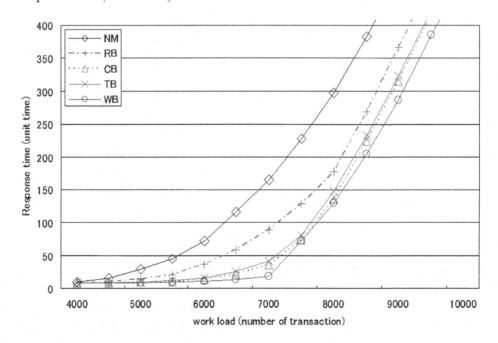

Figure 9. Response time (decentralized)

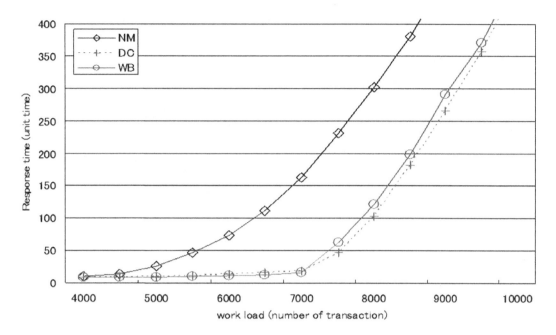

Figure 10. Comparison of the response time (poisson distribution)

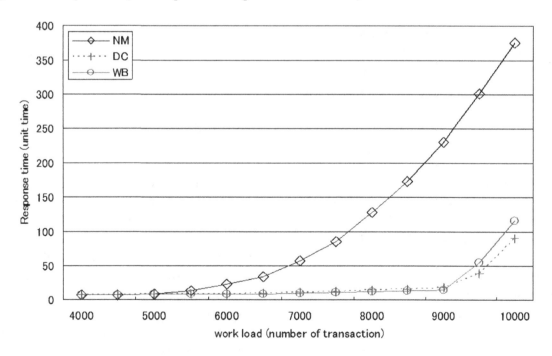

Figure 11. Comparison of the response time (uniform distribution)

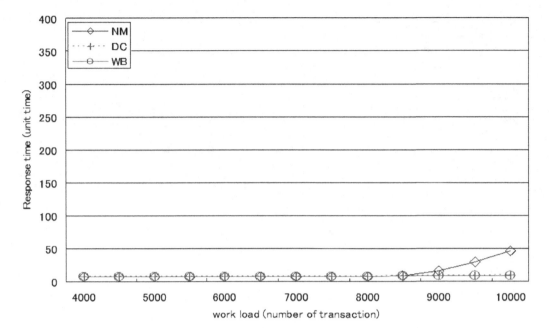

7000 in the Normal distribution, and around 9000 in the Poisson distribution.

Figure 12 shows the migration domain of the applications, which was obtained from Figure 9, 10 and 11. It indicates the migration area of transactions. The migration area of transactions changes according to the transaction distribution patterns and the workloads of transactions. When the shape of transactions is similar to the Normal distribution pattern and the workloads of the transactions are between 4000 and 7000, both migration algorithms, the DC and BW, work efficiently. When the workloads of transactions are 7000, each transaction will have about 9 times better response time than the NM, if the migration were performed. When the workload exceeds 7000, both algorithms get worsen exponentially, so it had better not to migrate the transactions. When the transactions arrive as a Poisson distribution pattern and the workloads of transactions are between 4500 and 9000, the migration works efficiently. It will have 15 times better response time than the NM. When transactions arrive as a

Uniform distribution pattern, the migration will have tremendous effect. Though the NM has the threshold point at 8500, the migration methods do not have the threshold point. It works over the threshold point continuously.

Simulation3: Performance Comparison of Response Time Varying Grid Scales

The computing sites are scaled up to 500 sites from 50 sites, and the same simulations are performed. Figure 13 shows the response time of each site in the case of 50 sites. Figure 14 shows the response time scaling up the sites to 500. It can be observed that the increase of sites does not affect the response time at all. Scaling up sites did not affect the response time of each site. Even though the sites increase, the average response time in the grids will not change in our model, if the computing scales were in the order of hundreds.

Figure 12. Migration domain

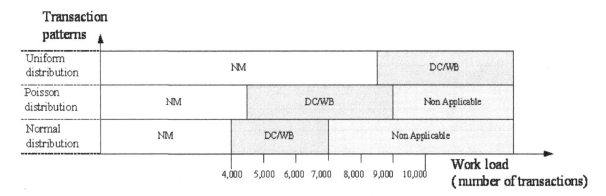

Simulation4: Performance Comparison of Response Time Varying Network Delay

To observe the influence of network delay, the transmission time is changed, and the response time is observed. The ratio of transmission time to processing time per transaction is ranged from 1:1 to 1:20. Figures 15 and 16 show the response time, obtained by changing the transmission time and the workload of transactions. The intersections of the NM and the others are shifting to the right side in the graph by increasing the workload.

When the workload of transactions is 4000 and the network delay is less than the 10 times of the processing time per transaction, the migration works effectively. When the workload of transactions is 5000 and the network delay is less than the 20 times of the processing time per transaction, the migration works effectively.

As the network delay increases, it get worsen the response time lineally. The equation for the response time graph can be described as follows.

```
<network delay> / 2 + C (1)
```

Figure 13. Response time (50 sites)

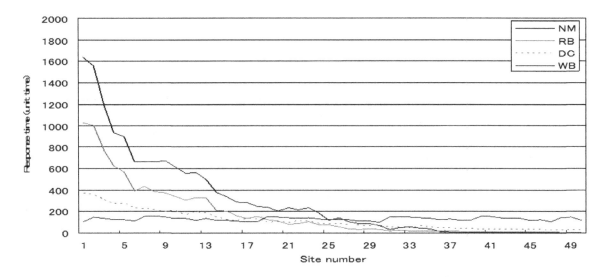

Figure 14. Response time (500 sites)

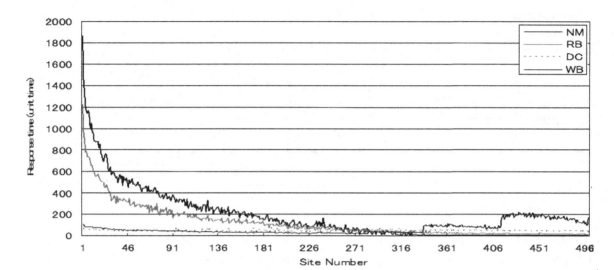

Network delay is the relative time unit compared to the processing time. C is the constant value determined by the workload of transactions. Given the network delay and C, the upper bound of the migration domain can be obtained by the equation. If the value obtained by the equation (1) is greater than the non-migrating response time, then migration should not be performed, or the constant value C has to be adjusted. Given the network delay and the value of C, we can calculate the response time and compare with the anticipated response time.

Figure 15. Response time (4000 transaction /site assumed)

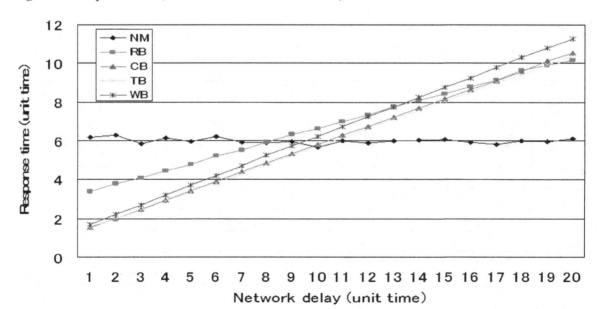

Figure 16. Response time(5000 transactions/site assumed)

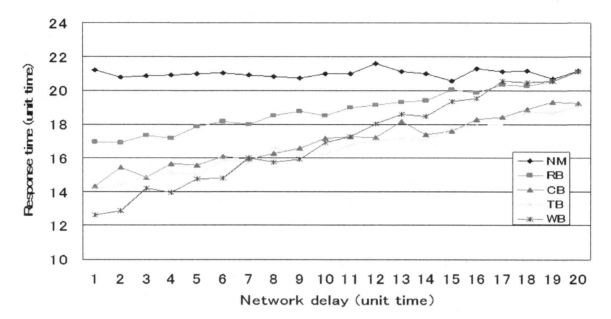

Simulation Results

The results of the simulations are summarized as follows.

1. Several load balancing algorithms were evaluated and compared with the non migration algorithm (NM). The effective order of the location policy algorithms for response time is as follows.

```
(good) DC > WB> {TB,CB} > RB > NM
(bad)
```

On comparing the threshold points that the response time get worse, we observed that the WB algorithm is 8.8 times faster than the NM algorithm. Moreover, the DC algorithm is 34% faster than the WB algorithm.

2. A pattern of transactions affects the response time of the system tremendously. The effective order of the transaction patterns for response time can be observed as follows.

```
(good) Uniform > Poisson > Normal
(bad)
```

The workload of transactions affects the response time tremendously. It is possible to improve the response time 41.8 times faster when the workload of transactions is appropriately controlled and the transactions are migrated appropriately.

3. The increase of sites in our model does not affect the response time of transactions at each site when the grid scales were in the order of hundreds.

4. When the network delay is very large compared to the processing time of a transaction, it is useless to migrate the transaction. The migration must be designed in relation to the network delay and the response time of a transaction.

DESIGN METHODOLOGIES

The language and the design methodologies for the desktop computing grids are described (Yoshida & Kojima, 2010).

Language Designed

We designed the language, DIST that can specify the domains of the transactions for load balancing. The domain defines the effective sites of transactions for the migration in computing grid, and can be used not only for the purpose of load balancing but also for fault tolerant or any other purposes.

Figure 17 (a) shows the syntax of the language, and (b) shows the BNF notation. In the language, one of the four parameters must be selected:" ALL", "domain names"," direct address" or

"NULL". If "ALL" is selected, the migration request is notified to all the sites in the computing grid. If "domain names" is selected, the migration request is multicasted to the sites that the domain involves. The address of the sites must be included into the domain name in advance. If "direct address" is selected, the request is sent to the address directly described. If "NULL" is selected, the request is not sent to anywhere, and be executed in its own site.

Design Methodologies

This section describes the design methodologies derived from the simulation results. The schema of the design methodology is shown in Figure 18. We based the following policies to formulate the design methodology.

Figure 17. Language syntax for distributed computing (a) DIST syntax (b) BNF notation

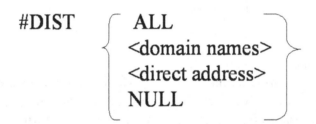

$$
\#DIST \quad \left\{ \begin{array}{l} ALL \\ \text{<domain names>} \\ \text{<direct address>} \\ NULL \end{array} \right\}
$$

(a)

```
DIST::= #DIST {ALL | <domain names> | <direct address> | NULL}
<domain names>::= <domain name> | <domain name>,<domain names>
<domain name>::= <direct address> | <direct address>,<domain name>
<direct address>::= <IP address> | <symbolic address>
<symbolic address>::= <IP address> | <IP address>, <symbolic address>
```

(b)

Figure 18. Design schema

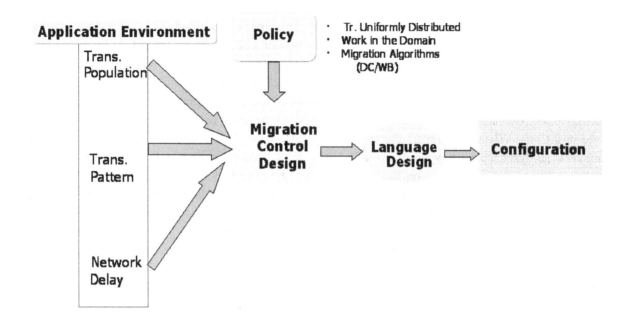

1. The Migration State Table, which carries out the transfer policy for migration, must be constantly maintained by the agent, and must be situated at each site.
2. Transactions had better be distributed uniformly in the computing grids.
3. The relationship between the average network delay and the average processing time of transactions must be observed. It defines the boundary of the migration domain. The simulation result indicated that the network delay should be less than the 20 times of the processing time of a transaction when the number of sites is in the order of hundreds.
4. If the number of grid sites is in the order of hundreds and the traffics are within the migration domain, the distributed algorithm for decentralized control and the working buffer algorithm for centralized control are the best solution to be applied.

The following is the design methodologies we derived from the simulation results.

1. Before designing the migration, trace the workload of transactions, and analyze the average workload of transactions and the pattern of transactions at each site.
2. Obtain the Migration State Table for transfer policy, by tracing or designing the workload of transactions.
3. Define the boundary of the migration domain. Analyzing the network delay, workload of transactions, anticipating response time, we can define the boundary of the migration for transactions.
4. Design the migration domain of each site. Group the sites into the same domain to have the uniform distribution of the workloads.
5. Define the domain of each site grouped by the distributed language proposed.
6. Select the load balancing algorithm for location policy. Either the DC algorithm for distributed control or the WB algorithm for centralized control had better be selected. If it does not have powerful machines for servers, select the DC algorithm.

7. Configure the distributed desktop computing grids, and execute the platform as is shown in Figure 19.

Figure 19 shows the platform of the distributed desktop computing grids. It consists of several agents. MST agent maintains the Migration State Table, and code execution agent executes the object code in the site. When a job enters the system, the syntax analyzer checks the syntax of the DIST language. If it requests the migration, the transfer policy agent, looking at the MST, calls either the code execution agent or the location policy agent. The location policy agent is called when the current MST is in the busy state, and the object code will be transferred to the server.

CONCLUSION

This article described the performance evaluation of load balancing control, and proposed the design methodologies of workload management in distributed computing grids. These are derived from the code migration experiments and from the simulation results. Several factors define the migration of transactions. The migration state table, transaction patterns, transaction workload and network delay were parameterized in the simulations, and the relations of these factors were analyzed. The workload design in the computing grids was formalized as a design methodology. The distributed language, the DIST language, was also introduced.

The validation of the system we described is our next research topic. We are now implementing the platform of the distributed desktop computing grids.

Figure 19. Platform system

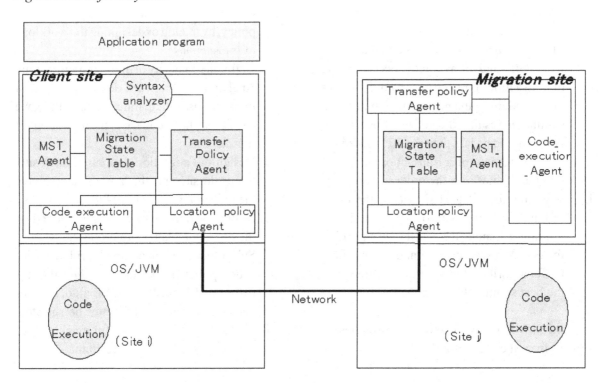

REFERENCES

Choi, S., Kim, H., Buyya, E., Baik, M., Gil, J., & Park, C. (2008). *A taxonomy of desktop grids and its mapping to state-of-the-art systems* (Tech. Rep. No. GRIDS-TR-2008-3). Melbourne, Australia: University of Melbourne.

Coulouris, G., Dollirnore, J., & Kindberg, T. (2005). *Distributed systems, coulouris, G.: Distributed systems: Concepts and design*. Reading, MA: Addison-Wesley.

Krauter, K., Buyya, R., & Maheswaran, M. (2002). A taxonomy and survey of grid resource management systems for distributed computing. *Software, Practice & Experience, 32*.

Santos, P. P. L. (1996). *Load distribution: A survey* (Tech. Rep. No. UM/DI/TR/96/03). Braga, Portugal: Universidade do Minho.

Shah, R., Veeravalli, B., & Misra, M. (2007). On the design of adaptive and decentralized load balancing algorithms with load estimation for computational grid environments. *IEEE Transactions on Parallel and Distributed Systems, 18*(12), 1675–1685. doi:10.1109/TPDS.2007.1115

Venugopal, S., Buyya, R., & Ramamohanarao, K. (2006). A taxonomy of data grids for distributed data sharing, management, and processing. *ACM Computing Surveys, 38*(1). doi:10.1145/1132952.1132955

Yoshida, M., & Kojima, K. (2010). Design methodologies of workload management through code migration in distributed desktop computing grids. In *Proceedings of the International Symposium on Frontiers of Parallel and Distributed Computing* (pp. 100-111).

Yoshida, M., & Sakamoto, K. (2007). Code migration control in large scale loosely coupled distributed systems. In *Proceedings of the 4th International Conference on Mobile Technology, Applications and Systems* (pp. 32-38).

Yoshida, M., & Sakamoto, K. (2008). Performance comparison of load balancing algorithms through code migration in distributed desktop computing grids. In *Proceedings of the 3rd IEEE Asia Pacific Services Computing Conference* (pp. 781-788).

This work was previously published in the International Journal of Grid and High Performance Computing, Volume 3, Issue 4, edited by Emmanuel Udoh and Ching-Hsien Hsu, pp. 53-70, copyright 2011 by IGI Publishing (an imprint of IGI Global).

Chapter 13
Parallelization of Littlewood–Richardson Coefficients Computation and its Integration into the BonjourGrid Meta–Desktop Grid Middleware

Heithem Abbes
University of Tunis, Tunisia

Franck Butelle
LIPN/UMR 7030 - Université Paris 13, France

Christophe Cérin
LIPN/UMR 7030 - Université Paris 13, France

ABSTRACT

This paper shows how to parallelize a compute intensive application in mathematics (Group Theory) for an institutional Desktop Grid platform coordinated by a meta-grid middleware named BonjourGrid. The paper is twofold: it shows how to parallelize a sequential program for a multicore CPU which participates in the computation; and it demonstrates the effort for launching multiple instances of the solutions for the mathematical problem with the BonjourGrid middleware. BonjourGrid is a fully decentralized Desktop Grid middleware. The main results of the paper are: a) an efficient multi-threaded version of a sequential program to compute Littlewood-Richardson coefficients, namely the Multi-LR program and b) a proof of concept, centered around the user needs, for the BonjourGrid middleware dedicated to coordinate multiple instances of programs for Desktop Grids and with the help of Multi-LR. In this paper, the scientific work consists in starting from a model for the solution of a compute intensive problem in mathematics, to incorporate the concrete model into a middleware and running it on commodity PCs platform managed by an innovative meta Desktop Grid middleware.

DOI: 10.4018/978-1-4666-2065-0.ch013

1. INTRODUCTION

Desktop Grid (DG) have been successfully used to address large applications with significant computational requirements, including search for extraterrestrial intelligence -SETI@Home (Anderson, Cobb, Korpela, Lebofsky, & Werthimer, 2002), global climate predication (Climatprediction.net,Anderson, 2004), and cosmic rays study (XtremWeb, Fedak, Germain, Néri, & Cappello, 2001; Cappello, Djilali, Fedak, Herault, Magniette, Néri, & Lodygensky, 2005). While the success of these applications demonstrates the potential of Desktop Grid, existing systems are often centralized and suffer from relying always on an administrative staff who guarantees the continuous running of the master. Moreover, although, in practical, the crash of the master is not frequent and replication techniques can solve this problem when it occurs, we still believe in the need to decentralized approaches. We justify this by the fact that since all institutions have not the same financial means to guarantee high levels of equipments robustness, the community should offer solutions to institutions which have not sufficient facilities to avoid the central element crash for instance. Thus, we believe in the importance of collaborative and decentralized solutions for the setting of Desktop Grid middleware.

In this context, Abbes, Cérin and Jemni have proposed a novel approach, called BonjourGrid (Abbes, Cérin, & Jemni, 2008, 2009), which enables to establish a specific execution environment for each user. Indeed, BonjourGrid constructs, dynamically and in a decentralized way, a Computing Element (CE – a CE is a set of workers managed by one master, or an instance of a local Desktop Grid middleware) when a user needs to run an application. BonjourGrid orchestrates multiple instances of CEs in a decentralized manner. Our approach does not rely on a unique static central element in the whole system, since we dedicate a temporary central element for each running application, in a dynamic way.

Furthermore, it is important to note that BonjourGrid is not only a decentralized approach to orchestrate and coordinate local DG (Desktop Grid) but it is also a system which is able, contrarily to classical DG, to construct specific execution environment on-demand (based on any combination of XtremWeb, Boinc, Condor middleware), in a decentralized, dynamic and autonomous way. This is the originality of the BonjourGrid system. We consider that it is a novel approach, a step forward regarding Desktop Grid systems.

The application that we investigate in this paper to explain our approach is a compute intensive applicationin the field of Group Theory. To our knowledge, there has been no attempt in the past to derive a multi-threaded solution of the computation of Littlewood–Richardson coefficients for desktop grid, especially for those based on multicore processors. We give an original and efficient solution to this difficult problem because it is hard to predict on the fly the space where the solution is located in as we will see later in the paper.

Therefore, the paper is mainly organized according to two central discussions: first of all the threading of the computation of LR coefficients and second the integration of the solution into BonjourGrid. The typical use case underlying our work is the following: a mathematician needs to guess the property of some numbers. Usually it uses the PCs in its institution to 'compute' the properties of the objects with the sequential implementation of Schur1 while colleagues work on others problems. He requires also that it could be done with a minimal effort for him (minimum of deployment, minimum of line codes to launch the application) because he is not an expert in grid middleware. This user belongs to the community ofBoinc users, so he wants to use this middleware whereas one of his colleague belongs to the Condor community and he wants to use Condor. Our solution allows any user to run the multi-threaded release of the Schur application that we introduce in this paper on its favorite middleware.

We do not fully describe the adaptation of the application on the BonjourGrid infrastructure because it is out of the scope and will require too much space. BonjourGrid is a large project consisting in coordinating, simultaneously major desktop grid middleware such as Condor, Boinc and XtremWeb instances.

This idea, while closely related to the concept of "Infrastructure on demand" concept central to the Cloud Computing paradigm and thus not completely new, may help in widening the spread of the Desktop Grid approach. The article strives to demonstrate the feasibility of the solution using the application from mathematics namely the computation of LR coefficients because we still need to validate BonjourGrid through 'real applications' and not emulation as we have already done. We choose the LR coefficients application because it is used by people in our laboratory, and because it is a central piece in the Schur package that is a tool to 'guess' properties of polynomials for instance.

Again, the main result of this paper is not about a new Desktop Grid middleware because in this case we need also to address, for the sake of completeness, the problems of volatility (host churn) and heterogeneity but it is about a multi-threaded code for the computation of LR coefficients. The ultimate goal is not to beat records in speed but to demonstrate that BonjourGrid is able to coordinate multiple instances of the same application on multiple instances of an innovative grid middleware deployed over an institution and also that a non experimented user may use this new environment.

2. A COMPUTATIONAL PROBLEM IN GROUP THEORY

2.1. Mathematical Background

In order to be self content we need some standard definitions and vocabulary from group theory

(MacDonald, 1995). A partition of a positive integer n is a way of writing n as a sum of non increasing strictly positive integers. For example ë = (4,2,2,1) and ì = (2,1) are partitions of n = 9 and n′ = 3 respectively. We write ë ⊢ n and ì ⊢ n′ or |ë| = n and |ì| = n′.

The Ferrers diagram $F^ë$ associated to a partition ë = (ë$_1$,ë$_2$,-, ë$_p$) consists of |ë| = n boxes, arranged in l(ë) = p left-justified rows of lengths ë$_1$, ë$_2$, -, ë$_p$. Rows in $F^ë$ are oriented downwards. $F^ë$ is called the shape of ë.

A semi-standard Young tableau of shape $F^ë$ (SSY $T^ë$) is a numbering of the boxes of $F^ë$ with entries from {1,2,-, n}, weakly increasing across rows and strictly increasing down columns. A tableau is standard (SY $T^ë$) if all its entries are different. Skew tableaux are defined in an analogous way. For example, for ë = (4,2,2,1) and ì = (2,1), $F^ë$ and SSY $T^ë$ are as follows:

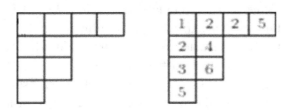

A Symmetric Function is a function which is symmetric or invariant under permutation of its variables.

$$f(x_{\sigma(1)}, x_{\sigma(2)},...,x_{\sigma(n)}) = f(x_1, x_2,...,x_n)$$

where ó is any permutation of the symmetric group S$_n$. The Schur function s$_ë$ is the symmetric function defined as:

$$s\lambda(x) = \sum_{T \in Tab(\lambda)} x^T$$

where Tab(ë) is the set of all tableaux of shape ë and x^T is the product of the x$_i$ for all i appearing in the tableau T. For example, for $ì = (2,1)$ there are 8 semi-standard tableaux of shape $ì$ using $\{1,2,3\}$:

The associated Schur function is therefore:

1	1
2	
1	3
2	

1	1
3	
1	3
3	

1	2
2	
2	2
3	

1	2
3	
2	3
3	

$$s_{21}(x_1, x_2, x_3) = \begin{aligned} &x_1^2 x_2 + x_1^2 x_3 + x_1 x_2^2 + x_1 x_2 x_3 \\ &+ x_1 x_2 x_3 + x_1 x_3^2 + x_2^2 x_3 + x_2 x_3^2 \end{aligned}$$

The Littlewood-Richardson coefficients $c_{ëì}^{i}$ are defined as the structure constants for the multiplication in the basis of the Schur functions. So if $ë \vdash n$ and $ì \vdash m$:

$$s_\lambda s_\mu = \sum_{v \vdash n+m} c_{\lambda\mu}^{v} s_v$$

Example:

$s_{4221}s_{21} = s_{6321} + s_{622} + s_{62211} + s_{5421} + s_{5331}$
$+ 2s_{5322} + 2s_{53211} + s_{4431} + s_{4422}$
$+ s_{44211} + 2s_{52221} + s_{4332} + 2s_{43221}$
$+ s_{522111} + s_{43311} + s_{432111} + s_{42222}$
$+ s_{422211}$

Thus $c_{4221,21}^{5322} = c_{4221,21}^{43221} = 2$ and $c_{4221,21}^{6321} = c_{4221,21}^{422211} = 1$.

2.2. The Hives Model

Littlewood-Richardson coefficients $c_{ëì}^{i}$ have a polynomial growth with respect to the dilatation factor N:

$$c_{N\lambda, N\mu}^{Nv} = P_{\lambda\mu}^{v}; \; P_{\lambda\mu}^{v}(0) = 1$$

where $P_{ëì}^{i}$ is a polynomial in N with non negative rational coefficients depending on $ë$, $ì$ and $í$. This was first conjectured in King, Tollu, and Toumazet (2004). A partial proof (existence of

$P_{ëì}^{i}$ and rationality of coefficients) was given in (Rassart, 2004). Those polynomials (King, Tollu, & Toumazet, 2004) are obtained considering a model known as the hive model. An n-integer-hive is a triangular array of non negative integers a_j^i with $0 \le i,j \le n$ where neighboring entries define three distinct types of rhombus, each with its own constraint condition.

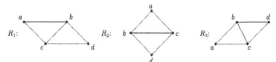

In each case, with the labeling as shown, the hive condition takes the form:

b+c≥a+d (1)

A LR-hives (King, Tollu, & Toumazet, 2004) is an integer hive satisfying the hive condition (1) for all its constituent rhombic of type R_1, R_2 and R_3, with border labels determined by the partitions $ë$, $ì$ and $í$, such that:

$$\begin{cases} a_0^0 = 0; \; a_j^j = \lambda_1 + \lambda_2 + ... + \lambda_j \\ \qquad\qquad \forall j \in \{1, ..., n\} \\ a_0^i = v_1 + v_2 + ... + v_i \\ \qquad\qquad \forall i \in \{1, ..., n\} \\ a_{n-k}^k = a_n^0 + \mu_1 + \mu_2 + ... + \mu_k \\ \qquad\qquad \forall k \in \{1, ..., n\} \end{cases}$$

with $l(ë)$, $l(ì)$, $l(í) \le n$ and $|ë| + |ì| = |í|$.

For example, for n = 4, LR-hives will be sketched as:

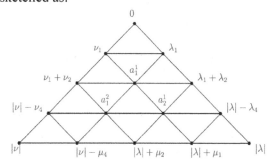

The Littlewood-Richardson coefficient $c_{ëì}^{i}$ is the number of LR-hives with border labeled as above by ë, ì and í. So c_{ei}^i is the number of triples (a_1^1, a_1^2, a_2^1) satisfying (1) for all rhombic of type R_1, R_2 and R_3. That is the number of integer solutions to the system of inequalities obtained by writing (1) for all rhombic. The degree of the polynomial $P_{ei}^i(N)$ is always bounded by $(n-1)(n-2)/2$, the number of interior points of the hive, but if any of the partitions, ë, ì or í has repeated parts then it is possible to use the hive inequalities to improve this bound with some maxDeg $< (n-1)(n-2)/2$. We compute $c_{Ne,Ni}^{Ni}$ for any $N \in N$ with N increasing, and compute the interpolating polynomial for the points $(N, c_{Ne,Ni}^{Ni})$. The computation is stopped when two successive interpolating polynomials are equal. As stated by theory, actually the number of computed coefficients is often less than $(n-1)(n-2)/2$.

2.3. A Parallel Computation

The aim of this section is to explain the different ways we compute the LR coefficients in parallel. Two kinds of parallelization is under concern in this article which are the parallelization on a single machine (multicore CPU) and the parallelization at the grid level. The goal is to replace the current sequential code provided with Schur2 by a multi-threaded one able to be integrated into a DG middleware. Schur is recognized to be a powerful and efficient tool for calculating properties of Lie groups and symmetric functions. Developing a parallel version of Schur is challenging and we restrict our study to the computation of LR coefficients in parallel

2.3.1. Parallelization on a Single Machine: The Multi-LR Code

The ways we are computing the Littlewood-Richardson coefficients allows us to split the enumeration process of the feasible space in several parts. To do this, we use the Pthread API, and divide the enumeration process in two pieces:

- We assume that only n threads are allowed for the process. The first step of the enumeration is to divide the feasible space in n parts. Since the enumeration space is made of a product of intervals, we divide the first interval in min(nb_thread,interval_size) of the same size, and for each part we attach a thread.

- Each thread uses an optimized method to explore the feasible space and returns the number of solutions. Once the enumeration is done for all the threads, the main thread sends the result to the user.

2.3.2. Parallelization Using a Desktop Grid

The computation of LR polynomials can be achieved using the multiple machine on a local network. The idea is to compute the Littlewood-Richardson coefficients on various machines for a set of dilatation coefficients and to collect the results to build the interpolating polynomial. The time needed to compute one LR coefficient depends on the partitions given to the program and on the dilatation coefficient.

The four input parameters $(ë, ì, í, N)$ are given to the program, where N is the dilatation coefficient. For each computer on the network, a unique dilatation coefficient is given. The result of each computation is the Littlewood-Richardson coefficient $c_{Ne,Ni}^{Ni}$. Thus many interpolation points $(N, c_{Ne,Ni}^{Ni})$ are computed. Each time a new interpolation point is produced, a new interpolating polynomial is computed using all the values available. Thus, a sequence of polynomials is built:

$$P_{1\lambda\mu}^v(N), P_{2\lambda\mu}^v(N), ..., P_{k\lambda\mu}^v(N), ...$$

The computation is stopped when the sequence becomes stationary. That means that $P_{iei}^i = P_{(i+1)ei}^i$ for some i and it holds for any j greater than i.

Figure 1. Computation time with respect to the dilatation coefficient. The partitions are ë = (5,3,2,2,1), ì = (4,3,2,2,1) and í = (7,5,4,4,3,2)

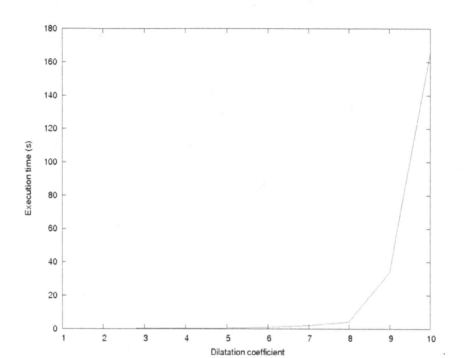

The complexity of the algorithm used to compute each Littlewood-Richardson coefficient is:

$$C(N) = \left(\prod_{k=1}^{m} | I_k | \right) N^m$$

where m is the number of intervals in the hive, $|I_k|$ is the number of elements in the interval I_k and N is the dilatation coefficient. Thus, the time needed to compute a Littlewood-Richardson coefficient has a polynomial growth of order m (Figure 1). This means that for high values of m, the time needed to compute the coefficient N + 1 will be greater than the time needed to compute all the coefficients up to N. In other words, for large values of m, the time needed for the whole computation (all coefficients) is more or less the time needed to compute the last one.

2.4. Experimental Results

2.4.1. Performance Gain on a Single Machine

The use of threads to compute the Littlewood-Richardson coefficients leads to improvement in the execution time. To compare the gain in performance, we use a multi-core processor. In the remainder of the section, computations are done on a Bi-AMD Opteron dual core at 2.8GHz, which means that 4 cores were available for the computation.

The computation of Littlewood-Richardson coefficients was done for various partitions and variable maximum number of threads. The first remark is that the gain in time depends on the first interval (which is divided to create the threads) and on the symmetry of the problem. For example if the first interval is a single value, only one thread is launched, and the time needed for the computation is the same than without threads.

The "symmetry" of the feasible space is also important for the enumeration. To understand this, the algorithm has to be explained again. As said before, the enumeration method used by each thread is optimized, so that the whole feasible space is not searched. Each step of the algorithm corresponds to one point of the hive. For each feasible value of a point, the feasible space is computed again so that useless values are not tried. Therefore, the number of feasible values tried by each thread depends on the interval it received from the first step, and some threads are faster than other. This phenomenon can be observed on Figure 2, which shows the results for the partitions ($\lambda = (5,5,3,2,1,1)$, $\mathrm{i} = (6,6,4,2,1)$ and $\nu = (6,6,6,5,5,3,2,2,1)$) and ($\lambda = (7,6,5,4)$, $\mathrm{i} = (7,7,7,4)$, $\nu = (12,8,8,7,6,4,2)$). The computation time for the dilatation coefficient $N = 7$ does not decrease when the number of threads increases.

However, the majority of the practical cases shows that threading the program is useful. The computation time is divided by a factor of 3.5, and nearly four in thebest cases, depending on the "symmetry" of the problem. In fact, we could think that the results should be similar for any number of threads greater than 4. But as we can see on the first diagram of Figure 2, the time needed for the computation is stationary for a number of threads greater than 10. This is explained by the fact that for less than 10 threads, one of the threads is slower than the others because the number of values it deals with is bigger than for the other threads.

For a very large number of threads, the performance mainly depends on the operating system's scheduler. We are using the Linux scheduler, and even with a great number of threads (over 200 threads), the results are impressive.

3. PORTING THE PARALLEL CODE ON A DEKTOP GRID PLATFORM

3.1. Introduction to BonjourGrid

BonjourGrid is a meta Desktop Grid middleware meaning that it is able to instantiate multiple Desktop Grid middleware in the same infrastructure. As referenced in many other works (Domingues, Andrzejak, & Silva, 2006; Kondo, Chien, & Casanova, 2004), this kind of environment is called Institutional Desktop Grid or Enterprise Desktop Grid (e.g., located in the same institution). The principle of the proposed approach is to create, dynamically and in a decentralized way, a specific execution environment for each user to execute any type of applications without any system administrator intervention. An environment do not affect another one if it fails.

This section aims at demonstrating the potential of BonjourGrid and it serves as a proof of concept. The BonjourGrid protocol has been validated in Abbes, Cérin, and Jemni (2009) and Abbes, Cérin, Jemni, and Saad (2010) but the goal was to show that BonjourGrid is able to behave "like" a job scheduler. Here we are deploying a real application on top of BonjourGrid. Moreover, in this section we do not evaluate the application performance on the Grid, but we explain, from a user point of view, what is the work to accomplish to run a code on top of the middleware.

Details about BonjourGrid follow and the software is available on sourceForge3. Each user, behind its desktop machine in his office, can submit an application. BonjourGrid deploys a master (coordinator), locally on the user machine, and requests for participants (workers). Negotiations to select them should now take place. Using a publish/subscribe infrastructure, each machine publishes its state (idle, worker or master) when changes occur as well as information about its local load or its "utilization cost", in order to provide useful metrics for the selection of participants by the BonjourGrid middleware. Under these assump-

Figure 2. Evolution of the computation time needed with the number of threads allowed for partitions

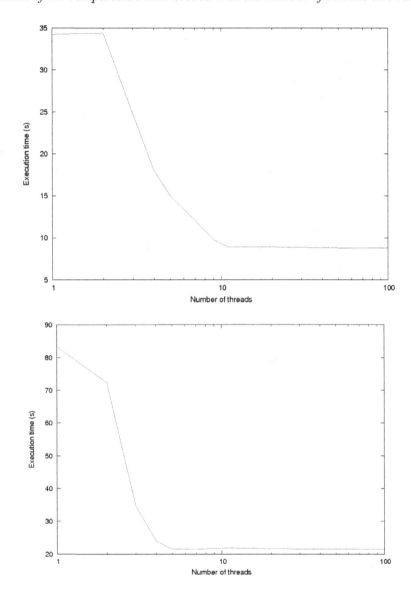

tions, the master can select a subset of workers nodes according to a strategy that could balance the "power" of the node and the "price" of its use. The master and the set of selected workers build the Computing Element (CE) which will execute, manage and control the user application. When a CE finishes the application, its master becomes free, returns in idle state and releases all workers to return also to the idle state. When no application is submitted, all machines are in the idle state.

The main technologies used in BonjourGrid are publish/subscribe systems (Eugster, Felber, Guerraoui, & Kermarrec, 2003) and ZeroConf protocol (Steinberg & Cheshire, 2005). In a previous work (Abbes & Dubacq, 2008), we tackled the following questions: Can a system based on publish/subscribe protocols be "powerful"? Can it be scalable? What is the response time to publish a service? What is the discovery time of a service? We carried out experiments on various protocols such as Bonjour protocol, on the GdX node of Grid5000 (Bolze et al., 2006) platform using more than 300 machines (AMD Opterons connected with a 1Gb/s network). Measures show that Bonjour is reliable and very powerful in resources discovery. Indeed, Bonjour discovers more than 300 services published simultaneously in less than 2 seconds with 0% of loss. These evaluations support and justify our choice to use Bonjour as a basis for the discovery protocol in BonjourGrid system. Moreover, we believe that using an existing and tested protocol for the industry (Bonjour is available on Macintosh machines), to evaluate its usability in Desktop Grid environment is, in itself, of great value and very useful for the community.

The advantages in using a publication/subscription (Pub-Sub) (Eugster, Felber, Guerraoui, & Kermarrec, 2003) mechanisms come from the asynchronous nature of the paradigm. The Pub-Sub paradigm is an asynchronous mode for communicating between entities. Some users, namely the subscribers or clients or consumers, express and record their interests under the form or subscriptions, and are notified later by another event produced by other users, namely the producers.

This communication mode is thus multipoint, anonymous and implicit. It is a multipoint mode (one-to-many or many-to-many) because events are sent to the set of clients that have declared an interest into the topic. It is an anonymous mode because the provider does not know the identity of clients. It is an implicit mode because the clients are determined by the subscriptions and not explicitly by the providers.

It is also known that this asynchronous communicating mode allows spatial deco upling (the interacting entities do not know each other), and time decoupling (the interacting entities do not need to participate at the same time). This total decoupling between the production and the consumption of services increases the scalability by eliminating many sorts of explicit dependencies between participating entities. Eliminating dependencies reduces the coordination needs and

consequently the synchronizations between entities. These advantages make the communicating infrastructure well suited to the management of distributed systems and simplify the development of a middleware for the coordination of DGs.

The key idea of BonjourGrid is to rely on existing Institutional Desktop Grid middleware, and to orchestrate and coordinate multiple instances, i.e multiple CEs, through a publish/subscribe system (Figure 3). Each CE will be owned by the user who has started the master on his machine. Then this CE is responsible for the execution of one or many applications for the same user. As shown in Figure 3, in the user level, a user A (resp. B) deploys his application on his machine and the execution seems to be local. Level 1 (middleware layer) shows that, actually, a CE with 4 (resp. 5) workers has been dynamically created, specifically for the user A (resp. B). Level 0 shows that all machines are interconnected and under the availability of any user.

3.2. Implementation

BonjourGrid is entirely implemented using Python. We have used Bonjour-py package that offers a python interface to interact with Bonjour protocol. When a machine joins our system, information about its characteristics (i.e., MHZ, CPU, RAM, Hostname, IP address, average load) are automatically collected and stored in a Python dictionary. This information is useful for the selection of the suitable machines that match the application requirements. For instance, one would like to select workers according to the CPU metric only; another one would like to select workers that have been being idle for a long time. In our system, we can easily plug a new policy in order to select workers. We can also imagine, in the future, to make an economic model based choice of the suitable policy; the coding effort is not important, thanks to the Python abstractions.

Figure 3. BonjourGrid abstract layers

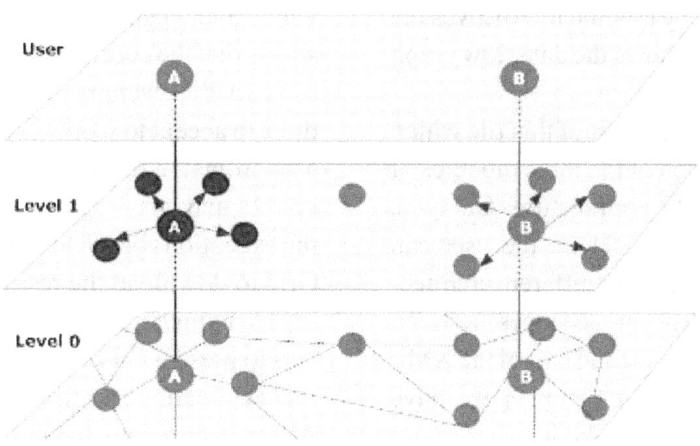

3.2.1. Running the XtremWeb Services

In this paper, we choose to use XW (XtremWeb) as a middleware for the CE. To run or deactivate an XW service (coordinator or worker), the environment should be already installed. The procedure to install a XW-Coordinator, in particular, is not currently simple enough, so we have improved it. We would not like to make user spends his time in configuring and installing the various files and modules necessary to the XW installation. An installation procedure consists in installing a MySQL server, Java Development Kit, creating a specific database for XW, making several directories and configuring system files. Consequently, we set up an automatic installation of all the necessary packages. Such facilities were not included in the current distribution of XW.

3.3. Experiments and Validation of BonjourGrid

From a user point of view, deploying an application on BonjourGrid starts with preparing the executable code and data that are archived in a compressed file. BonjourGrid enables the execution of applications with precedence between tasks.

Indeed, the user can describe the precedence of a data flow graph using a XML description; this is not trivial, especially, for complex applications.

SDAD is the system of deployment that we have developed and it helps the user in describing the data flow graph of his application according to an XML syntax using a graphical interface (for simple applications, see Figure 9) or an advanced wizard (for complex ones, see Figure 10). It also helps user to put the different files of his applications (i.e., binary and data files) in the right path of his package. SDAD generates a compressed package ready to be deployed on BonjourGrid system. Now, the user can submit his application to BonjourGrid. He can specify the size of the computing element (CE) and the middleware (XtremWeb in this case study) to run the application. BonjourGrid, then, will construct the CE according to the criteria mentioned in the XML file.

To summarize, using the SDAD tool, the user can draw the task graph and put binary and data files in the suitable path in the application tree. Thereafter, SDAD will generate the XML description of the application which is used by XW and BonjourGrid. As described in subsection 2.3, the first module of the application Hives can be divided in several parallel tasks. The outputs of these tasks are forwarded to the so called Build-Inter module. Finally, the module Interp gives the interpolation. Figure 4 shows the data flow graph of the Hives application.

Figure 5 shows the first part of this file which illustrates the description of the three modules of the application (i.e., OS architecture, OS type, location of binary files…). Here, the user can provide several binary files for different architectures and OS types. The precedences between tasks are illustrated in the second part of the XML file shown in Figure 6. On Figure 6 we have simplified the XML file to make it easier to understand (we drawn only two parallel tasks for the Hives module).

Now, Hives is ready to be submitted to the BonjourGrid system. In the following, we illustrate snapshots picked out from a Hives execution using the Orsay node of Grid5000. Specifically for this demo, we are going to dissociate the CE building phase from the effective submission to illustrate the different steps. First, we initiate machines in idle state. We launch the coordinator, on any machine, to start the building phase of a suitable CE. Figure 7 shows the outputs of a construction of a CE with 2 workers (just for the sake of clarity of reading). Indeed, the coordinator is started on the gdx-5 node, requiring two

workers as shown in the Figure 7. For that, the coordinator gdx-5 searches for idle machines which match the tasks requirements. Figure 7 shows that the coordinator gdx-5 discovers in this test two idle machines gdx-9 and gdx-17 and asks them to accept to work for it. Thereafter, the gdx-5 coordinator receives two confirmations from gdx-17 and gdx-9 as depicted in Figure 8. When the execution completes, we can invoke Bonjour-Grid to download the results.

To summarize, the objective of this experiment was to present a use case of BonjourGrid using a real application and from the user point of view. Abbes, Cérin, and Jemni have already done experiments to analyze the performance of Bonjour-Grid in Abbes, Cérin, and Jemni (2008, 2009) and Abbes and Dubacq (2008) but the scope of this work is to demonstrate how BonjourGrid can help users to construct, dynamically and without any intervention of a system administrator, their own environments to deploy and perform out a parallel application.

4. RELATED WORK ON ADVANCED DESKTOP GRID ARCHITECTURES

Before concluding, we compare BonjourGrid with others systems. OurGrid (Cirne, Brasileiro,

Figure 4. Description of the data flow graph of Hives composed with 3 modules; Hives, BuildInter and Interp

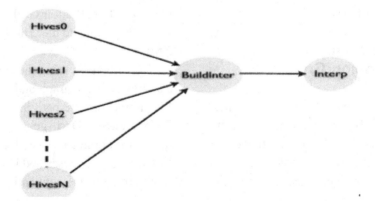

Figure 5. Description of the flow data graph of the application Hive

```
<Deployment>
    <Application ApplicationDescription="monapp" Client="heithem">
        <Module ModuleDescription="hives" ModuleDirIn="/bin/">
            <Binary BinaryCpuType="amd64" BinaryExecutable="hives"
                    BinaryOsName="Linux" BinarySubFolder="linux"/>
        </Module>
        <Module ModuleDescription="buildinter" ModuleDirIn="/bin/">
            <Binary BinaryCpuType="amd64" BinaryExecutable="buildinter"
                    BinaryOsName="Linux" BinarySubFolder="linux"/>
        </Module>
        <Module ModuleDescription="interp" ModuleDirIn="/bin/">
            <Binary BinaryCpuType="amd64" BinaryExecutable="interp"
                    BinaryOsName="Linux" BinarySubFolder="linux"/>
        </Module>
    </Application>
```

Andrade, Costa, Andrade, Novaes, & Mowbray, 2006) system avoids the centralized server by creating the notion of the home machine from which applications are submitted; the existence of several home machines reduces the impact of failures at the same time. Moreover, OurGrid provides an accounting model to assure a fair resources sharing in order to attract nodes to join the system. However, the originality of BonjourGrid comparing to OurGrid is that it supports distributed applications with precedence between tasks as well as Bag-of-Tasks (BOT), while OurGrid supports only BOT

Figure 6. Description of the precedences between tasks in Hive application

```
<Table>
    <Task Application="monapp" ApplicationModule="hives"
        Description="hives1" DirIn="/hives/" FileIn="dir.zip" Final="0">
        <Input InputName="x1"/>
        <Output OutputName="y1"/>
        <cmdLine>11,10,8,5 20,17,3 26,25,8,8,7 out1 1</cmdLine>
        <QoS>
            <Power NbMax="0" ErrorMargin="0.2">3000.0</Power>
        </QoS>
    </Task>

    <Task Application="monapp" ApplicationModule="hives"
        Description="hives2" DirIn="/hives/" FileIn="dir.zip" Final="0">
        <Input InputName="x2"/>
        <Output OutputName="y2"/>
        <cmdLine>11,10,8,5 20,17,3 26,25,8,8,7 out2 2 </cmdLine>
        <QoS>
            <Power NbMax="0" ErrorMargin="0.2">3000.0</Power>
        </QoS>
    </Task>

    <Task Application="monapp" ApplicationModule="buildinter"
        Description="build" DirIn="/hives/" FileIn="dir.zip" Final="0">
        <Input InputName="y1"/>
        <Input InputName="y2"/>
        <Output OutputName="y3"/>
        <cmdLine>2 out interresult  </cmdLine>
        <QoS>
            <Power NbMax="0" ErrorMargin="0.2">3000.0</Power>
        </QoS>
    </Task>

    <Task Application="monapp" ApplicationModule="interp"
        Description="interp" DirIn="/hives/" FileIn="dir.zip" Final="1">
        <Input InputName="y3"/>
        <Output OutputName="y4"/>
        <cmdLine>interresult 2 finalresult </cmdLine>
        <QoS>
            <Power NbMax="0" ErrorMargin="0.2">3000.0</Power>
        </QoS>
    </Task>

</Table>
</Deployment>
```

Figure 7. Construction of a new CE with 2 workers

```
mpi@gdx-5:~/BG3$ python startmaster.py 2

[BG:INFO] Automatic generation of the machine features

[BG:INFO] (STATUS=MASTER) Your machine is a Master now

[BG:STAT] master : gdx-5.orsay.grid5000.fr

[BG:INFO] Your master is looking for idle machines

[BG:SYS] ServiceAdd : gdx-9\.orsay\.grid5000\.fr._idle._tcp.local.gdx-9.orsay.grid5000.fr.
2222

[BG:INFO] -- gdx-9.orsay.grid5000.fr -- is just discovered as Idle machine

[BG:INFO] -- gdx-9.orsay.grid5000.fr -- is requested for working

[BG:SYS] ServiceAdd: gdx-17\.orsay\.grid5000\.fr._idle._tcp.local.gdx-17.orsay.grid5000.fr.
2222

[BG:INFO] -- gdx-17.orsay.grid5000.fr -- is just discovered as Idle machine

[BG:INFO] -- gdx-17.orsay.grid5000.fr -- is requested for working

[BG:INFO] Checking if all the requested Idle machines are reserved by your Master
```

applications (BOT applications are independent divisible tasks). WaveGrid (Zhou & Lo, 2006) is a P2P middleware which uses a timezone-aware overlay network to indicate when hosts have a large block of idle time. This system reinforces the idea of BonjourGrid concept since changing from a set of workers to another one depending on the time zone (Wave Grid) is analogous to the principle of creating a CE from an application to another one in BonjourGrid, and depending on users requirements.

Approaches based on publish/subscribe systems to coordinate or decentralise Desktop Grid infrastructures are not very numerous according

Figure 8. Confirmation of two idle machines to work for the master gdx-5

```
[BG:SYS] ServiceAdd: gdx-17\.orsay\.grid5000\.fr._gdx-5orsaygrid5000fr-master._tcp.local.
gdx-17.orsay.grid5000.fr. 3333

[BG:INFO] -- gdx-17.orsay.grid5000.fr -- has accepted to work for you

[BG:STAT] worker : gdx-17.orsay.grid5000.fr

[BG:SYS] ServiceAdd: gdx-9\.orsay\.grid5000\.fr._gdx-5orsaygrid5000fr-master._tcp.local.
gdx-9.orsay.grid5000.fr. 3333

[BG:INFO] -- gdx-9.orsay.grid5000.fr -- has accepted to work for you

[BG:STAT] worker : gdx-9.orsay.grid5000.fr

[BG:INFO] Lucky : All requested machines are workers for your Master
```

Figure 9. One snapshot of SDAD tool which depicts the graphical interface to draw the Hives data flow graph

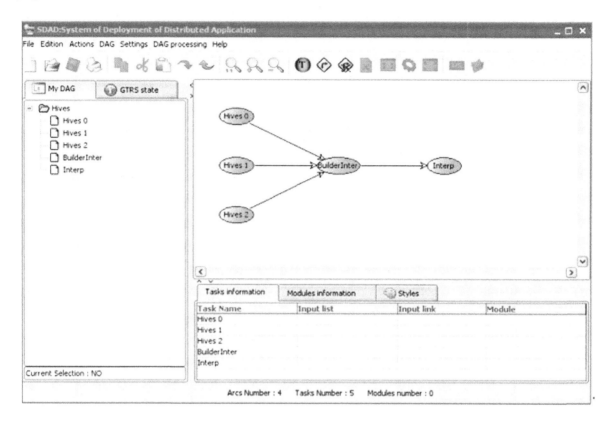

to our knowledge. A similar project to our project is the Xgrid project (Kramer & MacInnis, 2004). In Xgrid system, each agent (or worker) makes itself available to a single controller. It receives computational tasks and returns the results of these computations to the controller. Hence, the whole architecture relies on a single and static component which is the controller. Moreover, Xgrid runs only on MacOS systems. In contrast with Xgrid, in BonjourGrid, the coordinator is not static and is created in a dynamic way. Furthermore, Bonjour-Grid is more generic since it is possible to "plug" on it any computing system (XW, Boinc, Condor) while Xgrid has its own computing system. The key advantage of bonjourGrid is that the user is free to use his favorite desktop grid middleware.

5. CONCLUSION AND FUTURE WORK

In this work, we have proposed a novel algorithm to compute Littlewood-Richardson coefficients (by the Hive method) in parallel and we have shown how to run the code on top of BonjourGrid. The aim of BonjourGrid is to orchestrate multi-instances of computing elements, in a decentralized manner. BonjourGrid creates, dynamically, a specific environment for the user to run his application. There is no need for a system administrator. Indeed, BonjourGrid is fully autonomous and decentralized. We have conducted several experimentations to show that BonjourGrid operates well with a real world application. Therefore BonjourGrid has shown its usefulness. Moreover, the deployment of the Hive code on BonjourGrid, demonstrates

Figure 10. One snapshot of SDAD tool showing the advanced mode where the user needs 100 parallel tasks of the Hives module

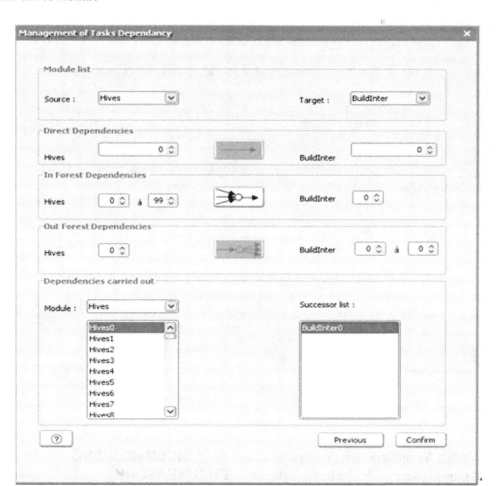

that BonjourGrid may help users to create several independent environments. Then, mathematicians, for instance, can create their Desktop Grid easily to run their parallel applications.

Several issues must be taken into account in our future work about meta-Desktop Grid middleware. The first issue is to build a fault-tolerant system for the coordinators. In fact, it is important to continue the execution of the application when the coordinator (user machine) fails (it is disconnected for instance). This issue has been solved and it is currently tested overand validated on Grid'5000 testbed. Condor, Boinc plugins have also been built and are currently tested with the

Hive code, especially but not only. The second issue is the reservation of participation: in the current version, BonjourGrid allocates available resources for a user without any reservation rules. Thus, BonjourGrid may allocate to a single user all the available resources. The third issue is to pass to a wide area network.

In order to be widely adopted by the community, we are currently working also on the following issues. First, BonjourGrid is still working on top of Bonjour which is a local-area network. The wide area-Bonjour4 is available but requires some work to configure it. The goal is to deploy our protocol over the Internet and not over a local network. After installing Wide Area Bonjour, the experimental work could not really be about performance because they cannot be reproducible over Internet. The setting of a large platform of volunteers is more challenging and the experimental work would be to show that the system can handle large configurations of PC.

Another choice is to implement our protocol over another Pub-Sub tool. The target language may take the form of a popular language on the Internet such as XMPP5. In fact, many libraries support the publish-subscribe mechanism are being deployed (e.g., Jetty), including the forthcoming HTML5 standard. The danger is reimplementing the protocol is to forget some implementation details that make the protocol correct. We are currently working on the specification of our coordination protocol by using Petri Net tools in order to isolate the main properties of our protocol but also the main knowhow in using Pub-sub systems. Petri Net is a formal tool to reasoning about the specification in order to check fundamental properties of the design such as safety ("nothing bad happens") for which the absence of deadlock is an example and liveness ("something good eventualy happens").

Any grid middleware should also support a security level. Even if you are sure that communications will not be decrypted you must ensure the authentication of the participants. Conventionally authentication in grids is via X509 certificates. In the case of BonjourGrid, we also need an orchestration of certificates to ensure for example that two Boinc coordinators can exchange participants. Who says X509 certificates also said VO (Virtual Organizations) that allow the federation of resources. The problem will be to manage various VOs.

We are also working on the adaptation of BonjourGrid principles for data management. The main challenge is to resume the protocol to coordinate data servers by introducing a new state in the Protocol to mean that a node can become a data server. This new state impacts the protocol with respect to fault tolerance. It will be necessary to revise the protocol to manage data backup and servers backup.

We hope that this work helps to understand what is a possible future for Desktop Grid middleware as well as the new efforts that users should make to use such systems.

REFERENCES

Abbes, H., Cérin, C., & Jemni, M. (2008). BonjourGrid as a decentralised job scheduler. In *Proceedings of the IEEE Asia-Pacific Services Computing Conference* (pp. 89-94).

Abbes, H., Cérin, C., & Jemni, M. (2009, May 29). BonjourGrid: Orchestration of multi-instances of grid middleware on institutional desktop grid. In *Proceedings of the 3rd Workshop on Desktop Grid and Volunteer Computing Systems in conjunction with IPDPS*, Roma, Italy (pp. 1-8).

Abbes, H., Cérin, C., Jemni, M., & Saad, W. (2010). Fault tolerance based on the publish-subscribe paradigm for the BonjourGrid Middleware. In *Proceedings of the 11th ACM/IEEE International Conference on Grid Computing*, Brussels, Belgium (pp. 57-64).

Abbes, H., & Dubacq, J. C. (2008). Analysis of peer-to-peer protocols performance for establishing a decentralized desktop grid Middleware. In E. César, M. Alexander, A. Streit, J. L. Träff, C. Cérin, A. Knüpfer, D. Kranzlmüller, & S. Jha (Eds.), *Proceedings of the Euro-Par Workshops on Parallel Processing* (LNCS 5415, pp. 235-246).

Anderson, D. P. (2004). BOINC: A system for public-resource computing and storage. In *Proceedings of the IEEE International Conference on Grid Computing* (pp. 4-10).

Anderson, D. P., Cobb, J., Korpela, E., Lebofsky, M., & Werthimer, D. (2002). SETI@home: An experiment in public-resource computing. *Communications of the ACM, 45*(11), 56–61. doi:10.1145/581571.581573

Bolze, R., Cappello, F., Caron, E., Daydé, M. J., Desprez, F., & Jeannot, E. (2006). A large scale and highly reconfigurable experimental grid testbed. *International Journal of High Performance Computing Applications, 20*(4), 481–494. doi:10.1177/1094342006070078

Cappello, F., Djilali, S., Fedak, G., Herault, T., Magniette, F., Néri, V., & Lodygensky, O. (2005). Computing on large scale distributed systems: XtremWeb architecture, programming models, security, tests and convergence with grid. *Future Generation Computer Science, 21*(3), 417–437. doi:10.1016/j.future.2004.04.011

Cirne, W., Brasileiro, F., Andrade, N., Costa, L., Andrade, A., Novaes, R., & Mowbray, M. (2006). Labs of the world, unite!!! *Journal of Grid Computing*, 225–246. doi:10.1007/s10723-006-9040-x

Domingues, P., Andrzejak, A., & Silva, L. M. (2006). Using checkpointing to enhance turnaround time on institutional desktop grids. *eScience, 73.*

Eugster, P. T., Felber, P. A., Guerraoui, R., & Kermarrec, A. M. (2003). The many faces of publish/subscribe. *ACM Computing Surveys, 35*(2), 114–131. doi:10.1145/857076.857078

Fedak, G., Germain, C., Néri, V., & Cappello, F. (2001). Xtremweb: A generic global computing system. In *Proceedings of the IEEE International Symposium on Cluster Computing and the Grid* (pp. 582-587).

King, R. C., Tollu, C., & Toumazet, F. (2004). Stretched Littlewood-Richardson and Kostka coefficients. In Winternitz, P., Harnard, J., Lam, C. S., & Patera, J. (Eds.), *Symmetry in physics: In memory of Robert T. Sharp* (pp. 99–112). Providence, RI: American Mathematical Society.

Kondo, D., Chien, A. A., & Casanova, H. (2004). Resource management for rapid application turnaround on enterprise desktop grids. In *Proceedings of the ACM/IEEE Conference on Supercomputing* (p. 17).

Kramer, D. A., & MacInnis, M. (2004). Utilization of a local grid of mac OS X-based computers using Xgrid. In *Proceedings of the 13th IEEE International Symposium on High Performance Distributed Computing* (pp. 264-265).

MacDonald, I. G. (1995). *Symmetric functions and hall polynomials* (2nd ed.). Oxford, UK: Clarendon Press.

Rassart, E. (2004). A polynomiality property for Littlewood-Richardson coefficients. *Journal of Combinatorial Theory Series A, 107*, 161–179. doi:10.1016/j.jcta.2004.04.003

Steinberg, D., & Cheshire, S. (2005). *Zero configuration networking: The definitive guide.* Sebastopol, CA: O'Reilly Media.

Thain, D., & Livny, M. (2003). Condor and the grid. In Berman, F., Hey, A. J. G., & Fox, G. (Eds.), *Grid computing: Making the global infrastructure a reality.* New York, NY: John Wiley & Sons.

Zhou, D., & Lo, V. (2006). WaveGrid: A scalable fast-turnaround heterogeneous peer-based desktop grid system. In *Proceedings of the 20th IEEE International Symposium on Parallel and Distributed Processing* (p. 1-10).

This work was previously published in the International Journal of Grid and High Performance Computing, Volume 3, Issue 4, edited by Emmanuel Udoh and Ching-Hsien Hsu, pp. 71-86, copyright 2011 by IGI Publishing (an imprint of IGI Global).

Chapter 14
Structural Outlooks for the OTIS–Arrangement Network

Ahmad Awwad
Fahad Bin Sultan University, Saudi Arabia

Jehad Al-Sadi
Arab Open University, Jordan

Bassam Haddad
University of Petra, Jordan

Ahmad Kayed
Fahad Bin Sultan University, Saudi Arabia

ABSTRACT

Recent studies have revealed that the Optical Transpose Interconnection Systems (OTIS) are promising candidates for future high-performance parallel computers. This paper presents and evaluates a general method for algorithm development on the OTIS-Arrangement network (OTIS-AN) as an example of OTIS network. The proposed method can be used and customized for any other OTIS network. Furthermore, it allows efficient mapping of a wide class of algorithms into the OTIS-AN. This method is based on grids and pipelines as popular structures that support a vast body of parallel applications including linear algebra, divide-and-conquer types of algorithms, sorting, and FFT computation. This study confirms the viability of the OTIS-AN as an attractive alternative for large-scale parallel architectures.

INTRODUCTION

The choice of network topology for parallel systems is a critical design decision that involves inherent trade-offs in terms of efficient algorithms support and network implementation cost. For instance, networks with large bisection width allow

fast and reliable communication. However, such networks are difficult to implement using today's electronic technologies that are two dimensional in nature (Wang & Sahni, 2002). In principle, free-space optical technologies offer several fronts to improve this trade-off. The improved transmission rates, dense interconnects, power consumption, and signal interference are few examples on these fronts (Agelis, 2005; Akers et al., 1977; Dally,

DOI: 10.4018/978-1-4666-2065-0.ch014

1988; Day & Tripathi, 1990; Hendrick et al., 1959; Wang & Sahni, 2001; Yayla et al., 1998).

In this paper, we focus on Optical Transpose Interconnection Systems Arrangement Networks-(OTIS-AN) which was proposed by Al-Sadi that can be easily implemented using free-space optoelectronic technologies (Agelis, 2005; Al-Sadi & Awwad, 2010). In this model, processors are partitioned into groups, where each group is realized on a separate chip with electronic inter-processor connects. Processors on separate chips are interconnected through free space interconnects. The philosophy behind this separation is to utilize the benefits of both the optical and the electronic technologies.

The advantage of using OTIS as optoelectronic architecture lies in its ability to maneuver the fact that free space optical communication is superior in terms of speed and power consumption when the connection distance is more than few millimeters (Dally, 1988). In the OTIS-AN, shorter (intra-chip) communication is realized by electronic interconnects while longer (inter-chip) communication is realized by free space interconnects.

Extensive modeling results for the OTIS have been reported in (Day & Tripathi, 2002). The achievable Terra bit throughput at a reasonable cost makes the OTIS-AN a strong competitive to the to its factor network (Dally, 1988; Krishnamoorthy et al., 1992; Marsden et al., 1993).

These encouraging findings prompt the need for further testing of the suitability of the OTIS-AN for real-life applications. A number of recent studies have been conducted in this direction (Al-Sadi, 2004; Awwad & Al-Ayyoub, 2001; Chatterjee & Pawlowski, 1999; Day & Al-Ayyoub, 2002). Awwad (2005) have presented and evaluated various algorithms on OTIS-networks such as basic data rearrangements, routing, selection and sorting. They have also developed algorithms for various matrix multiplication operations and image processing (Sahni & Wang, 1997; Wang & Sahni, 2000). Zane et al. (2000) have shown that the

OTIS-mesh efficiently embeds four-dimensional meshes and hypercubes.

Aside from the above mentioned works, the study of algorithms on the OTIS is yet to mature (Sahni, 1999). In this paper we contribute towards filling this gap by presenting a method for developing algorithms on the OTIS-AN. These methods is based on grid and pipeline as popular a structure that supports a vast body of applications ranging from linear algebra to divide-and-conquer type of algorithms, sorting, and FFT computation. The proposed methods are discussed in the sequel, but first we give the necessary definitions and notation

PRELIMINARY NOTATIONS AND DEFINITIONS

Let n and k be two integers satisfying $1 \leq k \leq n-1$ and let us denote $<n> = \{1, 2, \ldots, n\}$ and $<k> = \{1, 2, \ldots, k\}$. Let P_k^n taken k at a time, the set of arrangements of k elements out of the n elements of $<n>$. The k elements of an arrangements p are denoted $p_1, p_2, \ldots, p_k$.

Definition 1 (Arrangement Graph):

The (n,k)-arrangement graph $A_{n,k} = (V, E)$ is an undirected graph given by:

$$V = \{ p_1 p_2 \cdots p_k | p_i \text{ in} <n> \text{ and } p_i \neq p_j \text{ for } i \neq j\} = P_k^n,$$
$$\ldots \qquad (1)$$

and

$$E = \{(p,q) \mid p \text{ and } q \text{ in } V \text{ and for some } i \text{ in } <k>,$$
$$p_i \neq q_i \text{ and } p_j = q_j \text{ for } j \neq i\}. \ldots \qquad (2)$$

That is the nodes of $A_{n,k}$ are the arrangements of k elements out of n elements of $<n>$, and the edges of $A_{n,k}$ connect arrangements which differ exactly in one of their k positions. For example in $A_{5,2}$ the node $p=23$ is connected to the nodes 21, 24, 25, 13, 43, and 53. An edge of $A_{n,k}$ connecting two arrangements p and q which differ only in one position i, it is called i-edge. In this case, p and q is called the (i,q)-neighbour of p. $A_{n,k}$ is therefore a regular graph with degree $k(n-k)$ and $n!/(n-k)!$ nodes. As an example of this network Figure 1 shows $A_{4,2}$ arrangement with size of 12 nodes and a symmetric degree of 4.

Since OTIS-networks are basically constructed by "multiplying" a known topology by itself. The set of vertices is equal to the Cartesian product on the set of vertices in the factor network. The set of edges consists of edges from the factor network and new edges called the *transpose* edges. The formal definition of OTIS-networks is given below.

Definition 2 (*OTIS-Network*):

Let $G_0 = (V_0, E_0)$ be an undirected graph representing a factor network. The OTIS-$G_0 = (V, E)$ network is represented by an undirected graph obtained from G_0 as follows $V = \{\langle x, y \rangle \mid x, y \in V_0\}$ and $E = \{(\langle x, y \rangle, \langle x, z \rangle) \mid \text{if } (y, z) \in E_0\} \cup \{(\langle x, y \rangle, \langle y, x \rangle) \mid x, y \in V_0 \text{ and } x \neq y\}$.

The set of edges E in the above definition consists of two subsets, one is from G_0, called G_0-type edges, and the other subset contains the *transpose* edges. The OTIS-AN approach suggests implementing *Arrangement*-type edges by electronic links since they involve intra-chip short links and implementing transpose edges by free space optics. Throughout this paper the terms "*electronic move*" and the "*OTIS move*" (or "*optical move*") will be used to refer to data transmission based on electronic and optical technologies, respectively.

Definition 3 (Cross Product):

The cross product $G = G_1 \otimes G_2$ of two undirected connected graphs $G_1 = (V_1, E_1)$ and $G_2 = (V_2, E_2)$ is the undirected Graph $G = (V, E)$, where V and E are given by:

Figure 1. The arrangement graph $A_{4,2}$

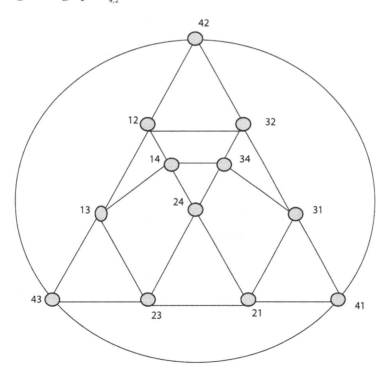

$V=\{\langle x_1, y\rangle \mid x_1 \in V_1 \text{ and } y \in V_2\}$ and

$E=\{(\langle x_1, y\rangle, \langle y_1, y\rangle) \mid (x_1, y_1) \in E_1\} \cup \{(\langle x, x_2\rangle, \langle x, y_2\rangle) \mid (x_2, y_2) \in E_2\}$.

So for any $u=\langle x_1, x_2\rangle$ and $v=\langle y_1, y_2\rangle$ in V, (u, v) is an edge in E if, and only, if either (x_1, y_1) is an edge in E_1 and $x_2 = y_2$, or (x_2, y_2) is an edge in E_2 and $x_1 = y_1$. The edge (u, v) is called a G_1-edge if (x_1, y_1) is an edge in E_1, and it is called G_2-edge if (x_2, y_2) is an edge in E_2. The size, degree, diameter and number of links of the cross product of two networks are defined next.

Definition 4: (Topological properties of cross product networks)

If G_1 and G_2 are two undirected connected graphs of respective size s_{l1} and s_2 and have respective diameters δ_1 and δ_2, then (Day & Al-Ayyoub, 2002):

1. $G_1 \otimes G_2$ connected.
2. The diameter δ of $G_1 \otimes G_2$ is $\delta = \delta_1 + \delta_2$.
3. The size s of $G_1 \otimes G_2$ is given by s = $s_1.s_2$.
4. The degree of a node $u = \langle x_1, x_2\rangle$ in $G_1 \otimes G_2$ is equal to the sum of the degrees of vertices x_1 and x_2 in G_1 and G_2, respectively.
5. Number of links for the product network, is given by (size·degree)/2.

TOPOLOGICAL PROPERTIES OF OTIS-AN

This section reviews some of the basic topological properties of the OTIS-Arrangement network including size, degree, diameter, number of links, and shortest distance between 2 nodes (Day & Tripathi, 1992; Al-Sadi & Awwad, 2010).

The topological properties of the OTIS-Arrangement network along with those of the Arrangement network are discussed below.

We will refer to g as the group address and p as the processor address. An intergroup edge of the form $(\langle g, p\rangle, \langle p, g\rangle)$ represents an optical link and will be referred to as OTIS or optical move. Note that also we will be using the following notations are defined:

* $|A_{n,k}|$ = size of the graph $A_{n,k}$.
* $|\text{OTIS-}A_{n,k}|$ = size of the graph OTIS-$A_{n,k}$.
*   Deg. $A_{n,k}(p)$ = Degree of the graph $A_{n,k}$ at node p.
*   Deg. OTIS-$A_{n,k}(g, p)$ = Degree of the graph OTIS-$A_{n,k}$ at node address $<g, p>$.
*   Dist-$A_{n,k}(p_1, p_2)$ = The length of a shortest path between the two nodes p_1 and p_2 in Arrangement graph.
*   Dist. OTIS-$A_{n,k}(p_1, p_2)$ = The length of a shortest path between the two nodes $<g_1, p_1>$ and $<g_2, p_2>$ in OTIS-Arrangement.

In the OTIS-Arrangement the notation $\langle g, p\rangle$ is used to refer to the group and processor addresses respectively. Figure 2 shows that as an example of OTIS-$A_{3,2}$. The figure shows that two nodes $\langle g_1, p_1\rangle$ and $\langle g_2, p_2\rangle$ are connected if and only if $g_1 = g_2$ and $(p_1, p_2) \in E_0$ (such that E_0 is the set of edges in Arrangement network) or $g_1 = p_2$ and $p_1 = g_2$, in this case the two nodes are connected by transpose edge. The distance in the OTIS-Arrangement is defined as the shortest path between any two processors, $\langle g_1, p_1\rangle$ and $\langle g_2, p_2\rangle$, and involves one of the following forms:

1. When $g_1 = g_2$ then the path involves only electronic moves from source node to destination node.
2. *When* $g_1 \neq g_2$ and if the number of optical moves is an even number of moves and more than two, then the paths can be compressed into a shorter path of the form: $\langle g_1, p_1\rangle \xrightarrow{E} \langle g_1, p_2\rangle \xrightarrow{O} \langle p_2, g_1\rangle \xrightarrow{E} \langle p_2, g_2\rangle \xrightarrow{O} \langle g_2, p_2\rangle$ here the symbols

Figure 2. OTIS-$A_{3,2}$ network

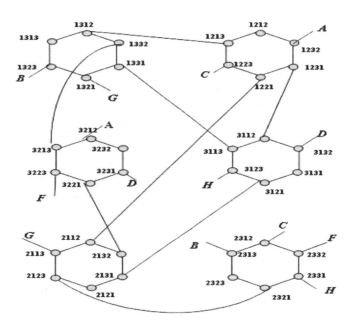

O and E stand for optical and electronic moves respectively.

When $g_1 \neq g_2$, and the path involves an odd number of OTIS moves. In this case the paths can be compressed into a shorter path of the form:

$$\langle g_1, p_1 \rangle \xrightarrow{E} \langle g_1, g_2 \rangle \xrightarrow{O} \langle g_2, g_1 \rangle \xrightarrow{E} \langle g_2, p_2 \rangle.$$

The following are the basic topological properties for the OTIS-Arrangement. For instance if the factor Arrangement network is of size $n!/(n-k)!|$, degree is n-1 and diameter is $\lfloor 1.5\, k \rfloor$ (Day & Tripathi, 1992).

Then the size, the degree, the diameter, number of links, and the shortest distance of OTIS-Arrangement network are as follows:

- Size of $|OTIS\text{-}A_{n,k}| = |n!/(n-k)!|^2$.
- Degree of $OTIS\text{-}A_{n,k} = Deg.(A_{n,k})$, if $g = p$.
- Deg. $(A_{n,k}) + 1$, if $g \neq p$.
- Diameter of $OTIS\text{-}A_{n,k} = 2\lfloor 1.5\, k \rfloor +1$.

- Number of Links: Let N_0 be the number of links in the $A_{n,k}$ and let M be the number of nodes in the $A_{n,k}$. The number of links in the $OTIS\text{-}A_{n,k} = (M^2 - M)/2 + N_0^2$. For instance, the number of links in the $OTIS\text{-}A_{4,2}$ consisting of 144 processors is $= (12^2 - 12)/2 + 23_0^2 = 595$

- Dist. of $OTIS\text{-}A_{n,k} =$

$$\begin{bmatrix} \min(\ d(p_1, g_2) + d(g_1, p_2) \\ + 1, d(p_1, p_2) + d(g_1, g_2) + 2) & \text{if } g1 \neq g2 \\ \text{Dist. } (p1, p2) & \text{if } g1 = g2 \end{bmatrix}$$

Theorem 1:

The length of the shortest path between any two processors $\langle g_1, p_1 \rangle$ and $\langle g_2, p_2 \rangle$ in OTIS-Arrangement is $d(p_1, p_2)$ when $g_1 = g_2$ and min$\{d(p_1, p_2) + d(g_1, g_2) + 2, d(p_1, g_2) + d(g_1, p_2) + 1\}$ when $g_1 \neq g_2$, where $d(p, g)$ stands for the shortest distance between the two processors p and g using any of the possible shortest paths as seen in the above forms 1, 2 and 3 (Awwad, 2005).

It is obvious from the above theorem that when $g_1 = g_2$, then the length of the path between the two processors $\langle g_1, p_1 \rangle$ and $\langle g_2, p_2 \rangle$ is $d(p_1, p_2)$. From the shortest path construction methods in (2) and (3) above, it can be easily verified that the length of the path equal min $\{d(p_1, p_2) + d(g_1, g_2) +2, d(p_1, g_2) + d(g_1, p_2) + 1$ when $g_1 \neq g_2\}$.

To send a message M from the source node $\langle g_1, p_1 \rangle$ to the destination node $\langle g_2, p_2 \rangle$ it must follow a route along one of the three possible paths *1, 2,* and *3*. The length of the shortest path between the nodes $\langle g_1, p_1 \rangle$ and $\langle g_2, p_2 \rangle$ is one of the forms (as seen in Box 1).

Where $d(p_1, p_2)$ is the length of the shortest path between any two processors $\langle g_1, p_1 \rangle$ and $\langle g_1, p_2 \rangle$. If δ_0 is the diameter of the factor network $A_{n,k}$ then from (1I) it follows that the diameter of the OTIS-$A_{n,k}$ is $2\delta_0 + 1$. The diameter of OTIS-$A_{n,k}$ is the *Max* $(\delta_0, 2\delta_0 + 1)$ which is equal to $2\delta_0 + 1$. The proof of the above theorem is a direct result from (I).

GRID STRUCTURAL OUTLOOK FOR OTIS-ARRANGEMENT NETWORK

In this section the hierarchical structure of the OTIS-AN is discussed. The properties of a new decomposition method for the OTIS-AN presented and proved. These properties are then used in the subsequent sections to develop grids and pipelines as methods for developing various parallel algorithms on the OTIS-AN.

An OTIS-AN based computer contains N^2 processors partitioned into N groups with N processors each. A processor is indexed by a pair $\langle x, y \rangle$, $0 \leq x, y < N$ where x is the group index and y is the processor index. Processors within a group are connected by a certain interconnecting topology; while inter-group links are achieved by transposing group and processor indexes (Sahni, 1999; Wang & Sahni, 2002).

The OTIS-AN constructed by "multiplying" the arrangement factor topology by itself. The vertex set is equal to the *Cartesian* product on the vertex set in the arrangement network. The edge set consists of edges from the arrangement network and new edges called the *transpose* edges.

The address of a node $u = \langle x, y \rangle$ from V is composed of two components: the first, denoted by $\gamma(u)=x$, designates the group address and the second, denoted by $\rho(u)=y$, designates the processor address within that group.

The network OTIS-AN can be decomposed into $|V_0|$ disjoint copies of AN. This decomposition can be achieved by fixing the group address and varying the processor address. Another way of decomposing the OTIS-AN is by fixing the processors $_{address}$ and varying the group address. These two decomposition methods are given below.

Definition 5 (row-subgraph):

Let Ψ_i for all $i \in V_0$, be the subgraph induced by the set of nodes from V having the form $\langle i, x \rangle \; \forall x \in V_0$.

Definition 6 (column-subgraph):

Box 1.

$$
\text{Length} =
\begin{cases}
d(p_1, p_2) \text{ if } g_1 = g_2 \\
\\
min(d(p_1, g_2) + d(g_1, p_2) + 1, d(p_1, p_2) + d(g_1, g_2) + 2) \; o.w.
\end{cases}
$$

(3)

Let Φ_j, for all $j \in V_0$, be the subgraph induced by the set of nodes from V having the form $\langle x, j \rangle$ for all $x \in V_0$.

Given a graph G, for simplicity we denote by V_G the set of vertices, E_G the set of edges, $d_G(u, v)$ the length of a shortest path connecting u and v, and δ_G the diameter of G. Finally, any two graphs G_1 and G_2 are said to share *perfect matching* if there exists a bijective function between V_{G1} and V_{G2}.

Definition 7 (perfectly matching):

Let $G_\Psi = (V_{G\Psi}, E_{G\Psi})$ be the graph obtained from OTIS-AN_0 by clustering Ψ_i into a single vertex labeled by i and having a link between i and j if Ψ_i and Ψ_j share a prefect matching, i.e. $V_{G\Psi} = V_0$ and $E_{G\Psi} = \{(i, j) \mid \Psi_i \text{ perfectly matches } \Psi_j\}$.

Theorem 2:

The two Ψ and Φ decomposition methods of the OTIS-AN_0 have the following properties:

1. Ψ_i is isomorphic to AN_0.
2. $V_{\Psi i} \cap V_{\Phi j} = \{\langle i, j \rangle\}$.
3. Ψ_i and Φ_i share perfect matching for all i values.
4. Ψ_i and Ψ_j share perfect matching for all i and j values and hence G_Ψ is a complete graph. (Figure 3)

Proof:

Property 1 is a direct consequence of Definition 7. The function ρ maps nodes from $V_{\Psi i}$ to V_0. In fact, the set $\{\rho(u) \mid u \in \Psi_i\}$ is equal to V_0 for any i. Since any two neighboring nodes u and v in Ψ_i should have $\gamma(u) = \gamma(v)$ and since $(\rho(u), \rho(v))$ is an edge in E_0; the subgraph Ψ_i is isomorphic to AN_0.

Property 2 states that for any two labels i and j from V_0, the two subgraphs Ψ_i and Φ_j have exactly one node in common. Since, $V_{\Psi i} = \{\langle i, x \rangle \mid x \in V_0\}$ and $V_{\Phi j} = \{\langle x, j \rangle \mid x \in V_0\}$, the intersection $V_{\Psi i} \cap V_{\Phi j}$ contains only the node $\langle i, j \rangle$.

Let $f_i: V_{\Psi i} \to V_{\Phi i}$ be a function that maps nodes form Ψ_i into Φ_i for all i values defined as follows: $f_i(\langle x, y \rangle) = \langle y, x \rangle$. First we have $|V_{\Psi i}| = |V_{\Phi i}|$ for all i and j. For any two distinct nodes u and v in $V_{\Psi i}$ we have $f_i(\langle \gamma(u), \rho(u) \rangle) = \langle \rho(u), \gamma(u) \rangle \neq f_i(\langle \gamma(v), \rho(v) \rangle) = \langle \rho(v), \gamma(v) \rangle$; because $\rho(u) \neq \rho(v)$. Hence the function f_i is on-to-one and onto. Thus property 3 follows.

Let $t_{ij}: V_{\Psi i} \to V_{\Psi j}$ be a function that maps nodes form Ψ_i into Ψ_j, for any i and j, as follows: $t_{ij}(\langle i, x \rangle) = \langle j, x \rangle$. For any two distinct nodes u and v from $V_{\Psi i}$ we have $t_{ij}(\langle i, \rho(u) \rangle) = \langle j, \rho(u) \rangle \neq t_{ij}(\langle i, \rho(v) \rangle) = \langle j, \rho(v) \rangle$. Since $|V_{\Psi i}| = |V_{\Psi j}|$ it follows that Ψ_i and Ψ_j share perfect matching for all i and j values and hence G_Ψ is a complete graph.

Lemma 1: G_Ψ can be embedded into OTIS-AN_0 with dilation $\delta_{AN0} + 2$.

Proof:

Since G_Ψ is complete, any two distinct *nodes* i and j in $V_{AN\Psi}$ are neighbors. The "virtual" path between $\langle i, x \rangle$ and $\langle j, x \rangle$ in OTIS-AN_0 that corresponds to the edge (i, j) in $E_{AN\Psi}$ is constructed as follows: $\langle i, x \rangle \to \langle x, i \rangle \parallel \pi_{G0}(i, j) \parallel \langle x, j \rangle \to \langle j, x \rangle$. An arrow represents an edge connecting the two nodes and the operation "$\parallel$" means appending two paths (i.e. connecting the last node in the left path to first node in the right path). Notice that the choice of x from V_0 does not affect the construction of this path nor its length. The path segment $\pi_{G0}(i, j)$ is an isomorphic copy to the optimal length path from i to j in AN_0. It can be verified that the above constructed path is of optimal length equal to $d_{AN0}(i, j) + 2$. Hence, the longest such path cannot exceed $\delta_{AN0} + 2$.

PIPELINE STRUCTURE FOR THE OTIS-ARRANGEMENT NETWORK

The structural outlooks are based on grid and pipeline views as popular structures that support

Figure 3. The grid structural for OTIS-AN

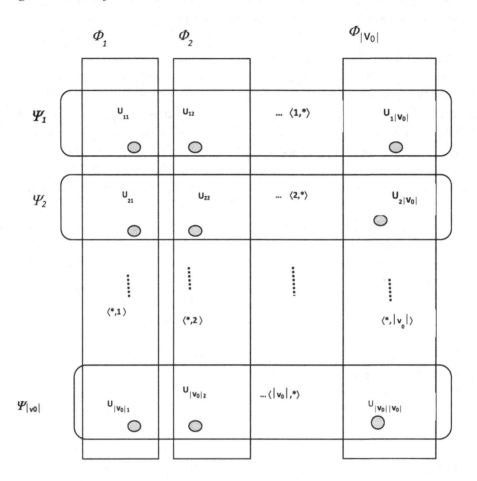

a vast body of applications that are encountered in many areas of science and engineering, including matrix computation, divide-and-conquer type of algorithms, sorting, and Fourier transforms. The proposed structural outlooks are applied to the OTIS, notably the OTIS-AN network.

The pipeline structure is a well-known structural outlook that is suitable for real applications It is known from the literature that the Arrangement graph can be structured according to a pipelined view where the OTIS-AN can be arranged as a sequence of (n)-Arrangement forming an n-stage pipeline. However, the structural outlook based on the pipeline view for the Arrangement graph is insufficient as it generates a large number of nodes in each pipeline stage (Saika & Sen, 1995, 1996).

The OTIS-AN graph possesses a structural outlook that provides a pipelined structure in a more balanced manner. From the literature (Day & Tripathi, 1992; Jwo et al., 1991), we know that the arrangement graph is Hamiltonian. Therefore, the pipeline structure can be issued for the OTIS-AN graph in: by the graph $A_{n,k}$ and the Hamiltonian path OTIS or vice versa (Day & Al-Ayyoub, 1992). We have full control over the number of stages and the size of each stage by tuning the parameters n, m, k.

The broadcasting across stages is the cost in one stage plus the cost of shifting the data to the next stage for the pipeline structure as a performance measure. The results will be reported for different network sizes and a fixed message of length M =1024 byte (Graham & Seidel, 1993).

For the structure, we estimate the communication cost of broadcasting across a row plus the communication cost across a column (Day & Tripathi, 1992; Jwo et al., 1991; Graham & Seidel, 1993). To estimate the broadcasting in both directions we use the lower bound formula that has been extensively used in existing similar studies (Al-Ayyoub & Day, 1997; Graham & Seidel, 1993):

$$\left(\sqrt{\frac{M.a}{\beta\Delta}} + \sqrt{\delta - 1} \right)^2 \beta .$$

The parameters Δ and δ are the degree and diameter of the graph respectively and the symbols M, a, and β are the message length, unit transmission cost and the message latency cost. The values of these parameters are set to 1024 byte, 1 μs and 1000 μs respectively.

The broadcasting cost based on the pipeline structure can be estimated in two different ways; by shifting the data through the Hamiltonian cycle of $A_{n,k}$ or by shifting the data through the Hamiltonian cycle of *OTIS*. The lower bound of the broadcasting cost in the pipelined structure is equal to the lower bound of the broadcasting cost in the arrangement graph across one stage plus the cost of shifting the data to the next stage or vice versa. The cost of shifting the data to the next stage is equal to $\delta(\beta+Ma)$, where the parameters M, β and a are as defined previously (Al-Ayyoub & Day, 1997).

Theorem 3: If $A_{n,k}$ is Hamiltonian, OTIS- $A_{n,k}$ embeds a pipeline consisting of $|V_0|$ stages of size $|V_0|$ nodes each. Stages are $A_{n,k}$-configured and interstage distance is 3.

Proof: OTIS-$A_{n,k}$ network can be decomposed into $|V_0|$ disjoint copies of Ψ_x sub-networks. The Ψ_x subnetworks form the different pipeline stages. By Theorem 2 each of the Ψ_x's is isomorphic to $A_{n,k}$. We arrange the pipeline stages (the Ψ_x's) according the rank of x in a Hamiltonian cycle of $A_{n,k}$. Let $h: V_0 \rightarrow \{1, 2, ..., |V_0|\}$ be a function that defines the node's rank in the Hamiltonian cycle of $A_{n,k}$. So, the jth stage consists of the set of nodes $\{\langle h^{-1}(j), y \rangle \mid y \in V_0\}$. The node $\langle h^{-1}(j), y \rangle$ in the jth stage is coupled with the node $\langle h^{-1}(j+1), y \rangle$ in the $(j+1)^{st}$ stage of the pipeline. These two nodes are connected by the path $\langle h^{-1}(j), y \rangle \rightarrow \langle y, h^{-1}(j) \rangle \rightarrow \langle y, h^{-1}(j+1) \rangle \rightarrow \langle h^{-1}(j+1), y \rangle$. Notice that $h^{-1}(j)$ and $h^{-1}(j+1)$ are neighbours in $A_{n,k}$.

Corollary 1: If $A_{n,k}$ is Hamiltonian, OTIS- $A_{n,k}$ can embed a two-dimensional wraparound mesh with dilation 3.

The above pipeline structural outlook exemplifies circular pipelines. Changing the number of stages or stage configuration (linear, circular, tree, etc.) in the above pipeline structure is straightforward. This can be done by characterising a path, cycle, or tree of size equal to the required number of stages in the new pipeline. Stages in the new pipeline are then ordered according to the ranks of the nodes in the characterised path, cycle, or tree. The interstage distance is 3 in all these cases. In fact, the result in Theorem 3 can be extended so that we have control over the stage structure as well. The stage can be $A_{n,k}$ or any network embedded in $A_{n,k}$.

CONCLUSION

The study of algorithms on the Optical Transpose Interconnection Systems (OTIS) is still far from being matured. In this paper, we have contributed towards filling this gap by proposing a method for algorithm development on OTIS-AN network. This method is based on the grid and pipeline structure as popular framework for supporting vast body of important real-world parallel applications. Utilizing this method to develop parallel algorithms for linear algebra will be discussed as a future case study.

Several topological properties including size, degree, diameter, number of links and shortest distance between any two nodes have been discussed. The proposed OTIS-AN shown to be an attractive alternative for its factor network in terms of routing by utilizing both electronic and optical technologies. As a future research work we could utilize the proposed framework in solving real life problems on OTIS-AN including Matrix problems and Fast Fourier transforms.

REFERENCES

Agelis, S. (2000). Optoelectronic router with a reconfigurable shuffle network based on micro-optoelectromechanical systems. *Journal of Optical Networking*, *4*(1), 1–10. doi:10.1364/JON.4.000001

Akers, S. B., Harel, D., & Krishnamurthy, B. (1987). The star graph: An attractive alternative to the n-Cube. In *Proceedings of the International Conference on Parallel Processing* (pp. 393-400).

Al-Ayyoub, A., & Day, K. (1997). Matrix decomposition on the star graph. *IEEE Transactions on Parallel and Distributed Systems*, *8*(8), 803–812. doi:10.1109/71.605767

Al-Ayyoub, A., & Day, K. (1998). The hyperstar interconnection network. *Journal of Parallel and Distributed Computing*, *48*(2), 175–199. doi:10.1006/jpdc.1997.1414

Al-Sadi, J., & Awwad, A. (2010). *A new efficient interconnection network*. International Arab Journal of Information Technology.

Al-Sadi, J., Awwad, A., & AlBdaiwi, B. (2004). Efficient routing algorithm on OTIS-Star network. In *Proceedings of the IASTED International Conference on Advances in Computer Science and Technology* (pp. 157-162).

Awwad, A., Al-Ayyoub, A., Ould-Khaoua, M., & Day, K. (2001). Solving linear systems equations using the grid structural outlook. In *Proceedings of the 13th IASTED Parallel and Distributed Computing and Systems* (pp. 365-369).

Awwad, A. M. (2005). OTIS-star an attractive alternative network. In *Proceedings of the 4th WSEAS International Conference on Software Engineering, Parallel & Distributed Systems* (p. 37).

Chatterjee, S., & Pawlowski, S. (1999). Enlightening the effects and implications of nearly infinite bandwidth. *Communications of the ACM*, *42*(6), 75–83.

Dally, W. J. (1988). Performance analysis of k-ary n-cubes interconnection networks. *IEEE Transactions on Computers*, *39*(6), 775–785. doi:10.1109/12.53599

Day, K., & Al-Ayyoub, A. (1999). The cross product of interconnection networks. *IEEE Transactions on Parallel and Distributed Systems*, *8*(2), 109–118. doi:10.1109/71.577251

Day, K., & Al-Ayyoub, A. (2002). Topological properties of OTIS-Networks. *IEEE Transactions on Parallel and Distributed Systems*, *13*(4), 359–366. doi:10.1109/71.995816

Day, K., & Tripathi, A. (1992). Arrangement graphs: A class of generalised star graphs. *Information Processing Letters*, *42*, 235–241. doi:10.1016/0020-0190(92)90030-Y

Day, K., & Tripathi, A. (1992). *Embedding of cycles in arrangement graphs (Tech. Rep. No. TR 91-58)*. Minneapolis, MN: University of Minnesota.

Graham, S., & Seidel, S. (1993). The cost of broadcasting on star graphs and k-ary hypercubes. *IEEE Transactions on Computers*, *42*(6), 756–759. doi:10.1109/12.277296

Hendrick, W., Kibar, O., & Esener, S. (1959). *Modeling and optimisation of the optical transpose interconnection system*. Ithaca, NY: Cornell University.

Jwo, J., Lakshmivarahan, S., & Dhall, S. (1991). Embedding of cycles and grids in star graphs. *Journal of Circuits, Systems, and Computers*, *1*(1), 43–74. doi:10.1142/S0218126691000215

Krishnamoorthy, A., Marchand, P., Kiamilev, F., & Esener, S. (1992). Grain-size considerations for optoelectronic multistage interconnection networks. *Applied Optics*, *31*(2), 5480–5507. doi:10.1364/AO.31.005480

Marsden, G., Marchand, P., Harvey, P., & Esener, S. (1993). Optical transpose interconnection system architecture. *Optics Letters*, *18*(13), 1083–1085. doi:10.1364/OL.18.001083

Sahni, S. (1999). Models and algorithms for optical and optoelectronic parallel computers. In *Proceedings of the International Symposium on Parallel Algorithms and Networks* (pp. 2-7).

Sahni, S., & Wang, C. (1997). *BPC permutations on the OTIS-mesh optoelectronic computer* (Tech. Rep. No. 97-008). Gainesville, FL: University of Florida.

Saika, D., & Sen, R. K. (1990). Two ranking schemes for efficient computation on the star interconnection network. *IEEE Transactions on Parallel and Distributed Systems*, *96*(7), 321–327.

Saika, D., & Sen, R. K. (1995). Order preserving communication on a star network. *Parallel Computing*, *21*, 1292–1300.

Wang, C., & Sahni, S. (2000). Image processing on the OTIS-mesh optoelectronic computer. *IEEE Transactions on Parallel and Distributed Systems*, *11*(2), 97–109. doi:10.1109/71.841747

Wang, C., & Sahni, S. (2001). Matrix multiplications on the OTIS-mesh optoelectronic computer. *IEEE Transactions on Computers*, *40*(7), 635–646. doi:10.1109/12.936231

Wang, C., & Sahni, S. (2002). Computational geometry on the OTIS-Mesh optoelectronic computer. In *Proceedings of the International Conference on Parallel Processing* (pp. 501-507).

Yayla, G., Marchand, P., & Esener, S. (1998). Speed and energy analysis of digital interconnections: Comparison of on-chip, off-chip, and free-space technologies. *Applied Optics*, *37*(2), 205–227. doi:10.1364/AO.37.000205

Zane, F., Marchand, P., Paturi, R., & Esener, S. (2000). Scalable network architecture using the optical transpose interconnection system (OTIS). *Journal of Parallel and Distributed Computing*, *60*, 521–538. doi:10.1006/jpdc.2000.1627

This work was previously published in the International Journal of Grid and High Performance Computing, Volume 3, Issue 2, edited by Emmanuel Udoh and Ching-Hsien Hsu, pp. 59-68, copyright 2011 by IGI Publishing (an imprint of IGI Global).

Chapter 15
Energy Efficient Packet Data Service in Wireless Sensor Network in Presence of Rayleigh Fading

Arnab Nandi
National Institute of Technology Durgapur, India

Sumit Kundu
National Institute of Technology Durgapur, India

ABSTRACT

Energy level performances of three packet delivery schemes in Wireless Sensor Networks (WSN) are evaluated in presence of Rayleigh fading. Three different information delivery mechanisms are investigated using regenerative relays with or without error correction capability. Energy consumption for successful delivery of a data packet for each mechanism is evaluated and compared under several conditions of node density, bit rate, transmit power, and channel fading. Energy efficiencies of different retransmission schemes are also evaluated. Further, an optimal packet length based on energy efficiency is derived. Impact of optimal packet size on average number of retransmission and total energy expenditure is analyzed for each delivery scheme.

INTRODUCTION

Recent advances in wireless communication technologies led to great interest in wireless sensor networks (WSNs). WSN consists of wireless interconnection of several sensor nodes which comprise of sensor devices with wireless communication facilities (Akyildiz et al., 2002). Most

of the research work on WSN assumes idealized radio propagation models without considering fading and shadowing effects. However network performance degrades due to shadowing and fading (Goldsmith, 2005). Relayed transmission is a promising technique that helps in attaining broader coverage and in combating the impairment of the wireless channel. Relaying information on several hops reduces the need of large transmitter power and distributes the use of power throughout

DOI: 10.4018/978-1-4666-2065-0.ch015

the hops which results in extended battery life and lowered level of interference (Raghunathan, 2002). Energy conservation is one of the most important issues in WSN, where nodes are likely to rely on limited battery power. The connectivity of WSN mostly depends on the transmission power of the source nodes. If the transmission power is not sufficiently high there may be single or multiple link failure. Further transmitting at high power reduces the battery life and introduces excessive inter node interference. Given that the sensors have limited energy, buffer space, and other resources, different MAC protocols are being developed by several researchers (Dam & Langendoen, 2003; Kwon et al., 2006). Most of the previous research work in this field assumes free-space radio link model and Additive White Gaussian Noise (AWGN) (Bettstetter & Zangl, 2002; Panichpapiboon et al., 2006; Tseng & Chen, 2004). However signal fading due to multipath propagation severely impairs the performance of wireless link. Several approaches have been proposed in literature to prolong network lifetime. Sooksan et al. evaluated Bit Error Rate (BER) performance and optimal power to preserve the network connectivity considering only path-loss and thermal noise (Panichpapiboon et al., 2006). In Bettstetter and Zangl (2002) Bettstetter et al. derived the transmission range for which network is connected with high probability considering free-space radio link model. In Tseng and Chen (2004) the relationships between transmission range, service area and network connectedness is studied in a free space model. Narayanaswamy et al. (2002) proposed a protocol that extends battery life through providing low power routes in a medium with path loss exponent greater than two. In Mansouri et al. (2005) a new method is proposed utilizing a diversity scheme to reduce power consumption in large scale sensor networks.

In this paper, Energy level performances of three different information delivery mechanisms are evaluated in presence of Rayleigh fading. In all the three schemes, message packet is sent on hop-by-hop basis. Further in scheme I message is corrected at every hop. While in the other two schemes, message is corrected at the destination. However in case II, ACK/NACK propagates from destination to source via multiple hops through intermediate nodes while in case III it propagates directly. Further we derived energy efficiency of those retransmission mechanisms. Energy requirement for successful delivery of a packet is evaluated under several conditions of network such as node density. Impact of Rayleigh fading on energy requirement is also investigated. We propose a scheme utilizing optimal size packets to reduce energy consumption in WSN. An optimal packet length which corresponds to highest energy efficiency for a particular set of network conditions is evaluated for each packet delivery scheme. The impact of optimal size packet on energy consumption is indicated for Rayleigh fading channel. The energy requirement also depends on routing and the Medium Access Control (MAC) protocol used (Ferrari & Tonguz; Perkins, 2001, 2003).

SYSTEM MODEL

A square grid network architecture is considered as in (Panichpapiboon et al., 2006). Figure 1 shows a two tier sensor network using square grid topology (Hong & Hua, 2006; Panichpapiboon et al., 2006). Distance between two nearest neighbor is d_{link}. It is assumed that N numbers of nodes are distributed over a region of area A obeying square grid topology. The node spatial density ρ_{sq} is defined as number of nodes per unit area i.e., $\rho_{sq} = N/A$. The minimum distance between two consecutive neighbors is given by (Panichpapiboon et al., 2006)

$$d_{link} = \frac{1}{\sqrt{\rho_{sq}}} \tag{1}$$

When the node density increases, minimum distance between two nodes decreases following (1).

Here we assume a simple routing strategy such that a packet is relayed hop-by-hop, through a sequence of nearest neighboring nodes, until it reaches the destination (Perkins, 2001). Therefore, we assume that a route between source and destination exists.

Further we consider a simple reservation-based MAC protocol, called reserve-and-go (RESGO) following (Ferrari & Tonguz, 2003; Perkins, 2001). In this protocol, a source node first reserves intermediate nodes on a route for relaying its packets to the destination. A transmission can begin after a route is discovered and reserved. If the destination node is busy, it waits for an exponential random back-off time before transmitting or relaying each packet again. When the random back-off time expires, node starts transmitting a packet. The random back-off time helps to reduce interference among nodes in the same route and also among nodes in different routes. Throughout this paper, we assume that the random back-off time is exponential with mean $1/\lambda_t$, where λ_t is the packet transmission rate.

The major perturbations in wireless transmission are large scale fading and small scale fading (Goldsmith, 2005; Sklar, 1997). Large scale fading represents the average signal power attenuation or path loss due to motion over large areas. This phenomenon is affected by prominent terrain contours (hills, forests, billboards, clumps of buildings, etc.) between the transmitter and receiver. However small-scale fading exhibits rapid changes in signal amplitude and phase as a result of small changes (as small as a half-wavelength) in the spatial separation between a receiver and transmitter. The rate of change of these propagation conditions accounts for the fading rapidity. Small-scale fading is also called Rayleigh fading because if the multiple reflective paths are large in number and there is no line-of-sight signal component, the envelope of the received signal is statistically described by a Rayleigh pdf given:

$$p(r) = r/\sigma^2 \exp\left[-r^2/2\sigma^2\right] \text{ for } r \geq 0$$
$$= 0 \quad \text{otherwise} \tag{2}$$

here r is the envelope amplitude of the received signal and $2\sigma^2$ is the pre-detection mean power of the multipath signal. When there is a dominant non-fading signal component present, the small scale fading envelope is described by a Rician pdf. In the present work we consider the presence of Rayleigh fading in addition to path loss.

It can be assumed without loss of generality that source node is at the center of the network (Figure 1). If a destination node is selected at random, the minimum number of hops to reach the destination can vary from 1 to $2i_{max}$, where i_{max} is the maximum tier order. Counting the number of hops on a route from the source to each destination node and finding the average value we determine the average number of hops. Assuming that each destination is equally likely, the average number of hops on a route can be written as (Panichpapiboon et al., 2006)

Figure 1. Sensor nodes in square grid topology

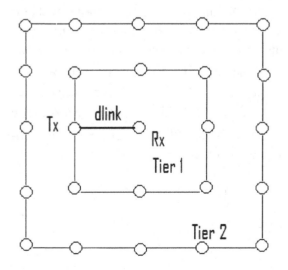

$$\bar{n}_{hop} \cong \sqrt{N}/2 \qquad (3)$$

The received signal at the receiver is the sum of three components (1) the intended signal from a transmitter, (2) interfering signals from other active nodes, and (3) thermal noise. Since the interfering signals come from other nodes, we assume that total interfering signal can be treated as an additive noise process independent of thermal noise process. The received signal in the antenna, Y during each bit period can be expressed as (Panichpapiboon et al., 2006)

$$Y = hS_{rcv} + \sum_{j=1}^{N-2} S_j + n_{thermal} \qquad (4)$$

where h is the channel on the receive antenna, S_{rcv} is the desired signal in the antenna, S_j is the interference from the other nodes and $n_{thermal}$ is the thermal noise signal.

The power received at the receiving end is given by Frii's transmission equation (Goldsmith, 2005)

$$P_{rcv} = \frac{P_t G_t G_r c^2}{\left(4\pi\right)^2 f_c^2 d_{link}^{\alpha}} \qquad (5)$$

where P_t is the transmit power, G_t is the transmitting antenna gain, G_r is the receiving antenna gain, f_c is the carrier frequency, α is the path-loss exponent and c is the velocity of light. Here we considered omni directional ($G_t=G_r=1$) antennas at the transmitter and receiver. The carrier frequency is in the unlicensed 2.4 GHz band. Assuming Binary Phase Shift Keying (BPSK) modulation, there can be two cases for the amplitude of the S_{rcv}

$$S_{rcv} = \sqrt{\frac{P_{rcv}}{R_{bit}}} = \sqrt{E_{bit}} \text{ for a +1 transmission}$$

$$= -\sqrt{\frac{P_{rcv}}{R_{bit}}} = -\sqrt{E_{bit}} \text{ for a -1 transmission} \qquad (6)$$

where R_{bit} is the bit rate and $\sqrt{E_{bit}}$ is the bit energy of the received signal considering only path loss.

The interference power received from node j can be written using Frii's transmission equation (Goldsmith, 2005; Panichpapiboon et al., 2006)

$$P_{int\,j} = \frac{P_{rcv}}{\left(\nu_j\right)^{\alpha}} \qquad (7)$$

ν_j is the multiplicative factor depends on the position of the interfering node. It is observed that the significant part of the inter-node interference comes from the first two tires only. So we consider inter-node interference from first two tires only.

For each interfering node j, the amplitude of the interfering signal can be of three types (Panichpapiboon et al., 2006):

$$S_j = \sqrt{\frac{P_{int\,j}}{R_{bit}}} \text{ for a +1 transmission}$$

$$= -\sqrt{\frac{P_{int\,j}}{R_{bit}}} \text{ for a -1 transmission}$$

$$=0 \text{ for no transmission of node j} \qquad (8)$$

The probability that an interfering node will transmit and cause interference depends on the MAC protocol used. Considering the RESGO MAC protocol and assuming that each node transmits packets with length L_{pkt}, the interference probability is equal to the probability that an interfering node transmits during the vulnerable interval of duration L_{pkt}/R_{bit}. This probability can be written as (Ferrari & Tonguz, 2003)

$$p_{trans} = 1 - e^{-\frac{\lambda_t L_{pkt}}{R_{bit}}} \qquad (9)$$

Thus S_j appears with different probabilities of transmission as given below

$$S_j = \sqrt{\frac{P_{int\, j}}{R_{bit}}} \text{ with probability } \frac{1}{2}P_{trans}$$

$$= -\sqrt{\frac{P_{int\, j}}{R_{bit}}} \text{ with probability } \frac{1}{2}P_{trans}$$

$$= 0 \text{ with probability } \left(1 - P_{trans}\right) \qquad (10)$$

Size of the interference vector $\vec{S}_j$ increases as the number of nodes increases in the network. The thermal noise power can be written as

$$P_{thermal} = FkT_0 B \qquad (11)$$

where F is the noise figure, $k = 1.38 \times 10^{-23} J/K$ is the Boltzmann's constant, T_0 is the room temperature and B is the transmission bandwidth. The received thermal noise signal is simply

$$n_{thermal} = \sqrt{FkT_0 B} \qquad (12)$$

Next we derive the energy spent in successfully transmitting a data packet considering three different retransmission schemes between a pair of source and destination nodes. Figure 2 shows three different packet delivery mechanisms.

Scheme I is based on hop-by-hop retransmission, as shown in Figure 2a following (She et al., 2009), where at every hop the receiver checks the correctness of the packet and requests for a retransmission with a NACK packet to previous node until a correct packet is received. ACK packet is sent to the transmitter indicating a successful transmission.

Scheme II is based on multi-hop delivery with intermediate nodes, performing as digital repeaters (Taddia & Mazzini, 2004) as shown in Figure 2b. The packet is checked only at destination for correctness; retransmissions are requested to source, with a NACK coming back from destination to source via intermediate nodes through multi-hop path.

Scheme III is based on multi-hop delivery with intermediate nodes, performing as digital repeaters (She et al., 2009) as shown in Figure 2c. The packet is checked at the destination for correctness. However retransmissions are requested to source, with a NACK coming back to source directly from destination (without multi-hop).

It is assumed that each packet consists of header, message and trailer as shown in Figure 3. So, transmitted packet length can be expressed as (Sankarasubramaniam et al., 2003),

$$L_{pkt} = l_h + l_m + l_t \qquad (13)$$

where l_h, l_m and l_t are the header length, message length and trailer length respectively. So, the energy required to transmit a single packet is

$$E_t = \frac{P_t L_{pkt}}{R_{bit}} \qquad (14)$$

Here it is assumed that 75% of the transmit energy is required to receive a packet (Kleinschmidt et al., 2007). So, energy required to communicate, i.e. transmit and receive a single packet is given by

$$E_{packet} = \frac{P_t(L_{pkt} + l_{ack})}{R_{bit}} \times 1.75 + E_d \qquad (15)$$

Figure 2. Different information delivery mechanisms

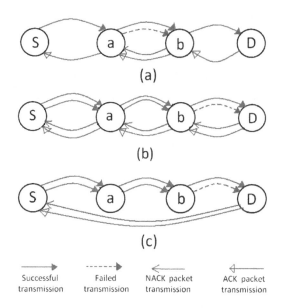

(a)

(b)

(c)

where E_d is the decoding energy to decode a single packet and l_{ack} is the acknowledge frame length. Since Forward Error Correction (FEC) technique is not used here, decoding energy and trailer length both are assumed zero (Sankarasubramaniam et al., 2003). Thus the energy to communicate a single packet is:

$$E_{packet} = \frac{P_t(l_h + l_m + l_{ack})}{R_{bit}} \times 1.75 \qquad (16)$$

The minimum energy required to communicate a packet is the energy required to transmit and receive the message bits (l_m) only. Thus minimum energy is given by the following expression:

$$E_{\min} = \frac{P_t l_m}{R_{bit}} \times 1.75 \qquad (17)$$

Now we consider the energy requirement for three different information delivery mechanisms as mentioned above to communicate a data packet from source to destination node until it is received successfully.

Scheme I

Average probability of error at packet level at each hop is expressed as (Kleinschmidt et al., 2007)

$$PER_{link} = 1 - (1 - BER_{link})^{L_{pkt}} \qquad (18)$$

where, BER_{link} is the link BER in presence of Rayleigh fading. The probability of 'n' retransmissions is the product of failure in the (n-1) transmissions and the probability of success at the nth transmission:

$$P_I[n] = (1 - PER_{link})(PER_{link})^{n-1} \qquad (19)$$

Average number of retransmissions for scheme I, assuming an infinite ARQ (Nandi & Kundu, 2010)

$$R_I = \sum_{n=1}^{\infty} P_I[n].n = \frac{PER_{link}}{(1 - PER_{link})} \qquad (20)$$

We consider only path loss in reverse link. Further we assume that ACK/NACK from receiving

Figure 3. Simple structure of a packet

Header (l_h bits)	Message Bits (l_m bits)	Trailer (l_t bits)

237

node is instantaneous and error free. Considering receiver sensitivity S_i, the required transmit power for reverse link is given by (Goldsmith, 2005)

$$P_{tI} = \frac{S_i \left(4\pi f\right)^2 d_{link}^2}{G_t G_r c^2} \qquad (21)$$

The energy consumed per packet at the end of $\bar{n}_{hop}$ number of hops is considered as the energy spent in forward transmission of information and reverse transmission for NACK/ACK as in Kleinschmidt et al. (2007)

$$E_I = \frac{1.75 \times (1 + R_I) \times \bar{n}_{hop}}{R_{bit}} \left[P_t \left(l_h + l_m\right) + P_{tI} \, l_{ack}\right] \qquad (22)$$

Scheme II

Average probability of error at packet level at the end of multihop route is given as

$$PER_{route} = 1 - \left(1 - PER_{link}\right)^{\bar{n}_{hop}} \qquad (23)$$

Average number of retransmissions for scheme II is given by

$$R_{II} = \sum_{n=1}^{\infty} P_{II}[n].n = \frac{PER_{route}}{\left(1 - PER_{route}\right)} \qquad (24)$$

where $P_{II}[n]$ is the probability of n retransmissions considering Scheme II. The energy consumed per packet at the end of $\bar{n}_{hop}$ number of hops is given by

$$E_{II} = \frac{1.75 \times (1 + R_{II}) \times \bar{n}_{hop}}{R_{bit}} \left[P_t(l_h + l_m) + P_{tII} l_{ack}\right] \qquad (25)$$

where P_{tII} is the transmit power of reverse link and same as P_{tI}.

Scheme III

The energy consumed per packet at the end of $\bar{n}_{hop}$ number of hops using Scheme III is given by

$$E_{III} = \frac{1.75 \times (1 + R_{III}) \times \bar{n}_{hop}}{R_{bit}} \left[P_t(l_h + l_m) + P_{tIII} l_{ack}\right] \qquad (26)$$

where average number of retransmissions, R_{III} is same as R_{II}. Reverse link transmit power P_{III} is given as

$$P_{tIII} = \frac{S_i \left(4\pi f\right)^2 d_{avg}^2}{G_t G_r c^2} \qquad (27)$$

where d_{avg} is the average distance between source and destination.

Now the energy efficiency (η) of each scheme can be expressed as (Kleinschmidt et al., 2007):

$$\eta = \frac{E_{min}}{\text{Energy Required for that Scheme}} \qquad (28)$$

SIMULATION MODEL

We now present our simulation model developed in MATLAB to evaluate the performance of three different information delivery mechanisms:

- At first digital data 1 and 0 with equal probability is generated for BPSK modulation. Our transmitted signal is +1 or -1 corresponding to data 1 or 0.
- The desired message signal is affected by Rayleigh fading, thermal noise and interference from other nodes. The signal re-

ceived by the receiving antenna in destination node is generated following (4).

- Rayleigh distributed random variables with 0 mean and normalized variance 1 is generated to indicate the channel.

- The received signal Y as given in (4) is then detected considering the threshold level at 0. If the received signal is greater than the threshold level 0 then it is detected as 1. Otherwise it is detected as 0.

- Each received bit is then compared with the transmitted bits. If there is mismatch an error counter is incremented. Now dividing the error count by the total number of transmitted bits, link BERs is obtained.

- The energy efficiency for three information delivery mechanisms is evaluated using equn. (28).

- The energy consumption of the three retransmission schemes is evaluated using equn. (22), (25) and (26).

- Optimal size packet for a particular set of network condition is derived.

- Energy consumption for optimal size packet and fixed size packet is compared using (22), (25) and (26).

RESULTS AND DISCUSSION

Table 1 shows the important network parameters used in the simulation study

Figure 4 shows the link BER, denoted as BER_{link} for different values of node spatial density considering different bit rates and transmit power over a Rayleigh faded channel. It is observed that BER_{link} performance improves with the increase in node spatial density. However it is seen that beyond a certain node density the BER_{link} does not change with further increase in node spatial density and a floor in BER_{link}, as denoted by BER_{floor} appears. The desired signal power as well as the inter-node interference increases with increase in node density. As a result we obtain the

Table 1. Network parameters used in the simulation

Parameter	Values
Path loss exponent (γ)	2
Number of nodes in the network (N)	289
Node spatial Density (ρ_s)	$10^{-9} - 10^{-2}$
Packet arrival rate at each node (λ_t)	0.5 pck/s
Career frequency (f_c)	2.4 GHz
Noise figure (F)	6dB
Room Temperature (T_0)	300k
Transmission Power (P_{Tx})	10 mW, 100 mW
Receiver Sensitivity (S_i)	-60 dBm

BER_{floor}. This is expected because, increasing node spatial density beyond a certain limit no longer improves the signal to noise ratio (SNR), as the interfering nodes also become close enough to the receiver. It is also seen that BER_{link} performance degrades as bit rate decreases. This is due to increase in vulnerable interval with decrease of bit rate (Panichpapiboon et al., 2006). As a result, transmission probability of the interfering nodes increases. For a data rate of 10 Mbps and node spatial density of 10^{-4} BER_{link} is 3.9×10^{-4}, while it increases to 3.15×10^{-3} for a bit rate of 2 Mbps. Further it is observed that BER floor appears earlier with the increase in transmit power for a fixed bit rate.

Figure 5 shows the energy efficiency as a function of packet length for different information delivery mechanisms. It is seen that there exists a peak value of efficiency for a given packet size. The message length corresponding to maximum efficiency is optimal packet size from energy efficiency perspective (Sankarasubramaniam et al., 2003). Thus there exists an optimal packet size for a particular network condition. Further optimal packet length increases with the increase in node spatial density. For example, in case of scheme II at node density of 6.12×10^{-6}, optimal packet size is 56 bit but it increase to 71 bit when node density increases to 3×10^{-4}. It is seen that the energy efficiency shows a steep drop for message

Figure 4. Link BER as a function of Node Spatial Density for different bit rate and transmit power

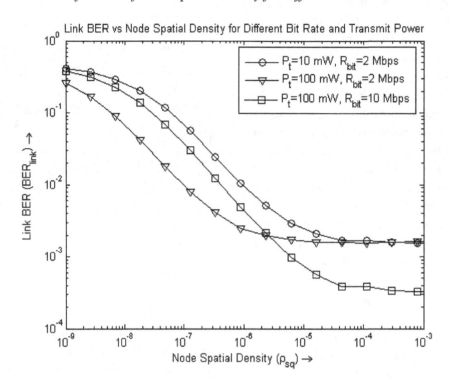

lengths smaller than the optimal length. This behavior can be attributed to the higher overhead and start-up energy consumption of smaller packets (Sankarasubramaniam et al., 2003). On the other hand, for message length larger than the optimal length, the drop in energy efficiency is much slower due to increase in average retransmission. With the increase of packet length the vulnerable interval increases and the probability of transmission of an interfering node becomes high. It is observed that energy efficiency degrades in presence of Rayleigh fading. Further energy efficiency improves with increase in node spatial density. It is seen that Scheme I is the most energy efficiency information delivery system. This is because in case of Scheme I, average number retransmission is less compared to other two schemes. Further among the three retransmission schemes, Scheme I has the highest optimum packet size.

Figure 6 shows the energy required to successfully deliver a fixed packet of size of 100 bit considering three different information delivery mechanisms. Energy consumption in presence of Rayleigh fading is compared with that of path loss case only. It is seen that in presence of Rayleigh fading energy requirement increases. Further it is observed that scheme I is the best retransmission scheme in energy consumption perspective. Further it is observed that Scheme I and Scheme II consume nearly same amount of energy in high node density region. However Scheme II performs better in low node spatial density region. For example in presence of Rayleigh fading and at a node density of 6×10^{-6}, required energy to communicate 100 bit of data is 50 μJ for Scheme II while it is 95 μJ for Scheme III.

Figure 7 shows the impact of node spatial density on optimal packet size. Initially as node spatial density increases the optimum packet size also increases. However the optimal packet size

Figure 5. Energy efficiency as a function of packet length for different retransmission schemes; $P_t=100\,mW$

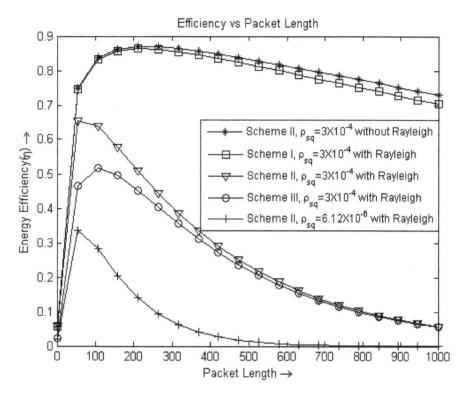

Figure 6. Energy consumption to communicate a packet of length 100 bit vs node spatial density for different retransmission schemes; $R_{bit}=10\,Mbps$ and $P_t=100\,mW$

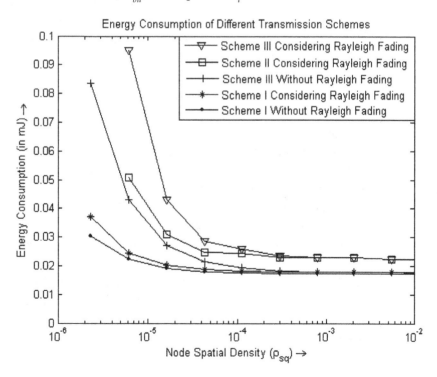

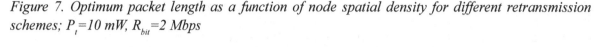

Figure 7. Optimum packet length as a function of node spatial density for different retransmission schemes; $P_t=10$ mW, $R_{bit}=2$ Mbps

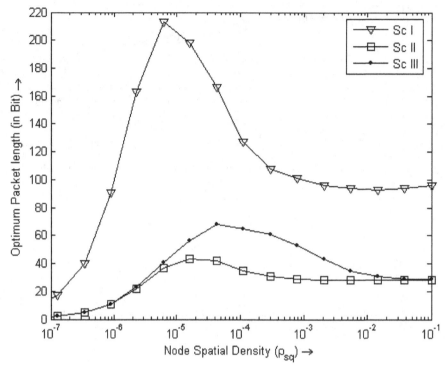

(L_{opt}) attains a peak at a particular node density. Beyond this node density L_{opt} decreases gradually and attains a floor finally. The initial behavior of L_{opt} is due to improvement in BER with increase in node spatial density which allows transmission of higher packet size. However beyond a particular node density the internode interference becomes comparable with the received signal component which causes allowable packet size to reduce. Hence optimum packet length decreases from a peak level. With further increase in node spatial density, the BER attains a floor as seen in Figure 4. Thus average number of retransmission required to successfully deliver a packet remains same with increase in node density for the region where BER attains a floor. As a result energy associated with retransmission remains same as node density increases which causes a floor in optimum packet length.

Figure 8 shows the average retransmission as a function of node spatial density. It is seen that average number of retransmissions increase abruptly in case of low node density region. This is due to degradation of BER performance in that region. Further use of optimum size packet reduces average number of retransmissions significantly. For example, in Scheme II, at a node spatial density of 8×10^{-4}, the average number of retransmission reduces by 80% in optimum packet based scheme as compared to fixed packet based transmission in case of a 100 bit packet.

Figure 9 shows the energy required to successfully deliver a file of size 10^6 bit with different packet sizes using Scheme I and II. Energy consumption for optimal packet based transmission scheme is compared with fixed packet size based transmission. In case of optimal packet based

Figure 8. Average number of retransmission as a function of node spatial density for different retransmission schemes and packet size; P_t=10 mW, R_{bit}=2 Mbps

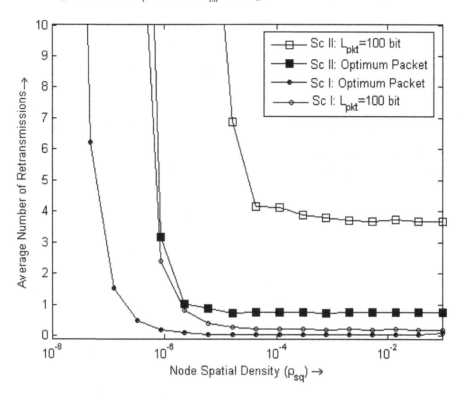

Figure 9. Energy consumption as a function of node spatial density for fixed and optimal packet size; P_t=10 mW, R_{bit}=2 Mbps

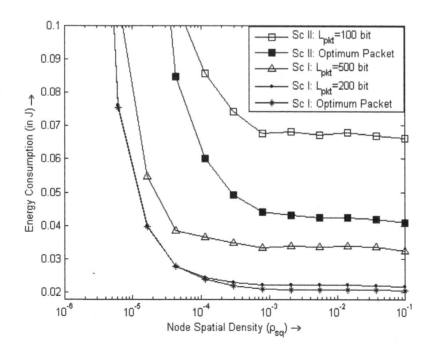

transmission, an optimal packet size corresponding to the particular node density and network condition has been used. For example, in case of Scheme II and at a node spatial density of 3×10^{-4} the optimum size packet is 53 bit [Figure 5]. It is seen that energy requirement increases with increase in packet size. Further use of optimal size packets reduces energy requirement significantly. In scheme II at a node density of 3×10^{-4}, required energy to transfer the file is 49 mJ using optimal size packet, while it increases to 74 mJ for a fixed packet of size 100 bit.

CONCLUSION

Energy level performances of three information delivery schemes are evaluated. Further, a scheme utilizing optimal size packet is analyzed. A simulation test bed has been developed to assess the performance of such network in terms of energy consumption, energy efficiency and bit error rate. Energy consumption using three different types of information delivery schemes are studied and compared. It is seen that Scheme I performs better than the other two schemes. Further Scheme II consumes less energy than Scheme III in low node density region. However at higher node spatial density energy consumption in Scheme I and Scheme II are same. It is also seen that Scheme I provides highest energy efficiency compared to other schemes. An optimum packet length, which maximizes energy efficiency, is also derived. It is seen that optimum packet size increases as node spatial density increases. However the optimal packet size attains a peak at a particular node density. Beyond this node density optimum packet size decreases gradually and attains a floor. Further it is observed that scheme I yields highest size of optimum packet compared to other two schemes. Decoding and retransmission for error correction at every node in multi-hop path seems to be more energy efficient compared to other mechanisms. Optimal packet size based scheme reduces average number of retransmissions. Optimal packet size based transmission also consumes less energy than fixed packet size based transmission.

REFERENCES

Akyildiz, I. F., Weilian, S., Sankarasubramaniam, Y., & Cayirci, E. (2002). A survey on sensor networks. *IEEE Communications Magazine*, *40*(8), 102–114. doi:10.1109/MCOM.2002.1024422

Bettstetter, C., & Zangl, J. (2002, September). How to achieve a connected ad hoc network with homogeneous range assignment: An analytical study with consideration of border effects. In *Proceedings of the 4th International Workshop on Mobile and Wireless Communications Network*, Stockholm, Sweden (pp. 125-129).

Dam, T. V., & Langendoen, K. (2003, November). An adaptive energy efficient MAC protocols for wireless sensor networks. In *Proceedings of the 1st International Conference on Embedded Networked Sensor Systems*, Los Angeles, CA.

Ferrari, G., & Tonguz, O. K. (2003, December). Performance of ad hoc wireless networks with aloha and PR-CSMA MAC protocols. In *Proceedings of the IEEE Global Telecommunications Conference*, San Francisco, CA (Vol. 5).

Goldsmith, A. (2005). *Wireless communications*. Cambridge, UK: Cambridge University Press.

Hong, K., & Hua, Y. (2006, July). Throughput of large wireless networks on square, hexagonal and triangular grids. In *Proceedings of the Fourth IEEE Workshop on Sensor Array and Multichannel Processing*, Waltham, MA.

Kleinschmidt, J. H., Borelli, W. C., & Pellenz, M. E. (2007, June). An analytical model for energy efficiency of error control schemes in sensor networks. In *Proceedings of the IEEE International Conference on Communications*, Glasgow, UK (pp. 3895-3900).

Kwon, H., Hyun Kim, T. H., Choi, S., & Lee, B. G. (2006). A cross-layer strategy for energy-efficient reliable delivery in wireless sensor networks. *IEEE Transactions on Wireless Communications*, *5*(12), 3689–3699. doi:10.1109/TWC.2006.256992

Mansouri, V. S., Ghiassi-Farrokhfal, Y., Nia-Avval, M., & Khalaj, B. H. (2005, October). Using a diversity scheme to reduce energy consumption in wireless sensor networks. In *Proceedings of the 2nd International Conference on Broadband Networks*, Boston, MA.

Nandi, A., & Kundu, S. (2010, November). Energy level performance of retransmission schemes in wireless sensor networks over Rayleigh fading channel. In *Proceedings of the IEEE International Conference on Computational Intelligence and Communication Networks*, Bhopal, India (pp. 220-225).

Narayanaswamy, S., Kawadia, V., Sreenivas, R. S., & Kumar, P. R. (2002, February). Power control in ad-hoc networks: Theory, architecture, algorithm and implementation of the COMPOW protocol. In *Proceedings of the European Wireless Conference Next Generation Wireless Networks: Technologies, Protocols, Services and Applications*, Florence, Italy.

Panichpapiboon, S., Ferrari, G., & Tonguz, O. K. (2006). Optimal transmit power in wireless sensor networks. *IEEE Transactions on Mobile Computing*, *5*(10), 1432–1447. doi:10.1109/TMC.2006.155

Perkins, C. E. (2001). *Ad hoc networking: An introduction*. Reading, MA: Addison-Wesley.

Raghunathan, V., Schurgers, C., Park, S., & Srivastava, M. B. (2002). Energy-aware wireless microsensor network. *IEEE Signal Processing Magazine*, *19*(2), 40–50. doi:10.1109/79.985679

Sankarasubramaniam, Y., Akyildiz, I. F., & McLaughlin, S. W. (2003, May). Energy efficiency based packet size optimization in wireless sensor networks. In *Proceedings of the First IEEE International Workshop on Sensor Network Protocols and Applications*, Anchorage, AK (pp. 1-8).

She, H., Lu, Z., Jantsch, A., Zhou, D., & Zheng, L.-R. (2009 April). Analytical evaluation of retransmission schemes in wireless sensor networks. In *Proceedings of the IEEE 69th Vehicular Technology Conference*, Barcelona, Spain (pp. 1-5).

Sklar, B. (1997). Rayleigh fading channels in mobile digital communication systems part I: Characterization. *IEEE Communications Magazine*, *35*(7), 90–100. doi:10.1109/35.601747

Taddia, C., & Mazzini, G. (2004, September). On the retransmission methods in wireless sensor networks. In *Proceedings of the IEEE 60th Vehicular Technology Conference*, Los Angeles, CA (Vol. 6).

Tseng, C.-C., & Chen, K.-C. (2004, March). Power efficient topology control in wireless ad hoc networks. In *Proceedings of the IEEE Wireless Communications and Networking Conference*, Atlanta, GA (Vol. 1).

This work was previously published in the International Journal of Grid and High Performance Computing, Volume 3, Issue 3, edited by Emmanuel Udoh and Ching-Hsien Hsu, pp. 31-44, copyright 2011 by IGI Publishing (an imprint of IGI Global).

Chapter 16
Cost Efficient Implementation of Multistage Symmetric Repackable Networks

Amitabha Chakrabarty
Dublin City University, Ireland

Martin Collier
Dublin City University, Ireland

ABSTRACT

Symmetric rearrangeable networks (SRN) (Chakrabarty, Collier, & Mukhopadhyay, 2009) make efficient use of hardware, but they have the disadvantage of momentarily disrupting the existing communications during reconfiguration. Path continuity is a major issue in some application of rearrangeable networks. Using repackable networks (Yanga, Su, & Pin, 2008) is a solution to the path continuity problem in SRN. These networks provide functionality comparable to that of strict sense no blocking networks (SNB) but with minimum increase in the hardware than SRN. This paper proposes an efficient implementation of multistage symmetric repackable networks requiring optimum hardware cost than the method proposed in the literature. Cost optimization is achieved through the use of minimum number of bypass link(s). Investigated method works for networks built with more than three switching stages and shows promise of scalability.

INTRODUCTION

Repackable networks allow the path continuity even though it's built on top of rearrangeable network. Basic structure of these networks contain bypass links, which route requests where paths

DOI: 10.4018/978-1-4666-2065-0.ch016

need to be rearranged of those requests, one at a time or all together through those bypass links for continuation of the ongoing communication. After the necessary rearrangements, requests through the bypass links are put back into their new rearranged routes hence the term repackable used for these networks. Addition of bypass links increases the hardware cost than a similar size rearrangeable network but this provides a performance close to SNB networks (Busi & Pattavina, 1998). Today's high performance communication systems require fast switching so that requested connecting paths can be established quickly. In optical networks, these switches typically require multistage implementation for capacities larger than 16x16. The choice between blocking networks (Wu & Feng, 1980; Lawrie, 1975; Feng, 1974) and rearrangeable (Hwang, Lin, & Lioubimov, 2006; Yeh & Feng, 1992) or strict sense nonblocking (Busi & Pattavina, 1998) networks involve a tradeoff between the complexity of rearrangeable routing and the cost of strict nonblocking networks. In a blocked state, rearranging the connections is the basic operation principle of a rearrangeable network. These rearrangements disrupt the existing communication through the candidate links. But it is possible to imply some efficient method to make rearrangeable network much more efficient, such as modifying the rearrangement process in a blocking state and make rearrangeable networks more effective in high performance communications. Use of repkable method can allow modification in the rearrangement process of the rearrangeable networks. We used most popular rearrangeable network to design our proposed repack method, which is Beneš network. Beneš network is an N input-output network build with 2x2 switching elements (SEs) (Beneš, 1965).

RELATED WORK

Most proposals for repkable networks are based on 3-stage Clos networks. Ackroyed (1979) first introduced the concept of repacking for 3-stage networks. He proposed using one of the middle stage subnetworks for routing all the requests. This is generally termed as packing. If this packing technique results in blocking, the other subnetwork is used to route the blocked request. At a later time, that request is rerouted via the packed subnetwork. Jajszczyk and Jekel (1993) provided

the basic condition for a 3-stage Clos network to be repackable. If n and m being the input and output for the each input (output) stage switching elements and r being the number of switching elements in the input (output) stage} respectively then repackable condition is, $m \geq 2n - \lceil n / (r - 1) \rceil$ Jajszczyk and Jekel (1993) explained that using a repackable network, it is always possible to establish connecting paths between an input and output. His proposed method routes requests from the less used subnetwork to the most used one before the arrival of a new request.

Schehrer (1999, 2000, 2001, 2007) proposed two method of reswitching in a repackable network (1) sequential (2) simultaneous. The term reswitching is different than rearrangement, as it means putting requests through the bypass network or paths, and put back to rearrangeable network once paths have been rearranged and making the bypass network or paths free for future use. In sequential reswitching paths need to be rearranged are selected sequentially and put through the bypass paths. Once the paths are rearranged in the rearrangeable network they are put back to their new routes and then new set of paths are selected for the reswitching. On the other hand, simultaneous reswitching selects the smallest number of paths needs to be rearranged and then put them to the bypass links or network. Once the paths are rearranged in the rearrangeable network, they are put back to their new routes together.

OUR CONTRIBUTION

As mentioned earlier that most of the repackable works pro-posed in the literature are mainly for 3-stage Clos networks. In this paper we propose repacking method for the Beneš networks which is a very popular symmetric rearrangeable network. In this paper we proposed method that utilizes the basic method of using bypass network proposed by Schehrer (1999, 2000, 2001, 2007). Our method requires less overall cross points then Schehrer's method for (2logN-1) stages symmetric rearrangeable networks. This paper investigates the minimum required bypass links for different size of networks, hence achieving optimize cost for the network. It provides an indepth analysis of required number of crosspoints for different size of networks. We explore the prospect of using two different repackable topologies in the same network. It is known that the symmetric rearrangeable networks are built as a combination of smaller subnetworks. If it can be shown that smaller subnetworks require less bypass links compare to the bigger ones, total crosspoints requirement can be reduced considerably. Symmetric networks have the option to change the structure in the middle stage, which can save considerable amount of required crosspoints. So this paper presents a required number crosspoints comparison of rearrangeable and proposed repackable network and also symmetric rearrangeable networks with modified middle stages. The method proposed in this work is based on Beneš network but can be applied to any symmetric rearrangable network just by changing the fixed permutations between stages.

PRELIMINARIES

This section presents the notation used throughout the paper:

- **Chain:** Chains are used to identify the loop that needs to be broken, i.e the set of input-output pairs for which the switching element settings need to be changed. The length of the chain is the total number of paths forming the loop.

  If a candidate chain has r paths in it then the length of the chain is r. The length of the chain determines the number of rearrangement required for each blocked request.

Figure 1 shows an example of such a chain. Input 5 requests a connecting path to output 6. With the existing switching element state the free links at the input-output switching elements connect to two different middle stage switching elements, and so cannot be used to establish connecting paths between input port 5 and output port 6. The solution to this problem is to rearrange the chain having a loop $0 \rightarrow 3; 2 \rightarrow 2; 3 \rightarrow 0; 4 \rightarrow 1$. Rearranging this chain will give both blocked switching elements access to a common middle switch.

- **Blocking State:** A blocking state inside a network results when more than one request is competing for the same output link. This puts the network into a state where paths rearrangement of ongoing communication are required to bring the network into a state where it is possible to establish path for the blocked request.

  For a 3-stage network this can arise because of unavailability of connecting link from one middle stage switching element to the requested output switching element. For longer depth networks, it can happen because of the fact that required inner stage link is already occupied by some other request. For example in Figure 1 the request by input 5 for connection to output 6 is blocked because of the current state of the network.

- **Isolated Links:** If two inputs from the same switching element in the input stage are connected to two different output stage switching elements, and they are the only requests for those switching elements, the two paths are called isolated paths. Similarly if two inputs of two different switching elements in the input stage are connected to the same output stage switching element, and they are the only requests from those switching elements they are called isolated links.

  In Figure 2 two isolated links are from inputs 6 and 7.

Figure 1. Chain with length 4

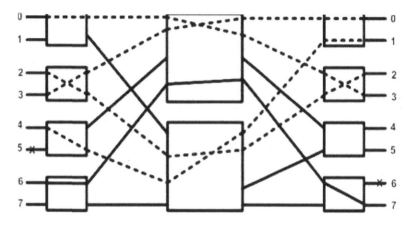

Figure 2. Two isolated links from inputs 6 and 7

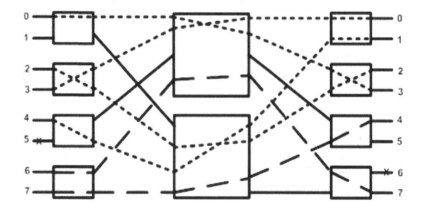

GENERAL REARRANGEMENT SCENARIO

This section describes the blocking scenario and rearrangement process in rearrangeable networks. Basic operation of blocking resolution in a rearrangeable network has two parts. One is to identify the chain related to the blocked request and the other one is to rearrange the chain and setup path for blocked request.

Figure 2 demonstrates a blocking scenario for a request from the input 5 and the output 6. Network goes into the blocking state because input switching element 2 has one free link going to upper middle stage switching element (U). Similarly, output switching element 3 has one free

link coming from lower middle stage switching element (L). This tells that there are no free links available sharing same middle stage switching element that can establish path for the request. To setup path for the request the network goes through rearrangement and finds path for the new request. Part of Table 1 explains the input-output path map before rearrangement for the scenario presented in Figure 2, where the symbol "X" indicates input request is blocked.

Now let's identify the paths forming chains and also the isolated paths from the Figure 2. Input-output paths forming the chain are as follows: $0 \rightarrow U \rightarrow 3, 2 \rightarrow L \rightarrow 2, 3 \rightarrow U \rightarrow 0$ and $4 \rightarrow L \rightarrow 1$. And existing isolated paths are $6 \rightarrow U \rightarrow 7$ and $7 \rightarrow L \rightarrow 4$. To unblock the blocked

Table 1. Path map for input-output request

Input	Before Rearrangement		After Rearrangement	
	Network	Output	Network	Output
0	U	3	U	3
2	L	2	L	2
3	U	0	U	0
4	L	1	L	1
5	X	6	U	6
6	U	7	L	7
7	L	4	U	4

request $5 \rightarrow 6$, the connecting paths forming the chain or the isolated paths need to be rearranged. Number of isolated paths is smaller than exiting chain length, hence selected for required re-arrangement. Once the isolated paths have been rearranged, two links are available that share upper middle stage switching element, hence a path is established between the input 5 and the output 6. Table 1 explains the paths map after required rearrangements. The rearrangement process is carried out by treading off the path continuity of existing communications. Repackable network is used to overcome this path continuity issue of rearrangeable networks and discussed in detail in next sections.

PRINCIPLE OF REPACKABLE NETWORKS

The complexity of a repackable network is a function of the minimum possible length chain. This also depends on whether operations are performed on all effected paths simultaneously, or are performed sequentially which requires intelligent selection of paths.

A. **Network Architecture:** Repackable networks that can perform simultaneous re-switching, accommodate the maximum length of the smallest chain, on the other

hand for sequential reswitching it requires intelligent algorithm to select candidate paths to be reswitched. Figure 3 shows a general block diagram of a symmetric repackable network capable of simultaneous reswitching. This network has N inputs and outputs and uses 2x3 switching elements and bypass network of size $\frac{N}{2} + \frac{N}{2}$ at the out most stage. The architecture of the network follows a recursive structure, hence each sub-networks is built with similar switching elements as well as similar bypass structure. As it can be seen that the complexity of the bypass networks is $0(N^2)$, which is similar to crossbar network of size N. This repackable network is not cost effective, as the crosspoints count exceeds that of crossbar network of similar size. Thus simultaneous reswitching is not an efficient repackable structure for symmetric rearrangeable networks. Hence possible sequential reswitching structures from symmetric rearrangeable networks will be looked in detail in this paper.

B. **Sequential Reswitching Structures:** Sequential reswitching structure requires intelligent identification of the required bypass links. The minimum number of bypass links required is repoted in the literature to be two (Schehrer, 2007). In sequential reswitching,

Figure 3. Symmetric repackable network for simultaneous reswitching

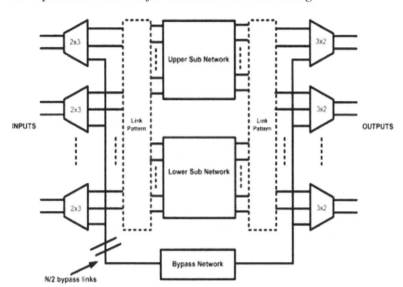

the paths in the chain are reswitched consecutively, so that the bypass network only requires capacity for two bypass links. Paths in the smallest chain are numbered following a topdown or bottom up approach. Then paths with the odd numbers are reswitched first then the even ones or vice versa. Detail of this reswitching algorithm can be found in (Schehrer, 1999, 2007). Figure 4 shows a repackable network having two bypass links. Sequen-tial structure saves considerable number of crosspoints in building a symmetric repackable network, detail on the number of crosspoints requirement discussed in crosspoints requirements section. The operation of sequential reswitching can be described by the below example:

Example: To start with, let's assume a network with N=8 and in a blocking state as in Figure 5. This particular state of the network has two chains of similar length:

$$0 \rightarrow U \rightarrow 5, 3 \rightarrow L \rightarrow 4, 2 \rightarrow U \rightarrow 0 \text{ and }$$
$$5 \rightarrow L \rightarrow 2, 6 \rightarrow U \rightarrow 3, 7 \rightarrow L \rightarrow 7$$

Presented state of the network requires rearrangement to find path for the new request 4 → 1, as there are no two links sharing a common middle stage switching element that can be used for the blocked request. In this case first chain has been selected for necessary sequential reswitching with repackable network having two bypass links. Paths are numbered and the second path in the chain is chosen for reswitching and put through the bypass path. This state of the network can described as below:

$$0 \rightarrow U \rightarrow 5$$
$$2 \rightarrow U \rightarrow 0 \text{ and }$$
$$3 \rightarrow \text{Bypass} \rightarrow 4$$

Putting the path through the bypass link give the rearrangeable network chance to do the following rearrangements:

$$2 \rightarrow L \rightarrow 0 \text{ and }$$
$$0 \rightarrow L \rightarrow 5$$

These rearrangements give the chance to reswitch request 3 → 4 through upper middle stage switching elements, these set of operations

251

Figure 4. Repackable network with 2 bypass links

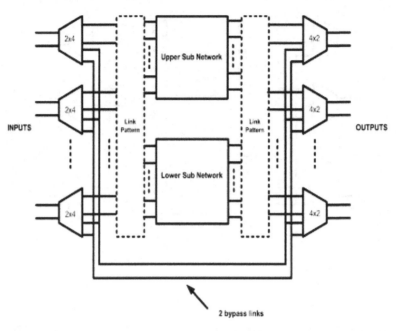

Figure 5. Blocking state in the network for request 4 →1

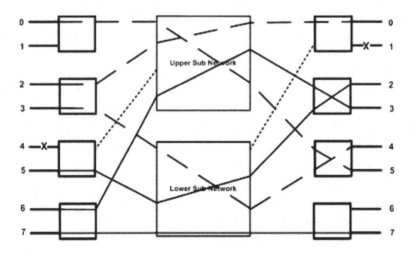

allow two free links that are sharing upper middle stage switching element, hence a path has been established for request $4 \rightarrow 1$. Final path map is described in Table 2.

This section discusses possible modifications to the sequential reswitching structure in repackable networks. This will highlight the link level modifications that can reduce the required number of crosspoints in building the networks. This modification will address the reduction on number of links required in the bypass network. Number of bypass links required in a repackable network is directly related to the maximum length of the smallest chain. Maximum length of a chain a blocking state can be as long as $\frac{(N-2)}{2}$. This

Table 2. Path map for input-output requests after reswitching

Input	Network	Output
0	L	5
3	U	4
2	L	0
4	U	1
5	L	2
6	U	3
7	L	7

Table 3. Worst case chain length

Network Size	Length
8	3
16	7
32	15
64	31
128	63
256	127
512	255
1024	511

is due to that fact that there can be at maximum $N-2$ active requests in the network to have a blocking for any new request. And also in worst case there will be only two chains with equal length. Table 3 shows the worst case chain lengths for different network size.

For a chain length of over 3, reswitching algorithm selects two paths with consecutive odd or even numbering from two different switching elements and puts them through the bypass links. This allows other two paths of those switching elements to rearrange in the network and then the paths in the bypass links are put back to their new positions in the rearrangeable network. But with a chain length of 3, reswitching algorithm has two options, one is to put two even numbered paths on the bypass links or put the odd numbered one to the bypass link. Putting the odd numbered one to one of the bypass links gives other two paths free links to switch their middle stage switching elements. This process only required one bypass link rather than two. This shows that networks of size N = 8 give the option to modify the sequential reswitching link structure.

Inner most stages of these networks are built with 8×8 subnetworks, as a result replacing inner repackable networks built with two bypass links with one will save considerable number of crosspoints. A network of size $2^{\log N} \times 2^{\log N}$, will have a total of $2^{(\log N - 3)}$ subnetworks of size 8x8.

Figure 6 shows repackable network build with one by pass link. The next section discusses details on the required number of crosspoints for different repackable networks.

CROSSPOINT REQUIREMENTS

Required crosspoints is not an accurate metric of implementation cost for to-day's communication switches and routers, since components will rarely be implemented as discrete entities. However in the absence of implementation specific information on cost, crosspoints count requirements are useful indicators of overall switch complexity. An in-depth study of switch depth and the size of the building blocks has been presented in Beneš (1965). According to that study, an optimal network should have a depth of (2M-1), where M is the sum of the prime factors of N (the number of switch inlets). It was recommended that the middle stage should have larger building blocks compared to the other stages. Using a recursive construction technique to build symmetric rearrangeable networks re-quire number of crosspoints can be given as (4NlogN-2N). The required crosspoints count a for strict sense nonblocking network is $\left(6N^{3/2} - 3N\right)$. The required crosspoints count per input varies depends on the switching element size.

Figure 6. Repackable network with one bypass link

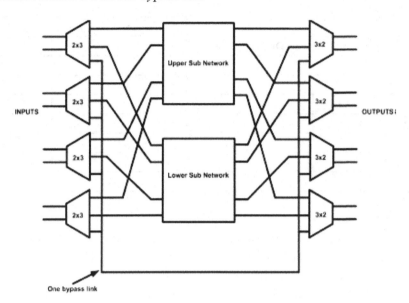

Networks built with larger switching elements have stages smaller than net-works built 2x2 switching elements; this allows the input signals to travel less number of stages to reach output port. In general a network of input size N has ($2\log_k N$-1) stages, where k= switching elements input size. This also saves required number of crosspoints per input in the network (but this increases complexity of routing). To understand the required number of crosspoints comparisons, let's assume a network with N=2048 built with 2x2 switching elements. This network will have 21 stages in total with a total required crosspoints of 86016 which gives 42 crosspoints per input. A network with N=2187 constructed with 3x3 switching elements will have 13 stages. This network will require a total of 85293 crosspoints, requiring 39 crosspoints per input. A network built with 4x4 switching elements and N = 4096 will have a total of 11 stages. This network will require a total of 180224 crosspoints, requiring 44 crosspoint per input. An-other network built with 5x5 switching elements and N=3125 will have a total of 9 stages. This network will con-

sume a total of 140625 crosspoints, requiring 45 crosspoints per input.

It is of particular interest to investigate situations when only a fraction of available numbers of input-output are active in a network. These investigations are particularly important where it is always the case that some of the switching elements will always remain unused, where little modifications in the structure can eliminate unused switching elements from the network. To explain this more specifically, let's assume a network that requires 100 active input-output ports. This situation will be discussed in respect of networks built with different size switching elements. Starting with a network built with 2x2 switching elements, current scenario requires a rearrangeable network of size N=128 to satisfy the requirement. In this network bottom 28 inputs will remain unused, hence 14 switching elements will be idle in for first two stages of the network. Similar scenario will happen for two stages starting from the output stage towards middle stage (because of the recursive structure of the network). Immediate stage after the second stage (stage 2), have three idle switching elements and one with

Figure 7. (a). 4x4 rearrangeable network. (b). 4x4 crossbar

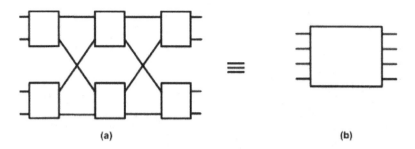

(a)   (b)

a size of (1x2) in each subnetwork, similar situation at stage 10. At stage three 3 will be one idle switching element and one of size (1x2) at each subnetwork, at output half (stage 9) the network will have similar configuration. Following stage of the network will have three switching elements of size 2x2 and one 1x2 in each subnetwork, same applies to the output half of the network. A rearrangeable net-work of size 100x100 built from 128x128 can be constructed. The new network will have total crosspoints of 1320, which give 23.2 crosspoints per input.

Similar required input size of the network can be build with 5x5 switching elements. To start with, it is required to trim down a network of size N=125 to a network of size N^1=125.This network will have 5 stages in total and requires 20 switching elements in input and output stage respectively. At stages 1 and 3 there will be five subnetworks with four switching elements each with size 5x5. The middle stage will have 25 switching elements with a size of 4x4. Total required crosspoints for this network is 2400, which gives 24 crosspoints per input.

For symmetric rearrangeable networks built exclusively using 2x2 switching elements, the required crosspoint count per input can be reduced by using 4x4 crossbar switches in the middle stage. This also reduces the network stages by 2. A crossbar network equivalent to 4x4 rearrangeable network is shown in Figure 7. The crosspoint count in Figure 7 (a) is 8x3=24 and in Figure 7 (b) it is 4x4. Thus 8 crosspoints are saved, i.e.,

two crosspoints per input. The crosspoint count per input for a rearrangeable network built from 2x2 switching elements with 2^{logN} input-output is (4NlogN-2N). Each network have a total of 2^{logN-2} subnetworks built with 4x4 rearrangeable networks. For example, a network size of N=16, a recursive construction results in each input require 14 crosspointss but with (4x4) crossbar in middle stages this count reduced to 12. Similarly for N=32 the numbers are 18 and 16 respectively. Replacing middle stages with 4x4 crossbar gives overall required crosspoints as in Equation 1.1, and Figure 8 shows a modified 16x16 network.

Using 2 bypass links for outer subnetworks and 1 for all 8x8 subnetworks and 4x4 crossbars to replace the 3 middle stages will require a total number of crosspoints, C_{mb} is given by Equation 1.2 and shown in Figure 9, these networks will be called networks with mixed bypass (mb) links.

$$C_{rearr}=(4NlogN-2N)-(8x2^{logN-2})$$
$$=(4NlogN-2N)-2^{logN+1}... \qquad 1.1$$

In this network first (logN-3) stages will have two bypass links and then the following stage will have only one bypass link. Next three middle stages will be replaced by 4x4 crossbars, hence the equation can be given as:

$$C_{mb}=8N(logN-3)+6N+16x2^{logN-2}$$
$$=8NlogN-6N+2^{logN+2}$$
$$=8NlogN-18N+2^{logN+2}.... \qquad 1.2$$

Figure 8. 16x16 Beneš network with 4x4 crossbar in the middle stage

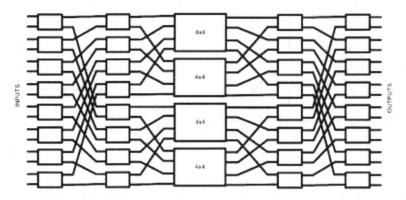

Figure 9. Mixed bypass links repackable network

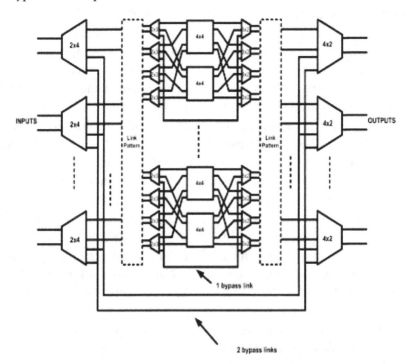

A Repackable network with two bypass links (with rearrangeable middle stages) will need a total crosspoint count given by Equation 1.3:

$$C_{2b}=4N(2logN-2)+2N=8NlogN-6N... \qquad 1.3$$

Crosspoints requirement per input can be given by Table 4. In this table a comparison is made between rearrangeable networks, repackable networks with mixed bypass which is combination of 2 and 1 bypass links also with repackable network with 2 bypass links have been carried out. It shows considerable savings in the required number of crosspoints per input in using mixed bypass method rather than 2 bypass.

Table 4. Crosspoint requirement per input for various size of networks

Size	Rearrangeable	Mixed Bypass	2 Bypass
16	14	18	26
32	18	26	34
64	22	34	42
128	26	42	50
256	30	50	58
512	34	58	66
1024	38	66	74

CONCLUSION

Symmetric rearrangeable networks show promise for use in optical crossconnect (OXC) networks. Suitable switch elements of compact size and low insertion loss are emerging (e.g., using MEMS technology (Fan, Lin, Chiang, Chen, Chung, & Yang, 2009) and the use of multi-stage techniques has been validated experimentally (e.g., the thermo-optic 32 x 32 ma-trix switch (Sohma, Watanabe, Ooba, Itoh, Shibata, & Takahashi, 2006). Multi-stage switch architectures have also been proposed in the related area of on-chip optical interconnection (Wu & Feng, 1980). If these networks are to be agnostic to the signal format of the data they bear, they must treat all signals as analog signals, and thus require path continuity. In other words, unless the timing of a discrete-timed or sampled-data signal being transported through the net-work is known, there is no safe time at which the signal path can be disconnected other than during connection setup and teardown. The techniques described in this chapter allow the Beneš architecture (which features the minimum known number of stages for a fully-connected switch) to be modified to feature path continuity during rearrangement with only a modest increase in network complexity (less than twice to be precise), thus allowing a repackable network to be constructed at relatively low cost. Such a network provides performance indistinguishable from that of a strictly non-blocking network, provided requests arrive at a rate sufficiently low to allow the computation of the required rearrangement to repack the network, and for the sequence of switch state changes required to effect the rearrangement to be executed.

REFERENCES

Ackroyd, M. H. (1979). Call repacking in connecting networks. *IEEE Transactions on Communications, 27*(3). doi:10.1109/TCOM.1979.1094428

Beneš, E. (1965). *Mathematical theory of connecting networks and telephone traffic.* New York, NY: Academic Press.

Busi, I., & Pattavina, A. (1998). Strict-sense non-blocking conditions for shuffle/exchange networks with vertical replication. In *Proceedings of the Seventeenth Annual Joint Conference INFOCOM*, San Francisco, CA (pp. 126-133).

Chakrabarty, A., Collier, M., & Mukhopadhyay, S. (2009, November 15-20). Matrix based routing algorithm for Beneš networks. In *Proceedings of the International Conference on Future Computational Technologies and Applications*, Athens, Greece.

Fan, K., Lin, W., Chiang, L., Chen, S., Chung, T., & Yang, Y. (2009). A 2 × 2 mechanical optical switch with a thin MEMS mirror. *Journal of Lightwave Technology, 27*(9).

Feng, T. (1974). Data manipulating functions in parallel processors and their implementations. *IEEE Transactions on Computers, 23*(3), 309–318. doi:10.1109/T-C.1974.223927

Hwang, F. K., Lin, W., & Lioubimov, V. (2006). On noninterruptive rearrangeable networks. *IEEE/ACM Transactions on Networking, 14*(5). doi:10.1109/TNET.2006.882846

Jajszczyk, A., & Jekel, G. (1993). A new concept-repackable networks. *IEEE Transactions on Communications, 41*(8). doi:10.1109/26.231967

Lawrie, D. H. (1975). Access and alignment of data in an array processor. *IEEE Transactions on Computers, 24*(12), 1145–1155. doi:10.1109/T-C.1975.224157

Schehrer, R. G. (1999, September). Investigation of networks with rearrangement by means of simple methods. In *Proceedings of the Sixth German-Russian Seminar on Flow Control and Integrated Communication Systems*, Dortmund, Germany.

Schehrer, R. G. (2000, October 27). On a class of non-blocking networks with repacking. In *Proceedings of the 6ᵗʰ International Informatization Forum on Informational Networks and Systems*, St. Petersburg, Russia (p. 6077).

Schehrer, R. G. (2001, October 24). On rearrangeable networks with at most one reswitching. In *Proceedings of the Seventh International Conference on Information Networks, Systems and Technologies*, Minsk, Russia.

Schehrer, R. G. (2007). On non-blocking multistage switching networks with rearrangement or repacking. *International Journal of Electronics and Communications*, 423-432.

Sohma, S., Watanabe, T., Ooba, N., Itoh, M., Shibata, T., & Takahashi, H. (2006, September). Silica-based PLC type 32×32 optical matrix switch. In *Proceedings of the European Conference on Optical Communications* (pp. 24-28).

Wu, C., & Feng, T. (1980). On a class of multistage interconnection networks. *IEEE Transactions on Computers, 29*(8), 694–702. doi:10.1109/TC.1980.1675651

Yanga, J., Su, X., & Pin, X. (2008). A module design of rearrange-able nonblocking double omega optical network using binary optics elements. *Optics & Laser Technology, 40*(5).

Yeh, Y., & Feng, T. (1992). On a class of rearrangeable networks. *IEEE Transactions on Computers, 41*(11).

This work was previously published in the International Journal of Grid and High Performance Computing, Volume 3, Issue 4, edited by Emmanuel Udoh and Ching-Hsien Hsu, pp. 1-13, copyright 2011 by IGI Publishing (an imprint of IGI Global).

Chapter 17
Using Machine Learning Techniques for Performance Prediction on Multi-Cores

Jitendra Kumar Rai
ANURAG, Hyderabad, India

Atul Negi
University of Hyderabad, India

Rajeev Wankar
University of Hyderabad, India

ABSTRACT

Sharing of resources by the cores of multi-core processors brings performance issues for the system. Majority of the shared resources belong to memory hierarchy sub-system of the processors such as last level caches, prefetchers and memory buses. Programs co-running on the cores of a multi-core processor may interfere with each other due to usage of such shared resources. Such interference causes co-running programs to suffer with performance degradation. Previous research works include efforts to characterize and classify the memory behaviors of programs to predict the performance. Such knowledge could be useful to create workloads to perform performance studies on multi-core processors. It could also be utilized to form policies at system level to mitigate the interference between co-running programs due to use of shared resources. In this work, machine learning techniques are used to predict the performance on multi-core processors. The main contribution of the study is enumeration of solo-run program attributes, which can be used to predict concurrent-run performance despite change in the number of co-running programs sharing the resources. The concurrent-run involves the interference between co-running programs due to use of shared resources.

DOI: 10.4018/978-1-4666-2065-0.ch017

INTRODUCTION

Multi-core has become the dominant processor architecture at present. Majority of the computing systems are based on multi-core processors, which include both the desktops as well as servers. In future the number of cores on a single processor chip is going to increase with the upcoming generations of processors. Most of the recent multi-core processors have last level caches, which are shared among the cores (Intel Corporation; Kongetira, Aingaran, & Olukotun, 2005; Golla, 2006). Programs co-running on the cores of multi-core processors also share other resources such as hardware prefetch unit, Front Side Bus (FSB) and memory controller along with last level caches. Along with the growth in number of cores per chip with the generations of processors, future multi-core based systems are poised to witness increased degree of sharing of the resources.

The interference between programs co-running on the cores sharing the resources causes degradation in the performance of systems based on multi-core processors. For example a process on one core may cause the eviction of data belonging to process on the other core, with which it shares the cache space. Such interference between co-running programs due to use of shared cache space can cause the performance of simultaneous running processes to get affected by each other. We measured the performance of some of programs from SPEC cpu2006 benchmark suite (SPEC, 2006) on our Intel quad-core Xeon X5482 processor based experimental platform (described in section named EXPERIMENTAL PLATFORMS) for their solo-run as well as concurrent-run. The values of solo-run and concurrent-run performance for those programs in terms of cycles per instruction (CPI) are mentioned in Table 1.

The performance results shown in Table 1 indicate towards degradation in performance of the programs in concurrent-run as compared to their solo-run (i.e., increase in concurrent-run CPI as compared to solo-run CPI). It can be seen that concurrent-run performance of the same program differs when it is run along-with different co-runner programs. In Table 2 we mention the co-runner based performance degradation of the programs mentioned in Table 1. The co-runner based performance degradation results are also shown in Figure 1.

The degradation in performance results from the interactions of program and its co-runner behaviors with respect to usage of resources shared by the cores. In our previous work (Rai et al., 2010) we used the solo-run attributes of the programs to predict their concurrent-run performance on multi-core processors. The methodology proposed in the work to build the model utilized machine learning techniques. The trained model predicts concurrent-run performance of a program

Table 1. Solo-run and concurrent-run performance of some of the SPEC cpu2006 programs on Intel Xeon X5482 processor

Program Names	Performance in terms of CPI, for			
	Solo-run	Concurrent-run, when co-runner is		
		429.mcf	433.milc	459.GemsFDTD
429.mcf	5.89	8.37	10.15	10.04
433.milc	2.41	2.89	3.46	3.54
459.GemsFDTD	1.62	1.98	2.21	2.39
462.libquantum	1.67	2.24	3.05	3.06
410.bwaves	1.17	1.36	1.45	1.53

Table 2. Percentage degradation in performance of some of the SPEC cpu2006 pro-grams, observed during concurrent-run as compared to their solo-run on Intel Xeon X5482 processor

Program Names	Percentage degradation in performance during concurrent-run, when co-runner is		
	429.mcf	**433.milc**	**459.GemsFDTD**
429.mcf	42.13	72.34	70.49
433.milc	20.33	43.83	47.07
459.GemsFDTD	21.87	35.92	47.07
462.libquantum	34.41	82.55	83.39
410.bwaves	16.64	24.36	31.22

by taking the solo-run attributes of that program and its co-runner. For example consider programs A and B co-scheduled on cores of a multi-core processor to run in paired manner. In this paired-run both utilize and contend for the shared resources. The model f to predict the paired-run performance of program A can be expressed in the form of equation shown below:

$$f((a_{1A}, a_{2A}, \ldots a_{nA}), (a_{1B}, a_{2B}, \ldots a_{nB})) \rightarrow p\_CPI_A$$

Figure 1. Percentage degradation in performance of some of the SPEC cpu2006 programs, observed during concurrent-run as compared to their solo-run on Intel Xeon X5482 processor

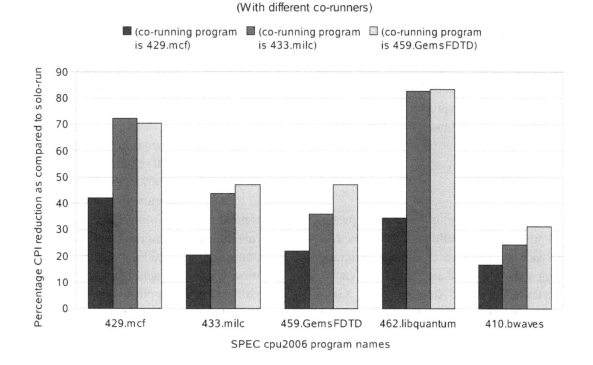

Where p_CPI_A is paired-run (concurrent-run) performance of program A in terms of cycles per instructions (CPI) and $(a_{1A}, a_{2A},....., a_{nA})$ and $(a_{1B}, a_{2B},....., a_{nB})$ are set of solo-run program attributes of A and B respectively. This implies that the model needs to be re-built if the number of co-running programs sharing the resources is more than two. For example on Intel Xeon E5630 processor (Intel Corporation) four cores share the last level cache.

The main contribution of this paper is enumeration of solo-run program attributes, which can be used to predict concurrent-run performance on multi-core processors despite change in the number of co-running programs sharing the resources. The concurrent-run involves the interference between co-running programs due to use of shared resources. We also provide results on prediction accuracy as well as transferability of trained models generated by various machine learning algorithms. The paper begins with of the brief description of related work. Next to this we give overview of machine learning and mention the algorithms used in the work. We conducted experiments on the platforms to generate the data-sets to train the machine learning algorithms as well as to test the regression models (which were built by training the machine learning algorithms). We provide details of the experimental platforms and the methodology used to generate the train-set and test-set data. Next to details of methodology, we mention the results on prediction accuracy and transferability of trained models and conclude.

RELATED WORK

A large portion of previous research on performance prediction on multi-core is focused on interference between the co-running programs resulting from use of shared last level caches (Zhuravlev et al., 2010; Xu et al., 2010; Xie & Loh, 2008; Lin et al., 2008; Moreto et al., 2007; Qureshi & Patt, 2006; Chandra et al., 2005). It involves development of techniques and methods

to understand and predict the program behaviors with respect to utilization of shared last level cache and associated performance implications. The program behaviors can manifest in two kinds of performance implications, which arise because of interference due to use of resources shared by the cores of the processor:

1. The extent by which a program suffers with performance degradation due to interference with its co-runner.
2. The extent by which a program can degrade performance of its co-runner.

Previous studies on program behaviors resulted in classification schemes for understanding the performance as well as workload creation (Moreto et al., 2007; Lin et al., 2008; Qureshi & Patt, 2006). We give brief overview of previous program classification schemes.

Moreto et al. (2007) explained the speedups, which can be achieved by cache partitioning. The metrics used in their study to classify the programs, requires comparison against the performance when using full L2 cache, which in turn requires a complete redundant execution of the programs.

Chandra et al. (2005) proposed three analytical models for predicting miss rates for processes sharing the same cache. These models require the reuse distance or stack distance profiles for each thread to predict the inter thread cache contention. Getting a reuse distance or stack distance profile for every program is a costly operation. Zhuravlev et al. (2010) obtained it using MICA (Hoste & Eeckhout, 2007), a Pin (Luk et al., 2005) based binary instrumentation tool. Running one benchmark program from SPEC cpu2006 under Pin instrumentation require one to two days.

Qureshi and Patt (2006) studied the problem of partitioning a shared cache between multiple concurrently executing applications. They observed that a higher demand for cache resources does not always correlate with a higher performance from additional cache resource. They proposed utility-based cache partitioning (UCP), which uses Utility Monitor (UMON) a special kind of counters implemented in hardware.

Lin et al. (2008) studied the cache partitioning using operating system level page coloring. As part of their work they classified programs into four classes by considering the performance degradation observed when running a program using only a 1MB L2 cache compared to the baseline configuration with 4 MB cache. Their classification scheme does not involve prediction task. It is post-facto kind of scheme for creation of workloads.

Xie and Loh (2008) performed animalistic classification of program memory behaviors. Their classification scheme requires use of special performance counters implemented in hardware.

Zhuravlev et al. (2010) performed Pain classification of programs based on cache sensitivity and intensity. By combining the sensitivity and intensity of two applications "pain" estimate of a co-schedule is made. Sensitivity of a program was obtained from its stack distance profile, obtaining which using Pin binary instrumentation (Luk et al., 2005; Hoste & Eeckhout, 2007) is very time consuming. They also studied contention for other shared resources such as hardware prefetch unit, Front Side Bus (FSB) and memory controller. As all other shared resources studied belong to memory subsystem, they used last level (L2) cache miss rate as metric for characterizing the programs behaviors.

Xu et al. (2010) proposed shared cache aware performance model for multi-core processors. It estimates the performance degradation due to cache contention of processes running on multicores. Their model uses reuse distance diagram of the program. Their method to obtain the reuse distance diagram involves multiple runs of the given program with a synthetic benchmark called stressmark.

We used machine learning to predict the performance degradation for co-running programs on multi-core processors. The machine learning generated model uses solo-run performance data of programs to predict the paired-run performance on multi-core processors.

Machine learning technique have been used in workload characterization (Richard et al., 2006; Pusukuri & Negi, 2004) and improving scheduling (Pusukuri & Negi, 2005), on single-core processors. The focus of the study in Pusukuri and Negi (2004) was on understanding the behavior of programs from their previous execution history and executable file format (ELF) attributes.

Among recent works Ould-Ahmed-Vall et al. (2007a) compared machine learning algorithms for predicting the performance in terms of Instructions Per Cycle (IPC) using the event data collected from hardware performance counters. In their subsequent work (Ould-Ahmed-Vall et al., 2007a), model trees have been used in performance evaluation. Here the generated tree was used to gain insights into bottlenecks affecting processor performance. In their study the model was developed to understand the solo-run performance. It differs from the focus of our study i.e., the prediction of paired-run performance using solo-run program attributes on multi-core processors.

Ramazan et al. (2008) proposed implementation of artificial neural networks based framework in hardware to coordinate the management of multiple interacting resources in chip multiprocessors. In our recent work (Rai et al., 2009) we used model tree to characterize the L2 cache behavior so that the linear models at the leaf of the generated tree can be used to help intelligent scheduling of programs on multi-core processors.

In this study we trained machine learning algorithm to predict the paired-run performance on multi-core processors. We used hardware performance counter data from exiting Intel quad-core Xeon X5482 processor for training.

The use of machine learning technique does not require specialized hardware support as required in some of the previous studies (Xie & Loh, 2008; Qureshi & Patt, 2006). It can reduce the time required for performance prediction as a trained model could be used for performance prediction afterwards, thus amortizing the efforts required for training the algorithm to build the model. It does not require time-consuming program run under binary instrumentation (Zhuravlev et al., 2010; Hoste & Eeckhout, 2007; Luk et al., 2005) for collecting the information about program behaviors in the form of stack distance profiles for generating the performance prediction model.

OVERVIEW OF MACHINE LEARNING

We used supervised learning (Mitchel, 1997), where we train the machine learning algorithms with supplied data-set (also called train-set) to build the models. On training the machine learning algorithms generate regression models, which later on can be used for predicting the variable of interest in a real world scenario. The process of regression consists of fitting a model that relates a dependent variable y to a set of independent variables x_1, x_2, ..., x_n expressed in the form of equation shown below:

$$y = f(x_1, x_2, ... x_n)$$

Different machine learning algorithms correspond to different concept description spaces searched with different biases. Some problems are served well by different description languages and biases, while others are not served well or even served badly. This entails the study of various machine learning algorithms belonging to different families to check their efficacy to solve a given problem across various scenarios (Witten & Frank, 2005).

The machine learning algorithms used in the study are: Linear Regression (LR), Artificial Neural Networks (ANN), Model Trees (M5'), K-nearest neighbors classifier (IBK), KStar (K*) and Support Vector Machines (SVM).

Linear regression (Witten & Frank, 2005) performs least-squares linear regression. Artificial neural networks (Mitchel, 1997) are based on the mechanism of co-operative processing of information, as done by neurons in the brain. In a multilayer neural network, there is an input layer, an output layer and a number of hidden layers. Each layer has a number of neurons (nodes) organized in it. The input layer takes the information to be processed as input. The first hidden layer takes the results from input layer as its inputs and forwards its results as inputs to the next layer. The output layer takes the results of the last hidden layer as inputs and produces the prediction result. In this study back-propagation was used to train feed-forward multilayer neural network.

K-nearest neighbors classifier (IBK) and KStar (K*) (Mitchel, 1997; Aha & Kibler, 1991; Cleary & Trigg, 1995) are lazy or instance-based learning algorithms. In this case a new regression equation is fitted each time, when the model needs to predict on a new instance (i.e., a new query point).

Model trees are a kind of regression tree (Breiman et al., 1984). We chose M5' algorithm (Wang & Witten, 1997), which is an improved version of original M5 algorithm invented by Quinlan (1992). Model trees recursively partition the input space until the linear models at the leaf nodes can explain the remaining variability in those partitions.

Support Vector Machines (SVM) (Smola & Scholkopf, 1998) tries to find instances that are at the boundary of the classes. These instances are called support vectors. Then it generates functions that discriminate those vectors as widely as possible. For training the support vector machine, a generalization of Sequential Minimal Optimization algorithm (SMO) by Shevade et al. (1999) is used.

In this study we used weka-3.6.2 machine learning workbench (Witten & Frank, 2005). We used default settings of the parameters to the above-mentioned machine learning algorithms in weka-3.6.2.

EXPERIMENTAL PLATFORMS

We performed experiments on two platforms. The first platform is a dual-socket DELL Precision T7400 workstation with two Intel quad-core Xeon X5482 processors (3.2 GHz) and 32 GB of memory. Data generated from the first experimental platform are used to train the machine learning algorithms to build the regression models.

The second platform is a single socket DELL Precision 390 workstation with one Intel dual-core Core2 6300 processor (1.86 GHz) and 2 GB of memory. Data collected from the second experimental platform are used to assess the transferability of the regression models, (which are built using the data collected from first experimental platform based on Intel Xeon X5482 processor). The operating system kernel on both experimental platforms was Linux-2.6.30. For collecting data from the hardware performance counters we used perfmon2 (Eranian, 2006) interface.

WORKLOAD

We used benchmark programs from SPEC cpu2006 suite (SPEC 2006) in our experiments. The SPEC cpu2006 benchmark suit consists of 12 integer programs and 17 floating point programs. We used reference inputs. With reference inputs the total workload consists of 35 integer programs and 20 floating point programs i.e., total 55 programs.

HARDWARE PERFORMANCE COUNTERS

Data collected from the hardware performance counters of the processors present on the experimental platforms were used to generate the datasets for training the machine learning algorithms to build the regression models as well as testing the built regression models. Modern processors have Performance Monitoring Unit (PMU) for measuring various performance related events such as number of instructions retired, L2 cache misses etc. Hardware performance counters (Intel Corporation, n. d.) are special registers, by reading which the performance related events can be measured for programs running on the processors.

PROCESSOR CACHE ORGANIZATION ON EXPERIMENTAL PLATFORMS

In this section we describe the difference between the processors of two experimental platforms with respect to their cache organization to have a view of differences in the scenarios the two platforms offer viz. training the model and testing the trained model.

On both Intel quad-core Xeon X5482 and Intel dual-core Core2 6300 processors there is separate level-1 (L1) instruction and data cache, each of size 32KB per core. Both of the processors have unified level-2 (L2) cache shared between two cores. The level-2 (L2) cache is the last level cache on both processors. The sharing of last level (L2) cache between cores of Intel Xeon X5482 and Intel Core2 6300 processors are shown in Figure 2 and Figure 3 respectively. Table 3 shows the L2 cache related data (Intel Corporation, n. d.) for both the processors. There is difference in the L2 cache organization of the two processors in terms of cache size and ways of associativity.

In next section we describe the experiments performed on the experimental platforms to generate the data for training-set and test-set.

SOLO-RUN EXPERIMENT

In this experiment we ran each program from SPEC cpu2006 benchmark suite on a core and disallowed scheduling programs on other core sharing last level (i.e., L2 cache) with the previous core. The hardware performance counter data for

Figure 2. Last level (L2) cache sharing on Intel Xeon X5482 processor

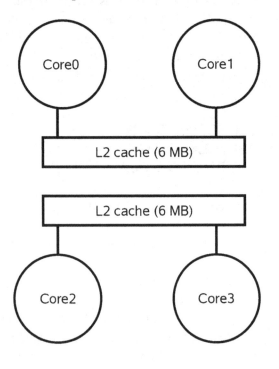

Figure 3. Last level (L2) cache sharing on Intel Core2 6300 processor

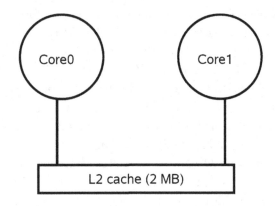

SOLO-RUN PROGRAM ATTRIBUTES

In our previous work (Rai et al., 2010) the proposed model needed solo-run attributes of both programs (i.e., program and its co-runner) as inputs for performance prediction. Thus a model trained for two programs sharing the resources, will not be usable for predicting the performance, when the number of co-running programs sharing the resources are more than two (e.g., on Intel Xeon E5630 processor (Intel Corporation, n. d.) four cores share the last level cache). Hence in such cases we need to again perform solo-run and concurrent run experiments on the new platform to collect the data to train the machine learning algorithms to generate the model for the new scenario (last level cache organization).

To overcome this limitation, we propose new solo-run program attributes. These attributes use fractional values of the hardware performance data. In this case the trained model needs fractional values of the solo-run program attributes of the program under consideration with its co-runners. Hence the model trained once for two programs sharing the resources can also be used for making performance predictions when the number of co-running programs varies. The event data generated from the solo-run of the programs were used to calculate the solo-run program attributes:

complete run of each program were collected. The various performance event data collected from hardware performance counters of Intel Xeon X5482 processor are described in section with heading SOLO-RUN PROGRAM ATTRIBUTES.

PAIRED-RUN EXPERIMENT

In this case the programs from SPEC cpu2006 benchmark suite were run on the cores sharing L2 cache and the hardware performance counter data for complete run of each program were collected. Each of these programs takes different amount of time for completion. Hence one of the co-scheduled programs was run till completion. The other program was run in an infinite loop to execute it again as it finished and was stopped only as the first program finished.

Table 3. Last level (L2) cache related data of Intel Xeon X5482 and Intel Core2 6300 processors

Processor	No of cores sharing last level (L2) cache	Size (MB) shared between the cores	Ways of associativity
Xeon X5482	2	6	24
Core2 6300	2	2	8

- INSTRUCTIONS_RETIRED: Number of instructions completed
- UNHALTED_CORE_CYCLES: Number of core cycles completed
- LAST_LEVEL_CACHE_REFERENCES: Number of references to last level cache
- LAST_LEVEL_CACHE_MISS: Number of misses occurring at last level cache

The class variable (i.e., the dependent variable to be predicted later) is concurrent-run cycles per instruction (concurrent_run_CPI) for each program for its complete run. The list of the solo-run program attributes calculated from the aforementioned performance event data is given:

- LAST_LEVEL_CACHE_REFERENCES_PKI: Number of references to last level cache per kilo instructions.
- LAST_LEVEL_CACHE_MISS_PKI: Number of misses occurring at last level cache per kilo instructions.
- LAST_LEVEL_CACHE_MISS_PK_LAST_LEVEL_CACHE_REFERENCES: Number of misses occurring at last level cache per kilo references. This gives a rough estimate of cache re-referencing property of the program at last level cache.
- Fr_LAST_LEVEL_CACHE_REFERENCES_PKI: Fraction of number of references to last level cache per kilo instructions of the program as compared to its co-running programs.
- Fr_LAST_LEVEL_CACHE_MISS_PKI: Fraction of number of misses to last level cache per kilo instructions of the program as compared to its co-running programs.
- Fr_CPI: Fraction of cycles per instruction of the program as compared to its co-running programs. It encapsulates the effect of overall resource utilization behavior of the program as compared to its co-running programs.
- solo_run_CPI: Cycles per instruction of the program for its solo run. It encapsulates the effect of overall resource utilization behavior of the program.

The generated model f to predict the concurrent-run performance of program A can be expressed in the form of equation shown:

$$f(a_{1A}, a_{2A}, a_{3A}, a_{4A}, a_{5A}, a_{6A}, a_{7A}) \rightarrow concurrent\_run\_CPI_A$$

Where $a_{1A}, a_{2A}, ..., a_{7A}$ are seven solo-run attributes for program A as mentioned.

PREDICTION ACCURACY OF TRAINED REGRESSION MODELS

We used 10-fold cross validation (Kohavi, 1995) to evaluate the prediction accuracy of the machine learning algorithm. The total number of instances used in the study is 3025. The values of prediction accuracy metrics (Witten & Frank, 2005) observed in the study are mentioned in Table 4.

The prediction accuracy metrics obtained as shown in Table 4, indicate that the best performing algorithms are KStar (K*) and Model Trees (M5').

Table 4. Prediction accuracy observed in 10-fold cross validation for performance prediction on Intel Xeon X5482 processor

Algor-ithms	Prediction Accuracy Metrics				
	Correlation coefficient (C)	Mean absolute error (MAE)	Root mean squared error (RMSE)	Relative absolute error (RRSE %)	Root relative squared error (RAE %)
LR	0.97	0.18	0.31	24.99	21.06
ANN	0.99	0.14	0.20	16.41	15.82
IBK	0.98	0.11	0.22	17.63	12.80
K*	0.99	0.08	0.20	15.72	9.73
M5'	0.99	0.09	0.17	13.95	10.66
SVM	0.97	0.15	0.33	26.82	17.52

Transferability of Trained Regression Models

To assess the transferability of the trained regression models, we use test-set data, which were generated by performing solo-run and concurrent-run experiments on other experimental platform based on Intel Core2 6300 processor. Please note that Intel Core2 6300 processor has different memory hierarchy (e.g., last level cache organization) as compared to Intel Xeon X5482 (performance counter data from which was used to train the regression models). The size of train-set data collected for the pairs formed by SPEC cpu2006 benchmark programs on Intel Xeon X5482 processor is 3025 (i.e., 55X55). The number of instances of test-set data generated from Intel Core2 6300 processor is 418. These numbers of test instances are generated based on the availability of the platforms for performing experiments. We used prediction accuracy metrics and statistical tests to assess the transferability of trained regression models. The assessment for transferability of trained regression models across two different cache organizations was performed for the three best performing algorithms in 10-fold cross validation i.e., KStar (K*), Model Trees (M5') and K-nearest neighbors classifier (IBK). The prediction accuracy metrics of the trained regression models on the test data-set are shown in Table 5.

The prediction accuracy metrics obtained for the test data shown in Table 5 indicate that the regression models trained by data from Intel Xeon X5482 processor are reasonable for performing performance predictions on other processor i.e., Intel Core2 6300 and the Model Trees (M5') algorithm seem to perform best.

Now we describe the statistical methods (Walpole et al., 2007) to compare two alternatives; which were used for assessing the transferability of trained regression models. These methods fall in two categories parametric and non-parametric. Parametric methods include t-test, where the data are assumed to be normally distributed. If there is any reason to doubt the assumption of normality of data, then we can use a distribution free test i.e., Wilcoxon test, which falls under non-parametric methods. First we test about the normality of the data and then test about the difference between predicted and actual values of the class variable concurrent_run_CPI.

Testing for Normality of Data

We test the normality of class variable (actual values of concurrent_run_CPI), as well as predicted values of concurrent_run_CPI for the test data-set. The predicted values are produced by three best performing algorithms observed during 10-fold cross validation (described in previous section)

Table 5. Prediction accuracy for test data from Intel Core2 6300 processor for performing performance prediction

Algorithms	Prediction Accuracy Metrics		
	Correlation coefficient (C)	Mean absolute error (MAE)	Root mean squared error (RMSE)
IBK	0.93	0.29	0.51
K*	0.95	0.20	0.33
M5'	0.93	0.17	0.35

i.e., KStar (K*), K-nearest neighbors classifier (IBK) and Model Trees (M5').

We test the normality of the data by three methods: quantile-quantile (Q-Q) plot, Kolmogorov-Smirnov test and Shapiro-Wilk test (R Development Core Team, 2004). The Q-Q plot for the actual values of concurrent_run_CPI observed on Intel Core2 6300 processor is shown in Figure 4(a). The Quantile-quantile (Q-Q) plots shown in Figures 4(b), 4(c), and 4(d) are for concurrent_run_CPI predicted by model trained (with data collected from Intel Xeon X5482 processor) using KStar (K*), K-nearest neighbors classifier (IBK) and Model Trees (M5') machine learning algorithms respectively. In the Q-Q plot, the sampled data is shown as circles against theoretical quantiles (i.e., from normal distribution) shown as straight line. If the sampled data comes from normal distribution then it should follow the theoretical quantiles on quantile-quantile (Q-Q) plot.

The calculated p-values from tests for normality (Kolmogorov-Smirnov test and Shapiro-Wilk test) are much below threshold (0.05). That indicates towards rejection of the null hypothesis (i.e., the data follows normal distribution).

The Q-Q plots shown in Figure 4 (i.e., points shown as circles v/s straight line) also indicate towards rejection of the null hypothesis (i.e., the data follows normal distribution). Hence we observe that there is doubt to assume that the data come from normal distribution.

Testing for Difference Between Actual and Predicted Values of Solo-Run Last Level Cache Stress

We have two samples to compare against each other for the presence of any significant difference between them. First sample consists of predicted and the other sample consists of actual values of concurrent_run_CPI on Intel Core2 6300 processor. The parametric method (t-test) assumes the data to have normal distribution.

The number of instances in test data-set 418 is quite large, so that the parametric method (t-test) becomes robust enough to be used for non-normal data (Non parametric test with small and large samples, Choosing between parametric non-parametric tests, http://www.graphpad.com). Hence to assess the transferability we use both parametric method (t-test) as well as non-parametric method (Wilcoxon test).

The acceptance of null hypothesis indicates the absence of significant difference between the predicted and actual values. In other words we can say that the given regression model used to predict concurrent_run_CPI is transferable across the two processors viz. one on which it was trained and the other on which it was used to make predictions.

The results of p-values for t-test as well as Wilcoxon test are shown in Table 6 against the machine learning algorithms trained to generate regression models. For Model Trees (M5') algorithm the p-values for both tests are greater than threshold (0.05), indicating the acceptance of the null hypothesis, which says there is no significant difference between actual and predicted values of class variable concurrent_run_CPI. Thus the Model Trees (M5') algorithm seems to have better transferability across the two architectures for predicting concurrent_run_CPI.

Figure 4. Q-Q plot for actual and predicted values of the concurrent_run_CPI values for Intel Core2 6300 processor

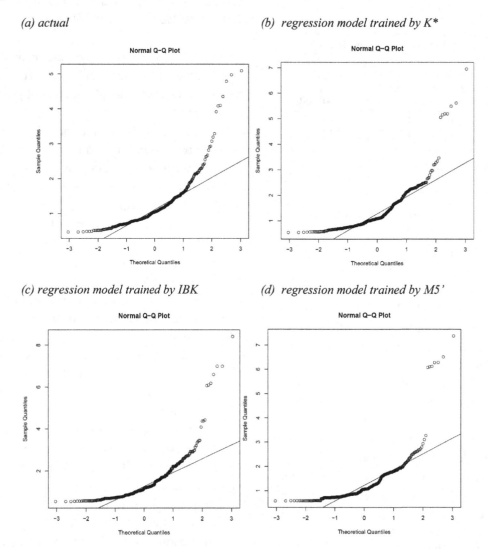

(a) actual

(b) regression model trained by K*

(c) regression model trained by IBK

(d) regression model trained by M5'

CONCLUSION

In this study we used machine learning to predict the paired-run performance of programs running on multi-core processor. The results show that machine learning technique could be utilized to predict the paired-run performance with reasonable accuracy. The work presented here has potential application for creation of workloads to perform performance studies on multi-core processors. We plan to investigate the use of such techniques to implement the policies at system level to alleviate the contention for shared resources on multi-core processors.

Table 6. p-values from t-test and Wilcoxon tests

Algorithm Trained	p-value for t-test	p-value for Wilcoxon test
IBK	0.000071	0.000952
K*	0.001589	0.005152
M5'	0.1023	0.2694

REFERENCES

Aha, D., & Kibler, D. (1991). Instance-based learning algorithms. *Machine Learning, 6,* 37–66. doi:10.1007/BF00153759

Breiman, L., Friedman, J., Olshen, R., & Stone, C. (1984). *Classification and regression trees.* Cleveland, OH: Wadsworth International Group.

Chandra, D., Guo, F., Kim, S., & Solihin, Y. (2005). Predicting inter-thread cache contenton on a chip multi-processor architecture. In *Proceedings of the 11th International Symposium on High Performance Computer Architecture*, San Francisco, CA (pp. 340-351).

Cleary, J. G., & Trigg, L. E. (1995). K*: An instance-based learner using an entropic distance measure. In *Proceedings of the 12th International Conference on Machine Learning* (pp. 108-114).

Eranian, S. (2006). Perfmon2: The hardware-based performance monitoring interface for Linux. In *Proceedings of the Linux Symposium, 1,* 269–288.

Golla, R. (2006). *Niagara2: A highly threaded server-on-a-chip.* Retrieved from http://www.opensparc.net/pubs/preszo/06/04-Sun-Golla.pdf

GraphPad Software. (2009). *Choosing between parametric non-parametric tests: Does it matter?* Retrieved from http://www.graphpad.com

GraphPad Software. (2009). *Non parametric test with small and large samples.* Retrieved from http://www.graphpad.com

Hoste, K., & Eeckhout, L. (2007). Microarchitecture-independent workload characterization. *IEEE Micro, 27*(3), 63–72. doi:10.1109/MM.2007.56

Intel Corporation. (n. d.). *Intel® 64 and IA-32 architectures software developer's manuals.* Retrieved from http://www.intel.com/products/processor/manuals

Kohavi, R. (1995). A study of cross-validation and bootstrap for accuracy estimation and model selection. In *Proceedings of the 14th International Joint Conference on Artificial Intelligence* (pp. 1137-1143).

Kongetira, P., Aingaran, K., & Olukotun, K. (2005). Niagara, a 32-way multithreaded sparc processor. *IEEE Micro,* 21–29. doi:10.1109/MM.2005.35

Lin, J., Lu, Q., Ding, X., Zhang, Z., & Sadayappan, P. (2008). Gaining insights into multicore cache partitioning: Bridging the gap between simulation and real systems. In *Proceedings of the 14th International Symposium on High Performance Computer Architecture*, Salt Lake City, UT (pp. 367-378).

Luk, C. K., Cohn, R., Muth, R., Patil, H., Klauser, A., Lowney, G., et al. (2005). Pin: Building customized program analysis tools with dynamic instrumentation. In *Proceedings of the ACM SIGPLAN Conference on Programming Language Design and Implementation* (pp. 190-200).

Mitchel, T. (1997). *Machine learning.* New York, NY: McGraw-Hill.

Moreto, M., Cazorla, F., J., Ramirez, A., & Valero, M. (2007). Explaining dynamic cache partitioning speed ups. *Computer Architecture Letters, 6*(1).

Ould-Ahmed-Vall, E., Woodlee, J., Yount, C., & Doshi, K. A. (2007a). On the comparison of regression algorithms for computer architecture performance analysis of software applications. In *Proceedings of the First Workshop on Statistical and Machine Learning Approaches Applied to Architectures and Compilation*, Ghent, Belgium.

Ould-Ahmed-Vall, E., Woodlee, J., Yount, C., Doshi, K. A., & Abraham, S. (2007b). Using model trees for computer architecture performance analysis of software applications. In *Proceedings of the IEEE International Symposium on Performance Analysis of Systems & Software* (pp. 116-125).

Pusukuri, K. K., & Negi, A. (2004). Character-izing process execution behavior using machine learning techniques. In *Proceedings of the HiPC International Conference*, Bangalore, India.

Pusukuri, K. K., & Negi, A. (2005). Applying machine learning techniques to improve GNU/Linux process scheduling. In *Proceedings of the IEEE Tencon Conference* (pp. 393-398).

Quinlan, R. (1992). Learning with continuous classes. In *Proceedings of the 5th Australian Joint Conference on Artificial Intelligence*.

Qureshi, M. K., & Patt, Y. N. (2006). Utility-based cache partitioning: A low-overhead, high-perfor-mance, runtime mechanism to partition shared caches. In *Proceedings of the 39th International Symposium on Microarchitecture*, Orlando, FL (pp. 423-432).

R Development Core Team. (2004). *R: A language and environment for statistical computing*. Vienna, Austria: R Foundation for Statistical Computing.

Rai, J. K., Negi, A., Wankar, R., & Nayak, K. D. (2009). Using machine learning to characterize L2 cache behavior of programs on multicore processors. In *Proceedings of the International Conference on Artificial Intelligence and Pattern Recognition*, Orlando, FL (pp. 301-306).

Rai, J. K., Negi, A., Wankar, R., & Nayak, K. D. (2010). Performance prediction on multi-core processors. In *Proceedings of the IEEE Interna-tional Conference on Computational Intelligence, Communication Systems and Networks*, Bhopal, India (pp. 633-637).

Ramazan, B., Engin, I., & Martinez, J. F. (2008). Coordinated management of multiple interacting resources in chip multiprocessors: A machine learning approach. In *Proceedings of the Inter-national Symposium on Microarchitecture*, Lake Como, Italy (pp. 318-329).

Richard, M. Y., Han, L., Kingsum, C., & Hsien-Hsin, S. L. (2006). Constructing a non-linear model with neural networks for workload char-acterization. In *Proceedings of the International Symposium on Workload Characterization* (pp. 150-159).

Shevade, S. K., Keerthi, S. S., Bhattacharyya, C., & Murthy, K. R. K. (1999). *Improvements to SMO algorithm for SVM regression* (Tech. Rep. No. CD-99-16). Singapore: Control Division Depart-ment of Mechanical and Production Engineering.

Smola, A. J., & Scholkopf, B. (1998). A tuto-rial on support vector regression. *Statistics and Computing*, *14*(3), 199–222. doi:10.1023/B:STCO.0000035301.49549.88

SPEC. (2006). *Standard performance evaluation corporation*. Retrieved from http://www.spec.org/cpu2006/

Walpole, R. E., Myers, R. H., Myers, S. L., & Ye, K. (2007). *Probability and statistics for engineer and scientists* (8th ed., pp. 413–467). Delhi, India: Pearson Education.

Wang, Y., & Witten, I. (1997). Inducing model trees for continuous classes. In *Proceedings of the 9th European Conference on Machine Learning*.

Witten, I. H., & Frank, E. (2005). *Data mining: Practical machine learning tools and techniques* (2nd ed.). San Francisco, CA: Morgan Kaufmann.

Xie, Y., & Loh, G. H. (2008). Dynamic classifi-cation of program memory behaviors in CMPs. In *Proceedings of the 2nd Workshop on Chip Multiprocessor Memory Systems and Intercon-nects in conjunction with the 35th International Symposium on Computer Architecture*, Beijing, China.

Xu, C., Chen, X., Dick, R. P., & Mao, Z. M. (2010). Cache contention and application performance prediction for multi-core systems. In *Proceedings of the IEEE International Symposium on Performance Analysis of Systems and Software*, White Plains, NY (pp. 76-86).

Zhuravlev, S., Blagodurov, S., & Fedorova, A. (2010). Addressing shared resource contention in multicore processors via scheduling. In *Proceedings of the 15th International Conference on Architectural Support for Programming Languages and Operating Systems*, Pittsburgh, PA (pp. 129-142).

This work was previously published in the International Journal of Grid and High Performance Computing, Volume 3, Issue 4, edited by Emmanuel Udoh and Ching-Hsien Hsu, pp. 14-28, copyright 2011 by IGI Publishing (an imprint of IGI Global).

Chapter 18
Performance Evaluation of Full Diversity QOSTBC MIMO Systems with Multiple Receive Antenna

Hardip K. Shah
Dharmsinh Desai University, India

Tejal N. Parmar
Dharmsinh Desai University, India

Nikhil Kothari
Dharmsinh Desai University, India

K. S. Dasgupta
Indian Institute of Space Science and Technology, India

ABSTRACT

Multipath fading is inherent in wireless communication systems. Diversity is the technique which takes advantage of multipath to mitigate the effect of fading and increase signal strength. Space Time Block codes (STBC) are used in MIMO systems to improve the performance by maximizing transmit and/or receive diversity. Among different schemes based on STBC, Quasi Orthogonal Space Time Block Code (QOSTBC) is able to achieve full rate transmission for more than two transmit antennas. Constellation Rotation QOSTBC (CR-QOSTBC) achieves full diversity and improves performance further along with full rate, to overcome the limitation of QOSTBC, which is unable to maintain orthogonality amongst the codes transmitted by different antennas. Higher diversity can be achieved by increasing uncorrelated paths between transmitter and receivers using higher number of receive antennas. This paper examines improvement in BER with reference to a number of receive antennas. Simulations were carried out under ideal as well as realistic environments, using least square technique with four antennas at transmitter side and variable receive antennas. Results of simulations presented in this paper indicate performance improvement of CR-QOSTBC over QOSTBC in flat fading channel environment. Simulation results also show performance degradation in BER when channel is estimated at the receiver.

DOI: 10.4018/978-1-4666-2065-0.ch018

INTRODUCTION

Apart from channel noise, performance of wireless communication is also restricted by factors like multipath fading, as it affects correct reception of information. The increasing need for high data rate transmission over wireless channels has spurred much research effort into new communication technique, which has better resistance against multipath fading effects (Paulraj, Gore, & Nabar 2004).

Channel coding, Equalization and Diversity are main techniques for minimizing the effect of multipath fading (Sharma & Papadias, 2003). Multipath effects can be reduced using diversity without decreasing data rates and incurring expenditure in transmission time or bandwidth. Space diversity techniques rely on transmitting and/or receiving the signal over multiple independently fading paths in space. These kinds of systems employ more than one transmit as well as receive antennas creating Multiple Input Multiple Output (MIMO) systems. Apart from the diversity at the receiver the transmit diversity can be used by using different space time codes (Guey, Fitz, Bell, & Kuo, 1996; Alamouti, 1998; Tarokh, Seshadri, & Calderbank, 1998, 1999).

Initial Space time codes designed in form of Space Time Trellis Code (STTC) enjoy large diversity and coding gain simultaneously. However, they inherently involve Viterbi decoders causing large decoding complexity with the transmission rate and diversity order. This discourages the use of large number of transmit antennas (Dalton & Georghiades, 2005). To minimize its decoding complexity, Alamouti has proposed STBC scheme (Alamouti, 1998). The orthogonal structure of code matrix in Alamouti scheme offers full diversity when complex symbol wise Maximum Likelihood (ML) decoding is applied. Alamouti scheme generalized later on for more than two transmit antennas, is called orthogonal STBC (Zheng & Burr, 2003). OSTBC scheme provides full diversity because of its orthogonal design.

Unfortunately, OSTBCs suffer from a reduced code rate when complex signal constellations and more than two transmit antennas are used (Zheng & Burr, 2003; Ganesan & Stoica, 2001; Lu, Fu, & Xia, 2004).

Therefore, STBC designs that can achieve full transmit diversity and a higher code rate is desirable. Quasi Orthogonal STBC (Jafarkhani, 2001) is the structure that offers full rate but partial diversity. Eliminating the disadvantage of partial diversity, constellation rotation of complex symbols is performed and the modified technique is known as Constellation Rotation Quasi Orthogonal STBC (Tirkkonen, 2001; Weifeng & Xiang-Gen, 2004; Liang & Huaping, 2005).

Performance of CR-QOSTBC has been evaluated previously (Sharma & Papadias, 2003). We investigate the performance of CR-QOSTBC MIMO systems. Simulations were carried out for different combinations of SNR and number of receive antennas to observe impact on BER over *flat fading* channels with QOSTBC and CR-QOSTBC. Results of simulations indicate that BER performance of CR-QOSTBC improves with multiple receive antennas. We also discuss relative performance of CR-QOSTBC with respect to QOSTBC for different number of antennas.

The results are observed with the assumption that *channel state information* (CSI) is perfectly known to the receiver, which is not true in real environments. Various channel estimation techniques have been proposed in literature to measure CSI at receiver (Portier, Baudais, & Hélard, 2004; Sand, Raulefs, & Auer, 2005). The simulation results of QOSTBC and CR-QOSTBC schemes with Least Square (LS) channel estimation method is presented in this paper.

Rest of the paper is organized as follow. Various Space-Time Block Code schemes are presented. We describe the theory of CR-QOSTBC. The simulation results and discussion of observation are presented and finally, conclusions are drawn.

RELATED WORK

As discussed earlier QOSTBC and CR-QOSTBC schemes have been appreciated for improving BER performance over MIMO channels. In this section QOSTBC and CR-QOSTBC are described briefly (Jafarkhani, 2001; Weifeng & Xiang-Gen, 2004).

We consider a wireless communication system with N antennas at the transmitter and M antennas at the receiver. This MIMO system can achieve maximum diversity order (full diversity) MN (Zheng & Tse, 2003). The channel is assumed to be a *flat fading* channel. The path gain from transmit antenna n to receive antenna m is defined to be $h_{n,m}$. The path gains are modeled as samples of independent complex Gaussian random variables. The wireless channel is assumed to be quasi-static so that the path gains are constant over a frame of length T and vary from one frame to another. In this MIMO system at time t, received signal at antenna m is given by

$$r_{t,m} = \sum_{n=1}^{N} h_{n,m} C_{t,n} + \eta_{t,m} \tag{1}$$

Here, the code matrix (C) of different STBC varies as described below.

Orthogonal structure of code matrix of alamouti scheme illustrated in Equation (2) allows ML decoding and achieves full diversity. It has been generalized for four transmit antennas, as given in Equation (3) which is recognized as OSTBC.

$$C_{t,n} = \begin{bmatrix} C1 & C2 \\ -C2* & C1* \end{bmatrix} \tag{2}$$

$$C_{t,n} = \begin{bmatrix} c_1 & c_2 & c_3 & c_4 \\ -c_2 & c_1 & -c_4 & c_3 \\ -c_3 & c_4 & c_1 & -c_2 \\ -c_4 & -c_3 & c_2 & c_1 \\ c_1^* & c_2^* & c_3^* & c_4^* \\ -c_2^* & c_1^* & -c_4^* & c_3^* \\ -c_3^* & c_4^* & c_1^* & -c_2^* \\ -c_4^* & -c_3^* & c_2^* & c_1^* \end{bmatrix} \tag{3}$$

It appears from code matrix, OSTBC require 8 time slots to transmit 4 symbols. While achieving good performance, transmission rate is compromised. However, QOSTBC retain full rate for more than two antennas where the code matrix is shown in Equation (4) (Jafarkhani, 2001). Here columns 1 and 2 are orthogonal and 3 and 4 are orthogonal, but no orthogonality otherwise. This requires that ML decoding should be performing for two symbols at a time, e.g., c_1 and c_4 is to be detected simultaneously and c_2 and c_3 simultaneously. Due to this, performance is degraded. Hence, QOSTBC achieves full rate with partial diversity. Further to improve the performance and obtain full diversity a modification to QOSTBC is suggested by Weifeng and Xiang-Gen (2004). The modified scheme is known as CR-QOSTBC. It is found that it transmits the signal at full rate for more than two transmit antennas and achieve full diversity as well.

$$C_{t,n} = \begin{bmatrix} c_1 & c_2 & c_3 & c_4 \\ -c_2^* & c_1^* & -c_4^* & c_3^* \\ -c_3^* & -c_4^* & c_1^* & c_2^* \\ c_4 & -c_3 & -c_2 & c_1 \end{bmatrix} \tag{4}$$

QUASI-ORTHOGONAL STBC WITH FULL DIVERSITY

It is shown in Weifeng and Xiang-Gen (2004) that CR-QOSTBC achieves full diversity by modified transmit symbols of QOSTBC. While mapping from group of bits to symbol, a complex number from the signal constellation is chosen. In case of BPSK modulation, the constellation diagram is shown in Figure 1(a) and its rotated version is shown in Figure 1(b). Weifeng and Xiang-Gen (2004) have reported that out of four complex symbols, if two are selected from Figure 1(a) and other two are selected from Figure 1(b), full diversity can be achieved. The optimum value of constellation rotation angle is found to be π/M for M-PSK constellation (Liang & Huaping, 2005).

Results presented in Weifeng and Xiang-Gen (2004) show that when four transmit and one receive antennas are used, there is 6db improvement in SNR for CR-QOSTBC as compared to QOSTBC. It is also reported that at lower SNR, CR-QOSTBC and QOSTBC perform similar but at higher SNR they start differing. If we increase number of receive antennas for achieving higher diversity, performance will definitely improve. In this paper, we extend the work which has been reported in Weifeng and Xiang-Gen (2004), by using multiple receive antennas. Of course, the code matrix used in this work is as shown in Equation (5) which is different from the one used in Weifeng and Xiang-Gen (2004). This code matrix is modification to the code matrix of Equation (4) as per the theory of Weifeng and Xiang-Gen (2004).

$$\begin{bmatrix} c_1 & c_2 & c_3 e^{j\theta} & c_4 e^{j\theta} \\ -c_2^* & c_1^* & (-c_4 e^{j\theta})^* & (c_3 e^{j\theta})^* \\ (-c_3 e^{j\theta})^* & (-c_4 e^{j\theta})^* & c_1^* & c_2^* \\ (-c_4 e^{j\theta})^* & (-c_4 e^{j\theta})^* & -c_2 & c_1 \end{bmatrix}$$

(5)

Table 1 shows comparison of various schemes (Dipl & Biljana, 2005) based on rate of transmission, decoding complexity and diversity order. Decoding complexity of CR-QOSTBC is same as QOSTBC. Since, transmitted symbols from each antenna are orthogonal to each other; decoder can decode each symbol individually. As a result, complexity of OSTBC linearly varies with constellation size. Transmitted symbols in QOSTBC and CR-QOSTBC are non-orthogonal to each other requires decoder to decode two symbols simultaneously. Consequently complexity of non-orthogonal STBC has exponential relationship with constellation size. This fact is described in Table 1. It is obvious from the table that CR-QOSTBC has performance same as OSTBC, at the same time its transmission rate and decoding delay are lower than OSTBC. Performance of CR-QOSTBC and QOSTBC is evaluated through simulations and the results are discussed in next section.

SIMULATION RESULTS AND DISCCUSION

In order to examine the performance of CR-QOSTBC and QOSTBC, a MIMO system with N transmit (4) and M receive antenna (1, 2, 3, 4) is implemented as shown in Figure 2 in a simulated environment, which uses QPSK modulation scheme. The wireless channel between the transmitter and receiver is a *Rayleigh flat fading*

Figure 1. Constellation rotation of BPSK constellation set

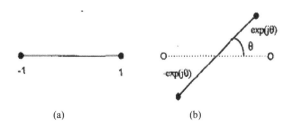

(a)   (b)

Table 1. Comparison of OSTBC, QOSTBC and CR-QOSTBC

Parameters	OSTBC	QOSTBC	CR- QOSTBC
Rate= K/T	½	1	1
Diversity Order	NxM	2xM	NxM
Complexity	KB	B^K	B^K
Decoding delay	8	4	4

K=Number of Information Symbols in One Frame, T=Number of Time Slots in One Frame, N=Number of Tx antenna, M=Number of Rx antenna, B=Constellation size.

channel and quai-static so that the path gains are constant over a frame of length *T* and vary from one frame to another. The path gain from transmit antenna *n* to receive antenna *m* is defined to be $h_{n,m}$. The path gains are modeled as samples of independent complex Gaussian random variables. The transmission code matrix of CR-QOSTBC is described in (5) and that of QOSTBC is shown (4) of previous section.

The objective of this paper is to verify relative improvement in BER in CR-QOSTBC as compared to QOSTBC with multiple receive antennas as increase in number of receive antennas would also increase diversity order. Simulations are carried out for evaluating performance with different SNR values. We varied number of antennas at the receiver. In the first phase of simulations, the receiver has perfect CSI.

Simulations are repeated in the second phase with an estimated CSI at the receiver to observe the performance of CR-QOSTBC in a realistic situation, as usually the channel condition is not perfectly known at the receiver. This obviously results in to degradation in BER performance.

A. Phase I Perfect CSI at Receiver

Figure 3 shows BER performance of CR-QOSTBC with multiple (i.e., 1, 2, 3 and 4) receive antennas. Here, the number of transmit antennas is fixed i.e., 4 and SNR is varied from 0 to 25 dB. The error probability decreases as the dth power of SNR, corresponding to a slope of −d in the error

Figure 2. MIMO system with N transmit and M receive antennas

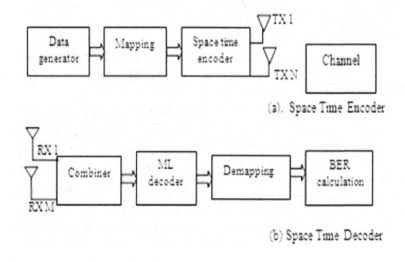

(a). Space Time Encoder

(b) Space Time Decoder

Figure 3. Performance of CR QOSTBC

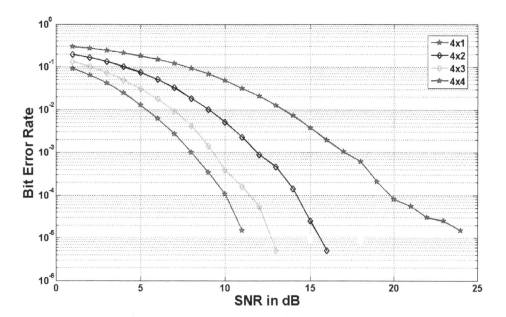

probability vs. SNR curve in dB/dB scale. Thus, the BER achieved by a space-time code with higher diversity order decreases faster than the BER of a space-time code with lower diversity order when the SNR increases. As a result, the plots corresponding to higher number of receive antennas are observed to be steeper in Figure 3, which indicates significant performance improvement. It can also be observed that there is 6dB improvement in SNR of 4X2 system as compared to 4x1 systems in case of the same BER i.e., 1 x 10^{-4}. Greater performance improvement is obvious with increased SNR.

As can be seen in Figure 4, at 5 dB SNR, addition of an antenna reduces BER from 0.18 to 0.08, as the diversity order is doubled. Note that with one more antenna, i.e., 4x3 system, will not improve the diversity order in the same order. Hence, the BER reduces by 0.03. In case of higher SNRs BER reduces drastically in general. In real communication systems, receive SNR is usually 15 dB and the BER is expected to be nearly zero. It is apparent from Figure 4 that BER

is very low for 15 dB SNR. The difference in performance is marginal.

Since CR-QOSTBC is a modified version of QOSTBC, we also compare the performance of MIMO systems with either schemes with multiple receive antennas to examine relative improvement in CR-QOSTBC. As discussed in previous section, because of higher diversity order, slope of BER vs

SNR curve of CR-QOSTBC has to be steeper than slope of same curve for QOSTBC. Hence, the performance of CR-QOSTBC is much better than QOSTBC at higher SNR. This can be seen in Figure 5. At lower SNR, performance plots of QOSTBC and CR-QOSTBC are found to be overlapping. From SNR around 12 dB onwards, the performances start departing. However, it is important to note that the performance difference in QOSTBC and CR-QOSTBC decreases with higher number of receive antennas. There are 3 dB performance improvements for single receive antenna in CR-QOSTBC as compared to QOSTBC. This difference continuously decreases with increase in number of receive antennas.

Figure 4. BER performance vs. number of receive antennas

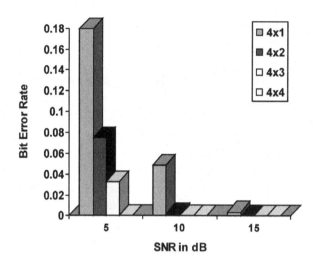

In order to examine the relative performance improvement with CR-QOSTBC as compared to QOSTBC, we next plot the SNR values with reference to number of receive antenna. It can be seen from Figure 6 that there is 3 dB performance improvements for single receive antenna in CR-QOSTBC. This difference in SNR of either scheme continuously decreases with increase in number of receiver antennas.

The above results are with assumption that channel state information is perfectly known to the receiver, which does not happen in real environment. It might be interesting to investigate the performance degradation when the CSI is estimated. We perform channel estimation which may include some error. We utilize these estimated parameters to decode the symbols. The corresponding simulations are discussed.

B. Phase II: Estimated CSI

In this paper, channel is estimated using Least Square method. For channel estimation, pilot symbols are sent in the form of diagonal matrix. This pilot symbol matrix is multiplied with received signal at the receiver, from this we get estimated

channel matrix. Figure 7 shows the simulation result of CR-QOSTBC with estimated CSI at the receiver using multiple receive antennas. Here, variation in BER vs. SNR curve with estimated channel matrix is found similar to perfect channel knowledge at receiver. As number of receive antenna increases, diversity order increases, which makes the curve steeper. Figure 8 illustrates comparison of CR-QOSTBC with perfect CSI known to the receiver and estimated CSI using Least Square channel estimation method at the receiver, at BER of 10^{-4}.

There is 2db degradation in SNR due to estimation error. This continuous 2 db performance gap is observed in each case of 4x1, 4x2, 4x3, 4x4 MIMO systems. Nevertheless, CR-QOSTBC has been found to be superior as compared to QOSTBC in either condition at the receiver.

CONCLUSION

CR-QOSTBC improves BER performance of MIMO systems suffering from multipath fading by offering full rate and full diversity. However, CR-QOSTBC has been previously evaluated using

Figure 5. Performance comparison of QOSTBC and CR-QOSTBC

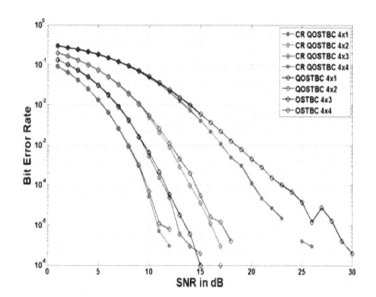

multiple transmit single receive (MISO) system with perfect CSI at Receiver.

In this paper, we approach performance evaluation of CR-QOSTBC in flat fading realistic channel condition using Least Square Channel estimation. Additionally, simulations incorporated different

number of receive antennas to observe its impact on further improvement in BER.

Simulation results for CR-QOSTBC show gradual performance improvement with increasing number of receive antenna. The performance improvement is inversely proportional to SNR^{-d} at

Figure 6. SNR Improvement at BER=10^{-4}

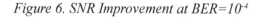

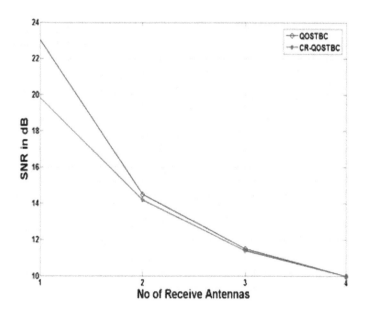

Figure 7. Performance of CR QOSTBC with estimated CSI

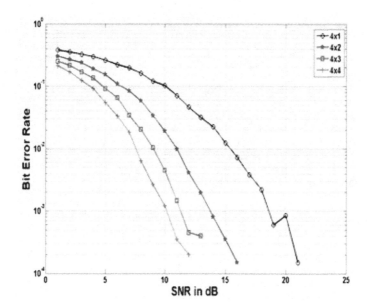

higher values of SNR. This has been confirmed through simulations. Since diversity order of CR-QOSTBC is higher, it performs better than QOSTBC at higher SNR. At SNR lower than 12 dB performance of both the schemes are nearly same.

Diversity order of QOSTBC is lower than CR-QOSTBC, whereas the decoding complexities of both are same. Thus, CR-QOSTBC offers better performance without increasing any complexity at receiver and without any additional bandwidth as well as power requirement at transmitter.

Figure 8. CR-QOSTBC with Perfect CSI and Estimated CSI at BER 10^{-4}

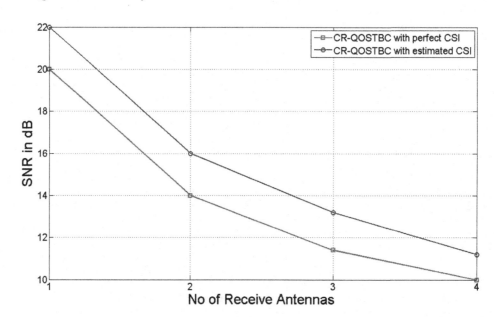

REFERENCES

Alamouti, S. (1998). A simple transmit diversity technique for wireless communications. *IEEE Journal on Selected Areas in Communications, 16*, 1451–1458. doi:10.1109/49.730453

Dalton, A., & Georghiades, N. (2005). A full-rate, full-diversity four-antenna quasi-orthogonal space-time block code. *IEEE Transactions on Wireless Communications, 4*(2). doi:10.1109/TWC.2004.842945

Dipl, I., & Biljana, B. (2005). *Space-time block coding for multiple antenna systems.* Unpublished doctoral dissertation, Technischen Universität Wien, Wien, Germany.

Ganesan, G., & Stoica, P. (2001). Space–time block codes: A maximum SNR approach. *IEEE Transactions on Information Theory, 47*(4), 1650–1656. doi:10.1109/18.923754

Guey, J., Fitz, M., Bell, M., & Kuo, W. (1996). Signal design for transmitter diversity wireless communication systems over Rayleigh fading channels. *IEEE Transactions on Communications, 47*(4), 527–537. doi:10.1109/26.764926

Jafarkhani, H. (2001). A quasi orthogonal space-time block code. *IEEE Transactions on Communications, 49*, 1–4. doi:10.1109/26.898239

Liang, X., & Huaping, L. (2005). Optimal rotation angles for quasi-orthogonal space-time codes with PSK modulation. *IEEE Communications Letters, 9*(8), 676–678. doi:10.1109/LCOMM.2005.1496579

Lu, K., Fu, S., & Xia, X. (2004). Close forms designs of complex orthogonal space–time block codes of rates $(k+1)/(2k)$ for $2k-1$ or $2k$ transmit antennas. In *Proceedings of the IEEE International Symposium on Information Theory* (p. 307).

Ning, Y. (2008). *A family of space-time blocks codes for wireless communication.* Boston, MA: Northeastern University.

Paulraj, A., Gore, D., & Nabar, R. (2004). An overview of MIMO communications - A key to gigabit wireless. *Proceedings of the IEEE, 92*(2), 198–218. doi:10.1109/JPROC.2003.821915

Portier, F., Baudais, J., & Hélard, J. (2004). Performance of STBC MC CDMA systems over outdoor realistic MIMO channels. In *Proceedings of the 60th IEEE Conference on Vehicular Technology* (Vol. 4, pp. 2409-2413).

Sand, S., Raulefs, R., & Auer, G. (2005). Iterative channel estimation for high mobility broadband MC-CDMA systems. In *Proceedings of the IEEE International Conference on Communications* (pp. 2139-2144).

Sharma, N., & Papadias, C. (2003). Improved quasi-orthogonal codes through constellation rotation. *IEEE Transactions on Communications, 51*(3), 332–335. doi:10.1109/TCOMM.2003.809753

Tarokh, V., Jafarkhani, H., & Calderbank, A. (1999). Space–time block codes from orthogonal designs. *IEEE Transactions on Information Theory, 45*, 1456–1467. doi:10.1109/18.771146

Tarokh, V., Seshadri, N., & Calderbank, A. (1998). Space–time codes for high data rate wireless communication: Performance criterion and code construction. *IEEE Transactions on Information Theory, 44*, 744–765. doi:10.1109/18.661517

Tirkkonen, O. (2001). Optimizing space–time block codes by constellation rotations. In *Proceedings of the Finnish Wireless Communications Workshop.*

Tirkkonen, O., Boariu, A., & Hottinen, A. (2000). Minimal nonorthogonality rate 1 space-time block code for 3+ Tx antennas. In *Proceedings of the IEEE 6th International Symposium on Spread-Spectrum Techniques and Applications* (pp. 429-432).

Weifeng, S., & Xiang-Gen, X. (2004). Signal constellations for quasi- orthogonal space–time block codes with full diversity. *IEEE Transactions on Information Theory*, *50*(10), 2331–2347. doi:10.1109/TIT.2004.834740

Zheng, F., & Burr, A. (2003). Receiver design for orthogonal space-time block coding for four transmit antennas over time-selective fading channels. In *Proceedings of the IEEE Conference on Global Telecommunications*, *1*, 128–132.

Zheng, L., & Tse, D. (2003). Diversity and multiplexing: A fundamental tradeoff in multiple-antenna channels. *IEEE Transactions on Information Theory*, *49*(5), 1073–1096. doi:10.1109/TIT.2003.810646

This work was previously published in the International Journal of Grid and High Performance Computing, Volume 3, Issue 4, edited by Emmanuel Udoh and Ching-Hsien Hsu, pp. 45-68, copyright 2011 by IGI Publishing (an imprint of IGI Global).

Section 5
Applications

Chapter 19

On Construction of Cluster and Grid Computing Platforms for Parallel Bioinformatics Applications

Chao-Tung Yang
Tunghai University, Taiwan

Wen-Chung Shih
Asia University, Taiwan

ABSTRACT

Biology databases are diverse and massive. As a result, researchers must compare each sequence with vast numbers of other sequences. Comparison, whether of structural features or protein sequences, is vital in bioinformatics. These activities require high-speed, high-performance computing power to search through and analyze large amounts of data and industrial-strength databases to perform a range of data-intensive computing functions. Grid computing and Cluster computing meet these requirements. Biological data exist in various web services that help biologists search for and extract useful information. The data formats produced are heterogeneous and powerful tools are needed to handle the complex and difficult task of integrating the data. This paper presents a review of the technologies and an approach to solve this problem using cluster and grid computing technologies. The authors implement an experimental distributed computing application for bioinformatics, consisting of basic high-performance computing environments (Grid and PC Cluster systems), multiple interfaces at user portals that provide useful graphical interfaces to enable biologists to benefit directly from the use of high-performance technology, and a translation tool for converting biology data into XML format.

DOI: 10.4018/978-1-4666-2065-0.ch019

1. INTRODUCTION

Bioinformatics is a combination of biology and information technology and includes any computational tools and methods for managing, analyzing and manipulating large sets of biology data. Thus, computing technologies are vital for bioinformatics applications (Konishi et al., 2002; Trelles et al., 1998). For example, biology problems often require repeating the same task millions of times such as when searching for sequence similarities in existing databases or comparing groups of sequences to determine evolutionary relationships. In such cases, the high-performance computers to process this information are indispensable. Biological information is stored on many computers around the world. The easiest way to access this information is to join these computers together through networking. Such activities require high-performance computing infrastructures (Prodan & Fahringer, 2002) with access to huge databases of information.

The major advances in computer technology and computer science over the past 30 years have dramatically changed much of our society. Currently, many parallel versions of bioinformatics applications can be used to conduct computing tasks on Linux PC Cluster or Grid systems, including, HMMer (http://hmmer.wustl.edu/), FASTA (ftp://ftp.virginia.edu/pub/fasta/), mpiBLAST (http://mpiblast.lanl.gov/index.html), ClustalW-MPI (Li, 2003), FastDNAml (Stewart et al., 2001), and TREE-PUZZLE (Schmidt et al., 2992). Using these parallel versions of bioinformatics software for sequence alignment or analysis can always save enormous amounts of time and cost. The use of parallel software versions and cluster system is cost-effective and it will become more and more popular in the near feature.

Computing technologies today represent promising future possibilities. Currently, it is still very difficult for researchers who are not specialized in Information Technology (IT) to fully utilize these high-performance computing technologies.

IT engineers are therefore playing an important role in improving the research environment. The mission imposed on us is to provide user-friendly interfaces for researchers who are not specialists in IT to be able to benefit directly from the use of high-performance technology. The user portal enables interactions between application users and applications obtaining parametric inputs for problems and reporting results upon execution completion (Pierce, 2002; Stocker, 2004; Sturn, 2003; Suzumura, 2004).

Large quantities of biological data have been made accessible to the scientific community through numerous genome websites such as the National Center for Biotechnology Information (NCBI) (http://www.ncbi.nlm.nih.gov) and the Protein Data Bank (PDB) (http://www.rcsb.org/pdb/index.html), and many of these genome websites distribute large datasets as flat files (e.g., tab-delimited files). Flat files are text files lacking any form of markup language. The tasks of automating the processes of information retrieval and integration of heterogeneous biological data are difficult due to their unstructured formats. The data involved may range from nucleic acid and protein sequences, to three-dimensional protein structures, and relationships among various metabolic pathways. Furthermore, different approaches are used for data modeling, storage, analysis, and querying purposes. Therefore, Molecular Biology databases have only a few widely accepted schemas.

As a consequence, integration and inter-operability of Molecular Biology databases are issues of considerable importance. The eXtensible Markup Language (XML) (http://www.w3.org/XML/) proposed by the World Wide Web Consortium (W3C) (http://www.w3.org) has emerged as a popular format for representing and exchanging information over the Web. XML was originally designed to overcome the limitations of HTML and flat files. In this paper, we present an approach to converting data from various databanks into XML format for storage in XML database management systems. Our system uses an open-source project called BioJava (http://www.biojava.org/) to translate biological data into XML format, simplifying biological data translation. The details are described below.

In the present study, THUBioGrid, an experimental distributed computing application for bioinformatics (BioGrid) is proposed (Yang, Hsiung, & Kan, 2005a, 2005b; Yang, Kuo, & Lai, 2004, 2005; Yang, Kuo, Li, & Gaudiot, 2004). THUBioGrid incorporates directory services (data and software), grid computing methods (security, authentication, data transport and remote jobs), and gene sequence/genomic data processing methods. It uses Java CoG Kit plus bioinformatics Java packages to perform various computational tasks. The performance of THUBioGrid has been tested by executing the FASTA and mpiBLAST programs for protein sequence alignment applications. Results demonstrate the speed-up effects with increasing number of processors used in the computations. Recently, biological applications interest the field of high performance computation. Therefore, a number of BioGrid projects are initiated, as listed in Table 1.

This work is motivated by the fact that activities of bioinformatics require high-performance computing power to search through and analyze huge amounts of data. Therefore, this paper proposes an approach to solving this problem using cluster and grid computing technologies. The problem is to find powerful tools to handle the complex and difficult task of integrating these heterogeneous biological data. The challenge of this problem lies in implementing an experimental distributed computing application for bioinformatics consisting of basic high-performance computing environments (Grid and PC Cluster systems), multiple interfaces at user portals that provide useful graphical interfaces to enable biologists who are not IT specialists to benefit directly from the use of high-performance technology, and a translation tool for converting biology data into XML format.

Table 1. BioGrid projects examples

Project	WebSite
NCBioGRID	http://www.ncbiogrid.org
APBioGRID	http://www.apbionet.org/grid/
EuroGRID	http://www.eurogrid.org
Canadian BioGRID	http://cbr-rbc.nrc-cnrc.gc.ca/
MyGRID	http://www.mygrid.org.uk
BioGRID	http://www.biogrid.jp/
BIRN	http://www.nbirn.net/
Illinois BioGrid	http://illinoisbiogrid.org/

The rest of this paper is organized as follows. In Section 2, we state the current state of high-performance computing technology. Then, a brief overview of bioinformatics is provided. Next, we report on relationships between biology data and XML technology. After that, details of parallel bioinformatics software are introduced. In Section 3, we describe the implementation of our system. In Section 4, we present the experimental environment and performance evaluation. Finally, conclusions are given in Section 5.

2. BACKGROUNDS

2.1 Cluster Computing and Grid Computing

A Beowulf cluster (Sterling et al., 1999) is a form of parallel computer that uses more than one processor. The many kinds of parallel computer are distinguished by the processors they use and the way in which those processors exchange data. They take advantage of two commodity components: fast CPUs designed primarily for the personal computer market and techniques for connecting personal computers in so-called local-area networks or LANs. Beowulf clusters provide effective and low-cost means of delivering enormous computational powers to applications and are now used virtually everywhere. More specifically, a Beowulf cluster is a high-performance, high-throughput, and high-availability computing platform (Wilkinson & Allen, 2004; Yang et al., 2001).

To make use of multiple processes each executed on a separate processor, we need to apply parallelism computing algorithms. There are two common types of parallelism: MPI (http://www.lam-mpi.org/) and PVM (http://www.epm.ornl.gov/pvm).

- **PVM:** This is a master-worker approach and is the simplest and easiest to implement. It relies on being able to break computations into independent tasks. A master then coordinates completion of these independent tasks by worker processes.
- **MPI:** This is for use when computations cannot (or cannot easily) be broken into independent tasks. In this kind of parallelism, the computation is broken down into communicating, inter-dependent tasks. We used LAM/MPI for our cluster system.

Grid Computing (Foster & Kesselman, 1999; Foster, 2002) enables virtual organizations to share geographically distributed resources as they pursue common goals, assuming the absence of central location, central control, omniscience, and an existing trust relationship. Some features of Grid Computing are listed below.

- Flexible, secure, coordinated resource-sharing among dynamic collections of individuals, institutions, and resources
- Transparent, secure, and coordinated resource-sharing and collaboration across sites
- The ability to form virtual, collaborative organizations that share applications and data in an open heterogeneous server environment in order to work on common problems

- The ability to aggregate large amounts of computing resources which are geographically dispersed to tackle large problems and workloads as if all the servers and resources are located in a single site
- A hardware and software infrastructure that provides dependable, consistent, pervasive, and inexpensive access to computational resources
- The Web provides us information -- the grid allows us to process it.

The Globus Project provides software tools that make it easier to build computational grids and grid-based applications. These tools are collectively called The Globus Toolkit (http://www.globus.org/). We adopted it as infrastructure for our BioGrid. The toolkit includes software for security, information infrastructure, resource management, data management, communication, fault detection, and portability.

The composition of the Globus Toolkit can be pictured as three pillars: Resource Management, Information Services, and Data Management. Each pillar represents a primary component of the Globus Toolkit and makes use of a common foundation of security. The Globus Resource Allocation Manager (GRAM) implements a resource management protocol, the Metacomputing Directory Service (MDS) implements an information services protocol, and GridFTP implements a data transfer protocol. They all use the GSI security protocol at the connection layer.

GRAM provides an API for submitting and canceling job requests, as well as checking the statuses of submitted jobs. The specifications are written by the Resource Specification Language (RSL), and processed by GRAM as part of each job request.

MDS is the information services component of the Globus Toolkit and provides information about available resources on the Grid and their statuses. Via the default LDAP schema distributed with Globus, it gives current information about the Globus gatekeeper including CPU type and number, real memory, virtual memory, file systems and networks.

GridFTP is a high-performance, secure, reliable data transfer protocol optimized for high-bandwidth wide-area networks. GridFTP protocol is based on FTP, the highly-popular Internet file transfer protocol.

Java CoG (Commodity Grid Kit) (http://www-unix.globus.org/cog/) combines Java technology with Grid Computing to develop advanced Grid Services and accessibility to basic Globus resources. It allows easier and more rapid application development by encouraging collaborative code reuse and avoiding duplication of effort among problem-solving environments, science portals, Grid middlewares, and collaborative pilots.

2.2 Bioinformatics and High-Performance Computing

Computer technology is used at nearly every stage of the drug development process for pre-clinical testing, research, and development. Bioinformatics allows researchers to analyze the terabytes of data produced by the Human Genome Project (http://www.ornl.gov/sci/techresources/Human_Genome/home.shtml). Bioinformatics is the discipline of obtaining information about genomic or protein sequence data. It may involve searching databases for sequence similarities, comparing an unidentified sequence to database sequences, or making predictions about a sequence based on current knowledge of similar sequences. Various databases of gene/protein sequences, gene expression, and related analysis tools help scientists determine whether and how a particular molecule is directly involved in a disease process. That, in turn, aids in the discovery of new and better drug targets (Bala, Pytlinski & Nazaruk, 2002; Moreau et al., 2002).

Database handle sequence similarity search queries using alignment algorithms and returning the highest scoring sequences. Examples of such

software tools are the BLAST (Bayer, Campbell & Virdee, 2004; Satish & Joshi, 2004), FASTA, and Smith-Waterman algorithms. BLAST and FASTA provide very fast searches within sequence databases.

Multiple alignments illustrate relationships among two or more sequences. When the sequences involved are diverse, conserved residues are often keys associated with maintenance of structural stability or biological function. Multiple alignments can reveal many clues about protein structures and functions. The most commonly used software for multiple alignments is the ClustalW package.

Biological data is generally stored as text in flat files. Flat files are text files lacking any form of markup structure, the hidden instructions that dictate how text is displayed on screen and in printed documents. XML is a new standard markup language that allows files to be described in terms of the types of data they contain. As a replacement for HTML, XML has the advantage of controlling not only how data is displayed on a WWW page, but also how the data is processed by other programs and database management systems.

Some advantages of XML are described below. XML is a simple, very flexible text format derived from SGML (http://xml.coverpages.org/sgml.html). Originally designed to meet the challenges of large-scale electronic publishing, XML is also playing an increasingly important role in the exchange of a wide variety of data in the biology community. XML is considered the format of choice for the exchange of information among various applications on the Internet. The popularity of XML is mainly due to its flexibility for representing many kinds of information. The use of tags makes XML data self-describing, and the extensible nature of XML makes it possible to define new kinds of documents for specialized purposes.

As XML increases in importance, a series of standards is growing up around it, many of which are defined by the World Wide Web Consortium.

For example, XML Schema provides a notation for defining new types of elements and documents; XML Path Language (XPath) provides a notation for selecting elements within XML documents; Extensible Stylesheet Language Transformation (XSLT) provides a notation for transforming XML documents from one representation to another; XQuery is becoming the standard query language for XML databases; Document Object Model (DOM) and Simple Application Program Interface (API) for XML (SAX) have been developed to facilitate the handling of XML documents. These XML technologies allow XML documents to be converted into HTML, postscript, pdf, Scalable Vector Graphics (SVG), and other document formats for various purposes.

Bioinformatics is typically a cross-platform discipline in which computers are used to integrate and manage data from a variety of sources. Popular programming, scripting, and markup language in bioinformatics reflect this versatility, and include the programming language Java, the scripting language JSP, and the markup language XML. We used an open-source project called Biojava for our biology data parser. BioJava is dedicated to providing a Java framework for processing biological data. It includes objects for manipulating bio-molecular sequences, file parsers, a DAS client and server support, access to the BioSQL and Ensembl databases, and powerful analysis and statistical routines, including a dynamic programming toolkit. BioJava runs on any computer with a Java virtual machine that complies with the Java 2 Standard Edition (J2SE) 1.3 (or later) specifications. It is suitable for Linux, Windows, and Solaris.

2.3 Parallel Bioinformatics Software

The most popular tool for searching sequence databases is a program called BLAST (Basic Local Alignment Search Tool), which compares any two arbitrary sequences by trying to align them with a database. The algorithm starts by looking for exact matches, and then expands the aligned regions by allowing for mismatches. It performs pair-wise comparisons of sequences, seeking regions of local similarity, rather than optimal global alignments between whole sequences.

mpiBLAST is an MPI-based parallel implementation of NCBI BLAST (Satish & Joshi, 2004). It consists of a pair of programs that replace formatdb and blastall with versions that execute BLAST jobs in parallel on a cluster of computers with MPI installed. There are two primary advantages to using mpiBLAST versus traditional BLAST. First, mpiBLAST splits the database across each node of the Grid. Because each node's segment of the database is smaller it can usually reside in the buffer-cache, yielding a significant speedup due to elimination of disk I/Os. Second, it allows BLAST users to take advantage of this efficiency. The four main executable programs in the BLAST distribution are:

- [blastall]: performs BLAST searches using one of five BLAST programs: blastn, blastp, blastx, tblastn, or tblastx. (Table 2 summarizes the query, database sequence, and alignment types for the various BLAST commands.);
- [blastpgp]: performs searches in PSI-BLAST or PHI-BLAST mode; blastpgp performs gapped blastp searches and can be used for iterative searches in psi-blast and phi-blast mode;
- [bl2seq]: performs local alignment of two sequences, allows compareson of two known sequences using the blastp or blastn programs; most bl2seq command-line options are similar to those of blastall;
- [formatdb]: used to format protein or nucleotide source databases; converts a FASTA-format flat file sequence database into a BLAST database.

Another popular tool for searching sequence databases is a program called FASTA, which

Table 2. Descriptions of five BLAST programs

Program	Query sequence type	Database sequence type	Alignment sequence type
blastn	nucleotide	nucleotide	nucleotide
blastp	protein	protein	protein
blastx	nucleotide	protein	protein
tblastn	protein	nucleotide	protein
tblastx	nucleotide	nucleotide	protein

compares any two arbitrary sequences by trying to align them with a database. FASTA can deliver very fast search results from sequence databases.

The FASTA distribution contains search programs analogous to the main BLAST modes, with the exception of PHI-BLAST and PSI-BLAST, as well as programs for global and local pair-wise alignments and other functions. The FASTA programs listed here can all be compiled easily on a Linux system.

- [fasta]: compares a protein sequence against a protein database or a DNA sequence against a DNA database using the FASTA algorithm;
- [ssearch]: compares a protein sequence against a protein database or DNA sequence against a DNA database using the Smith-Waterman algorithm;
- [fastx/fasty]: compares a DNA sequence against a protein database, performing translations on the DNA sequence;
- [tfastx/tfasty]: compares a protein sequence against a DNA database, performing translations on the DNA sequence database;
- [align]: computes the global alignment between two DNA or protein sequences;
- [lalign]: computes the local alignment between two DNA or protein sequences.

The FASTA package contains many programs inconveniently named after the version number of the package and the parallel programming library

used to build them. Nicknames are provided for most programs in Table 3.

ClustalW is a general-purpose multiple-sequence alignment program for DNA and proteins, and has become the most popular such program. It produces biologically meaningful multiple-sequence alignments of divergent sequences, calculates the best matches for selected sequences, and lines them up to show identities, similarities and differences.

3. IMPLEMENTATION

Our implementation is divided into three parts: basic high-performance computing environment, user portal, and biology data translation.

3.1 High-Performance Computing Environment

Our high-performance computing environment comprises the BioGrid and BioCluster systems, both of which have three developed bioinformat-

Table 3. Descriptions of FASTA functions

Nickname(s)	Binary
fasta	mp34compfa
ssearch	mp34compsw
fastx	mp34compfx
fasty	mp34compfy
tfastx	mp34comptfx
tfasty	mp34comptfy

ics packages: mpiBLAST, FASTA and ClustalW. Our hardware architecture is shown in Figure 1.

We constructed a BioGrid testbed that includes four separate nodes. Each node has the Globus Toolkit 3.0 installed for Grid infrastructure, and MPICH-G2 installed for message-passing in parallel computing.

The Redhat 9.0 Linux distribution has been installed on each node. The idea of the Linux cluster is to maximize the performance-to-cost ratio of computing by using low-cost commodity components and free-source Linux and GNU software to assemble parallel and distributed computing systems. Software support includes the standard Linux/GNU environment, including compilers, debuggers, editors, and standard numerical libraries. Coordination and communication among the processing nodes is a key requirement in parallel-processing clusters. In order to accommodate this coordination, developers have created software to carry out coordination, and hardware to send and receive the coordinating messages. Messaging architectures such as the

Message Passing Interface (MPI) and the Parallel Virtual Machine (PVM) allow programmers to ensure that control and data messages occur as needed during operation.

3.2 User Portal

The user portal enables interactions between the application user and the application, obtaining parametric inputs for problems and reporting results upon application execution completion. Our portal uses three interfaces for easy control of the Parallel Bioinformatics Software: Java-based Application, JSP web page, and Pocket PC. We have also developed various basic services for the Grid and Cluster systems.

The Java-based Application uses the Java CoG kit to connect to the Grid system. Key characteristics include: GridProxyInit, a JDialog for submitting pass phrases to Grid to extend certificate expiration dates, GridConfigureDialog uses the UITool in the CoG Kit to enable users to configure process numbers and host names of

Figure 1. Our system hardware architecture

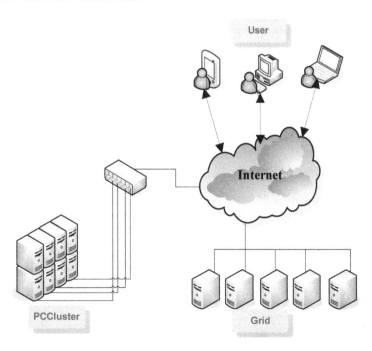

Grid servers, and GridJob, which creates GramJob instances. This class represents a simple gram job and allows for submitting jobs to a gatekeeper, canceling them, sending signal commands, and registering and unregistering from callbacks. GetRSL, RSL provides a common interchange language to describe resources.

The various components of the Globus Resource Management architecture manipulate RSL strings to perform their management functions in cooperation with the other components in the system. GetRSL combines RSL strings. JobMonitor uses two parameters, Gridjob and RSL, to start GlobusRun and monitor job processing. Globus-Run is a factory method for creating previously

exported credentials, submitting jobs to the Grid server and receiving its responses. GridFTP can upload DNA sequences to the Grid System. Added to the functions provided by the Java CoG kit, are API we developed for our system. For example, ProxyDestroy destroys CA files to protect the Grid system. We can configure the machinefile for the Grid system from the application site (see Figure 2).

We also developed a series of capabilities for the cluster system. We wrote a program called CommandClient for the server site that receives commands from the client. Users can configure the cluster system from the application site, including how many CPUs to use, lam/mpi locations,

Figure 2. Configure the machinefile for the Grid system

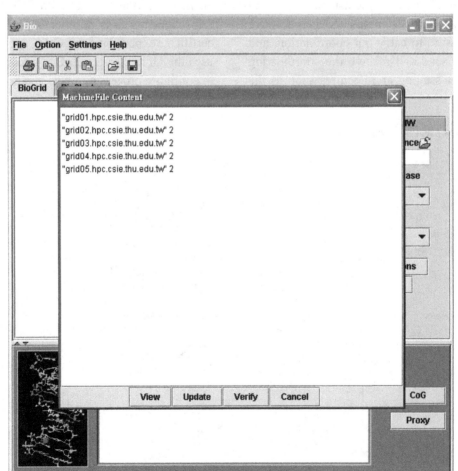

PVM locations, and lamhost file locations. We can also monitor CPU and memory information to know which machines in our cluster system are alive, and we have lamboot and lamhalt capabilities from remote sites (see Figure 3).

We implemented GUIs for the Grid and Cluster system bioinformatics software applications. Figure 4 shows the software architecture of our system. Only the application service interface is visible, implementation details such as distributed processing and parallel processing are invisible to users.

The JSP web page employs a variety of advanced technologies such as JavaServer Pages, HTML, JavaScript, ActionScript (in Flash), and Tomcat. The portal consists of three parts: Machine

Monitor, Bioinformatics Software Application and Job Submission. The Machine Monitor, shown in Figure 5, displays the status of our Grid system, including critical information such as whether a remote machine is working or idle and whether the Java CoG kit is installed on the machine. If the machine halts unexpectedly, the Error Log shows details of relevant information (see Figure 6). The Error Log also displays certificate expiration dates.

Figure 7 shows the GUI of Bioinformatics Application Software. It is divided into two parts: BioGrid and BioCluster. The server side also employs CommandClient (described above) to receive job commands submitted to the cluster. We developed GridJob to submit jobs to the Grid

Figure 3. Lamboot and lamhalt capabilities from a remote site

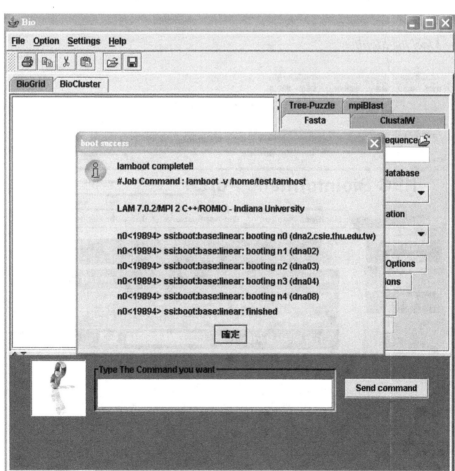

Figure 4. The software architecture of our system

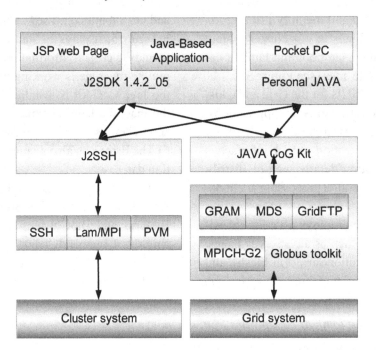

Figure 5. The Machine Monitor

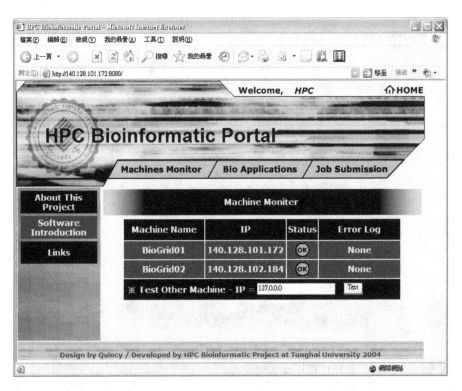

Figure 6. Error log example

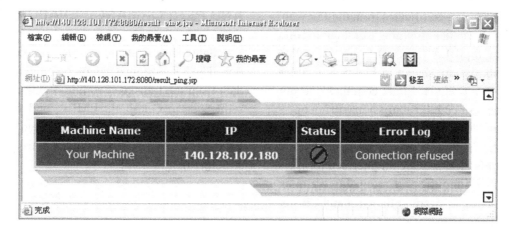

Figure 7. The Bioinformatics application software

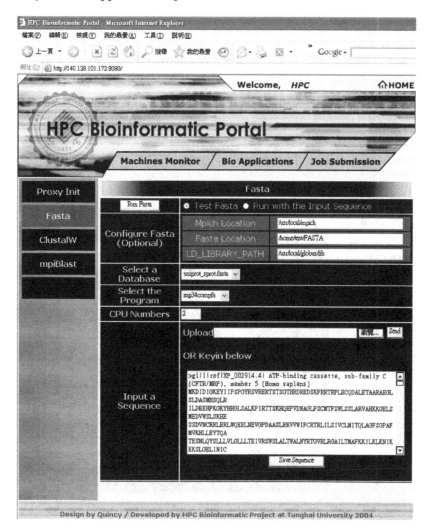

system, and use SimpleCreateProxy to extend the expiration dates of certificates from the JSP web. Three bioinformatics programs are integrated into our system, mpiBLAST, FASTA, and ClustalW.

Job Submission, shown in Figure 8, enables users to submit regular Linux commands to our Grid system. Since Job Submission will not operate without intact Globus RSL, the interface offers various RSL hotkeys to users. The main function of Pocket PC is to provide an interface for a researcher that simplifies operating the complex Bioinformatics software in the Grid and Cluster systems. It can also configure CPU numbers and server IP addresses, as shown in Figure 9.

4. EXPERIMENTAL ENVIRONMENTS AND PERFORMANCE EVALUATION

We adapted the NR database for our experimentation. The NR Protein database contains sequence data from the translated coding regions of DNA sequences in GenBank, EMBL, and DDBJ as well as protein sequences submitted to PIR, SWISSPROT, PRF, PDB (sequences from solved structures).

Figure 8. Job submission

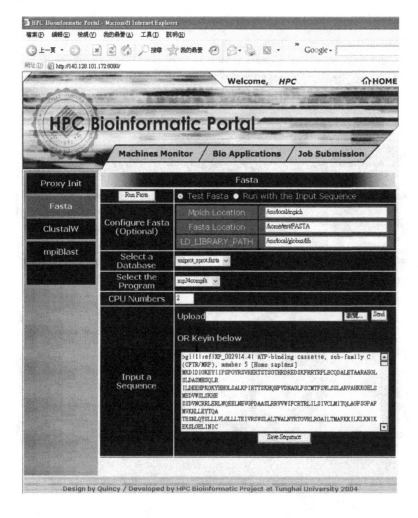

Figure 9. System configuration and bioinformatics software application on Pocket PC

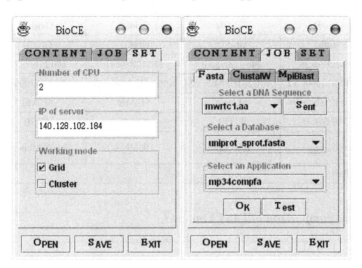

Figure 10. mpiBLAST performance comparison

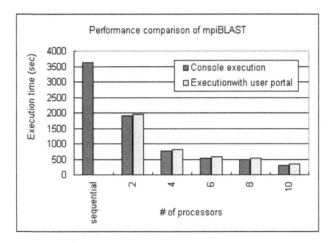

Figure 11. Problem size performance comparison using FASTA

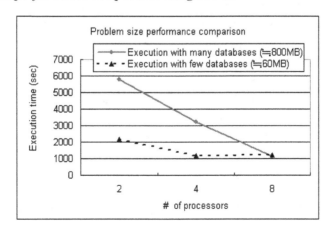

Table 4. Hardware configuration of our Grid system

	Grid01	**Grid02**	**Grid03**	**Grid04**	**Grid05**
Host Name	Grid01	Grid02	Grid03	Grid04	Grid05
IP Address	140.128.98.39	140.128.98.40	140.128.98.41	140.128.98.42	140.128.98.43
CPU	AMD MP 2000+ x2	AMD MP 2000+ x2	AMD MP 2000+ x2	AMD MP 2000+ x2	AMD MP 2000+ x2
RAM	512MB	512MB	512MB	512MB	512MB
Hard Disk	40 GB	40 GB	40 GB	40 GB	40 GB
Network Interface Card	100Mbps	100Mbps	100Mbps	100Mbps	100Mbps
Switch HUB	100Mbps				

Figure 12. Performance comparison of FASTA on grid

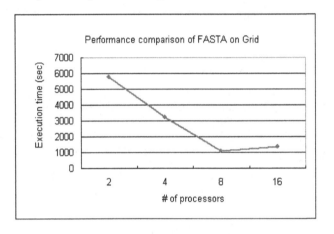

4.1 BioGrid

We assessed the performance of the BioGrid by executing mpiBLAST using 2, 4, 6, 8, and 10 processors, as well as sequential execution. Table 4 shows the hardware configuration of our BioGrid. In order to obtain more accurate data, we performed five executions per experiment and calculated average times. Figure 10 shows a comparison of sequential BLAST performance vs. that of mpiBLAST. The results show that mpiBLAST cut the execution time of sequential BLAST nearly in half. This figure also shows a comparison between executing from the console end and from the user portal. The results show that the user portal performed less efficiently than the console. However, the user-friendly interface can reduce the time needed for biologists to access the bioinformatics tools. We also tested performance on few vs. many databases using the FASTA program. Figure 11 and Figure 12 show that accessing many databases with more processors does indeed reduce execution times, but accessing few databases with many processors does not. We must examine the network communication (Wroe et al., 2004).

4.2 BioCluster

We experimented with a 16-processor Linux PC cluster. Table 5 shows the hardware configuration of our BioCluster. Figure 13 shows experimental results for the parallel versions of all bioinformatics applications. All applications were executed

Table 5. Hardware configuration of our PCCluster system

	Server Node	Client Node
Host Name	DNA01	DNA02~DNA08
IP Address	192.168.10.1	192.168.10.2~ 192.168.10.8
CPU	AMD MP 2000 + x2	AMD MP 2000+ x2
RAM	512MB x2	512MB
Hard Disk	80 GB x1, 60 GB x1	80 GB
Network Interface Card	100Mbps	100Mbps
Switch HUB	100Mbps	

Figure 13. Average execution times for all parallel versions using 2 to 16 processors

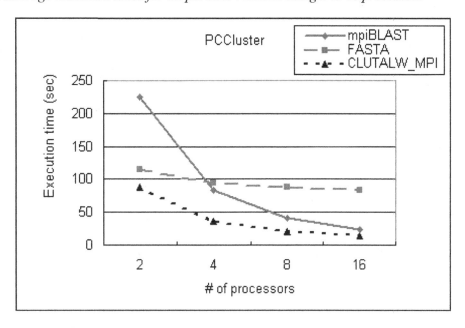

using from 2, 4, 8, and 16 processors to compare execution times. In order to obtain more accurate data, we performed five executions per experiment and calculated average times. The results clearly show that the parallel system reduced the execution time required to perform the sequence alignment.

4.3 Biology Data Translation

Many types of databases are available to researchers in the field of biology. These include primary sequence databases for storing new experimental data, secondary databases that contain information on sequence patterns and motifs, and organism-specific databases tailored for researchers working on a particular species. Unfortunately, the majority of database data formats are heterogeneous. Therefore, we developed a general framework to support heterogeneous data integration. The datasets that we attempted to interoperate using XML involved BLAST and FASTA output data. It is well-known that these data sources are complex and lack structured formats. Thus, a powerful tool is needed to maintain these various data.

Figure 14. The snapshot of the XML translation

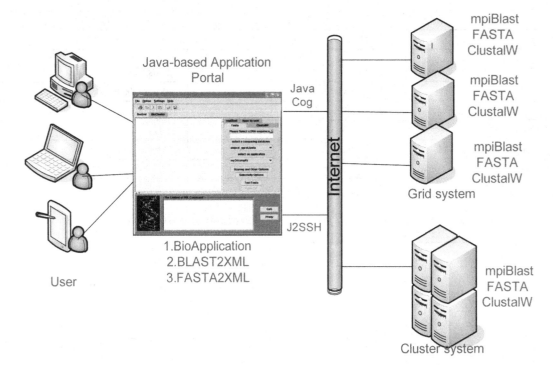

We used BioJava to develop an XML translation tool for each data format, as shown in Figure 14. Since different data sources may provide data in the same format, the same wrapper can be used to access and extract data from various sources. A wrapper can parse the data retrieved from a source data object and process SQL queries to extract desired data values. On use, BioJava parses a data file (a tab-delimited flat file) and converts it into an XML document. The integration system also reports on integration status, displays results on the user interface, and stores them directly into a native XML database.

There are two main translation programs in our system: BLAST2XML and FASTA2XML show in Figure 15. Their main function is to convert native outputs from sequence search tools into XML format. The main BioJava APIs in our system are listed below.

- **BlastLikeToXMLConverter:** converts the raw output from a variety of bioinfor-

matics programs into XML format that will validate against the biojava: BlastLikeDataSetCollection DTD; receives the native output from mpiBlast, then creates a parser for conversion to XML;

- **FastaSearchSAXParser:** SAX2-compliant parser for the '-m 10' output format from the FASTA search program;

- **SimpleXMLEmitter:** a simple XML DocumentHandler that processes SAX2 events to create a sensibly formatted XML as it parses without populating objects with data.

The mpiBlast matches the input (query) sequence "test" with the database "yeast.nt". Figure 16 demonstrates typical XML output formatting consisting of the following information: (i) BLAST program and version used (e.g., blastn 2.6.6 is used for nucleotide sequence searching); (ii) genome sequence database used for matching

Figure 15. The function of XML translation

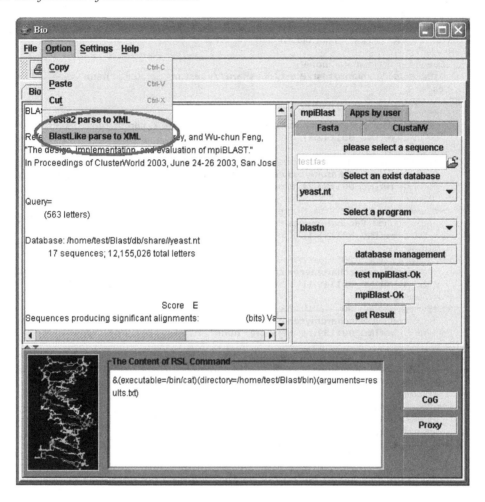

the query or input sequences; (iii) query sequence description; (iv) parameters used to perform the BLAST search; (v) descriptions of matches or hits, and statistics.

Figure 17 shows native mpiBlast program output and translation results to illustrate mpiBlast XML formatted output.

5. CONCLUSION

The development of grid and cluster environments made the high-performance computing power needed for complex biological tasks available to every scientist and research engineer. Faster data searching across numerous large-scale databases, coupled with parallel processing and improved modeling methods will bring significant improvements to drug discovery and development processes. In the paper, we have built the basic platform for a Cluster and Grid Computing environment using the Linux PC clusters. In the Grid environment, Globus Toolkit (GT) which serves as middleware is used for message transfer and communication between various Grid platforms and Sun Grid Engine (SGE) is responsible for task assignment.

Results show that the THUBioGrid indeed saves significant time in sequence alignment problems with increasing number of processors

Figure 16. Example of XML formatting

```
<?xml version="1.0" ?>
- <BlastLikeDataSet program="ncbi-blastn" version="2.2.6">
  - <Header>
      <QueryId id="" metaData="none" />
      <DatabaseId id="/home/test/Blast/db/share//yeast.nt" metaData="none" />
    </Header>
  - <Summary>
    - <HitSummary score="32" expectValue="0.38">
        <HitDescription>Saccharomyces cerevisiae chromosome X, complete...</HitDescription>
        <HitId id="ref|NC_001142.1|" metaData="none" />
      </HitSummary>
    - <HitSummary score="32" expectValue="0.41">
        <HitDescription>Saccharomyces cerevisiae chromosome IV, complet...</HitDescription>
        <HitId id="ref|NC_001136.2|" metaData="none" />
      </HitSummary>
    - <HitSummary score="32" expectValue="0.42">
        <HitDescription>Saccharomyces cerevisiae chromosome XIII, compl...</HitDescription>
        <HitId id="ref|NC_001145.1|" metaData="none" />
      </HitSummary>
    - <HitSummary score="30" expectValue="0.40">
        <HitDescription>Saccharomyces cerevisiae chromosome XVI, comple...</HitDescription>
        <HitId id="ref|NC_001148.1|" metaData="none" />
      </HitSummary>
    - <HitSummary score="30" expectValue="1.5">
        <HitDescription>Saccharomyces cerevisiae chromosome VII, comple...</HitDescription>
        <HitId id="ref|NC_001139.1|" metaData="none" />
      </HitSummary>
    - <HitSummary score="30" expectValue="1.6">
        <HitDescription>Saccharomyces cerevisiae chromosome II, complet...</HitDescription>
        <HitId id="ref|NC_001134.1|" metaData="none" />
      </HitSummary>
    - <HitSummary score="30" expectValue="1.6">
        <HitDescription>Saccharomyces cerevisiae chromosome XV, complet...</HitDescription>
        <HitId id="ref|NC_001147.1|" metaData="none" />
      </HitSummary>
```

Figure 17. Example of flat file formatting and its corresponding XML output

```
Flat File format

>ref|NC_001142.1| Saccharomyces cerevisiae chromosome X,complete chromosome sequence
        Length = 745440

 Score = 32.3 bits (16), Expect = 0.38
 Identities = 16/16 (100%)
 Strand = Plus / Plus


 Query: 70     cagcttctgaactggt 85
               ||||||||||||||||
 Sbjct: 530705 cagcttctgaactggt 530720
```

```
XML format
- <Hit sequenceLength="745440">
    <HitId id="ref|NC_001142.1|" metaData="none" />
    <HitDescription>Saccharomyces cerevisiae chromosome X, complete chromosome sequence</HitDescription>
  - <HSPCollection>
    - <HSP>
        <HSPSummary hitStrand="plus" queryStrand="plus" score="32.3" alignmentSize="16" percentageIdentity="100"
          numberOfIdentities="16" expectValue="0.38" />
      - <BlastLikeAlignment>
          <QuerySequence startPosition="70" stopPosition="85">CAGCTTCTGAACTGGT</QuerySequence>
          <MatchConsensus xml:space="preserve">||||||||||||||||</MatchConsensus>
          <HitSequence startPosition="530705" stopPosition="530720">CAGCTTCTGAACTGGT</HitSequence>
        </BlastLikeAlignment>
      </HSP>
```

used in the computations. However, the biological data derived from various biology tools are heterogeneous. XML serves as a standard language for integrating heterogeneous data formats. We took advantage of XML to establish a framework for biology data integration. If these data are distributed in XML format, users can easily perform functional gene comparisons between species, and thus realize key discoveries of new biological knowledge. The user portal we developed also enables biologists to easily control bioinformatics software, as well as the Grid and Cluster systems. Multiple interfaces allow users to work with bioinformatics software anywhere. In the near future, more processors will be added to the experimental design to yield more data points. Also, we will conduct more extensive surveys to explain the usability of this system in the future work.

REFERENCES

Bala, P., Pytlinski, J., & Nazaruk, M. (2002). BioGRID – An European Grid for Molecular Biology. In *Proceedings of the 11th IEEE International Symposium on High Performance Distributed Computing* (p. 412).

Bayer, M., Campbell, A., & Virdee, D. (2004). A GT3 based. BLAST grid service for biomedical research. In *Proceedings of the UK e-Science All Hands Meeting 2004*, Nottingham, UK. Retrieved from http://www.allhands.org.uk/2004/proceedings/papers/141.pdf

Foster, I. (2002). The Grid: A New Infrastructure for 21st Century Science. *Physics Today*, *55*(2), 42–47. doi:10.1063/1.1461327

Foster, I., & Kesselman, C. (1999). *The Grid 2: Blueprint for a New Computing Infrastructure* (2nd ed.). San Francisco, CA: Morgan Kaufmann.

Konishi, F., Yamamoto, T., Fukuzaki, A., Defago, X., Satou, K., & Konagaya, A. (2002). OBIGrid: A New Computing Platform for Bioinformatics. *Genome Informatics*, *13*, 484–485.

Li, K. B. (2003). ClustalW-MPI: ClustalW Analysis Using Distributed and Parallel Computing. *Bioinformatics (Oxford, England)*, *19*(12), 1585–1586. doi:10.1093/bioinformatics/btg192

Moreau, L., et al. (2002). On the Use of Agents in a BioInformatics Grid. In *Proceedings of the Network Tools and Applications in Biology Conference (NETTAB 2002)*. Retrieved from http://www.ecs.soton.ac.uk/~mml/papers/nettab02-b.pdf

Pierce, M., Fox, G., Youn, C., Mock, S., Mueller, K., & Balsoy, O. (2002). Interoperable Web services for computational portals. In *Proceedings of the 2002 ACM/IEEE Conference on Supercomputing*, Baltimore, MD (pp. 1-12).

Prodan, R., & Fahringer, T. (2002). ZENTURIO: An Experiment Management System for Cluster and Grid Computing. In *Proceedings of the IEEE International Conference on Cluster Computing (CLUSTER '02)*, Chicago, IL (pp. 9-18).

Satish, K. M., & Joshi, R. R. (2004). GBTK: A Toolkit for Grid Implementation of BLAST. In *Proceedings of the Seventh International Conference on High Performance Computing and Grid in Asia Pacific Region, (HPCAsia '04)*, Tokyo, Japan (pp. 378-382).

Schmidt, H. A., Strimmer, K., Vingron, M., & von Haeseler, A. (2002). TREE-PUZZLE: maximum likelihood phylogenetic analysis using quartets and parallel computing. *Bioinformatics (Oxford, England)*, *18*(3), 502–504. doi:10.1093/bioinformatics/18.3.502

Sterling, T. L., Salmon, J., Backer, D. J., & Savarese, D. F. (1999). *How to Build a Beowulf: A Guide to the Implementation and Application of PC Clusters*. Cambridge, MA: MIT Press.

Stewart, C. A., Hart, D., Berry, D. K., Olsen, G. J., Wernert, E. A., & Fischer, W. (2001). *Parallel implementation and performance of fastDNAml – a program for maximum likelihood phylogenetic inference.* Retrieved from http://www.sc2001.org/papers/pap.pap191.pdf

Stocker, G., Rieder, D., & Trajanoski, Z. (2004). ClusterControl: A Web Interface for Distributing and Monitoring Bioinformatics Applications on a Linux Cluster. *Bioinformatics (Oxford, England)*, *20*(5), 805–807. doi:10.1093/bioinformatics/bth014

Sturn, A., Mlecnik, B., Pieler, R., Rainer, J., Truskaller, T., & Trajanoski, Z. (2003). Client-Server Environment for High-Performance Gene Expression Data Analysis. *Bioinformatics (Oxford, England)*, *19*(6), 772–773. doi:10.1093/bioinformatics/btg074

Suzumura, T., Matsuoka, S., Nakada, H., & Casanova, H. (2004). GridSpeed: A Web-based Grid Portal Generation Server. In *Proceedings of the Seventh International Conference on High Performance Computing and Grid in Asia Pacific Region, (HPCAsia'04)*, Tokyo, Japan (pp. 26-33).

Trelles, O., Andrade, M. A., Valencia, A., Zapata, E. L., & Carazo, J. M. (1998). Computational Space Reduction and Parallelization of a new Clustering Approach for Large Groups of Sequences. *Bioinformatics (Oxford, England)*, *14*(5), 439–451. doi:10.1093/bioinformatics/14.5.439

Wilkinson, B., & Allen, M. (2004). *Parallel Programming: Techniques and Applications Using Networked Workstations and Parallel Computers* (2nd ed.). Upper Saddle River, NJ: Prentice Hall.

Wroe, C., Goble, C., Greenwood, M., Lord, P., Miles, S., & Papay, J. (2004). Automating experiments using semantic data on a bioinformatics grid. *IEEE Intelligent Systems*, *19*(1), 48–55. doi:10.1109/MIS.2004.1265885

Yang, C.-T., Hsiung, Y.-C., & Kan, H.-C. (2005a, June 27-30). Implementation of a Biology Data Translation System on Grid Environments. In *Proceedings of the 3rd International Conference on Information Technology: Research and Education (ITRE 05)*, Hsinchu, Taiwan.

Yang, C.-T., Hsiung, Y.-C., & Kan, H.-C. (2005b, March 28-30). Implementation and Evaluation of a Java Based Computational Grid for Bioinformatics Applications. In *Proceedings of the International Conference on Advanced Information Networking and Applications (AINA 2005)*, Taipei, Taiwan (Vol. 1, pp. 298-303).

Yang, C.-T., Hung, C.-C., & Soong, C.-C. (2001). Parallel Computing on Low-Cost PC-Based SMPs Clusters. In *Proceedings of the 2001 International Conference on Parallel and Distributed Computing, Applications, and Techniques (PDCAT 2001)*, Taipei, Taiwan (pp. 149-156).

Yang, C.-T., Kuo, Y.-L., & Lai, C.-L. (2004, March 28-31). Design and Implementation of a Computational Grid for Bioinformatics. In *Proceedings of the 2004 IEEE International Conference on e-Technology, e-Commerce and e-Service (EEE 04)*, Taipei, Taiwan (pp. 448-451).

Yang, C.-T., Kuo, Y.-L., & Lai, C.-L. (2005). Designing Computing Platform for BioGrid. *International Journal of Computer Applications in Technology*, *22*(1), 3–13. doi:10.1504/IJCAT.2005.006798

Yang, C.-T., Kuo, Y.-L., Li, K.-C., & Gaudiot, J.-L. (2004, December 27-30). On Design of Cluster and Grid Computing Environments for Bioinformatics Applications. In A. Sen, N. Das, S. K. Das, et al. (Eds.), *Distributed Computing: IWDC 2004: 6th International Workshop*, Kolkata, India (LNCS 3326, pp. 82-87).

This work was previously published in the International Journal of Grid and High Performance Computing, Volume 3, Issue 1, edited by Emmanuel Udoh and Ching-Hsien Hsu, pp. 69-88, copyright 2011 by IGI Publishing (an imprint of IGI Global).

Chapter 20
Migrating Android Applications to the Cloud

Shih-Hao Hung
National Taiwan University, Taiwan

Jeng-Peng Shieh
National Taiwan University, Taiwan

Chen-Pang Lee
National Taiwan University, Taiwan

ABSTRACT

Recently, smartphone technologies have evolved quickly and offered end users the computing power and networking capabilities required to perform useful network and multimedia applications. However, due to limited physical sizes and battery capacities, the current generation of smartphones cannot yet fulfill the requirements of sophisticated applications of which personal computers are capable. One way to solve this problem is to minimize the workload on a smartphone as much as possible by offloading portions of an application to a server. The solution is particularly attractive today as cloud computing provides the needed server resources at relatively low costs. This paper proposes a novel, lightweight application migration mechanism for the users of smartphones to suspend the execution of applications and offload them to the cloud. The authors also developed a framework to perform Android applications efficiently with virtual phones in the cloud with a virtual storage. This paper discusses the migration mechanism and evaluates its effectiveness on the Android smartphone. This approach may effectively offload workload for Android applications even with low-speed mobile network.

INTRODUCTION

Smartphones have evolved rapidly during the last three years. Thanks to the advances in processor, memory, flash storage, mobile communication, and software, smartphones have enabled sophis-

ticated applications for mobile users. The current leading brands for smartphones in the market, Apple iPhone, Microsoft Window Mobile, Black-Berry RIM, and Google Android, all support applications such as multimedia playback, Internet browsing, email, voice mail, social networks and location-based services. Still, the limited hardware resources and the constrained battery capacities

DOI: 10.4018/978-1-4666-2065-0.ch020

have strongly impacted their user experiences (Chun & Maniatis, 2009).

On the other hand, in a modern datacenter, cloud computing has changed the infrastructure of computation, data storage, networking, and software architecture, as well as the business model for providing the resources and applications to the users. Numerous innovative and powerful cloud-based services have been pushed to the public with low amortized operational costs (Armbrust et al., 2009). For example, Google has made many useful services available to users: Gmail, Google Map, Goggle Docs, YouTube, etc., and many of them are free.

Today, many smartphone users take advantage of low-cost or free cloud-based services. The combination of smartphone and cloud-based service has worked quite successfully and has become very popular, as it essentially offloads computational workload and data storage from the user's smartphone. That way, an application could consume less power by having most of the application workload performed by a cloud-based service.

However, as cloud-based services become popular, security and privacy issues have also been raised. Many users would not use a cloud-based service to handle their critical data and tasks, unless the service provider can guarantee the security of their data and protect their privacy. Facebook has long been criticized for privacy risks. Thus, mechanisms besides public services are needed for offloading workloads for smartphone applications.

Depending on how a cloud infrastructure is exposed as a service to the user, there are so called service models which are commonly used to categorize a cloud-based service. For example, *infrastructure as a service*, also known as *IaaS*, is a type of service which delivers a computational infrastructure - typically in the form of a virtualization environment or a virtual machine.

One could take advantage of the low infrastructure cost offered by IaaS to set up an environment and perform computation on-demand.

This approach may offer a secure and private environment as the user controls the environment and may protect the work and data handled in the environment with security measures. Following this model, we have developed a framework for facilitating a virtual environment, called virtual phone, to perform smartphone applications via IaaS.

Many previous research works were focused on the partitioning of application workloads or re-design of applications (Balan, Flinn, Satyanarayanan, Sinnamohideen, & Yang, 2002; Cuervo et al., 2010; Flinn, Narayanan, & Satyanarayanan, 2001). Our framework is designed to (1) make it easy to deploy application to the cloud by the control of end user, (2) allow users to create a virtual phone in the cloud (3) provide a lightweight method to migrate application states between Android and the cloud, (4) keep the data storage synchronized at best and reduce unnecessary network traffic, (5) offer an end-to-end secure communication channel and encrypted file system to protect user data.

Application migration and data synchronization are key issues in our framework. For offloading smartphone applications, these key issues are sensitive to the characteristics of a mobile network, e.g. bandwidth, latency, connectivity, and cost. Thus, traditional solutions developed to offload desktop applications or migrating server workloads may not work well.

In this paper, we discuss our migration mechanism, the performance issues and data storage associated application migration, and evaluate its effectiveness on the Android smartphone. By July of 2010, there had been more than 100000 Android applications developed as claimed by AndroLib (TechCrunch, 2010), and migrating these existing applications with no code modifications was quite challenging.

The rest of the paper is organized as the following. We discuss the characteristics of Android applications in Section *Android Applications*. The design of our migration scheme is described in Section *Migrating Android Applications*. We

ANDROID APPLICATIONS

Before we discuss the details about our design and implementation, it is necessary to review the way applications are managed by the operating environment on an Android smartphone. Typically, Android applications are written in Java and are compiled into a package with an .apk suffix. A package contains the Java bytecode, resource files, and data. Each application is executed on a virtual machine, called *Dalvik*, with its own states and memory space apart from other applications. Each application has a unique Linux user ID for permission setting. This user ID is assigned when the application is installed on the device, and remains during its existence on that device. Thereof, an application is isolated from touching other applications.

As shown in Figure 1, the Android software stacks include (1)application framework, to offer the developers to build rich and innovative applications, (2)libraries, implemented in C/C++ programming language, and exposed to developers through application framework, (3)Android runtime, bundled with a core libraries and Dalvik virtual machine on which Android application runs in its own process, (4)Linux kernel, to support Android for its core system services such as security, process management, networking and device drivers.

As an optimization for smartphone applications, the Android operating environment manages applications differently from traditional operating environments. There are four key application components in the Android framework, namely *activities, services, broadcast receivers* and *content providers*. An application may consist of one or more activities, each of which presents a graphics user interface to the user. A service does not have any visual interface, and it just runs on behalf of application in the background for a long period of time. A broadcast receiver does nothing but react to broadcast events. And content provider shares its application specific data to other applications. Since we found activity is the driving force of Android application, it is the interface for application interacting with users. It will issues services to run on demands, responds to broadcast events and accesses the data needed from content provider. And also the activity life cycle is defined clear on its states, so we focus on Activities in this paper for offloading execution purpose.

Android system may kill a process when the system falls short of memory. To decide which processes to kill, Android places each process into an "importance hierarchy" with the running components and its states. There are five levels in the hierarchy. (1) A *foreground* process is one that is working for what the user is doing. And they are killed only when available memory is too low to support its running. (2) A *visible* process is one that does not have any components, but affects what the user sees. It is still important and kept alive unless necessary to free resource for foreground one. (3) A *service* process is one that is a running service that does not belong to the above two categories. They will be killed to favor two higher processes. (4) A *background* process is one holding an activity invisible to the user. They do not have any direct impact on user experience. They will be killed to reclaim resource for the above three. They are kept in an LRU list and make sure the recent activity associated with it is the last to be killed. (5) An *empty* process is one that does not associate with active components. These processes are often killed to balance the system workload. Based on the importance hierarchy, Android ranks a process at the highest level.

Figure 1. System architecture of Android smartphones

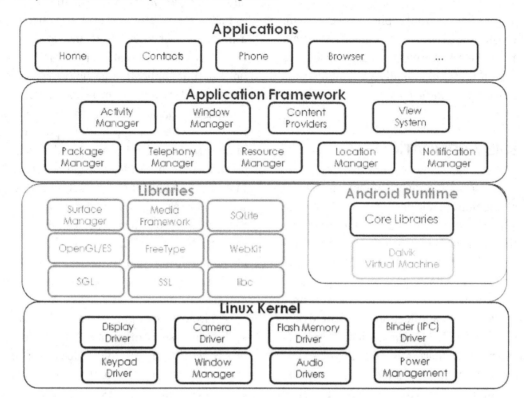

The *life cycle* of an activity is illustrated in Figure 2. There are seven methods which are involved in the entire lifecycle of an activity. A developer can monitor by implementing them with three nested loops:

1. The entire lifetime of an application begins with the *onCreate()* method to perform initialization and ends with the *onDestroy()* method to release allocated resources.
2. The *visible* lifetime is between *onStart()* and *OnStop()*, where the user can see the activity on-screen, whether the application is in the foreground or not.
3. The *foreground* lifetime is between *onResume()* and *onPause(),* which is the point we are interested in. During this time, the activity is active and shown on the screen and is interacting with the user.

To conserve the energy on the smartphone, the Android operating environment suspends an application when the smartphone goes to sleep or when a new activity is issued. When an application receives the request to suspend, its *onPause()* method is called to commit unsaved state changes to persistent data and stop animations and/or other operations that may consume CPU time. When an activity gets the focus by user's action or a new intent is delivered, its *onResume()* method is called. Since the application may be killed by the Android operating environment during the suspension time, the *onResume()* method should include the instructions to restore the application state before the activity gets ready to receive input from the user.

On an Android phone, only one application is actively running on the foreground, and the other applications are either running in the background or suspended in the stack. Thus, application devel-

Figure 2. Illustration of Android application activities

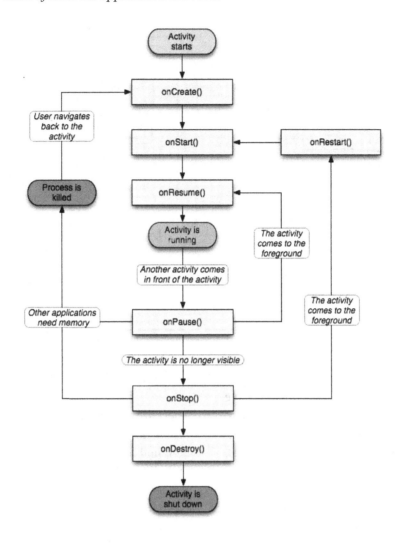

opers are advised to use the pause-resume scheme provided by the Android to save *application states* in the persistent storage so that the application can resume later. Since most Android applications follow this programming paradigm, we leveraged the application *pause-resume* scheme to design our application migration scheme. The concept of our application migration scheme is actually quite simple: suspend the application on phone A, transfer the saved application state to phone B, and then resume the application on phone B. The design of our migration scheme is further discussed in the next section.

MIGRATING ANDROID APPLICATIONS

In Section *Introduction*, we have introduced the concept of virtual phones for executing applications in the cloud. For executing Android application, the operating environment of a virtual phone is different from traditional virtual machines. Since Android is a cross-platform operating environment, there are binary compatibility issues which affects the portability and performance. In Subsection A, we will first explain the software architecture of a virtual phone for running Android

Figure 3. Illustration of application migration and virtual storage of virtual phones

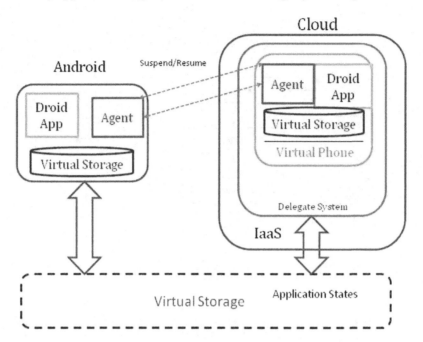

application in the cloud as shown in Figure 3. After establishing a virtual phone, we can migrate a live application to the virtual phone. The procedure for deploying Android applications to the virtual phone in our approach is described in Subsection B.

In addition, the network connection between a physical phone and a virtual phone can be slow or unreliable, and our framework needs to address these issues. Subsection C discusses the method for synchronizing data between two phones. For that, we have developed a user space filesystem and designed a synchronization protocol. We show how a lazy synchronization protocol can save the network traffic and techniques to improve the time for migrating an application.

Finally, when an application is executed on a virtual phone, security and privacy issues are serious concerns. The data transmitted over the network need to be protected as well as the data stored on the virtual phone. The virtual phone itself may not be secure as attacks could come from insiders. Subsection D talks about security and privacy measures that can be included to enhance our design.

A. Establishing a Virtual Phone

There are a variety of processor architectures (i.e. *instruction set architectures*, or *ISA*) which can be found on today's Android phones and tablets, including ARM, MIPS, VIA, and Intel Atom. While the developers of Android applications have been advised to write application codes in Java and take advantage of the library functions provided by the Android Framework, some applications were still written in part with C or assembly codes for performance. In fact, the Android framework provide the *Java Native Interface (JNI)* to allow Java code running in the Dalvik virtual machine (DVM) to interact with native applications and libraries which are written in other languages, such as C, C++ and assembly.

For an Android application which is written completely in Java and uses only the standard libraries provided by the Android framework, its portability should be less of a problem, as the application can run on any Android platforms without any modifications. On the other hand, if an application contains native codes or uses non-standard libraries, the virtual phone would need to address these portability issues in order to execute the application correctly.

In our framework, we use the Android Emulator (http://www.android-x86.org/) to address the binary compatibility issues. The Android Emulator is included in the Android Software Development Kit (SDK) to support the development of Android applications. The Android emulator allows a user to prototype, develop, and test Android applications on an x86-based computer without using a physical device. It mimics the hardware and software features of an ARM-based Android phone.

While it seems that Android Emulator can be used directly as a virtual phone for executing Android applications in the cloud, there are a couple of technical issues. First, it only supports specific processor architecture in the ARM family, i.e. ARM926EJ-S. Secondly, the Android Emulator can be significantly slower than a physical phone as it takes time to translate ARM instructions into x86 instructions.

Internally, the Android Emulator uses an open-source machine virtualization called QEMU (Bellard, 2005). QEMU supports full system emulation in which a complete and unmodified operating system is run in a virtual machine and Linux user mode emulation where a Linux process compiled for one target CPU can be run on another CPU. Besides of CPU emulation, it also provides a set of genetic devices and emulated peripherals.

QEMU is an active and fast evolving open source project. More and more emulated CPUs and devices are added into QEMU source tree. So far, QEMU supports a range of processor models, including MIPS, x86, PowerPC, etc., and one may patch the processor model in the QEMU for a virtual phone to support new processor architectures.

On the other hand, regular Android applications, i.e. those which do not use non-standard native library functions, can be performed well by an x86-based computer running a version of Android compiled for the x86 processor. It will reduce a lot of virtualization overhead, since Dalvik

bytecodes could be translated to x86 instructions which is executed natively on the PC servers in the cloud. That will speed up the computation and enhance the scalability of our framework. We had some evaluation to compare with the performance of different computing devices in later section. It showed that an entry-level Intel Atom processor still outperformed the Google G1 phone by 4.9 to 6.4 times.

Thus, in our current scheme, we use Android-x86 to serve as a virtual phone and automatically invoke the Android Emulator to execute those applications which use JNI to interact with non-standard native library functions. This allows a virtual phone to execute regular Android applications efficiently and overcome portability issues when necessary.

B. Migrating an Application

In our design, the user of an Android phone only needs to download the agent that we have developed and uses it to set up a virtual phone in the cloud. To quickly establish a virtual phone, it is necessary to reduce the amount of data needed for the virtual phone to become operational. This is important as transferring the entire Android operating environment to a virtual phone can take a long time. The memory and data storage have reached the range of gigabytes in today's Android phones, and it would be impractical for the virtual phone to clone the entire contents in the physical phone.

To speed up the establishment of a virtual phone, our framework prepares the images for standard Android operating environments. As of today, the major versions of Android have been 1.5, 1.6, 2.0, 2.1, and 2.2. When the agent first sets up a virtual phone, it installs our standard image for the same version of Android as the physical phone. Our standard image also contains an agent program which runs in the background when the virtual phone comes to life. After that, the two

Figure 4. Illustration of application migration to the cloud

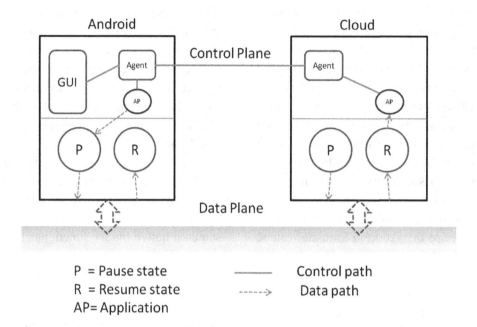

P = Pause state   ——— Control path
R = Resume state   -----> Data path
AP= Application

agents communicate to transfer needed programs/ data and synchronize any changes.

The agents serve for our scheme for migrating an application between two phones. The procedures for offloading an application are illustrated in Figure 4. On the left-hand side: (1) The user issue a request-to-resume by GUI program and has its target application enter the *OnPause* function. (2) Its target application saves the states in the *OnPause* function. (3) The agent sends request-to-resume to the agent on the other side. Then, on the right-hand side: (4) The agent gets request-to-resume and restarts the target application. (5) The application resumes by calling the *OnResume* function and (6) resumes the execution after restoring the application states.

Via the scheme, we can send the application's activity back and forth between a physical phone and a virtual phone in the cloud. Actually, this scheme may also be used to migrate applications between two physical phones. The user may pause an application any time and decide where an application should be executed. Note that, during the migration, the application states are saved and

restored via the synchronized file storage which is discussed in the next subsection.

For the virtual phone to operate in a public cloud, it is important to encrypt the user data storage and the communication traffic between the physical phone and the virtual phone. This aspect will also be described later in this section.

C. Synchronizing Data

While an Android application is migrated from one machine to another machine, it is necessary to clone its application states and data in the storage system. Conceptually, the local storage in the mobile device needs to be synchronized with the storage in the virtual phone, so that the migrated application cannot tell the differences in these two operating environments. However, the costs associated with data synchronization can be prohibitively high over a mobile network. In this subsection, we analyze this problem and describe the data synchronization protocol that we developed specifically for migrating Android applications.

A brute-force way for synchronizing data between two phones is to maintain identical data for all files in their file systems. For that, the data must be updated as soon as one phone makes changes to any file, which incur *network traffic*. Also, the applications on one phone may need to wait for the completion of any synchronization operation if a strict synchronization protocol (Bernstein, Hadzilacos, & Goodman, 1987) is used, which would cause a long delay as the *communication latencies* can be quite high between the two phones. Thus, it is necessary to reduce the amount of data required to be communicated, and it should reduce the wait time if each application does not need to wait for the synchronization operations which have no effects on the application.

First, we divide the data storage into three categories: *system image*, *system-wide data*, and *application data*. When a virtual phone is initialized, its filesystem is loaded with the system image and application packages which are on a standard operating environment image, as mentioned in the previous subsection. Since the system image of a physical Android phone is usually stored as a *firmware* in the flash memory, the system image is changed only when the user or the vendor upgrades the firmware on the phone. Once the user starts to use the phone, the activities on the phone would add/modify the data files that belong to the latter two categories.

Synchronizing the system image is quite straightforward, and reducing the traffic for that is generally not a critical issue. Once a new firmware is released, both the physical phone and the virtual phone will download the firmware from the vendor and upgrade their system images at the same time. The synchronization should only incur a small amount of communication traffic between the two phones, and the virtual phone should not cause further delay here as it is connected to a high-bandwidth network in the cloud. It would also be an interesting option for a user who wishes to experiment with a new firmware before adopting it on a physical phone. The user

may choose to upgrade the system image on a virtual phone to test if the existing applications still work.

System-wide data refers to those files which record system-wide information and/or would affect the operations of the system and applications. On the other hand, application data refers to those files which are owned by one application. Libraries are examples of system data. Modifying a library may affect multiple applications running on the system. When a physical phone makes a change to its system data, it often stops the applications which might be affected and sometimes requires the system to reboot. Similarly, its virtual phone counterpart should follow the same procedure.

As far as application data is concerned, the synchronization can be done on per-application basis during the course of application migration. Running the same application on multiple phones would make the synchronization more complicate, and our current framework does not support that. Thus, it does not require a coherence protocol (Bayer, Heller, & Reiser, 1980) to synchronize the application data all the time. Instead, we apply lazy and on-demand policies (Gray, Lorie, Putzolu, & Traiger, 1994) to synchronize the data upon the request of an application. Some heuristics can also be used to speed up the response time by analyzing the file access patterns of an application.

However, there are services which are critical to the operations of an Android phone. For example, *Contact Provider* offers contact information to all the applications on the phone. Once an application calls Contact Provider to add/modify/delete an entry, it would affect other applications. In our framework, we allow some of these critical services to execute simultaneously on each phone. The file accesses, performed by these services, are monitored by a protocol to ensure the coherence of data.

Our framework also aims to provide the capability for backing up filesystems and cloning the virtual phone. For that purpose, we need to synchronize the entire filesystem. In a conventional file system, a disk image consists of many blocks and meta-data for file descriptions. Some implementations support content-based sharing that shares identical blocks in the disk images in order to reduce the size of the occupied physical disk blocks. They support copy-on-write mechanisms for data access in the same physical disk blocks. Those methods can reduce the usage of physical disks and can also reduce the communication load to clone those disk images. However, it cannot resolve the version conflict of disk branches, while all files are stored in the same disk (Pfaff, Garfinkel, & Rosenblum, 2006). Figure 5 shows an example of version conflict in disk branches. The local machine clones its disk image to the remote machine, and then both machines update their own disk images respectively. Disk-cloning cannot be done in a straightforward way, while there are branches in the disk images.

To simplify the disk version conflict problem, putting data of each application on different disk images is proposed. Besides, the following assumptions are given. Although the conditions are relaxed, it still satisfies most of application scenarios.

1. **No common data between different applications:** If no data are accessed by different applications, then there are no data conflicts between different applications.
2. **No parallel copies of the same application running in different machines:** When no parallel copies of one application run in parallel in different machines, then there are no data conflicts due to this application.

The following describes the implementation of our data synchronization protocol for the Android phones. In a Linux system, a file system is a collection of file trees. A disk partition is mounted as a directory as well as file trees. The disk partition can be either physical disk partition or logical disk partition. A logical partition is a file in the native file system, and the file is mounted as a directory in the native file system. Therefore, application data can be put in many logical partitions respectively, but are not mixed in a single partition. During the course of application migration, we just need to synchronize the logical partitions associated with the application, but not the entire physical partition. The version

Figure 5. Version conflicts in disk branches

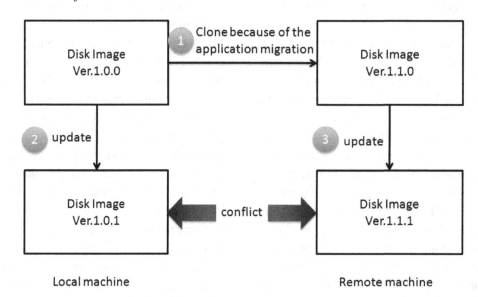

conflict issues can thus be simplified and do not affect the applications.

In addition, the content-based sharing mechanism also applies to reduce the occupied space in the logical disk. The copy-on-write mechanism helps to record what blocks are modified in the meta-data and makes it easier to synchronize the modified blocks via metadata. In the content-based sharing mechanism, a finer granularity exposes more redundancy than a coarser granularity but requires more meta-data to track modified blocks. Hence, a proper block size needs to be evaluated with real applications. In a previous study, the content-based sharing mechanism take relatively small space by 4K bytes of block size with popular Linux applications in an enterprise-scale evaluation (Nath et al., 2006).

Several new components need to be added into Android. The system architecture is shown in Figure 6. Their functions are summarized as the following:

1. **Immigrant disk image for the logic disk:** Record modified blocks in meta-data and support extendible disks.
2. **Immigrant disk manager:** Transmit modified blocks to the destination machine and find out identical blocks to reduce the communication load. In Figure 6, the implementation is based on FUSE (n.d.), file system in user space. Thus we can avoid implementing any new components in the kernel space.

The stages of the storage synchronization are briefed as the following:

1. **At the first time of application execution:** Create a new logical disk image in the native file system and mount the logical disk for the data storage of the application.
2. **Writing data to the storage:** Enlarge the logic disk image by the copy-on-write mechanism, and record the modified blocks

in meta-data for data synchronization in next steps.
3. **Application migration:** Transmit modified blocks to the destination machine based on meta-data and reduce the communication load, if any identical blocks already exist in the destination.

D. Security and Privacy Measures

Since a virtual phone may operate in a public cloud, it is important to protect the user data with an end-to-end secure communication channel. In addition, choosing a trustworthy IaaS provider is critical to deploy a virtual phone. A strong authentication and encryption scheme is needed to set up the secure storage and the secure channel for storing private keys and exchanging master encryption keys. Later communications can be done via a secure channel such as the *virtual private network* (VPN) (Schmidt, Kuntze, & Kasper, 2008) as shown in Figure 7. For stronger level of trust, *Trusted Platform Module (TPM)* (Sevinc, Strasser, & Basin, 2007) could be integrated to enhance the trust level on both sides, offering hardware mechanisms to store the encryption keys and perform cryptographic operations on sensitive data.

While a variety of secure threats are raised by virtual computing environments (Garfinkel & Rosenblum, 2005), we believe the operations on a virtual phone hosted by an IaaS provider should still be more secure than having personal data processed and stored on *software as a service* (SaaS) provider. As the layers of virtual machines help protect the virtual phone, it is far more difficult for an employee working for the service provider to peek into the virtual phone.

To further prevent the intervention from the service provider or attackers, sensitive data in the memory and the storage could be encrypted. Our prototype includes an encrypted virtual storage to both the physical phone and the virtual phone over a FUSE-based encrypted filesystem (FUSE,

Figure 6. Software architecture of virtual storage

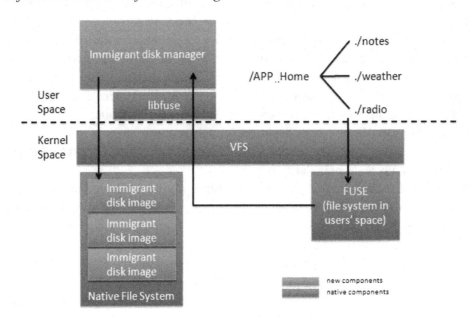

n. d.). Since the files are encrypted and hashed, attackers from another virtual machine on the same host or in the middle of the network will be harder to retrieve and manipulate the contents in the files. Again, TPM could be used to store the master encryption keys and perform the encryption procedure to keep the encryption keys away from the eavesdroppers.

EVALUATION

In this section, we first use a *peer-to-peer* (P2P) file exchange application program, *androidtorrent* (Google Inc., 2011) as an example to illustrate the application migration procedure. P2P is a distributed network for participants to share their resources without a centralized coordinator.

The working set in the P2P application can be quite large as the user exchanges many files with many peers, which also consumes a lot of resources on the processor, the storage, and the network. It is obvious that the workload would be better handled by a virtual phone in the cloud. The agent transferred the states saved by *android-*

torrent, approximately 320 Kbytes of data, to the virtual phone in a few seconds over a 3G mobile network. In our experiment, *androidtorrent* was migrated to the virtual phone and resumed execution in 3.8 seconds, and we defined a policy for the agent not to synchronize the *temporal files* (i.e. incomplete downloads) as these data in these file should be re-acquired anyway.

In our experiment, we used the Intel Atom-based system host Android-x86 as virtual phone in the cloud. As shown in Figure 8, the 1.6GHz Intel Atom processor was already 4.9 to 6.4 times faster than the 528MHz ARM processor found on a mid-range Android phone. The results suggested that the virtual phones might be powered by servers equipped with low-end processors and still provided sufficient performance for average applications. For compute-intensive application, the user may migrate the application to a faster server for better performance.

In comparison, for migrating an application, a traditional approach, such as (Satyanarayanan et al., 2007) would need to transfer the state of the entire phone by taking a snapshot of the memory. Assuming an Android phone with 512MB

Figure 7. Building a trusted environment with VPN and encrypted storage

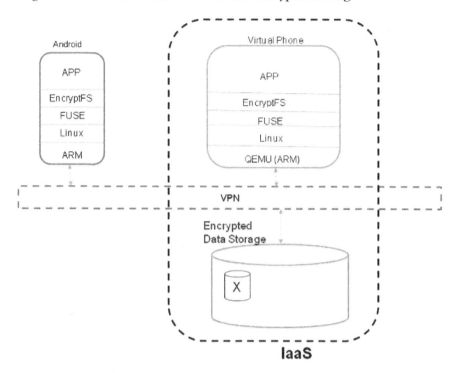

of system memory, it would take more than one hour to transfer the snapshot. With our approach, it would only take milliseconds to transfer the state files saved by Android applications. In the case of *YouTube*, even when we transfer the cache buffers, the latency is still far less than the traditional approach.

RELATED WORK

It was shown in earlier work that remote execution saved a large amount of power for mobile computers (Rudenko, Reiher, Popek, & Kuenning, 1998; Chun & Maniatis, 2009). While there were different approaches proposed, program partitioning for remote execution has been a challenge for researchers. Spectra (Flinn, Narayanan, & Satyanarayanan, 2001) proposed to monitor the current resource availability and dynamically determine the best remote execution plan for an application.

Cyber foraging (Balan, Flinn, Satyanarayanan, & Sinnamohideen, 2002) used surrogates to improve the performance of interactive applications and distributed file systems on mobile clients. MAUI (Cuervo et al., 2010) proposed to reduce the programming efforts by automating program partitioning with the combination of code portability, serialization, reflection, and type safety.

Without application partitioning, methods have been developed to migrate the entire application execution to a remote server. Process migration and virtual machine migration have been two common approaches to migrate execution across the network. The ISR system (Satyanarayanan et al., 2007) emulated the capabilities of suspend/resume functions in a computer system and migrate the system by storing the snapshot image of a virtual machine in a distributed storage system. Zap (Osman, Subhraveti, Su, & Nieh, 2002) introduced a pod (PrOcess Domain) abstraction, which provided a collection of processes with a

Figure 8. Normalized benchmark performance

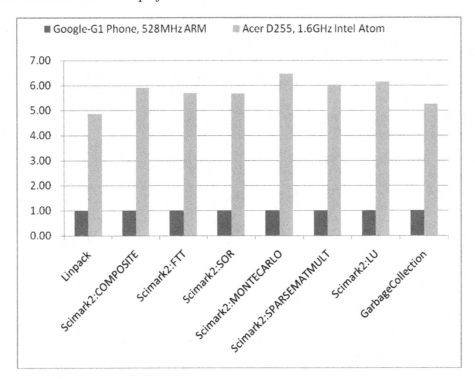

host-independent virtualized view of the operating system, so as to support a general-purpose process migration functionality, but it did not allow live migration. Live VM migration (Keir et al., 2005) achieved rapid movement of workloads within clusters and data centers with minimal service downtime by continuously pre-copying page changes in a virtual machine to another system, but on highly demand of network bandwidth.

However, most of the previous works did not specially address the need for smartphone applications to offload workloads in a pervasive environment with limited network bandwidth. Nor did they address the control/privacy/secure issues surfaced in today's cloud services as extensively we did in our framework. While virtual machines (Smith & Nair, 2005) have been widely used to isolate individual applications consolidate servers, and amortize the operation costs, a variety of secure threats are raised by virtual computing environments (Garfinkel & Rosenblum, 2005).

Meanwhile, virtualization were utilized to support the detection of vulnerabilities (Wilander & Kamkar, 2003) and network intrusion (Chen, Hung, & Lee, 2010; Qin, Wang, Li, Kim, Zhou, & Wu, 2006).

CONCLUSION

In this paper, we introduced the framework that we developed for Android users to offload applications to virtual phones in the cloud. The framework automates the creation of a virtual phone and migrates live Android application faster than traditional methods. Compared to a conventional scheme, our approach does not require the developers to redesign their applications, and we offer several effective techniques to migrate applications and data over a mobile network, with security measures included to address security and privacy issues.

Our preliminary experimental results showed that our virtual phones were capable of intensive workloads and our efficient application-level migration method was suitable for mobile network. The strategies that we developed to reduce the network traffic for application migration and data synchronization were important to the user experience as the latency for completing a live migration and communication costs were significantly reduced.

With more computational resources and virtualization technologies, we showed that a virtual phone could be equipped with security measures to protect the system against network attacks. More functionalities, such as remote backup, file sharing, virus scan, and malware detection, can be conveniently integrated into our framework to make a virtual phone more capable and secure.

We are in the progress to refine our framework and extend the framework to support more applications and systems. We envision that developers take advantage of our framework in the future and create collaborative pervasive applications which run across a range of systems, from small embedded devices to servers in the cloud.

REFERENCES

Armbrust, M., Fox, A., Griffith, R., Joseph, A. D., Katz, R. H., Konwinski, A., et al. (2009). *Above the clouds: A Berkeley view of cloud computing* (Tech. Rep. No. UCB/EECS-2009-28). Berkeley, CA: University of California.

Balan, R., Flinn, J., Satyanarayanan, M., Sinnamohideen, S., & Yang, H.-I. (2002). The case for cyber foraging. In *Proceedings of the 10th ACM SIGOPS European Workshop* (pp. 87-92).

Bayer, R., Heller, H., & Reiser, A. (1980). Parallelism and recovery in database systems. *ACM Transactions on Database Systems*, *5*, 139–156. doi:10.1145/320141.320146

Bellard, F. (2005). QEMU, a fast and portable dynamic translator. In *Proceedings of the Annual USENIX Technical Conference* (pp. 41-46).

Bernstein, P. A., Hadzilacos, V., & Goodman, N. (1987). *Concurrency control and recovery in database systems*. Reading, MA: Addison-Wesley.

Chen, C. C., Hung, S. H., & Lee, C. P. (2010). Protection of buffer overflow attacks via dynamic binary translation. *Reliable and Autonomous Computational Science*, *2*, 305–324.

Chun, P., & Maniatis, B. G. (2009). Augmented smartphone applications through clone cloud execution. In *Proceedings of the 12th Workshop on Hot Topics in Operating Systems* (p. 8).

Cuervo, E., Balasubramanian, A., Cho, D.-K., Wolman, A., Saroiu, S., Chandra, R., et al. (2010). MAUI: Making smartphones last longer with code offload. In *Proceedings of the 8ᵗʰ International Conference on Mobile Systems, Applications, and Services* (pp. 49-62).

Flinn, J., Narayanan, D., & Satyanarayanan, M. (2001). Self-tuned remote execution for pervasive computing. In *Proceedings of the 8ᵗʰ Workshop on Hot Topics in Operating Systems* (pp. 61-66).

FUSE. (n. d.). *Filesystem in userspace*. Retrieved from http://fuse.sourceforge.net/

Garfinkel, T., & Rosenblum, M. (2005). When virtual is harder than real: Security challenges in virtual machine based computing environments. In *Proceedings of the 10th Conference on Hot Topics in Operating Systems* (Vol. 10).

Google Inc. (2011). *Google code project*. Retrieved from http://code.google.com/

Gray, J. N., Lorie, R. A., Putzolu, G. R., & Traiger, I. L. (1994). Granularity of locks and degrees of consistency in a shared data base. In Stonebraker, M. (Ed.), *Readings in database systems* (2nd ed., pp. 181–208). San Francisco, CA: Morgan Kaufmann.

Keir, C. C., Clark, C., Fraser, K., Hand, S., Hansen, J. G., Jul, E., et al. (2005). Live migration of virtual machines. In *Proceedings of the 2nd ACM/USENIX Symposium on Networked Systems Design and Implementation* (pp. 273-286).

Nath, P., Kozuch, M. A., O'Hallaron, D. R., Harkes, J., Satyanarayanan, M., Tolia, N., et al. (2006). Design tradeoffs in applying content addressable storage to enterprise-scale systems based on virtual machines. In *Proceedings of the USENIX Annual Technical Conference* (pp. 363-378).

Osman, S., Subhraveti, D., Su, G., & Nieh, J. (2002). The design and implementation of Zap: A system for migrating computing environments. In *Proceedings of the Fifth Symposium on Operating Systems Design and Implementation* (pp. 361-376).

Pfaff, B., Garfinkel, T., & Rosenblum, M. (2006). Virtualization aware file systems: Getting beyond the limitations of virtual disks. In *Proceedings of the 3rd Symposium of Networked Systems Design and Implementation* (pp. 353-366).

Qin, F., Wang, C., Li, Z., Kim, H. S., Zhou, Y., & Wu, Y. (2006). Lift: A lowoverhead practical information flow tracking system for detecting security attacks. In *Proceedings of the 39th Annual IEEE/ACM International Symposium on Microarchitecture* (pp. 135-148).

Rudenko, A., Reiher, P., Popek, G. J., & Kuenning, G. H. (1998). Saving portable computer battery power through remote process execution. *SIGMOBILE Communication Review, 2*, 19–26. doi:10.1145/584007.584008

Satyanarayanan, M., Gilbert, B., Toups, M., Tolia, N., Surie, A., & O'Hallaron, D. (2007). Pervasive personal computing in an internet suspend/resume system. *IEEE Internet Computing, 11*(2), 16–25. doi:10.1109/MIC.2007.46

Schmidt, A., Kuntze, N., & Kasper, M. (2008). On the deployment of mobile trusted modules. In *Proceedings of the Wireless Communications and Networking Conference* (pp. 3169-3174).

Sevinc, P. E., Strasser, M., & Basin, D. (2007). Securing the distribution and storage of secrets with trusted platform modules. In *Proceedings of the First IFIP TC6/WG8.8/WG11.2 International Conference on Information Security Theory and Practices: Smart Cards, Mobile and Ubiquitous Computing Systems* (pp. 53-66).

Smith, J., & Nair, R. (2005). *Virtual machines: Versatile platforms for systems and processes*. San Francisco, CA: Morgan Kaufmann.

TechCrunch. (2010). *100,000 android applications submitted to date, AndroLib claims*. Retrieved from http://techcrunch.com/2010/07/30/android-market-100000/

Wilander, J., & Kamkar, M. (2003). A comparison of publicly available tools for dynamic buffer overflow prevention. In *Proceedings of the Network and Distributed System Security Symposium* (pp. 4-15).

This work was previously published in the International Journal of Grid and High Performance Computing, Volume 3, Issue 2, edited by Emmanuel Udoh and Ching-Hsien Hsu, pp. 14-28, copyright 2011 by IGI Publishing (an imprint of IGI Global).

Chapter 21
A Grid and Cloud Based System for Data Grouping Computation and Online Service

Wing-Ning Li
University of Arkansas, USA

Jonathan Baran
University of Arkansas, USA

Donald Hayes
University of Arkansas, USA

Cameron Porter
Acxiom Corporation, USA

Tom Schweiger
Acxiom Corporation, USA

ABSTRACT

Record linkage deals with finding records that identify the same real world entity, such as an individual or a business, from a given file or set of files. Record linkage problem is also referred to as the entity resolution or record recognition problem. To locate those records identifying the same real world entity, in principle, pairwise record analyses have to be performed among all records. Analytical operations between two records vary from comparing corresponding fields to enhancing records through large knowledge bases and querying large databases. Hence, these operations are complex and take time. To reduce the number of pairwise record comparisons, blocking techniques are introduced to partition the records into blocks. After that records in each block are analyzed against one and another. One of the effective blocking methods is the closure approach, where a "related" equivalence relation is used to partition the records into equivalence classes. This paper introduces the closure problem and describes the design and implementation of a parallel and distributed closure prototype system running in an enterprise grid.

DOI: 10.4018/978-1-4666-2065-0.ch021

1. INTRODUCTION

A record may be viewed conceptually as consisting of a set of fields. When unique identifiers are unavailable or do not exist in records, determining records that represent the same real world entity is an important and challenging problem, which has many applications. For instance, it addresses data quality issues such as "data accuracy, redundancy, consistency, currency and completeness" (Li, Zhang, & Bheemavaram, 2006). Ensuring data quality is becoming a critical issue that impacts organizational performance(Ballou, Wang, & Pazer, 1998; Ballou, 1999; Delone & Mclean, 1992; Redman, 1998) This problem is also referred to in the literature as record linkage problem (Fellegi & Sunter, 1969; Newcombe, 1988), data cleaning problem (Do & Rahm, 2002), object identification problem (Tejada, Knoblock, & Minton, 2001; Tejada, Knoblock, & Minton, 2002), or entity resolution problem (Benjelloun, Garcia-Molina, Su, & Widom, 2005). All these research efforts deal with the fundamental question of how to effectively identify record "duplicates" when unique identifiers are unavailable or do not exist in records. The main idea is to rely on matching of other fields in records such as name, address, and so on. It is not uncommon for a record having over hundred fields in real data files. Therefore only a relatively small subset of fields is used to carry out the matching. The set of fields selected is application dependent and is often referred to as keys.

1.1. Motivation for Closure Computation

The most basic application is to identify duplicates within a single file or between two files. In the single file situation, in principle, each record must be checked against every other record in the same file in order to find its duplicates. Similarly, in the two files scenario, each record in one file must be compared against every record in the other file.

Both schemes amount to carrying out all pairwise analyses among records and have a time complexity that is quadratic to the number of records (the input size of an algorithm). The methods used by analytical tools to decide if two records is a match vary from comparing corresponding keys (fields selected for matching) to enhancing records (correcting certain fields, appending additional fields, etc.) through large knowledge bases and querying large databases. Since analytical tools are complex and time consuming, each pairwise analysis takes much more time than that of a simple instruction. For large files having hundreds of millions to billions of records, the performance of such a scheme is unacceptable.

To overcome the poor performance, the total number of pairwise record analyses must be reduced. To understand how this could be done, let us consider the case where records are in a single file. Conceptually each record may be viewed as being associated with a potential set of records from which to find its duplicates. Records not in the potential set are guaranteed not to be duplicates, and therefore need not be compared with. Hence, pairwise analyses are needed only between records in the same potential set. For a record, a straightforward way of defining its potential set is to let all other records in the file to be its potential set. This leads to the quadratic pairwise comparisons. Now imagine that a scheme exists that reduces the potential set from the whole file to a small fraction of that. Furthermore, this scheme can be carried out efficiently. What the scheme does is that it effectively partitions the records in the input file into many relatively small groups within which all pairwise record analyses are needed. The scheme that reduces the record pairs to be compared is called blocking in the literature (Baxter & Christen, 2003). Closure operation, of which the definition is given in the preliminary section, is one of the blocking schemes. This paper presents a parallel and distributed, grid based prototype that carries out the closure operation.

Closure operation is not only useful in reducing the number of pairwise comparisons in single file record linkage applications but also in applications that involve multiple files. For instance, sometimes two files are provided as input, where file A has the distinct records (no duplicates) and file B contains potential "duplicate" records of file A, and the goal is to find the "duplicate" records in file B for each record in file A.

To apply the same idea introduced earlier, for each record in file A, we need to know its potential set or closure in file B. One way to solve this problem is to combine the two files into a single file and then perform the closure (blocking or partitioning) operation. Once this is done, each record in file A is associated with a closure (a potential set) that could contain some records from file B. Notice that records in file B are partitioned into closures and each closure could be associated with some record in file A. To determine its duplicates in file B, a record of file A only needs to be checked with those records of file B that are in the same closure in which the record of file A also belongs. Other record linkage applications that involve multiple files can use the closure idea to reduce the number of record analyses in a similar way.

Since the primary objective of a blocking scheme such as closure is to reduce the time and space complexity of an overall process of record linkage, the blocking scheme must be implemented efficiently. To this end, it is necessary to investigate the question of how to design efficient algorithms and systems that implement these algorithmic ideas to realize any proposed blocking method. For the closure method, efficient sequential algorithms are proposed and empirical studies are carried out in (Li, Zhang, & Bheemavaram, 2006). A parallel and distributed algorithm is proposed and implemented in MPI (Bheemavaram, 2006; Li et al., 2007; Li, Bheemavaram, & Zhang, 2010). A graph theoretic view of the closure problem is also introduced in Li, Zhang, and Bheemavaram (2006) and Bheemavaram (2006). The grid based closure

prototype system described in this paper adopts the parallel and distributed closure algorithm proposed in Bheemavaram (2006) to a service based grid environment. The system is developed in C++ with pthread and Corba libraries, and runs in an enterprise grid. The system can either produces in a batch fashion a closure file, where records are partitioned into closures or runs as a service where upon receiving a record it returns the closure of that record. Preliminary experiment indicates the approach is efficient and scalable.

1.2. Blocking Approach Literature Review

The grouping process is often referred to as "blocking methods" in the literature (Baxter & Christen, 2003), which have been found beneficial in solving problems such as record linkage, data cleaning, data purging/merging, and data enhancement. The notion of "grouping" or "blocking" is to divide the whole data set into relatively smaller subsets for which pairwise record analysis is performed. One of the requirements of the subsets is that the sum of the number of pairwise analysis within each subset, over all subsets, is minimized. Notice that if each subset contains a single element, then this sum is zero since no pairwise analysis is ever performed within each subset. On the other hand, another contrary requirement of the subsets is that all pairwise comparisons within each subset are sufficient to discover records, usually from different data sources and without a unique identifier or primary key, identifying the same real world entity (e.g., a customer, a patient, a business, or an organization) in the whole data set. Notice that if the only subset is the input data source itself, then it is ensured that all pairwise comparisons within each subset (there is only one subset which is the set itself) are sufficient since all possible pairs are compared. In addition to the two requirements, the third requirement has to be met as well. This requirement states that the subsets, meeting the two requirements above, must be computed much more efficiently relative to performing pairwise analysis over all pairs. The transitive closure formulation of the grouping problem is a new "blocking" method suggested by our project sponsor that satisfactory meeting the first two requirements in practice. The prototype reported in this paper demonstrates the third requirement can be also met by using clever algorithm design, implementation, and parallel and distributed grid processing.

The "blocking methods" could be categorized as Standard Blocking (Jero, 1989), Sorted Neighborhood (Hernandez & Stolfo, 1998), Bigram Indexing (Baxter & Christen, 2003), and Canopy Clustering with TFIDF (Term Frequency/Inverse Document Frequency) (McCallum, Nigam, & Ungar, 2000). In Standard Blocking, records are grouped together because they share the identical blocking key value. A blocking key could be a single attribute or composed of several attributes and is application dependent. For example, the name attribute could be the blocking key or the first four characters of the name attribute could be the blocking key. In Sorted Neighborhood, records are sorted based on a sorting key. Similar to the concept of blocking key, a sorting key could be a single attribute or composed of several attributes. Once the records are sorted, a window of a certain size, which is also application dependent just as the sorting key, is moved along the records. The records fall into a window form a group implicitly and are paired with each other in the detailed analysis step.

In Bigram Indexing, the blocking key as introduced in the standard blocking is first transformed into a set of bigrams (all sub-strings of length two). For example, a key value "baxter" will result in a bigram set (ba, ax, xt, te, er). The resulting bigram set is then used to derive it's all possible subsets of a certain size. The size of subset is determined by some application dependent size factor. For example, if size factor is 0.8, the size of the subset, in the above example, is $5 \times 0.8 = 4$ (notice that the number of bigrams in (ba,

ax, xt, te, er) is 5). The new subsets are (ax, xt, te, er), (ba, xt, te, er), (ba, ax, te, er), (ba, ax, xt, er), (ba, ax, xt, te). Two records are compared if the corresponding lists of subsets of the two records contain a common element. The subsets become the conceptual blocking keys to increase the number of record pair analyses compared to standard blocking.

In Canopy Clustering with TFIDF (Term Frequency/Inverse Document Frequency), records are group together if they are in the same canopy cluster. Picking a record at random from a candidate set of records, which is initialized to all records, and then including all records within a certain "loose-threshold" distance to it forms a canopy cluster. The record chosen at random and any records within a certain "tight-threshold" distance to it are removed from the candidate set. Then the above process is repeated with the current candidate set, and continues until the current candidate set is empty. Notice that blocking process is in essence a clustering process. Empirical studies of the various blocking methods are reported in Baxter and Christen (2003).

The blocking technique considered here is similar to the standard blocking in that records with the same blocking key are grouped. Unlike the standard blocking, the transitive closure blocking method allows the consideration of multiple keys at the same time and relates different keys through transitivity. The final groupings are obtained by a transitive closure computation. The precise formulation is given next.

2. PRELIMINARY AND BACKGROUND

The development of the prototype system is based on previous research efforts on the closure problems (Li, Zhang, & Bheemavaram, 2006; Bheemavaram, 2006; Li et al., 2007; Li, Bheemavaram & Zhang, 2010), where the reader will find more information about the transitive closure problem and the parallel and distributed algorithm that has been adopted and implemented in grid architecture in this paper. Nonetheless, a brief description is provided in the subsection to make the paper self-contained.

2.1. The Closure Problem

Since the application of a blocking scheme such as Transitive Closure is basically the same for a single file or multiple files, in the sequel, a single file is assumed. A file contains a sequence of records. Each record contains a sequence of fields. Each record also has a record identifier, which typically is an alphanumeric string of fixed length. Certain fields or some combinations of fields are chosen as keys. The selection of fields to be designated as keys depends on the types of record linkage and could vary from applications to applications.

Once keys are selected, two records are defined as *directly related* if for some key the two records have the same value. Note that we interpret the same value as identical value for illustrative purpose. In real world application, same value could mean a match based on an approximated string matching or other matching logic (Anathakrishna, Chaudhuri, & Ganti, 2002; Bertolazzi, Santis, & Scannapieco, 2003; Bilenko & Mooney, 2003; Chaudhuri, Ganti, & Motwani, 2005; Larsen & Rubin, 2001) For example, if name and address fields are the keys, two records A and B with the same name values "John Doe" and different address values "723 main street" and "123 main street", respectively, are *directly related* because of same value "John Doe" in the name key.

Two records X and Y are defined as *transitively related* if there is a sequence of records of which each adjacent pair is directed related and X and Y are directly related to the first and last records in the sequence respectively. Let us expand the above example by introducing records C, where C has name value "Jane Doe" and address value "123 main street". In the example, A and C are *transitively related* because A and B are directly related (through name key with value "John Doe") and B and C are directly related (through address key with value "123 main street"). In this simple example, the sequence in the definition of transitively relatedness has only one record (record B) even though in reality the sequence may contain many records.

Two records are defined as *related* if and only if either they are *directly related* or *\transitively related*. The notion of relatedness just introduced as a relation is reflexive, symmetric and transitive. Therefore, it is an equivalence relation, which could be used to partition elements in the relation into equivalence classes. Based on the relatedness just introduced, records in the input file are partitioned into groups (equivalence classes) in the closure computation, where all related records are in one group, which is called a *closure*. Typically, a closure is a set of record identifiers instead of a set of physical records with all the fields. When the context is obvious clear, record is used instead of record identifier in the sequel.

2.2. A Graph Model View of the Closure Problem

The closure problem has a graph theoretic model. In this model, each vertex represents a record. Each edge represents the direct relatedness of two records, which correspond to the two vertices connected by the edge, namely the direct relatedness defined earlier. Of course, some computation is needed to determine if an edge exists between two record vertices. Nonetheless, given a set of records and a set of keys, an undirected graph can be constructed conceptually. We already know that edges represent direct relatedness. It is not hard to see that paths of length two or more between two record vertices indicate transitive relatedness between the corresponding records. Then it follows that closures correspond to connected components of the graph thus defined. Two records are related if and only if their corresponding vertices belong to the same connected component. The graph model view provides another perspective of the closure problem.

The connected components problem is a well known graph theoretic problem. Many researchers have investigated the question of how to solve the problem efficiently using parallel algorithms. Some algorithms (Hirschberg, Chandra, & Sarvate, 1979; Shiloach & Vishkin, 1982; Han & Wagner, 1990; Chong & Lam, 1993) have been developed for the theoretical PRAM model where processors may read the same memory cell concurrently. As for writing to the same memory cell certain model allows concurrent write while other only allows exclusive write. Since the model is a theoretical model, the number of processors used by the algorithms could be larger than, sometimes much larger than, the input size of the problem instance in order to achieve the best time complexity. Other algorithms (Goddard, Kumar, & Prins, 1995; Woo & Sahni, 1989) have been developed for special multiprocessor architectures such as hypercube and mesh. Several theoretical algorithms have been implemented on the available parallel computers and studied empirically (Greiner, 1994).

All algorithms in the literature assume the graph is available either as an adjacency matrix or an adjacency list in the memory or in the input file. In other words, the graph is explicitly represented. However, the input to the closure problem is not an explicit graphical representation. Additional computation is required to obtain an explicit graphical representation. In essence the direct relatedness information is implicitly given between records.

2.3. Input Preprocessing

The input to the transitive closure problem is a file of records and chosen keys, in the batch-processing mode, the output is a set of closures. In a service-oriented mode, a file of records and chosen keys are given once to set up the closure service. Afterwards each record in the file may be sent to the service. Upon receiving a record, the service returns the closure associated with the record. The design and implementation of the closure software to be presented support both modes of operations.

Even though the transitive closure problem is defined in terms of a file of records containing many fields of which some are chosen as keys, the input to the prototype system is not a file of records. Instead it is a file of pairs of record identifiers. From the graph model perspective, it is a set (or more precise multiset) of edges where some edges of the graph could appear several times. Each pair of record identifiers signifies that the corresponding records are directly related. For any two directly related records at least one pair of the corresponding record identifiers exists in the input file. The reason for the change of input is as follows.

It has been observed in Bheemavaram (2006) and Li, Bheemavaram, and Zhang (2010), the process of parallel and distributed computation of closure may be broken into two steps: in step one all directly related pair of records are computed; in step two upon getting the result from step one all closures are computed. From the graph model perspective, step one derives the edges of the graph from records and step two determines the connected components.

The idea of how step one can be carried out in a massively parallel fashion is as follows. We will view the processing in stages even though stages could overlap. Suppose we have data records with three key fields. Then we use 3 processors (one for each key in this illustration) in the first stage. Each processor reads the input file in parallel using some parallel file system such as PVFS and extracts the required information from the file. That is, each processor will extract the value of the key for which it is responsible and the record identifier. The key value and the record identifier form a pair, which is distributed to the processors in the next stage. Each processor in the first stage has exclusive control over 'n' processors in the second stage, where n controls the degree of parallelism in the second stage. The distribution is based on the hashed value of the key modulo n. Hence, for a key, all key value and record identifier pairs with key values that are equal are sent to the same processor, although not all the pairs received by a process may have the same key value due to the effect of hashing and modulo operations.

With 3 processors in the first stage and each processor having exclusive control over n processors, a total of 3n processors work in the second stage in parallel. These processors collect key value and record pairs, do some internal sorting, and generate the directly related pairs (i.e., pairs of record identifiers) for which key values match. Since keys are processed independently, the distributed process may generate duplicated record pairs. The reader is referred to Bheemavaram (2006) and Li, Bheemavaram, and Zhang (2010) for details of the above distributed processing parallel algorithm and its variations, as well as the discussion of efficiency and scalability.

Since step one can be computed efficiently using a parallel and distributed processing algorithm that is scalable (Bheemavaram, 2006; Li, Bheemavaram, & Zhang, 2010), the focus of this research effort aims at step two. For this reason, the input to the prototype is preprocessed as a file of pairs of record identifiers. Conceptually the two parallel and distributed solutions of steps one and two can be easily combined into a single system where the input to the system is a file of records and chosen keys.

2.4. The Basic Parallel and Distributed Algorithm

The basic parallel and distributed algorithmic idea and algorithm that the prototype uses are provided in Bheemavaram (2006), Li, Bheemavaram, and Zhang (2010), and Hayes (2008). The main ideas are recapped as follows.

First hashing is used to evenly assign records to processors conceptually. A record identifier is an alphanumeric string. The string's hash value modulo of the number of processors is the ID of the processor that owns the record. Records owned to a processor are called local records with respect to that processor. Once this is done, record pairs (directly related records) in the input file are classified with respect to each processor as local pairs, global pairs, and irrelevant pairs. A record pair is said to be a local pair of a processor if both records in the pair are local to the processor, a global pair if only one of the records is local to the processor, and an irrelevant pair if none are local to the processor.

In parallel, processors read the record pairs from the input file, where local pairs are processed immediately using disjoint set find and union data structures (Cormen, Leiserson, Rivest, & Stein, 2002) (the two records are directly related and should be in the same closure or the same set), global pairs are stored so they may be processed after all the pairs are read, and irrelevant pairs are ignored (note an irrelevant pair to one processor is always a local pair or a global pair to some other processor). The disjoint set data structures maintain that the local records that belong to the same closure are grouped together as a set, called a local cluster. Once the reading of the input file is finished, in parallel each processor goes through its global pairs to generate new local pairs and new global pairs for other processors. Then in parallel the processors interchange new local pairs and global pairs among themselves. The new local edges are processed first using the disjoint set data structures that allow more local records in a closure to be grouped together (combining local clusters determined in the previous iteration together). Once the new local pairs are processed, the new global pairs are examined to generate new local and global pairs for the next phase in the iteration. After that global pairs are collapsed or reduced. Each phase is synchronized and within a phase communication and computation among the processors are asynchronous or concurrent. The number of iteration is logarithmically related to the number of processors (Bheemavaram, 2006).

Note that after processing the local pairs, no local pair is stored. And after processing the global pairs, each local cluster has at most one global pair from its processor to another processor. The rest of the global pairs are thrown away. The existence of global pairs indicates that records in a closure are assigned to different processors by the hashing scheme. At the end, all local records belonging to a closure form a single local cluster. And local clusters in different processors are linked to each other by global pairs to establish a closure. The disjoint sets (local clusters) and the associated global pair structures allow the generation of closure file and support the closure query service.

The algorithm is realized in the prototype of which the design is given next. For a more detailed description and examples of the algorithm the reader is referred to Bheemavaram (2006), Li, Bheemavaram, and Zhang (2010), and Hayes, (2008).

One more thing should be noted before describing the design. The efficient implementation of disjoint set find and union requires that integer values be the members of the set (Li, Zhang, & Bheemavaram, 2006; Cormen, Leiserson, Rivest, & Stein, 2002). On the other hand record identifiers are alphanumeric strings in general, and this is particularly true for the real data files where record identifiers contain both letters and digits. To bridge the gap, a mapping scheme is needed that maps each alphanumeric string to a unique integer in the range from 1 to n, where n is the number of records. The mapping scheme is also used to convert pairs of strings to pair of integers. Once the conversion is done, the computation of closures is based on integer pairs, which have much smaller memory foot print and reduce computation time as well as communication time of the parallel and distributed algorithm outlined earlier. An empirical study of the time reduction in computation and communication by using integer pairs is conducted in Bheemavaram (2006).

Even though the mapping operation is expensive, as shown in experimentation (Setup pair), the time and space reduction it brings to the overall computation outweighs its initial cost.

3. ARCHITECTURE DESIGN

The system runs on a set of grid nodes, which may be thought of as processors in a parallel computer conceptually. Multiple threads are used to carry out the processing in each grid node. The system uses Client-Server architecture to implement the parallel and distributed closure algorithm. In particular, the architecture addresses the no blocking communication between processors so that computation and communication can be concurrent within a phase of the algorithm. The client and server are separate threads in the same grid node so that computation and communication are carried out concurrently. The current design uses one thread for the client and one thread for the server. Each grid node has a server, which is a remote object to clients running on other grid nodes. The server provides remote procedure calls for clients. These procedures allow a remote client to send the new local and global pairs derived in each iteration (push the data to grid node running the server) and to query the string to integer mapping information of the local records of the gird node.

Each grid node spawns a client thread and keeps the main thread running as a server. The client thread does the majority of processing and makes remote procedure calls to servers running on other grid nodes. The server thread handles incoming requests from remote clients and delivers the data to the client thread via shared memory between the two threads.

Each gird node has three major data structures: A) for mapping between local alphanumeric record identifiers and integers from 1 to n (n is the total number of records), B) for supporting disjoint set find and union, and C) for relating global pairs and local clusters. The current design delegates the mapping structures to the server thread, and the other two structures to the client thread. It is conceivable that the mapping operation may be separated as a grid service to reduce the memory requirement of each grid node in closure computation. The current design makes that transition easier to implement.

For batch processing, the system has three phases to go through: the assignment phase, the closure computation phase, and output phase. For service processing, the only change is to have the output phase replaced by a repeated query-processing phase.

In the assignment phase, the local records of each grid node are determined and mapped to integers. At the end of the assignment phase, a single communication occurs in which all grid nodes communicate the largest integer used in the local map. The information is used to establish a global map consisting of all the local maps (each grid node adds an offset to its local map). The global map is used to map string pairs to integer pairs. The information is needed so that remote records (an integer) can be mapped back to the grid node to which they are assigned. The client thread of each grid node sends the largest integer used information to all servers (server threads) on other grid nodes. Once a grid node receives this communication from all other grid nodes, it has the assignment information and the next phase begins.

During closure computation phase, in each grid node, the client thread goes through the record pairs (first local pairs then global pairs) of the current iteration by combining local clusters, generating local and global pairs for other grid nodes, and sending new pairs generated to other grid nodes (remote servers) for the next iteration. The server thread receives record pairs from remote clients and gathers all the pairs received so that pairs are delivered when the client is ready for the next iteration

The problem of handling communication between multiple, simultaneously running programs in each grid node is solved by using multiple threads. The client thread is used for processing while the server thread is used to handle incoming messages. The server thread handles incoming messages by storing the data (pairs) in a temporary buffer and then writing to a shared data structure at the end of a closure computation phase. This allows the client thread to continue processing while information is being received. This threading approach realizes a significant practical improvement from the single threaded MPI implementation in Bheemavaram (2006). The communication between grid nodes is logically a fully connected network; each grid node communicates with every other grid node. More detailed discussions of the design are given in Hayes (2008).

4. SYSTEM IMPLEMENTATION

The software is implemented in C++ programming language using a multi-threaded client-server architecture. Each grid node runs the same copy of the program. POSIX Pthread library is used to implement multithreading and CORBA library is used to implement remote objects allowing communication between servers and clients running on different grid nodes. Each grid node has a client thread that does the bulk of the processing. A separate server thread is started in each grid node in order to asynchronously receive data from remote grid nodes. The specific communication API used is CORBA. CORBA was selected in order to allow the software to conform to the current grid architecture of the project sponsor and to be more easily adapted to a service-oriented architecture in the future (for instance closure query service).

The total number of grid nodes and the ID of the current grid node must be provided to the program, to be executed by the current grid node, as a command line parameter. A potential improvement would be to move this information to a configuration file. In either case, the number of running grid nodes is known. The total number of grid nodes and the ID of the current grid node running the program are required by the program for the implemented algorithm to perform correctly.

MD5 is used as the hashing function in the assignment phase. The mapping structure is implemented using C++ map class in the standard template library. The mapping object maps the alphanumeric strings (record identifiers) to integers. Records may be inserted into the object. After all initial records are inserted, the object must be finalized. This finalization is done for performance reasons, as the object is read only after finalization and does not require further locking. The local server reads this object in order to map incoming record identifiers (alphanumeric strings) to integers. During the output phase, a reverse map is also constructed to allow the string records to be output after completion of the entire algorithm or to support closure service.

A two-pass scan of the input file is used in this particular implementation. The first scan assigns records to grid nodes and establishes the mapping object in each grid node. The second scan converts string pairs from the input file to an integer pairs. The mapping object of each grid node, which is established in the first scan, is used to realize the conversion step. To be more specific, the local mapping object will be consulted twice to convert a local pair. The local mapping object and a remote mapping object are consulted to convert a global pair. Since consulting remote mapping objects involves remote procedure calls, bulk lookup was implemented and used to improve efficiency. In bulk lookup an array of strings is provided as input and an array of integers is returned as output. More detailed discussions of the implementation are given in Hayes (2008).

5. EXPERIMENTAL RESULTS

Preliminary tests are conducted for the system. The tests were run on dual core Intel Pentium III 1.266 Ghz dual core machines with 4 GB of memory using 100 Mbit Ethernet for grid node connection. The operating system was CentOS 4.5 with the 2.6.9-55.0.2.ELsmp linux kernel. Two grid nodes were run on each machine. Hence, each grid node has a maximum of 2GB memory.

In Tables 1 through 3, each column except the first one identifies a grid node and shows the resources used by the grid node, in various steps in the computation. The second row shows the peak memory usage. For example, in Table 1, memory at 8M means the global pairs array was allocated for a maximum of 8 million record pairs and node 0 peak memory usage is 276 MB. As mentioned in Hayes (2008), CORBA does not define or make available its memory allocation and deallocation routines. As such, the memory usage is more indicative of the implementation than of the algorithm. All times are in seconds.

The third row labeled by "Max pair" is the largest number of global pairs that existed at any point in the processing, though this usually oc-

Table 1. Synthetic data of 7.3 million pairs

Node ID	0	1	2	3	4	5
Memory at 8M	276 MB	274 MB	281 MB	268 MB	280 MB	271 MB
Max Pair	2130875	2044955	2204346	1837045	2317816	1968969
Scan Time	14	13	14	16	16	16
Pair Set-up	27	28	28	25	30	27
Compute Closure	11	10	11	14	9	12
Total Time	52	51	53	55	55	55

Table 2. Real data of 26.9 million pairs on 2 node

Node ID	0	1
Memory at 14M	1.8 GB	1.8 GB
Max Pair	13549308	13549308
Scan Time	159	159
Pair Set-up	225	225
Compute Closure	39	39
Total Time	423	423

curred during the first pass. The fourth row labeled by "Scan time" gives the time to complete the initial pass of reading the file. The fifth row labeled by "Pair Set-up" gives the time to convert string pairs to integer pairs and to process the initial local pairs. "Compute Closure" is the time to process initial global pairs, to generate and send new local and global pairs in all iterations.

Table 1 contains the results of a synthetic data set running on six grid nodes. Tables 2 and 3 contain the results from running a real data set on two and six grid nodes. The average runtime on two grid nodes is 423 seconds, compared to 345 seconds on six grid nodes. The memory usage for two grid nodes is 1.8 GB of memory, but only 1.1GB of memory when using six grid nodes. This shows the speed and memory benefits of parallelism.

Note that the large portion of the time is related to alphanumeric string pair to integer pair conversion process in all tests. Note also that in the two grid node test, both grid nodes are in the same machine and the measured time (commu-

nication portion) could be shorter than that of the two grid nodes running on different machines.

The closure query service uses the results and structures of the closure computation and has two major steps. Upon receiving a record identifier for closure service, the service grid node uses the hash function to determine which grid node owns the record as its local record. Once the grid node is determined, the service grid node performs an initial fetch by sending the record identifier to the grid node, which returns a list of processor ID and remote key pairs. The processor ID tells us the processor that has some of the records in the closure as its local records. The remote key is the corresponding mapped integer value of one local record in the closure. The list is derived from the mapping object and the global pairs of the local cluster to which the queried record identifier belongs. Next for each pair in the list, the service grid node sends the remote key to the processor, identified by the processor ID, which returns all the record identifiers of the local cluster to which

Table 3. Real data of 26.9 million pairs

Node ID	0	1	2	3	4	5
Memory at 14M	1.1 GB	1.1 GB	1.1 GB	1.1 GB	1.1 GB	1.1 GB
Max Pair	7482705	7481988	7488032	7474246	7477869	7489096
Scan Time	101	101	102	102	98	99
Pair Set-up	179	178	173	179	180	183
Compute Closure	62	66	70	67	64	64
Total Time	342	345	345	348	342	346

Table 4. Closure queries to 2 million records (1472 records retrieved)

Nodes to maintain closure	0	1	2	3	4	5
Average fetch time	0.0420	0.0730	0.0720	0.0680	0.0560	0.6080
Average busy time	0.0420	0.0365	0.0240	0.0170	0.0112	0.0101
Reduced work time $t_n - t_{n-1}$	-	0.0055	0.0125	0.0070	0.0058	0.0011

the remote key belongs. The returned information is derived from the disjoint set and mapping object structures. When every queried processor returns, the service grid node has all the records in the closure corresponding to the query record identifier and performs a return.

The closure query service is evaluated by a synthetic data set; the same data set that Table 1 is based. It has about two millions of records and 7.3 million pairs.

This data was processed by the transitive closure solution, and subsequently queried by the service addition to select a known closure of 1,472 members for the purpose of timing comparison. The timing method was composed of repeating a request for an entry 1,000 times and recording the average request timer for the fetch process. This was performed for multiple members of the closure, and using one to six processors to maintain the distributed closure. The process was timed for both the initial process fetch that returns the processor id and the remote key pairs for a given record identifier, and for the subsequent queries of transitive closure components. The initial fetch was noted as negligible, as it did not require more than one value search into its local data, and returned at most 2n integers, with n being the number of processes (nodes in the grid) in the system.

The time spent for a query to each processor was averaged for the 1000 attempts, and then grouped by processor count to record the average amount of time that was spent on each processor.

As shown in Table 4, independent to the number of grid nodes used, the average fetch time remains more or less the same. This is expected as the service node runs a sequential process, which is the bottleneck. However, the average busy time per process decreases as more nodes are used. It suggests that nodes in the closure solution are not very busy when more nodes are use. It seems that this could support multiple service nodes to query the closure solution in parallel and maintain average fetch time for each service node.

6. CONCLUSION

A parallel and distributed transitive closure prototype system running in an enterprise grid was developed. The system could speed up various record linkage applications. The design and implementation is based on a novel parallel and distributed closure algorithm, multithreading, and Corba-based client and server model. The system can either produce all closures to a file in a batch fashion or run as a service where upon receiving a record it returns the closure of that record. Preliminary experiment results are encouraging and seem to indicate the approach is efficient and scalable.

A more thorough evaluation of the prototype is needed in the future so it may be fine tuned and enhanced for efficiency and scalability

ACKNOWLEDGMENT

This research was supported in part by Acxiom Corporation through the Acxiom Laboratory for Applied Research.

REFERENCES

Anathakrishna, R., Chaudhuri, S., & Ganti, V. (2002). Eliminating fuzzy duplicates in data warehouses. In *Proceedings of the Conference on Very Large Data Bases* (pp. 586-597).

Ballou, D. (1999). Enhancing data quality in data warehousing environment. *Communications of the ACM, 42*(1), 73–78. doi:10.1145/291469.291471

Ballou, D., Wang, H., & Pazer, G. (1998). Modeling information manufacturing systems to determining information product quality. *Management Science, 44*(4), 462–484. doi:10.1287/mnsc.44.4.462

Baxter, R., Christen, P., & Churches, T. (2003). A comparison of fast blocking methods for record linkage. In *Proceedings of the ACM SIGKDD Workshop on Data Cleaning, Record Linkage, and Object Consolidation*, Washington, DC (pp. 25-27).

Benjelloun, O., Garcia-Molina, H., Su, Q., & Widom, J. (2005). *Swoosh: A generic approach to entity resolution*. Stanford, CA: Stanford University InfoLab.

Bertolazzi, P., Santis, L. D., & Scannapieco, M. (2003). Automatic record matching in cooperative information systems. In *Proceedings of the Workshop on Data Quality in Cooperative Information Systems* (pp. 13-20).

Bheemavaram, R. (2006). *Parallel and distributed grouping algorithms for finding related records of huge data sets on cluster grid*. Unpublished master's thesis, University of Arkansas, Fayetteville, AK.

Bilenko, M., & Mooney, R. (2003). Adaptive duplicate detection using learnable string similarity metrics. In *Proceedings of the ACM Conference on Knowledge Discovery and Data Mining* (pp. 39-48).

Chaudhuri, S., Ganti, V., & Motwani, R. (2005). Robust identification of fuzzy duplicates. In *Proceedings of the International Conference on Data Engineering* (pp. 865-876).

Chong, K., & Lam, T. (1993). Finding connected components in o(log n log log n) time on EREW PRAM. In *Proceedings of the 4th ACM-SIAM Symposium on Discrete Algorithms* (pp. 11-20).

Cormen, T., Leiserson, C., Rivest, R., & Stein, C. (2002). *Introduction to algorithms*. New York, NY: McGraw-Hill.

Delone, W., & Mclean, E. (1992). Information systems success: The quest for the independent variable. *Information Systems Research, 3*(1), 60–95. doi:10.1287/isre.3.1.60

Do, H., & Rahm, E. (2002). Coma -a system for flexible combination of schema matching approaches. In *Proceedings of the ACM Conference on Knowledge Discovery and Data Mining*.

Fellegi, I., & Sunter, A. (1969). A theory for record linkage. *Journal of the American Statistical Association, 64*, 1183–1210. doi:10.2307/2286061

Goddard, S., Kumar, S., & Prins, J. F. (1995, October 17-19). Connected components algorithms for mesh-connected parallel computers. In *Proceedings of the 3rd DIMACS Series Workshop on Parallel Algorithms Science* (pp. 43-58).

Greiner, J. (1994). A comparison of parallel algorithms for connected components. In *Proceedings of the 6th ACM Symposium on Parallel Algorithms and Architectures* (pp. 16-23).

Han, Y., & Wagner, R. (1990). An efficient and fast parallel-connected component algorithm. *Journal of the ACM, 73*(3), 626–642. doi:10.1145/79147.214077

Hayes, D. (2008). *A corba-based distributed and multithreaded algorithm finding related records in a large data set.* Unpublished master's thesis, University of Arkansas, Fayetteville, AK.

Hernandez, M., & Stolfo, S. (1998). Real-world data is dirty: Data cleansing and the merge/purge problem. *Journal of Data Mining and Knowledge Discovery, 1*(2), 9–37. doi:10.1023/A:1009761603038

Hirschberg, D., Chandra, A., & Sarvate, D. (1979). Computing connected components on parallel computers. *Communications of the ACM, 22*(8), 461–464. doi:10.1145/359138.359141

Jero, M. (1989). Advances in record linkage methodology as applied to matching the 1985 census of Tempe, Florida. *Journal of the American Statistical Society, 84*(406), 414–420.

Larsen, M., & Rubin, D. (2001). Alternative automated record linkage using mixture models. *Journal of the American Statistical Association, 79*, 32–41. doi:10.1198/016214501750332956

Li, W., Bheemavaram, R., & Zhang, J. (2010). Transitive closure of data records. In Chan, Y., Talburt, J., & Talley, T. (Eds.), *Data engineering: Mining, information and intelligence* (pp. 39–74). New York, NY: Springer.

Li, W., Zhang, J., & Bheemavaram, R. (2006). Efficient algorithms for grouping data to improve data quality. In *Proceedings of the International Conference on Information and Knowledge Engineering* (pp. 149-154).

McCallum, A., Nigam, K., & Ungar, L. (2000). Efficient clustering of high-dimensional data sets with application to reference matching. In *Proceedings of the 6th ACM SIGKDD International Conference on Knowledge Discovery and Data Mining* (pp. 169-178).

Newcombe, H. (1988). *Handbook of record linkage: Methods for health and statistical studies, administration, and business.* Oxford, UK: Oxford University Press.

Redman, T. (1998). The impact of poor data quality on the typical enterprise. *Communications of the ACM, 41*(2), 79–82. doi:10.1145/269012.269025

Shiloach, Y., & Vishkin, U. (1982). An o(log n) parallel connectivity algorithm. *Journal of Algorithms, 3*, 57–67. doi:10.1016/0196-6774(82)90008-6

Tejada, S., Knoblock, C., & Minton, S. (2001). Learning object identification rules for information extraction. *Information Systems, 26*(8), 607–633. doi:10.1016/S0306-4379(01)00042-4

Tejada, S., Knoblock, C., & Minton, S. (2002). Learning domain-independent string transformation for high accuracy object identification. In *Proceedings of the Conference on Very Large Data Bases* (pp. 610-621).

Woo, J., & Sahni, S. (1989). Hypercube computing: Connected components. *The Journal of Supercomputing, 3*, 209–234. doi:10.1007/BF00127829

This work was previously published in the International Journal of Grid and High Performance Computing, Volume 3, Issue 4, edited by Emmanuel Udoh and Ching-Hsien Hsu, pp. 39-52, copyright 2011 by IGI Publishing (an imprint of IGI Global).

Compilation of References

Abbes, H., & Dubacq, J. C. (2008). Analysis of peer-to-peer protocols performance for establishing a decentralized desktop grid Middleware. In E. César, M. Alexander, A. Streit, J. L. Träff, C. Cérin, A. Knüpfer, D. Kranzlmüller, & S. Jha (Eds.), *Proceedings of the Euro-Par Workshops on Parallel Processing* (LNCS 5415, pp. 235-246).

Abbes, H., Cérin, C., & Jemni, M. (2008). BonjourGrid as a decentralised job scheduler. In *Proceedings of the IEEE Asia-Pacific Services Computing Conference* (pp. 89-94).

Abbes, H., Cérin, C., & Jemni, M. (2009, May 29). BonjourGrid: Orchestration of multi-instances of grid middleware on institutional desktop grid. In *Proceedings of the 3rd Workshop on Desktop Grid and Volunteer Computing Systems in conjunction with IPDPS*, Roma, Italy (pp. 1-8).

Abbes, H., Cérin, C., Jemni, M., & Saad, W. (2010). Fault tolerance based on the publish-subscribe paradigm for the BonjourGrid Middleware. In *Proceedings of the 11th ACM/IEEE International Conference on Grid Computing*, Brussels, Belgium (pp. 57-64).

Abdelsalam, H. S., Maly, K., Mukkamala, R., Zubair, M., & Kaminsky, D. (2009). Analysis of energy efficiency in clouds. In *Proceedings of Computation World: Future Computing, Service Computation, Cognitive, Adaptive, Content* (pp. 416–421). Patterns. doi:10.1109/ComputationWorld.2009.38

Abdullah, A., Ramly, N., Muhammed, A., & Derahman, M. N. (2008). Performance comparison study of routing protocols for mobile grid environment. *International Journal of Computer Science and Network Security, 8*(2), 82–88.

Ackroyd, M. H. (1979). Call repacking in connecting networks. *IEEE Transactions on Communications, 27*(3). doi:10.1109/TCOM.1979.1094428

Agelis, S. (2000). Optoelectronic router with a reconfigurable shuffle network based on micro-optoelectromechanical systems. *Journal of Optical Networking, 4*(1), 1–10. doi:10.1364/JON.4.000001

Aggarwal, M., & Aggarwal, A. (2006). A Unified Scheduling Algorithm for Grid Applications. In *Proceedings of the International Symposium on High Performance Computing in an Advanced Collaborative Environment (HPCS'06)* (pp. 1-7).

Aggarwal, M., & Kent, R. (2005). An Adaptive Generalized Scheduler for Grid Applications. In *Proceedings of the 19th Annual International Symposium on High Performance Computing Systems and Applications (HPCS'05)* (pp. 15-18).

Aggarwal, M., Kent, R. D., & Ngom, A. (2005). Genetic Algorithm Based Scheduler for Computational Grids. In *Proceedings of the 19th International Symposium on High Performance Computing Systems and Applications (HPCS'05)* (pp. 209-215). Washington, DC: IEEE Computer Society.

Aha, D., & Kibler, D. (1991). Instance-based learning algorithms. *Machine Learning, 6*, 37–66. doi:10.1007/BF00153759

Ahmad, I., & Kwok, Y. (1994). A New Approach to Scheduling parallel Programs Using Task Duplication. In. *Proceedings of the International Conference on Parallel Processing, 2*, 47–51.

Ahmed, I., & Kwok, Y. (1998). On exploiting task duplication in parallel program scheduling. *IEEE Transactions on Parallel and Distributed Systems*, *9*, 872–892. doi:10.1109/71.722221

Akers, S. B., Harel, D., & Krishnamurthy, B. (1987). The star graph: An attractive alternative to the n-Cube. In *Proceedings of the International Conference on Parallel Processing* (pp. 393-400).

Akyildiz, I. F., & Su, W., Sankarasubramaniam, & Cayirci, E. (2002). Wireless sensor networks: A survey. *Computer Networks*, *38*(4), 393–422. doi:10.1016/S1389-1286(01)00302-4

Akyildiz, I. F., Weilian, S., Sankarasubramaniam, Y., & Cayirci, E. (2002). A survey on sensor networks. *IEEE Communications Magazine*, *40*(8), 102–114. doi:10.1109/MCOM.2002.1024422

Alamouti, S. (1998). A simple transmit diversity technique for wireless communications. *IEEE Journal on Selected Areas in Communications*, *16*, 1451–1458. doi:10.1109/49.730453

Al-Ayyoub, A., & Day, K. (1997). Matrix decomposition on the star graph. *IEEE Transactions on Parallel and Distributed Systems*, *8*(8), 803–812. doi:10.1109/71.605767

Al-Ayyoub, A., & Day, K. (1998). The hyperstar interconnection network. *Journal of Parallel and Distributed Computing*, *48*(2), 175–199. doi:10.1006/jpdc.1997.1414

Al-Kazemi, B., & Mohan, C. K. (2002). Training feed forward neural networks using multi-phase particle swarm optimization. In *Proceedings of the 9th International Conference on Neural Information* (Vol. 5).

Al-Sadi, J., Awwad, A., & AlBdaiwi, B. (2004). Efficient routing algorithm on OTIS-Star network. In *Proceedings of the IASTED International Conference on Advances in Computer Science and Technology* (pp. 157-162).

Al-Sadi, J., & Awwad, A. (2010). *A new efficient interconnection network*. International Arab Journal of Information Technology.

Amaki, H., Kita, H., & Kobayashi, S. (1996). Multiobjective Optimization by Genetic Algorithms: A Review. In *Proceedings of the IEEE International Conference on Evolutionary Computation* (pp. 517-522). Washington, DC: IEEE Computer Society.

Anastasi, G., Borgia, E., Conti, M., & Gregori, E. (2003). IEEE 802.11: Ad-hoc networks: Performance measurements. In *Proceedings of the IEEE Workshop on Mobile and Wireless Networks* (pp. 758-763).

Anathakrishna, R., Chaudhuri, S., & Ganti, V. (2002). Eliminating fuzzy duplicates in data warehouses. In *Proceedings of the Conference on Very Large Data Bases* (pp. 586-597).

Anderson, D. P. (2004). BOINC: A system for public-resource computing and storage. In *Proceedings of the IEEE International Conference on Grid Computing* (pp. 4-10).

Anderson, D. P., Cobb, J., Korpela, E., Lebofsky, M., & Werthimer, D. (2002). SETI@home: An experiment in public-resource computing. *Communications of the ACM*, *45*(11), 56–61. doi:10.1145/581571.581573

Armbrust, M., Fox, A., Griffith, R., Joseph, A. D., Katz, R. H., Konwinski, A., et al. (2009). *Above the clouds: A Berkeley view of cloud computing* (Tech. Rep. No. UCB/EECS-2009-28). Berkeley, CA: University of California.

Armbrust, M., Fox, A., Griffith, R., Joseph, A. D., Katz, R., & Konwinski, A. (2010). A view of cloud computing. *Communications of the ACM*, *53*(4), 50–58. doi:10.1145/1721654.1721672

Awwad, A. M. (2005). OTIS-star an attractive alternative network. In *Proceedings of the 4th WSEAS International Conference on Software Engineering, Parallel & Distributed Systems* (p. 37).

Awwad, A., Al-Ayyoub, A., Ould-Khaoua, M., & Day, K. (2001). Solving linear systems equations using the grid structural outlook. In *Proceedings of the 13th IASTED Parallel and Distributed Computing and Systems* (pp. 365-369).

Bae, I.-H. (2007). An adaptive location service on the basis of diamond quorum for MANETs. In *Proceedings of the Third IEEE International Conference on Natural Computation* (p. 781).

Bain, S. A., Read, I., Thomas, J. J., & Merchant, F. (2009). *Advantages of a dynamic infrastructure: A closer look at Private Cloud TCO, from IBM Rep.* Retrieved from http://ftp://public.dhe.ibm.com/common/ssi/ecm/en/zsw03126usen/ZSW03126USEN.PDF

Bala, P., Pytlinski, J., & Nazaruk, M. (2002). BioGRID – An European Grid for Molecular Biology. In *Proceedings of the 11th IEEE International Symposium on High Performance Distributed Computing* (p. 412).

Balan, R., Flinn, J., Satyanarayanan, M., Sinnamohideen, S., & Yang, H.-I. (2002). The case for cyber foraging. In *Proceedings of the 10th ACM SIGOPS European Workshop* (pp. 87-92).

Ballou, D. (1999). Enhancing data quality in data warehousing environment. *Communications of the ACM, 42*(1), 73–78. doi:10.1145/291469.291471

Ballou, D., Wang, H., & Pazer, G. (1998). Modeling information manufacturing systems to determining information product quality. *Management Science, 44*(4), 462–484. doi:10.1287/mnsc.44.4.462

Baruah, S., Koren, G., Mishra, B., Raghunath, A., Roiser, L., & Shasha, D. (1991). On-line scheduling in the presence of overload. In *Proceedings of the 32nd Annual Symposium on Foundations of Computer Science* (pp. 100-110).

Baruah, S., Funk, S., & Goossens, J. (2003). Robustness results concerning EDF scheduling upon uniform multiprocessors. *IEEE Transactions on Computers, 52*(9), 1185–1195. doi:10.1109/TC.2003.1228513

Baruah, S., & Goossens, J. (2004). Rate-monotonic scheduling on uniform multiprocessors. *IEEE Transactions on Computers, 52*(7), 966–970. doi:10.1109/TC.2003.1214344

Basagni, S., Chlamtac, I., Syrotiuk, V., & Woodward, A. B. (1998). A distance routing effect algorithm for mobility (dream). In *Proceedings of the 4th Annual ACM/IEEE International Conference on Mobile Computing and Networking* (pp. 76-84).

Baxter, R., Christen, P., & Churches, T. (2003). A comparison of fast blocking methods for record linkage. In *Proceedings of the ACM SIGKDD Workshop on Data Cleaning, Record Linkage, and Object Consolidation*, Washington, DC (pp. 25-27).

Bayer, M., Campbell, A., & Virdee, D. (2004). A GT3 based. BLAST grid service for biomedical research. In *Proceedings of the UK e-Science All Hands Meeting 2004*, Nottingham, UK. Retrieved from http://www.allhands.org.uk/2004/proceedings/papers/141.pdf

Bayer, R., Heller, H., & Reiser, A. (1980). Parallelism and recovery in database systems. *ACM Transactions on Database Systems, 5*, 139–156. doi:10.1145/320141.320146

Bell, W. H., Cameron, D. G., Capozza, L., Millar, A. P., Stockinger, K., & Zini, F. (2003). Optorsim: A grid simulator for studying dynamic data replication strategies. *International Journal of High Performance Computing Applications.*

Bellard, F. (2005). QEMU, a fast and portable dynamic translator. In *Proceedings of the Annual USENIX Technical Conference* (pp. 41-46).

Beloglazov, A., & Buyya, R. (2010). Energy efficient allocation of virtual machines in cloud data centers. In *Proceedings of the 10th IEEE/ACM International Conference on Cluster, Cloud and Grid Computing* (pp. 577-578).

Beneš, E. (1965). *Mathematical theory of connecting networks and telephone traffic.* New York, NY: Academic Press.

Benjelloun, O., Garcia-Molina, H., Su, Q., & Widom, J. (2005). *Swoosh: A generic approach to entity resolution.* Stanford, CA: Stanford University InfoLab.

Berman, F., Wolski, R., Figueira, S., Schopf, J., & Shao, G. (1996). Application-Level Scheduling on Distributed Heterogeneous Networks. In *Proceedings of the 1996 ACM/IEEE Conference on Supercomputing* (p. 39).

Bernstein, P. A., Hadzilacos, V., & Goodman, N. (1987). *Concurrency control and recovery in database systems.* Reading, MA: Addison-Wesley.

Bertis, V., Ferreira, L., & Amstrong, J. (2002). Introduction to grid computing with Globus. In *IBM RedBook.* Armonk, NY: IBM.

Bertolazzi, P., Santis, L. D., & Scannapieco, M. (2003). Automatic record matching in cooperative information systems. In *Proceedings of the Workshop on Data Quality in Cooperative Information Systems* (pp. 13-20).

Bettstetter, C., & Zangl, J. (2002, September). How to achieve a connected ad hoc network with homogeneous range assignment: An analytical study with consideration of border effects. In *Proceedings of the 4th International Workshop on Mobile and Wireless Communications Network*, Stockholm, Sweden (pp. 125-129).

Bheemavaram, R. (2006). *Parallel and distributed grouping algorithms for finding related records of huge data sets on cluster grid*. Unpublished master's thesis, University of Arkansas, Fayetteville, AK.

Bilenko, M., & Mooney, R. (2003). Adaptive duplicate detection using learnable string similarity metrics. In *Proceedings of the ACM Conference on Knowledge Discovery and Data Mining* (pp. 39-48).

Blackburn, M. (2008). *Five ways to reduce data center server power consumption*. Retrieved from http://www.thegreengrid.org/en/sitecore/content/Global/Content/white-papers/Five-Ways-to-Save-Power.aspx

Bolze, R., Cappello, F., Caron, E., Daydé, M. J., Desprez, F., & Jeannot, E. (2006). A large scale and highly reconfigurable experimental grid testbed. *International Journal of High Performance Computing Applications*, *20*(4), 481–494. doi:10.1177/1094342006070078

Borst, S., Mandelbaum, A., & Reiman, M. I. (2004). Dimensioning large call centers. *Operations Research*, *52*(1), 17–34. doi:10.1287/opre.1030.0081

Bose, P., Morin, P., Stojmenovic, I., & Urrutia, J. (2001). Routing with guaranteed delivery in ad-hoc wireless networks. *Wireless Networks*, *7*(6). doi:10.1023/A:1012319418150

Box, G., Jenkins, G. M., & Reinsel, G. C. (1994). *Time Series Analysis: Forecasting and Control* (3rd ed.). Upper Saddle River, NJ: Prentice-Hall.

Boyer, W. F., & Hura, G. S. (2005). Non evolutionary algorithm for scheduling dependent tasks in distributed heterogeneous computing environments. *Journal of Parallel and Distributed Computing*, *65*, 1035–1046. doi:10.1016/j.jpdc.2005.04.017

Braun, T. D., & Siegel, H. J. (1998). A taxonomy for describing matching and scheduling heuristics for mixed-machine heterogeneous computing systems. In *Proceedings of the Seventeenth IEEE Symposium on Reliable Distributed Systems,* West Lafayette, IN (pp. 330-335).

Breiman, L., Friedman, J., Olshen, R., & Stone, C. (1984). *Classification and regression trees*. Cleveland, OH: Wadsworth International Group.

Broch, J., Maltz, D. A., & Johnson, D. B. (1998). A performance comparison of multi-hop wireless ad-hoc network routing protocols. In *Proceedings of the 4th Annual ACM/IEEE Conference on Mobile Computing and Networking* (pp. 85-97).

Busi, I., & Pattavina, A. (1998). Strict-sense non-blocking conditions for shuffle/exchange networks with vertical replication. In *Proceedings of the Seventeenth Annual Joint Conference INFOCOM*, San Francisco, CA (pp. 126-133).

Buyya, R., & Vazhkudai, S. (2001). Compute Power Market: Towards a Market-Oriented Grid. In *Proceedings of the 1st International Symposium on Cluster Computing and the Grid* (p. 574).

Buyya, R., Abramson, D., & Giddy, J. (2000). Nimrod/G: An architecture for a resource management and scheduling system in a global computational grid. In *Proceedings of the 4th International Conference and Exhibition on High Performance Computing in the Asia-Pacific Region* (Vol. 1, pp. 283-289).

Buyya, R. (1999). *High performance cluster computing: systems and architectures*. Upper Saddle River, NJ: Prentice Hall.

Buyya, R., & Murshed, M. (2002). Gridsim: A toolkit for the modeling and simulation of distributed resource management and scheduling for grid computing. *Journal of Concurrency and Computation: Practice and Experience*, *14*, 13–15.

Buyya, R., Yeo, C. H., Venugopal, S., Broberg, J., & Brandic, I. (2009). *Future generation computer system*. Amsterdam, The Netherlands: Elsevier.

Camp, T., Boleng, J., & Wilcox, L. (2001). Location information services in mobile ad hoc networks. In *Proceedings of the IEEE International Conference on Communications* (pp. 3318-3324).

Camp, T., Bolengm, J., & Davies, V. (2002). A survey of mobility models for ad hoc network research. *Wireless Communications and Mobile Computing*, *2*(5), 483–502. doi:10.1002/wcm.72

Cao, J., Spooner, D. P., Jarvis, S. A., & Nudd, G. R. (2005). Grid load balancing using intelligent agents. *Future Generation Computer Systems*, *21*(1), 135–149. doi:10.1016/j.future.2004.09.032

Cappello, F., Djilali, S., Fedak, G., Herault, T., Magniette, F., Néri, V., & Lodygensky, O. (2005). Computing on large scale distributed systems: XtremWeb architecture, programming models, security, tests and convergence with grid. *Future Generation Computer Science, 21*(3), 417–437. doi:10.1016/j.future.2004.04.011

Casanova, H., Kim, M., Plank, J., & Dongarra, J. (1999). Adaptive Scheduling for Task Farming with Grid middleware. *International Journal of Supercomputer Applications and High-Performance Computing, 13*(3), 231–240. doi:10.1177/109434209901300306

Catteddu, D., & Hogben, G. (2009). *Cloud computing, benefits, risks and recommendations for information security.* Retrieved from http://www.net-security.org/secworld.php?id=8531

Chakrabarty, A., Collier, M., & Mukhopadhyay, S. (2009, November 15-20). Matrix based routing algorithm for Beneš networks. In *Proceedings of the International Conference on Future Computational Technologies and Applications*, Athens, Greece.

Chakrabarty, K., Iyengar, S. S., Qi, H., & Cho, E. (2002). Grid coverage for surveillance and target location in distributed sensor networks. *IEEE Transactions on Computers, 51*(12). doi:10.1109/TC.2002.1146711

Chandra, D., Guo, F., Kim, S., & Solihin, Y. (2005). Predicting inter-thread cache contenton on a chip multiprocessor architecture. In *Proceedings of the 11th International Symposium on High Performance Computer Architecture*, San Francisco, CA (pp. 340-351).

Chang, P. C., Wu, I. W., Shann, J. J., & Chung, C. P. (2008). ETAHM: An energy-aware task allocation algorithm for heterogeneous multiprocessor. In *Proceedings of the 45th Conference on Design Automation* (pp. 776-779).

Chatterjee, S., & Pawlowski, S. (1999). Enlightening the effects and implications of nearly infinite bandwidth. *Communications of the ACM, 42*(6), 75–83.

Chaudhuri, S., Ganti, V., & Motwani, R. (2005). Robust identification of fuzzy duplicates. In *Proceedings of the International Conference on Data Engineering* (pp. 865-876).

Chellappan, S., Bai, X., Mam, B., & Xuan, D. (2005). Mobility limited flip-based sensor networks deployment. *IEEE Transactions on Parallel and Distributed Systems, 18*(2), 199–211. doi:10.1109/TPDS.2007.28

Chen, T., Zhang, B., & Hao, X. (2008). A dependent tasks scheduling model in grid. In Y. Zhang, G. Yu, E. Bertino, & G. Xu (Eds.), *Proceedings of the 10th Asia-Pacific Conference on Progress in WWW Research and Development* (LNCS 4976, pp. 136-147).

Chen, C. C., Hung, S. H., & Lee, C. P. (2010). Protection of buffer overflow attacks via dynamic binary translation. *Reliable and Autonomous Computational Science, 2*, 305–324.

Cheng, C. T., Lemberg, H. L., Philip, S. J., van den Berg, E., & Zhang, T. (2002). SLALoM: A scalable location management scheme for large mobile adhoc networks. In *Proceedings of the IEEE Conference on Wireless Communications and Networking* (pp. 574-578).

Cheng, H., Cao, J., & Chen, H. H. (2007). GrLS: Group-based location service in mobile ad hoc networks. In *Proceedings of the IEEE International Conference on Communications* (pp. 4734-4740).

Choi, S., Kim, H., Buyya, E., Baik, M., Gil, J., & Park, C. (2008). *A taxonomy of desktop grids and its mapping to state-of-the-art systems* (Tech. Rep. No. GRIDS-TR-2008-3). Melbourne, Australia: University of Melbourne.

Chong, K., & Lam, T. (1993). Finding connected components in o(log n log log n) time on EREW PRAM. In *Proceedings of the 4th ACM-SIAM Symposium on Discrete Algorithms* (pp. 11-20).

Chong, C. Y., & Kumar, S. P. (2003). Sensor networks: Evolution, opportunities, and challenges. *Proceedings of the IEEE, 91*(8), 1247–1256. doi:10.1109/JPROC.2003.814918

Chtepen, M., Dhoedt, B., Turck, F. D., & Demeester, P. (2008). Scheduling of dependent grid jobs in absence of exact job length information. In *Proceedings of the 4th IEEE/IFIP International Workshop on End-to-end Virtualization and Grid Management*, Samos Island, Greece (pp. 185-196).

Chun, P., & Maniatis, B. G. (2009). Augmented smartphone applications through clone cloud execution. In *Proceedings of the 12th Workshop on Hot Topics in Operating Systems* (p. 8).

Chung, Y., & Ranka, S. (1992). Applications and Performance Analysis of a Compile-time Optimization Approach for List Scheduling Algorithms on Distributed Memory Multiprocessors. *Proceedings of the Conference on Supercomputing* (pp. 512-521).

Cirne, W., Brasileiro, F., Andrade, N., Costa, L., Andrade, A., Novaes, R., & Mowbray, M. (2006). Labs of the world, unite!!! *Journal of Grid Computing*, 225–246. doi:10.1007/s10723-006-9040-x

Cleary, J. G., & Trigg, L. E. (1995). K*: An instance-based learner using an entropic distance measure. In *Proceedings of the 12th International Conference on Machine Learning* (pp. 108-114).

Cloud Security Alliance. (2010). *Top threats to cloud computing.* Retrieved from http://www.cloudsecurity-alliance.org/topthreats/csathreats.v1.0.pdf

Cormen, T., Leiserson, C., Rivest, R., & Stein, C. (2002). *Introduction to algorithms.* New York, NY: McGraw-Hill.

Coulouris, G., Dollirnore, J., & Kindberg, T. (2005). *Distributed systems, coulouris, G.: Distributed systems: Concepts and design.* Reading, MA: Addison-Wesley.

Creel, M., & Goffe, W. (2008). Multi-core CPUs, Clusters, and Grid Computing: A Tutorial. *International Journal of Computational Economics*, *32*(4), 353–382. doi:10.1007/s10614-008-9143-5

Cuervo, E., Balasubramanian, A., Cho, D.-K., Wolman, A., Saroiu, S., Chandra, R., et al. (2010). MAUI: Making smartphones last longer with code offload. In *Proceedings of the 8th International Conference on Mobile Systems, Applications, and Services* (pp. 49-62).

Dai, Y. S., Xie, M., & Poh, K. L. (2002). Reliability Analysis of Grid Computing Systems. In *Proceedings of the Pacific Rim International Symposium on Dependable Computing (PRDC '02)* (p. 97).

Dally, W. J. (1988). Performance analysis of k-ary n-cubes interconnection networks. *IEEE Transactions on Computers*, *39*(6), 775–785. doi:10.1109/12.53599

Dalton, A., & Georghiades, N. (2005). A full-rate, full-diversity four-antenna quasi-orthogonal space-time block code. *IEEE Transactions on Wireless Communications*, *4*(2). doi:10.1109/TWC.2004.842945

Dam, T. V., & Langendoen, K. (2003, November). An adaptive energy efficient MAC protocols for wireless sensor networks. In *Proceedings of the 1st International Conference on Embedded Networked Sensor Systems*, Los Angeles, CA.

Daoud, M., & Kharma, N. (2008). Research Note: A high performance algorithm for static task scheduling in heterogeneous distributed computing systems. *International Journal of Parallel and Distributed Computing*, *68*(4), 399–409. doi:10.1016/j.jpdc.2007.05.015

Darpa. (2007). *Creating & preventing strategic surprise.* Retrieved from http://www.darpa.mil/default.aspx

Das, S. M., Pucha, H., & Hu, Y. C. (2005). Performance comparison of scalable location service for geographic ad hoc routing. In *Proceedings of the 24th Annual IEEE Joint Conference INFOCOM* (pp. 1228-1239).

Davis, L. (1991). *Handbook of Genetic Algorithms.* New York, NY: Van Nostrand Reinhold.

Day, K., & Al-Ayyoub, A. (1999). The cross product of interconnection networks. *IEEE Transactions on Parallel and Distributed Systems*, *8*(2), 109–118. doi:10.1109/71.577251

Day, K., & Al-Ayyoub, A. (2002). Topological properties of OTIS-Networks. *IEEE Transactions on Parallel and Distributed Systems*, *13*(4), 359–366. doi:10.1109/71.995816

Day, K., & Tripathi, A. (1992). Arrangement graphs: A class of generalised star graphs. *Information Processing Letters*, *42*, 235–241. doi:10.1016/0020-0190(92)90030-Y

Day, K., & Tripathi, A. (1992). *Embedding of cycles in arrangement graphs (Tech. Rep. No. TR 91-58).* Minneapolis, MN: University of Minnesota.

Delone, W., & Mclean, E. (1992). Information systems success: The quest for the independent variable. *Information Systems Research*, *3*(1), 60–95. doi:10.1287/isre.3.1.60

Dertouzos, M., & Ogata, K. (1974). Control robotics: The procedural control of physical process. In *Proceedings of the IFIP Congress* (pp. 807-813).

Deza, E., & Deza, M. (2006). *Dictionary of Distances*. Amsterdam, The Netherlands: Elsevier.

Dhillon, S. S., Chakrabarty, K., & Iyengar, S. S. (2002). Sensor placement for grid coverage under imprecise detections. In *Proceedings of the Fifth International Conference on Information Fusion* (Vol. 2, pp. 1581-1587).

Dhillon, S. S., & Chakrabarty, K. (2003). Sensor placement for effective coverage and surveillance in distributed sensor networks. *IEEE Wireless Communications and Networking, 3*, 1609–1614.

Dipl, I., & Biljana, B. (2005). *Space-time block coding for multiple antenna systems.* Unpublished doctoral dissertation, Technischen Universität Wien, Wien, Germany.

Do, H., & Rahm, E. (2002). Coma -a system for flexible combination of schema matching approaches. In *Proceedings of the ACM Conference on Knowledge Discovery and Data Mining*.

Domingues, P., Andrzejak, A., & Silva, L. M. (2006). Using checkpointing to enhance turnaround time on institutional desktop grids. *e-Science, 73*.

Dorigo, M., & Caro, G. (1999). The ant colony optimization metaheuristic. In Corne, D., Dorigo, M., & Glover, G. (Eds.), *New ideas in optimization*. New Delhi, India: McGraw-Hill.

Dorigo, M., & Gambardella, L. M. (1997). Ant colony system: A cooperative learning approach to the traveling salesman problem. *IEEE Transactions on Evolutionary Computation, 1*(1), 53–66. doi:10.1109/4235.585892

Dorigo, M., Maniezzo, V., & Colorni, A. (1996). The ant system: Optimization by a colony of cooperative agents. *IEEE Transactions on Systems, Man, and Cybernetics. Part B, Cybernetics, 26*(1), 29–41. doi:10.1109/3477.484436

Dorigo, M., & Stutzle, T. (2004). *Ant colony optimization*. Cambridge, MA: MIT Press.

Dumitrescu, C. L., & Foster, I. (2005). Gangsim: A simulator for grid scheduling studies. In *Proceedings of the Fifth IEEE International Symposium on Cluster Computing and the Grid* (Vol. 2, pp. 1151-1158).

Dutta, S., & Shekhar, S. (1994). Bond rating: a non consecutive application of neural networks. In *Proceedings of the IEEE International Conference on Neural Networks* (pp. 527-554).

Eranian, S. (2006). Perfmon2: The hardware-based performance monitoring interface for Linux. In *Proceedings of the Linux Symposium, 1*, 269–288.

Eugster, P. T., Felber, P. A., Guerraoui, R., & Kermarrec, A. M. (2003). The many faces of publish/subscribe. *ACM Computing Surveys, 35*(2), 114–131. doi:10.1145/857076.857078

Falzon, G., & Li, M. (2010). Enhancing list scheduling heuristics for dependent job scheduling in grid computing environments. *Journal of Supercomputing*.

Fan, K., Lin, W., Chiang, L., Chen, S., Chung, T., & Yang, Y. (2009). A 2 × 2 mechanical optical switch with a thin MEMS mirror. *Journal of Lightwave Technology, 27*(9).

Fatos, X., Alba, E., & Dorronsoro, B. (2007). Efficient Batch Job Scheduling in Grids using Cellular Memetic Algorithms. In *Proceedings of the IEEE International Symposium on Parallel and Distributed Processing (IPDPS 2007)* (pp. 1-8).

Fausett, L. (1994). *Fundamentals of Neural Network: Architecture, Algorithms and Applications*. Upper Saddle River, NJ: Prentice Hall.

Fedak, G., Germain, C., Néri, V., & Cappello, F. (2001). Xtremweb: A generic global computing system. In *Proceedings of the IEEE International Symposium on Cluster Computing and the Grid* (pp. 582-587).

Fellegi, I., & Sunter, A. (1969). A theory for record linkage. *Journal of the American Statistical Association, 64*, 1183–1210. doi:10.2307/2286061

Feng, T. (1974). Data manipulating functions in parallel processors and their implementations. *IEEE Transactions on Computers, 23*(3), 309–318. doi:10.1109/T-C.1974.223927

Ferrari, G., & Tonguz, O. K. (2003, December). Performance of ad hoc wireless networks with aloha and PR-CSMA MAC protocols. In *Proceedings of the IEEE Global Telecommunications Conference*, San Francisco, CA (Vol. 5).

Firip, H. A., & Goodman, E. (2004). Swarmed feature selection. In *Proceedings of the 33rd Applied Imagery Pattern Recognition Workshop* (pp. 112-118).

Flinn, J., Narayanan, D., & Satyanarayanan, M. (2001). Self-tuned remote execution for pervasive computing. In *Proceedings of the 8th Workshop on Hot Topics in Operating Systems* (pp. 61-66).

Flury, R., & Wattenhofer, R. (2006). MLS: An efficient location service for mobile ad hoc networks. In *Proceedings of the 7th ACM Conference on Mobile Ad Hoc Networking and Computing* (pp.226-237).

Foster, I. (2005). Globus toolkit version 4: Software for service oriented systems. In H. Jin, D. Reed, & W. Jiang (Eds.), *Proceedings of the International Conference on Network and Parallel Computing*, Beijing, China (LNCS 3779, pp. 2-13).

Foster, I., Roy, A., & Sander, V. (2000). A Quality of Service Architecture that Combines Resource Reservation and Application Adaptation. In *Proceedings of the International Workshop on Quality of Service* (pp. 181-188).

Foster, I. (2002). The Grid: A New Infrastructure for 21st Century Science. *Physics Today*, *55*(2), 42–47. doi:10.1063/1.1461327

Foster, I., & Kesselman, C. (1999). *The Grid 2: Blueprint for a New Computing Infrastructure* (2nd ed.). San Francisco, CA: Morgan Kaufmann.

Fujimoto, N., & Hagihara, K. (2004). A Comparison among Grid Scheduling Algorithms for Independent Coarse-Grained Tasks. In *Proceedings of the 2004 Symposium on Applications and the Internet-Workshops (SAINT 2004 Workshops)* (p. 674).

Funk, S., Goossens, J., & Baruah, S. (2001). On-line scheduling on uniform multiprocessors. In *Proceedings of the IEEE Real-Time Systems Symposium* (pp. 183-192).

FUSE. (n. d.). *Filesystem in userspace*. Retrieved from http://fuse.sourceforge.net/

Gage, D. W. (1992). Command control for many-robot systems. In *Proceedings of the 19th Annual AUVS Technical Symposium*.

Ganesan, G., & Stoica, P. (2001). Space–time block codes: A maximum SNR approach. *IEEE Transactions on Information Theory*, *47*(4), 1650–1656. doi:10.1109/18.923754

Gao, Y., Rong, H., & Huang, J. Z. (2005). Adaptive Grid Job Scheduling with Genetic Algorithms. *Future Generation Computer Systems*, *21*(1), 151–161. doi:10.1016/j.future.2004.09.033

Garfinkel, T., & Rosenblum, M. (2005). When virtual is harder than real: Security challenges in virtual machine based computing environments. In *Proceedings of the 10th Conference on Hot Topics in Operating Systems* (Vol. 10).

Geetha, J., & Gopinath, G. (2007). Ad hoc mobile wireless networks routing protocols – A review. *Journal of Computer Science*, *3*(8), 574–582. doi:10.3844/jcssp.2007.574.582

Gerasoulis, A., & Yang, T. (1992). A comparison of clustering heuristics for scheduling directed acyclic graphs on multiprocessors. *Journal of Parallel and Distributed Computing*, *16*(4), 276–291. doi:10.1016/0743-7315(92)90012-C

Goddard, S., Kumar, S., & Prins, J. F. (1995, October 17-19). Connected components algorithms for mesh-connected parallel computers. In *Proceedings of the 3rd DIMACS Series Workshop on Parallel Algorithms Science* (pp. 43-58).

Goldberg, D. E. (2007). *Genetic Algorithms in Search, Optimization & Machine Learning*. Upper Saddle River, NJ: Pearson Education.

Goldsmith, A. (2005). *Wireless communications*. Cambridge, UK: Cambridge University Press.

Golla, R. (2006). *Niagara2: A highly threaded server-on-a-chip*. Retrieved from http://www.opensparc.net/pubs/preszo/06/04-Sun-Golla.pdf

Google Inc. (2009). *App engine*. Retrieved from http://code.google.com/status/appengine

Google Inc. (2010). *Security whitepaper Google Apps messaging and collaboration products*. Retrieved from http://static.googleusercontent.com/external_content/untrusted_dlcp/www.google.com/zh-TW//a/help/intl/en/admins/pdf/ds_gsa_apps_whitepaper_0207.pdf

Google Inc. (2011). *Google code project.* Retrieved from http://code.google.com/

Google Inc. (2011a). *Security and privacy.* Retrieved from http://www.google.com/support/a/bin/answer.py?answer=60762

Google Inc. (2011b). *The JRE class white list.* Retrieved from http://code.google.com/appengine/docs/java/jre-whitelist.html

Gowrishankar, S., Basavaraju, T. G., & Sarkar, S. K. (2007). Effect of random mobility models pattern in mobile ad hoc networks. *International Journal of Computer Science and Network Security, 7*(6), 160–164.

Graham, S., & Seidel, S. (1993). The cost of broadcasting on star graphs and k-ary hypercubes. *IEEE Transactions on Computers, 42*(6), 756–759. doi:10.1109/12.277296

GraphPad Software. (2009). *Choosing between parametric non-parametric tests: Does it matter?* Retrieved from http://www.graphpad.com

GraphPad Software. (2009). *Non parametric test with small and large samples.* Retrieved from http://www.graphpad.com

Gray, J. N., Lorie, R. A., Putzolu, G. R., & Traiger, I. L. (1994). Granularity of locks and degrees of consistency in a shared data base. In Stonebraker, M. (Ed.), *Readings in database systems* (2nd ed., pp. 181–208). San Francisco, CA: Morgan Kaufmann.

Greiner, J. (1994). A comparison of parallel algorithms for connected components. In *Proceedings of the 6th ACM Symposium on Parallel Algorithms and Architectures* (pp. 16-23).

Grosan, C., Abraham, A., & Helvik, B. (2007). *Multi-objective Evolutionary Algorithms for Scheduling Jobs on Computational Grids.* Retrieved from http://www.softcomputing.net/ac2007_2.pdf

Guey, J., Fitz, M., Bell, M., & Kuo, W. (1996). Signal design for transmitter diversity wireless communication systems over Rayleigh fading channels. *IEEE Transactions on Communications, 47*(4), 527–537. doi:10.1109/26.764926

Halfin, S., & Whitt, W. (1981). Heavy-traffic limits for queues with many exponential servers. *Operations Research, 29*(3), 567–588. doi:10.1287/opre.29.3.567

Hamm, L., Brorsen, B. W., & Sharda, R. (1993). Futures trading with a neural network. In *Proceedings of the NCR-134 Conference on Applied Commodity Analysis, Price Forecasting and Market Risk Management* (pp. 486-496).

Han, Y., Jiang, C., & Luo, X. (2005). Resource Scheduling Model for Grid Computing Based on Sharing Synthesis of Petri Net. In *Proceedings of the Ninth International Conference on Computer Supported Cooperative Work in Design* (pp. 367-372).

Han, Y., & Wagner, R. (1990). An efficient and fast parallel-connected component algorithm. *Journal of the ACM, 73*(3), 626–642. doi:10.1145/79147.214077

Hayes, D. (2008). *A corba-based distributed and multi-threaded algorithm finding related records in a large data set.* Unpublished master's thesis, University of Arkansas, Fayetteville, AK.

He, L., Jarvis, S., Spooner, D., Bacigalupo, D., Tan, G., & Nudd, G. (2005). Mapping DAG-based Applications to Multiclusters with Background Workload. In *Proceedings of the IEEE International Symposium on Cluster Computing and the Grid (CCGrid'05)* (pp. 855-862).

He, K., & Zhao, Y. (2008). Clustering and scheduling method based on task duplication. *Wuhan University Journal of Natural Sciences, 12*(2), 260–266. doi:10.1007/s11859-006-0028-y

Hendrick, W., Kibar, O., & Esener, S. (1959). *Modeling and optimisation of the optical transpose interconnection system.* Ithaca, NY: Cornell University.

Hernandez, M., & Stolfo, S. (1998). Real-world data is dirty: Data cleansing and the merge/purge problem. *Journal of Data Mining and Knowledge Discovery, 1*(2), 9–37. doi:10.1023/A:1009761603038

Hevner, A. R., March, S. T., Park, J., & Ram, S. (2004). Design science in information systems research. *Management Information Systems Quarterly, 28*(1), 75–105.

Hirschberg, D., Chandra, A., & Sarvate, D. (1979). Computing connected components on parallel computers. *Communications of the ACM, 22*(8), 461–464. doi:10.1145/359138.359141

Holden, K., Peel, D. A., & Thompson, J. L. (1990). *Economic Forecasting: an Introduction.* New York, NY: Cambridge University Press.

Hong, K., & Hua, Y. (2006, July). Throughput of large wireless networks on square, hexagonal and triangular grids. In *Proceedings of the Fourth IEEE Workshop on Sensor Array and Multichannel Processing*, Waltham, MA.

Hoste, K., & Eeckhout, L. (2007). Microarchitecture-independent workload characterization. *IEEE Micro*, *27*(3), 63–72. doi:10.1109/MM.2007.56

Hsin, C. (2005). On The Design of Task Scheduling in The Heterogeneous Computing Environments. In *Proceedings of the Computers and Signal Processing Conference (PACRIM 2005)* (pp. 396-399).

Huedo, E., Montero, R. S., & Llorente, I. M. (2006). Evaluating the Reliability of Computational Grids from the End User's Point of View. *Journal of Systems Architecture*, 727–736. doi:10.1016/j.sysarc.2006.04.003

Hwang, F. K., Lin, W., & Lioubimov, V. (2006). On noninterruptive rearrangeable networks. *IEEE/ACM Transactions on Networking*, *14*(5). doi:10.1109/TNET.2006.882846

Hwang, J. J., Chow, Y. C., & Anger, F. D. (1989). Scheduling Precedence Graphs in Systems with Inteprocessor Communication Costs. *SIAM Journal on Computing*, *18*(2), 244–257. doi:10.1137/0218016

Iavarasan, E., Thambidurai, P., & Mahilmannan, R. (2005). Performance Effective Task Scheduling Algorithm for Heterogeneous Computing System. In *Proceedings of the 4th International Symposium on Parallel and Distributed Computing* (pp. 28-38).

Ilavarasan, E., & Thambidurai, P. (2007). Low complexity Performance Effective Task Scheduling Algorithm for Heterogeneous Computing Environments. *Journal of Computer Science*, *3*, 94–103. doi:10.3844/jcssp.2007.94.103

Indu, S., Chaudhury, S., Mittal, N. R., & Bhattacharyya, A. (2009). Optimal sensor placement for surveillance of large spaces. In *Proceedings of the Third International Conference on Digital Object Identifier* (pp. 1-8).

Intel Corporation. (n. d.). *Intel® 64 and IA-32 architectures software developer's manuals.* Retrieved from http://www.intel.com/products/processor/manuals

International Organization for Standardization. (2005). *ISO/ IEC 27001: Information technology -- Security techniques -- Information security management systems -- Requirements.* Retrieved from http://www.iso27001security.com/html/27001.html

International Organization for Standardization. (2007). *ISO/ IEC 27002: Information technology - Security techniques - Code of practice for information security management.* Retrieved from http://www.iso.org/iso/catalogue_detail?csnumber=50297

International Organization for Standardization. (2008). *ISO/ IEC 27005: Information technology -- Security techniques -- Information security risk management.* Retrieved from http://www.27001.com/products/155

Jaeger, T., & Schiffman, J. (2010). Outlook: Cloudy with a chance of security challenges and improvements. *IEEE Security & Privacy*, *8*(1), 77–80. doi:10.1109/MSP.2010.45

Jafarkhani, H. (2001). A quasi orthogonal space-time block code. *IEEE Transactions on Communications*, *49*, 1–4. doi:10.1109/26.898239

Jajszczyk, A., & Jekel, G. (1993). A new concept-repackable networks. *IEEE Transactions on Communications*, *41*(8). doi:10.1109/26.231967

Jen, M., & Yuan, F. (2009). Service-oriented grid computing system for digital rights management (GC-DRM). *International Journal of Expert Systems with Applications*, *36*(7), 10708–10726. doi:10.1016/j.eswa.2009.02.066

Jens, V., Martin, W., & Roman, B. (2009). Services Grids in Industry - On-Demand Provisioning and Allocation of Grid-based Business Services. *International Journal of Business & Information Systems Engineering*, *1*(2), 177–184. doi:10.1007/s12599-008-0009-0

Jero, M. (1989). Advances in record linkage methodology as applied to matching the 1985 census of Tempe, Florida. *Journal of the American Statistical Society*, *84*(406), 414–420.

Jiang, W., Baumgarten, M., Zhou, Y., & Jin, H. (2009). A bipartite model for load balancing in grid computing environments. *Frontiers of Computer Science in China*, *3*(4), 503–523. doi:10.1007/s11704-009-0036-0

Jomeiri, A., & Dehghan, M. (2008). Performance improvement of a grid based location service in manet. In *Proceedings of the Second IEEE International Conference on Mobile Ubiquitous Computing, Systems, Services, and Technologies* (pp. 165-170).

Jwo, J., Lakshmivarahan, S., & Dhall, S. (1991). Embedding of cycles and grids in star graphs. *Journal of Circuits, Systems, and Computers, 1*(1), 43–74. doi:10.1142/S0218126691000215

Kadav, A., & Sanjeev, K. (2006). A workflow editor and scheduler for composing applications on computational grids. In *Proceedings of the 12th International Conference on Parallel and Distributed Systems* (pp. 127-132).

Kamalam, G. K., Maharajan, R., & Maheish Sundhar, K. P. (2010). Min mean: A static scheduling algorithm for mapping meta-tasks on heterogeneous computing systems. In *Proceedings of the International Conference on Information Science and Applications*, Chennai, India.

Kanas, A. (2001). Neural network linear forecasts for stock returns. *Financial Economics, 6*, 245–254.

Keir, C. C., Clark, C., Fraser, K., Hand, S., Hansen, J. G., Jul, E., et al. (2005). Live migration of virtual machines. In *Proceedings of the 2nd ACM/USENIX Symposium on Networked Systems Design and Implementation* (pp. 273-286).

Kennedy, J., & Eberhart, R. C. (1995). Particle swarm optimization. In *Proceedings of the IEEE International Conference on Neural Networks* (pp. 1942-1948).

Kennedy, J., & Eberhart, R. C. (1997). A discrete binary version of the particle swarm algorithm. In *Proceedings of the Conference on Systems, Man, and Cybernetics* (pp. 4104-4108).

Khanbary, L. M. O., & Vidyarthi, D. P. (2008). A GA-Based Effective Fault-Tolerant Model for Channel Allocation in Mobile Computing. *IEEE Transactions on Vehicular Technology, 57*(3), 1823–1833. doi:10.1109/TVT.2007.907311

Khanbary, L. M. O., & Vidyarthi, D. P. (2009). Modified Genetic Algorithm with Threshold Selection. *International Journal of Artificial Intelligence, 2*(9), 126–148.

Khezri, S., Meybodi, M., & Osmani, A. (2011). Fuzzy adaptive PBIL based sensor placement in WSN. In *Proceedings of the International Symposium on Computer Networks and Distributed Systems* (pp. 216-221).

Khezri, S., Osmani, A., & Gholami, M. (2011). Estimation of distribution algorithm based on learning automata for sensors placement in wireless sensor networks. In *Proceedings of the 3nd National Conference on Computer/ Electrical and IT Engineering*.

Kimito, T., Asakawa, K., & Takeoka, N. (1990). Stock market prediction system with modular neural networks. In *Proceedings of the IEEE International Joint Conference on Neural Networks* (pp. 11-16).

Kim, S. J., & Browne, J. C. (1998). A general approach to mapping of parallel computation upon multiprocessor architectures. In *Proceedings of the International Conference on Parallel Processing, 2*, 1–8.

King, R. C., Tollu, C., & Toumazet, F. (2004). Stretched Littlewood-Richardson and Kostka coefficients. In Winternitz, P., Harnard, J., Lam, C. S., & Patera, J. (Eds.), *Symmetry in physics: In memory of Robert T. Sharp* (pp. 99–112). Providence, RI: American Mathematical Society.

Kinyanjui, K. (2009 August 13). *High speed Internet exposes Kenya to cybercrime.* Retrieved from http://www.businessdailyafrica.com

Kiran, M., Hassan, A., Kuan, L., & Yee, Y. (2009). Execution Time Prediction of Imperative Paradigm Tasks for Grid Scheduling Optimization. *International Journal of Computer Science and Network Security, 9*(2), 155–163.

Kleinschmidt, J. H., Borelli, W. C., & Pellenz, M. E. (2007, June). An analytical model for energy efficiency of error control schemes in sensor networks. In *Proceedings of the IEEE International Conference on Communications*, Glasgow, UK (pp. 3895-3900).

Kohavi, R. (1995). A study of cross-validation and bootstrap for accuracy estimation and model selection. In *Proceedings of the 14th International Joint Conference on Artificial Intelligence* (pp. 1137-1143).

Kolesar, P., & Green, L. (1998). Insights on service system design from a normal approximation to Erlang's formula. *Production and Operations Management, 7*(3), 289–293.

Kondo, D., Chien, A. A., & Casanova, H. (2004). Resource management for rapid application turnaround on enterprise desktop grids. In *Proceedings of the ACM/IEEE Conference on Supercomputing* (p. 17).

Kongetira, P., Aingaran, K., & Olukotun, K. (2005). Niagara, a 32-way multithreaded sparc processor. *IEEE Micro*, 21–29. doi:10.1109/MM.2005.35

Konishi, F., Yamamoto, T., Fukuzaki, A., Defago, X., Satou, K., & Konagaya, A. (2002). OBIGrid: A New Computing Platform for Bioinformatics. *Genome Informatics*, *13*, 484–485.

Koppe, N. (n. d.). *Ektosym*. Retrieved from http://www.ektosym.com/

Koren, G., & Shasha, D. (1995). DOver: An optimal on-line scheduling algorithm for overloaded real-time systems. *SIAM Journal on Computing*, *24*, 318–339. doi:10.1137/S0097539792236882

Kotecha, K., & Shah, A. (2008). Efficient dynamic scheduling algorithms for real-time multiprocessor system. In *Proceedings of the International Conference on High Performance Computation Networking and Communications* (pp. 21-25).

Kousalya, K., & Balasubramanie, P. (2008). An Enhanced ant algorithm for grid scheduling problem. *International Journal of Computer Science and Network Security*, *8*(4), 262–271.

Kramer, D. A., & MacInnis, M. (2004). Utilization of a local grid of mac OS X-based computers using Xgrid. In *Proceedings of the 13th IEEE International Symposium on High Performance Distributed Computing* (pp. 264-265).

Krauter, K., Buyya, R., & Maheswaran, M. (2002). A taxonomy and survey of grid resource management systems for distributed computing. *Software, Practice & Experience*, *32*.

Krishnamoorthy, A., Marchand, P., Kiamilev, F., & Esener, S. (1992). Grain-size considerations for optoelectronic multistage interconnection networks. *Applied Optics*, *31*(2), 5480–5507. doi:10.1364/AO.31.005480

Kruatrachue, B., & Lewis, T. G. (1998). Grain Size Determination for Parallel Processing. *IEEE Software*, *5*(1), 23–32. doi:10.1109/52.1991

Kshetri, N. (2010). Cloud computing in developing economies. *IEEE Computer*, *43*(10), 47–55.

Kumar, V., & Das, S. R. (2004). Performance of dead reckoning-based location service for mobile ad hoc networks. *Wireless Communications and Mobile Computing*, *4*(2), 189–202. doi:10.1002/wcm.163

Kumar, V., Grama, A., Gupta, A., & Karypis, G. (1994). *Introduction to Parallel Computing*. Redwood City, CA: Benjamin/Cummings.

Kwok, Y., & Ahmad, I. (1996). Dynamic Critical-Path Scheduling: An Effective Technique for Allocating Task Graphs to Multiprocessors. *IEEE Transactions on Parallel and Distributed Systems*, *7*(5), 506–521. doi:10.1109/71.503776

Kwok, Y.-K., & Ahmad, I. (1999). Static scheduling algorithms for allocating directed task graphs to multiprocessors. *ACM Computing Surveys*, *31*, 406–471. doi:10.1145/344588.344618

Kwon, H., Hyun Kim, T. H., Choi, S., & Lee, B. G. (2006). A cross-layer strategy for energy-efficient reliable delivery in wireless sensor networks. *IEEE Transactions on Wireless Communications*, *5*(12), 3689–3699. doi:10.1109/TWC.2006.256992

Larsen, M., & Rubin, D. (2001). Alternative automated record linkage using mixture models. *Journal of the American Statistical Association*, *79*, 32–41. doi:10.1198/016214501750332956

Lawrie, D. H. (1975). Access and alignment of data in an array processor. *IEEE Transactions on Computers*, *24*(12), 1145–1155. doi:10.1109/T-C.1975.224157

Leal, K., Huedo, E., & Llorente, I. M. (2009). A decentralized model for scheduling independent tasks in Federated Grids. *Future Generation Computer Systems*, *25*, 840–852. doi:10.1016/j.future.2009.02.003

Lee, W., Squicciarini, A., & Bertino, E. (2009). The Design and Evaluation of Accountable Grid Computing System. In *Proceedings of the 29th IEEE International Conference on Distributed Computing Systems (ICDCS '09)* (pp. 145-154).

Legrand, A., Marchal, L., & Casanova, H. (2003). Scheduling distributed applications: The simgrid simulation framework. In *Proceedings of the 3rd IEEE/ACM International Symposium on Cluster Computing and the Grid* (pp. 138-145).

Leng, S., Zhang, L., Rao, J., & Yang, J. (2006). A novel k-hop cluster-based location service protocol for mobile ad hoc networks. In *Proceedings of the 6th IEEE International Conference on ITS Telecommunications* (pp. 695-700).

Li, J., Jannotti, J., De Couti, D. S. J., Karger, D. R., & Morris, R. (2000). A scalable location service for geographic ad hoc routing. In *Proceedings of the 6th Annual ACM International Conference on Mobile Computing and Networking* (pp. 120-130).

Li, W., Zhang, J., & Bheemavaram, R. (2006). Efficient algorithms for grouping data to improve data quality. In *Proceedings of the International Conference on Information and Knowledge Engineering* (pp. 149-154).

Liang, X., & Huaping, L. (2005). Optimal rotation angles for quasi-orthogonal space-time codes with PSK modulation. *IEEE Communications Letters*, *9*(8), 676–678. doi:10.1109/LCOMM.2005.1496579

Li, K. B. (2003). ClustalW-MPI: ClustalW Analysis Using Distributed and Parallel Computing. *Bioinformatics (Oxford, England)*, *19*(12), 1585–1586. doi:10.1093/bioinformatics/btg192

Li, M., & Hadjinicolaou, M. (2008). Curriculum Development on Grid Computing. *International Journal of Education and Information Technology*, *1*(2), 71–78.

Limaye, K., Leangsuksun, B., Liu, Y., Greenwood, Z., Scott, S. L., Libby, R., & Chanchio, K. (2005). Reliability-Aware Resource Management for Computational Grid/Cluster Environments. In *Proceedings of the Sixth IEEE/ACM International Workshop on Grid Computing* (pp. 211-218).

Lin, J., & Wu, H. (2005). A Task Duplication Based Scheduling Algorithm on GA in Grid Computing Systems. In *Advances in Natural Computation* (LNCS 3612, pp. 225-234).

Lin, J., Lu, Q., Ding, X., Zhang, Z., & Sadayappan, P. (2008). Gaining insights into multicore cache partitioning: Bridging the gap between simulation and real systems. In *Proceedings of the 14th International Symposium on High Performance Computer Architecture*, Salt Lake City, UT (pp. 367-378).

Lin, F. Y. S., & Chiu, P. L. (2005). A near-optimal sensor placement algorithm to achieve complete coverage/discrimination in sensor networks. *IEEE Communications Letters*, *9*(1), 43–45.

Lip, H. B., Tang, Y. Y., Meng, J., & Jp, Y. (2004). Neural networks learning using vbest model particle swarm optimization. In *Proceedings of the 3rd International Conference on Machine Learning and Cybernetics* (pp. 3157-3159).

Little, J. D. C. (1961). A proof for the queuing formula $L = \lambda W$. *Operations Research*, *9*, 383–387. doi:10.1287/opre.9.3.383

Liu, L., Yang, Y., Lian, L., & Wanbin, S. (2006). Using Ant Optimization for Super Scheduling in Computational Grid. In *Proceedings of the IEEE Asia-pacific Conference on Services Computing*.

Liu, T. N., & Hwang, S. I. (2006). On design of an efficient hierarchical location service for ad hoc network. In *Proceedings of the 1st IEEE International Symposium on Wireless Pervasive Computing* (pp. 1-6).

Liu, W. S. (2001). *Real-time systems*. New Delhi, India: Pearson Education.

Li, W., Bheemavaram, R., & Zhang, J. (2010). Transitive closure of data records. In Chan, Y., Talburt, J., & Talley, T. (Eds.), *Data engineering: Mining, information and intelligence* (pp. 39–74). New York, NY: Springer.

Locke, C. D. (1986). *Best effort decision making for real-time scheduling.* Unpublished doctoral dissertation, Carnegie-Mellon University, Pittsburgh, PA.

Lopez, J. M., Diaz, J. L., & Garcia, D. F. (2004). Minimum and maximum utilization bounds for multiprocessor rate monotonic scheduling. *IEEE Transactions on Parallel and Distributed Computing*, *15*(7), 642–653. doi:10.1109/TPDS.2004.25

Lu, K., Fu, S., & Xia, X. (2004). Close forms designs of complex orthogonal space–time block codes of rates (k+1)/(2k) for 2k − 1 or 2k transmit antennas. In *Proceedings of the IEEE International Symposium on Information Theory* (p. 307).

Luk, C. K., Cohn, R., Muth, R., Patil, H., Klauser, A., Lowney, G., et al. (2005). Pin: Building customized program analysis tools with dynamic instrumentation. In *Proceedings of the ACM SIGPLAN Conference on Programming Language Design and Implementation* (pp. 190-200).

Lundberg, L. (2002). Analyzing fixed-priority global multiprocessor scheduling. In *Proceedings of the Eighth IEEE Real-Time and Embedded Technology and Applications Symposium* (pp. 145-153).

Luo, X., Camp, T., & Navidi, W. (2005). Predictive methods for location services in mobile ad hoc networks. In *Proceedings of the 19th IEEE International Symposium on Parallel and Distributed Processing* (p. 6).

MacDonald, I. G. (1995). *Symmetric functions and hall polynomials* (2nd ed.). Oxford, UK: Clarendon Press.

Maheswaran, M., Ali, S., Siegel, H. J., Hensgen, D., & Freund, R. F. (1999). Dynamic mapping of a class of independent tasks onto heterogeneous computing systems. *Journal of Parallel and Distributed Computing, 59*, 107–121. doi:10.1006/jpdc.1999.1581

Mainwaring, A., Polastre, J., Szewczyk, R., Culler, D., & Anderson, J. (2002). Wireless sensor networks for habitat monitoring. In *Proceedings of the 1st ACM International Workshop on Wireless Sensor Networks and Applications* (pp. 88-97).

Makridakis, S., & Wheelright, S. (1978). *Forecasting Methods and Applications*. New York, NY: John Wiley & Sons.

Malone, W., Fikes, R., Grant, R., & Howard, M. (1988). A Market-Like Task Scheduler for Distributed Computing Environments. In *Ecology of Computation* (pp. 177–205). Enterprise.

Mansouri, V. S., Ghiassi-Farrokhfal, Y., Nia-Avval, M., & Khalaj, B. H. (2005, October). Using a diversity scheme to reduce energy consumption in wireless sensor networks. In *Proceedings of the 2nd International Conference on Broadband Networks*, Boston, MA.

Marsden, G., Marchand, P., Harvey, P., & Esener, S. (1993). Optical transpose interconnection system architecture. *Optics Letters, 18*(13), 1083–1085. doi:10.1364/OL.18.001083

Mather, T., Kumaraswamy, S., & Latif, S. (2009). *Cloud security and privacy*. Sebastopol, CA: O'Reilly Media.

Mauve, M., Widmer, J., & Hartensteinm, H. (2001). A survey on position-based routing in mobile ad hoc networks. *IEEE Network, 15*(6), 30–39. doi:10.1109/65.967595

McCallum, A., Nigam, K., & Ungar, L. (2000). Efficient clustering of high-dimensional data sets with application to reference matching. In *Proceedings of the 6th ACM SIGKDD International Conference on Knowledge Discovery and Data Mining* (pp. 169-178).

McCulloch, W. S., & Pitts, W. (1998). A logical calculus of the ideas imminent in nervous activity. In Anderson, J., & Rosenberg, E. (Eds.), *Neurocomputing: Foundations and Research* (pp. 18–28). Cambridge, MA: MIT Press.

Meguerdichian, S., Koushanfar, F., Potkonjak, M., & Srivastava, M. B. (2001). Coverage problems in wireless ad-hoc sensor networks. In *Proceedings of the International Conference on Mobile Computing and Networking* (pp. 1380-1387).

Mell, P., & Granc, T. (2009 Oct 7). *The NIST definition of cloud computing v15*. Retrieved from http://www.nist.gov/itl/cloud/upload/cloud-def-v15.pdf

Mendel, J. M. (1995). Fuzzy logic systems for engineering: A tutorial. *Proceedings of the IEEE, 83*(3), 345–377. doi:10.1109/5.364485

Mendel, J. M. (2001). *Uncertain rule-based fuzzy logic systems*. Upper Saddle River, NJ: Prentice Hall.

Microsoft. (2010). *Information security management system for Microsoft cloud infrastructure-online services security and compliance*. Retrieved from http://www.globalfoundationservices.com/security/documents/InformationSecurityMangSysforMSCloudInfrastructure.pdf

Miller, K. W., Voas, J., & Laplante, P. (2010). In trust we trust. *IEEE Computer, 43*(10), 85–87.

Mitchell, M. (1999). *An Introduction to Genetic Algorithms*. Cambridge, MA: MIT Press.

Mitchel, T. (1997). *Machine learning*. New York, NY: McGraw-Hill.

Mok, A. (1983). *Fundamental design problems of distributed systems for the hard-real-time environment*. Unpublished doctoral dissertation, Massachusetts Institute of Technology, Cambridge, MA.

Moreau, L., et al. (2002). On the Use of Agents in a Bio-Informatics Grid. In *Proceedings of the Network Tools and Applications in Biology Conference (NETTAB 2002)*. Retrieved from http://www.ecs.soton.ac.uk/~mml/papers/nettab02-b.pdf

Moreto, M., Cazorla, F., J., Ramirez, A., & Valero, M. (2007). Explaining dynamic cache partitioning speed ups. *Computer Architecture Letters, 6*(1).

Murthy, C. S. R., & Manoj, B. S. (2004). *Ad hoc wireless networks architectures and protocols*. Upper Saddle River, NJ: Prentice Hall.

Nakechbandi, M., Colin, J.-Y., Gashumba, J. B. (2007). An efficient fault tolerant scheduling algorithm for precedence constrained tasks in heterogeneous distributed systems. *Innovations and Advanced Techniques in Computer and Information Sciences and Engineering*, 301-307.

Nandi, A., & Kundu, S. (2010, November). Energy level performance of retransmission schemes in wireless sensor networks over Rayleigh fading channel. In *Proceedings of the IEEE International Conference on Computational Intelligence and Communication Networks*, Bhopal, India (pp. 220-225).

Narayanaswamy, S., Kawadia, V., Sreenivas, R. S., & Kumar, P. R. (2002, February). Power control in ad-hoc networks: Theory, architecture, algorithm and implementation of the COMPOW protocol. In *Proceedings of the European Wireless Conference Next Generation Wireless Networks: Technologies, Protocols, Services and Applications*, Florence, Italy.

Naserian, M., Tepe, K. E., & Tarique, M. (2005, August). Routing overhead analysis for reactive routing protocols in wireless ad hoc networks. In *Proceedings of the IEEE International Conference on Wireless and Mobile Computing, Networking, and Communications*, Windsor, ON, Canada (Vol. 3, pp. 87-92).

Nath, P., Kozuch, M. A., O'Hallaron, D. R., Harkes, J., Satyanarayanan, M., Tolia, N., et al. (2006). Design tradeoffs in applying content addressable storage to enterprise-scale systems based on virtual machines. In *Proceedings of the USENIX Annual Technical Conference* (pp. 363-378).

Nebro, A. J., Alba, E., & Luna, F. (2006). *Multi-objective optimization using Grid Computing*. Berlin, Germany: Springer Verlag.

Newcombe, H. (1988). *Handbook of record linkage: Methods for health and statistical studies, administration, and business*. Oxford, UK: Oxford University Press.

Nilsson, T. (2005). *Resource allocation and service differentiation in wireless local area networks*. Umea, Sweden: Umea University.

Ning, Y. (2008). *A family of space-time blocks codes for wireless communication*. Boston, MA: Northeastern University.

Niyato, D., Chaisiri, S., & Bu Sung, L. (2009). Optimal power management for server farm to support green computing. In *Proceedings of the 9th IEEE/ACM International Symposium on Cluster Computing and the Grid* (pp. 84-91).

Oh, Y., & Son, S. H. (1995). Allocating fixed-priority periodic tasks on multiprocessor systems. *Real-Time Systems, 9*(3), 207–239. doi:10.1007/BF01088806

Osman, S., Subhraveti, D., Su, G., & Nieh, J. (2002). The design and implementation of Zap: A system for migrating computing environments. In *Proceedings of the Fifth Symposium on Operating Systems Design and Implementation* (pp. 361-376).

Osmani, A., & Haghighat, A. T. (2010). SALAM: Scalable @ location advertisement management in ad hoc networks. In *Proceedings of the Second IEEE International Conference on Computational Intelligence, Communication Systems and Networks* (pp. 355-360).

Osmani, A., Dehghan, M., Pourakbar, H., & Emdadi, P. (2009). Fuzzy-based movement-assisted sensor deployment method in wireless sensor networks. In *Proceedings of the International Conference on Computational Intelligence, Communication Systems and Networks* (pp. 90-95).

Osmani, A., Haghighat, A. T., & Khezri, S. (2010). Performance improvement of two ble location services in MANET. In *Proceedings of the IEEE International Conference on Computational Intelligence and Communication Networks* (pp. 172-176).

Osmani, A., Haghighat, A. T., Dehghan, M., & Emdadi, P. (2010). FSPNS: Fuzzy sensor placement based on state. In *Proceedings of the International Conference on Computer Modeling and Simulation.*

Ould-Ahmed-Vall, E., Woodlee, J., Yount, C., & Doshi, K. A. (2007a). On the comparison of regression algorithms for computer architecture performance analysis of software applications. In *Proceedings of the First Workshop on Statistical and Machine Learning Approaches Applied to Architectures and Compilation*, Ghent, Belgium.

Ould-Ahmed-Vall, E., Woodlee, J., Yount, C., Doshi, K. A., & Abraham, S. (2007b). Using model trees for computer architecture performance analysis of software applications. In *Proceedings of the IEEE International Symposium on Performance Analysis of Systems & Software* (pp. 116-125).

OWASP. (2010)... *Top (Madrid)*, *10*, Retrieved from http://www.owasp.org/index.php/Top_10_2010-Main.

Padmavathi, M., Yong, R., & Yelena, Y. (2006). Key frame-based video summarization using Delanunay clustering. *International Journal on Digital Libraries*, *6*, 219–232. doi:10.1007/s00799-005-0129-9

Panichpapiboon, S., Ferrari, G., & Tonguz, O. K. (2006). Optimal transmit power in wireless sensor networks. *IEEE Transactions on Mobile Computing*, *5*(10), 1432–1447. doi:10.1109/TMC.2006.155

Parikh, T. S. (2009). Engineering rural development. *Communications of the ACM*, *52*(1), 54–63. doi:10.1145/1435417.1435433

Park, G., Shirazi, B., & Marquis, J. (1997). DFRN: A New Approach for Duplication Based Scheduling for Distributed Memory Mulitiprocessor Systems. In *Proceedings of the International Conference on Parallel Processing* (pp. 157-166).

Paulraj, A., Gore, D., & Nabar, R. (2004). An overview of MIMO communications - A key to gigabit wireless. *Proceedings of the IEEE*, *92*(2), 198–218. doi:10.1109/JPROC.2003.821915

Perkins, C. E., Royer, E. M. B., & Das, S. R. (2003). *Ad hoc on-demand distance vector (AODV) routing.* Retrieved from http://www.ietf.org/rfc/rfc3561.txt

Perkins, C. E. (2001). *Ad hoc networking: An introduction.* Reading, MA: Addison-Wesley.

Petrowski, A., Dreyfus, G., & Girault, C. (1993). Performance analysis of a pipelined backpropagation parallel algorithm. *IEEE Transactions on Neural Networks*, *4*(6), 970–981. doi:10.1109/72.286892

Pfaff, B., Garfinkel, T., & Rosenblum, M. (2006). Virtualization aware file systems: Getting beyond the limitations of virtual disks. In *Proceedings of the 3rd Symposium of Networked Systems Design and Implementation* (pp. 353-366).

Philip, S. J., Ghosh, J., & Qiao, C. (2005). Performance evaluation of a multilevel hierarchical location management protocol for ad hoc networks. *Computer Communications*, *28*(10), 1110–1122. doi:10.1016/j.comcom.2004.07.015

Pierce, M., Fox, G., Youn, C., Mock, S., Mueller, K., & Balsoy, O. (2002). Interoperable Web services for computational portals. In *Proceedings of the 2002 ACM/IEEE Conference on Supercomputing*, Baltimore, MD (pp. 1-12).

Pirzada, A. A., McDonald, C., & Datta, A. (2006). Performance comparison of trust based reactive routing protocols. *IEEE Transactions on Mobile Computing*, *5*(6), 695–710. doi:10.1109/TMC.2006.83

Portier, F., Baudais, J., & Hélard, J. (2004). Performance of STBC MCCDMA systems over outdoor realistic MIMO channels. In *Proceedings of the 60th IEEE Conference on Vehicular Technology* (Vol. 4, pp. 2409-2413).

Pottie, G. J. (1998). Wireless sensor networks. In *Proceedings of the Information Theory Workshop* (pp. 139-140).

Pottie, G. J., & Caiser, W. (2000). Wireless sensor networks. *Communications of the ACM, 43*(5). doi:10.1145/332833.332838

Prabhu, C. S. R. (2008). *Grid and Cluster Computing.* PHI Learning Private Limited.

Prodan, R., & Fahringer, T. (2002). ZENTURIO: An Experiment Management System for Cluster and Grid Computing. In *Proceedings of the IEEE International Conference on Cluster Computing (CLUSTER'02),* Chicago, IL (pp. 9-18).

Prodan, R., & Ostermann, S. (2009). A survey and taxonomy of infrastructure as a service and web hosting cloud providers. In *Proceedings of the 10th IEEE/ACM International Conference on Grid Computing* (pp. 17-25).

Pusukuri, K. K., & Negi, A. (2004). Characterizing process execution behavior using machine learning techniques. In *Proceedings of the HiPC International Conference,* Bangalore, India.

Pusukuri, K. K., & Negi, A. (2005). Applying machine learning techniques to improve GNU/Linux process scheduling. In *Proceedings of the IEEE Tencon Conference* (pp. 393-398).

Qi, H., Iyengar, S. S., & Chakrabarty, K. (2001). Distributed sensor fusion – a review of recent research. *Journal of the Franklin Institute, 338,* 655–668. doi:10.1016/S0016-0032(01)00026-6

Qin, F., Wang, C., Li, Z., Kim, H. S., Zhou, Y., & Wu, Y. (2006). Lift: A lowoverhead practical information flow tracking system for detecting security attacks. In *Proceedings of the 39th Annual IEEE/ACM International Symposium on Microarchitecture* (pp. 135-148).

Quinlan, R. (1992). Learning with continuous classes. In *Proceedings of the 5th Australian Joint Conference on Artificial Intelligence.*

Qureshi, M. K., & Patt, Y. N. (2006). Utility-based cache partitioning: A low-overhead, high-performance, runtime mechanism to partition shared caches. In *Proceedings of the 39th International Symposium on Microarchitecture,* Orlando, FL (pp. 423-432).

Qu, Y., Soininen, J.-P., & Nurmi, J. (2007). Static scheduling techniques for dependent tasks on dynamically reconfigurable devices. *Journal of Systems Architecture, 53,* 861–876. doi:10.1016/j.sysarc.2007.02.004

R Development Core Team. (2004). *R: A language and environment for statistical computing.* Vienna, Austria: R Foundation for Statistical Computing.

Raghunathan, V., Schurgers, C., Park, S., & Srivastava, M. B. (2002). Energy-aware wireless microsensor network. *IEEE Signal Processing Magazine, 19*(2), 40–50. doi:10.1109/79.985679

Rahman, M. O., Razzaque, M. A., & Hong, C.-H. S. (2007). Probabilistic sensor deployment in wireless sensor network: A new approach. In *Proceedings of the 9th International Conference on Advanced Communication Technology* (pp. 12-14).

Rai, J. K., Negi, A., Wankar, R., & Nayak, K. D. (2009). Using machine learning to characterize L2 cache behavior of programs on multicore processors. In *Proceedings of the International Conference on Artificial Intelligence and Pattern Recognition,* Orlando, FL (pp. 301-306).

Rai, J. K., Negi, A., Wankar, R., & Nayak, K. D. (2010). Performance prediction on multi-core processors. In *Proceedings of the IEEE International Conference on Computational Intelligence, Communication Systems and Networks,* Bhopal, India (pp. 633-637).

Rajagopalan, R., Niu, R., Mohan, C. K., Varshney, P. K., & Drozd, A. L. (2008). Sensor placement algorithms for target localization in sensor networks. In *Proceedings of the IEEE Radar Conference* (pp. 1-6).

Ramamritham, K., & Stankovik, J. A. (1994). Scheduling algorithms and operating support for real-time systems. *Proceedings of the IEEE, 82*(1), 55–67. doi:10.1109/5.259426

Ramamritham, K., Stankovik, J. A., & Shiah, P. F. (1990). Efficient scheduling algorithms for real-time multiprocessor systems. *IEEE Transactions on Parallel and Distributed Systems, 1*(2), 184–190. doi:10.1109/71.80146

Ramazan, B., Engin, I., & Martinez, J. F. (2008). Coordinated management of multiple interacting resources in chip multiprocessors: A machine learning approach. In *Proceedings of the International Symposium on Microarchitecture*, Lake Como, Italy (pp. 318-329).

Ramos, V., Muge, F., & Pina, P. (2002). Self-organized data and image retrieval as a consequence of inter-dynamic synergistic relationships in artificial ant colonies. In *Proceedings of the Second International Conference on Hybrid Intelligent System*, Santiago, Chile (pp. 500-512).

Ranjan, R., Harwood, A., & Buyya, R. (2006). SLA-Based Coordinated Superscheduling scheme for Computational Grids. In *Proceedings of the IEEE International Conference on Cluster Computing* (pp. 1-8).

Rassart, E. (2004). A polynomiality property for Littlewood-Richardson coefficients. *Journal of Combinatorial Theory Series A*, *107*, 161–179. doi:10.1016/j.jcta.2004.04.003

Ratnasamy, S., Karp, B., Yin, L., Yu, F., Estrin, D., Govindan, R., & Shenker, S. (2002). GHT: A geographic hash table for data-centric storage in sensornets. In *Proceedings of the 1st ACM International Workshop on Wireless Sensor Networks and Applications* (pp. 78-87).

Raza, Z., & Vidyarthi, D. P. (2008a). A Fault Tolerant Grid Scheduling Model to Minimize Turnaround Time. In *Proceedings of the International Conference on High Performance Computing, Networking and Communication Systems (HPCNCS'08)*, Orlando, FL.

Raza, Z., & Vidyarthi, D. P. (2008b). *Maximizing Reliability with Task Scheduling in a Computational Grid*. Paper presented at the Second International Conference on Information Systems Technology and Management, Dubai, UAE.

Raza, Z., & Vidyarthi, D. P. (2010a). *Reliability Based Scheduling Model (RSM) for Computational Grids*.

Raza, Z., & Vidyarthi, D. P. (2009a). A Computational Grid Scheduling Model To Minimize Turnaround Using Modified GA. *International Journal of Artificial Intelligence*, *3*(A9), 86–106.

Raza, Z., & Vidyarthi, D. P. (2009b). GA Based Scheduling Model for Computational Grid to Minimize Turnaround Time. *International Journal of Grid and High Performance Computing*, *1*(4), 70–90. doi:10.4018/jghpc.2009070806

Raza, Z., & Vidyarthi, D. P. (2009c). Maximizing Reliability with Task Scheduling In a Computational Grid Using GA. *International Journal of Advancements in Computing Technology*, *1*(2), 40–47.

Raza, Z., & Vidyarthi, D. P. (2010b). A Scheduling Model with Multi-Objective Optimization for Computational Grids using NSGA-II. *International Journal of Applied Evolutionary Computation*, *1*(2), 74–94. doi:10.4018/jaec.2010040104

Redman, T. (1998). The impact of poor data quality on the typical enterprise. *Communications of the ACM*, *41*(2), 79–82. doi:10.1145/269012.269025

Rewini, H., & Lewis, T. G. (1990). Scheduling Parallel Program Tasks onto Arbitrary Target Machines. *Journal of Parallel and Distributed Computing*, *9*, 138–153. doi:10.1016/0743-7315(90)90042-N

Richard, M. Y., Han, L., Kingsum, C., & Hsien-Hsin, S. L. (2006). Constructing a non-linear model with neural networks for workload characterization. In *Proceedings of the International Symposium on Workload Characterization* (pp. 150-159).

Rich, E., & Knight, K. (1993). *Artificial Intelligence*. New Delhi, India: Tata McGraw Hill.

Ristenpart, T., Tromer, E., Shacham, H., & Savage, S. (2009). Hey, you, get off of my cloud: Exploring information leakage in third-party compute clouds. In *Proceedings of the 16th ACM Conference on Computer and Communication Security*, Chicago, IL (pp. 199-212).

Rostami, M., & Nezam Abadi, H. (2006). Modified binary PSO. In *Proceedings of the IEEE 14th International Conference on Electrical Engineering*, Iran.

Rowe, G., & Wright, G. (1999). The Delphi technique as a forecasting tool: issues and analysis. *International Journal of Forecasting*, *15*(4), 353–375. doi:10.1016/S0169-2070(99)00018-7

Rudenko, A., Reiher, P., Popek, G. J., & Kuenning, G. H. (1998). Saving portable computer battery power through remote process execution. *SIGMOBILE Communication Review*, *2*, 19–26. doi:10.1145/584007.584008

Rzadca, K., Tryatram, D., & Wierzbicki, A. (2007). Fair Game-Theoretic Resource Management in Dedicated Grids. In *Proceedings of the IEEE International Conference on Cluster Computing and the Grid (CCGrid'07)* (pp. 343-350).

Saad, E. M., Adawy, M. E., & Habashy, S. M. (2006). Reconfigurable parallel processing system based on a modified ant colony system. In *Proceedings of the 23ʳᵈ National Conference on Radio Science*, Menoufiya, Egypt (pp. 1-11).

Sacerdoti, F., Katz, M., Massie, M., & Culler, D. (2003). Wide area cluster monitoring with Ganglia. In *Proceedings of the IEEE International Conference on Cluster Computing* (pp. 289-298).

Sahni, S. (1999). Models and algorithms for optical and optoelectronic parallel computers. In *Proceedings of the International Symposium on Parallel Algorithms and Networks* (pp. 2-7).

Sahni, S., & Wang, C. (1997). *BPC permutations on the OTIS-mesh optoelectronic computer* (Tech. Rep. No. 97-008). Gainesville, FL: University of Florida.

Saika, D., & Sen, R. K. (1990). Two ranking schemes for efficient computation on the star interconnection network. *IEEE Transactions on Parallel and Distributed Systems*, *96*(7), 321–327.

Saika, D., & Sen, R. K. (1995). Order preserving communication on a star network. *Parallel Computing*, *21*, 1292–1300.

Saini, G. (2005). Application of fuzzy-logic to real-time scheduling. In *Proceedings of the 14ᵗʰ IEEE Real-Time Conference* (pp. 60-63).

Salcedo-Sanz, S., Xu, Y., & Yao, X. (2006). Hybrid meta heuristics algorithms for task assignment in heterogeneous computing systems. *Computers & Operations Research*, *33*, 820–835. doi:10.1016/j.cor.2004.08.010

Saleh, M. A., Deldari, H., & Dorri, B. M. (2008). Balancing load in a computational grid applying adaptive, intelligent colonies of ants. *Informatica*, *32*, 327–335.

Sand, S., Raulefs, R., & Auer, G. (2005). Iterative channel estimation for high mobility broadband MC-CDMA systems. In *Proceedings of the IEEE International Conference on Communications* (pp. 2139-2144).

Sankarasubramaniam, Y., Akyildiz, I. F., & McLaughlin, S. W. (2003, May). Energy efficiency based packet size optimization in wireless sensor networks. In *Proceedings of the First IEEE International Workshop on Sensor Network Protocols and Applications*, Anchorage, AK (pp. 1-8).

Santos, P. P. L. (1996). *Load distribution: A survey* (Tech. Rep. No. UM/DI/TR/96/03). Braga, Portugal: Universidade do Minho.

Sarker, B. K., Tripathi, A. K., Vidyarthi, D. P., Rani, K., & Uehara, K. (2002). Comparative Study of Task Allocation Algorithms based on A* and GA in a Distributed Computing System. In *Proceedings of the Third International Conference on Parallel and Distributed Computing, Applications and Technologies,* Kanazawa, Japan (pp. 116-121).

Sasikumar, P., Vasudevan, S. K., Vivek, C., & Subashri, V. (2009). Heuristic approaches with probabilistic management for node placement in wireless sensor networks. *International Journal of Recent Trends in Engineering*, *2*(4).

Satish, K. M., & Joshi, R. R. (2004). GBTK: A Toolkit for Grid Implementation of BLAST. In *Proceedings of the Seventh International Conference on High Performance Computing and Grid in Asia Pacific Region, (HPCAsia'04)*, Tokyo, Japan (pp. 378-382).

Satyanarayanan, M., Gilbert, B., Toups, M., Tolia, N., Surie, A., & O'Hallaron, D. (2007). Pervasive personal computing in an internet suspend/resume system. *IEEE Internet Computing*, *11*(2), 16–25. doi:10.1109/MIC.2007.46

Schehrer, R. G. (1999, September). Investigation of networks with rearrangement by means of simple methods. In *Proceedings of the Sixth German-Russian Seminar on Flow Control and Integrated Communication Systems*, Dortmund, Germany.

Schehrer, R. G. (2000, October 27). On a class of non-blocking networks with repacking. In *Proceedings of the 6ᵗʰ International Informatization Forum on Informational Networks and Systems*, St. Petersburg, Russia (p. 6077).

Schehrer, R. G. (2001, October 24). On rearrangeable networks with at most one reswitching. In *Proceedings of the Seventh International Conference on Information Networks, Systems and Technologies*, Minsk, Russia.

Schehrer, R. G. (2007). On non-blocking multi-stage switching networks with rearrangement or repacking. *International Journal of Electronics and Communications*, 423-432.

Schmidt, A., Kuntze, N., & Kasper, M. (2008). On the deployment of mobile trusted modules. In *Proceedings of the Wireless Communications and Networking Conference* (pp. 3169-3174).

Schmidt, H. A., Strimmer, K., Vingron, M., & von Haeseler, A. (2002). TREE-PUZZLE: maximum likelihood phylogenetic analysis using quartets and parallel computing. *Bioinformatics (Oxford, England)*, *18*(3), 502–504. doi:10.1093/bioinformatics/18.3.502

Seet, B.-C., Pan, Y., Hsu, W.-J., & Lau, C.-T. (2005). Multi-home region location service for wireless ad hoc networks: An adaptive demand-driven approach. In *Proceedings of the 2nd IEEE Annual Conference on Wireless On-demand Network Systems and Services* (pp. 258-263).

Sevinc, P. E., Strasser, M., & Basin, D. (2007). Securing the distribution and storage of secrets with trusted platform modules. In *Proceedings of the First IFIP TC6/WG8.8/WG11.2 International Conference on Information Security Theory and Practices: Smart Cards, Mobile and Ubiquitous Computing Systems* (pp. 53-66).

Shah, A., & Kotecha, K. (2010). Dynamic scheduling algorithm for real-time operating system using ACO. In *Proceedings of the International Conference on Computing Intelligence and Communication Networks* (pp. 617-621).

Shah, R., Veeravalli, B., & Misra, M. (2007). On the design of adaptive and decentralized load balancing algorithms with load estimation for computational grid environments. *IEEE Transactions on Parallel and Distributed Systems*, *18*(12), 1675–1685. doi:10.1109/TPDS.2007.1115

Sharma, N., & Papadias, C. (2003). Improved quasi-orthogonal codes through constellation rotation. *IEEE Transactions on Communications*, *51*(3), 332–335. doi:10.1109/TCOMM.2003.809753

She, H., Lu, Z., Jantsch, A., Zhou, D., & Zheng, L.-R. (2009 April). Analytical evaluation of retransmission schemes in wireless sensor networks. In *Proceedings of the IEEE 69th Vehicular Technology Conference*, Barcelona, Spain (pp. 1-5).

Shevade, S. K., Keerthi, S. S., Bhattacharyya, C., & Murthy, K. R. K. (1999). *Improvements to SMO algorithm for SVM regression* (Tech. Rep. No. CD-99-16). Singapore: Control Division Department of Mechanical and Production Engineering.

Shiloach, Y., & Vishkin, U. (1982). An o(log n) parallel connectivity algorithm. *Journal of Algorithms*, *3*, 57–67. doi:10.1016/0196-6774(82)90008-6

Sih, D. C., & Lee, E. A. (1993). A Compile-Time Scheduling heuristic for Interconnection-Constrained Heterogeneous Processor Architectures. *IEEE Transactions on Parallel and Distributed Systems*, *4*(2), 175–186. doi:10.1109/71.207593

Silberschatz, A., Galvin, P., & Gagne, G. (2005). *Operating System Concepts*. New York, NY: John Wiley & Sons.

Sklar, B. (1997). Rayleigh fading channels in mobile digital communication systems part I: Characterization. *IEEE Communications Magazine*, *35*(7), 90–100. doi:10.1109/35.601747

Smith, J., & Nair, R. (2005). *Virtual machines: Versatile platforms for systems and processes*. San Francisco, CA: Morgan Kaufmann.

Smola, A. J., & Scholkopf, B. (1998). A tutorial on support vector regression. *Statistics and Computing*, *14*(3), 199–222. doi:10.1023/B:STCO.0000035301.49549.88

Sohma, S., Watanabe, T., Ooba, N., Itoh, M., Shibata, T., & Takahashi, H. (2006, September). Silica-based PLC type 32×32 optical matrix switch. In *Proceedings of the European Conference on Optical Communications* (pp. 24-28).

SPEC. (2006). *Standard performance evaluation corporation*. Retrieved from http://www.spec.org/cpu2006/

Steinberg, D., & Cheshire, S. (2005). *Zero configuration networking: The definitive guide*. Sebastopol, CA: O'Reilly Media.

Sterling, T. L., Salmon, J., Backer, D. J., & Savarese, D. F. (1999). *How to Build a Beowulf: A Guide to the Implementation and Application of PC Clusters.* Cambridge, MA: MIT Press.

Stewart, C. A., Hart, D., Berry, D. K., Olsen, G. J., Wernert, E. A., & Fischer, W. (2001). *Parallel implementation and performance of fastDNAml – a program for maximum likelihood phylogenetic inference.* Retrieved from http://www.sc2001.org/papers/pap.pap191.pdf

Stocker, G., Rieder, D., & Trajanoski, Z. (2004). Cluster-Control: A Web Interface for Distributing and Monitoring Bioinformatics Applications on a Linux Cluster. *Bioinformatics (Oxford, England)*, *20*(5), 805–807. doi:10.1093/bioinformatics/bth014

Stojmenovic, I. (1999). *A scalable quorum based location update scheme for routing in ad hoc wireless network* (Tech. Rep. No. TR-99-09). Ottawa, ON, Canada: University of Ottawa.

Stojmenovic, I., Liu, D., & Jia, X. (2008). A scalable quorum based location service in ad hoc and sensor networks. *International Journal of Communication Networks and Distributed Systems*, *1*(1), 71–94. doi:10.1504/IJCNDS.2008.017205

Sturn, A., Mlecnik, B., Pieler, R., Rainer, J., Truskaller, T., & Trajanoski, Z. (2003). Client-Server Environment for High-Performance Gene Expression Data Analysis. *Bioinformatics (Oxford, England)*, *19*(6), 772–773. doi:10.1093/bioinformatics/btg074

Sun Microsystems Inc. (2009). *Introduction to cloud computing architecture.* Retrieved from http://webobjects.cdw.com/webobjects/media/pdf/Sun_CloudComputing.pdf

Sundararajan, N., & Saratchandran, P. (1998). *Parallel Architectures for Artificial Neural Networks-Paradigms and Implementation.* Los Alamitos, CA: IEEE Computer Society Press.

Suzumura, T., Matsuoka, S., Nakada, H., & Casanova, H. (2004). GridSpeed: A Web-based Grid Portal Generation Server. In *Proceedings of the Seventh International Conference on High Performance Computing and Grid in Asia Pacific Region, (HPCAsia '04),* Tokyo, Japan (pp. 26-33).

Taddia, C., & Mazzini, G. (2004, September). On the retransmission methods in wireless sensor networks. In *Proceedings of the IEEE 60th Vehicular Technology Conference,* Los Angeles, CA (Vol. 6).

Takefuji, Y. (1992). *Neural Network Parallel Computing.* Norwell, MA: Kluwer Academic.

Takefusa, A., Matsuoka, S., Aida, K., Nakada, H., & Nagashima, U. (1999). Overview of a performance evaluation system for global computing scheduling algorithms. In *Proceedings of the Eighth IEEE International Symposium on High Performance Distributed Computing.*

Tanenbaum, A. S., & van Steen, M. (2001). *Distributed systems: Principles and paradigms.* Upper Saddle River, NJ: Prentice Hall.

Tarokh, V., Jafarkhani, H., & Calderbank, A. (1999). Space–time block codes from orthogonal designs. *IEEE Transactions on Information Theory*, *45*, 1456–1467. doi:10.1109/18.771146

Tarokh, V., Seshadri, N., & Calderbank, A. (1998). Space–time codes for high data rate wireless communication: Performance criterion and code construction. *IEEE Transactions on Information Theory*, *44*, 744–765. doi:10.1109/18.661517

Tarricone, L., & Esposito, A. (2005). *Grid Computing for Electromagnetics.* Norwood, MA: Artech House.

Taylor, I. J., & Harrison, A. (2009). *From P2P and Grids to Services on the Web- Evolving Distributed Communities* (2nd ed.). New York, NY: Springer.

TechCrunch. (2010). *100,000 android applications submitted to date, AndroLib claims.* Retrieved from http://techcrunch.com/2010/07/30/android-market-100000/

Tejada, S., Knoblock, C., & Minton, S. (2002). Learning domain-independent string transformation for high accuracy object identification. In *Proceedings of the Conference on Very Large Data Bases* (pp. 610-621).

Tejada, S., Knoblock, C., & Minton, S. (2001). Learning object identification rules for information extraction. *Information Systems*, *26*(8), 607–633. doi:10.1016/S0306-4379(01)00042-4

Thain, D., & Livny, M. (2003). Condor and the grid. In Berman, F., Hey, A. J. G., & Fox, G. (Eds.), *Grid computing: Making the global infrastructure a reality*. New York, NY: John Wiley & Sons.

The National Institute of Standards and Technology. (2008). *NIST 800-39: Managing risk from information systems, an organization perspective*. Retrieved from http://www.nist.gov/index.html

Tian, G.-Z., & Yu, J. (2008). Grid Workflow Scheduling Based on the Resource Combination Reliability. In *Proceedings of the Fourth International Conference on Natural Computing* (Vol. 1, pp. 207-211).

Tirkkonen, O. (2001). Optimizing space–time block codes by constellation rotations. In *Proceedings of the Finnish Wireless Communications Workshop*.

Tirkkonen, O., Boariu, A., & Hottinen, A. (2000). Minimal nonorthogonality rate 1 space-time block code for 3+ Tx antennas. In *Proceedings of the IEEE 6th International Symposium on Spread-Spectrum Techniques and Applications* (pp. 429-432).

Topcuoglu, H., Hariri, S., & Wu, M. Y. (2002). Performance effective and low-complexity task scheduling for heterogeneous computing. *IEEE Transactions on Parallel and Distributed Systems, 13*, 262–274. doi:10.1109/71.993206

Trelles, O., Andrade, M. A., Valencia, A., Zapata, E. L., & Carazo, J. M. (1998). Computational Space Reduction and Parallelization of a new Clustering Approach for Large Groups of Sequences. *Bioinformatics (Oxford, England), 14*(5), 439–451. doi:10.1093/bioinformatics/14.5.439

Tripathi, A. K., Sarker, B. K., Kumar, N., & Vidyarthi, D. P. (2000). A GA Based Multiple Task Allocation Considering Load. *International Journal of High Speed Computing, 11*(4), 203–214. doi:10.1142/S0129053300000187

Trippi, R., & Turban, E. (1993). *Neural Networks in Finance and Investing*. Chicago, IL: Probus.

Tsai, M.-J., & Hung, Y.-K. (2009). Distributed computing power service coordination based on peer-to-peer grids architecture. *International Journal of Expert Systems with Applications, 36*(2), 3101–3118. doi:10.1016/j.eswa.2008.01.050

Tseng, C.-C., & Chen, K.-C. (2004, March). Power efficient topology control in wireless ad hoc networks. In *Proceedings of the IEEE Wireless Communications and Networking Conference*, Atlanta, GA (Vol. 1).

Tseng, L., Chin, Y., & Wang, S. (2009). A minimized makespan scheduler with multiple factors for Grid computing systems. *International Journal of Expert Systems with Applications, 36*(8), 11118–11130. doi:10.1016/j.eswa.2009.02.071

Tseng, L., Chin, Y., & Wang, S. (2009). The anatomy study of high performance task scheduling algorithm for Grid computing system. *International Journal of Computer Standards & Interfaces, 31*(4), 713–722. doi:10.1016/j.csi.2008.09.017

T-Systems. (2010). *White paper security in the cloud*. Frankfurt, Germany: T-Systems International GmbH.

Turneo, A., Pilato, C., Ferrandi, F., Sciuto, D., & Lanzi, P. L. (2008). Ant colony optimization for mapping and scheduling in heterogeneous multiprocessor systems. In *Proceedings of the International Conference on Embedded Computer Systems: Architectures, Modeling and Simulation* (pp. 142-149).

Uçar, B., Aykanat, C., Kaya, K., & Ikinci, M. (2006). Task assignment in heterogeneous computing systems. *Journal of Parallel and Distributed Computing, 66*, 32–46.

Ullman, J. D. (1973). Polynomial complete scheduling problems. *Operating Systems Review, 7*(4), 96–101. doi:10.1145/957195.808055

Usop, M., Abdullah, A., & Abidin, A. (2009). Performance evaluation of AODV, DSDV & DSR routing protocol in grid environment. *International Journal of Computer Science and Network Security, 9*(7), 261–268.

Venugopal, S., Buyya, R., & Ramamohanarao, K. (2006). A taxonomy of data grids for distributed data sharing, management, and processing. *ACM Computing Surveys, 38*(1). doi:10.1145/1132952.1132955

Vidyarthi, D. P., Tripathi, A. K., Sarker, B. K., & Rani, K. (2003). Comparative Study of Two GA based Task Allocation Models in Distributed Computing System. In *Proceedings of the Fourth International Conference on Parallel and Distributed Computing, Applications and Technologies*, Chengdu, China.

Vidyarthi, D. P., Sarker, B. K., Tripathi, A. K., & Yang, L. T. (2009). *Scheduling in distributed computing systems analysis, design and models*. New York, NY: Springer. doi:10.1007/978-0-387-74483-4

Vidyarthi, D. P., & Tripathi, A. K. (2001). Maximizing Reliability of Distributed Computing System with Task Allocation using Simple Genetic Algorithm. *Journal of Systems Architecture*, *47*(6). doi:10.1016/S1383-7621(01)00013-3

Vidyarthi, D. P., Tripathi, A. K., & Sarker, B. K. (2001). Allocation Aspects in Distributed Computing Systems. *IETE Technical Review*, *18*, 449–454.

Vidyarthi, D. P., Tripathi, A. K., Sarker, B. K., & Yang, L. T. (2005). Performance Study of Reliability Maximization and Turnaround Minimization with GA based Task Allocation in DCS. In Yang, L. T., & Guo, M. (Eds.), *Scheduling and Resource Management, High Performance Computing: Paradigm and Infrastructure* (pp. 349–360). New York, NY: John Wiley & Sons.

Waldspurger, C., Hogg, T., Huberman, B., Kephart, O., & Stornetta, S. (1992). Spawn: A Distributed Computational Economy. *IEEE Transactions on Software Engineering*, *18*, 103–177. doi:10.1109/32.121753

Walpole, R. E., Myers, R. H., Myers, S. L., & Ye, K. (2007). *Probability and statistics for engineer and scientists* (8th ed., pp. 413–467). Delhi, India: Pearson Education.

Wang, C., & Sahni, S. (2002). Computational geometry on the OTIS-Mesh optoelectronic computer. In *Proceedings of the International Conference on Parallel Processing* (pp. 501 -507).

Wang, G., Cao, G., & La Porta, T. (2004). Proxy-based sensor deployment for mobile sensor networks. In *Proceedings of the 1st IEEE International Conference on Mobile Ad-hoc and Sensor Systems* (pp. 493-502).

Wang, Y., & Witten, I. (1997). Inducing model trees for continuous classes. In *Proceedings of the 9th European Conference on Machine Learning*.

Wang, C., & Sahni, S. (2000). Image processing on the OTIS-mesh optoelectronic computer. *IEEE Transactions on Parallel and Distributed Systems*, *11*(2), 97–109. doi:10.1109/71.841747

Wang, C., & Sahni, S. (2001). Matrix multiplications on the OTIS-mesh optoelectronic computer. *IEEE Transactions on Computers*, *40*(7), 635–646. doi:10.1109/12.936231

Wang, G., Cao, G., & La Porta, T. (2006). Movement-assisted sensor deployment. *IEEE Transactions on Mobile Computing*, *5*(6). doi:10.1109/TMC.2006.80

Weifeng, S., & Xiang-Gen, X. (2004). Signal constellations for quasi- orthogonal space–time block codes with full diversity. *IEEE Transactions on Information Theory*, *50*(10), 2331–2347. doi:10.1109/TIT.2004.834740

Weigend, A. S., Abu-Mostafa, Y. S., & Refenes, A. P. N. (1997). *Decision Technologies for Financial Engineering*. New York, NY: World Scientific.

White, H. (1990). Economic prediction using neural networks: the case of IBM daily stock returns. In *Proceedings of the IEEE International Conference on Neural Networks* (pp. 451-458).

Wilander, J., & Kamkar, M. (2003). A comparison of publicly available tools for dynamic buffer overflow prevention. In *Proceedings of the Network and Distributed System Security Symposium* (pp. 4-15).

Wilkinson, B., & Allen, M. (2004). *Parallel Programming: Techniques and Applications Using Networked Workstations and Parallel Computers* (2nd ed.). Upper Saddle River, NJ: Prentice Hall.

Winkler, K. (2010). *Green clouds*. Retrieved from http://interconnectedworld.typepad.com/my_weblog/2009/10/green-clouds.html

Witten, I. H., & Frank, E. (2005). *Data mining: Practical machine learning tools and techniques* (2nd ed.). San Francisco, CA: Morgan Kaufmann.

Wolski, R., Spring, N., & Hayes, J. (1999). The Network Weather Service: A Distributed Resource Performance Forecasting Service for Metacomputing. *International Journal of Future Generation Computing Systems*, *15*(5-6), 757–768. doi:10.1016/S0167-739X(99)00025-4

Woo, J., & Sahni, S. (1989). Hypercube computing: Connected components. *The Journal of Supercomputing*, *3*, 209–234. doi:10.1007/BF00127829

Woo, S.-C. M., & Singh, S. (2001). Scalable routing protocol for ad hoc networks. *Wireless Networks*, *7*(5), 513–529. doi:10.1023/A:1016726711167

Wroe, C., Goble, C., Greenwood, M., Lord, P., Miles, S., & Papay, J. (2004). Automating experiments using semantic data on a bioinformatics grid. *IEEE Intelligent Systems*, *19*(1), 48–55. doi:10.1109/MIS.2004.1265885

Wu, C., & Feng, T. (1980). On a class of multistage interconnection networks. *IEEE Transactions on Computers*, *29*(8), 694–702. doi:10.1109/TC.1980.1675651

Wu, M., & Gajski, D. (1990). Hyprotocol: A Programming Aid for Message Passing Systems. *IEEE Transactions on Parallel and Distributed Systems*, *1*, 330–334. doi:10.1109/71.80160

Wu, X., Cho, J., Auriol, B. J. D., & Lee, S. (2007). Mobility-assisted relocation for self-deployment in wireless sensor networks. *IEICE Transactions on Communications*, *90*(8), 2056–2069. doi:10.1093/ietcom/e90-b.8.2056

Xie, Y., & Loh, G. H. (2008). Dynamic classification of program memory behaviors in CMPs. In *Proceedings of the 2nd Workshop on Chip Multiprocessor Memory Systems and Interconnects in conjunction with the 35th International Symposium on Computer Architecture*, Beijing, China.

Xu, C., Chen, X., Dick, R. P., & Mao, Z. M. (2010). Cache contention and application performance prediction for multi-core systems. In *Proceedings of the IEEE International Symposium on Performance Analysis of Systems and Software*, White Plains, NY (pp. 76-86).

Yadav, N. S., & Yadav, R. P. (2007). Performance comparison and analysis of table-driven and on-demand routing protocols for mobile ad hoc networks. *International Journal of Information Technology*, *4*(2), 101–109.

Yagoubi, B., & Meddeber, M. (2010). Distributed load balancing model for grid computing. *Revue Africaine de la Recherche en Informatique et Mathématiques Appliquées*, *12*, 43–60.

Yan, H., Shen, X., Li, X., & Wu, M. (2005). An Improved Ant Algorithm for Job Scheduling in Grid Computing. In *Proceedings of the IEEE International Conference on Machine Learning and Cybernetics* (pp. 2957-2961).

Yang, C.-T., Hsiung, Y.-C., & Kan, H.-C. (2005a, June 27-30). Implementation of a Biology Data Translation System on Grid Environments. In *Proceedings of the 3rd International Conference on Information Technology: Research and Education (ITRE 05)*, Hsinchu, Taiwan.

Yang, C.-T., Hsiung, Y.-C., & Kan, H.-C. (2005b, March 28-30). Implementation and Evaluation of a Java Based Computational Grid for Bioinformatics Applications. In *Proceedings of the International Conference on Advanced Information Networking and Applications (AINA 2005)*, Taipei, Taiwan (Vol. 1, pp. 298-303).

Yang, C.-T., Hung, C.-C., & Soong, C.-C. (2001). Parallel Computing on Low-Cost PC-Based SMPs Clusters. In *Proceedings of the 2001 International Conference on Parallel and Distributed Computing, Applications, and Techniques (PDCAT 2001)*, Taipei, Taiwan (pp. 149-156).

Yang, C.-T., Kuo, Y.-L., & Lai, C.-L. (2004, March 28-31). Design and Implementation of a Computational Grid for Bioinformatics. In *Proceedings of the 2004 IEEE International Conference on e-Technology, e-Commerce and e-Service (EEE 04)*, Taipei, Taiwan (pp. 448-451).

Yang, C.-T., Kuo, Y.-L., Li, K.-C., & Gaudiot, J.-L. (2004, December 27-30). On Design of Cluster and Grid Computing Environments for Bioinformatics Applications. In A. Sen, N. Das, S. K. Das, et al. (Eds.), *Distributed Computing: IWDC 2004: 6th International Workshop*, Kolkata, India (LNCS 3326, pp. 82-87).

Yanga, J., Su, X., & Pin, X. (2008). A module design of rearrange-able nonblocking double omega optical network using binary optics elements. *Optics & Laser Technology*, *40*(5).

Yang, C.-T., Kuo, Y.-L., & Lai, C.-L. (2005). Designing Computing Platform for BioGrid. *International Journal of Computer Applications in Technology*, *22*(1), 3–13. doi:10.1504/IJCAT.2005.006798

Yang, S., Li, M., & Wu, J. (2007). Scan-based movement-assisted sensor deployment methods in wireless sensor networks. *IEEE Transactions on Parallel and Distributed Systems*, *18*(8).

Yang, T., & Gerasoulis, A. (1994). DSC: Scheduling parallel tasks on an unbounded number of processors. *IEEE Transactions on Parallel and Distributed Systems*, 5(9), 951–967. doi:10.1109/71.308533

Yan, K. Q., Wang, S. C., Chang, C. P., & Lin, J. S. (2007). A hybrid load balancing policy underlying grid computing environment. *Computer Standards & Interfaces*, 29, 161–173. doi:10.1016/j.csi.2006.03.003

Yayla, G., Marchand, P., & Esener, S. (1998). Speed and energy analysis of digital interconnections: Comparison of on-chip, off-chip, and free-space technologies. *Applied Optics*, 37(2), 205–227. doi:10.1364/AO.37.000205

Yeh, Y., & Feng, T. (1992). On a class of rearrangeable networks. *IEEE Transactions on Computers*, 41(11).

Yoon, Y., & Swales, G. (1993). A comparison of discriminate analysis vs. artificial neural network. *Operational Research Society*, 1, 51–60.

Yoshida, M., & Kojima, K. (2010). Design methodologies of workload management through code migration in distributed desktop computing grids. In *Proceedings of the International Symposium on Frontiers of Parallel and Distributed Computing* (pp. 100-111).

Yoshida, M., & Sakamoto, K. (2007). Code migration control in large scale loosely coupled distributed systems. In *Proceedings of the 4th International Conference on Mobile Technology, Applications and Systems* (pp. 32-38).

Yoshida, M., & Sakamoto, K. (2008). Performance comparison of load balancing algorithms through code migration in distributed desktop computing grids. In *Proceedings of the 3rd IEEE Asia Pacific Services Computing Conference* (pp. 781-788).

Zane, F., Marchand, P., Paturi, R., & Esener, S. (2000). Scalable network architecture using the optical transpose interconnection system (OTIS). *Journal of Parallel and Distributed Computing*, 60, 521–538. doi:10.1006/jpdc.2000.1627

Zeng, X., Bagrodia, R., & Gerla, M. (1998). Glomosim: A library for parallel simulation of large scale wireless networks. *ACM SIGSIM*, 28(1), 154–161. doi:10.1145/278009.278027

Zhang, S., Zhang, S., Chen, S., & Huo, X. (2010). Cloud computing research and development trend. In *Proceedings of the Second International Conference on Future Networks* (pp. 93-97).

Zheng, F., & Burr, A. (2003). Receiver design for orthogonal space-time block coding for four transmit antennas over time-selective fading channels. In. *Proceedings of the IEEE Conference on Global Telecommunications*, 1, 128–132.

Zheng, L., & Tse, D. (2003). Diversity and multiplexing: A fundamental tradeoff in multiple-antenna channels. *IEEE Transactions on Information Theory*, 49(5), 1073–1096. doi:10.1109/TIT.2003.810646

Zhou, D., & Lo, V. (2005). Wave Scheduler: Scheduling for Fast Turnaround Time in Peer-based Desktop Grid Systems. In *Proceedings of the 11th International Workshop on Job Scheduling Strategies for Parallel Processing* (pp. 194-218).

Zhou, D., & Lo, V. (2006). WaveGrid: A scalable fast-turnaround heterogeneous peer-based desktop grid system. In *Proceedings of the 20th IEEE International Symposium on Parallel and Distributed Processing* (p. 1-10).

Zhuravlev, S., Blagodurov, S., & Fedorova, A. (2010). Addressing shared resource contention in multicore processors via scheduling. In *Proceedings of the 15th International Conference on Architectural Support for Programming Languages and Operating Systems*, Pittsburgh, PA (pp. 129-142).

Zomaya, A. Y., & Teh, Y. H. (2001). Observations on Using Genetic Algorithms for Dynamic Load-Balancing. *Proceedings of IEEE Transactions on Parallel and Distributed Systems*, 12(9), 899–911. doi:10.1109/71.954620

Zomaya, A. Y., & Wright, M. (2002). Observation on Using Genetic Algorithms for Channel Allocation in Mobile Computing. *IEEE Transactions on Parallel and Distributed Systems*, 13(9), 948–962. doi:10.1109/TPDS.2002.1036068

Zou, Y., & Chakrabarty, K. (2004). Sensor deployment and target localization in distributed sensor networks. *IEEE Transactions on Embedded Computer Systems, 3*(1).

About the Contributors

Emmanuel Udoh is a Professor of Computer Science at the Indiana Institute of Technology, USA. He received his PhD degree in Information Technology and Master of Business Administration (MBA) degree from Capella University, USA. Moreover, he is also a PhD holder in Geology from the University of Erlangen, Germany.

* * *

Amrit Kumar Agrawal did B.Sc. in 2000, B.Tech. (CSE) in 2005 from the Institute of Engineering & Technology, Purvanchal University, Jaunpur, India, and M.Tech. (CSE) in 2010 from Jaypee University of Information Technology, Solan, India. He served as a Lecturer in the Dept. of CSE in IET, Purvachal University from July 2006 to June 2008. Since July 2010 he is working as an Assistant Professor in the Dept. of CSE in Apollo Institute of Technology, Kanpur, India.

Sarita S. Bhadauria was born in 1961 in Gwalior, Madhya Pradesh, India, received B.E. degree in Electronics Engineering from Madhav Institute of Technology& Science, Gwalior, Madhya Pradesh, India in 1985, M.Tech. degree in Computer Science & Tech. from University of Roorkee, Roorkee, Uttar Pradesh, India, in 1993 and Ph.D. in Computer Science and Engineering from Rajiv Gandhi Technological University, Bhopal, Madhya Pradesh, India. She is currently working as Professor in Electronics Engineering Department at Madhav Institue of Technology, Gwalior, Rajiv Gandhi Technological University, Bhopal, M.P., India. She is life member of Institution of Electronics and Telecommunication Engineers (IETE), India, life member of Computer Society of India (CSI), India, life Member of the Indian Society for Technical Education (ISTE), India and associate member of the Institution of Engineers (IE), India. Her research interests are Image Processing, Networking.

Amitabha Chakrabarty received his B.Sc in Computer Science and Technology and M.Sc in Computer Science and Engineering from University of Rajshahi, Bangladesh. He received another M.Sc in Telecommunication engineering from Independent University, Bangladesh. Currently, he is perusing his PhD at School of Electronic Engineering, Dublin City University, Ireland. His research interests include switching theory, wireless networking and handover management in cellular networks.

Pranay Chaudhuri is currently a Professor of Computer Science and Engineering at Jaypee University of Information Technology, Solan, India. Prior to joining Jaypee University of Information Technology, Professor Chaudhuri was holding a Chair Professorship in Computer Science at the University of the West Indies, Cave Hill Campus, Barbados (2000-2009). Professor Chaudhuri has also held faculty positions at the Indian Institute of Technology at Kharagpur, James Cook University of North Queensland, University of New South Wales and Kuwait University. Professor Chaudhuri's research interests include Parallel and Distributed Computing, Grid Computing, Self-stabilization and Algorithmic Graph Theory. In these areas, he has extensively published in leading international journals and conference proceedings. He is also the author of a book titled, *Parallel Algorithms: Design and Analysis* (Prentice-Hall, Australia, 1992). Professor Chaudhuri has been involved with numerous international conferences in various capacities across the globe and most recently served as General Chair of the IEEE Sponsored 2010 1st International Conference on Parallel, Distributed and Grid Computing (PDGC-2010), organized during 28-30 October 2010 in India.

Martin Collier (S'87–M'93) received the B.Eng. and M.Eng. degrees in electronic engineering from the National Institute for Higher Education, Dublin, Ireland, in 1986 and 1988, respectively, and the Ph.D. degree from Dublin City University (DCU), Dublin, Ireland, in 1993. Currently, he is a Senior Lecturer with DCU, where he runs the Switching and Systems Laboratory. He established the Research Institute for Networks and Communications Engineering (RINCE), DCU, in 1999. His research interests include programmable networks, quality of service, and advanced switching techniques.

K. S. Dasgupta received his B.E. in Electronics & Telecommunications and his Master's degree in Computer Science from Jadavpur University in *1st class with Honours in 1972 and 1973 respectively.* He obtained his Ph.D. in Electrical Engineering from Indian Institute of Technology Bombay in 1990. Dr. K S Dasgupta joined Space Applications Centre in 1974 and contributed significantly in the field of Image Processing and Satellite Communications, which honored him with a recognition of Outstanding/Distinguished Scientist. Before joining as Director of Indian Institute of Space Technology in December, 2010, he was the Deputy Director of SATCOM and Navigation Payload Area (SNPA) and Former Director-DECU (Development & Educational Communication Unit) of Indian Space Research Organization (ISRO). Dr. Dasgupta is senior member of IEEE, CSI and Fellow IETE. He has been awarded for excellent performance in year 2009 by ISRO.

Don Hayes received a BS in Computer Engineering in 2004 and an MS in Computer Science in 2009, both from the University of Arkansas. Since receiving his undergrad in 2004, he has worked as a software engineer for a number of companies ranging from university start-ups to Fortune 500 corporations. Currently he works as a software engineer at a major online retailer in Seattle. His research interests include distributed and cloud computing, service-oriented architecture, and computational complexity.

Kazumine Kojima received the B.S. and M.S. degrees in information and computer engineering from Okayama University of Science in 2009 and 2011, respectively. His research interests include grid computing and P2P computing. He is a member of the IPSJ.

Nikhil J. Kothari received the degree in electronics engineering from Sardar Patel University, Vallabh Vidyanagar, Gujarat in 1985, the M.E. degree from the Gujarat University, Gujarat, in 1994, and the Ph.D. degree from Dharmsinh Desai University, Gujarat, in 2010. He joined the Department of Electronics & Communication Engineering, Dharmsinh Desai University, Nadiad, as a Lecturer in 1989, and has been a Professor since 2001. His current research interests are in wireless networks, satellite networks, and Internet Congestion Control.

Wing Ning Li received the B.S. degree from the University of Iowa in 1982 and the M.S and Ph.D. degrees from the University of Minnesota in 1985 and 1989 respectively, all in computer science. Presently he is Professor of Computer Science and Computer Engineering Department at the University of Arkansas. His research interests include design and analysis of algorithms, grid and cloud computing, design automation, and combinatorial optimization.

Atul Negi, is working as Associate Professor at Dept. of Computer and Information Sciences at University of Hyderabad, India. Formerly he was Director at Prestige Institute of Engineering and Science at Indore, India. He has about 20 years of research and teaching experience. Dr. Negi took his Doctorate from the University of Hyderabad and his M.Sc.(Engg.) from the Indian Institute of Science, Bangalore, India. He is a graduate with distinction in Electronics and Communication Engineering from the Osmania University Hyderabad, India. He has varied research interests in Pattern Recognition and its applications to Systems Security, and Systems Research and has authored over 50 publications. Tejal N. Parmar received the degree in Electronics Engineering from Sardar Patel University, Vallabh Vidyanagar, Gujarat, India, in 2006, the M.E. degree in Electronics & Communication Systems from Dharmsinh Desai University, Nadiad, and Gujarat in 2010. From 2006 to 2008, she was Lecturer in Parul Institute of Engineering & Technology, Waghodia, Vadodara, Gujarat. Her current research interests include Space time coding for MIMO- OFDM.

Rashedur M. Rahman received his Ph.D. Degree in Computer Science from University of Calgary, Canada in November, 2007. He had his M.Sc. degree from University of Manitoba, Canada in 2002 and Bachelor degree from Bangladesh University of Engineering and Technology (BUET) in 2000 respectively. He is currently working as an Assistant Professor in North South University, Dhaka, Bangladesh. He has authored more than 30 international journal and peer reviewed conference papers in the area of parallel, distributed, grid computing and knowledge and data engineering. He has been serving as reviewers for leading journals and conferences in the area of high performance computing, data mining and knowledge engineering. He has been serving as technical committee members of several conferences. His current research interest is in data mining especially on financial, educational and medical surveillance data, data replication on Grid, and application of fuzzy logic for grid resource and replica selection.

Jitendra Kumar Rai is M.Tech. in Computer Science from Department of Computer Science, University of Pune, India. He is a graduate in Chemical Engineering, with Gold Medal from Government Engineering College, Ujjain, India. He worked on systems software especially operating systems. He is currently working as scientist at Advanced Numerical Research and Analysis Group (ANURAG), Hyderabad, India. He is also a Ph.D. student at Department of Computer and Information Sciences, University of Hyderabad,India. His research interests include processor architecture, operating systems, computer system modeling, performance and power analysis, prediction techniques and tools. Zahid Raza is currently an Assistant Professor in the School of Computer and Systems Sciences, Jawaharlal Nehru University, India. He has a Master degree in Electronics as well as Computer Science and is pursuing Ph.D. from Jawaharlal Nehru University. Prior to joining Jawaharlal Nehru University, he served as a Lecturer in Banasthali Vidyapith University, Rajasthan, India. His research interest is in the area of Grid Computing and has proposed a few models for job scheduling in a Computational Grid. He is a member of IEEE.

Ahmed Ibrahim Saleh received his B.Sc. in the department of Computer Engineering and Systems Department in the faculty of Engineering in Mansoura university, with general grade Excellent. He got the master degree in the area of Mobile agents. He has a good knowledge in networks Hardware and Software. Currently he is working as a Teacher at the faculty of Engineering, Mansoura University, Egypt. His interests are (Programming Languages, Networks and System Administration, and Database).

Hardip Shah received the degree in Electronics, from Sardar Patel University, Vallabh Vidhyanagar,Gujarat, India in 1997, the M.E. degree in Electronics & Communication Systems from Dharmsinh Desai University, Nadiad, Gujarat, in 2004 and in the same university he is currently working toward the Ph.D. degree. Since 2000, he is with Dharmsinh Desai University, where he is Associate Professor at present. His research interests are signal processing for wireless communications.

Laxmi Shrivastava was born in 1970 in Mathura, Uttar Pradesh, India, received B.Tech. degree in Electronics and Communication Engineering from Govind Ballabh Pant University of Agriculture and Technology, Pantnagar, Nainital, India in 1993, M.Tech. degree in Electronics and Comuunication (Microwave Engineering) from Madhav Institue of Technology, Gwalior, Rajiv Gandhi Prodyogiki Vishwavidyala, Bhopal, M. P., India in 2006 and pursuing Ph.D. from the same university. She is currently working as Lecturer(Selection Grade) in Electronics Engineering Department at Madhav Institue of Technology, Gwalior, Rajiv Gandhi Prodyogiki Vishwavidyala, Bhopal, M.P., India. She is associate member of Institution of Electronics and Telecommunication Engineers (IETE), India and life member of Computer Society of India (CSI), India. Her research interests are development of algorithm for congestion in Mobile Adhoc Networks and security of these networks.

Parimala Thulasiraman received B.Eng. (Honors) and M.A.Sc. degrees in Computer Engineering from Concordia University, Montreal, Canada and obtained her Ph.D. from University of Delaware, Newark, DE, USA after finishing most of her formalities in McGill University, Montreal, Canada. She is now an Associate Professor with the Department of Computer Science, University of Manitoba, Winnipeg, MB, Canada. The focus of her research is on the design, development, implementation and performance evaluation of scalable parallel algorithms for multicore heterogeneous processors in computational science applications such as computational biology, computational finance, medical imaging or computational medicine on advanced architectures. Over the past few years, she has moved towards developing distributed algorithms for wireless networks using nature inspired algorithms such as Ant Colony Optimization techniques. She has published several papers in the above areas in leading journals and conferences and has graduated many students. Parimala has organized conferences as local chair, program chair and tutorial chair. She has been serving as a reviewer and program committee member for many conferences. She has also been a reviewer for many leading journals. She is a member of the ACM and IEEE societies.

Ruppa K Thulasiram (Tulsi) is an Associate Professor with the Department of Computer Science, University of Manitoba, Winnipeg, Manitoba. He received his Ph.D. from Indian Institute of Science, Bangalore, India and spent years at Concordia University, Montreal, Canada; Georgia Institute of Technology, Atlanta; and University of Delaware as Post-doc, Research Staff and Research Faculty before moving to University of Manitoba as an Assistant Professor. Tulsi has undergone training in Mathematics, Applied Science, Aerospace Engineering, Computer Science and Finance during various stages of his education and post doctoral training. Tulsi's current primary research interest is in the emerging area of Computational Finance. Tulsi has developed a curriculum for cross-disciplinary computational finance course at University of Manitoba and currently teaching this at both graduate and undergraduate level. His other research interests include Scientific Computing, Ad-hoc Networking for M-Commerce applications, and Mathematical Finance. He has published number of papers in the areas of High Temperature Physics, Gas Dynamics, Scientific Computing and Computational Finance in leading journals and conferences. Tulsi has been serving in many conference technical committees related to parallel and distributed computing, Neural Networks, Computational Finance and has been a reviewer for many conferences and journals. He has started a workshop "Intl. Workshop on Parallel and Distributed Computing in Finance" in conjunction with the IPDPS. He is a member of the ACM, IEEE and SIAM societies.

Geetam Singh Tomar (IEEE M' 2002), received his UG, PG, and Ph. D. degrees in electronics engineering from reputed universities of India. He is presently Principal, Malwa Institute of Technology & Management, Gwalior, India. He is actively involved in research and consultancy with Machine Intelligence Research Labs (USA), India section, Gwalior. He is guiding Ph.D. Students in the area of air interface for cellular and mobile ad-hoc networks, Antenna design and fabrication, wireless sensors networks and underwater communication. He is actively involved in IEEE activities and is chief editor of international journals.

Deo Prakash Vidyarthi, received Master Degree in Computer Application from MMM Engineering College Gorakhpur and PhD in Computer Science from Banaras Hindu University, Varanasi. He was associated with the Department of Computer Science of Banaras Hindu University, Varanasi for more than 12 years. Joined JNU in 2004 and currently working as Associate Professor in the School of Computer & Systems Sciences, Jawaharlal Nehru University, New Delhi. Dr. Vidyarthi has published around 50 research papers in various peer reviewed International Journals and Transactions (including IEEE, Elsevier, Springer, World Scientific, IGI, Inderscience etc.) and around 25 research papers in the proceedings of peer-reviewed International conferences in India and abroad. Research interest includes Parallel and Distributed System, Grid Computing, Mobile Computing.

Rajeev Wankar is working as a Reader in the Department of Computer and Information Sciences at University of Hyderabad, India since July 2004. Before joining this University he was serving as a Lecturer in the Department of Computer Sciences of North Maharashtra University Jalgaon, India for ten years. He earned Ph.D. in Computer Science from the Department of Computer Science, Devi Ahilya University, Indore, India. In 1998, the German Academic Exchange Service awarded him "Sandwich Model" fellowship. He was working in the Institut für Informatik, Freie Universität, Berlin, Germany and had collaboration with Scientists of Konrad Zuse Institut für Informationstechnik (ZIB), a Supercomputing Laboratory in Berlin, for almost two years. Currently he is working in the area of Parallel Computing, especially Parallel Algorithms design using Reconfigurable Bus System, Distributed Shared Memory Computing, Grid Computing and Multi Core Computing. He is also an Associate Faculty in the University Center for Earth and Space Sciences at University of Hyderabad and working for parallel implementations for many grand challenge problems like weather forecasting, ocean modeling etc. He is actively participating in an International Geo-Grid activity known as GEON with San Diego Supercomputing Center, University of California, San Diego, USA. He served as a program committee member in many prestigious conferences such as HiPC-07, TEAA, and ICDCIT.

Makoto Yoshida received the B.S. degree in computer science from Yamanashi University, Japan, in 1977, and the M.S. in information and computer science from Georgia Institute of Technology, Atlanta, in 1980. From 1980 to 2003, he joined OKI Electric Industry Co., Ltd., and engaged in research and development of distributed systems. He received his Ph.D. degree in information engineering at Hiroshima City University in 2003, and joined the Department of information and computer engineering at Okayama University of Science, in 2004. He is currently an associate professor in information and computer engineering at Okayama University of Science, Japan. His research interests include grid computing, cloud computing, distributed system architecture and software engineering. He is a member of the IPSJ and JSAI.

Index